INTANGIBLE CULTURAL HERITAGE AND INTELLECTUAL PROPERTY

INTANGIBLE CULTURAL HERITAGE AND INTELLECTUAL PROPERTY

Communities, Cultural Diversity and Sustainable Development

Toshiyuki Kono
(ed.)

intersentia
Antwerp – Oxford – Portland

Distribution for the UK:
Hart Publishing Ltd.
16C Worcester Place
Oxford OX1 2JW
UK
Tel.: +44 1865 51 75 30
Fax: +44 1865 51 07 10

Distribution for Switzerland and Germany:
Schulthess Verlag
Zwingliplatz 2
CH-8022 Zürich
Switzerland
Tel.: +41 1 251 93 36
Fax: +41 1 261 63 94

Distribution for the USA and Canada:
International Specialized Book Services
920 NE 58th Ave Suite 300
Portland, OR 97213
USA
Tel.: +1 800 944 6190 (toll free)
Tel.: +1 503 287 3093
Fax: +1 503 280 8832
Email: info@isbs.com

Distribution for other countries:
Intersentia Publishers
Groenstraat 31
BE-2640 Mortsel
Belgium
Tel.: +32 3 680 15 50
Fax: +32 3 658 71 21

Intangible Cultural Heritage and Intellectual Property. Communities, Cultural Diversity and Sustainable Development
Toshiyuki Kono (ed.)

Cover photographs: iStockphoto.com/Amer Kapetanovic – 'Whirling Dervishes from Kony' and iStockphoto.com/Stephan Hoerold – 'Tea ceremony'

ISBN 978-90-5095-758-8
D/2009/7849/2
NUR 828

ACKNOWLEDGEMENTS

The main idea behind this edited volume entered my mind in the course of participating in several fora held by the United Nations Educational, Scientific and Cultural Organization (UNESCO) and the World Intellectual Property Organization (WIPO). As I personally participated in drafting the *Convention for the Safeguarding of the Intangible Cultural Heritage* (ICH Convention), I became intimately acquainted with the issues and problems involved in the safeguarding of intangible cultural heritage and the solutions that have been proposed thus far.

After attending several of the UNESCO and WIPO fora, I was left with the impression that there was inadequate cooperation between UNESCO and WIPO and a lack of mutual understanding of the main problems involved in the safeguarding of intangible cultural heritage. My impression on the lack of mutual understanding and inadequate cooperation between UNESCO and WIPO in the safeguarding of intangible cultural heritage persists even though there has been a long tradition of fruitful cooperation between these organizations.

To efficiently achieve the same goal – safeguarding intangible cultural heritage – I believe that a greater exchange of ideas and views is necessary amongst those involved in safeguarding activities, whether they are involved in the various publicly funded programs or use legal measures to protect traditional knowledge and cultural traditions from misappropriation. The need for greater cooperation is especially salient when one takes into account that different approaches to safeguarding employ similar concepts, instruments and mechanisms, such as intangible cultural heritage inventories, obtaining prior informed consent from concerned communities for any use of their cultural traditions and active community involvement in the safeguarding.

To make a small but steady step to remedy the unfortunate lack of cooperation and mutual understanding, Kyushu University, together with the Asia/Pacific Cultural Centre for UNESCO (ACCU), the Council of Scientific and Industrial Research (CSIR) and the National Institute of Science Communication and Information (NISCAIR), co-organized an international conference entitled *Intangible Cultural Heritage and Intellectual Property under the 2003 Convention: Seeking a Collaborative Interface between ICH and IP,* which was held on 25–26 March 2007 in New Delhi, India. The main idea behind the conference was to provide a forum for discussion and cooperation by people with a variety of expertise in the field of protection and safeguarding of cultural traditions, *e.g.*

archivists, anthropologists, ethnomusicologists, lawyers, policy makers, academics and others. The contributions of the conference speakers were very valuable that fuelled vibrant discussions between respective experts, making the conference a success, in my view. It seemed apparent to me that this view was also widely shared by other conference participants. Given the success of the conference, we thought it would be worthwhile to publish individual extended conference papers in a collected volume; the result is the book which is currently before the reader.

A book such as this could not be put together by one person alone, but requires the work of many people. I owe a debt of gratitude to each of the conference participants for their valuable discussions before, during, and after the conference. Their contributions greatly influenced the organization of this volume as well as the content of the introductory notes. Special thanks also go to my colleagues Branislav Hazucha and Steven Van Uytsel, from Kyushu University, for supporting and assisting me during preparations for the conference and in putting this volume together. My research associate Carlo C. Osi's hard work in organizing the conference thousands of miles from Japan was priceless. I also owe many thanks for the painstaking editing by Joel-David R. Dalibard, Dean L. Dalke, Nadav Weg and Samuel Reuben Vandegrift. In addition, I am grateful to Tom Scheirs and his colleagues from Intersentia for their patience and understanding while waiting months for the completion of the manuscript.

Last, but not least, thanks are also due to the Asia/Pacific Cultural Centre for UNESCO (ACCU) for their generous funding, without which this volume would never see the light of day.

Toshiyuki Kono
Fukuoka, August 2008

FOREWORD

The *Convention for the Safeguarding of the Intangible Cultural Heritage* (ICH Convention), which was adopted by the Member States of UNESCO in October 2003, could welcome its hundredth State Party as early as the summer of 2008. The Convention, which entered into force in April 2006, became fully operational in June 2008, when the second session of the General Assembly of its States Parties approved a set of *Operational Directives* aimed at guiding its implementation. Eagerly awaited among these were the Directives concerning criteria and procedures for: inscribing elements on the Lists of the Convention; the use of the Fund of the Convention; and the accreditation of non-governmental organizations that are to provide consultative assistance to the Intergovernmental Committee.

It was the 24-member Intergovernmental Committee, elected by the General Assembly at it first session, that prepared these first Operational Directives. It did so at the request of – and for approval by – the General Assembly, the sovereign organ of the Convention. The Committee no doubt will be asked to continuously adapt and expand the set of Directives, in response to future experiences and new developments in thinking about intangible heritage and its safeguarding. Such expansions and adaptations will have to be submitted to the General Assembly for its approval.

The ICH Convention presents an open definition of intangible cultural heritage that may be interpreted differently over time, and the text, as a rule, does not define many of the terms it introduces nor does it provide a detailed framework for each of the measures it imposes or proposes. The governmental experts who prepared the draft text of the Convention acknowledged that thinking about intangible heritage varies from region to region and over time. Furthermore, they recognized that the field of safeguarding living heritage is relatively new. In line with this, the Convention requests the Intergovernmental Committee to select and disseminate programmes, projects and activities that best reflect the principles and objectives of the Convention. The Committee, which time and again has underscored that safeguarding is the main objective of the Convention, elaborated in the framework of the Operational Directives extensive procedures and criteria for the selection and dissemination of best practices for safeguarding.

The first set of Operational Directives, as recently approved, allows the Committee to start inscribing elements on the two Lists of the Convention, to select best safeguarding practices, to use the Fund of the Convention (for instance for granting international assistance), and for organizing consultative assistance.

While the Operational Directives are much more specific than the Convention, many issues remain to be discussed, either by the Committee itself, or at its request by expert meetings. States Parties to the Convention regularly pose questions to the secretariat of the Convention, but many of those questions cannot really be answered by the secretariat, as it is the prerogative of the Committee to pronounce on certain questions or choose to leave them unanswered. Such questions may include, for instance, how to elaborate inventories of intangible heritage, how to define communities, or how to apply intellectual property rights to intangible cultural heritage. Fortunately, expert meetings are continually organized and individual experts continue to study questions related to the implementation of the Convention. The UNESCO Secretariat, which also acts as the secretariat of the Convention, tries to provide all available relevant information concerning such activities on its website (www.unesco.org/culture/ich).

The present volume is a welcome addition to the scarce studies on the ICH Convention conducted thus far. While the question of intellectual property rights on intangible cultural heritage constitutes its *leitmotiv*, the present volume also pays due attention to the concept of community, a notion left undefined by the Convention and not yet tackled by the Intergovernmental Committee. Some contributions discuss and elaborate on the requirement of consent by the community, group or individuals concerned. This is appropriate, since the Operational Directives are quite insistent on the requirement of consent as a prerequisite for almost any action of a State concerning its intangible heritage. Various contributions also deal with inventory making, another significant aspect of the Convention, which obliges all States Parties to establish one or more inventories of the intangible cultural heritage present in their territory in a manner geared to their own situation. If a State Party intends to provide extensive documentation with inventoried elements, then the question of intellectual property rights may indeed become urgent. Providing extensive documentation for inventoried elements is, however, not an obligation under the Convention, which clearly distinguishes between inventorying and documentation; in fact, extensive documentation might even go against the spirit of the Convention if it would contribute to establishing canonical versions of intangible heritage expressions or practices, or to defining community membership in strict terms.

It is my pleasure to recommend this volume of papers by fine experts which were presented at a meeting timely convened by Prof. Toshiyuki Kono and held in New Delhi, India, in March 2007.

Rieks Smeets
First Secretary of the ICH Convention

TABLE OF CONTENTS

PART FOUR COMMUNITY'S PRIOR INFORMED CONSENT

PART ONE
SAFEGUARDING OF INTANGIBLE CULTURAL HERITAGE AND INTELLECTUAL PROPERTY

CONVENTION FOR THE SAFEGUARDING OF INTANGIBLE CULTURAL HERITAGE

Unresolved Issues and Unanswered Questions

Toshiyuki KONO*

The *Convention for the Safeguarding of Intangible Cultural Heritage* (ICH Convention)[1] was adopted to safeguard intangible cultural heritage of concerned communities, groups and individuals; to ensure respect for it; to raise awareness at the local, national and international levels of its importance and importance of ensuring mutual appreciation thereof; and to establish a necessary foundation for international cooperation and assistance.[2] Since achieving these objectives is not always a simple, straightforward or painless effort, the Convention provides, in some regards, only a framework and often leaves solving controversial or

* Professor of Law, Kyushu University Faculty of Law. The author expresses his many thanks to Carlo C. Osi and Miriam Rose L. Pereira for their research support in the early stages of drafting this Chapter.

1 Convention for the Safeguarding of the Intangible Cultural Heritage, 17 October 2003, U.N. Doc. MISC/2003/CLT/CH/14 (2003), *available at* http://unesdoc.unesco.org/images/0013/001325/132540e.pdf (last visited 31 July 2008) [hereinafter "ICH Convention"].

2 *See id.*, Article 1.

contentious issues to later stages of implementation and application. One issue that was left to future interpretation is the mutual relationship and interaction among the various regimes that are focused on safeguarding of intangible cultural heritage.[3] This Chapter identifies the issues that have been left for future implementation and application, and attempts to provide some background for the more focused and profound analyses that follow in later chapters of the present volume.

Before examining individual issues, one-by-one, it is essential to understand how they evolved. This Chapter thus commences with an inquiry into the main rationales and historical circumstances surrounding the adoption of the ICH Convention, and aims to uncover and illuminate the background behind, and foundations of, unanswered questions and unresolved issues. This Chapter continues by scrutinizing the individual issues and questions that arose in the design of the ICH Convention and that are likely to arise in implementing the safeguarding measures under the ICH Convention. These questions relate to designing and operating intangible cultural heritage inventories, as well as recognizing intangible cultural heritage and its ownership, possession or

---

3 In addition to the regime established by the ICH Convention, there are other regimes that also aim to protect traditional knowledge and cultural traditions from misappropriation. Some regimes are already in force while others are still in the preparatory stages. For the activities taking place under the auspices of the World Intellectual Property Organization (WIPO), *see* WIPO, Intergovernmental Committee on Intellectual Property and Genetic Resources, Traditional Knowledge and Folklore, *The Protection of Traditional Knowledge: Draft Objectives and Principles*, WIPO/GRTKF/IC/10/5 (2 October 2006), *available at* www.wipo.int/edocs/mdocs/tk/en/wipo_grtkf_ic_10/wipo_grtkf_ic_10_5.pdf (last visited 31 July 2008) [hereinafter "*Draft TK Principles*"]; WIPO, Intergovernmental Committee on Intellectual Property and Genetic Resources, Traditional Knowledge and Folklore, *The Protection of Traditional Cultural Expressions/Expressions of Folklore: Draft Objectives and Principles*, WIPO/GRTKF/IC/10/4 (2 October 2006), *available at* www.wipo.int/edocs/mdocs/tk/en/wipo_grtkf_ic_10/wipo_grtkf_ic_10_4.pdf (last visited 31 July 2008) [hereinafter "*Draft TCE Principles*"]. For an overview of national and other measures, *see* WIPO, Intergovernmental Committee on Intellectual Property and Genetic Resources, Traditional Knowledge and Folklore, *The Protection of Traditional Knowledge: Revised Outline of Policy Options and Legal Mechanisms*, WIPO/GRTKF/IC/9/INF/5 (27 March 2006), *available at* www.wipo.int/edocs/mdocs/tk/en/wipo_grtkf_ic_9/wipo_grtkf_ic_9_inf_5.doc (last visited 31 July 2008) [hereinafter "*Revised Draft TK Legal Mechanisms*"]; WIPO, Intergovernmental Committee on Intellectual Property and Genetic Resources, Traditional Knowledge and Folklore, *The Protection of Traditional Cultural Expressions/Expressions of Folklore: Updated Draft Outline of Policy Options and Legal Mechanisms*, WIPO/GRTKF/IC/9/INF/4 (27 March 2006), *available at* www.wipo.int/edocs/mdocs/tk/en/wipo_grtkf_ic_9/wipo_grtkf_ic_9_inf_4.pdf (last visited 31 July 2008) [hereinafter "*Updated Draft TCE Legal Mechanisms*"]; United Nations Conference on Trade and Development (UNCTAD), *Analysis of Options for Implementing Disclosure of Origin Requirements in Intellectual Property Applications*, UNCTAD/DITC/TED/2005/14 (15 February 2006) (*prepared by* J.D. Sarnoff and C.M. Correa), *available at* www.unctad.org/en/docs/ditcted200514_en.pdf (last visited 31 July 2008) (discussing various available policy options).

custodianship. This inquiry, however, does not rest with the identification of unresolved issues and unanswered questions. For adequate and sufficient understanding of these challenges to the implementation of the ICH Convention, it is vital to address possible consequences of safeguarding measures on affected communities and their intangible cultural heritage.

Despite an array of potentially negative consequences, even amongst well-intentioned safeguarding measures, this Chapter concludes with a certain degree of optimism. It acknowledges potential shortcomings in the ICH Convention's safeguarding of intangible cultural heritage, yet counters with the assertion that the ICH Convention's safeguarding measures are necessary to protect the global diversity of intangible cultural heritage for future generations – the dangers of our modern age demand it. In this respect, the ICH Convention is undoubtedly one of the first groundbreaking steps on a long road to the final goal of achieving sustainable living heritage. Its provisions exhibit great potential for success and shall be tested and vetted through their application.

1. CONTEXT OF THE ICH CONVENTION

The character of the ICH Convention significantly impacts ways particular issues and questions are framed, and how respective solutions and answers should be designed. For this reason, it is important to understand the context and characteristics of the ICH Convention. This section examines three primary characteristics of the ICH Convention. The first main characteristic of the ICH Convention is that it recognizes the importance of safeguarding intangible cultural heritage as a mainspring of cultural diversity and as vital to achieving sustainable development. Another characteristic of the final text of the ICH Convention is that it addresses shortcomings in the safeguarding of intangible cultural heritage as it has developed thus far in the field of international cultural heritage law. Finally, this Section addresses the relationship between safeguarding intangible cultural heritage and intellectual property law. Intellectual property laws have conventionally considered cultural traditions to be in public domain. Hence, communities' interests in safeguarding their intangible cultural heritage have, until recently, not been taken into account while drafting intellectual property laws and regulations. However, the need for achieving efficient safeguarding of intangible cultural heritage requires proper and adequate understanding of intellectual property related aspects concerning intangible cultural heritage and its safeguarding.

1.1. IMPORTANCE OF INTANGIBLE CULTURAL HERITAGE AND ITS SAFEGUARDING

Several provisions in the ICH Convention expressly recognize the importance of intangible cultural heritage and its safeguarding.[4] The dire need for efficient safeguarding of intangible cultural heritage is highlighted by defining it "as a mainspring of cultural diversity and a guarantee of sustainable development".[5] In this way, the Convention emphasizes the close link between heritage, cultural diversity, and sustainable development. Such wording clearly suggests that development should not only be seen in economic or financial terms; that is, it should not be restricted merely to growth and rapid expansion of productivity. To consider changes only through a financial lens short-changes the enormity of human considerations and repercussions that development entails. Therefore, the Convention clearly acknowledges that development should not bring only economic benefits, but it should also provide individuals with the "opportunity to choose a full, satisfying, valuable, and valued way of living together."[6] The Convention stems from a standpoint that the quality of human life should be at the centre of developmental agendas by understanding the economic and human dimensions of such development.

The broader understanding of its concept also expects that development should occur only in such a way that "meets the needs of the present without compromising the ability of future generations to meet their own needs."[7] Although the concept of sustainable development is an offshoot of anxieties recognized by ecologists and environmental scientists of depletion and overexploitation of natural resources, it relates equally to needs future generations possess to enjoy the marvels of traditional cultural expressions, practices and other social processes. Partial or complete disappearance either as a result of its abuse or misuse by non-members of concerned communities, or of its disuse or abandonment by their members looms as a danger to intangible cultural heritage. The ICH Convention avows such threats by stating, "the processes of globalization and social transformation ... also give rise, as does the phenomenon of intolerance, to grave threats of deterioration, disappearance and destruction of the intangible cultural heritage".[8]

Acknowledging the importance of incorporating safeguarding of intangible cultural heritage into sustainable development reflects the fact that traditional

4 *See*, *e.g.*, ICH Convention, *supra* note 1, Preamble, 2 and 10, and Article 1(c).

5 ICH Convention, *supra* note 1, Preamble, 2.

6 L. Arizpe, "The Intellectual History of Culture and Development Institutions", in V. Rao and M. Walton (eds.), *Culture and Public Action* 2004, 163, 178.

7 World Commission on Environment and Development, *Our Common Future*, at 24, A/42/427, Annex (4 August 1987).

8 *See* ICH Convention, *supra* note 1, Preamble, 4.

knowledge, cultural expressions and practices play an important role in everyday life among diverse communities all around the world. Communities actively carried out these practices for times immemorial. One of their main roles, as also acknowledged in the definition of intangible cultural heritage in Article 2(1) of the ICH Convention, is that they provide communities and their members with the sense of identity and continuity.[9] In this way, it is conceded that intangible cultural heritage has a considerable, daily impact on communities. Traditional cultural expressions and traditional environmental, agricultural, and medicinal knowledge represent essential survival tools especially within Indigenous and traditional communities.[10] Although Westerners may view such cultural expressions, practices and knowledge as arcane, many individuals utilize such methods in their ordinary lives.[11] One of the main goals of the ICH Convention is to prevent deterioration of existing cultural traditions, and to help improve imperfect situations[12], especially since intangible cultural heritage fundamentally shapes the way of life held by millions of people worldwide.[13]

Economic development accompanied with contemporary social phenomena such as modernization, industrialization, urbanization, migration and globalization, takes its tolls. Intangible cultural heritage slowly, but steadily, withers. Numbers within new generations who can actively practice and employ individual traditional cultural expressions and traditional knowledge is fast declining. Many are lured to cities by prospects of employment and money, and consequently adjust their customs, habits and values to those held by the wider population. A further threat to intangible cultural heritage is posed by modern popular culture. Its popularity often overshadows traditional cultural expressions presenting a flashy alternative to practices seen as out-dated and unattractive by

---

9 *Id.*, Article 2(1) (stipulating that intangible cultural heritage "provides [communities and groups] with a sense of identity and continuity").

10 *See* R.J. Coombe, "Protecting Traditional Environmental Knowledge and New Social Movements in the Americas: Intellectual Property, Human Right, or Claims to an Alternative Form of Sustainable Development?", 17 *Fla. J. Int'l L.* 115 (2005) (noting that "most of the worlds' poorest people depend upon their traditional environmental, agricultural, and medicinal knowledge for their continuing survival, given their marginalization from market economies and the inability of markets to meet their basic needs of social reproduction.").

11 *See* United Nations Educational, Scientific and Cultural Organization (UNESCO) and the Asia/Pacific Cultural Centre for UNESCO (ACCU), *UNESCO-ACCU Expert Meeting on Transmission and Safeguarding of Intangible Cultural Heritage through Formal and Non-formal Education* (21–23 February 2007), *available at* www.accu.or.jp/ich/en/pdf/b2007Expert.pdf (last visited 31 July 2008).

12 *See* ICH Convention, *supra* note 1, Articles 1 and 2(3).

13 Indigenous and tribal peoples constitute about 5% of the world's population – around 370 million people worldwide; *see* Rural Poverty Portal, *Statistics and Key Facts about Indigenous Peoples*, www.ruralpovertyportal.org/english/topics/indigenous/statistics.htm (last visited 31 July 2008).

young generations. Thus traditional knowledge and cultural expressions often lose ground and are replaced by a standardized dominant global culture.[14]

On the other hand, commercialization of traditional cultural practices often results in adaptation of custom to fit the taste of potential consumers, be they tourists or general public. Some even argue that commercialization may destroy, or at least dilute, the sanctity of concerned heritage especially in cases where traditional cultural expressions habitually used for religious purposes are used for commercial ones.

By ultimately changing the customs, habits, skills, cultural expressions and other social practices endorsed and maintained by significant parts of affected communities, the abovementioned contemporary social phenomena may unwittingly and unintentionally relegate various elements of intangible cultural heritage, partially or completely, to oblivion. The problem is further magnified when we take into account that negative consequences of this kind may be irreversible, especially in cases where the transfer of traditions from their bearers to younger generations is disrupted in some way. A death of an elder, guardian of community's traditional knowledge and traditional cultural expressions, may cause such a loss. This leads some to equate the death of elders to the "loss of a library by fire".[15] Due to the fragility of relations between communities and their intangible cultural heritage, the ICH Convention underscores the importance of enabling continuous transmission of knowledge between generations for its safeguarding in a living form.[16]

As intangible cultural heritage can be lost forever, if it is ignored or abandoned, its continued preservation and respect amongst communities worldwide is essential. To prevent negative outcomes, effective safeguarding regimes should require proper and adequate education and building of social awareness concerning these issues.[17] Youth must be educated and inspired to be the tradition bearers for future generations. The ICH Convention thus attempts to create a framework that will enable numerous communities worldwide to become aware

---

14 *See* Institute of Historic Building Conservation, *Implications for IHBC and Preservation of Craft Skills*, www.ihbc.org.uk/Unesco/intangible_assets.html (last visited 8 March 2007).

15 *See, e.g.*, "UNESCO Unified over Diversity", *Yomiuri Shimbun* 7 November 2003 ("If a wise man dies in an African village, the cultural loss is said to be equal to the loss of a library by fire. With the trend toward modernization, there are many instances in which folklore and folksongs indigenous to a locality are lost because they are not passed down generation to generation.").

16 *See* ICH Convention, *supra* note 1, Articles 1 and 2(3) (safeguarding of intangible cultural heritage is defined as "measures aimed at ensuring the *viability* of the intangible cultural heritage, including the identification, documentation, research, preservation, protection, promotion, enhancement, *transmission*, particularly through formal and non-formal education, as well as the *revitalization* of the various aspects of such heritage" (emphasis added)).

17 *See* ICH Convention, *supra* note 1, Preamble, 10.

of the existence, practice and importance of intangible cultural heritage despite the attacks of Western cultures, traditions and media.

Applied to environmental concerns, sustainable development implies that present economic use of natural resources must not wipe out entire species of fauna or flora, but rather, allow future generations equal enjoyment. Applied to cultural traditions, it requires ongoing re-creation of traditional cultural expressions, practices and other social processes innate in a community, for the benefit of future generations. Through appropriate safeguarding of intangible cultural heritage, the welfare of a community advances in an efficient and sustainable way. Of course, it is difficult to develop quantifiable indicators to measure how a community's well-being is furthered. It is beyond the scope of purely economic assessments, since measuring the impact of songs, dances, chants, traditional processes and rituals on peoples' satisfaction, happiness or emotions cannot happen with bullet-proof empiricism. However, the importance of intangible cultural heritage and its safeguarding can be quantified even in economic terms. For example, it is estimated that the value of plant-based medicines sold per year is worth several hundred billion U.S. dollars.[18] At the same time, it should be kept in the mind that economic estimates take into consideration only the sales of related goods and services, not the impact of intangible cultural heritage on the practicing community, cultural diversity and sustainable development.

Measurable or not, the relationship of intangible cultural heritage and sustainable development is clear under the ICH Convention. Present community needs – sense of identity, respect of elders, happiness through traditional performances, knowledge of millennia-old information, environmental knowledge, and wisdom about plants and kindred spirits – must be met without compromising the ability of future generations to meet similar needs. The only way for future generations to meet community needs would be to ensure that intangible cultural heritage is passed on from generation to generation, as a living trust, whereby history is re-experienced and reconstituted.

1.2. SOLUTION TO HISTORICAL SHORTCOMINGS

Calls to safeguard intangible cultural heritage are not a recent phenomenon whether on the national[19] or international level. On the latter level, the United

18 *See, e.g., Economic Value of Medicinal Plants and Plant Based Drugs*, www.medicinalplants-kr.org/ECONOMIC_VALUE_OF_MEDICINAL3.HTM (last visited 31 July 2008).

19 *See* R. Kurin, "Tangible Progress: A response to "Safeguarding the Intangible," a Cultural Comment essay by Michael F. Brown", *Cultural Commons* December 2003, *available at* www.culturalcommons.org/kurin.htm (last visited 31 July 2008) ("A variety of international programs in the ICH arena trace their roots to the post-World War II Japanese programs

Nations Educational, Scientific and Cultural Organization (UNESCO) plays an important role. During the last 40 years, UNESCO has continued a relentless struggle to achieve up-to-date protection of intangible cultural heritage as an integral and vital part of cultural heritage as a whole. But it took time until the importance of intangible cultural heritage was fully acknowledged through a legally binding multilateral instrument.

For a long period of time, intangible cultural heritage has not been sufficiently protected because of the absence of any international instrument and lack of sufficient issue awareness. Early foundations for current international protections of cultural heritage were laid down more than 100 years ago[20], but such documents setting up legally binding international standards for cultural heritage protection mainly protected tangible aspects.[21] In this spirit, Article 1 of the 1972 *Convention Concerning the Protection of the World Cultural and Natural Heritage* (World Heritage Convention)[22] defined "cultural heritage" as monuments,[23] groups of buildings[24] and sites.[25] Once in place, the World Heritage Convention indeed protected and preserved cultural heritage, but only those parts with material existence. Yet, performances, traditions, chants and other intangible parts of

---

which have continued through the present. Declaring cultural practitioners as 'living treasures,' and viewing folk traditions as 'valuable intangible cultural heritage' predates current concerns about intellectual property rights. Such programs grew in reaction to the fear that local traditions would disappear in the face of modernization and thus diminish national identity.").

20 Convention with Respect to the Laws and Customs of War on Land, 29 July 1899, Article 56, 32 Stat. 1803 (providing that "[a]ll seizure of, and destruction, or intentional damage done to such institutions, to historical monuments, works of art or science, is prohibited, and should be made the subject of proceedings."); Convention Respecting the Laws and Customs of War on Land, 18 October 1907, Article 27, 36 Stat. 2277 (requiring that "[i]n sieges and bombardments all necessary steps must be taken to spare, as far as possible, buildings dedicated to religion, art, science, or charitable purposes, historic monuments ..., provided they are not being used at the time for military purposes.").

21 *See, e.g.*, Convention for the Protection of Cultural Property in the Event of Armed Conflict, 14 May 1954, 249 U.N.T.S. 240 (1954); Convention on the Means of Prohibiting and Preventing the Illicit Import, Export and Transfer of Ownership of Cultural Property, 14 November 1970, 823 U.N.T.S 231, 10 I.L.M. 289 (1971); Convention Concerning the Protection of the World Cultural and Natural Heritage, 16 November 1972, 1037 U.N.T.S. 151, 11 I.L.M. 1358 (1972) [hereinafter "World Heritage Convention"].

22 World Heritage Convention, *supra* note 21.

23 *Id.*, Article 1 (defining "monuments" as "architectural works, works of monumental sculpture and painting, elements or structures of an archaeological nature, inscriptions, cave dwellings and combinations of features, which are of outstanding universal value from the point of view of history, art or science").

24 *Id.* (defining "groups of buildings" as "groups of separate or connected buildings which, because of their architecture, their homogeneity or their place in the landscape, are of outstanding universal value from the point of view of history, art or science").

25 *Id.* (defining "sites" as "works of man or the combined works of nature and man, and areas including archaeological sites which are of outstanding universal value from the historical, aesthetic, ethnological or anthropological point of view").

cultural heritage also hold importance equal to landscapes, monuments and other tangible structures. It is no less vital in the web of any civilization.[26]

The fact that the World Heritage Convention neglected an important part of cultural heritage was considered from its adoption a shortcoming of international regimes focusing on protection of cultural heritage. During its drafting and immediately after its adoption, several initiatives focusing on protection of intangible cultural heritage were proposed.[27] For instance, in a 1973 solution for regulating the conservation, promotion and diffusion of folklore and oral heritage[28], the Bolivian government suggested the adoption of a protocol to the *Universal Copyright Convention*[29], which would incorporate protection for these traditions within the copyright regime. Over the last three decades other initiatives to fill the gaps in the international cultural heritage protection regime in relation to the safeguarding of intangible components occurred. This led to the adoption of several recommendations and declarations[30], and to the organization of plentiful regional seminars.[31]

During this period, in addition to the persistent need to protect cultural heritage in its entirety, further deficiencies of traditional approaches to the protection of cultural heritage emerged. Amongst them, a mere listing of traditional cultural expressions and their properties was perceived to be insufficient. Many thus called for a switch in focus from regimes protecting cultural heritage to instead establishing clear-cut activities, projects and programs that would ensure safeguarding cultural traditions in a living form. The perception of necessary changes dominated the 1999 international conference co-organized by UNESCO and the Smithsonian Institution in Washington, D.C.[32] At that time, Lyndel V. Prott put it tersely, "Current anthropological studies emphasize that it

26 *See* G. Pinna, "Intangible Heritage and Museums", *ICOM News*, No. 4 (2003), *available at* http://icom.museum/pdf/E_news2003/p3_2003-4.pdf (last visited 31 July 2008).

27 *See, e.g.*, UNESCO, *Brief History of the Convention for the Safeguarding of the Intangible Cultural Heritage (2003)*, www.unesco.org/culture/ich/index.php?pg=00007 (last visited 31 July 2008).

28 *See, e.g.*, J. Early and P. Seitel, "UNESCO Draft Convention For Safeguarding Intangible Cultural Heritage: "No Folklore Without the Folk"", *Talk Story* Fall 2002, No. 22:19, *available at* www.folklife.si.edu/resources/center/cultural_policy/pdf/TSFall2002EarlySeitel.pdf (last visited 31 July 2008).

29 Universal Copyright Convention, opened for signature 6 September 1952, 943 U.N.T.S. 311 (revised 24 July 1971).

30 *See, e.g.*, Recommendation on the Safeguarding of Traditional Culture and Folklore, 15 November 1989, *available at* http://portal.unesco.org/en/ev.php-URL_ID=13141&URL_DO=DO_TOPIC&URL_SECTION=201.html (last visited 31 July 2008); Universal Declaration on Cultural Diversity, 9 November 2001, *available at* http://unesdoc.unesco.org/images/0012/001271/127160m.pdf (last visited 31 July 2008); and the Istanbul Declaration of 2002 adopted by the Third Round Table of Ministers of Culture.

31 This, of course, takes into consideration UNESCO's programme of the *Proclamation of Masterpieces of the Oral and Intangible Heritage of Humanity* which was begun in 1997.

32 *See* P. Seitel (ed.), *Safeguarding Traditional Cultures: A Global Assessment*, 2001.

is social process that needs to be preserved, rather than merely the items produced, to ensure the continued creation of these valued products."[33] The catchphrase, "There is no Folklore without the Folk," showed this understanding. It also embodied the importance of involving communities as tradition bearers in safeguarding of their own intangible cultural heritage.

The culmination of such collaborative efforts by international organizations, national governments, nongovernmental organizations (NGOs), activist groups, people's organizations, academics, experts and individuals to recognize the importance of intangible cultural heritage and its safeguarding resulted in two major achievements: (i) the 1994 *Proclamation of Masterpieces of the Oral and Intangible Heritage of Humanity* program[34], and (ii) a 2003 binding convention focusing on safeguarding of intangible cultural heritage – the ICH Convention.[35] The adoption of the Convention on 17 October 2003 is a milestone in the field of international cultural heritage law. The field's main shortcoming, the narrow concept of cultural heritage covering only tangible aspects, was rectified when the ICH Convention entered into force, after ratification by Romania as the 30th UNESCO member state, on 20 April 2006.

At the ICH Convention, drafters and UNESCO sought to further embolden the abovementioned manifest through safeguarding traditional cultural expressions, practices and other social processes[36] that are habitually performed and transmitted in oral form. Since its adoption, cultural heritage no longer remains associated just with physical works like churches, bridges and other monumental constructions, but also with songs, oral epics and poems, woodcarvings and other traditional cultural expressions and practices. Michael F. Brown characterizes this adoption as "a manifestation of growing concern about the fate of the intangible elements of cultural heritage: language, stories, art styles, music, dance, religious beliefs – in other words, those aspects of culture not

---

33 L.V. Prott, "Some Considerations on the Protection of the Intangible Heritage: Claims and Remedies", in P. Seidel (ed.), *Safeguarding Traditional Cultures: A Global Assessment,* 2001, 104.

34 *See* UNESCO, *Proclamation of the Masterpieces of the Oral and Intangible Heritage of Humanity (2001–2005),* www.unesco.org/culture/ich/index.php?pg=00103 (last visited 31 July 2008).

35 At its 32nd session, the General Conference of UNESCO finally adopted a binding international document – the ICH Convention; *see* ICH Convention, *supra* note 1, Preamble, par. 8 (noting "that no binding multilateral instrument as yet exists for the safeguarding of the intangible cultural heritage").

36 *See* D.W. Papuga, *A Taste of Intangible Heritage: Food Traditions Inside and Outside of the Museum* (2–8 October 2004) (paper presented at the ICOM 2004 General Conference, Seoul, South Korea), *available at* http://museumsnett.no/icme/icme2004/papuga.html (last visited 31 July 2008) ("As nourishment, food consists of tangible, material substances which humans consume. But the knowledge and practice of food preparation, etiquette of eating and symbolic meanings tied to various foods are all intangible.").

directly embodied in material things."[37] Janet Blake further vocalizes such importance and likens the "[r]ecognition of 'intangible heritage' as a subject for protection ... [to] one of the most significant recent developments of international cultural heritage law".[38]

However, the ICH Convention should not be seen simply as a remedial measure to fix inefficiencies and shortcomings of the World Heritage Convention reflected mainly in its narrow focus on only tangible, material heritage. To a certain extent, the ICH Convention was drafted to address these inadequacies, but it should also be viewed as a complementary international document that cements the importance of intangible aspects of cultural heritage in international consciousness. It manifests escalating global support of holistic approaches to the protection of cultural heritage[39] by shifting "attention to safeguarding the knowledge, skills, and values behind tangible culture, concentrating on the people and social processes that sustain it."[40]

There is no doubt that the ICH Convention has an enormous potential to improve safeguarding intangible cultural heritage worldwide. Nevertheless, it is hard to say that the Convention answers most questions, or provides all the solutions, to associated problems. In fact, the ICH Convention is very general. It does not use clearly defined terminology and is not sufficiently rigid in certain areas. As Rieks Smeets puts it succinctly, "[the ICH] Convention text is carved in stone and general."[41]

Although it is commendable that the text does not include the ominously ambiguous phrase "best efforts" – as a reference to the dilution of State Parties' mandatory obligations – still the use of "shall endeavour" may mean the same thing. One explanation for such a language might be that using stronger language of clearly drafted obligations would turn off countries and would lead to a systemic withdrawal of their support. However, using a highly diluted form of "obligations" leaves the State Parties the freedom to decide to comply with the ICH Convention depending on the country's national interests. The use of a strong, mandatory language may, to a certain extent, offend some nations and impinge upon their

37 M.F. Brown, "Safeguarding the Intangible", *Cultural Commons* November 2003, *available at* www.culturalcommons.org/comment-print.cfm?ID=12 (last visited 31 July 2008).

38 J. Blake, "Safeguarding Traditional Culture and Folklore: Existing International Law and Future Developments", in P. Seidel (ed.), *Safeguarding Traditional Cultures: A Global Assessment*, 2001, at 149.

39 *See, e.g.*, A. Galla, *Museums and Intangible Heritage, available at* http://rspas.anu.edu.au/papers/heritage/museums_%20Intangible_Heritage_ARTery.pdf (last visited 31 July 2008).

40 C. Kreps, "Indigenous Curation as Intangible Cultural Heritage: Thoughts on the Relevance of the 2003 UNESCO Convention", *Theorizing Cultural Heritage*, Vol. 1(2), at 5, *available at* www.folklife.si.edu/resources/center/cultural_policy/pdf/ChristinaKrepsfellow.pdf (last visited 31 July 2008).

41 This note was made by R. Smeets during discussion at the *UNESCO-ACCU Expert Meeting on Transmission and Safeguarding of Intangible Cultural Heritage through Formal and Non-formal Education*, Chiba, Japan, 21–23 February 2007.

sovereignty. But providing the Convention with false teeth significantly weakens it. In drafting binding international instruments, governments are usually inclined to weaken "shall" obligations into "shall endeavour" obligations for a simple reason: They seek to avoid constraints that force actions seen as incompatible with their own national agenda. If a contracting party is required only to try achieving of some goals, it will suffer no penalties or other punitive consequences for failing to do so. Trying one's best is quite different from meeting concrete benchmarks.

Put differently, the ICH Convention provides an outline, a framework for the safeguarding processes that leaves many issues and questions for later stages, *i.e.* its implementation and application. There are several reasons for such solution. Many of these issues and questions remain controversial, and therefore, achieving necessary consensus amongst delegations from different countries was not easy. In addition, solutions and answers in question often heavily depend upon circumstances of a particular safeguarding measure, thus they change on a case-by-case basis and over time. The text of the ICH Convention would thus easily become outdated and obsolete causing its inoperability, if it provided detailed solutions and answers to all possible issues and questions. It is especially true when one takes into account the extreme difficulty in amending international conventions. Certainly, this applies to the text of the ICH Convention under Article 38.

In order to address some of the issues and questions discussed above, operational directives for the implementation of the ICH Convention were adopted in mid-2008.[42] They are supposed to guide the proper implementation of the Convention. But at the same time, they are envisaged to evolve much like intangible cultural heritage, that is, to exist in constant "re-creation".

1.3. SAFEGUARDING INTANGIBLE CULTURAL HERITAGE AND INTELLECTUAL PROPERTY

Issues concerning various aspects of protecting intangible cultural heritage attracted more than just UNESCO's attention. Other international organizations also hold a stake in ensuring mutual appreciation of, and respect for, various forms of intangible cultural heritage. For instance, several bodies[43], established

---

42 *See* UNESCO, *Operational Directives for the implementation of the Convention for the Safeguarding of the Intangible Heritage*, www.unesco.org/culture/ich/index.php?pg=00026 (last visited 31 July 2008).

43 There are several bodies established under the CBD, *infra* note 44, such as the Conference of the Parties to the Convention on Biological Diversity, Working Group on ABS and Working Group on Article 8(j).

under the *Convention on Biological Diversity* (CBD)[44], focus on how to "respect, preserve and maintain knowledge, innovations and practices of indigenous and local communities embodying traditional lifestyles relevant for the conservation and sustainable use of biological diversity and promote their wider application with the approval and involvement of the holders of such knowledge, innovations and practices and encourage the equitable sharing of the benefits arising from the utilization of such knowledge, innovations and practices"[45], as an indispensable part of the *in-situ* conservation of ecosystems and natural habitats.[46] The World Intellectual Property Organization (WIPO)[47] tackles "legal mechanisms and practical tools concerning the protection of traditional knowledge and traditional cultural expressions (folklore) against misappropriation and misuse, and the intellectual property aspects of access to and benefit-sharing in genetic resources."[48] Similarly, within the framework of the World Trade Organization (WTO), the Council for Trade-Related Aspects of Intellectual Property Rights attempts to address and ameliorate intricate relationships between the *Agreement on Trade-Related Aspects of Intellectual Property Rights* (TRIPS Agreement)[49] and the CBD in order to provide sufficient protection of traditional knowledge and folklore in relation to trade related aspects of intellectual property regulations. There are also other international organizations and bodies, which handle various developmental aspects of intellectual property and protection of intangible cultural heritage.[50]

In order to avoid inconsistency between the various regulations for the protection of intangible cultural heritage, Article 3(b) of the ICH Convention provides that "[n]othing in this Convention may be interpreted as ... affecting the

---

44 Convention on Biological Diversity, 5 June 1992, 31 I.L.M. 818, *available at* www.biodiv.org/convention/convention.shtml (last visited 31 July 2008) [hereinafter "CBD"].

45 *Id*, Article 8(j).

46 *Id*, Article 2 (defining "in-situ conservation" as "the conservation of ecosystems and natural habitats and the maintenance and recovery of viable populations of species in their natural surroundings and, in the case of domesticated or cultivated species, in the surroundings where they have developed their distinctive properties").

47 In October 2000, the WIPO General Assembly established the WIPO Intergovernmental Committee on Intellectual Property and Genetic Resources, Traditional Knowledge and Folklore.

48 WIPO, *Traditional Knowledge, Genetic Resources and Traditional Cultural Expressions/Folklore*, www.wipo.int/tk/en/(last visited 31 October 2007).

49 Agreement on Trade-Related Aspects of Intellectual Property Rights, 15 April 1994, Marrakesh Agreement Establishing the World Trade Organization, Annex 1C, Legal Instruments – Results of the Uruguay Round, 33 I.L.M. 1125 (1994) [hereinafter "TRIPS Agreement"].

50 *See, e.g.*, G. Dutfield, *Protecting Traditional Knowledge: Pathways to the Future*, at 16–18 (June 2006), *available at* www.iprsonline.org/unctadictsd/docs/Graham%20final.pdf (last visited 31 July 2008) (referring to activities of several international organizations and bodies); United Nations Conference on Trade and Development (UNCTAD), *Traditional Knowledge(TK)*, www.unctad.org/trade%5Fenv/topicTK.asp (last visited 31 July 2008) (listing recent meetings discussing traditional knowledge issues under UCTAD).

rights and obligations of State Parties deriving from any international instrument relating to intellectual property rights or to the use of biological and ecological resources to which they are parties."[51] However, international instruments usually set up only minimal standards of protection, and contracting parties are often allowed to adopt a higher standard of protection within their jurisdictions. Furthermore, the abovementioned efforts within the framework of the CBD, WIPO and WTO are, basically, in advanced stages of international policy debates, which could lead to the development of new legally binding multilateral instruments. At the same time, several countries have already independently adopted some forms of protection for traditional knowledge and cultural expressions against their misappropriation.[52] Consequently, a variety of questions arise concerning relationships between safeguarding intangible cultural heritage under the ICH Convention and other means of preserving cultural traditions. Does the Convention address and solve all possible conundrums, clashes and inconsistencies, which may occur during the safeguarding of intangible cultural heritage in relation to aspects related to intellectual property or the use of biological and ecological resources, just by excluding some of them[53] from the scope of its application?

The issue becomes even more perplexing considering that two main purposes of the ICH Convention stipulated in Article 1 refer to the "respect for the intangible cultural heritage". The Convention requires State Parties "to ensure respect for the intangible cultural heritage of the communities, groups and individuals concerned"[54] and at the same time "to raise awareness at the local, national and international levels of the importance ... of ensuring mutual appreciation thereof".[55] From these provisions, further questions emerge. Does respect and appreciation of intangible cultural heritage also include recognizing rights communities, groups and individuals hold? What relationships exist between any entitlements to intangible cultural heritage held by communities and intellectual property rights related to intangible goods stemming from traditional knowledge and cultural expressions?

Intellectual property rights are temporary privileges over intellectual creations and other intangible goods, such as literary works, music, songs, inventions and brand names. These rights determine who holds exclusive rights to commercial exploitation of such expressions of ideas or other results of human intellectual

51 ICH Convention, *supra* note 1, Article 3(b).

52 *See, e.g., Revised Draft TK Legal Mechanisms, supra* note 3; *Updated Draft TCE Legal Mechanisms, supra* note 3.

53 ICH Convention, *supra* note 1, Article 3(b) (excluding only any impact of the ICH Convention on "the rights and obligations of States Parties deriving from any international instrument" in this regard).

54 *Id.*, Article 1(b).

55 *Id.*, Article 1(c).

and creative labour. Copyrights encompass literary and artistic works such as writings, drawings, computer software and databases, among others. Patents vest the exclusive rights in inventors for the use, development, control and marketing of novel and inventive products and industrial processes. Trademarks, for their part, lend protection to brand names that distinguish goods or services with an established market identity or presence.

However, one must ask whether any part of intangible cultural heritage can ever be an eligible subject matter of intellectual property rights held by individuals or communities. While individual specimens of traditional craft and performance may be protected by intellectual property laws when they satisfy general requirements for copyrightability or registration, in many cases, intangible cultural heritage, including traditional ecological, agricultural, medicinal knowledge and traditional cultural expressions, go beyond the scope of intellectual property protection. Collective knowledge, ideas, innovations, creativity, traditional cultural expressions, practices and other social processes of numerous communities worldwide go beyond the concerns of intellectual property laws. Characteristics like collective and communal ownership and passage between generations define such heritage, yet these traits lack recognition by intellectual property laws.[56]

In terms of copyright, creativity and originality of expressions are paramount for obtaining exclusive rights. Copyright mandates the identification of an individual author or a group of authors. It is the converse of the collective nature of traditional cultural expressions and other expressions of folklore. For many Indigenous and traditional communities, the entire community is the actual owner, steward or custodian of intangible cultural heritage. No single person actually claims authorship. In addition, tracing the history of such creative practices to one person is virtually impossible.

The derivative and inter-generational transmissibility of intangible cultural heritage further impedes protections via copyright regulations because copyright applies only to original and creative works. Obtaining copyrights in some jurisdictions requires that the expression be fixed in a material, tangible form. This again goes against the very nature of intangible cultural heritage which is transmitted frequently only in oral form.[57] Preserved or ancient documents do not necessarily exist, nor are in use for transmission purposes.

A further incompatibility between intangible cultural heritage and intellectual property is the time-limited nature of intellectual property rights. Intangible

---

56 An exemption are geographical indications, "which identify a good as originating in the territory ..., where a given quality, reputation or other characteristic of the good is essentially attributable to its geographical origin"; *see* TRIPS Agreement, *supra* note 49, Article 22(1).

57 *See* J. Blake, *Developing a New Standard-setting Instrument for the Safeguarding of Intangible Cultural Heritage: Elements for consideration*, at 8, CLT-2001/WS/8 Rev. (2002), *available at* http://unesdoc.unesco.org/images/0012/001237/123744e.pdf (last visited 31 July 2008).

cultural heritage is continuously evolving and adapting throughout the centuries, and setting up a maximum number of years for proprietary interests may, in many cases, not be in the best interests of affected communities. Time limitation of intellectual property rights is in sharp contrast to these expressions that may have been re-created over centuries and millennia.

Thus, possible consequences of safeguarding intangible cultural heritage under such intellectual property laws are a bit perplexing. On the one side, intellectual property rights potentially could help promote and safeguard the future of intangible cultural heritage. They contribute to the enrichment of society through the availability of socially useful goods and services, while creating an atmosphere of refined economic activity premised on the production, marketing and distribution of cultural goods and services. On the other, these protections might restrict the freedoms of intangible cultural heritage bearers and constrict their abilities to evolve, re-create and adapt. Since traditional cultural expressions, practices or other social processes fall outside of intellectual property rights (and thus cannot be obtained by concerned communities), they are considered public domain and are available for everyone's use and appropriation.

Simultaneously, a non-member of an affected community can co-opt its intangible cultural heritage as free inspiration for his own creative endeavours. This causes friction in many cases. The Indian legal battles over several patents that concerned turmeric, Basmati rice and neem are good examples of such misappropriation of traditional ecological, agricultural and medicinal knowledge by non-members of affected communities. In 1995, the US Patent Office granted a patent on the wound-healing properties of turmeric.[58] In 1998, another was granted to new strains of rice similar to Basmati rice, which is traditionally planted in India. The turmeric patent was revoked in 1997 and the Basmati rice patent in 2002. Also in 1995, another legal battle was fought before the European Patent Office against the patent issued on an anti-fungal product derived from the neem tree. The patent was successfully revoked in 2005. Bandana Shiva clarifies this issue as follows:

> All production based on biodiversity and biological resources are a co-production by nature and communities working in harmony with nature. Negating this co-production simultaneously robs resources from people while allowing corporations to claim "novelty" where only parasitism is taking place.[59]

---

58 In March 1995, two expatriate Indians at the University of Mississippi Medical Center were granted a patent for turmeric for wound healing.

59 B. Shiva, "The Very Basis of World Food Production Is at Stake", *Humanscape Magazine* August 2004, *available at* www.humanscape.org/Humanscape/new/aug04/thevery.htm (last visited 11 March 2007) (emphasis added).

In addition to moral implications of cross-cultural misappropriation of cultural traditions deemed by affected communities as stealing of their past and identity, there are other negative practical implications of such activities. For example, a pharmaceutical company holding a patent over a specific medicinal plant may prevent local communities, even the traditional knowledge holders themselves, from producing the same goods, which they produced for generations. Such monopolistic control, at the behest of the patent holder, may be prioritized over other important public interests, the rights to health, nutrition and access to, and transmission of, knowledge. This may even ultimately lead to the loss of biodiversity and the extinction of essential parts of intangible cultural heritage, thus having a negative impact on the livelihood and culture of affected communities.

Consequently, the level of intellectual property protection considerably affects how much control communities have over their traditional cultural expressions, be they arts (legends, epic stories, fairytales, songs, carvings or paintings), traditional ecological or agricultural knowledge, herbal or other traditional medicines and other matters pertinent to the community's well-being and survival. Clearly, obtaining proprietary rights to intellectual creations and other intangible goods, which are claimed through copyrights, patents, trademarks or other intellectual property rights by the non-members of concerned communities, are deemed by many as a pernicious threat to traditional cultural expressions and traditional ecological, agricultural and medicinal knowledge.

Conventionally, intellectual property rights are premised on the idea of balance or reconciliation between private interests and public benefits. They protect the interests of creators or authors, and further induce production of more creative and innovative things.[60] This line of justification is based on the premise that granting exclusive rights to an individual or corporation to exploit specific products of human ingenuity spurs further creativity. However, this limits access to information by, and to broad dissemination of information to, the general public. When law successfully strikes a balance between these two seeming competing interests, intellectual property can lead to further creativity, while protecting other important public interests recognized by society.

Many, however, argue that intellectual property laws often lack adequate and just balance. They suggest that private interests benefit more from time-limited proprietary rights than the public. Intellectual property laws are criticized for making the rich richer and the poor poorer. The critics of a never-ending expansion of intellectual property law refer to several colourful examples, where public interests vividly lose out to private interests.[61] For example, rising prices of drugs

---

60 *See, e.g.*, W.M. Landes and R.A. Posner, *The Economic Structure of Intellectual Property Law*, 2003.

61 *See, e.g.*, S.K. Sell, *Private Power, Public Law: The Globalization of Intellectual Property Rights*, 2003.

and limiting the development of generic drugs led to an international outcry. But a partial reassessment of the patent law in favour of public health occurred only after a long and harsh struggle.[62] Similar condemnation exists regarding misappropriation of intangible cultural heritage by the non-members of concerned communities.

A further criticism of the current level of intellectual property protection is that intellectual property rights go far beyond their intended scope. This prevents the realization of other human rights guaranteed by international instruments.[63] Some even argue that the intellectual property regimes may easily conflict with fundamental economic, social and cultural rights and thus have a considerable negative impact on local communities, their traditional knowledge and cultural expressions. Such negative consequences occur despite the fact that intellectual property rights are also considered as human rights. For instance, the *International Covenant on Economic, Social and Cultural Rights*[64], namely Article 15(1)(c), provides "the right of everyone to benefit from the protection of the moral and material interests resulting from any scientific, literary or artistic production of which he is the author." The United Nations (UN) High Commissioner for Human Rights affirmed that provision is in accordance with Article 27(2) of the *Universal Declaration of Human Rights*.[65] But at the same time, he confirmed "[that] there are apparent conflicts between the intellectual property rights regime embodied in the TRIPS Agreement, on the one hand, and international human rights law, on the other."[66] UN Special Rapporteurs J. Oloka-Onyango and Deepika Udagama previously also questioned the paradox that the TRIPS Agreement, imposed on by international economic law, goes against the basic principles of liberalization and favours monopolistic restriction and control.[67] They emphasized "[that] actual or potential conflicts exist between the implementation of the TRIPS Agreement and the realization of economic, social and cultural rights."[68]

---

62 *See, e.g.*, P. Drahos and J. Braithwaite, *Information Feudalism: Who Owns the Knowledge Economy?*, 2002, 208–9, 217.

63 *See, e.g.*, P.L.C. Torremans (ed.), *Copyright and Human Rights: Freedom of Expression – Intellectual Property – Privacy*, 2004; P.K. Yu, "Ten Common Questions About Intellectual Property and Human Rights", 23 *Ga. St. U. L. Rev.* 709 (2007).

64 International Covenant on Economic, Social and Cultural Rights, 16 December 1966, 993 U.N.T.S. 3 (1966).

65 Universal Declaration of Human Rights, 10 December 1948, G.A. Res. 217A(III), U.N. Doc. A/810 at 71 (1948).

66 UN High Commissioner for Human Rights (UNHCHR), *Intellectual Property Rights and Human Rights: Sub-Commission on Human Rights resolution 2000/7*, www.unhchr.ch/Huridocda/Huridoca.nsf/0/c462b62cf8a07b13c12569700046704e?Opendocument (last visited 31 July 2008).

67 *See* J. Oloka-Onyango and D. Udagama, *The Realization of Economic, Social and Cultural Rights: Globalization and Its Impact on the Full Enjoyment of Human Rights*, U.N. Doc. E/CN.4/Sub.2/2000/13 (2000).

68 *See* UNHCHR, *supra* note 66.

Intellectual property laws should therefore take into account these important public concerns when balancing private and public interests. Accordingly, Laurence R. Helfer observes that human rights and intellectual property, once dialectical opposites, are now becoming strange intimate bedfellows. He argues that the international community has, for the last few years, commenced identifying previously unchartered intersections, shared goals and other points of commonality between the two international regimes. The co-existence approach, *vis-à-vis* the conflict approach, allows human rights to influence intellectual property and trade issues, enhancing individual rights and global economic welfare in general.[69] Going even further, given the importance of cultural diversity and sustainable development, successful safeguarding of intangible cultural heritage for future generations must be considered as an important public interest that must be taken into account in the design of intellectual property laws. Intellectual property rights should thus become a tool rather than an obstacle for the achievement of these common goals.

2. ISSUES AND QUESTIONS SURROUNDING THE CONVENTION

Although protecting intellectual property and safeguarding intangible cultural heritage raise a myriad of possible issues, three main groups of unresolved questions emerge under the ICH Convention. The Convention requires State Parties to safeguard components of intangible cultural heritage by establishing inventories within their jurisdictions. Their establishment, operation and maintenance bring several controversies. They include specific intellectual property issues related to the operation of inventories, the relationship of already established lists to the inventories required under the Convention and finally, restrictions for recognizing intangible cultural heritage under the Convention and possible impacts on affected intangible cultural heritage and its ownership.

Second, the ICH Convention tacitly recognizes the communities' rights to their intangible cultural heritage. However, squabbles exist in defining ownership of ICH amongst communities, and in how to define communities as holders of intangible cultural heritage. Further questions arise regarding community's involvement and prior informed consent to safeguarding measures.

Finally, even the most benevolent and well-designed safeguarding measures inadvertently produce negative outcomes and consequences. The question then arises whether such safeguarding measures and regimes benefit communities and

---

69 *See* L.R. Helfer, "Human Rights and Intellectual Property: Conflict or Coexistence?", 5 *Minn. Intell. Prop. Rev.* 47 (2003).

their intangible cultural heritage long-term. For instance, an inventory of intangible cultural heritage can represent a rich source of materials for misappropriation by intellectual property related industries. In such a way, information held in secrecy by Indigenous, traditional or local communities for generations can become publicly available and may fall into public domain. An array of other possible negative consequences exists, not the least of which may be the stunting of development of communities and of their intangible cultural heritage.

2.1. INTANGIBLE CULTURAL HERITAGE AND ITS INVENTORYING

Three main groups of controversies related to intellectual property occur in relation to the inventorying of intangible cultural heritage. First, the establishment, operation and maintenance of these inventories bring specific intellectual property issues related to their operation. Second, there are currently several inventory lists of various parts in different countries.[70] They were set up for different purposes, mainly protection against the misappropriation of protected heritage by the non-members of affected communities. What is the relationship between these established lists and databases to new inventories required under the ICH Convention? Finally, the ICH Convention sets up the conditions under which it recognizes intangible cultural heritage. How will these parameters affect communities' integrity, identity and any would-be entitlements to their intangible cultural heritage? Since the first two groups of controversies receive detailed attention later in the present volume[71], the following enquiry will mainly focus on the third group of problems.

Without doubt, some traditional cultural expressions and practices go against values considered universal by humankind, such as sustainable development and other important public interests, including human rights, tolerance, mutual respect and dialogue between various communities and their cultures. To balance such public values with safeguarding intangible cultural heritage, the ICH Convention requires that protected units be compatible with existing human rights instruments and other important public interests to receive safeguarding under the provided regime.[72] The importance of compatibility with existing human rights instruments is stressed by the opening statement of the Convention:

70 *See* Chapter [WENDLAND] of the present volume.

71 *See* Part on "Designing a Means for the Safeguarding Intangible Cultural Heritage", presented later in the present volume.

72 ICH Convention, *supra* note 1, Article 2(1) ("consideration will be given solely to such intangible cultural heritage as is compatible with existing international human rights instruments").

"Referring to existing international human rights instruments, in particular to the Universal Declaration on Human Rights of 1948, the International Covenant on Economic, Social and Cultural Rights of 1966, and the International Covenant on Civil and Political Rights of 1966."[73] Furthermore, the definition of intangible cultural heritage itself goes even further: "[C]onsideration will be given solely to such intangible cultural heritage as is compatible with existing international human rights instruments, as well as with the requirements of mutual respect among communities, groups and individuals, and of sustainable development."[74] Undoubtedly, the ICH Convention only sanctions and safeguards those traditional cultural expressions, practices and knowledge that are consistent with human rights and other important public interests, and not those deemed inimical to them.

Such mandatory compatibility, which is prerequisite for inclusion into inventory and ensuing safeguarding, is a deep-seeded issue requiring additional clarification. It presents an obstacle to overcome before formal recognition of intangible cultural heritage takes place. State Parties may encounter difficulties advancing certain traditional expressions and practices that seem contrary to human rights and other public interests, yet these often represent a community's intangible heritage. A paradox may then exist: A traditional cultural expression, practice or social process is clearly a part of intangible cultural heritage in the eyes of the practitioners and community, but it violates human rights or other public interests from a Western viewpoint. What is the solution then? Will specific community cultural traditions be the foremost concern? Can State Parties censure, from their generated lists, practices perceived as inconsistent with human rights or other public interests? Shall the intent of the framers be followed despite protests from communities or members? Can non-recognition of intangible cultural heritage alter or otherwise affect cultural traditions of the affected community?

While drafting the ICH Convention, there was an intense debate about including a compatibility requirement into the definition of intangible cultural heritage. The majority of the delegates believed the requirement should be included since it will work to weed out intangible cultural heritage that is prejudicial, discriminatory, malevolent, violent and insensible. The minority view was that intangible cultural heritage should be defined without any reference to international human rights standards or other public interests, but that its consistency with them could be provided through a separate provision. The minority's rationale was that intangible cultural heritage should first be defined without contextualizing it through the lens of Western values reflected in international human rights instruments and other recognized public interests.

[73] *Id.*, Preamble, par. 1.
[74] *Id.*, Article 2(1).

The abovementioned deliberations during the drafting of the ICH Convention clearly reflected a debate prevailing in the field of international human rights protection and the recognition of the rights of minority cultures. It is the debate between universalism of human rights, on the one side, and cultural relativism, on the other.[75] Universalism connotes global respect for, and observance of, human rights and fundamental freedoms without discrimination to race, sex, language or religion. It argues that all peoples of the world should be provided with the common standard of human rights protection. It stresses that the rights contained in the Universal Declaration of Human Rights are universally binding and applicable without exception. In any conflict between international human rights standards and domestic norms, the former always trumps.

This viewpoint sharply contrasts to cultural relativism. Relativists believe that national norms and perspectives must prevail. The international community and international documents should not interfere with domestic practices. Relativists put forward that no one should be a judge of other peoples' culture, even those that pertain to their intangible cultural heritage. As outsiders, extraneous individuals or groups should not be allowed to claim the superior right of determination whether a particular traditional cultural expression or practice is compatible with, or in violation of, international human rights instruments or other important public interests. Accordingly, traditions, communal practices and social processes should be exempted from any criticism or comment from outsiders. Human rights and other recognized public interests should not be circumscribed by the standards of any single culture or determined by any single people.[76]

It is apparent this clash of ideas cannot be disregarded. In this regard, universalists fear that cultural relativism, as a doctrine, will justify oppression and inevitable violations of human rights and other important public interests. They also decry the threat of nihilism. Cultural relativists, on the other hand, view universalism as an opportunity for continued oppression, via Western legal ideals, through a force-feeding of "universal" principles inconsistent with domestic norms pervading in other countries. Thus, a compromise is now being sought. Some theoreticians currently further the thought for modified universal approaches that take local culture into consideration, or a diminished relativist position that admits a universal basis for human rights and other important public interests. The compromise approach argues that local circumstances must be taken into consideration when scrutinizing human rights and other public

75 *See, e.g.*, M.F. Brown, "Cultural Relativism 2.0", 49 *Current Anthropology* 363 (2008).

76 *See, e.g.*, American Anthropological Association, "Statement on Human Rights", 49 *Am. Anthropologist* 539 (1947); J. Rüssen, "Human Rights from the Perspective of a Universal History", in W. Schmale (ed.), *Human Rights and Cultural Diversity: Europe, Arabic-Islamic World, Africa, China*, 1993, 28, 29–30.

interests, and that discretion must be given to local authorities. The applicability of international human rights instruments or other public interests need then not be forsaken, but the extremism involved either in a pure universalism or pure relativism can be discarded.

Despite achieving a fragile compromise when deciding whether an intangible cultural heritage should be recognized, there still seems to be considerable difficulties in practice. Discrimination in terms of gender, banned by international human rights and other antidiscrimination instruments, is not the exception but the rule in many parts of the world. For instance, the Office of the High Commissioner for Human Rights points out "harmful traditional practices" such as female genital mutilation, forced-feeding of women, early marriages, taboos or practices which prevent women from controlling their own fertility, nutritional taboos and traditional birth practices, son preference and its implications for the status of born girl child, female infanticide, early pregnancy and dowry price.[77] The reason for objections against, or even a ban on, such traditions is discrimination against women and bias in favour of men.

Some severe forms of female circumcision can be taken as an example of traditional cultural practices, which cause huge international and cross-cultural controversy, debate and outcry. Female circumcision is a time-honoured custom in certain countries whereby some parts of the female genital organ are removed or even infibulated in case of Pharaonic circumcision. Still commonly practiced in many sub-Saharan African countries, some form of female circumcision is a prerequisite rite of passage in ceremonies to mark female coming of age. The most controversial forms of female circumcision are those where its aim is to control the sexual desires of the child, ensuring her chastity for her future marriage. Similar traditions were, however, also found in other countries and cultures, such as metal rings attached to slaves in ancient Rome to prevent procreation, metal chastity belts in old England, Pharaonic circumcision in Egypt and Sudan, and as a cure for psychological disorders in America and England. The Western view on female circumcision, often called as female genital mutilation, may be summed up as follows:

> [Female genital mutilation] is rooted in discrimination against women. It is an instrument for socializing girls into prescribed roles within the family and community. It is therefore intimately linked to the unequal position of women in the political, social, and economic structures of societies where it is practised.[78]

---

77 *See* UNHCHR, *Fact Sheet No.23, Harmful Traditional Practices Affecting the Health of Women and Children*, www.unhchr.ch/html/menu6/2/fs23.htm (last visited 31 July 2008).

78 Amnesty International, *Female Genital Mutilation and International Human Rights Standards*, ACT 77/014/97 (1 October 1997), *available at* www.amnesty.org/en/library/asset/ACT77/014/1997/en/dom-ACT770141997en.html (last visited 31 July 2008).

Based on compatibility with human rights instruments and other important public interests, respect for, and non-discrimination against, women and its relationship with the health and well-being of women, female genital mutilation is inimical to them and should not be recognized as intangible cultural heritage entitled to safeguarding. Such practices are viewed with extreme scepticism and contempt by Western, or Western-inspired, thought models. The problem is that the communities practicing female circumcision do not regard it as discriminatory; rather, a mere rite of passage in the way that male circumcision is practiced elsewhere. The concerned communities, through the relativist lens, do not believe that outsiders should interfere with their practices.

Nonetheless, there are many traditional cultural expressions and practices, which are considered controversial from the view of other cultures. For instance, from a Japanese point of view, female genital mutilation is, of course, a reproachable practice. It is antithetical to gender equality and subordinates women. But there is a traditional cultural expression, a part of Japanese intangible cultural heritage, which characteristics are not as violent or virulent as female genital mutilation. Nonetheless, it may be subject to a similar debate on its appropriateness because of gender discrimination.

The *kabuki* theatre is a traditional Japanese theatre wherein characters wear intricate make-up and portray drama. Despite *kabuki*'s tradition of male-only performance, in November 2005 UNESCO proclaimed it a masterpiece of traditional performing arts in the *Third Proclamation of Oral and Intangible Heritage of Humanity*.[79] The history of the *kabuki* theatre can be traced to 1603 when a young woman in the service of a Shinto shrine began performing a new style of dramatic dance in Kyoto. Female performers played both men and women in comical portrayals of daily life. Unfortunately, *kabuki* performances were often used as an opportunity to solicit the services of the female performers for prostitution. So in 1629, female participation on *kabuki* performances was banned to protect public morals. From 1629 to 1652, young male actors took over the roles of the women. Their subsequent availability for prostitution led the shogunate to also ban their performances. Consequently, since 1653 only matured male actors have been allowed to perform *kabuki*.

Compared to female genital mutilation, the matured men-only *kabuki* theatre seems rather harmless, with entertainment as the sought end. However, both are cultural expressions and practices. Can it, therefore, be said that the *kabuki* theatre is antagonistic to gender sensitivity and equality since it banned women from performing? Is it in violation of international human rights instruments or other important public interests so that it should not be recognized as an intangible cultural heritage entitled to its safeguarding under the ICH Convention? For the Japanese, *kabuki* is a part of life, an intricate fabric of being Japanese, a sort of a

---

79 Third Proclamation of Oral and Intangible Heritage of Humanity, 25 November 2005.

rite of passage for younger generations to experience the richness of the Japanese culture. It is the intangible cultural heritage that should be recognized, inventoried and safeguarded. But it may well be objected by other peoples and nations advocating gender equality. Is the *kabuki* theatre contradictory to the principle of ban on sex discrimination, or the equal right of men and women to the enjoyment of economic, social and cultural rights? Richard Kurin succinctly expressed this controversy as follows:

> UNESCO does not want to support or encourage practices inimical to human rights such as slavery, infanticide, or torture. Yet, the standard is not without controversy. Is female genital mutilation a legitimate part of intangible cultural heritage to be recognized by the Convention or not? Is a religious tradition that includes Brahmins, but excludes non-Brahmins disqualified as intangible cultural heritage because of a discriminatory quality? Is a musical tradition where only men play instruments and only women sing inequitable, and thus contrary to human rights accords?[80]

This unresolved issue must receive further attention from UNESCO, individual State Parties, NGOs and the communities themselves. Communities practicing so-called "harmful" intangible cultural heritage can easily defend their actions by illustrating how the questioned cultural expressions and practices are traditions passed on from generation to generation. Further, they may argue that criticisms against such traditional cultural expressions, practices and other social processes are simply imbued and fraught with the Western value judgments, which are reflected in many international human rights and other instruments. Attempting to find the borderline, Peter Turner summarizes the issue as follows:

> Culture is the means by which people articulate meaning. The only limits that ought to be placed on this expression is to ensure that one person or group's expression does not do harm to others. It is fitting, then, that the heritage movement is linked historically to the international human rights movement.[81]

Each intangible cultural heritage must be examined case-by-case to determine whether it is "safeguardable" under the ICH Convention. Justifications based upon the length of time during which a community practices traditional cultural expression are not sufficient by themselves to merit recognition under the Convention. There must be a connection or nexus between the human right or other public interest considered violated and the main objectives of the intangible

80 R. Kurin, "Safeguarding Intangible Cultural Heritage in the 2003 Convention: A Critical Appraisal", 56 *Museum Int'l* 66, 70 (2004).

81 P. Turner, *Report on the Pocantico Conference for the International Journal of Cultural Property, available at* www.williams.edu/AnthSoc/IJCP/Synopsis.htm (last visited 31 July 2008).

cultural heritage. Those espousing Western legal thought may speculate that little connection exists between the infringement of women's rights during female genital mutilation and its objective, which is the rite of passage. They would say that it is always mutilation. But the same can be said about the Japanese *kabuki* theatre. Potential prostitution by female actors resulted in their exclusion for centuries. There is no reason to prevent the resurgence of female *kabuki* theatre actors today.

Choosing who makes these decisions lies central to resolving this argument. At the first level, national governments must survey their respective jurisdictions for intangible cultural heritage during the inventory-making purposes. Thus, State Parties should provide the first line of defence against the entry of traditional cultural expressions, practices and other social processes, which violate international human rights standards or other important public interests recognized by the ICH Convention. Of course, consultations with the affected communities and organizations must take place before the decision is made. The consultations mitigate adverse consequences of granting the government sole discretion over what to protect as intangible cultural heritage and when to act. If a State Party excludes components the community feels is not contradictory to any human right or other public interests, what remedy can the members of affected community employ? The matter is, unfortunately, left solely for the State Parties to decide. The ICH Convention, operational directives and other international documents can assist decision-making, but the sovereignty of all State Parties remains sacrosanct. Since the ICH Convention texts fail to specifically outline how communities may effectively influence governmental policies, the issue remains unclear.

Once a State Party proposes listing an intangible cultural heritage under the ICH Convention, can it be rejected on basis of supposed violations of international human rights standards or other recognized public interests? As before, it is not plain in the text of the Convention if the General Assembly of the State Parties to the ICH Convention or the Intergovernmental Committee for the Safeguarding of the Intangible Cultural Heritage (Committee), as the organs of the ICH Convention, are empowered to do so. If the Committee is uncertain, can it seek the assistance from, or turn the matter over, to the General Assembly or another international body? Can the UNESCO step in? If a listed intangible cultural heritage is later found incompatible with international human rights instruments or other public interests, is there any mechanism to de-list it, completely or partially, or to allow only a "sanitized" version to stay as listed? Before any removal from the list, can a dialogue be initiated between the State Party, the concerned community, the alleged victims of the abuse of rights, and the Committee?[82]

---

82 *See* T. Kono and J. Cornett, "What is Intangible Cultural Heritage? An Analysis of the Convention for the Safeguarding of Intangible Cultural Heritage and the Requirement of

One might argue non-recognition due to incompatibilities with sustainable development, human rights, tolerance, mutual respect and dialogue between various communities and their cultures can detrimentally affect the concerned community. Unchecked, unknowns could compromise community integrity, identity and any would-be entitlements to safeguard intangible cultural heritage. These issues are addressed in more details below.

2.2. COMMUNITY AND ITS INTANGIBLE CULTURAL HERITAGE

Active community involvement in safeguarding intangible cultural heritage promotes efficient operation and achievement of expected outcomes. The ICH Convention attempts to stimulate this in several ways. Among methods covered in this Chapter, promoting respect for intangible cultural heritage fosters recognition of communities and their members "as those who identify, enact, recreate and transmit the intangible or living heritage".[83] Designing and implementing individual safeguarding measures on a case-by-case basis requires involvement of communities, various groups and even individuals. As mentioned above, youths should be also engaged in this process as current practitioners, apprentices and future transmitters of intangible cultural heritage.[84] Accordingly, the ICH Convention stipulates that Indigenous, traditional and local populations are to be consulted in the decision-making processes on several levels and in a wide-ranging manner.[85] However, despite heated debate during its drafting, the Convention lacks operational definitions, clear answers and workable solutions to identify the holder, owner or steward of intangible cultural heritage. This flaw may cause misinterpretations by State Parties that unduly cater to local conditions and safeguarding mechanisms.

Despite the prevalence of community-oriented provisions, critics argue that national governments become sole owners and stewards of intangible cultural heritage under the Convention because individual State Parties are the members of the ICH Convention. There is no mention in the Convention whether the State

---

Compatibility with Human Rights", in J. Blake (ed.), *Safeguarding Intangible Cultural Heritage: Challenges and Approaches*, 2007, 143.

83 UNESCO, *Intangible Heritage*, http://portal.unesco.org/culture/en/ev.php-URL_ID=2225&URL_DO=DO_TOPIC&URL_SECTION=201.html (last visited 5 March 2007).

84 ICH Convention, *supra* note 1, Preamble, 10 ("[c]onsidering the need to build greater awareness, especially among the younger generations, of the importance of the intangible cultural heritage and of its safeguarding") and Article 14(a)(i).

85 *Id.*, Preamble, par. 6 ("[r]ecognizing that communities, in particular indigenous communities, groups and, in some cases, individuals, play an important role in the production, safeguarding, maintenance and re-creation of the intangible cultural heritage, thus helping to enrich cultural diversity and human creativity") and Articles 11(b), 14(a)(ii) and 15.

Parties only represent the communities, groups and in some cases, individuals as owners or stewards of their intangible cultural heritage. Put it otherwise, it is not apparent whether a State Party representing its national territory also holds, under the Convention, the exclusive rights over the entire intangible cultural heritage found within its jurisdiction. Paul Kuruk, a member of the Committee of Experts assigned to produce its preliminary draft, bewails that despite the efforts of like-minded advocates, "[a]s currently worded, the ICH Convention leaves the impression that the State has exclusive rights to intangible cultural heritage found within its territories and ignores the rights of others, including indigenous groups."[86]

Many, however, argue that the community owns intangible cultural heritage. Neither the state nor local government should exercise ownership rights. How can the state exercise ownership when traditional cultural expressions, practices and other related social processes are intangible and transmitted almost exclusively by oral traditions within communities? The state can neither possess them as tangible properties, nor can it hold mastery, power or pre-eminence over contemporary forms of their performance, their evolutionary nature or modes of their transmission. These and a multitude of other rights pertain solely to communities. Kurin advances that position stating "intangible cultural heritage, the traditions exist outside the museum, in the community ... [and] reside under the authority of the people who practices them."[87]

Before deciding whether the community owns intangible cultural heritage, it is vital to identify a community as the *holder* of intangible cultural heritage. The ICH Convention fails to define the terms such as "communities" and "groups of people". There is, of course, a host of explanations and definitions despite their absence in the text, but certainly the baseline and the main unifying feature of communities would be the peoples' common history. A community is best characterized as a group of people with a shared historical connectedness, which is traceable to their continuous use and inter-generational transmission of their intangible cultural heritage. Quite noticeably, in addition to the references to communities and groups, the ICH Convention employs the term "individuals". In this way, its drafters have foreseen the situations, where only a solitary practitioner is the bearer of both the memory and practice of traditions.

A useful tool in plugging certain holes in the definitions under the ICH Convention can be, although it pre-dates the drafting and adoption of the

86 *See* P. Kuruk, "Cultural Heritage, Traditional Knowledge and Indigenous Rights: An Analysis of the Convention for the Safeguarding of Intangible Cultural Heritage", 1 *Macquarie J. Int'l & Comp. Env'l. L.* 111 (2004), *available at* www.austlii.edu.au/au/journals/MqJICEL/2004/5.html (last visited 31 July 2008).

87 R. Kurin, "Museums and Intangible Heritage: Culture Dead or Alive?", *ICOM News*, No. 4, at 7 (2004), *available at* http://palimpsest.stanford.edu/icom/pdf/E_news2004/p7_2004-4.pdf (last visited 31 July 2008).

Convention, a glossary of terms related to intangible cultural heritage, which was generated by a small meeting of terminological experts organized by the UNESCO from 10–12 June 2002. For example, the glossary defines the following terms:

> **Community** [as] [p]eople who share a self ascribed sense of connectedness. This may be manifested, for example, in a feeling of identity or in a common behaviour, as well as in activities and territories. Individuals can belong to more than one community.[88]
>
> **Indigenous Community** [as] a community whose members consider themselves to have originated in a certain territory. This does not exclude the existence of more than one indigenous community in the same territory.[89]

A glossary of useful intangible cultural heritage terms might shackle the creativity or evolving nature associated with intangible cultural heritage. However, largely because of confusion created by a lack of adequate definitions, the 2002 glossary will appear in a UNESCO Manual to be published in 2008 as a form of guidance comprising approximately 40 words.

In March 2006, experts met in Tokyo at a community involvement meeting and worked to correct this lack of an operational guide. UNESCO and the Asia/Pacific Cultural Centre for UNESCO (ACCU) called the meeting as part of their groundwork efforts to implement the ICH Convention. The UNESCO-ACCU Expert Meeting on Community Involvement in Safeguarding Intangible Cultural Heritage addressed, in a vigorous debate, several key issues. These included the definition and identification of "communities", the level of involvement of communities in the inventory making, as well as their participation in the preparation of the two lists of intangible cultural heritage required by the Convention for the safeguarding at the international level.

There were intense discussions on the practice of intangible cultural heritage. Who are the actual practitioners? Who are the people who facilitated the practice but do not directly take part? Who are other stakeholders? The experts took into consideration the sense of community and its identity founded on having a common or shared intangible cultural heritage. In this line, Diana Baird N'Diaye put succinctly that a community consists of "groups of people who have shared history, shared experience, shared practice, shared knowledge, shared values, and shared aesthetics."[90] A "group" was, meanwhile, said to be a subset of the

---

88 UNESCO, *Frequently Asked Questions: Convention for the Safeguarding of the Intangible Cultural Heritage (2003)*, http://portal.unesco.org/culture/en/ev.php-URL_ID=21593&URL_DO=DO_TOPIC&URL_SECTION=201.html (last visited 8 March 2007).

89 *See id.*

90 D.B. N'Diaye, *Community in the Context of UNESCO's Convention on Intangible Cultural Heritage*, at 3 (13–15 March 2006) (paper presented at *UNESCO/ACCU Expert Meeting on Community Involvement in Safeguarding Intangible Cultural Heritage: Towards the*

community, which practices an intangible cultural heritage that is not necessarily communally shared. The individuals perform a specific role in intangible cultural heritage transmission as tradition bearers or custodians. The notion of apprentices was even taken into account in order to deal with necessary measures for achieving sustainability of the intangible cultural heritage. In the end, the experts agreed on the following definitions:

> **Communities** are networks of people whose sense of identity or connectedness emerges from a shared historical relationship that is rooted in the practice and transmission of, or engagement with, their ICH.
>
> **Groups** comprise people within or across communities who share characteristics such as skills, experience and special knowledge, and thus perform specific roles in the present and future practice, re-creation and/or transmission of their intangible cultural heritage as, for example, cultural custodians, practitioners or apprentices.
>
> **Individuals** are those within or across communities who have distinct skills, knowledge, experience or other characteristics, and thus perform specific roles in the present and future practice, re-creation and/or transmission of their intangible cultural heritage as, for example, cultural custodians, practitioners and, where appropriate, apprentices.[91]

Back to the issue concerning the ownership of intangible cultural heritage, a hint to cut this Gordian knot can be found in Article 11(b) of the ICH Convention, which demands State Parties, among taking other safeguarding measures, to "identify and define the various elements of the intangible cultural heritage present in its territory, with the participation of communities, groups and relevant non-governmental organizations."[92] This provision recognizes that State Parties must play an active role in safeguarding intangible cultural heritage through programs and activities. None the less, these are clearly safeguarding, identification and definition roles of State Parties and do not substantiate any proprietary claims to intangible cultural heritage by them. As Marilyn Strathern puts it tersely, the safeguarding programs and schemes are intended merely to "re-embed or recontextualize indigenous ownership in traditional knowledge,"[93] and not to

---

Implementation of the 2003 Convention, Tokyo, Japan), *available at* www.accu.or.jp/ich/en/pdf/c2006Expert_NDIAYE.pdf (last visited 31 July 2008).

91 UNESCO/ACCU, *Expert Meeting on Community Involvement in Safeguarding Intangible Cultural Heritage: Towards the Implementation of the 2003 Convention*, at 9 (13–15 March 2006), *available at* http://unesdoc.unesco.org/images/0014/001459/145919e.pdf (last visited 31 July 2008).

92 ICH Convention, *supra* note 1, Article 11(b).

93 M. Strathern, *Property, Substance, and Effect: Anthropological Essays on Persons and Things*, 1999, 167.

transfer ownership to states or local governments. Harriet Deacon develops the idea even further. She puts forward that:

> Communities earn the right to be involved in the definition and management of the ICH because they 'own' it. The notion of ownership here is more like intellectual property ownership than ownership of a thing, however. It emerges out of the development and practice of a particular form of ICH in that community over time ...[94]

This interpretation of communities' ownership of intangible cultural heritage, advocated by Deacon, may seem at odds with UNESCO's stand which makes all efforts towards clear and accurate defining.[95] Since the ICH Convention lacks specifics defining ownership, challenges arise between communal rights and potential restrictions on non-members seeking use of intangible cultural heritage. Intangible cultural heritage is conventionally considered to be in the public domain and thus accessible to, and appropriable by, anyone. Many scholars, communities, NGOs and international organizations recognize this as the current *status quo*. For instance, the UN Conference on Trade and Development (UNCTAD), together with the International Centre for Trade and Sustainable Development (ICTSD), admits that "[i]n most countries, all [traditional knowledge] anywhere in the world that has not been kept secret is generally treated as being the intellectual property of nobody."[96]

The critics of this situation put forward that, secret or not, traditional knowledge and traditional cultural expressions belong to those who are their custodians. Accordingly, Kuruk criticizes the ICH Convention since it could have "affirmed the inalienable rights of indigenous communities to their intangible cultural heritage."[97] Those who advocate for the proprietary rights of communities condemn the Convention as a failure to prevent any misappropriation of by the non-members of affected communities. However, it is beyond any doubt that the express recognition of communal proprietary rights to intangible cultural heritage evokes controversy. This is especially true since individual community ownership directly contradicts the ideal of universal ownership for the good of all humanity.

---

94 H. Deacon, *Expert Report: Harriet Deacon*, at 1 (13–15 March 2006) (paper presented at *UNESCO/ACCU Expert Meeting on Community Involvement in Safeguarding Intangible Cultural Heritage: Towards the Implementation of the 2003 Convention*, Tokyo, Japan), *available at* www.accu.or.jp/ich/en/pdf/c2006Expert_DEACON_1.pdf (last visited 31 July 2008).

95 *See* UNESCO, *supra* note 88 ("ownership of specific forms of intangible cultural heritage by groups or communities is difficult to define, and will be an important issue of discussion for the future Intergovernmental Committee for the Safeguarding of the Intangible Cultural Heritage").

96 ICTSD and UNCTAD, *Intellectual Property Rights: Implications for Development*, 2003, 118.

97 *See id.*

In addition to ownership, active participation by concerned communities, groups and individuals throughout all stages is another central requirement for efficient safeguarding measures and adequate achievement of expected outcomes. Thus, the ICH Convention calls for planning and executing safeguarding measures "with the participation of communities, groups and relevant non-governmental organizations."[98] Moreover, Article 15 recites that "[w]ithin the framework of its safeguarding activities of the intangible cultural heritage, each State Party shall endeavour to ensure the widest possible participation of communities, groups and, where appropriate, individuals that create, maintain and transmit such heritage, and to involve them actively in its management."[99] Yet the text again provides only a framework and lacks absolute precision and clarity.

At the UNESCO-ACCU Expert Meeting on Community Involvement in Safeguarding Intangible Cultural Heritage, the experts agreed the focus lie not with products but with the practices and processes creating those products. Accordingly, the practitioners must play a pivotal role in safeguarding their heritage. Under the Convention, there may be varied ways on how to generate inventories, but the various stakeholders should cooperate, since both bottom-up and top-down approaches are indispensable for adequate and efficient designing and implementing of safeguarding measures on the national and international levels.

Following much debate, the experts therefore agreed on how the State Parties should involve communities, groups and in certain cases, individuals in inventory-making through: (1) requiring proper identification of communities or groups and their representatives; (2) ensuring that only intangible cultural heritage that is recognized by communities and groups is inventoried, or proposed for listing; (3) ensuring that the permission of communities and groups is obtained for inventorying; (4) ensuring the prior consent of communities when involving non-community members; (5) respecting customary practices governing the access to intangible cultural heritage; and (6) ensuring the free, prior and informed consent of communities and groups for nominating their intangible cultural heritage for the lists of intangible cultural heritage under the ICH Convention. Although the results of the expert meeting summarized in the *Conclusions and Recommendations of the UNESCO-ACCU Expert Meeting*[100] can be used as helpful guidance in the implementation and application of the ICH Convention, there are still unsolved issues and unanswered questioned in relation to actual operation of cooperation between communities and agencies implementing safeguarding measures under the terms of prior informed consent granted by affected communities. How important is the community's prior informed consent in the process of inventory

98 ICH Convention, *supra* note 1, Article 11(b).

99 *Id.*, Article 15.

100 *See* UNESCO/ACCU, *supra* note 91, at 12–15.

making and even in research efforts? How can their prior informed consent be achieved in an adequate and efficient way? Who represents the community? And so on.

2.3. POSSIBLE IMPACTS ON COMMUNITIES AND THEIR HERITAGE

The drafters of the ICH Convention attempted to devise an operational document, yet several critiques examine potential shortcomings and measurable success. The Convention design concentrated not merely on listing traditional knowledge, cultural expressions and other practices but in the institutionalization of activities, projects and programs created to safeguard the continued practice of intangible cultural heritage. However, from the beginning, many opposed requiring State Parties to create their own inventories. Amongst others, Brown argues that reducing cultural heritage to a mere list of items represents a major flaw in the Convention. Doing so contradicts the ideal of safeguarding since heritage can never be equated to, much less encapsulated by, a list.[101] Sarah Zoogman puts it succinctly: "Documentation Doesn't Keep My Heritage Alive!"[102] Heritage is continuously moving, evolving, and codification might stifle the creativity and spontaneity associated with it. According to other scholars, documentation and archiving of intangible cultural heritage can fossilize and objectify traditional cultural expressions and practices as they are translated or embodied in films, texts, recordings and other tangible forms and media.[103] Others criticize it as the formalization or institutionalization of something supposedly intangible. They suggest that such, rather oxymoronic approach presents some kind of schizophrenia.

The logistics of documentation similarly worries many scholars and governmental bureaucrats. It can divert limited resources of cultural workers and governmental agencies from genuine safeguarding via substantial programs to bureaucratization of significant processes in identifying and listing traditional practices.

Another argument against inventorying is the vulnerability of the listed or documented intangible cultural heritage to misappropriation, knowledge theft or even bio-piracy which is defined by Graham Dutfield as "the ways that individuals and corporations from the developed world free ride on the genetic resources and

---

101 *See* Brown, *supra* note 37.

102 S. Zoogman, "Documentation Doesn't Keep My Heritage Alive!", *Tourist Productions*, 6 November 2005, *available at* www.nyu.edu/classes/bkg/touristblog/archives/2005/11/documentation_d.html (last visited 31 July 2008).

103 *See* Kreps, *supra* note 40.

traditional knowledge and technologies of the developing countries."[104] Among others, Brown warns that inventorying may lead to a situation where documented and inventoried intangible cultural heritage may be more "readily commandeered by musicians, novelists, pharmaceutical companies, the motion-picture industry – indeed, by anyone positioned to take advantage of an intellectual property system".[105] The WIPO also recognized the possible negative outcomes of inventory making, to wit:

> ICH inventory-making can inadvertently facilitate the misappropriation, misuse and commercialization of [traditional cultural expressions] to the detriment of their source communities and cultures; for example, digitizing and making accessible a traditional song can, while valuably contributing to the safeguarding of the song, enable the song to be copied and commercialized by a third party, so raising concerns as to its legal protection.[106]

The counterargument to these concerns is documenting intangible cultural heritage represents a better option than inaction. Videotaping traditional forms of singing, dancing or other performance may stem abandonment and certainly prevent outright disappearance. Rather than allowing a practice to vanish completely, recording provides a chance for future recovery. Exhibits, museum pieces and documentation through media may also raise the awareness of dying practices and inspire youth to bear the torch. This may also lead to increased support from the government, local authorities and organizations. In fact, there are situations where people who try to revive some parts of intangible cultural heritage are not based at all in the concerned community but are actually outsiders. If this is the case, can it still count as safeguarding of intangible cultural heritage when the non-members of affected community are the ones working towards re-creation?

A further possible negative impact of inappropriate measures in relation to intangible cultural heritage concerns communities themselves. Indigenous, traditional and other local communities are mostly informal, non-institutionalized groupings of people bound by ancestral lands, cultural spaces and traditions. In many such communities, there are no elections; rather, the oldest or wisest members of communities are heralded as spiritual leaders. Sometimes, a council of elders decides the fate of the group or charts its future. A system of governance

104 Dutfield, *supra* note 50, at ix.

105 Brown, *supra* note 37.

106 WIPO Secretariat, *Information Note*, at 2 (13–15 March 2006) (paper presented at *UNESCO/ACCU Expert Meeting on Community Involvement in Safeguarding Intangible Cultural Heritage: Towards the Implementation of the 2003 Convention*, Tokyo, Japan), *available at* www.accu.or.jp/ich/en/pdf/c2006Expert_UEMURA.pdf (last visited 31 July 2008).

may not necessarily be absent, but certainly it may seem primitive – at least in the eyes of Westerners or majority population – if compared to their standards.

As mentioned above, the ICH Convention mandates State Parties generate national inventories of intangible cultural heritage. Once the State Party sends out its field researchers and scholars into the countryside, these governmental agents will be forced to seek out the "leader" or "head" of a community to verify and document their existing intangible cultural heritage. Whether for an electronic database format or a simple written list, the State Party must coordinate its safeguarding activities with the communities in a grassroots manner. But there is a couple of remaining questions such as follows: Who will represent communities in case there are no leaders or if there is a plenitude of representatives? Who will be possible to prove beyond reasonable doubts that someone is the sovereign authority within a community? The hallmarks of democracy may not necessarily be found in deep intricacies of smaller or larger communities. Thus, even sincere efforts to implement the ICH Convention may force communities to formalize their structures or establish a hierarchy when originally they have neither. This poses a serious obstacle since the listing or itemizing of intangible cultural heritage may consequently lead to a change in the norms followed for centuries by affected communities.

However, the aforesaid dangers concerning the making, documenting and digitizing of intangible cultural heritage inventories may be eclipsed by the expected benefits of record making. For instance, in 2004, Cambodia published its first book on the inventory of its intangible cultural heritage. It describes in detail the diversity of Cambodian arts, such as performing arts, oral traditions, minority languages, folklore, poetry, artisan craftsmanship, literature, handicraft making and others. It resulted from enormous research work. UNESCO characterized it as a great initiative to revitalize the "outstanding cultural heritage of Cambodia, which was seriously damaged during the nearly thirty years of conflicts."[107] Given that most of the practitioners of intangible cultural heritage in Cambodia have disappeared[108], record keeping may be the best way, perhaps the only way, for Cambodian intangible cultural heritage to remain intact. Yes, there are dangers. But they are severely outweighed by the need to perpetuate intangible cultural heritage and to draw national and global awareness to their possible extinction.

Indonesia is another good example. With the largest Muslim population and the most islands, more than 17,000 islands, of any nation, Indonesia is very multi-

---

107 UNESCO, *Presentation of a New Book: An Inventory of the Intangible Cultural Heritage in Cambodia*, http://portal.unesco.org/en/ev.php-URL_ID=19674&URL_DO=DO_PRINTPAGE&URL_SECTION=201.html (last visited 12 March 2007).

108 *Id.* (claiming that "90% of the artists, musicians, actors, playwrights and poets perished during the Khmer Rouge period").

cultural and multi-ethnic, with 500 languages and more than 500 different cultures. Its government has not done much to protect intangible cultural heritage since it is concerned more with economic and political affairs. Regional governments are also rather helpless in this regard. Spearheaded by organizations and individuals, and backed by the central and provincial governments, list-making activities have, however, been underway. They are either in the form of inventories, monographs or encyclopaedias. Regional data collection and digitization of intangible cultural heritage, coordination with governmental cultural bodies and foreign researchers, uploading of the data collected into a system, and development of a new system of data gathering in the entire Indonesia are the steps of their intangible cultural heritage inventory-making schema.[109] In this regard, its documentation and digitization are the only options if intangible cultural heritage is to be kept afloat in such a highly dense country. It is apparent that inventory making, in most cases, is the boon to, not a bane of, the slow but steady disappearance of intangible cultural heritage in modern societies.

In view of both examples, State Parties face serious obstacles that require surmounting so the ICH Convention spirit becomes practice. UNESCO is clearly aware of challenges and potential flaws:

> The challenge is whether and, if yes, how documentation might contribute to continued transmission in traditional ways and how it may contribute to the development of new forms of transmission, in both types of cases without in the act freezing the element in question ... [I]t is often feared that documentation of a living tradition may contribute to its standardization. The establishment of, for instance, one canonical text for an epic tradition which knows a lot of variation and, in fact, is constantly recreated, would not be in the spirit of the Convention.[110]

Overall, the ICH Convention epitomizes a great effort on the part of international community in the recognition of the existence and need to protect intangible cultural heritage. It counterbalances the World Heritage Convention, which admittedly favours monumental or material heritage. However, it may potentially bring both benefits and disadvantages to communities. But, at the same time, certainly, it is a work in progress and each involved stakeholder has to do his best in order to efficiently safeguard the variety of intangible cultural heritage for future generations. Kuruk points out that "the instrument could best be seen as providing

---

109 S. Hastanto, *Inventory of Intangible Cultural Heritage in Indonesia* (13–16 December 2005) (paper presented at the Sub-Regional Experts Meeting in Asia on *Intangible Cultural Heritage: Safeguarding and Inventory-Making Methodologies*, Bangkok, Thailand), *available at* www.accu.or.jp/ich/en/pdf/c2005subreg_Indo.pdf (last visited 31 July 2008).

110 UNESCO, *Expert Meeting on Documenting and Archiving Intangible Cultural Heritage*, at 7, CLT/CH/ITH/DOCEM0106 (12–13 January 2006), *available at* http://unesdoc.unesco.org/images/0014/001445/144592e.pdf (last visited 31 July 2008).

general guidelines in the hope that contracting States would 'adopt appropriate legal, technical, administrative and financial' measures"[111], but definitely it is not a missed opportunity to advance the cause of the Indigenous people.

3. CONCLUSION

Despite being a member of the Japanese delegation significantly involved in drafting the ICH Convention, I have to sincerely acknowledge that its text suffers from peculiar flaws, which, while serious, can and must be overcome. The definitions found within the text are manifestly lacking both in specificity and substance, and the informal re-introduction of the Glossary is most needed. Admittedly, the "shall endeavour" types of obligations undertaken by State Parties weaken the overarching objectives of the ICH Convention and make it somewhat a best-efforts approach.

These shortcomings, however, do not detract from the fact that the ICH Convention is an important document for the future of intangible cultural heritage. It presents a viable tool for protecting the cultural traditions of individual communities and mankind. It steers attention away from mere monumental or material heritage to those that are intangible, invisible, spiritual. It emphasizes the plight of the Indigenous peoples – populations of long-neglected persons who have fervently practiced their intangible cultural heritage despite the fact that they have endured long time of colonization and cultural destruction. Indeed, the text of the ICH Convention suffers from certain cracks but these gaps can still be ameliorated through the collaborative efforts of the organs of the ICH Convention, State Parties, communities and individuals.

It is still a new document, and any form of experimentation almost always takes places. But given the passage of years and the gaining of experience, all of these international bodies, State Parties and other stakeholders will be able to coalesce and sail in the same direction. It may take some time, but democratized safeguarding does take time. To focus on the people who create and re-create intangible cultural heritage, despite the vast efforts and time needed, is critical. It is therefore on point to say that in the safeguarding and preserving of cultural heritage for future generations, we must not only focus on the masterpieces, but more importantly, on their masters and craftsmen.[112]

---

111 Kuruk, *supra* note 86 (quoting the ICH Convention, *supra* note 1, Article 13(d)).

112 *See* B. Kirshenblatt-Gimblett, "Intangible Heritage as Metacultural Production", 56 *Museum Int'l* 52 (2004).

PART TWO
DESIGNING A MEANS FOR THE SAFEGUARDING OF INTANGIBLE CULTURAL HERITAGE

INTANGIBLE CULTURAL HERITAGE IDENTIFIED

Inventories as an Essential Part of the Safeguarding Process

Steven VAN UYTSEL and Toshiyuki KONO*

Safeguarding intangible cultural heritage is only possible if the intangible cultural heritage is identified. Without proper and adequate identification of intangible cultural heritage, no steps can be taken to ensure its viability, regardless of the form it takes. The *Convention for the Safeguarding of the Intangible Cultural Heritage* (ICH Convention)[1] acknowledges this issue in two different ways. First, Article 2 of the ICH Convention puts forward a definition of what intangible cultural heritage is for the purposes of the Convention, thus establishing an internationally accepted standard to identify intangible cultural heritage. Second, Article 12 of the ICH Convention requires the State Parties to incorporate this identified intangible cultural heritage in inventories. Inventories in the context of safeguarding intangible cultural heritage have sparked quite some discussion, justifying it as a separate part of the present volume.

---

* STEVEN VAN UYTSEL, LL.B., LL.M. (University of Antwerp), LL.M., LL.D. (Kyushu University); Assistant Professor, Kyushu University Faculty of Law; TOSHIYUKI KONO, Professor of Law, Kyushu University Faculty of Law.

1 Convention for the Safeguarding of the Intangible Cultural Heritage, 17 October 2003, U.N. Doc. MISC/2003/CLT/CH/14 (2003), *available at* http://unesdoc.unesco.org/images/0013/001325/132540e.pdf (last visited 31 July 2008) [hereinafter "ICH Convention"].

This introductory Chapter to this Part begins by providing a brief overview of the antecedents of inventory making. It continues by outlining how inventory making is incorporated in the safeguarding regimes under the ICH Convention. Then, this introduction sketches out the different issues that are currently raised in relation to inventory making. Finally, the individual authors' contributions to this Part are introduced.

1. INVENTORY MAKING AND ITS ANTECEDENTS

The idea of establishing inventories of what would be now called intangible cultural heritage is nothing new.[2] Whether we refer to compilations of ancient mythologies, fables, legends, folktales or fairy tales, they all represent an early form of making inventories of what we would now call intangible cultural heritage. Some of these compilations, such as Homer's *Ilias*, Virgil's *Aneid*, *The Book on One Thousand and One Night*'s *Aladdin's Wonderful Lamp* or the Brother Grimm's *Children and Household Tales*, are still very popular and well-known these days. The main characteristic of these compilations – earlier forms of inventories, so to say – is that, with some exceptions, they originated and grew from private local initiatives. The ICH Convention differs. States now take on a binding legal obligation to make inventories. However, also here the ICH Convention has its precedents.

On the international level, early efforts of setting up an inventory of intangible cultural heritage can be traced back to the 1980s. At that time, the United Nations Educational, Scientific and Cultural Organization (UNESCO) made an attempt to establish an *International Directory of Non-physical Cultural Heritage* (International Directory).[3] However, these efforts ended in a deadlock caused by the fundamentally different scientific and research methods within respective fields of research, especially cultural anthropology and musicology. Whereas the object of study of cultural anthropologists is the traditional cultures in their entirety, folklorists mainly focus on the study of the forms in which these cultures are expressed. These methodological differences led to a disagreement between both groups of specialists about a universal standard typology and a universal classification system for non-physical cultural heritage. In the end, the disagreement showed itself to be insurmountable, and finally buried the entire endeavour.

2 *See* N. Aikawa, "Challenges for National Inventories of Intangible Cultural Heritage", in *2004 Workshop on Inventory-making for Intangible Cultural Heritage Management: Final Report*, 2005, 43, *available at* www.accu.or.jp/ich/en/pdf/2004_Tokyo.pdf (last visited 31 July 2008).

3 *See id.* at 43.

The efforts to provide adequate and sufficient protection to traditional cultures and folklore against the negative consequences of industrialization, modernization and other modern global social phenomena bore fruit in 1989, when UNESCO adopted the *Recommendation for the Safeguarding of Traditional Culture and Folklore* (Recommendation).[4] In the Recommendation, identification of traditional culture and folklore in regional and global registers was put forward as one of the six measures necessary to efficiently safeguard traditional cultures and folklore. National institutions active in the field of folklore were supposed to make inventories that could be incorporated into a regional or global register. For this purpose, it was essential to create and develop identification and recording systems in such a way that a coordinated classification approach within the different institutions could be established. Besides this, the Recommendation encouraged its Member States to create a standard typology of folklore.

Nevertheless, like the International Directory, the Recommendation was not a great success. It failed for several reasons. The insistence on regional or, if possible, universal classification of folklore obviously showed that few lessons were drawn from the failure of the International Directory. Moreover, it became obvious that the safeguarding techniques subscribed to in this Recommendation did not respond to the needs and the wishes of those to whom the traditional cultures and folklore (nowadays we speak about intangible cultural heritage) are precious. Rather than focusing on the participation of the communities, the Recommendation regarded the role of researchers as much more important.[5] Ironically enough for the inventory making issue, the latter would have meant a prominent role for the tangible form of intangible cultural heritage, such as archives and other documentation centres.[6]

A more moderate approach to creating a list of intangible cultural heritage was put forward in the UNESCO program of the *Proclamation of Masterpieces of Oral and Intangible Cultural Heritage of Humanity* (Proclamation of Masterpieces).[7] Under the Proclamation of Masterpieces, the *List of the Masterpieces of the Oral and Intangible Heritage of Humanity* (List of Masterpieces) was created. The List of Masterpieces did not aim at categorizing intangible cultural heritage according to universal criteria. Rather, its main purpose was to

4 Recommendation on the Safeguarding of Traditional Culture and Folklore, 15 November 1989, *available at* http://portal.unesco.org/en/ev.php-URL_ID=13141&URL_DO=DO_TOPIC&URL_SECTION=201.html (last visited 31 July 2008).

5 *See* A. McCann *et al.*, "The 1989 Recommendation Ten Years On: Towards a Critical Analysis", in P. Seitel (ed.), *Safeguarding Traditional Cultures: A Global Assessment*, 2001, 56.

6 *See* N. Aikawa, "An Historical Overview of the Preparation of the UNESCO International Convention for the Safeguarding of the Intangible Cultural Heritage", 56 *Museum* 140 (2004).

7 *See* United Nations Educational, Scientific and Cultural Organization (UNESCO), *The Oral Heritage of Humanity*, 12 November 1997, 29C/Resolution 23. *See also* UNESCO, *Proclamation of the Masterpieces of the Oral and Intangible Heritage of Humanity (2001–2005)*, www.unesco.org/culture/ich/index.php?pg=00103 (last visited 31 July 2008).

raise awareness by rewarding two types of expressions of intangible cultural heritage: popular and traditional cultural expressions and cultural spaces.[8] Due to the awareness raising purpose, the cultural expressions and cultural spaces proposed for the Proclamation of the Masterpieces could be judged without the need for selection criteria that rely on universal standards. The selection criteria did, for example, require only a demonstration of an outstanding value, and not a universal outstanding value.[9] In doing so, UNESCO provided some leeway for local elements to be given importance.

2. INVENTORYING UNDER THE ICH CONVENTION

Based upon the success of the Masterpieces program, the ICH Convention gave greater prominence and broader scope to the concept of making directories, recordings, collections, catalogues, transcripts, registers or lists as an important part of adequate and efficient safeguarding of intangible cultural heritage. As pointed out above, no efficient safeguarding measures can be taken without actual knowledge of the existence of a specific heritage. The heritage to be safeguarded has to be known. Hence, visibility has been stressed in order to take further steps in the safeguarding process. Depending on the level of safeguarding, the abovementioned concepts have been translated into "inventories" which are to include the entire intangible cultural heritage on the national level.[10] In addition, the *Representative List of Intangible Cultural Heritage of Humanity* (Representative List)[11] and the *List of Intangible Cultural Heritage in Need of Urgent Safeguarding* (List in Need of Urgent Safeguarding)[12] are established on the international level. The former is an obligation for the State Parties, while the latter two are an obligation for the international organs responsible under the ICH Convention.

All three concepts appear in an earlier instrument of UNESCO, the 1972 *Convention Concerning the Protection of the World Cultural and Natural Heritage*

---

8 *See* UNESCO, *Selection Procedure for the Masterpieces of the Oral and Intangible Heritage of Humanity (2001–2005)*, www.unesco.org/culture/ich/index.php?pg=00105 (last visited 31 July 2008).

9 *Compare* Convention Concerning the Protection of the World Cultural and Natural Heritage, Article 1, 16 November 1972, *available at* http://whc.unesco.org/en/conventiontext/(last visited 31 July 2008) [hereinafter "World Heritage Convention"].

10 *See* N. Aikawa-Faure, "UNESCO Convention for the Safeguarding of Intangible Cultural Heritage – from its Adoption to the First Meeting of the Intergovernmental Committee", in Kokuritsu Bunkazai Kikou, Tokyo Bunkazai Kenkyujo and Mukei Bunka Isanbu, *Safeguarding Intangible Cultural Heritage: International Cooperation and the Role of Japan,* 2008, 13, 21–25, *available at* www.tobunken.go.jp/~geino/pdf/sympo/07KeynoteSpeech 2Aikawa.pdf (last visited 31 July 2008).

11 ICH Convention, *supra* note 1, Article 16.

12 *See id.*, Article 17.

(World Heritage Convention).[13] The *World Heritage List*[14] and the *List of World Heritage in Danger*[15] correspond to the Representative List and the List in Need of Urgent Safeguarding, respectively. Contrary to the approach taken by international organizations, when national governments have addressed inventories in the two conventions they have negotiated, they give inventories a slightly different meaning. The World Heritage Convention requires national inventories of property forming part of cultural and natural heritage with a view to establishing the World Heritage List. Correspondingly, the inventories form part of the nomination process. In this capacity, inventories have not provoked any considerable controversy.[16] Even though it may be said that the national inventories in the ICH Convention are also part of the nomination process, the fact that they have to be created outside the framework of the nomination process for the respective lists suggests that the concept is part of a broader obligation for Member States under the ICH Convention.

3. CONTROVERSIES, CONCEPTUAL DILEMMAS AND INTELLECTUAL PROPERTY RIGHTS

The broader obligation to establish inventories of national intangible cultural heritage has provoked several controversies, created conceptual dilemmas, and raised concerns from an intellectual property rights perspective. The controversy mainly relates to the use of inventories as a means to safeguard heritage. On the one hand, this means of safeguarding has been described as outdated, while on the other hand it has been criticized for creating too much visibility of intangible cultural heritage. The conceptual dilemmas result in part from the absence of any criteria as to how the inventories should be framed. Concerns over intellectual property rights were raised as a logical consequence of creating instruments to which copyright applies. Beyond this conventional intellectual property issue, concerns have been formulated in relation to the proper legal protection of the rights and interests of local communities and Indigenous people to whom a specific intangible cultural heritage should be linked.

---

13 World Heritage Convention, *supra* note 9; *See also* Aikawa-Faure, *supra* note 9, at 21–25.

14 World Heritage Convention, *supra* note 9, Article 11(2).

15 *See id.*, Article 11(4).

16 The absence of controversy may be deduced from the fact that a similar concept of inventory was introduced in the first draft leading up to the ICH Convention, *supra* note 1. *See* UNESCO, *First Preliminary Draft of an International Convention for the Safeguarding of the Intangible Cultural Heritage*, Article 11, CLT-2002/CONF.203/3 (26 July 2002), *available at* http://unesdoc.unesco.org/ulis/cgi-bin/ulis.pl?catno=127018&gp=0&mode=e&lin=1 (last visited 31 July 2008).

3.1. THE REFLECTION OF THE SPECIFIC NEEDS OF INTANGIBLE CULTURAL HERITAGE IN THE INVENTORY

The usefulness of inventories as a means of safeguarding has been questioned on the basis that it is ill-suited to preserve intangible cultural heritage as a *living system*.[17] Based upon previous experiences with some government funded preservation efforts, there is a genuine fear that these inventories will have a freezing effect on intangible cultural heritage. Mainly for this reason, inventory making has been called a discredited methodology or "oddly reminiscent of early anthropology."[18] The opponents further argue that inventory making cannot lead to encouraging cultural vitality. They warn that inventories can divert too many resources, be they human, material or financial, from more urgent safeguarding activities. In addition, the scale of such projects may be so huge that they become never-ending tasks. This might be especially true for multiethnic states.

The opponents' critique towards inventory making may be caused by an oversimplification of why inventory making has to be included in the ICH Convention. Proponents have made a reference to other cultural property, especially monument and archaeological sites. For this kind of cultural property, they have concluded that inventory making has turned out to be successful.[19] They therefore have argued that inventory making could also be deemed as a rational way for identifying intangible cultural heritage. It is obvious that this reasoning by analogy does not address any of the problems identified by opponents of inventory making. To tackle these problems it is necessary to recognize the difference between tangible and intangible cultural heritage and the special needs that may flow from these differences.

The special needs in the safeguarding of intangible cultural heritage have been widely discussed during the drafting process of the ICH Convention. Without going into detail[20], this debate raised a conceptual dilemma of how to regulate the inventories and their operation under the Convention. The drafters could either put forward a rigid framework for intangible cultural heritage inventories or, on the contrary, they could be very vague about the required framework. Political and practical concerns seem to have driven them to the second option.[21] During

---

17 *See* M.F. Brown, "Heritage Trouble: Recent Work on the Protection of Intangible Cultural Heritage", 12 *Int'l J. Cult. Prop.* 48 (2005).

18 *Id.* at 48.

19 *See* J. Blake, *Commentary on the UNESCO 2003 Convention on the Safeguarding of Intangible Cultural Heritage*, 2006, 63.

20 These special needs include, among others, the living nature of intangible cultural heritage, participation of communities, or the sensitive nature of intangible cultural heritage.

21 *See* Blake, *supra* note 19, at 63–64.

the second session of the Intergovernmental Meeting of Experts on the *Preliminary Draft Convention for the Safeguarding of the Intangible Cultural Heritage*, several states made it clear that state sovereignty should be respected as much as possible when drafting the state's obligations.[22] An overly prescriptive framework for national inventories would not have complied with these concerns. Furthermore, it was also made clear that not all states have the same financial resources, making it difficult to work with a uniformly defined inventorying framework. Therefore, the ICH Convention reflects a flexible approach toward the instruments necessary for safeguarding intangible cultural heritage.

3.2. INTELLECTUAL PROPERTY CONCERNS IN RELATION TO AN INVENTORY

An issue indirectly addressed during the negotiation of the ICH Convention was intellectual property rights. This issue became much more visible in the 2005 *Expert Meeting on Inventorying Intangible Cultural Heritage*.[23] The keynote speech of the session on *Management and Ownership of Intangible Cultural Heritage* directly linked inventory making with intellectual property rights.[24] This link, as it appears, is quite complex. On the one hand, an inventory, depending on the content, may facilitate the misuse and misappropriation of intangible cultural heritage and thereby jeopardize any attempt to safeguard the intangible cultural heritage. Intellectual property law, eventually adjusted to the interests and the needs of bearers of the intangible cultural heritage, could prevent this from happening. On the other hand, these inventories may be used as a tool to prevent misuse and misappropriation. More specifically, the inventories could be used as proof of prior art in patent applications.

The discussions on how these intellectual property issues can be solved continue to be held within the World Intellectual Property Organization (WIPO). The discussions follow two different lines. First, the WIPO Intergovernmental Committee on Intellectual Property and Genetic Resources, Traditional Knowledge and Folklore concentrates on the debate of whether traditional cultural expressions and traditional knowledge needs a *sui generis*

---

22 *See id.* at 63.

23 UNESCO, *Report of the Expert Meeting on Inventorying Intangible Cultural Heritage* (17–18 March 2005), *available at* www.unesco.org/culture/ich/doc/src/00036-EN.pdf (last visited 31 July 2008).

24 *See id.* at 29–30 (containing the keynote speech by W.B. Wendland on management and ownership of intangible cultural heritage).

approach for its protection.[25] Second, through their *Creative Heritage Project*[26], WIPO is learning from real practices about the managing of intellectual property issues and options during the recording, digitization and dissemination of intangible cultural heritage. Based on these experiences, WIPO develops guidelines aiming to assist communities and cultural institutions to deal with the intellectual property issues. In doing so, they give advice on how to harmonize the *protection* aspect of intellectual property law with the *safeguarding* aspect of intangible cultural heritage law.

4. CONTRIBUTIONS

In this Part, the contributors address numerous of the above-mentioned, bewildering issues. Antonio A. Arantes's contribution deals with the necessity of having inventories as part of the safeguarding process. He further elaborates on the possible pitfalls to avoid when drawing up an intangible cultural heritage inventory.[27] Wend B. Wendland focuses on the intellectual property issues in relation to intangible cultural heritage and its inventory making. This contribution provides an overview of the activities WIPO is taking in this regard.[28] Vinod K. Gupta gives, by describing the Traditional Knowledge Digital Library (TKDL) project, an example of how an inventory can be used as a tool against misuse and misappropriation of intangible cultural heritage. At the same time, this chapter offers an insight in how an inventory can be constructed.[29] Steven Van Uytsel combines these different conclusions and scrutinizes them alongside the provisions of the ICH Convention to investigate the real scope of the Convention. This exercise is illustrated by reference to some earlier projects of compiling intangible cultural heritage, mainly the compilation of the Brothers Grimm, Perrault and Basile.[30]

---

25 The establishment of the WIPO Intergovernmental Committee on Intellectual Property and Genetic Resources, Traditional Knowledge and Folklore (Intergovernmental Committee) was agreed to at the 26th (12th Extraordinary) Session of WIPO's General Assembly, held from 25 September to 3 October 2000. All working documents, comments, papers, studies, databases, questionnaires, and other materials prepared for consideration by the Intergovernmental Committee, as well as comprehensive reports of its sessions, are publicly available, in English, French and Spanish; *see* WIPO, *Intergovernmental Committee*, www.wipo.int/tk/en/igc (last visited 31 July 2008).

26 *See* WIPO, *Creative Heritage Project: IP Guidelines for Documenting, Recording and Digitizing Intangible Cultural Heritage*, www.wipo.int/tk/en/folklore/culturalheritage/index.html (last visited 31 July 2008).

27 *See* Chapter [Arantes] of the present volume.

28 *See* Chapter [Wendland] of the present volume.

29 *See* Chapter [Gupta] of the present volume.

30 *See* Chapter [Van Uytsel] of the present volume.

HERITAGE AS CULTURE

Limits, Uses and Implications of Intangible Cultural Heritage Inventories

Antonio A. ARANTES*

1. INTRODUCTION

Inventories are a widely used and useful procedure of heritage policy both for tangible and intangible culture. However, they are a controversial topic among anthropologists, particularly in the case of performances, songs, narratives or traditional knowledge. This Chapter focuses on the difficult topic of inventory-

* B.A., M.Sc. (São Paulo University); PhD (Cambridge University); Social Anthropologist. The author has taught and developed research in Brazil, Argentina, Mexico, France, Portugal, United States and England. Past President of the Brazilian Anthropological Association (ABA), of the Latin American Anthropological Association (ALA), as well as of the São Paulo State Council for Historical Preservation (CONDEPHAAT) and of the National Institute for Historic and Artistic Heritage (IPHAN), where he implemented the creation of the Department of Immaterial Heritage and the National Program for Immaterial Heritage. As a consultant of cultural policies, he collaborated in several programs developed by governmental and non-governmental institutions, created the methodology and supervised the pilot project for the establishment of the National Inventory of Cultural References in Brazil, gave workshops on inventory methods in Madagascar and in Mozambique, and participated in several national and international experts' meetings, particularly in France, Japan and India, under the auspices of the United Nations Educational, Scientific and Cultural Organization (UNESCO) and the Asia/Pacific Cultural Centre for UNESCO (ACCU). Developed several academic research projects and published books, articles and technical reports about cultural heritage in the context of contemporary social experience, and on related subjects.

making methodology and discusses some conceptual issues raised by the *Convention for the Safeguarding of the Intangible Cultural Heritage* (ICH Convention)[1], as well as on the uses and consequences of cultural inventories regarding intellectual property rights.

Preservation can only be sustainable, and therefore effective, if the internationally agreed parameters set by multilateral conventions and the constraints, demands and possibilities existing in specific local and national contexts are adequately mediated. Consequently, even if sharing a common legal and conceptual background, methodologies and research strategies will vary according to the singular contexts in which they are implemented, not least of which include the local political priorities to which they should respond.

The present reflections derive from my participation in creating the tools and procedures that were adopted by the Brazilian National Inventory of Cultural References, as well as by the enlightening discussions that I carried on with Malagasy and Mozambican colleagues during workshops on inventory-making that I had the opportunity of performing in their countries. My previous experience in discussing these matters in international expert meetings and in various national contexts also provided important background for the delineation of some theoretical, technical and ethical issues that I will focus on in this Chapter and that appear to be widely recurrent.

2. PERSPECTIVES SET BY THE ICH CONVENTION

The ICH Convention is grounded on a theoretically refined understanding of cultural heritage and of its significance for the present world and its future. The very idea of *safeguarding* as ensuring the "viability"[2] of living and changeable practices to which specific human communities ascribe patrimonial value, as opposed to *preserving* cultural products, in defining its mission is a good example of that. One has to do here with social processes and the conditions under which they come into existence, not collections of frozen memorabilia.

Furthermore, according to the perspective set by *consideranda* of that legal document, the safeguarding of intangible cultural heritage responds to a "universal will and ... common concern"[3] based on the fact that its object is "a mainspring of cultural diversity"[4] and "a factor in bringing human beings closer together and

1 Convention for the Safeguarding of the Intangible Cultural Heritage, 17 October 2003, U.N. Doc. MISC/2003/CLT/CH/14 (2003), *available at* http://unesdoc.unesco.org/images/0013/001325/132540e.pdf (last visited 31 July 2008) [hereinafter "ICH Convention"].

2 ICH Convention, *supra* note 1, Article 2(3).

3 *Id.*, Preamble, par. 6.

4 *Id.*, Preamble, par. 3.

ensuring exchange and understanding among them".[5] These views are consistent with the idea that heritage concerns us all, individually and collectively, and that safeguarding it – as well as protecting cultural diversity and creativity – is a task to which the international community should contribute in a cooperative fashion, above local interests and constraints.

The ICH Convention assigns specific roles to States Parties as agents of the safeguarding process, since they have the prerogative of being members of its governing boards, namely the General Assembly of the States Parties and the Intergovernmental Committee for the Safeguarding of the Intangible Cultural Heritage (Committee).[6] As stated in Article 13, a country that ratifies the Convention becomes responsible for "the safeguarding, development and promotion of the intangible cultural heritage present in its [own] territory". As a pre-condition to the implementation of those measures at the national level, Article 11 establishes that each State Party shall "identify and define the various elements of the intangible cultural heritage present in its territory". Article 12(1) specifically requires the *identification* of the various elements of intangible cultural heritage by means of "regularly updated" inventories, drawn up "in a manner geared to its own situation". Article 15 requires that the ICH Convention be implemented with "the widest possible participation of the communities, groups and, where appropriate, individuals that create, maintain and transmit such heritage". Furthermore, the States Parties are expected to propose the inclusion of intangible cultural heritage elements existing in their territories in a *Representative List of the Intangible Cultural Heritage of Humanity*, and to request the adoption of specific measures for those in need of urgent safeguarding.[7]

The member-states' preservation institutions face important challenges when implementing these principles in practice. Some challenges result because not all cultural practices recognized as heritage by local or national cultural communities around the world necessarily fit the standards set by the Convention or by the recommendations and declarations that are reinforced by that instrument.[8] From the perspective set by the *Universal Declaration of Human Rights*[9], for example, which is perhaps the most important moral landmark of the ICH Convention, it is arguable whether the practice of female circumcision, which is not only practiced but highly valued in many societies as a strong symbol of identity, should be internationally recognized and proclaimed as an intangible cultural heritage item.

5 *Id.*, Preamble, par. 14.
6 *Id.*, Articles 4–9.
7 *Id.*, Articles 16 and 17, respectively.
8 As to other documents mentioned in the ICH Convention, *supra* note 1.
9 Universal Declaration of Human Rights, 10 December 1948, G.A. Res. 217A(III), U.N. Doc. A/810 at 71 (1948).

Another type of challenge has to do with what I would call the *politics of representation and decision-making* that effectively sets in motion the safeguarding programs and routines created by the Convention. Since not all social groups have equal access to the governmental institutions of their own countries, they may be inadequately represented – if at all – by the state's bureaucracy in the Convention's governing bodies. Besides that, how can diasporas or immigrant communities, living as minorities in host countries, benefit from that instrument and be represented in the human heritage mosaic produced by means of the Convention? How can one actually put in practice the moral principle that, as human beings and as members of the international community, the agents of such process share that "universal will and ... common concern" about cultural diversity?

These issues raise questions about what the cultural elements supported by this Convention are representative of, and about what contribution they can make to the common heritage of humanity. Consequently, these issues underlie the elaboration of lists of representative cultural elements, and are vital to inventory making.

Indeed, inventory making is a crucial step in the whole safeguarding process for two reasons. First, inventory making is crucial because it is the *finding* process of "cultural gems", so to say, or the means by which particular practices and forms of knowledge will – as others will not – be identified, set apart from the continuous flow of community life and eventually be (positively or negatively) affected by the actions implemented by this policy. Second, inventory making is crucial because it is, at least in two senses, the basis of the *founding* stage of heritage: it inaugurates the establishment of specific and continuous formal relationships between safeguarding agencies and cultural communities; and it must provide arguments and evidence for the legal-administrative process of formally ascribing heritage value to selected cultural items, on which depends their being legitimate registration, listing or classification as patrimony by the public authority.

The political constraints related to the recognition of representativeness of cultural items in their national contexts, and related to access to decision-making mechanisms and to the design and implementation of safeguarding policies, are dealt with by the ICH Convention in terms of "community participation". *Participation* is indeed an essential aspect of heritage preservation, as shall be argued in the following pages. It is stimulated by the abovementioned Article 15, whereas Article 9 creates an important – even if timid – practical mechanism for that purpose, opening the way for the accreditation of non-governmental organizations to act in an advisory capacity to the Committee.

3. INVENTORIES IN CONTEXT

Artefacts and art works, often classified as *material culture*, have long been targets of collectors' classifications, typologies, or taxonomies. Family assets, in their turn, are usually inventoried and evaluated before being effectively handed down from generation to generation, and collectors' taxonomies are often used for that purpose. In architectural and urban preservation, inventories also play a major role as tools for the identification of monuments, buildings, landscapes and sites of patrimonial value and therefore worthy of protection. The making of lists of material artefacts (movable goods or built structures) for the use of museums and other institutions dedicated to the conservation and promotion of documents or testimonies of cultural history is undoubtedly another well established procedure of this kind. But the spirit in which the ICH Convention was conceived requires a totally new approach to this topic in so far as it aims at protecting the processes by which cultures are produced in the context of the historical formations to which they belong – not just objects, but the social experiences that create and *nurture*[10] them; not only heritage value as attributed by external agencies (preservation institutions, academics or state bureaucracies), but also those ascribed by local cultures and embedded in cultural dynamics – this is what seems to be at stake when safeguarding is conceived as "ensuring the viability"[11] of living and changeable social practices. Both the products and their formation processes should be accounted for by cultural surveys and by the safeguarding action plans. This being the case, the following conceptual issues must be raised regarding heritage as part of cultural dynamics.

1. Cultures are not sets of *elements* or *cultural traits* relatively independent from one another as cultural policy planners might presume and diffusionists and evolutionists would have it in the last decades of the nineteenth century. Edward B. Tylor's *Primitive Culture*[12], published in 1871, and *The Golden Bough*[13], by Sir James George Frazer, published in 1922, are classical examples of these approaches. Modern anthropologists, in the early twentieth century, were critical of such views. Bronislaw Malinowski, who was one of the most influential of them, wrote in 1929:

---

10 I take this expression from K. Vatsyayan's lucid pronouncement at the opening session of the *Expert Meeting on the Lists Established by the 2003 Convention for the Safeguarding of the Intangible Cultural Heritage*, held in New Delhi, India, 2–4 April 2007.

11 ICH Convention, *supra* note 1, Article 2(3).

12 E.B. Tylor, *Primitive Culture: Researches into the Development of Mythology, Philosophy, Religion, Language, Art, and Custom*, 1871.

13 Sir J.G. Frazer, *The Golden Bough: A Study in Magic and Religion*, Macmillan, (abr. ed. 1922), 1890.

> The reconstructive theorist, whether evolutionary or diffusionist, is bound to regard every element of culture as extraneous to the context in which it is found. For the evolutionist is mainly interested in a fact as a survival from a past stage, while the diffusionist sees in it above all a mechanically conveyed importation from another geographical region. The one places it in a past time, the other in a distant place. But both remove the fact far from the actual surroundings where it now lives.[14]

Malinowsky's criticism to evolutionists and diffusionists became widely accepted by culture theorists. It implies, in relation to the present argument, that social practices, knowledge and forms of expression – having patrimonial value or not – are created, appropriated, amalgamated and developed, cherished or forgotten, by particular populations in specific times and places. Regardless of their origins, they provide the basic chart that gives meaning to peoples' shared experiences. Malinowsky's criticism also highlights the fact that cultural practices and their products pertain to *ways of life* and constitute the historical presents of real human beings; they are not fragments of past events, reminiscent of some golden age of cultural history. It suggests, furthermore, that the significance of these practices and products are grounded on the social contexts in which they are formed and transformed; in other words, on their systemic interrelations with other social practices.

These ideas lead to a central issue for inventory making, namely, that the identification of cultural references and their inclusion in heritage lists must take into account the practices with which they are interconnected as well as the resources (material and intellectual) that are needed for their production, reproduction and change in specific times and places.

2. The importance of contextual interconnections for the understanding of social realities was clearly formulated by Marcel Mauss, the celebrated author of the *Essai sur le don*.[15] His theory about social exchanges, published in the mid-1920s, introduces the idea that social facts condense at all levels of human experience. He puts it succinctly:

> Les faits que nous avons étudiés sont tous, qu'on nous permette l'expression, des faits sociaux *totaux* ... Tous ces phénomènes sont à la fois juridiques, économiques, religieux, et même esthétiques, morphologiques, etc.[16]

---

14 B. Malinowski, *The Sexual Life of Savages in North-Western Melanesia: An Ethnographic Account of Courtship, Marriage, and Family Life Among the Natives of the Trobriand Islands British New Guinea*, Routledge & Kegan Paul LTD, (edition 1968), (1929).

15 M. Mauss, "Essai sur le don", in M. Mauss (ed.), *Sociologie et anthropologie*, (3d ed., 1966) 145 (the essay was first published in *Année Sociologique*, Paris, 1924/25).

16 *Id.* at 274.

From the point of view of the specific issue discussed in this Chapter, this implies that the segmentation of any social fact must take into account the holistic nature of all things social, particularly its psychosocial dimension.

3. Indeed, the third premise to be taken into account in inventory making is that, as phrased by Mauss, "[d]ans les sociétés, on saisit plus que des idées ou des règles, on saisit des hommes, des groupes et leurs comportements. ... Nous apercevons des nombres d'hommes, des forces mobiles, et qui flottent dans leur milieu et dans leurs sentiments."[17] As Claude Lévi-Strauss stresses in his classical introduction to Mauss, total social facts are only observable in individual concrete experience, hence they necessarily incorporate subjectivity and sentiment, as well as history:

> [L]e fait total ne réussit pas à être tel par simple réintégration des aspects discontinus ... Il faut aussi que'il s'incarne dans une expérience individuelle, et cela ... d'abord dans une histoire individuelle que permette d'observer le comportement d'êtres totaux, et non divisés en facultés ...[18]
>
> Car la seule garantie que nous puissions avoir qu'un fait total correspond à la realité ... c'est qu'il soit saissable dans une expérience concrète.[19]

4. Furthermore, social realities should not be represented as static flashes, but as realities in motion, in at least two senses of the word: in the sense that they imply duration in time, and in the sense that they are changeable (not fixed) products of human agency. This implies that, as far as cultural processes are concerned, lists produced by surveys are necessarily dated and open-ended.

5. Inventories result from the segmentation of social reality *in flux* by classificatory systems of thought, which are intrinsically culturally biased.[20] Indeed, societies do not necessarily build theories about their own cultural practices, and do not sort out aspects of their social life in categories and types such as religion, art, economy, public ceremonies *etc.*, as Western thought has done for centuries. Pairs of clearly opposed categories such as material and immaterial, sacred and profane, religion and entertainment, politics and economy, do not necessarily make sense from the point of view of all cosmologies and worldviews. From the point of view of African traditions of thought, for example,

17 *Id.* at 276.
18 Cl. Lévi-Strauss, "Introduction à l'oeuvre de M. Mauss", in *Sociologie et anthropologie*, *supra* note 15, xxv (citation omitted).
19 *Id.* at xxvi.
20 *See* J. Goody, "Literacy and Classification: On Turning the Tables", in J. Goody (ed.), *The Domestication of the Savage Mind*, 1977, 52.

Olabiyi Babalola J. Yaï has made a clear statement about the inadequacy of such dichotomies: "[I]l faut se rendre à l'évidence que ces catégories aristotéliciennes ne sont pas des universaux philosophiques, et qu'elles cadrent mal avec le postulat de base des philosophies de la tradition africaine, pour lesquelles *tout est en tout* ... [ou] *l'immatériel est dans le matériel* ... [et] [l]es morts ne sont jamais morts non plus".[21] Similarly, know-how or artistic skills are not necessarily dissociated from other forms of participation in ritual performances, just as prayers and spells are not set apart from the activities in which people engage in their everyday life. Not all peoples reify the products of human agency as goods belonging to individual owners, as objects made for their aesthetic value or for commercial trade.

6. Cultures are reproduced and changed historically. The mechanisms by which the institutions, values and attitudes flow through time are not those of simple transmission of information from one generation to the next. Knowledge, forms of expression, beliefs, and sense of belonging are some ingredients embedded in social practice; they give the social structure its singular appearance.

So, the transmission of technologies, languages, codes and information are particular ways through which a social group reproduces and changes its structure and organization. It is not a universal aspect of the human condition that cultural specialists and interpreters should transmit to every member of the younger generations their wisdom, arts and crafts. There are often preferential rules and interdictions that make the somewhat simple process of transmitting information part of the complex, codified and ritualized practices of initiation and succession to office.

Another issue to be taken into account in this context is the idea of *tradition* that, in principle, is constitutive of the concept of heritage. This notion needs some relativization, particularly in the case of post-colonial nations like those in the Americas and the Caribbean. In these countries, present-day populations include large numbers of descendants of African slaves and immigrants from all continents, belonging to many distinct ethnic groups. Particularly in highly urbanized contexts or in cases where the native peoples and their cultures were practically decimated by colonial rule, the formation and transmission of cultural practices that are today considered distinctive of nations or of social groups within these nations, or their contemporary re-creation, involve the time depth of some decades, perhaps a few centuries and, consequently, not many generations. The same is true for the notion of *originality*, in many contexts deeply associated with that of "tradition". This idea quite often contradicts the cultural processes of fusion, mixture or *métissage* that are strongly characteristic of these cultures and

[21] O.B.J. Yaï, "Odo layé (éloge de la Vie-Fleuve): Perspectives Africaines sur le Patrimoine Culturel", in J. Blake (ed.), *Safeguarding Intangible Cultural Heritage: Challenges and Approaches*, 2007, 73, 75–76.

involve various ethnic, popular and, also, academic sources. The flexible idea of *historical continuity* is the notion adopted in Brazilian heritage legislation[22] to account for the varied time depth of items identified as intangible cultural heritage; other notions may be more adequate for other countries.

7. Intangible cultural heritage items are cultural constructions produced by negotiations between local social agencies and preservation institutions.[23] They are not necessarily seen as *heritage* in their contexts of origin, and they do not become such if not thus recognized by the proper institutional agencies (national or multilateral). So, one should take into account that the listing of cultural items depends on what I would call *process of cultural translation*, implying the mediation of, on the one hand, the parameters that underlie the local attribution of value by custodians, practitioners or members of cultural communities in general, with, on the other hand, those adopted by observers and cultural annalists for the construction of taxonomies and definition of priorities.

The holistic, systemic and processual perspective presented in this Chapter suggests that it is crucial for surveys to unveil the practical and symbolic links of intangible cultural heritage with territory and with the natural environment, as well as its social embedment and socio-psychological rooting – *i.e.*, its implications for self-esteem, personal identity and social identification. For that reason, inventories – and research instruments and methods, alike – should take into account not only what is highlighted by legal and administrative parameters, but also what is empirically indicated by fieldwork. This Chapter also points out that the segmentation of cultures is obviously not a matter of "butterfly collecting", but is rather a complex intellectual operation that requires specialized training. It should also be mentioned that the theories and methods applicable to inventorying cultural heritage are the object of much disagreement among professionals. Consequently, the subject matter of this Chapter is as polemical as it is strategically relevant both for the designing of the policies required by the ICH Convention, and for the evaluation of their challenges and consequences for local lives.

The perspective adopted by the ICH Convention is consistent with the conceptual perspective adopted in this Chapter. It defines intangible cultural heritage as the "practices, representations, expressions, knowledge, skills – as well as the instruments, objects, artefacts and cultural spaces associated therewith – that communities, groups and, in some cases, individuals recognize as part of

---

22 Federal Decree 3551, Article 1(2) ("The inscription in one of the Registry Books [of imaterial cultural heritage] will always have as reference the historical continuity of the item and its relevance – at a national level – for the memory, identity and formation of Brazilian society." (author's translation)).

23 *See* A.A. Arantes, "Cultural Diversity and the Politics of Difference in Safeguarding Intangible Cultural Heritage", in J. Blake (ed.), *Safeguarding Intangible Cultural Heritage: Challenges and Approaches*, 2007, at 85.

their cultural heritage."[24] In terms of the domains of cultural production in which intangible cultural heritage is manifested, that Convention singles out, without intending to be exhaustive, the following: (a) oral traditions and expressions, including language as a vehicle of the intangible cultural heritage; (b) performing arts; (c) social practices, rituals and festive events; (d) knowledge and practices concerning nature and the universe; and (e) traditional craftsmanship.[25] It becomes clear that these definitions adopt the widest possible view of the subject, since they include not only a vast domain of cultural practices but also the (material) artefacts and environmental resources that are associated with them.

According to the spirit of the Convention, inventories are supposed to identify and document the cultural items that are recognized by specific social groups as their patrimony, and by the safeguarding authorities as suitable for protection within the limits of the existing legislation. Consequently, its implementation requires tools and procedures that give adequate responses both to the demands implied by the conceptions underlying the whole safeguarding system, and to the historically accumulated experience, actual demands, constraints and possibilities that are proper to the specific national and local contexts in which safeguarding action plans are to be developed.[26] The short phrase of Article 12, according to which inventories should be drawn by the State Party "in a manner geared to its own situation", has very important implications from this point of view.

In brief, it suggests that the construction of internationally agreed safeguarding practices – and particularly inventories – demands the development of research and management strategies and methods that (i) raise questions on the basis of these general parameters and (ii) effectively illuminate issues and give answers to priorities that are put forth by the protagonists of heritage creation: the so-called *cultural communities*. It also leads to the understanding that inventories must be reasonably dense in terms of ethnographic and historic interpretation, because they are tools of strategic importance in mediating the cultural and political gap existing between the local, national and international levels. Consequently, they should be supported by in-depth ethnographies about the social realities targeted by safeguarding and by anthropological evaluations of their consequences on local lives.

In order to achieve this purpose, inventories should adopt an approach that I would qualify as *contextual* in at least two senses. First, since intangible cultural heritage elements are not detachable from the social life and history of the communities that have developed them, inventories should be contextual in the

---

24 ICH Convention, *supra* note 1, Article 2(1).

25 *Id.*, Article 2(2).

26 *See* A.A. Arantes, "Reconsidering the Social Aspects of Sustainability: Integrated Conservation and the Urban Environmental Heritage", in S.M. Zanchetti (ed.), *Conservation and Urban Sustainable Development: A Theoretical Framework* (1999).

sense of articulating any phenomenon of interest to the various relevant spheres of interaction and cultural genres practiced locally.[27] Second, in a broader sociological and historical sense, they should respond to the cultural and political issues and demands raised locally. Consequently, methodological issues should not be dealt with only in theoretical terms. Of course, questions of social theory and epistemology must be thought of in their own right, but matters of *politics of representation and decision-making* must be faced and resolved politically in concrete arenas. This is the central aspect of the inventory-making process for it provides a safe basis for designing realistic and socially sustainable safeguarding action plans.[28]

4. THE ROLE OF CULTURAL COMMUNITIES

According to the ICH Convention, safeguarding measures aim at "ensuring the viability of the intangible cultural heritage, including the identification, documentation, research, preservation, protection, promotion, enhancement, transmission,' particularly through formal and non-formal education, as well as the revitalization of the various aspects of such heritage."[29] They include drawing up one or more inventories in order to identify the intangible cultural heritage present in a territory "with the participation of communities, groups and relevant nongovernmental organizations".[30]

Since what is at stake in safeguarding intangible cultural heritage, as argued earlier, is the nurturing of current social practices and the fulfillment of their agents' capacity to constantly actualize them according to their changing social needs and motives; and considering that one of the main challenges is not to freeze these expressions of intellectual and poetic creativity, it becomes necessary to highlight in this definition the reference made to the role of communities, groups and individuals in the construction of intangible cultural heritage. The recognition by a social group of a certain practice, knowledge or form of expression as being their own patrimony is closely related to two other issues pointed out by the ICH Convention. One is the attribute of intangible

27 As argued by D. Ben-Amos, "folklore is a social interaction via the art media and differs from other modes of speaking and gesturing. This distinction is based upon sets of cultural conventions, recognized and adhered to by all the members of the group, which separate folklore from no art communication." *See* D. Ben-Amos, "Toward a Definition of Folklore in Context", in A. Paredes and R. Bauman (eds.), *Toward New Perspectives in Folklore,* 1972, 10. He later adds that "[i]t is a sphere of interaction in its own right." *Id.* at 15.

28 For empirical information about some processes conceptually outlined in this Section, *see* Appendix.

29 ICH Convention, *supra* note 1, Article 2(3).

30 *Id.*, Articles 11 and 12.

cultural heritage as providing the cultural community "with a sense of identity and continuity".[31] The other is the community's means of transmitting intangible cultural heritage from generation to generation, making possible its persistence to our days, *i.e.* intangible cultural heritage as a form of patrimony that is embedded in present day social practices of living sociological entities. Such perspective implies that safeguarding – *as a public policy* – interferes with social processes that (i) take place in the present, not in the past, and (ii) are developed by real and specific human collectivities, not by social entities or nations in the abstract: in contrast to brick and plaster or stone monuments, intangible cultural heritage is *living* heritage.

A preliminary point to be taken in consideration here is that social memory[32] and preserved heritage are not synonyms. Both concern the reproduction of social life by means of creating affective and cognitive landmarks that provide shared references to historical change and continuity. But one major difference between them lies in the fact that, if social memory mainly concerns social agencies and actors belonging to localized and often small scale social environments, cultural heritage, in the strict sense of the term, results from the already mentioned complex and often tense negotiations involving cultural mediators who belong to different cultural and social milieus. Examples of such intermediaries are: the cultural communities' representatives and cultural custodians; the technical and administrative personnel working for the preservation institutions; independent consultants, experts and political activists; and entrepreneurs and marketing experts interested in developing business opportunities on the basis of heritage as an economic resource. Whatever is classified and protected as heritage by a governmental institution is, in one-way or another, permeated by such negotiations. It is a cultural construction resulting from negotiations between agencies belonging to two distinct social spheres, namely, the cultural communities (sometimes significantly referred to as "source" communities) and the preservation institutions, whose actions are dictated and regulated by legal instruments and institutionalized administrative procedures.

From that perspective, inventories delineate the borders of the universe from which cultural items will be selected for official protection. Inventory making is the occasion when, and the context in which, decisions are made as to which cultural manifestations should be chosen for institutional protection, which should not, and why. But cultural inventories rarely occur as initiatives of the cultural communities themselves. Practices, knowledge and forms of expression classified by preservation agencies as intangible cultural heritage are usually embedded in everyday life or in ceremonial activities. They are frequently not systematized, and their transmission as well as their constant changes and

31 *Id.*, Article 2(1).

32 *See* P. Ricoeur, *Memory, History, Forgetting*, 2004.

adaptations to historical circumstances are regulated by established costume and common law, following the cultural logics proper to these communities' social organization.

This does not mean, however, that cultural differences between Indigenous and traditional peoples and the agents of preservation institutions cannot be overcome. Community celebrations, cultural performances, and local specialist activities can – and in fact are – recognized by the local people as activities that have a beginning, a foreseeable development and an end, specific associated narratives that make sense of them, as well as a certain *raison d'être*. They are subject matters that people talk about, and often dispute over. Besides this, there are a growing number of intellectuals and academic researchers among Indigenous peoples in all continents. Cultural differences aside, dialogues and disputes in the field of cultural rights are increasing and getting much deeper, and more sophisticated and well focused. Indigenous and traditional peoples' organizations have become visibly stronger nowadays in national and in international fora. This tendency can be exemplified by the evolving role played by so-called "marginal groups" in public policy decision making in Brazil since the 1980s. After a long period of authoritarianism, "participation" became, in the 1980s, the politically correct motto and eventually a recognized constitutional right in relation to policy making; today, "protagonism" and "empowerment" are perspectives that civil society organizations are struggling for in those matters. So, intercultural dialogue on heritage matters is absolutely viable in cultural and intellectual terms. The crucial issue here is the nature of the arena in which these negotiations take place, or the power relation of the local and external parties involved in them.

Policy decision-making in such matters may hopefully mean convergent recognition of (i) the value ascribed to some cultural achievement, (ii) the communities' rights of having their heritage protected, and (iii) the preservation institutions' commitment to providing the legal, administrative and material means for that protection to be effective. But this is not often the case.

Cultural preservation, as any other social practice, has its own history. In Brazil, at least, it is an historical fact that discussions regarding the production of heritage lists became more intense and passionate as the items proposed for preservation became less orthodox, including not only artefacts of historic and artistic value, but also intangible items: not only those referred to as high culture, but also an increasing number of items that primarily concern Indigenous and popular cultures. The construction of public policies in this sector tends to be biased by hegemonic values and conceptions about national cultures. This bias often favours elitist cultural perspectives; in the Brazilian context, for example, this has historically highlighted white, catholic and colonial cultural landmarks.

To my understanding, it is our responsibility – as critical professionals and specialists devoted to heritage issues – to help refine and regulate the political balance of such negotiations. The ICH Convention may produce, for various reasons, a very positive consequence on the strategic positioning of the cultural communities *vis-à-vis* the traditionally elitist bias of the criteria usually adopted by the preservation institutions. It reinforces, in the first place, the local communities' intellectual authority (the legitimacy of local knowledge); second, it reinforces their condition as protagonists (or at least as active participants) of the safeguarding action plans; and, mainly, it reinforces their self-determination in terms of building political strategies and deciding about priorities in relation to their own cultural development.

5. SAFEGUARDING CULTURAL PRACTICES AND PROTECTING INTELLECTUAL PROPERTY RIGHTS

The issues previously discussed take us to another point in our agenda: who is the intellectual property holder of intangible cultural heritage. The draft formulations of the World Intellectual Property Organization (WIPO), particularly those referring to traditional knowledge and traditional cultural expressions, are much clearer on this topic than the ICH Convention.[33] One of these documents, for example, defines as beneficiaries of intellectual property rights protection communities (Indigenous and traditional) as well as recognized individuals within these communities and peoples who generate, preserve and transmit the knowledge in a traditional and intergenerational context, who are associated with it and who culturally identify with it:

> as holding the knowledge through a form of custodianship, guardianship, collective ownership or cultural responsibility. This relationship may be expressed formally or informally by customary or traditional practices, protocols or laws.[34]

---

33 I refer especially to the documents underlying the discussions held in the Tenth Session of the Intergovernmental Committee on Intellectual Property and Genetic Resources, Traditional Knowledge and Folklore, held in Geneva, 30 November to 8 December 2006. *See* WIPO, Intergovernmental Committee on Intellectual Property and Genetic Resources, Traditional Knowledge and Folklore, *The Protection of Traditional Knowledge: Draft Objectives and Principles*, WIPO/GRTKF/IC/10/5 (2 October 2006), *available at* www.wipo.int/edocs/mdocs/tk/en/wipo_grtkf_ic_10/wipo_grtkf_ic_10_5.pdf (last visited 31 July 2008) [hereinafter "*Draft TK Principles*"]; WIPO, Intergovernmental Committee on Intellectual Property and Genetic Resources, Traditional Knowledge and Folklore, *The Protection of Traditional Cultural Expressions/Expressions of Folklore: Draft Objectives and Principles*, WIPO/GRTKF/IC/10/4 (2 October 2006), *available at* www.wipo.int/edocs/mdocs/tk/en/wipo_grtkf_ic_10/wipo_grtkf_ic_10_4.pdf (last visited 31 July 2008).

34 *Draft TK principles*, *supra* note 32, at 7.

Whatever the case may be, it seems clear that, in the spirit of both the UNESCO and WIPO formulations, the practices and criteria established by cultural communities are as valid and as legitimate as the external (technical, academic) ones in questions regarding the inclusion of cultural items in the safeguarding process. The same is true about the identification of their legitimate holders, whether collective or individual, for the sake of protection of intellectual property rights. Consequently, in practical terms, the perspective outlined in this Chapter, echoing what has become a strong worldwide political tendency, indicates and justifies the need for obtaining the community's informed consent prior to making inventories and starting the safeguarding process.

On the basis of the information produced by inventories, databases should systematically store information on intangible cultural heritage and make it available to the agencies that are responsible for designing, implementing and evaluating safeguarding programs and for enforcing its legal protection. They should also be accessible to the general public, as well as to the cultural communities, feeding back the open ended process of constant cultural invention and recreation. However, such accessibility can lead to the disclosure of cultural information that, if not sacred or secret, is not meant to become public. So, access to databases is another matter that should be regulated in dialogue with cultural communities and with their consent.

Local people do not usually have access to the research done in their territories and about their ways of life, although this may be crucial information for the construction of social identities, identifications and senses of belonging, as well as for cultural creation, reproduction and change. For that reason, the repatriation in original language of information produced by academics and experts, as well as making accessible bibliographic sources and relevant documentation gathered by inventories, may be one of the first priorities of safeguarding programs.

The safeguarding of intangible cultural heritage becomes more effective if complemented by a fair international legal regime designed to protect intellectual property rights associated with traditional knowledge and cultural expressions. By a "fair regime" I mean one that responds to the specificities and vicissitudes of intangible cultural heritage – taking into account its much varied and *sui generis* nature – and respects the beliefs, values and ways of transmission practiced by their creators and custodians. The social embedment of heritage in the life of concrete cultural communities is what sustains the vitality of its participation in the social reproduction and reinforces the historical continuity of the social groups from whose experience they derive.

Many countries are engaged in developing legal and administrative measures to protect socio-biodiversity and associated traditional knowledge. In January 2007, for instance, a new legal instrument entered into force in Brazil further protecting traditional knowledge in the process of patent authorization. But the protection of intellectual property rights associated with traditional knowledge and cultural expressions is not a matter that should be addressed exclusively by national legislation. There are several issues that may – and in fact should be – resolved by means of bilateral or multilateral agreements. Such is, for instance, the case for issues concerning ethnic groups and nations whose territories have been divided by international borders that are relatively recent in terms of the immemorial time depth of their histories. There are many examples of such situations on almost all continents.

Safeguarding is one of the emergent issues leading to the consolidation of the global cultural sphere.[35] Not only the preservation of practices and artefacts, but also – if not mainly – the protection of the associated intellectual property rights must be a global concern since contemporary national territories are inescapably permeated by global flows of people, signs and capital. This implies that new limits and parameters are progressively being set to the regulatory power of states over cultural processes and trade within their territories. The legal protection of rights (intellectual or other) must take into account this fundamental reality. For that reason, a legal regime enforced by the WIPO could provide not only a conceptual framework and legitimate precedents to local and specific agreements and conflict resolutions, but also general normative parameters for the regulation of processes that take place in the global market for intangible heritage commodities. A seemingly sensible recommendation in this regard would be that the implementation of such regime be monitored both for preventing or mitigating its undesirable consequences and as a way of constantly refining these instruments. The influence of the global sphere on local realities is inevitable; so also should the feed-back of the local be on the global.

In closing the present reflections, I would like to recall Claude Lévi-Strauss's claim in the essay about race and cultural diversity published by UNESCO in 1952. His point was that that there are no cultures in isolation, and that a culture's main contribution to civilization depends on the number and nature of the differences that it brings to developing *a common strategy* with other cultures. With that idea in mind, and taking into account the fact that, in our times, the formation and dissemination – as well as the neutralization – of cultural differences mainly take place in the context of global economy, it becomes clear that the need to provide agreed parameters for the global market of cultural commodities is as urgent as it is crucial to our common future. And, conversely, it leads to the conclusion that a hyper-local focus on cultural policies, as well as on cultural economic matters, may lead to hyper-particularism, or to parochialism.

---

[35] A.A. Arantes, "Diversity, Heritage and Cultural Politics", 24 *Theory, Culture & Society* 290, 293–94 (2007).

APPENDIX. A PLACE FOR INTANGIBLE CULTURAL HERITAGE IN OUR COMMON FUTURES*

The projects given awards in this contest of best practices offer important lessons for the implementation of UNESCO's 2003 Convention. They bring to our minds the imponderable vicissitudes that are faced by the agents of safeguarding activities when theories are turned into effective practice. They also demonstrate that cultural communities can develop creative and effective ways of coping with the difficulties that are faced when heritage is cultivated as present-day cultural practice, and nurtured as an asset to be handed down to younger generations. Last, but not least, they bring out the positive values that are attributed by youth groups, associations and individuals to this ever changing legacy.

The collective experiences developed and accumulated by these projects' participants suggest various relevant themes from the point of view of outlining a practical agenda for policy makers. I outline and comment on, in this Appendix, issues that seem to constitute a common basis of concern among these projects' participants. My hope that this can be a contribution to the critique, consolidation and development of these projects' strategies and achievements, as well as to the continuous elaboration of practical parameters for the application of the above mentioned Convention.

a) Diversity

The first lesson taught by these projects and by the discussions that took place after their presentations in the workshop sessions is that may be many differences in the nature of the cultural performances to which heritage values are attributed, as well as in the meanings attributed to them by the practitioners.

Diversity in terms of the nature of cultural performances

Some safeguarding projects aim at the transmission and development of highly codified artistic languages. This is the case of the Sanskrit dance theater *Kutiyattam*, as performed in the Ammannur Chachuchakyar Samaraka Gurukulam, in India; as well as of the classic shadow puppet theater *Nang Yai*, practiced at the Wat Kanon Temple, in Rajburi Province, Thailand; of *Kurokawa-Noh*, performed by the Kami-za and Shimo-za troupes and parishioners of the Kasuga Shinto Shrine of Tsuruoka City, Yamagata Prefecture, Japan; of the Shinto

* Originally published by ACCU and reprinted with its kind permission. *See* ACCU, *Workshop for Youth Participation for Safeguarding the Intangible Cultural Heritage and Community Development, Final Report*, at 41 (8–11 June 2007), *available at* www.accu.or.jp/ich/en/pdf/d2007Accenture.pdf (last visited 31 July 2008) (containing the author's comments on the projects awarded by the *Contest for Best Practices in Communities' ICH Revitalization* promoted by ACCU).

music and dance performance known as *Bangaku*, as developed by the Nekko Bangaku Hozonkai, in Kita-Akita City, Akita Prefecture, Japan; and of the *Joruri* puppet theater as developed by the Awaji Puppet Association in some cities of Hyogo Prefecture, Japan.

Other initiatives focus on rituals or aspects of communities' celebrations. This is the case of the Tanedori Festival held at Taketomi Island, Okinawa Prefecture and of the *Yatai-Bayashi* drum playing, which is a central feature of the *dashi* floats that take place during the festival held at the Chichibu City, in Saitama Prefecture, both in Japan. Another case in point is the Nama's *stapdans*, the music and dance performance practiced in Richtersveld, the World Heritage Site located on the South African and Namibian border.

Diversity of meanings attributed by the practitioners and their communities to cultural performance

ICH is consistently valued by these projects as an important – if not crucial – reference for the construction of social and personal identities, self-esteem, sentiments of belonging to a specific social environment, and social inclusion, particularly for the elderly and for migrant populations. It does not just persist in contemporary life as part of a group's social memory, but as an important symbolic and economic asset available to the present cultural community members, and as an element of their legacy to future generations.

Some of them are mostly concerned with the sociological value of heritage, i.e. with strengthening the processes by which senses of belonging and/or social inclusion are constructed or reinforced by means of these practices. The Tanedori Festival, that takes place at Taketomi Island, provides a good example. The island was severely depopulated in the last decades particularly because young adults, mostly male, left their birthplace to work and live elsewhere. The festival became an important opportunity for the villagers to reassemble former neighbors and relatives, as well as to reinforce the socialization of migrant villagers and initiate their mates and children in the Taketomi world-view, language and religion. Similar meanings and values are attributed to the performance of Nama *stapdans* in the Richtersveld, as well as to the drum playing at the Chichibu City parade; community participation seem to be the main focus of these performances, without neglecting technical and expressive standards of interpretation.

In other instances, such as the performances that are highly associated with Shinto rituals, of which *Kurokawa-Noh* is a strong example, or with cosmology and the performing arts as in the Sanskrit *Kutiyattam* dance theater, the aesthetic and spiritual values manifested by and reinforced through the practice of a particular genre seem to be the main concern of the practitioners.

b) Meanings and Priorities

As a consequence of the previous lesson, it would neither be realistic nor productive to think of developing a homogeneous set of parameters for policy making. Diversity of strategies and styles became explicit particularly in the discussions that took place after each project's presentation in the workshop. Whatever such parameters may be, they must be flexible in order to respond both to the specific characteristics of the cultural practices designated as ICH, and to the singular contexts in which they are transmitted, performed and safeguarded.

Diversity of priorities and strategies elected by the communities, according to their views about the nature and meaning of heritage, as well as to their perception of the difficulties faced in these practices

In relation to the production and transmission of ICH, the following problems were very frequently mentioned: (1) Insufficient material and financial resources for the production and reproduction of ICH; (2) Decreasing number of young practitioners and of participants of all ages in the supporting activities; (3) Decreasing public interest and lack of motivation due to strengthening of patterns of sociability and life-styles stimulated by the mass media, consumer society and information technology.

Demographic changes seem to be at the roots of some of the most serious difficulties faced by the continuous reproduction of these practices. Among them, the main ones seem to be (1) ageing of the population, (2) low birth-rates, and (3) migration of significant numbers of young adults, male and female, looking for better job opportunities.

The experiences described and discussed in the seminar indicate that the processes by which information technology, entertainment industries and mass media became such powerful cultural producers also undermine the reproduction and development of cultural performances.

Combinations of these tendencies put at risk the patterns and values that provide the sociological framework for the transmission of knowledge and skills associated with heritage (*transmission* was significantly referred to several times as *succession* by practitioners), as well as the organization of the supporting activities on which such performances rely.

However, safeguarding projects creatively respond to these difficulties in various ways. In Tanedori Festival, for example, it is vital to assemble an increasing number of performers and to widen, as much as possible, the network of those involved in providing the necessary background support to the performances. This implies fundraising and much actual work in the preparation of the site, food, and proms, *etc.*

The Nama music and dance project has another focus and strategy. Centered in the performance, transmission and promotion of a hybrid and fragmented musical language resulting from decades of colonial domination and apartheid, it aims at developing the self-esteem of a population that has diverse ethnic backgrounds, but that shares a territory and views about the future. Community pride and identification with their territory are at the center of this project's preoccupations.

The priorities for *Kutiyattam*, as developed in the tradition of the Chukyar and Nambiar families of Thrissur District, in Kerala, India are of a different kind. Their main challenges are the high production costs of performances and rehearsals, as well as providing adequate working space for masters and apprentices. The growing success of the film and television industries in that country is another challenge, in so far as it affects the interest and motivation of the young people either as audiences or as future practitioners of this art.

The *Ningyo Joruri* puppet theater, in its turn, was developed as one of the religious activities of Shinto shrines and relied for a long time on the professional work of practitioners assembled in several *zas*. However, they face a different kind of problem. The fall of the patronage system in the Meiji Period, as well as the social and economic changes that took place in Japan after World War II, seem to have seriously affected this activity as an economically viable way of life. In addition, children and adolescents became strongly IT minded, and gradually resistant to learn and appreciate this delicately "handmade" form of expression. Besides that, *Joruri* has had much less public exposure in the last decades than the related and apparently more entertaining genre of puppetry known as *Bunraku*. Activities consistently developed in schools, supported by young peoples' associations as well as by other forms of voluntary work that are so characteristic of Japan proved to be most beneficial in terms of facing the hegemony of mass media and information technology among young people and of making *Joruri* better known and appreciated by children, adolescents and the general public. A similar process took place in the case of *Nekko Bangaku* practiced in Akita Prefecture, in Japan, whose performers and producers developed viable means of support and transmission on the basis of voluntary associations.

Differences in priorities and strategies developed at a particular time and place for contextual purposes may become, in the long run, differences in styles of approach to safeguarding

In order to formulate this issue, one could start by making a schematic distinction between the main commitments that safeguarding projects might intend to respond to. In the case of the present seminar, there seems to be, on the one hand, the commitment to achieving the utmost technical and expressive development of a specific genre of cultural performance. On the other hand, there is the preoccupation of providing for the socio-political needs, future plans and intentions of a cultural community. I would refer to the former as an *aesthetical commitment*, and the latter as a *social commitment*. Obviously, safeguarding projects do not strictly fall in one of these two extreme categories. However, the workshop discussions suggested that, in one way or another, they all face a tension that can be formulated – in terms of this model – as a double commitment with the aesthetical, formal and technical aspects of heritage, as well as with the social dynamics of their bearing communities.

It seems that nothing would be less adequate, from the point of view of policy-making, as to go along the lines of "*either or*" – and not "*both and*" – on these matters. Stakeholders must decide by themselves, in terms of their needs, criteria, and effective possibilities, and according to the circumstances faced at a certain point in time, as to where to stand along this line, but they should also be careful in order not to transform situational choices in styles, dogmas or orthodoxies.

Kurokawa-Noh is a good example of a balanced and successful implementation of safeguarding measures that were intended to respond to the social as well the aesthetic (and religious) aspects of heritage. This 500 year-old Shinto ritual is presently performed by the Kami-za and Shimo-za troupes and by the Kasuga shrine parishioners, in Kurokawa area of Tsuruoka City, Japan. In facing the hardships of World War II as well as the country's deep post-war socio-economic changes, the local community was able not only to keep this ritual as one of the manifestations of their deep religious devotion, but also to develop new roots and blend it with fast changing community ways of life.

Apparently, there is no doubt that *Kurokawa-Noh* belongs to this local community. But in the last decades, practitioners faced a decreasing interest from the local community, particularly from the younger generations, in the complex and time-consuming training in the art of *Noh,* as well as a decreasing degree of commitment to the practical demands of performance production. The transmission of *Noh* (or *succession* in this art, as practitioners often phrase it) would have been seriously jeopardized if community leaders had been too strict in following the usual patterns of transmission and participation. Two particularly limiting aspects of these rules were that *Noh* should be transmitted within family groups, preferably to first-born male children, and that women had little if anything to do with this almost exclusively male art.

The long celebrated Ohgi Festival was the chosen context for the implementation of important changes in gender and age based on social patterns of participation in performances. An Executive Committee was set to improve the *Rosoku-Noh* (literally, candle lit *Noh*) as a special feature of this annual festival that will have its 15th consecutive edition in 2008. It became a new institutional space open to a wider involvement of community members, both male and female, as well as teenagers. As a result, there has been an increase in fundraising by means of public donations, as well as sponsorship by private corporations and development of complementary commercial activities in the Kasuga Shrine compound.

Another extremely important outcome was the strengthening of public support and interest in *Noh* as an art, and the growth of audiences in public performances without interfering with the more religiously exclusive rituals of which the practice of *Noh* is an important part. Indeed, making the rules of participation more flexible and adequate to present day social reality was vital to safeguarding the practice of *Noh* in its local and traditional setting, as well as its artistic quality and significance for the Kasuga Shinto Shrine parishioners.

c) Continuity and Change

The previous example strongly illustrates that historical circumstances may produce changes in the social basis of ICH transmission and/or production. It also suggests – as contradictory as this may seem – that the continuity of a certain practice may imply change in terms of the gender, age and social status of its performers and participants. In such cases, the challenge from the point of view of safeguarding is to find the right balance between continuity and change and to realize that, in concrete situations, these forces are not as conflicting as one might suppose in the abstract.

Contextual issues are not the only factors that induce change. Performers and producers develop new styles of interpretation, pieces of repertoire and technical skills out of their continuous practice; the same happens with community celebrations and religious rituals. It would not be realistic to assume that genres of cultural performance have sprung ready-made from the territories where they are presently found and that they have been kept unchanged throughout the times. Languages are historic, dynamic and changeable realities; the social significance attributed to cultural practices, the values and knowledge conveyed by them, and the social organization underlying their manifestation in actual performance are also historic, dynamic and changeable realities.

Changes in the meanings attributed to community celebrations can be exemplified in our projects by the transformation of the old days sowing seeds ritual of Taketomy Island in a festival where social inclusion and belonging are cultivated under the leadership of a Shinto woman priest, supported by a significant number of other women and most community members. Another instance would be the renaissance of the Nama community's celebration by means of the *stapdans* performance, the contemporary folk music played on modern instruments, sung in Afrikaans and still reflecting, from the community's point of view, "*the rhythm and tone of the past*".

In all these instances, it seems that tension between continuity and change can be culturally productive, rather than destructive. But, in order to strengthen the creative output of these forces, the protagonism of local people in social and cultural matters is absolutely essential. Safeguarding policies should avoid the implementation of externally induced innovations and give way to the activities, social structural principles, as well as knowledge and skills that nurture the recognition – by the heritage bearers – of a certain practice as a continuous reference to their identity, memory and social values. This is, in my view, one of the foundations of cultural sustainability.

d) Social Protagonism

Sustainability of safeguarding strategies requires the active involvement of heritage bearers. A population that claims a cultural landmark as its own, or as a valuable public expression of its identity, should develop sustainable means for reproducing it. Among other things, this implies, firstly, taking initiatives and having the means of implementing them; and secondly, which is not less important, not depending on patronage, either supported by public or by private funds.

Various projects discussed in this workshop indicate that, from this point of view, the best practices are those that widen, feed and strengthen the social rooting of cultural performances and those that improve the diversification of their material and political means of support. The way to do this surely varies from one country to another, and from one town to another since sustainability depends on the volume and nature of the available resources, as well as on how they are socially distributed. Still, the political empowerment of communities as well as capacity building – to know how to deal with funding agencies, supporting institutions, accountancy and tax incentives – are important instruments for raising and strengthening social protagonism.

It is relevant to highlight in this context the importance of voluntary work developed by organizations such as preservation and youth associations, community centers, arts groups, friendship clubs, as well as by schools and religious organizations. As attested by the projects, these institutions provide in different towns and countries not only the basic social fabric responsible for gathering the necessary financial and political resources that are needed for these activities to take place, but also the environment that stimulates the raising of future participants' motivation, that feeds public opinion and develops the capacity to appreciate these complex and often subtle forms of expression.

e) Education

The practice of ICH in schools, while feeding and inspiring both extracurricular and regular school activities, is essential for increasing the motivation of new practitioners and developing well informed appreciation by audiences and participants, particularly when heritage has lost visibility and relevance in public life. In addition to that, it provides extremely rich themes related to the historical, expressive and spiritual aspects of a culture that can be dealt with in multi-disciplinary educational activities. It also contributes to body language development, to health programs, and raises stamina and awareness among students.

Several projects are stories of success on this topic, but *Awaji Ningyo Joruri* and *Nekko Bangaku* should be highlighted in this context. In both cases, the preservation associations with the support of youth groups and children's voluntary associations were efficient enough to develop extra-curricular activities for elementary school, junior high school and high school students on a regular basis in several towns and villages of Japan.

f) Collective Intellectual Property Rights

In the cases of *Kurokawa-Noh*, *Awaji Ningyo Joruri* and *Kutiyattam*, issues concerning ownership rights in relation to plays and styles of interpretation were raised in the discussions. These rights, historically consolidated as common law, have important implications for the accessibility and transmission of ICH that are not in the public domain. They also raise questions about the need for further legal protection of these rights in addition to current customary practices, and to the safeguarding processes.

g) Universality and Singularity

The safeguarding of ICH faces an apparent contradiction: the more these cultural treasures are embedded in specific social contexts, the more they concern us all, as human beings. *Kutiyattam, Nang Yai* and *Kurokawa-Noh* are very good examples in this respect. These traditional expressions of high art seem to be well and deeply rooted in community life, and their publicly recognized importance has by far transcended the limits of the institutions, social groups and localities in which they are practiced and transmitted. They became part of the rich diversity that feeds human experience, part of the same human experience reflected in the other forms of artistic expression presented in this meeting.

Recognition of the importance of ICH beyond community boundaries by means of their designation as heritage by national states and by UNESCO may produce positive consequences for those community practices. In fact this has often been the case in relation to the projects that have received awards in this contest. Cultural communities may take advantage of the added symbolic value, legitimacy and visibility produced by such official proclamations (in symbolic, political and practical ways). They have often done so in the projects discussed in this meeting.

Concluding Remarks

I should like to end these comments emphasizing that the utmost aim of any ICH policy or project should be to contribute to building a sustainable cultural diversity for human development and understanding beyond community life. Diversity is the main treasure to be safeguarded for our successors in this planet and we do not have the moral right to deprive them of such beauty and transcendental experiences. In safeguarding cultural resources, our compass must be rooted in the present yet facing the future. Our minds should be attuned to those who will follow after us; that is why young people's participation in safeguarding ICH is so relevant. To design the ways and provide the means for these treasures to be handed down to our contemporary young fellows and to future generations is no simple task. Poverty, illiteracy, intolerance, war and forced migration make our task as difficult as it is urgent.

A. Appadurai has pointed out that sustainable diversity depends on the capacity of human beings to design their own cultural futures. Their "capacity to aspire", as the Indian anthropologist phrases it, links culture to development: to human development in general, not just economic. This common will is surely the life principle of *transmission*, which we outsiders tend to name "cultural reproduction", or *succession* as some practitioners have called it in this seminar, suggesting the importance of local social structures in organizing intergenerational matters. The psychosocial force of shared belonging is what brings together custodians and apprentices as practitioners and militants of the same art, as individuals who form the core of historic continuity, the guardians of their own villages' or people's heritage and of what is, or may be – shared by all of us, as human beings.

Cultural heritage is a planetary concern; no wonder institutions like UNESCO and ACCU, as well as broad-minded individuals like you have taken this mission as their own. Let us not forget that last lesson of our workshop!

MANAGING INTELLECTUAL PROPERTY OPTIONS WHEN DOCUMENTING, RECORDING AND DIGITIZING INTANGIBLE CULTURAL HERITAGE

Wend B. Wendland*

* B.A., LL.B., LL.M.; Attorney of the Supreme Court of South Africa; Head of the Traditional Creativity, Cultural Heritage and Cultural Expressions Section, World Intellectual Property Organization (WIPO), Geneva, Switzerland. The views expressed in this Chapter are not necessarily those of WIPO or any of its Member States. The author may be contacted at wend.wendland@wipo.int. An earlier version of parts of this Chapter appeared as "Intellectual Property Implications of Inventory-Making: Towards Intellectual Property Guidelines for Recording, Digitising and Disseminating Intangible Cultural Heritage", in J. Blake (ed.), *Safeguarding Intangible Cultural Heritage: Challenges and Approaches*, 2007, 129.

1. INTRODUCTION

The protection of intellectual property and the safeguarding of intangible cultural heritage have always had a somewhat uncertain and awkward relationship, stemming in large measure from an inherent ambiguity in the meaning of "protect" and a need to clarify the relationship between the *safeguarding* of cultural heritage and the *legal protection* of creativity against unauthorized use.

This conceptual ambiguity has marked the efforts made by the World Intellectual Property Organization (WIPO)[1] and the United Nations Educational, Scientific and Cultural Organization (UNESCO)[2] over the last 40 or so years to address questions related to intellectual property and intangible cultural heritage.[3] These include the 1967 amendment to the *Berne Convention for the Protection of Literary and Artistic Works*[4] to provide protection for the unpublished works of unknown authors at the suggestion of India[5], the 1976 *Tunis Model Law on Copyright*[6], the 1982 UNESCO-WIPO *Model Provisions for National Laws on the Protection of Expressions of Folklore Against Illicit Exploitation and Other Prejudicial Actions*[7], the 1984 *Draft Treaty for the Protection of Expressions of*

---

1 The World Intellectual Property Organization (WIPO) is the United Nations agency responsible for the promotion and protection of creative intellectual activity and for facilitating the transfer of technology in order to accelerate economic, social and cultural development. It has 184 Member States who decide on, direct and monitor its programme activities.

2 The United Nations Educational, Scientific and Cultural Organization (UNESCO) is a specialised agency of the United Nations and it promotes cooperation amongst its 193 Member States in the fields of education, science and culture.

3 *See generally* L.V. PROTT, "An International Legal Instrument for the Protection of Intangible Cultural Heritage?", in C.D. CLASSEN *et al.* (eds.), *In einem vereinten Europa dem Frieden der Welt zu dienen...: Liber amicorum Thomas Oppermann*, 2001; S. SHERKIN, "A Historical Study on the Preparation of the 1989 Recommendation on the Safeguarding of Traditional Culture and Folklore", in P. SEITEL (ed.), *Safeguarding Traditional Cultures: A Global Assessment*, 2001, 42.

4 Berne Convention for the Protection of Literary and Artistic Works, 9 September 1886, 828 U.N.T.S. 221 (amended 28 September 1979), *available at* www.wipo.int/export/sites/www/treaties/en/ip/berne/pdf/trtdocs_wo001.pdf (last visited 31 July 2008).

5 *See* WIPO, *The Berne Convention for the Protection of Literary and Artistic Works from 1886 to 1986*, 199, 206, 249–53 (1986) (containing the Records of Diplomatic Conference, Conference in Stockholm, 11 June to 14 July 1967).

6 "Tunis Model Law on Copyright", 10(2) *Copyright Bull.* 10 (1976), *available at* http://portal.unesco.org/culture/en/files/31318/11866635053tunis_model_law_en-web.pdf/tunis_model_law_en-web.pdf (last visited 31 July 2008) (adopted by the Committee of Governmental Experts convened by the Tunisian Government in Tunis from 23 February to 2 March 1976 with the assistance of WIPO and the United Nations Educational, Scientific and Cultural Organization (UNESCO)).

7 COMMITTEE OF GOVERNMENTAL EXPERTS ON THE INTELLECTUAL PROPERTY ASPECTS OF THE PROTECTION OF EXPRESSIONS OF FOLKLORE, "Model Provisions for National Laws on the Protection of Expressions of Folklore Against Illicit Exploitation and Other Prejudicial Actions", 16(1/2) *Copyright Bull.* 62 (1982) (convened by WIPO and UNESCO).

Folklore Against Illicit Exploitation and Other Prejudicial Actions,[8] the 1989 *Recommendation on the Safeguarding of Traditional Culture and Folklore*[9], the 2003 *Convention for the Safeguarding of the Intangible Cultural Heritage* (ICH Convention)[10] and the 2005 *Convention on the Protection and Promotion of the Diversity of Cultural Expressions.*[11]

The uncertain interface between the protection of creativity, including traditional creativity, and the safeguarding of intangible cultural heritage is particularly visible in relation to the recording and documentation of intangible cultural heritage. Many initiatives are underway – internationally, nationally and locally – to document, record and digitize intangible cultural heritage, and these play an invaluable role in preserving the rich cultural heritage of our planet, fostering educational opportunities and promoting respect for the cultural expressions, traditions and ways of life of the world's diverse peoples and cultural communities.

However, Indigenous peoples and local communities express concerns that documentation activities by museums, archives and other cultural agencies and institutions, as well as by individual researchers, sometimes do not take adequate account of their rights and interests, and that documenting and displaying intangible cultural heritage – for instance, the recording of a traditional song or a tribal symbol – may make intangible cultural heritage vulnerable to misappropriation.[12] There is particular concern over safeguarding activities for "traditional cultural expressions" (or, "expressions of folklore") and culturally

---

8 "Draft Treaty for the Protection of Expressions of Folklore Against Illicit Exploitation and Other Prejudicial Actions", 19(2) *Copyright Bull.* 34 (1985) (*prepared by* the Committee of Governmental Experts on the Intellectual Property Aspects of the Protection of Expressions of Folklore which was convened by WIPO and UNESCO).

9 Recommendation on the Safeguarding of Traditional Culture and Folklore, 15 November 1989, *available at* http://portal.unesco.org/en/ev.php-URL_ID=13141&URL_DO=DO_TOPIC&URL_SECTION=201.html (last visited 31 July 2008) (adopted by the General Conference of the UNESCO at its twenty-fifth session).

10 Convention for the Safeguarding of the Intangible Cultural Heritage, 17 October 2003, U.N. Doc. MISC/2003/CLT/CH/14 (2003), *available at* http://unesdoc.unesco.org/images/0013/001325/132540e.pdf (last visited 31 July 2008) [hereinafter "ICH Convention"].

11 Convention on the Protection and Promotion of the Diversity of Cultural Expressions, 20 October 2005, *available at* http://unesdoc.unesco.org/images/0014/001429/142919e.pdf (last visited 31 July 2008).

12 *See, e.g.*, Mataatua Declaration on Cultural and Intellectual Property Rights of Indigenous Peoples, 19 June 1993, U.N. Doc. E/CN.4/Sub.2/AC.4/1993/CRP.5 (1993); and UN Declaration on the Rights of Indigenous Peoples, 13 September 2007, G.A. Res. 61/295, U.N. Doc. A/RES/61/295 (2007) (developed with the strong involvement of Indigenous peoples and adopted by the UN General Assembly in 2007). *See also* T. Janke, *Our Culture: Our Future*, 1998 (report prepared for the Australian Institute of Aboriginal and Torres Strait Islander Studies); M. Solomon, *The Long Journey Home: Return of Our Ancestors* (12 November 2005) (paper presented at *World Archaeological Congress*, Auckland, New Zealand), *available at* www.wipo.int/export/sites/www/tk/en/folklore/creative_heritage/docs/solomon_maui_ancestors.pdf (last visited 31 July 2008).

sensitive materials, that may be perceived as "public domain" by conventional intellectual property laws.

Indigenous peoples and other local communities argue that they do not have adequate control over research conducted into their cultures, nor over how their cultures are recorded and presented to the public at large. The handling of secret and sacred materials held within such collections can be a source of particularly acute concern. The ethnographic collections of museums and other institutions often include invaluable, even unique, records of ancient traditions, lost languages and community histories which are integral to Indigenous peoples' identity and continuity. Yet the intellectual content of such material is often not owned by Indigenous people, but rather by the people who "made" the film, sound recording, photographs and manuscripts.[13] For instance, while a traditional song may be treated by intellectual property law as in the "public domain", recording that song creates new intellectual property rights in the recording, which are held by the person making the recording. How those new rights are exercised can significantly impact the interests of the tradition-bearing community, as well as other interested parties such as creators and the general public. A significant amount of Indigenous collections remains "unpublished" from a copyright perspective. As Jane Anderson writes, questions of access to, control over, and ownership of, those materials become critical in this context.[14] In other words, the very valuable process of *preserving* traditional cultural expressions can trigger concerns about their lack of legal *protection* against misappropriation and misuse.

It was with these concerns in mind that intellectual property related questions were raised during the preparation of the ICH Convention, in particular in respect of the obligation in the Convention that States Parties establish and publish inventories and lists of their intangible cultural heritage[15], as well as establish "documentation institutions for the intangible cultural heritage and facilitating access to them."[16] The Convention is more or less silent, however, on how such inventories ought to be compiled, to whom they should be made accessible and how intellectual property rights and interests, including of Indigenous peoples and other custodians of traditional cultural expressions, ought to be addressed. These are complex questions indeed.

The Convention does state that "[n]othing in this Convention may be interpreted as ... affecting the rights and obligations of States Parties deriving

---

13 *See* J. Anderson, *Access and Control of Indigenous Knowledge in Libraries and Archives: Ownership and Future Use*, at 4 (5–7 May 2005) (paper presented at the conference *Correcting Course: Rebalancing Copyright for Libraries in the National and International Arena*, Columbia University, New York, United States), *available at* www.conservationcommons.org/media/document/docu-i64cij.pdf (last visited 31 July 2008).

14 *Id.*

15 ICH Convention, *supra* note 10, Articles 12, 16 and 17.

16 *Id.*, Article 13(d)(iii).

from any international instrument relating to intellectual property rights ... to which they are parties"[17], and that States Parties should ensure "access to the intangible cultural heritage while respecting customary practices governing access to specific aspects of such heritage."[18] But larger questions remain as to authorship, control and intellectual ownership of intangible cultural heritage in documented form, and these questions require further thought.

2. SOME PRACTICAL EXAMPLES AS ILLUSTRATIONS

Perhaps some scenarios, drawing on actual examples, can best illustrate the issues at stake:

- The National Anthropological Archives (NAA) and the Human Studies Film Archives (HSFA) in the United States comprise a unique repository of ethnographic and anthropological materials, many of them unpublished, concerning North American Indian cultures and the discipline of anthropology. The NAA currently holds field notes, unpublished manuscripts, expedition logs, maps, photographs, drawings, correspondence, journals, sound recordings, film and video and other media produced by anthropologists. These include some 635,000 photographs, 11,400 sound recordings and 1,000 hours of original ethnographic audio-visual materials, some of which is believed to be the first recorded moving images of particular Indigenous peoples. The NAA and the HSFA have embarked on several digitization projects, some in collaboration with Indigenous peoples, organizations and museums. The digital copies are being made for preservation purposes and to facilitate the wider accessibility of the collections. Some of the field notes in the collection may not be disclosed, per the request of the anthropologist concerned; some photos depicting Navajo life include images of sacred ceremonies which the Navajo do not wish disclosed; and some other recordings and photos made many decades ago are considered "public domain" under US copyright law. In fact, almost each element in the vast collections of the NAA and the HSFA are subject to different cultural sensitivities and intellectual property considerations.[19]

---

17 *Id.*, Article 3(b).

18 *Id.*, Article 13(d)(ii).

19 *See* M. Skrydstrup, *Towards Intellectual Property Guidelines and Best Practices for Recording and Digitizing Intangible Cultural Heritage: A Survey of Codes, Conduct and Challenges in North America* (2006) (*prepared for* WIPO), *available at* www.wipo.int/export/sites/www/tk/en/folklore/culturalheritage/casestudies/skrydstrup_report.pdf (last visited 31 July 2008).

- In 1955, the famous American folksinger Peter Seeger put together a song *Where Have all the Flowers Gone?* the basic idea of which came from an old Russian folk song *Koloda Duda. Where Have all the Flowers Gone?* became an international hit. The Russian folk song had been recorded and made publicly available for safeguarding and promotional purposes, and it was therefore accessible to composers and performers such as Seeger. Seeger has since arranged for some royalties from the song to go to the national folk song archives in the Moscow library.[20] There are several similar examples of the use of ethnographic recordings of traditional music for commercial purposes, including the celebrated *Deep Forest* and *Return to Innocence* cases.[21]
- In the Pacific Northwest, a Skagit elder shared a personal story in a public meeting that was recorded and transcribed. It was later used in a classroom for teaching purposes. In the Skagit way, the story had been shared as a gift without any implied consent to the listeners to share it further, as it remained in custodianship of the elder. The derivative use of the story, even in the classroom for non-commercial purposes, was extremely offensive and hurtful to the elder.[22] Several other examples of the use of stories come to mind, such as Anne Cameron's children's books based on Westcoast (Canada) Indigenous stories but in which Cameron claimed sole authorship and gave no credit to the Indigenous origins of the stories.[23]
- In 2005, the Smithsonian Institution established the Smithsonian Global Sound initiative, a network of music audio archives that seeks to deliver the world's diverse cultural expressions via digital media. There are over 500 different cultural groups represented in the archive and the recordings date back to the 1930s. Whilst relevant permissions for the digital reproduction of these recordings have been sought, in many cases these permissions are

---

20 *See* WIPO, Intergovernmental Committee on Intellectual Property and Genetic Resources, Traditional Knowledge and Folklore, *Draft Report (Second Draft)*, at 60–61, par. 120, WIPO/GRTKF/IC/9/14. Prov.2 (5 November 2006), *available at* www.wipo.int/edocs/mdocs/tk/en/wipo_grtkf_ic_9/wipo_grtkf_ic_9_14_prov_2.pdf (last visited 31 July 2008) (statement by Peter Seeger, read on his behalf by Matt Callahan at its Ninth Session).

21 *See, e.g.*, H. Zemp, "The/An Ethnomusicologist and the Record Business" 28 *Yearbook for Traditional Music* 36 (1996) (discussing the *Deep Forest* case); A.R. Riley, "Recovering Collectivity: Group Rights to Intellectual Property in Indigenous Communities", 18 *Cardozo Arts & Ent. L.J.* 175 (2000) (discussing the *Return to Innocence* case).

22 *See* WIPO, Intergovernmental Committee on Intellectual Property and Genetic Resources, Traditional Knowledge and Folklore, *Second Draft Report*, at 63, par. 120, WIPO/GRTKF/IC/8/15. Prov. 2 (5 October 2005), *available at* www.wipo.int/edocs/mdocs/tk/en/wipo_grtkf_ic_8/wipo_grtkf_ic_8_15_prov_2.pdf (last visited 31 July 2008) (intervention by the *Tulalip* tribes presented at its Eighth Session).

23 *See* G. Younging, *Competing Jurisdictions over Traditional Knowledge in the Northern Americas*, at 12–13 (2006) (paper submitted to Tenth Session of WIPO Intergovernmental Committee on Intellectual Property and Genetic Resources, Traditional Knowledge and Folklore, Geneva, Switzerland), *available at* www.nationalimac.org/pt/Forums/tabid/59/Default.aspx?dnnbbfid=4&dnnbbtid=19 (last visited 31 July 2008).

impossible to obtain, as many artists were not originally documented and remain unidentified. In 2005, Smithsonian Global Sound unintentionally made available ceremonial material relating to an Indigenous group that was considered highly confidential. This was because the material pertained to certain men's religious or ceremonial practices. The claim, made by an anthropologist on behalf of the community, raised questions in regard to the Smithsonian's right to disclose this material, and what agreements the Smithsonian had entered with the anthropologist who had made the original recordings. The community had no legal rights to the material and hence no avenue to challenge the Smithsonian. The community in question was very concerned that whilst the recordings might legally constitute public domain material, this was contrary to the community's own beliefs, and that disclosure by uninitiated parties could have serious religious and spiritual consequences for the community. After ascertaining the provenance of the collection, and consulting historical records regarding the maintenance of and access to the collection, the Smithsonian resolved the dispute by taking the offending material off the website.[24]

- In 1984, a photographer from a local New Mexican newspaper flew over the Pueblo of Santo Domingo and photographed a ceremonial dance. The photos were published several times and the dance was described by the journalist as a "pow-wow". The dance was sacred and had to be kept secret under Pueblo customary laws.[25] The Pueblo wished to stop the use of the pictures to avoid future harm. The dance was not protected as a copyright work or a performance. The case was eventually settled out of court.
- At the Metropolitan Museum in New York an exhibition of ancient sculpture from West Mexico was on view from October 2004 to April 2005. A webpage with several images of sculptures from that exhibit remain available on the museum's website, and a hardback book entitled *Heritage of Power: Ancient Sculpture from West Mexico: The Andrall E. Pearson Family Collection*, accompanied the exhibition and remains for sale in the Metropolitan Museum's bookstore; the book includes 72 images; 64 of which are in full-colour. There are several parties with a legitimate interest in the presentation, treatment and archiving of these objects from West Mexico, all of which relate to intellectual property. The parties include the Pearson family that owns them; the Metropolitan Museum that is exhibiting them; the scholars and photographers who assembled the information and images providing the background for the exhibit, catalogue and hardback book; and the ancestors

---

24 *See* J. ANDERSON, working materials prepared for WIPO (on file with author).

25 *See* D. WÜGER, "Prevention of Misappropriation of Intangible Cultural Heritage through Intellectual Property Laws", in J.M. FINGER and P. SHULER (eds.), *Poor People's Knowledge: Promoting Intellectual Property in Developing Countries*, 2004, 183, 186.

of the West Mexican people who created these objects. If the objects themselves belonged to the museum, for example, the Pearson family interest would be eliminated. If the exhibit were centered on contemporary West Mexican artists instead of unidentifiable artists from an ancient culture, those artists' interests would come into play and the Museum would need to consider their individual concerns as opposed to the collective concerns of the *Comala, Ameca-Ezatlán* and *Ixtlán del Rio* peoples. Yet, even in such a case, the collective concerns of modern-day West Mexicans are at the heart of current calls for the protection of traditional cultural expressions against misappropriation and illegitimate use, and may need to be taken into account.[26]

- In 2004, the Museum of Victoria in Australia held an exhibition of previously un-exhibited Aboriginal bark paintings from collections held at the British Museum and the Royal Botanical Gardens in Kew. During the exhibition, the Dja Dja Warrung Aboriginal community in Central Victoria made ownership claims to the bark paintings and the intellectual property of the cultural expressions therein. The claims received significant publicity and tensions between community spokespeople and the Museum increased. Subsequently, an inspector acting under the *Aboriginal and Torres Strait Islander Heritage Protection Act (1984)* imposed a series of emergency declarations which prevented the museum from returning the items. The Museum of Victoria was unable to fulfil its contractual obligations to the British Museum. After several months of unsuccessful negotiations, which included a representative flown to Australia from the British Museum, the Museum of Victoria took the case to court and successfully challenged the legality of the emergency declarations. The inspector failed to make a permanent declaration to keep the objects in Australia and they were consequently returned. Whilst the dispute was resolved to the satisfaction of both the Museums, the Dja Dja Warrung community continues to make assertions regarding the ownership of the bark paintings and put forward arguments regarding the ongoing dispossession of cultural property.[27]

These are diverse examples, but they illustrate the variety of contexts within which intellectual property questions can arise and the range of intellectual property related concerns which there may be. They illustrate that the digitization and dissemination of traditional cultural expressions can lead to their

26 *See* M. Torsen, *Sustaining Creativity, Safeguarding Cultural Heritage and Protecting Traditional Cultural Expressions: The Management of Intellectual Property Issues and Options – A Practical Guide for Museums and Archives* (forthcoming, 2008) (*prepared for* WIPO) (manuscript on file with author).

27 *See* Anderson, *supra* note 24.

misappropriation and misuse. In some cases, well-intentioned safeguarding efforts have unwittingly led to the unauthorized disclosure or commercial exploitation of culturally sensitive materials. As a result, Indigenous organizations, museums and archives, and researchers (such as ethnomusicologists) have called for guidance on which intellectual property issues and options arise during recording and digitization initiatives.

2.1. CHANGING THE WAY MUSEUMS AND INDIGENOUS COMMUNITIES SEE EACH OTHER

The management of Indigenous collections raises unique issues for cultural institutions because of certain qualities that make them fundamentally different from other collections. These qualities include that: Indigenous materials were often collected by non-Indigenous researchers in the absence of the informed consent of the Indigenous communities; the informational content of the collections might be sacred or confidential and subject to restricted use under customary laws; the legal status of such materials under intellectual property law is often unclear (*e.g.*, are they "public domain"?); and, while there is a lack of information available to Indigenous peoples regarding the existence and location of collection items relating to themselves, Indigenous peoples and communities have a growing interest in being more directly involved in recording, presenting and representing their own cultures.[28]

The technological, political, legal and socio-cultural landscape within which cultural institutions, communities and other stakeholders operate is also under transformation. Digital technologies and the Internet are changing the way culture is preserved, produced and consumed. Politically, the resurgence of the Indigenous peoples movement has led to the recent adoption of a *United Nations Declaration on the Rights of Indigenous Peoples*.[29] There are changes too in how museums and communities see each other: communities are beginning to assert themselves not as the objects of study by others but as actively in control of if and how they are represented, while museums and cultural institutions worldwide increasingly see themselves not as "owners" but as "custodians" of their collections. Museums wish to work more directly and instrumentally with Indigenous communities, actively engaging Indigenous expertise, to foster new cross-cultural partnerships that can enrich museum work and benefit Indigenous communities.

---

28 *See* E. Hudson, *Cultural Institutions, Law and Indigenous Knowledge: A Legal Primer on the Management of Australian Indigenous Collections*, at 3–4 (2006), *available at* www.wipo.int/export/sites/www/tk/en/folklore/creative_heritage/docs/aiatsis_ipria.pdf (last visited 31 July 2008). *See also* Anderson, *supra* note 13.

29 United Nations Declaration on the Rights of Indigenous Peoples, 13 September 2007, G.A. Res. 61/295, U.N. Doc. A/RES/47/1 (2007).

In the legal and policy environment, there is a renewed focus on "culture" and, in particular, "intangible cultural heritage" and "cultural diversity". There are concerted calls for re-evaluating the "public domain" status of intangible cultural heritage and to extend intellectual property-like protection to "traditional knowledge" and "traditional cultural expressions". All this within an economic and trade-related environment in which cultural industries account for between 4% and 6% of world gross national product and international trade in cultural goods reached USD 60 billion in 2002. Yet, despite a growing international thirst for "local" and "authentic" cultural goods and services, developing countries account for less than 1% of global exports of cultural goods.[30]

With this context in mind, it seems that documentation initiatives could offer valuable opportunities for collaboration between documenting institutions (such as museums, archives and cultural agencies) and Indigenous and other local communities who are the bearers and practitioners of their heritage. If so, one might be prompted to ask: How can museums, libraries and archives respond to Indigenous peoples as new user groups? For their part, can Indigenous and local communities participate more directly in the recording, digitization and dissemination of their cultural expressions, for safeguarding, promotional and income-generating purposes? How might museums, libraries and archives and Indigenous communities collaborate in this regard? How might such new relationships be conceptualized and then operationalized in practice?[31] As Anderson observes, museums, libraries and archives emerge as pivotal spaces within which fundamental questions about access, control, ownership and authorship in Indigenous materials can be examined, negotiated and rebalanced.[32]

3. INTELLECTUAL PROPERTY BEST PRACTICES, PROTOCOLS AND GUIDELINES FOR RECORDING, DIGITIZING AND DISSEMINATING INTANGIBLE CULTURAL HERITAGE: WIPO'S CREATIVE HERITAGE PROJECT

Discussions continue at WIPO and elsewhere on calls for new intellectual property norms for the protection of traditional cultural expressions and traditional knowledge. Views diverge, however, on fundamental questions such as what is a

30 *See* UNESCO Institute for Statistics, International Flows of Selected Cultural Goods and Services, 1994–2003: *Defining and Capturing the Flows of Global Cultural Trade*, 2005, 9.

31 *See* Anderson, *supra* note 13, at 4.

32 *Id.*

"traditional" cultural expression, why should it be protected in an intellectual property sense and who should benefit from such protection. It is not clear at this stage which direction these discussions will take.[33]

In the interim, there is growing interest in using practical tools, such as protocols, codes of conduct, licensing and other agreements, to manage intellectual property issues and options during the recording, digitization and dissemination of intangible cultural heritage. Protocols, for example, can encourage ethical conduct and promote interaction based on good faith and mutual respect. While they differ from legal obligations, they can identify appropriate ways of using Indigenous materials and interacting with Indigenous communities.[34]

In response to a widely-felt need for technical advice and a sharing of experiences on these issues, WIPO is distilling and developing, through its *Creative Heritage Project*[35], "best practices" and guidelines for managing intellectual property issues and options during the recording, digitization and dissemination of intangible cultural heritage. These best practices and guidelines would aim to assist communities and cultural institutions to manage intellectual property options so as to both *preserve* cultural heritage and *protect* it against misappropriation and misuse. In other words, they would aim to support safeguarding initiatives in concert with the protection of creativity, signalling an inherent complementarity and mutual supportiveness between intellectual property protection and intangible cultural heritage safeguarding. They would also seek to play a part in facilitating the kinds of collaborations described above between institutions and communities.

As already alluded to, this WIPO project is a practical complement to the ongoing discussion of *sui generis* approaches to the protection of traditional cultural expressions and traditional knowledge taking place in several countries and regional organizations, and internationally at WIPO in the WIPO Intergovernmental Committee on Intellectual Property and Genetic Resources, Traditional Knowledge and Folklore (Intergovernmental Committee).[36] In Section 4, there is further information on this process.

---

33 For further information, *see supra* Section 4.

34 *See, e.g.*, Australia Council for the Arts, Performing Cultures: Protocols for Producing Indigenous Australian Performing Arts 2-3 (2002) *available at* www.wipo.int/export/sites/www/tk/en/folklore/creative_heritage/docs/performing_cultures.pdf (last visited 31 July 2008).

35 *See* WIPO, *Creative Heritage Project: IP Guidelines for Documenting, Recording and Digitizing Intangible Cultural Heritage*, www.wipo.int/tk/en/folklore/culturalheritage/index.html (last visited 31 July 2008).

36 The establishment of the WIPO Intergovernmental Committee on Intellectual Property and Genetic Resources, Traditional Knowledge and Folklore (Intergovernmental Committee) was agreed to at the 26th (12th Extraordinary) Session of WIPO's General Assembly, held from 25 September to 3 October 2000. All working documents, comments, papers, studies, databases, questionnaires, and other materials prepared for consideration by the Intergovernmental Committee, as well as comprehensive reports of its sessions, are publicly available, in English,

The project recognizes that new technologies provide communities with fresh opportunities to document and digitize expressions of their traditional cultures, meeting the strong desire of communities to preserve, promote and pass on their cultural heritage to succeeding generations. Indeed, the opportunities offered by digital technologies and computer networks – especially the Internet – are, quite simply, unprecedented. Expressions of traditional creativity and innovation can serve as springboards for new cultural expressions especially in the digital world. Digitized traditional music, designs and art can reach new audiences in niche markets for distinctive, diverse and "local" cultural goods and services, and, in so doing, promote community and rural economic and cultural development. New technologies also offer enhanced means to safeguard and restore intangible cultural heritage, especially elements in danger of erosion and disappearance. They can also facilitate educational and scholarly opportunities and enhanced cultural exchange. Yet, these new forms of documentation and digitization can leave this cultural heritage vulnerable to unwanted exploitation beyond the traditional circle.

The Creative Heritage Project is accordingly developing a suite of practical tools and resources to assist cultural institutions and communities. More specifically, the project:

- has established a **hands-on training program in cultural documentation** for Indigenous and local communities and museum staff of developing countries, in partnership with the American Folklife Centre (AFC) and the Centre for Documentary Studies (CDS), both in the United States of America. This program will provide communities and museum staff with hands-on training in documentary techniques and archival skills necessary for effective community-based cultural conservation. Staff from WIPO will provide related intellectual property training, and WIPO will also provide the community with a basic kit of audio and video equipment for its own use after the training. A pilot project of this program will take place in September 2008, and representatives of a Maasai community from Kenya and of the National Museums of Kenya (NMK) will participate in this pilot. This pilot program recognizes both the utility of technology for Indigenous communities and the paramount need to empower communities to make informed decisions about how to manage intellectual property issues in a way that corresponds with community values and development goals;
- is preparing a **compendium for museums, archives and libraries** on identifying and addressing intellectual property issues that arise in relation to

French and Spanish; *see* WIPO, *Intergovernmental Committee*, www.wipo.int/tk/en/igc (last visited 31 July 2008).

the management of access to, ownership of and control over Indigenous and other collections;
- is preparing a **guidebook for Indigenous and local communities** on the development by them of intellectual property protocols related to their own documentation of intangible cultural heritage. Some communities have already developed their own intellectual property protocols and the guidebook would assist others to do so. Intellectual property protocols can enable communities to manage rights to their documentation as they relate to third parties, such as researchers and commercial parties.

3.1. SURVEYS AND CONSULTATIONS: AN EMPIRICAL AND INCLUSIVE APPROACH

A need to manage intellectual property issues within the already complex legal, cultural and social environments within which museums, archives and libraries operate is perhaps an unwelcome burden for cultural specialists and institutions. As Wim van Zanten writes elsewhere in the present volume, research and fieldwork generally take place on the basis of relationships between researchers and source communities which are founded on ethical standards, common sense, trust and mutual confidence.[37] It could be argued that formalizing these relationships through excessive attention to legal questions could harm valuable safeguarding activities.[38] In addition, many institutions and professional associations already have well-established codes, protocols and practices – worked out in the very specific and complicated legal and cultural environments in which they operate – that deal with these complex issues, although many of them do not address intellectual property issues. The very diversity of the contexts within which each institution operates calls for a diversity of responses. Therefore, it is explicitly not the aim of Creative Heritage Project to establish norms or guidelines which would constrain institutions in how they deal with these issues, but rather to act as a source of ideas and options especially for those institutions which have less experience in this complex and evolving area.

Addressing intellectual property questions has perhaps become somewhat inevitable, especially with the advent of new technologies and other transformations referred to earlier. While new technologies offer exciting possibilities for enhancing access to and better preservation of ethnographic collections, concerns

---

37 *See* Chapter [VAN ZANTEN] of the present volume. *See also* W. VAN ZANTEN, *Prior Informed Consent, Experiences with Ethnomusicological Recordings in Indonesia* (*prepared for* WIPO), *available at* www.wipo.int/multimedia/en/cultural_heritage/wim_van_zanten/index.html (last visited 31 July 2008).

38 *Id.*

over access, ownership and control become even more pressing as museums and other institutions set up digital libraries of their collections. In addition, growing interest among research and other institutions in "open access" models, which enhance the dissemination of research, learning and other materials[39], highlights the need for the proper management of intellectual property rights and interests.

Such intellectual property related best practices and guidelines would need to strike careful balances between the interests of creators, communities, cultural institutions and the public at large, also taking into account the role, contours and boundaries of the "public domain", and their development must necessarily involve a wide range of stakeholders.

Many professional associations, institutions and communities have already developed valuable intellectual property related codes, protocols, policies and standard agreements relating to the safeguarding of, access to, ownership of and control over cultural heritage. These include the International Council of Museums (ICOM)[40], the Society for Ethnomusicology[41] and the Pacific Islands Museums Association (PIMA)[42], to name only a very few. These existing practices and experiences serve as a basis for the distillation and development of best practices, protocols and guidelines.

WIPO has therefore commissioned surveys of these existing resources and practices. The surveys, which were prepared by commissioned experts, are being progressively made available on WIPO's website.[43] A publicly-accessible database of guides, codes of conduct, protocols and standard agreements currently in use by museums, archives, libraries and researchers from around the world is also available.[44] A series of short case-studies has also been developed – these draw from the surveys to identify and describe particularly interesting practices and projects. For example, this work has documented the following initiatives[45]:

(a) the experiences of the Traditional Music Archive in Sudan which signs intellectual property related consents with communities before recording

---

39 *See* T. Vetter and E. Katz, *Access to Knowledge in the Information Society*, at 4 (September 2007) (*prepared for* International Institute for Sustainable Development), *available at* www.iisd.org/pdf/2007/igsd_access.pdf (last visited 31 July 2008).

40 *See* International Council of Museums, *ICOM Code of Ethics for Museums, available at* www.wipo.int/export/sites/www/tk/en/folklore/creative_heritage/docs/icom_code.pdf (last visited 31 July 2008).

41 *See* Chapter [van Zanten] of the present volume.

42 *See* Pacific Islands Museums Association, *PIMA Code of Ethics for Pacific Museums and Cultural Centres, available at* www.wipo.int/export/sites/www/tk/en/folklore/creative_heritage/docs/pima_code_ethics.pdf (last visited 31 July 2008).

43 *See* WIPO, *Surveys of Existing Practices, Protocols and Policies*, www.wipo.int/tk/en/folklore/culturalheritage/surveys.html (last visited 31 July 2008).

44 *See* WIPO, *Database of Existing Codes, Guidelines and Practices*, www.wipo.int/tk/en/folklore/creative_heritage/index.html (last visited 31 July 2008).

45 For the case studies and referred resources, *see* WIPO, *supra* note 35.

their cultural performances and subsequently gives the community 50% of the tapes made of the performances, as a form of benefit-sharing;

(b) the Sealaska Heritage Institute, founded by the Tlingit, Haida and Tsimshian communities of Alaska to promote and protect their cultures, has adopted a *Cultural and Intellectual Property Rights Policy*[46] regarding the protection of crests, songs, stories and names as well as a *Photography (Including Video and Film) Policy*[47] that limits commercial recordings of cultural celebrations and events;

(c) in Jamaica, the Rastafari community, represented by the Ethio-Africa Diaspora Union Millennium Council, has drawn up a draft intellectual property contract for the filming and recording of their performances and for other media activities;

(d) in Australia, the Mukurtu Wumpurrarni-kari Archive was established by the Warumungu community to house photos, digital video clips, audio files and digital reproductions of cultural artefacts and documents. Access to the digital archive is defined by access parameters based on a set of Warumungu cultural protocols for the viewing and distribution of cultural knowledge;

(e) the Hopi Tribe of Arizona has developed a *Protocol for Research, Publications and Recordings* that sets out how the Hopi people would like their intellectual resources and traditional cultural expressions to be used by others;

(f) the Ministry of Fijian Affairs, Culture and Heritage has developed guidelines for socio-cultural researchers, taking into account intellectual property issues; and

(g) a digitization project relating to Omaha traditional music which has been undertaken by the American Folklife Centre in close collaboration with the Omaha Tribal Council, in which intellectual property issues were jointly identified and managed with the full involvement of the tradition bearers concerned.[48]

These resources form a fact-based and inclusive foundation for the development and distillation of best practices and intellectual property guidelines. Such a next step would necessarily require the active involvement of all stakeholders: relevant governmental offices and intergovernmental bodies; archives, museums and other institutions; researchers; Indigenous and cultural communities; professional bodies; and intellectual property lawyers, to name only a few.

---

46 *See* Sealaska Heritage Institute, *Cultural and Intellectual Property Rights Policy*, *available at* www.wipo.int/export/sites/www/tk/en/folklore/creative_heritage/docs/sealaska_cultural_policy.pdf (last visited 31 July 2008).

47 *See* Sealaska Heritage Institute, *Photography (Including Video and Film) Policy*, *available at* www.wipo.int/export/sites/www/tk/en/folklore/creative_heritage/docs/sealaska_photo_policy.pdf (last visited 31 July 2008).

48 *See* Skrydstrup, *supra* note 19.

3.2. SPECIFIC INTELLECTUAL PROPERTY QUESTIONS RELATED TO INVENTORY MAKING

It might be useful to highlight certain intellectual property issues and implications associated with inventorying elements of intangible cultural heritage. The intellectual property implications depend to some degree on what "inventorying" means in practice, how and by whom it is carried out, and who has access to the inventories and on what terms. For example, the intellectual property issues raised by inventories which take the form only of "lists" are different from those which apply if inventorying involves the making of copies or other fixations of the elements of intangible cultural heritage being inventoried. For example, the intellectual property consequences of recording a performance of a traditional song and making that recording available to the public are distinct from those that arise if only the name of the song is entered into an inventory. In other words, an intellectual property analysis of inventory making can usefully examine the intellectual property implications of both the *making* of an inventory (what is inventoried and how this is carried out) and the *exploitation* of the inventory (what is made available and who has access to what and on which terms).

As has been mentioned before, the intellectual property implications of establishing and managing inventories of intangible cultural heritage impact directly on the interplay between measures for the intellectual property "protection" of creations and innovations, on the one hand, and the "safeguarding" or "preservation" of cultural materials, on the other. The intellectual property issues and implications associated with inventorying intangible cultural heritage are not obstacles to inventorying; however, they may require that some specific legal and practical steps be taken. Indeed, with appropriate coordination, measures for safeguarding intangible cultural heritage and for protecting the intellectual property therein could be mutually reinforcing and supportive.

Below are some of the main intellectual property related questions and issues that may arise during intangible cultural heritage inventory making. First, the process of inventorying intangible cultural heritage might establish new intellectual property rights (for example, new intellectual property rights might be established in recordings of intangible cultural expressions or in creating a database of materials embodying intangible cultural heritage). If so, how, if at all, should the intellectual property interests of the communities who are the bearers of the intangible cultural heritage be addressed? This question is important because the strategic management of new rights in a database or digitizations of materials otherwise in the "public domain" could benefit the communities who are the bearers of the intangible cultural heritage. For example, "public domain" rock paintings have been indirectly protected through exercise of copyright in photographs taken of the paintings.[49]

Second, inventories, databases and other information systems incorporating intangible cultural heritage or information about intangible cultural heritage could be useful in supporting claims by communities to enhanced protection of their intangible cultural heritage. For example, an inventory could provide valuable information on the identity of beneficiary communities, shed light on applicable customs, traditions and customary laws, identify culturally offensive uses and help to resolve claims to the same or similar expressions of folklore by more than one community. The information in an inventory is integral to the interpretation and implementation of many national and regional laws on the protection of traditional cultural expressions, as well as draft WIPO provisions for the *sui generis* protection of traditional cultural expressions.[50] For example, the draft WIPO provisions would protect traditional cultural expressions "characteristic of" a particular community against *offensive* uses, and share benefits according to "customary practices". Quaere whether cultural heritage inventories and databases could assist in interpreting and implementing provisions such as these. This discussion should not be taken to suggest that it is the role or responsibility of museums and other institutions to become directly involved, as interested parties, in dispute resolution processes. Rather, their valuable records could serve both preservation and protection objectives for the benefit of intangible cultural heritage practitioners and source communities.

Third, inventories could act as declaratory or constitutive registers of interests in traditional cultural expressions. For example, some national laws for the protection of traditional cultural expressions require or allow the registration of expressions for which protection is desired. Such a formality can provide certainty and transparency in relation to which expressions are claimed by which community. Perhaps a national intangible cultural heritage inventory or an inventory controlled and maintained by a tribe itself could also serve such a function. Furthermore, joint inventories established by more than one country could support claims by more than one country to a shared expression of traditional culture. Indeed, many cultural expressions in neighbouring countries have similar origins, and joint inventories could play a valuable role in pre-empting competing claims. The UNESCO program entitled the *Proclamation of Masterpieces of the Oral and Intangible Heritage of Humanity*[51] could provide

---

49 *See* T. Janke, *Minding Culture: Case Studies on Intellectual Property and Traditional Cultural Expressions* 9–27 (2003), *available at* www.wipo.int/tk/en/studies/cultural/minding-culture/studies/finalstudy.pdf (last visited 31 July 2008) (*prepared for* WIPO). *See also* Chapter [Janke] of the present volume.

50 *See infra* Section 4.2.

51 *See* UNESCO, *Proclamation of Masterpieces*, http://portal.unesco.org/culture/en/ev.php-URL_ID=2226&URL_DO=DO_TOPIC&URL_SECTION=201.html (last visited 31 July 2008).

some useful guidance here – the program allowed for multinational candidatures for forms of cultural expression shared by several Member States, and several Masterpieces have been proclaimed in the names of more than one country.[52]

Finally, inventory making complements and forms part of strategies aimed at documenting and publishing traditional knowledge so as to avoid the patenting of inventions derived from the knowledge. The documentation and publication of such knowledge could well vitiate a claim to novelty or non-obviousness and make it impossible for anyone to obtain a patent for an invention based upon or related to the knowledge. This may be desirable as part of a *defensive* strategy aimed at preventing the acquisition of intellectual property rights over traditional knowledge by parties other than the customary custodians of the knowledge. As Vinod K. Gupta describes elsewhere in the present volume, a growing number of initiatives, such as the Traditional Knowledge Digital Library (TKDL) in India, seek to use databases and registries of traditional knowledge as part of a defensive strategy, particularly in respect of previously disclosed and codified traditional medicinal knowledge.[53]

4. INTRODUCING WIPO'S WORK ON THE PROTECTION OF TRADITIONAL KNOWLEDGE AND CULTURAL EXPRESSIONS

4.1. WHAT IS "INTELLECTUAL PROPERTY PROTECTION"?

"Intellectual property protection" refers to the protection of the results of creative intellectual activity against misappropriation and misuse. Intellectual property systems are diverse in character, but they generally aim at: (i) giving the originators of intellectual works a say over whether, and if so how, their works are used by others; (ii) providing for acknowledgement and respect for originators; and (iii) appropriately sharing the benefits of use of their works. Intellectual property protection does not oblige the commercial exploitation of creative works, but rather offers a range of options for creators who may wish to disseminate their creative works while safeguarding against misleading attribution and deception of the public in the marketplace.

In this context, "protection" is distinct from but complementary to the concepts of "safeguarding", "conservation" and "preservation" in relation to cultural heritage, traditions and ways of life. Intellectual property "protection"

52 For example, the *Urtiin duu* or "long song" is a multinational Proclamation (China and Mongolia); *see* www.unesco.org/culture/ich/index.php?lg=EN&topic=mp&cp=MN#tocl (last visited 31 July 2008).

53 *See* Chapter [Gupta] of the present volume.

refers to the protection of intangible creations and innovations from illegitimate exploitation and misuse.

WIPO's work on traditional cultural expressions is concerned with the protection of traditional cultural expressions, as intellectual properties, against their copying, adaptation and use by unauthorized parties. On the other hand, the "safeguarding" of intangible heritage is more concerned with preserving the social processes and environments which have produced and continue to create traditional cultural expressions[54]; safeguarding is more directly concerned with the revitalization, transmission and maintenance of traditional cultural expressions than their legal protection in the intellectual property sense. Therefore, the protection of creativity and the safeguarding of cultural heritage seem to aim at different ends and address distinct harms. This does not mean they are at odds, however. Both are necessary for the holistic preservation, promotion and protection of intangible cultural heritage. They are, one may say, two sides of the same coin.

4.2. WIPO'S WORK ON THE PROTECTION OF TRADITIONAL KNOWLEDGE AND CULTURAL EXPRESSIONS AGAINST MISAPPROPRIATION AND MISUSE

WIPO first began examining the relationship between intellectual property and the protection, promotion and preservation of traditional knowledge and traditional cultural expressions several decades ago, often in cooperation with UNESCO. More recently, in 1998, WIPO embarked on extensive fact-finding and consultations with Indigenous peoples, local communities and other stakeholders, in order to learn first-hand of their intellectual property related needs and aspirations in relation to traditional cultural expressions and traditional knowledge.[55]

WIPO Member States have called for accelerated progress in this area, stressing the "international dimension" of these questions and emphasizing that no outcome of WIPO's work in this area is excluded, including the possible development of an international instrument or instruments. They have also

---

54 *See* PROTT, *supra* note 3, at 666–67.

55 *See* WIPO, *Intellectual Property Needs and Expectations of Traditional Knowledge Holders: WIPO Report on Fact-Finding Missions on Intellectual Property and Traditional Knowledge (1998–1999)* (April 2001), *available at* www.wipo.int/tk/en/tk/ffm/report/index.html (last visited 31 July 2008); W.B. WENDLAND, "Intellectual Property and the Protection of Cultural Expressions: The Work of the World Intellectual Property Organization (WIPO)", in F.W. GROSHEIDE and J.J. BRINKHOF (eds.), *Intellectual Property Law 2002: Articles on Cultural Expressions and Indigenous Knowledge*, 2002, 101 (2002).

underscored that WIPO's work should not prejudice developments in other forums.

The Intergovernmental Committee is currently examining draft provisions for the *sui generis* protection of traditional knowledge and traditional cultural expressions.[56] The draft *sui generis* instruments recognize, amongst other things, collective interests in traditional knowledge and expressions of traditional cultures which are "characteristic" of a distinct cultural identity. These interests would be respected for as long as a traditional community continues to be associated with the knowledge or cultural expressions. These drafts include compliance with the "free, prior and informed consent" principle in certain cases and the recognition of customary laws and practices. In line with the views of many Indigenous and traditional communities, the draft provisions do not require the assertion of new exclusive property rights over traditional knowledge or traditional cultural expressions, but accommodate this option if communities wish to take it up in accordance with applicable customary laws.

The draft on traditional cultural expressions is also explicitly intended to complement and support cultural heritage safeguarding programs and measures, and it contains specific provisions addressing the interface between the protection of traditional cultural expressions and their safeguarding. For example, the draft

---

56 There are two distinct sets of draft objectives and principles, the first dealing with traditional cultural expressions ("expressions of folklore") and the second with traditional knowledge as such. (In this context, "traditional cultural expressions" refers to tangible and intangible forms in which traditional knowledge and cultures are expressed, appear or are communicated. Traditional cultural expressions can include music, oral narratives and literature, art, crafts, names and symbols, designs, architectural forms and performances. "Traditional knowledge", on the other hand, refers to the content or substance of knowledge resulting from intellectual activity in a traditional context. It includes agricultural, environmental and medicinal knowledge, and knowledge associated with genetic resources.) This responds to the choice made in many cases to address distinctly the specific policy and legal questions raised by these two areas. The draft materials are prepared, though, in the understanding that for many communities these are closely related, even integral, aspects of respect for and protection of their cultural and intellectual heritage. The two sets of draft objectives and principles are therefore complementary. Some jurisdictions protect both traditional cultural expressions and traditional knowledge in a single instrument, while others use a range of laws and instruments to address the two areas, or specific aspects of them, distinctly. *See* WIPO, Intergovernmental Committee on Intellectual Property and Genetic Resources, Traditional Knowledge and Folklore, *The Protection of Traditional Knowledge: Draft Objectives and Principles*, WIPO/GRTKF/IC/10/5 (2 October 2006), *available at* www.wipo.int/edocs/mdocs/tk/en/wipo_grtkf_ic_10/wipo_grtkf_ic_10_5.pdf (last visited 31 July 2008); WIPO, Intergovernmental Committee on Intellectual Property and Genetic Resources, Traditional Knowledge and Folklore, *The Protection of Traditional Cultural Expressions/Expressions of Folklore: Draft Objectives and Principles*, WIPO/GRTKF/IC/10/4 (2 October 2006), *available at* www.wipo.int/edocs/mdocs/tk/en/wipo_grtkf_ic_10/wipo_grtkf_ic_10_4.pdf (last visited 31 July 2008) [hereinafter "*Draft TCE Principles*"]. For comments received on earlier drafts, *see* WIPO, *Draft Provisions on Traditional Cultural Expressions/Folklore and Traditional Knowledge*, www.wipo.int/tk/en/consultations/draft_provisions/draft_provisions.html (last visited 31 July 2008).

contains a provision to the effect that the measures for the protection of traditional cultural expressions in the draft would not apply to "non-commercial research or private study" or to "the making of recordings and other reproductions of [traditional cultural expressions/expressions of folklore] for purposes of their inclusion in an archive or inventory for non-commercial cultural heritage safeguarding purposes".[57] The draft also suggests that traditional cultural expressions of particular cultural or spiritual value for which strong property rights protection is sought should first be registered or notified to a public authority. In such a case, the draft provides:

> (i) To the extent that such registration or notification may involve the recording or other fixation of the traditional cultural expressions/expressions of folklore concerned, any intellectual property rights in such recording or fixation should vest in or be assigned to the relevant community.
> (ii) Information on and representations of the traditional cultural expressions/ expressions of folklore which have been so registered or notified should be made publicly accessible at least to the extent necessary to provide transparency and certainty to third parties as to which traditional cultural expressions/expressions of folklore are so protected and for whose benefit.[58]

The draft provisions, therefore, seek to complement, and respond to, the needs of safeguarding and the specific intellectual property aspects of registering and documenting traditional cultural expressions.

The drafts have not yet been adopted or endorsed by the Intergovernmental Committee and may be developed further. They draw upon a wide range of community, national and regional experiences[59], and have been developed over several years by and in consultation with Member States, Indigenous peoples and other traditional and cultural communities, civil society organizations and a range of other interested parties. Earlier drafts of the objectives and principles were the subject of open commenting processes established by the Intergovernmental Committee. Details of the background to these documents, and the wide range of materials and perspectives that shaped them, can be found on WIPO's website.[60]

While the draft objectives and principles have no formal status, they are already being used as points of reference in a range of national, regional and

57 *Draft TCE Principles*, *supra* note 56, Annex, Article 5(a)(iii).
58 *Id.*, Annex, Article 7(b).
59 *See* WIPO, *Legislative Texts on the Protection of Traditional Knowledge and Traditional Cultural Expressions (Expressions of Folklore) and Legislative Texts relevant to Genetic Resources*, www.wipo.int/tk/en/laws/index.html (last visited 31 July 2008) (containing a compilation of national and regional laws and legislative measures related to traditional cultural expressions and traditional knowledge).
60 *See* WIPO, *Draft Provisions*, *supra* note 56.

international policy discussions and standard-setting processes. Several processes in other policy areas are drawing directly from the draft WIPO provisions.

4.3. INTELLECTUAL PROPERTY AND TRADITIONAL CULTURAL EXPRESSIONS: A COMPLEX POLICY DEBATE

Traditional music, designs, rituals, performances, oral narratives, names, symbols and signs communicate a community's beliefs and values, embody skills and know-how, reflect a community's history, and define its cultural identity. Traditional cultural expressions such as these are valuable cultural assets of the communities who maintain, practice and develop them. They can also be economic assets – they are creations and innovations that can be traded or licensed for income generation and local economic development. They may equally serve as an inspiration to other creators and innovators who can adapt the traditional expressions and derive new creations and innovations.

In considering whether, and if so, how, to "protect" traditional cultural expressions in an intellectual property sense, it is appropriate to consider how such protection would affect important policy objectives such as the promotion of creativity, the preservation of cultural heritage and the promotion of cultural diversity. The possible intellectual property-like protection of expressions of traditional cultures also touches upon other important policy areas, such as (i) freedom of expression; (ii) respect for the rights, interests and claims of Indigenous and other traditional communities; (iii) recognition of customary laws, protocols and practices; (iv) "access to knowledge" and the scope of the "public domain"; and (v) the challenges of cultural pluralism and multiculturalism. How would proposals for the "protection" of traditional cultural expressions affect achievement of these valued policy goals? How would new intellectual property-like property rights over traditional cultural expressions affect creativity in a derivative culture? When does legitimate cultural borrowing become "misappropriation"? Which approach would best foster cultural diversity in this culturally pluralistic and socially, technologically and commercially interconnected world? Which approach best preserves the old while fostering the new?

The possible intellectual property-like protection of traditional cultural expressions is a deeply complex debate, and the Intergovernmental Committee has recently moved to discuss, in addition to the draft provisions, a list of core issues on intellectual property and traditional cultural expressions, in an effort to clarify key conceptual, policy and legal questions. While many are critical that the Intergovernmental Committee has not yet been able to agree on new international standards in this area, others call for caution and a greater understanding of *what* precisely would be protected, *why* there would be such protection and *how* any such protection would be provided.[61]

5. CONCLUDING REMARKS

Valuable safeguarding programs, including inventory making, could take into account relevant intellectual property issues, in particular, the wishes of Indigenous and cultural communities that their cultural heritage not be inadvertently misappropriated and misused. Mutually beneficial collaborations between collection and holding institutions and communities could promote creativity, community development, museum and archival services, and scientific and educational opportunities. Identifying relevant intellectual property issues and strategically managing intellectual property options could contribute to and enrich successful collaborations of this sort for the benefit of all. Clarity and certainty on intellectual property options could strengthen relationships between institutions and communities. Above all, managing intellectual property issues within intangible cultural heritage documentation programs could shed further light on the relationship between the legal protection of creativity and the safeguarding of intangible cultural heritage, and promote their relationship as one of complementarity and mutual supportiveness.

61 *See* W.B. Wendland, "It's a Small World (After All): Some Reflections on Intellectual Property and Traditional Cultural Expressions", in C.B. Graber and M. Burri-Nenova (eds.), *Intellectual Property and Traditional Cultural Expressions in a Digital Environment*, 2008, 150.

INDIA'S TKDL

Definition and Classification of Intangible Cultural Heritage and Traditional Knowledge in the Context of Inventory Making

Vinod K. GUPTA*

* Chairman, TKDL Task Force; Head, Information Technology Division, CSIR, Anusandhan Bhawan, 2 Rafi Marg, New Delhi-110 001, India; e-mail: vkg@csir.res.in.

1. INDIA'S TRADITIONAL KNOWLEDGE DIGITAL LIBRARY

The erroneous grant of patents to traditional medicines, which are either part of traditional knowledge or a minor variation thereof, has caused great concern in the developing world. In India, the origin of the Traditional Knowledge Digital Library (TKDL) goes back to the legal battle waged by India's Council of Scientific and Industrial Research (CSIR) for re-examination of patent No. US 5 401 504, which was granted to two Indians living in the United States for the wound-healing properties of turmeric. In a landmark decision, the United States Patent and Trademark Office (U.S. PTO) revoked the patent after ascertaining that there was no novelty in it, since turmeric had been used in India for centuries. This was the first time that a patent based on the traditional knowledge of a developing country had been successfully challenged. Since then, other patents have been successfully challenged on the basis of traditional knowledge. The revocation of the patent granted by the European Patent Office to W.R. Grace Company and the U.S. Department of Agriculture for neem (EPO patent No. 436 257) is another example. Following these experiences of wrongful patenting, the TKDL project was formally established in June 2001 in order to prevent further misappropriation of disclosed traditional knowledge.

At the outset, traditional knowledge documentation lacked a classification system. To meet this need, a modern classification system based on the structure of International Patent Classification (IPC) was developed. The classification system was named Traditional Knowledge Resource Classification (TKRC), and has already been applied to *ayurveda* and *unani*. The concepts of TKRC were presented in February 2001 at the Committee of Experts meeting of the Special Union for the International Patent Classification (IPC Union), which is a World Intellectual Property Organization (WIPO) task force composed of the United States Patent and Trademark Office, the European Patent Office, and representatives of China, Japan and India. The IPC Union studies the possibility of linking or integrating TKRC developed by India with IPC. In February 2002, the IPC Union recognized the need for a more detailed level of classification relating to medicinal plants and recommended adding a subclass named A61. In February 2003, the Committee of Experts further expanded the classification system by recommending (1) the inclusion of 200 subgroups on traditional knowledge, as opposed to the earlier single subgroup on medicinal plants (A61K 35/78); (2) the linkage of TKRC to IPC; and (3) continuation of work on biodiversity, traditional knowledge and traditional cultural expressions.

The Committee of Experts formally decided to link IPC and TKRC at its thirty fifth meeting, held in October 2004, as a result of the presentation made on the TKDL and the concordance table between IPC and TKRC. This development is likely to have a significant impact on the system of search and examination for patents in the area of traditional knowledge, thereby greatly reducing the possibility of granting erroneous patents to traditional knowledge.

2. PROBLEM DIMENSIONS IN THE INDIAN SCENARIO: SCALE OF MISAPPROPRIATION OF DISCLOSED TRADITIONAL KNOWLEDGE

2.1. BACKGROUND TO THE TKDL

As indicated by the Indian experience, defensive and positive protection of traditional knowledge should be fully integrated within a national traditional knowledge protection and documentation policy. The TKDL has an important function in each of these aspects.

2.2. TOOL FOR DEFENSIVE PROTECTION

Patent examiners use available resources for searching the appropriate non-patent literature sources, when considering the patentability of any claimed subject matter. Patent literature, however, is usually wholly contained in several distinctive databases and can be more easily searched and retrieved whereas non-patent literature *prior art* may be scattered diversely. Therefore, the TKDL serves as a more easily accessible non-patent literature database that deals with traditional knowledge subject matter.

2.3. TOOL FOR ACTIVE RESEARCH

It has the potential to act as a bridge between modern science, modern medicines and traditional knowledge, and can be used for international advanced research based on information on traditional knowledge for developing novel drugs. In fact, there are several examples where intensive research on traditional knowledge has successfully led to creation of drugs.

2.4. COMPLEMENTARITY WITH POSITIVE PROTECTION

Defensive protection of disclosed traditional knowledge through the TKDL is only the first step within a comprehensive traditional knowledge protection policy of India. Defensive measures must be supplemented by positive measures, such as benefit sharing, in order to provide adequate protection for traditional knowledge holders. Therefore, it was concluded at national and regional levels, that a positive legal protection framework should complement TKDL systems, in order to safeguard the interests of traditional knowledge holders. At national and regional levels, work is under way for *sui generis* protection frameworks, which will protect traditional knowledge, whether disclosed or undisclosed, against misappropriation in the form of commercial use without benefit sharing. Since biopiracy studies have shown that most misappropriation of Indian traditional knowledge occurs outside the region, use of the TKDL is being internationalized and thus *sui generis* protection must also be extended to the international level.

2.5. FEATURES AND FUNCTIONALITIES OF THE TKDL

2.5.1. Bridge Between Traditional Knowledge As Prior Art and Patent Examiners

The TKDL database acts as a bridge between ancient traditional knowledge in the original languages (which may be in Hindi, Sanskrit, Urdu, Persian, Arabic, Tamil, *etc.*) and a patent examiner at a global level, since the database will provide information on modern as well as local names in a language and format understandable to patent examiners. Thus the gap in *prior art* knowledge is minimized. The database has sufficient details on definitions, principles, and concepts to minimize the possibility of minor or insignificant modifications being accepted as novelty.

2.5.2. Traditional Knowledge Resource Classification

Traditional knowledge documentation lacked a classification system. Therefore, a modern classification was created based on the structure of IPC. This has been attempted for *ayurveda* and has been named as TKRC. It was essential to seek international recognition for this innovative effort. Therefore, linkages have been established with the IPC Union at WIPO Geneva as mentioned in the Introduction.

2.5.3. Knowledge Conversion

Documented knowledge available in local languages, *i.e.* Sanskrit, Hindi, Arabic, Persian, Urdu, Tamil *etc.*, is transcribed into TKRC symbols by experts. The patent examiner helps the experts prepare a concordance between TKRC and IPC, which is then a part of the software. The converted version of all the TKRC symbols is thereafter imported in the database. The knowledge available in local languages can presently be translated into five international languages, *i.e.* English, German, French, Japanese and Spanish. The converted version of the formulation can be easily understood by a layman.

TKDL software, with its associated classification system, converts the available documented knowledge into multiple languages. It may be noted that the software does not do transliteration rather it does knowledge based conversion, where data abstracted once is converted into several languages by using state of the art technology such as Unicode, XML and Metadata methodology. Software also converts traditional terminology into modern terminology, for example *Kumari* (local name) to *Aloe barbadensis Mill.*, *Masurika* (Sanskrit name of a disease) to small pox *etc.*

The primary objective in creating the TKDL database is the defensive protection and prevention of misappropriation of the disclosed traditional knowledge existing in India. The purpose of creating the database will be achieved only when the database is integrated into the international intellectual property office activity of search and examination of the prior art search systems. On the other hand, it is also essential to ensure that this database is used only for search purposes; it must not act as an easily available tool for enhancing bio-piracy. In view of the above, an access agreement has been prepared which sets out the obligations on part of the database provider and user, and needs to be signed by both the parties before access to the database is provided.

3. CURRENT STATUS OF THE TKDL

3.1. THE TKDL PROJECT TEAM FRAMEWORK

The TKDL integrates multidisciplinary skills in traditional knowledge, classification expertise, IPC, information technology, and expertise in the French, German, Spanish and Japanese languages. Therefore, the project team represents the above skill set. The information technology experts create the software, provide the software support system and develop the portal. The traditional knowledge experts identify the formulations, enter the formulations, and edit and verify the formulations. Patent examiners are responsible for determining the appropriate IPC codes and hence develop a concordance between the IPC and the TKRC for integration of the appropriate IPC codes for each of the formulations. Scientists validate the scientific names of the plants, which appear in the formulations. Technical officers carry out the scanning of formulations from the original texts for integrating these in the database, which appear along with the formulations. Eminent traditional knowledge experts who are retired traditional knowledge experts verify and validate each of the formulations that have been included in the TKDL database.

3.2. THE TKDL IN PROGRESS

The TKDL is being created on the codified traditional knowledge of Indian systems of medicine. In the creation of the TKDL, 148 books comprising 230 volumes of *ayurveda*, *unani*, *siddha* and *yoga* are being used. The formulations present in these texts are being transcribed in patent application format in five international languages, which are English, French, German, Spanish and Japanese. The images from the original texts are also being incorporated into the database. TKDL *ayurveda* is being created for 76,000 formulations from 64 books having 90 volumes. TKDL *unani* is also being created on 100,000 formulations from 19 books comprising 67 volumes in Urdu, Arabic and Persian in the same format and languages as that of *ayurveda*. TKDL *siddha* targets 12,000 formulations from 45 Tamil texts in 53 volumes. TKDL *yoga* will also be created for 1,500 postures from 20 books. So far about 24 million A4 sized pages of information have been created out of 31 million pages expected to be created by December 2007.

The TKDL database has been created for 170,000 formulations in *ayurvedic*, *unani* and *siddha* texts. The original verses from the traditional texts have been scanned and incorporated into the database. Images of 943 plant, animal and mineral resources used in the formulations have also been incorporated into the database.

3.3. LIKELY DATE OF COMPLETION

The project on TKDL *ayurveda*, *unani* and *siddha* is likely to be completed by December 2007 when the data will be included in the portal.

4. THE TKDL: TOOL FOR ACTIVE RESEARCH

4.1. BRIEF INTRODUCTION OF INDIAN SYSTEMS OF MEDICINE

Documentation of traditional knowledge in India has focused to date on the codified Indian systems of medicine with a view to break language barriers between the original languages in which these systems are codified and the patent examiners. The Indian systems of medicine consist of *ayurveda*, *yoga*, *unani*, *siddha* and naturopathy. These systems are Indigenous and have over the years become a part of Indian tradition. The *ayurveda* and *unani* systems of medicine are the oldest systems of medicine in the world, and are still popular and practiced in the Indian sub-continent and other parts of the world. They deal with both the preventive and curative aspects of life. The texts or knowledge of these systems is in various languages; for example, the *ayurveda* is in Sanskrit and while *unani* medicine is in Arabic, Persian or Urdu.

4.2. GOLDEN TRIANGLE OF MODERN SCIENCE, MODERN MEDICINE AND TRADITIONAL KNOWLEDGE

The TKDL database breaks the language and format barriers. Hence, the TKDL database is a valuable tool for carrying out advanced research for identifying novel drugs through the route of reverse pharmacology. This is possible by the integration of traditional knowledge with modern medicine and science. In fact, the CSIR has developed new drugs using the concept of the golden triangle. To give one example, the drug Asmon has been developed by Indian Institute of Chemical Biology, Kolkata, for the treatment of bronchial asthma. Simultaneously, based on Indian traditional knowledge, the TKDL is likely to serve as a valuable tool for carrying out advanced research. The Indian system of medicine includes well developed systems of traditional medicines, *i.e. ayurveda*, *unani* and *siddha*. These systems have been practised since origin of creation while documented knowledge dates back earlier than 1000 BC and 400 BC, respectively, and are quite proven. However, all these systems, though a part of the Indian system of medicine, have existed independently. The TKDL is a mechanism, which can validate these systems against each other. Thus likely to enhance active research potential based on traditional knowledge through reverse pharmacology by order of magnitude.

4.3. ACTIVE RESEARCH PROGRAM

There is scope for active research programmes based on the TKDL database. As per the policy of the country, the information collected in the TKDL can become the basis for development of new pharmaceutical products, which can bring major health care benefits to wide populations in India and abroad.

5. STRATEGY FOR PREVENTING ABUSE OF THE TKDL

5.1. ACCESS MECHANISM

The TKDL is a proprietary database and shall be available to patent offices for preventing misappropriation and for collaborative research.

5.2. PATENT OFFICES: NON-DISCLOSURE AGREEMENT

Access to patent offices will be provided freely. However, the access to patent offices will be based on signing an Access Agreement on Non-Disclosure, *i.e.*, forbidding third party disclosure unless it is essential for search purposes. In view of the above, an access agreement has been prepared.

5.3. USER OBLIGATIONS

The user obligations are:

- not to disclose the contents of the TKDL to third parties unless it is necessary for patent search and examination;
- to use TKDL information only for patent search and examination;
- to provide related information to the provider as and when the TKDL is utilized for prior art searches; and
- to give feedback on enhancing the features and functionality of the TKDL to the provider when considered necessary.

5.4. ACCESS FOR COLLABORATIVE RESEARCH

Access to the TKDL database shall be provided on the basis of a bilateral agreement, which shall include non-disclosure and non-compete clauses. The income generation model will be based on well-established principles of access and benefit sharing (ABS). The ABS model may be based on one or more of the following non-exhaustive conditions:

(a) collaborative research and development and/or marketing commercialization;
(b) joint ownership and licensing of intellectual property rights of the products to be created based on the contents of the TKDL, which may include a lump

sum initial payment and payment of periodic royalties on a mutually agreed basis, such as agreed percentage of gross turn over of the product(s) concerned;

(c) transfer of technologies including the categories:
technologies for conservation;
technologies for biotechnological research;
technologies for duplicating the biotechnological inventions;
laboratory techniques;
technologies for selection and screening of samples, but not limited to these technological options alone; and
any other terms and conditions that may be mutually beneficial.

6. APPLICATION OF TKDL TECHNOLOGY TO INTANGIBLE CULTURAL HERITAGE

The convention dealing with protection of intangible cultural heritage, the *Convention for the Safeguarding of the Intangible Cultural Heritage* (ICH Convention)[1] was unanimously adopted in 2003 and came into force in 2006 after ratification by 30 states. Currently, there are 75 states that have deposited their instruments of ratification, approval or acceptance to the Convention.

The ICH Convention defines intangible cultural heritage as the "practices, representations, expressions, knowledge, skills – as well as the instruments, objects, artefacts and cultural spaces associated therewith – that communities, groups and, in some cases, individuals recognize as part of their cultural heritage."[2] The Convention also provides guidelines to what could be probable ways of protecting it. Article 12(1) provides that

> [T]o ensure identification with a view to safeguarding, each State Party shall draw up, in a manner geared to its own situation, one or more inventories of the intangible cultural heritage present in its territory. These inventories shall be regularly updated.

One of the primary ways to protect, promote and also ensure benefit sharing would be proper documentation of the intangible cultural heritage so that the rightful owners are not divested of their culture nor distressed by the improper use of their traditions.

---

1 *See* Convention for the Safeguarding of the Intangible Cultural Heritage, 17 October 2003, U.N. Doc. MISC/2003/CLT/CH/14 (2003), *available at* http://unesdoc.unesco.org/images/0013/001325/132540e.pdf (last visited 10 August 2007) [hereinafter "ICH Convention"].

2 *Id.*, Article 2(1).

In order to create a technical framework for the potential intangible cultural heritage database, the objectives of creation of the intangible cultural heritage inventory are defined as:

- prevention of misuse of intangible cultural heritage;
- use of intangible cultural heritage expressions or craftsmanship, *etc.*, for commercial purpose under prior informed consent and access and benefit sharing agreements.

The definite objectives will serve as the premise on which the database is to be built.

The various categories of intangible cultural heritage as defined by the ICH Convention fall under the following manifestations:

- oral traditions and expressions, including languages as a vehicle of intangible cultural heritage;
- music, dance, drama and other performing arts;
- social practices concerning nature and the universe;
- foods and clothing; and
- traditional craftsmanship.

These broad areas may be used to define the structure of the classification. These may be further classified under more specific categories to get the final hierarchical structure.

The assimilated, available information relating to traditional and cultural heritage, such as art, dance, drama, languages, practices *etc.*, may be then put under the appropriate heads according to technical specifications of standards for the database creation. The description and data storage pattern will vary depending upon the type of intangible cultural heritage being stored.

Therefore, the project on intangible cultural heritage documentation needs to have defined objectives, *i.e.*, (i) preservation; (ii) prevention against misappropriation; and (iii) tool for wealth creation. For realizing these objectives, classification of intangible cultural heritage would be a pre-requisite which can impart structure to the unstructured details on intangible cultural heritage. Similarly, breaking of language barriers is equally essential so as to provide global opportunities in wealth creation to national heritage. It may also be recognized that documentation can act against the basic objective of defensive protection, in cases where holders of intangible cultural heritage are not empowered and adequate safeguards are not built into the system. Intangible cultural heritage inventorization with the consent of holders can become a vehicle for creating new intellectual property based on the traditional context of intangible cultural heritage. TKDL technology is fully capable and relevant for documenting or inventorizing intangible cultural heritage independent of the language or form in which it is available.

7. CONCLUSIONS

Based on the discussion in this Chapter, the following principles for designing intangible cultural heritage inventories may be put forward:

- Documentation of traditional knowledge and intangible cultural heritage is essential for the preservation and protection of, and wealth creation based on, traditional knowledge and intangible cultural heritage.
- Documentation requirements are different for disclosed and undisclosed knowledge.
- Before initiating documentation, it is necessary to establish appropriate classification schemes for structuring of knowledge.
- TKRC created by India has received wide international acceptance and has become a basis for enhancing IPC for medicinal plants. The TKRC framework is relevant and applicable to the classification of intangible cultural heritage.
- The TKDL has been a successful model resulting in the creation of several new technologies.
- Access to a database such as the TKDL or intangible cultural heritage must be regulated as per national requirements and policies.
- Traditional knowledge and intangible cultural heritage databases are vital resources for creating new intellectual property rights and new drug development and for creating new intellectual property related to intangible cultural heritage.
- Intangible cultural heritage and traditional knowledge are closely related since both are based on people and their creative talent; therefore, after addressing the issues of traditional knowledge documentation, the TKDL technology can be applied with an equal degree of success to intangible cultural heritage documentation and inventorization.

INVENTORY MAKING AND FAIRY TALES

Safeguarding of Intangible Cultural Heritage in Historical Perspective

Steven VAN UYTSEL*

1. INTRODUCTION

About 200 years ago, the Brothers Grimm undertook a huge effort to collect fairy tales. They invited storytellers and transcribed their oral tales. This resulted in 1812 in a collection of 86 German fairy tales in a volume titled *Kinder- und Hausmärchen*[1] (Children and Household Tales).[2] Two years later, another collection

* LL.B., LL.M. (University of Antwerp), LL.M., LL.D. (Kyushu University); Assistant Professor, Kyushu University Faculty of Law.

1 *See, e.g.*, BRÜDER GRIMM, *Kinder- und Hausmärchen* [Children and Household Tales] (18th ed., 1999).

2 *See* H. RÖLLEKE, *Entstehungs- und Veröffentlichungsgeschichte der Grimmschen Märchen* [The Origin and the Publication History of the Grimm's Fairy Tales], epilogue to BRÜDER GRIMM, *supra* note 1, at 840.

of 70 fairy tales followed.[3] Throughout the years, their collection grew to 200 fairy tales.[4] The Brothers Grimm, by far the best-known fairy tale collectors, were not the first to collect and publish fairy tales. In 1697, Charles Perrault published his *Histoire ou Contes de Temps passé* (Tales or Stories of the Past)[5], which were mostly adapted versions of earlier folk tales collected by Giambattista Basile. For a long time, Basile's Neapolitan fairy tales titled *Lo cunto de li cunti overo lo trattenemiento de peccerille* (The Tale of Tales, or Entertainment for Little Ones)[6], also known as the *Pentamerone* (1674), was the best and richest collection of folk tales.

The respective works of the Brothers Grimm, Perrault and Basile could be seen as an early example of inventorying intangible cultural heritage.[7] A recently adopted international legal instrument in relation to safeguarding intangible cultural heritage, the *Convention for the Safeguarding of Intangible Cultural Heritage* (ICH Convention)[8], resumes with this practice of inventory making. State Parties, according to Article 12(1) of the ICH Convention, must identify and inventory intangible cultural heritage within their territory.

This Chapter investigates the legal framework on inventory making under the ICH Convention through the lens of the Brothers Grimm, Perrault and Basile. This investigation does not attempt to critique these or any other collector of fairy tales. At the end, each deals with intangible cultural heritage within a specific time framework, with its own peculiarities. Rather, this investigation seeks to define boundaries set forth by the ICH Convention in relation to inventory making. Possible insights into the purpose of inventories, design, and administration of inventories, would endow secondary value to this Chapter.

---

3 *See id.* at 849 (mentioning that the Brothers Grimm collected a total of 156 fairy tales when they finished the two collections. Deducting the 86 first collection fairy tales from this number, one reaches a number of 70 fairy tales in the second collection).

4 Even though Wilhelm Grimm liked to keep the number of fairy tales at 200, a number reached in the 1857 edition, the collection of fairy tales is more extensive. Heinz Rölleke points out that some fairy tales in earlier editions were replaced, and that a list of 10 Children's Legends are counted separately from the fairy tales, even though they are a constitutive part of the last edition. Besides these 10 Children's Legends, the collection of fairy tales is supposedly 210 in total; *see id.* at 868–69. *Cf.* R.B. Bottigheimer, *Grimms' Bad Girls and Bad Boys: The Moral and Social Vision of the Tales*, 1987, Preface ix (reporting the number even at 211).

5 *See, e.g.*, Ch. Perrault, *Histoire ou Contes de Temp Passé* (P. Durand (ed.), Editions des Deux Coqs d'Or, 1971) (1679).

6 *See, e.g.*, G. Basile, *Der Pentamerone* (K. Ranke (ed.), F. Liebrecht (trans.), Georg Olm Verlag, 1973) (1846); G. Basile, *Stories from the Pentamerone* (E.F. Strange (ed.), J.E. Taylor (trans.), Macmillan, 1911) (1847).

7 This seems especially the case for the Brothers Grimm. During his search for a publisher, Jacob Grimm pointed out that he wanted to prevent German folklore from dying out. Hence, collecting and printing fairy tales would "salvage what was left of the priceless national resources." *See* M. Tatar, *The Hard Facts of the Grimms' Fairy Tales*, 1987, 11.

8 *See* Convention for the Safeguarding of the Intangible Cultural Heritage, 17 October 2003, U.N. Doc. MISC/2003/CLT/CH/14 (2003), *available at* http://unesdoc.unesco.org/images/0013/001325/132540e.pdf (last visited 31 July 2008) [hereinafter "ICH Convention"].

This Chapter is divided into four sections. Section 2 points out that inventory making presupposes a systematic analysis of the object of the inventory. It is argued that any form of inventorying is impossible without a clear delineation of this object. Examination of the ICH Convention illuminates how it can help State Parties in this respect. Section 3 illustrates how the much-advocated bottom-up approach of safeguarding, emphasizing the role of communities, is conceptualized in the ICH Convention. Specifically, we highlight the requirements provided in the ICH Convention for community involvement in inventory making. Section 4 investigates whether the ICH Convention prescribes something in relation to the scope of inventory making. More precisely, this section questions whether the inventory should provide for the broader environment in which the intangible cultural heritage is embedded. Section 5 elaborates on possible intellectual property law issues generated by inventories created for safeguarding intangible cultural heritage. It explores whether the Convention is completely silent on the issue.

2. A SYSTEMATIC APPROACH TOWARDS INTANGIBLE CULTURAL HERITAGE

Private initiatives, such those of the Brothers Grimm, Perrault or Basile, led to several valuable collections of fairy tales. These collections detail fairy tales transmitted orally for generations. However, it is imprudent to outrightly view these as an inventory of intangible cultural heritage. The Brothers Grimm's collection of fairy tales found its origin in a plan of Clemens Brentano, who wanted to devote a publication to fairy tales, a much-neglected form of folklore at that time. In doing so, the publication would follow the folk song collection *Des Knaben Wunderhorn* of Clemens Brentano and Achim von Arnim, to which the Brothers Grimm already contributed.[9] However, Brentano and von Arnim turned away from the planned publication of fairy tales to pursue their own individual projects. The Brothers Grimm, having already done a considerable amount of fieldwork, decided to publish this work under their name.[10] A second edition soon followed the first edition of the *Kinder- und Hausmärchen*. This continued until the Brothers Grimm gradually expanded their collection to 200 fairy tales, the number of fairy tales found in their seventh, and last, edition of the *Kinder- und Hausmärchen*.[11]

---

9 *See* Chr. Kamenetsky, *The Brothers Grimm and their Critics, Folktales and the Quest for Meaning*, 1992, 39.

10 *See id.* at 39–40.

11 *See supra* text accompanying note 4.

There are few criteria given by the Brothers Grimm identifying the specific collection sought, and what exists is scattered over different writings. Some appear in introductions to their fairy tale collection[12], others are part of their other books[13] and still others are letters to their friends.[14] The Brothers Grimm had a firm concept of fairy tales, and they set legends apart from this concept. Their collection intended to comprise old stories, poetic in nature that existed in of itself[15], while legends lack this attribute for they are "historically and geographically linked narratives."[16] They further restricted their collection to the geographical area of Hesse and immediate surroundings[17], and sought orally transmitted tales.[18] However it is noted, they admitted not adhering fully to this last criterion.[19] Even with such specific requirements, the Brothers Grimm should have been able to find more than the 200 fairy tales they collected.[20] However, Wilhelm Grimm wanted to keep it fixed at 200.[21] His desire to limit the collection shows they did not intend to engage in a systematic analysis of folkloric stories in order to deduct fairy tales and inventory them.

Likewise, Perrault and Basile lacked rigid collection standards. Neither put forward a well-defined framework explaining what kind of fairy tales they were interested in.[22] Perrault's collection of fairy tales reveals his devotion to educating his children and making folk culture part of modern France, rather than a profound study of fairy tales.[23] Basile, writing in a period in which the *Decamerone*

---

12 *See, e.g.*, BRÜDER GRIMM, *supra* note 1, at 31.

13 *See, e.g.*, BRÜDER GRIMM, *Deutsche Sagen [German Legends]*, Vol. I, 1–5 (D. WARD (trans.), 1981) (1816).

14 *See, e.g.*, S. NEUMANN, "The Brothers Grimm as Collectors and Editors of German Folktales", in J. ZIPES (ed.), *The Great Fairy Tale Tradition: From Straparola and Basile to the Brothers Grimm*, 2001, 969, 971 n.7.

15 *See* BRÜDER GRIMM, *supra* note 1, at 1–5. *See also* J.F. BRAADLAND, "Echoes of the Brothers Grimm from Thule: A Short Introduction to Andreas Faye (1802–1869) and his 'Norske Sagn' (1833)", in H. KUGLER, B. LAUER, F. PAUL, L. RÖHRICH and R. SCHMIDT-WIEGAND (eds.), *Jahrbuch der Brüder Grimm-Gesellschaft [Yearbook of the Brother's Grimm Association]*, 1995, 7, 16.

16 BOTTIGHEIMER, *supra* note 4, at 8.

17 *See infra* text accompanying note 44.

18 *See* BRÜDER GRIMM, *supra* note 1, at 31; NEUMANN, *supra* note 14, at 971 n. 7 (arguing that the orally transmitted fairy tales have to be faithfully transcribed).

19 *See* KAMENETSKY, *supra* note 9, at 151–153.

20 Officially, the collection consists of more than 200 fairy tales; *see The Great Fairy Tale Tradition*, *supra* note 14, at 831.

21 *See* RÖLLEKE, *supra* note 2, at 869 ("Diese Rundzahl wollte Wilhelm Grimm nicht mehr ausgeben..." ["Wilhelm Grimm did not want to give up this round figure anymore"] (author's translation)). Several unpublished fairy tales indicate that there are more than the 200 or 211 fairy tales, depending on the way of counting; *see* H. RÖLLEKE (ed.), *Grimms Märchen wie sie nicht im Buche Stehen* [Grimm's Fairy Tales as They are not Portrayed in the Books], 1993.

22 *See The Great Fairy Tale Tradition*, *supra* note 14, at 839; B. CROCE, "The Fantastic Accomplishment of Giambattista Basile and his Tale of Tales", in *The Great Fairy Tale Tradition*, *supra* note 14, at 879, 880–81.

23 *See The Great Fairy Tale Tradition*, *supra* note 14 at 839.

of Boccacio became the classic structure for stories, imagined weaving 49 stories into one overarching story.[24] It is doubtful these fifty stories emerged from a systematic analysis of a predetermined subset of traditional fairy tales from Venice, Sicily and Naples.[25] The lack of a protocol for the definition, delimitation or identification of works sought indicates these collections represent only an embryonic form of inventory making. A proper inventory process requires prior understanding on what shall be collected.[26] Such decisions would allow for a systematic approach towards collecting fairy tales by the respective authors.

The ICH Convention anticipates the identification problem, something with which these early collectors obviously struggled. Before imposing on the State Parties the duty to inventory, Article 2 of the ICH Convention defines intangible cultural heritage. This article firstly categorizes practices, representations, expressions, knowledge, skills, instruments, objects, artefacts and cultural spaces (hereinafter "practices") as intangible cultural heritage. These practices are further delineated by community identification. A community, a concept undefined by the ICH Convention, must recognize these practices as part of their cultural heritage. For the purposes of this Convention, mere recognition of a community is not sufficient. The ICH Convention necessitates community involvement towards the practices: (i) transmission of practices between generations of the same community; (ii) their recreation in ways reactive to communities' environments, nature and history; and (iii) their centrality to community identity and continuity. Outside the scope of community issues, Article 2 also stipulates that all practices complying with these criteria are intangible cultural heritage and relevant to the ICH Convention on the condition that they are compatible with existing human rights instruments[27] and meet the requirements of sustainable development and mutual respect for communities.[28]

---

24 *See* Croce, *supra* note 22, at 881.

25 *See id.* at 880–81 (in his enquiry into the reasons attracting Basile to make the Pentamerone, stating that "Basile does not take the whole thing seriously, nor does he treat it as a continuous jest, because this would become insipid; but he amuses himself by presenting the popular mind, and embroiders the presentation with humour.").

26 The object of intangible cultural heritage inventory should be defined in the countries' respective legislation which may considerably differ; *cf.* L.V. Prott and P.J. O'Keefe, *Law and Cultural Heritage: Discovery and Excavation*, 1984, 267 (stating that inventory making in relation to tangible cultural heritage may differ in various countries' legislation which defines the object of inventory).

27 *See* T. Kono and J. Cornett, "What is Intangible Cultural Heritage? An Analysis of the Convention for the Safeguarding of Intangible Cultural Heritage and the Requirement of Compatibility with Human Rights", in J. Blake (ed.), *Safeguarding Intangible Cultural Heritage: Challenges and Approaches*, 2008, 143.

28 *See* T. Kono, "UNESCO and Intangible Cultural Heritage from the Viewpoint of Sustainable Development", in A.A. Yusuf (ed.), *Normative Action in Education, Science and Culture: Essays in Commemoration of the Sixtieth Anniversary of UNESCO*, 2007, 237.

Still, this definition is broad. Moreover, some of the defining notions, such as "community", "human rights" or "sustainable development", may need further clarification. Without resolving these issues, for example in the *Operational Directives*[29], States may face problems when setting up national inventories. This is, at least, if States want to keep working under this definition of intangible cultural heritage. The ICH Convention, having left several things to be determined by its State Parties and thus having the character of a framework agreement[30], stipulates that, in case of the inventory making, a State can act "in a manner geared to its own situation."[31] This phrase was deliberately incorporated in the ICH Convention text to stress the sovereignty of States in identifying the intangible cultural heritage within their territory and the method for its inventorying.[32] Leaving methodology to States implies autonomous determination of what intangible cultural heritage is.[33] States may add more criteria to the definition in order to limit what is inventoried. Likewise, States may decide to reduce some of the defining notions of Article 2 of the ICH Convention, such as the human rights instruments or sustainable development. This reduction can, if a State deems it necessary, be combined with the incorporation of new criteria. However, adjusting

29 The Operational Directives adopted at the Second Session of the General Assembly of the States Parties (GA) from 16–19 June 2008 do not contain this kind of definitions; *see* GA, *Operational Directives for the implementation of the Convention for the Safeguarding of the Intangible Heritage*, 16–19 June 2008, *available at* www.unesco.org/culture/ich/index.php?pg=00026 (last visited 31 July 2008) [hereinafter "Operational Directives"]. Operational Directives are administrative acts created to steer the Intergovernmental Committee in its decision taking under the ICH Convention, *supra* note 8; *see* L. Boisson de Chazournes, "Treaty Law-Making and Non-Treaty Law-Making: The Evolving Structure of the International Legal Order", in R. Wolfrum and V. Röben (eds.), *Developments of International Law in Treaty Making*, 2005, 463, 473. The Operational Directives, not being a treaty, are soft law. A soft law instrument may have the advantage of being rapidly amendable; the disadvantage is its lack of bindingness. This principle would generally stand all the time, if it were not that soft law instruments very often have a dynamic interplay with hard law. Soft law rarely stands in isolation. The Operational Directives, for example, cannot be seen separate from the ICH Convention. The former elaborates and interprets the latter. This is not done on a voluntary basis. The ICH Convention, *supra* note 8, Article 7(e), gives the competence to the Intergovernmental Committee to undertake these tasks. This explicit reference to what could be part of a soft law instrument causes the soft law instrument to have binding force. Technically speaking, the Operational Directives are still soft law in form, but they have been hardened due to their interaction with the ICH Convention, out of which they derive their authority. *See* D. Shelton, "Introduction: Law, Non-Law and the Problem of 'Soft Law'", in D. Shelton (ed.), *Commitment and Compliance*, 2000, 1, 10.

30 A framework treaty is similar to any other treaty except that it provides a framework for later and more detailed treaties or national legislation. These treaties or national legislation will elaborate the principles declared in the framework treaty. *See* A. Aust, *Modern Treaty Law and Practice* (2nd ed.), 2007, 122.

31 ICH Convention, *supra* note 8, Article 12(1).

32 *See* J. Blake, *Commentary on the UNESCO 2003 Convention on the Safeguarding of Intangible Cultural Heritage*, 2006, 63.

33 *See id.* at 63–64.

the definition will most likely affect the chance of being listed in the *Representative List of the Intangible Cultural Heritage of Humanity* (Representative List).[34]

Having put forward what kinds of heritage a State wants to inventory, that State should take the necessary information down in relation to all *a priori* defined intangible cultural heritage. The inventory should give a complete picture of the presence of intangible cultural heritage within the boundaries of that State. During the negotiation of the ICH Convention, South Africa pointed out that all-encompassing inventories may require quite considerable financial resources from respective State Parties.[35] Cost may prohibit some State Parties from pursuing such a project. Besides, secrecy concerns of communities may also prevent inclusion of certain intangible cultural heritage. The above-described sovereignty-enforcing clause within Article 2 of the ICH Convention facilitates a realistic approach towards the inventory process. Whatever impediment exists, however, State Parties have the obligation to regularly update their inventories.[36] This forces State Parties to strive for complete inventories in two ways. First, the inventoried intangible cultural heritage has to be compared with the contemporary forms. Doing so recognizes the living nature such heritage. Second State Parties must strive to inventory intangible cultural heritage previously not included. Hence, the obligation to make an inventory should be seen as a continuous process rather than a static act.

3. INVENTORIZATION WITH RESPECT FOR COMMUNITY'S INTERESTS

3.1. COMMUNITY RECOGNITION

The fairy tales of *Cinderella*[37], *Rapunzel*[38], *Hansel and Gretel*[39], or *Sleeping Beauty*[40] are all well known to us. Nearly everyone links these tales directly with the Brothers Grimm. Not many of us spontaneously identify these fairy tales with Perrault, not to mention Basile. However, all these stories appear in their respective

---

34 The Operational Directives, *supra* note 29, ch. 1.2, provide the criteria for inscription in the Representative List. One of the criteria is quite obvious in regard to the definition of intangible cultural heritage, as it states that "[t]he element constitutes intangible cultural heritage as defined in Article 2 of the Convention for the Safeguarding of the Intangible Cultural Heritage." A similar criterion is stipulated for the inscription in the List of Intangible Cultural Heritage in Need for urgent Safeguarding in the Operational Directives, *supra* note 29, ch. 1.1.

35 *See* Blake, *supra* note 32, at 63.

36 *See* ICH Convention, *supra* note 8, Article 12(1).

37 *See The Great Fairy Tale Tradition*, *supra* note 14, at 444–73.

38 *See id.* at 474–91.

39 *See id.* at 699–716.

40 *See id.* at 684–98.

works. Perrault wrote in a French context[41], while Basile's work originated in Venice and Naples.[42] In this context, eagerness to portray the Grimm collection as part of German culture is awkward.[43] Obviously, many fairy tales have diffuse histories, preventing *ownership* limited to one, specific, legally recognized geographical territory. Therefore, presenting these works only as German culture prevents a fair account of the importance from elements of other cultures and communities.

Yet, the Brothers Grimm referred to the local character of their fairy tales. Frequent allusions attest to the fact that the fairy tales are all collected and rooted in the Hessian neighbourhood.[44] Praising Basile's collection of fairy tales in the third collection of their *Kinder- und Hausmärchen*, Wilhelm Grimm indicated that two-thirds of the principle incidents of the fairy tales came from Germany.[45] On one rare occasion, the Brothers Grimm marked these fairy tales as German. Contained within the second volume, the first edition (1815), the foreword to *Kinder- und Hausmärchen* had the following wording: "in these folktales lay old German Myths, which one thought were lost".[46]

Commentators and critics linked the reference to local character.[47] Ernst Siecke, underscoring the German and Hessian origin of the fairy tales, assessed that these tales significantly sustained and strengthened German national consciousness.[48] In the same vein, but more recently, Louis Snyder contends the

41 For Perrault's version of the works referred to in this paragraph; *see id.* at 449 (*Cinderella*), 688 (*Sleeping Beauty*), or 704 (*Little Thumbling*), respectively.

42 For Basile's version of the works referred to in this paragraph; *see id.* at 445 (*The Cat Cinderella*), 475 (*Petrosinella*), 685 (*Sun, Moon, and Talia*), respectively.

43 *See* Bottigheimer, *supra* note 4, at 14–15 (indicating through reference to E. Labes, H. Hesse and G. Textor that a nationalistic understanding of the fairy tales was created over time and that this process continued well into the twentieth century).

44 In the introduction to the *Kinder- und Hausmärchen* published in 1819, the Brothers Grimm wrote: "We have been collecting these fairy tales for nearly thirteen years ... in Hesse, in the regions of the Main and Kinzig of the County Hanau."; *see* Brothers Grimm, "Vorrede der Brüder Grimm [Introduction by the Brothers Grimm]", in *Kinder- und Hausmärchen, supra* note 1, at 31 ("Gesammelt haben wir an diesen Märchen seit etwa dreizehn Jahren ... nach und nach Hessen, in den Main- und Kinziggegenden der Grafschaft Hanau.") (author's translation). *See also* Kamenetsky, *supra* note 9, at 120.

45 *See* Croce, *supra* note 22, at 898–99; Kamenetsky, *supra* note 9, at 146 and 150 n. 59.

46 Brüder Grimm, *Kinder- und Hausmärchen*, Vol. II, VII f (1815) ("in diesen Volks-Märchen liegt lauter urdeutscher Mythus, den man für verloren gehalted") (author's translation). *See also* B. Lauer, "Die Brüder Jacob und Wilhelm Grimm im europäischen Kontext [The Brothers Jacob and Wilhelm Grimm in European Context]", in B. Lauer (ed.), *Die Brüder Grimm und die Geisteswissenschaften Heute [The Brothers Grimm and the Current Humanities]*, 1999, 146, 149.

47 *See, e.g.*, Kamenetsky, *supra* note 9; Bottigheimer, *supra* note 4; Tatar, *supra* note 7; J. Ellis, *One Fairy Story Too Many: The Brothers Grimm and the Tales*, 1983, 11.

48 *See* E. Siecke, "Über die Bedeuting der Grimmschen Märchen für unser Volksthum: Rede, gehalten in der Ortsgruppe Berlin des Alldeutschen Verbandes am 15. März 1895 [On the Significance of Grimm's Folktales for our Nation: Speech held at the Berlin of the Pan-Germanic League]", in R. Virchow and F. von Holtzendorff (eds.), *Sammlung*

Brothers Grimm used their fairy tale collection primarily to create a fanatic love for their fatherland.[49] Carl Franke, taking the argument even further, noted that the fairy tales enabled the German people to realize that they carry in themselves the power to extend the civilization of old times.[50] Once represented as the very essence of "Germandom"[51], differently described as "the remnants of an old faith shared by the German forefathers"[52], nothing could prevent an unfettered growth of a myth. It then should barely come as a surprise that the Nazi regime also reverted back to the Brothers Grimm's collection of fairy tales for their quest for national unity.[53] Although the Nazis exploited the collection to justify ideological goals, it should be noted that Nazi politicians were not the only group to use the Brothers Grimm in this way.[54]

The issue of the German national character of the fairy tales was also addressed outside Germany. The first English translation explicitly referred to the German character in the title. Edgar Taylor's assuredness of the purely German origin of the collection let to his translated title, *German Popular Stories*.[55] The translated prefaces of the collections always identify surrounding regions of Hesse and Main as origins for the tales. The conclusion reached by Taylor is not so awkward. More recently, John Ellis and Jack Zipes also contend the collection was German in its nature. Both authors believe the Brothers Grimm imposed their values on the fairy tales, either by pretending that various elements were German even if they were not[56] or by recomposing the fairy tales.[57]

---

gemeinverständlicher wissenschaftlicher Vorträge [Collection of Commonly Understandable Scientific Lectures], 1896.

49 *See* L.L. Snyder, *Roots of German Nationalism*, 1978.

50 *See* C. Franke, *Die Brüder Grimm: Ihr Leben und Werk [The Brothers Grimm: Their Life and Work]*, 1894.

51 Kamenetsky, *supra* note 9, at 238.

52 *Id.* at 239.

53 *See id.* at 241–48 and 294.

54 Emperor Wilhelm II did a great deal to revive the national folklore, including the Brothers Grimm's *Kinder- und Hausmärchen*, for the sake of enhancing patriotism and social values. The educational theorists, Georg Herbart and Tuiscon Ziller, were given to task of implementing a folk educational program focusing on Christian ideals and conventional morality and patriotic sentiments. *See, e.g.*, Kamenetsky, *supra* note 9, at 236–37. In a different time, the cultural policy of the Third Reich was designed in such a way that the Brothers Grimm were depicted as the forerunners of the Nazi Regime. Such an allusion was based on a very selective reading of the Brothers Grimm's fairy tales, leaving aside the comparative notes, erasing references to Christian legends or biblical elements, or ignoring some of the fairy tales at all; *see id.*, at 242–48. *See also* Chr. Kamenetsky, "Folklore as a Political Tool in Nazi Germany", 85 *Journal of American Folklore* 221–35 (1972).

55 *See* J. Grimm and W. Grimm, *German Popular Stories* (C. Baldwyn (ed.), E. Taylor (trans.), Scolar Press 1971) (1823).

56 *See* Ellis, *supra* note 47, at 35.

57 *See* J. Zipes, *The Trials and Tribulations of Little Red Riding Hood: Versions of the Tale in Sociocultural Context*, 1983; J. Zipes, "Dreams of a Better Bourgeois Life: The Psychological Origins of the Grimms' Tales", in M. McGlathery *et al.* (eds.), *The Brothers Grimm and*

Persistent emphasis on the German character of the Brothers Grimm's collection of fairy tales implies that no proper reference was made to the communities out of which these fairy tales originated. Consequently, the effort of the Brothers Grimm could be perceived as running counter to what has been advocated for in the 1999 Washington Conference, titled *A Global Assessment of the 1989 Recommendation on the Safeguarding of Traditional Culture and Folklore: Local Empowerment and International Cooperation*. This conference, jointly organized by the United Nations Educational, Scientific and Cultural Organization (UNESCO) and the Smithsonian Institution, concluded that effective safeguarding requires both the community and the intangible cultural heritage to be considered important.[58]

The community's importance in the safeguarding process links with the perception that intangible cultural heritage expresses the community's stance to various aspects of the outside world.[59] This reflection to the outside world is transmitted over generations; so intangible cultural heritage has become associated with the respective communities. Communities and intangible cultural heritage are thus mutually supportive to each other.[60] Because communities are increasingly aware of this situation, a growing claim exists towards rights on their intangible cultural heritage.[61] Recognition of this by the international community led to protections in several legally binding international instruments.[62] Drafters

---

Folktale, 1988, 205, 218; J. ZIPES, "The Grimms and the German Obsession with Fairy Tales", in R.B. BOTTIGHEIMER (ed.), *Fairy Tales and Society: Illusion, Allusion and Paradigm*, 1986, 272, 280–82.

58 *See* P. SEITEL (ed.), *Safeguarding Traditional Cultures: A Global Assessment,* 2001. *See also* N. AIKAWA, "An Historical Overview of the Preparation of the UNESCO International Convention for the Safeguarding of the Intangible Cultural Heritage", 56 *Museum* 137, 140 (2004).

59 *See, e.g.,* W.E.A. VAN BEEK and F. JARA, ""Granular Knowledge": Cultural Problems with Intellectual Property and Protection", in F.W. GROSHEIDE and J.J. BRINKHOF (eds.), *Intellectual Property Law 2002: Articles on the Legal Protection of Cultural Expressions and Indigenous Knowledge*, 2002, 35; U. KOCKEL, "Reflexive Traditions and Heritage Production", in U. KOCKEL and M.N. CRAITH (eds.), *Cultural Heritages as Reflexive Traditions*, 2007, 19, 28.

60 It could be held that early ancestors of that community have created, shaped and re-created the intangible cultural heritage. Very often this process happened in response to the outside world. Intangible cultural heritage may thus have originated from contacts with the natural environment, such as nature, landscape or climate. Intangible cultural heritage may also be a reflection of their reaction to the social environment, including their history or interactions with other communities and cultures. As the intangible cultural heritage shaped itself as a way to survive or to communicate, the ancestors have passed them through to future generations. As this process repeated itself, this intangible cultural heritage became associated with the communities.

61 *See* P.-T. STOLL and A. VON HAHN, "Indigenous Peoples, Indigenous Knowledge and Indigenous Resources in International Law", in S. VON LEWINSKY (ed.), *Indigenous Heritage and Intellectual Property: Genetic Resources, Traditional Knowledge and Folklore*, 2004, 5, 15–16.

62 *See, e.g.,* International Treaty on Plant Genetic Resources for Foods and Agriculture, 3 November 2001, *available at* ftp://ftp.fao.org/ag/cgrfa/it/ITPGRe.pdf (last visited 31 July 2008); Convention on Biological Diversity, 5 June 1992, 31 I.L.M. 818, *available at* www.biodiv.org/convention/convention.shtm (last visited 31 July 2008); Convention (No. 169) concerning

of the ICH Convention translated this claim as active involvement by a community in the process of safeguarding. Preceding such active involvement is community recognition.

Leaving aside the unlucky representation of the fairy tales as old German legends, the Brothers Grimm's emphasis of local character should in no way be interpreted as a rejection of community recognition. Rather, the opposite is true. The Brothers Grimm were aware that different versions of the fairy tales existed in various parts of Europe. To show their awareness, they added comparative notes indicating obvious and subtle similarities and differences. These comparative notes, some offered as comprehensive comparative analysis[63] meticulously attached to every tale, show that the Brothers Grimm never overlooked "the possible influences from other cultures or cross-cultural variants."[64] The most obvious languages, such as other Nordic Germanic languages, received their attention as did Jewish, Persian and other, older Indo-European language versions. Some of the variants cited even came from India.[65]

It would probably be incorrect to state that the Brothers Grimm framed their collection and comparative notes within the concept of communities. Together, both parts of the collection reveal the Brothers were conscious that the fairy tales they collected belonged to a wider environment from which they collected. The main part of their collection was local.[66] The comparative notes in turn delineated the locality of the main part. In this sense, the collection of the Brothers Grimm differed from the earlier collections of fairy tales. Others, including Perrault and Basile, failed to show how their collections belonged to their local environment.[67]

Indigenous and Tribal Peoples in Independent Countries, 27 June 1989, 28 I.L.M. 1382, *available at* www.ilo.org/ilolex/cgi-lex/convde.pl?C169 (last visited 31 July 2008). For a detailed explanation, *see* STOLL and VON HAHN, *supra* note 61, at 3–47.

63 Some of the comparative notes took even the form of a comprehensive comparative analysis, like the analysis of BASILE's tales in the 1822 edition; *see* BOTTIGHEIMER, *supra* note 4, at 5.

64 *See* KAMENETSKY, *supra* note 9, at 26–27.

65 *See id.* at 26.

66 The mainstream movement of the early nineteenth century, Romanticism, corresponds with an awakening interest for the native roots of a language, law or history of a nation. The Brothers Grimm's main emphasis on the local community's perception of the fairy tales is thus not entirely uncommon; *see id.* at 25. At the same time, it should be indicated that the locality of the stories was only one part of the Brother Grimm's interest. Like other scholars and writers in the Romantic movement, they developed a strong devotion to comparative research; *see id.* at 25.

67 The literature mentions that Perrault gets his information from storytelling of the popular mass and troubadours. The latter is most likely restricted to his direct environment. However, direct statements in this sense cannot be found; *see* L. SEIFERT, "The Marvellous in Context: The Place of the Conte de Fées in Late Seventeenth-Century France", in *The Great Fairy Tale Tradition*, *supra* note 14, at 902, 905, 907–8. It is even said that the French writers in general did not really care about this aspect; *see id.* at 904–5 ("none of the seventeenth-century *conteurs* and *conteuses* endeavored to transcribe folkloric narratives out of anything resembling ethnographic interest."). Hypotheses suggesting Perrault received inspiration from Basile are flawed because no translation from French existed and no textual convergences between the

It is only by taking the local versions of the fairy tales out of their comparative context[68] or by a selective reading of the whole picture[69], which would create the perception that the Brothers Grimm neglected the whole context to which the fairy tales belong. The smaller editions of the *Kinder- und Hausmärchen* without the comparative notes may have fuelled the feelings that the Brothers Grimm ignored the broader context of the time.[70]

The awareness that variations and parallel tellings of the same tales in different parts of Europe are important externalizes a close connection to the present day thinking of intangible cultural heritage belonging to a community. The recognition of communities is indirectly inscribed in the ICH Convention in Articles 11 and 15. While the latter deals with the soft obligation of State Parties to ensure the widest possible participation of the communities in the process of safeguarding[71],

two authors occurred; *see* I. Opie and P. Opie, *The Classic Fairy Tales*, 1974, 25. There seem to be indications that literary sources influenced Perrault's work, though; *see* H. Velten, "The Influence of Charles Perrault's Contes de ma Mère L'Oie on German Folklore", in *The Great Fairy Tale Tradition*, *supra* note 14, at 958, 959. Regarding Basile, the literature identifies his long residence in Venice and Naples, and therefore suggest these areas as his main source of fairy tales; *see* J. Zipes, "Cross-Cultural Connections and the Contamination of the Classical Fairy Tale", in *The Great Fairy Tradition*, *supra* note 14, at 845, 855. References to these cities in Basile's fairy tales only further support this view; *see id.* at 856. The literature also states his possible awareness of stories collected by Giovan Fransesco Straparola, even though there is no clear proof for that. However, this only fortifies belief that part of Basile's fairy tales came from Venice and its surroundings. It could also explain Basile's acquaintance with Oriental tales. Straparola, having spent his whole life in the thriving port city Venice, had come in contact with Oriental tales; *see id.* at 854–55.

68 Taylor, for example, did not translate the extensive comparative notes; *see* Grimm and Grimm, *supra* note 55. It was not until 1884, when Margaret Hunt translated the work of the Brothers Grimm that the comparative notes were made available to a public not fluent in German or who had limited access to the German complete edition of 1957; *see* J. Grimm and W. Grimm, *Grimm's Household Tales: with the Author's Notes*, Vol. I and II (M. Hunt (ed.) and G. Bell (transl.) 1892). It should be noted that the translation of Hunt was more accurate than the one made by Taylor; *see* Kamenetsky, *supra* note 9, at 312. Taylor liberally translated the works and later excused himself several times for that to the Brothers Grimm; *see id.* at 198 and 223–25; Bottigheimer, *supra* note 4, at 19. *See also* O. Hartwig, "Zur ersten englischen Übersetzung der Kinder- und Hausmärchen der Brüder Grimm [About the First English Translations of the Children and Household Tales]", XV *Zentralblatt für Bibliothekswesen [Central Magazine for Libraries]* 1 (1898).

69 *See* Kamenetsky, *supra* note 9, at 294; Bottigheimer, *supra* note 4, at 22; G. Schott, *Weissagung und Erfüllung im deutschen Volksmärchen [Fortune Telling and its Realization in German Folk Tales]*, 1936, 40 (describing how reading *Cinderella* required contextualizing within ideals of racial purity).

70 The smaller editions appeared on the market after the English translations without the comparative notes and with illustrations appeared to be a commercial success. The smaller editions were commercially more attractive than the large volumes with comparative notes. *See* Bottigheimer, *supra* note 4, at 20.

71 Even though this obligation is embedded in a treaty, which is usually seen as a form of hard law, the wording "endeavor to" renders it soft law; *see* Chr. Chinkin, "Normative Development in the International Legal System", in *Commitment and Compliance*, *supra* note 29, at 21, 25–26 (calling this phenomenon the fusion of "legal form with soft obligations").

the former demands from the States the participation of the communities to identify and define the various elements of the intangible cultural heritage present in its territory. This participation only materializes if the States recognize the community for whom the intangible cultural heritage is important. Like the Brothers Grimm, an indirect way to defining communities is to make a reference to different variants in the inventory. The advantage of this indirect way is that only few, if some at all, legal implications are attached. Recognition may occur in a direct way by granting the community rights in relation to the inventory or by actively involving the community in the activities surrounding inventory making.

3.2. COMMUNITY INVOLVEMENT

It was long thought that oral traditions of illiterate peasants, shepherds or other simple folk provided the main source of information for the Brothers Grimm, Perrault and Basile, to create their collection of fairy tales.[72] The belief romanticizes the notion of a collector who travelled to remote rural areas in order to gather the fairy tales. Building further on this belief, the fairy tale collectors then transcribed the stories as the storytellers told them. Regardless of the result, this would have meant an active participation of a geographically determined group of people sharing some common folk traditions. The belief thus wants that communities were obviously of utmost importance at the initial stage of setting up the different collections of fairy tales. However, studies of the last two to three decades have shown that this belief is a myth.[73] The Brothers Grimm, Perrault and to a lesser

72 *See* Croce, *supra* note 22, at 899 (referring to Wilhelm Grimm who noted that "Basile has not allowed himself to make any alteration, scarcely even any addition of importance, and that gives his work special value.") and 900 ("Basile culled his tales directly from the people, as is attested by the virgin freshness of their form."); Seifert, *supra* note 67, at 908 ("Whether they rely on the storytelling of the popular masses or the troubadours, both Perrault ... convey nostalgic and, thus, idealized visions of folklore."); Kamenetsky, *supra* note 9, at 113–14 ("[i]t used to be a misconception among critics that the Grimms made actual trips into the countryside to collect folktales from the common peasants so as to capture the living folk tradition."), 142(quoting words from Wilhelm Grimm stating that "Perrault has perceived the folktales in an undiluted form, and aside from some minor elements, has added nothing to them") and 201 ("his expression 'by word of mouth' was the phrase that many critics after his time mistook for the Grimms' sole method of recording tales").

73 *See* Zipes, *supra* note 67, at 855 ("Not only did he draw on an abundance of literary and historical sources to create his hilarious ironical tales"); Croce, *supra* note 22, at 891 (suggesting creative intervention by Basile by stating that "Basile managed ... to make the Neapolitan dialect even more Neapolitan than it really is"); Kamenetsky, *supra* note 9, at 67 ("From this perspective, to say that the Brothers Grimm looked for folktales 'among the peasants' is truly an understatement") and 114 ("The myth that the Grimms' informants had mainly been illiterate German peasant folk from rural areas of Hesse has now been largely dispelled."). Opposite of what seems to be the case for the Brothers Grimm and Basile, Perrault's

extent Basile[74] attributed themselves a prominent role in setting up the collections of fairy tales that was minimal, at best, and far from objective.

Rather than being impartial recorders of tales present in their environment, they engaged actively in the process of writing the fairy tales. Perrault outright created some of his fairy tales.[75] Jacob Grimm himself contributed not less than 17 fairy tales to the first edition of the *Kinder- und Hausmärchen*[76], and Wilhelm Grimm wrote 9 of the fairy tales to this edition.[77] Having enjoyed a university education[78], the Brothers Grimm certainly did not represent the illiterate peasants. Many of the other main informants, such as the family Wild, Hassenplug or von Haxthausen, came from the same educated middle class.[79] Not all other key informants belonged to this educated middle class, but most were certainly not peasants or shepherds as the myth wants us to believe. Frau Viehmänn, even though referred to as a peasant woman by the Brothers Grimm, was actually a poor widow of a tailor living in the rural area of Zwehrn.[80]

Furthermore, there is discussion in the literature of whether all of these informants were familiar with the fairy tales as they were told in Germany. The Huguenot background of several informants led critics to conclude that their fairy tale versions were influenced by the French tradition.[81] Though perhaps speculation or misconception, the Brothers Grimm do not conceal that some were tainted by the French tradition.[82] For example, doubtlessly Perrault's version of *Puss in the Boots* was the basis for the Brothers Grimm's version.[83] Less clear is the relationship between versions of *Little Red Riding Hood*.[84] As for the other fairy tales resembling Perrault's version, like *Cinderella*[85] or *Bluebeard*,[86] the Brothers Grimm made clear that, despite their close knowledge of that version, they were able to test its roots in the German oral tradition. Similarly, Perrault

collections seem not to have been embedded with the same amount of mythical power. Rather, it seems the opposite was proven, namely that he had some contacts with the popular mass; *see* L. Seifert, *supra* note 67, at 905 ("Soriano shows ... that Perrault himself was an avid but unsentimental observer of popular folklore.") and 905 n. 8 ("Perrault ... demonstrates a wide and detailed knowledge of folkloric narratives.").

74 *See* Croce, *supra* note 22, at 901 ("Nevertheless, this critic is still of the opinion that, after due comparison, it is evident that Basile wrote independently of Straparola.").

75 Wilhelm Grimm seems to speculate that Perrault invented some of his fairy tales; *see* Kamenetsky, *supra* note 9, at 142.

76 *See id.* at 114.

77 *See id.*

78 *See id.* at 14–17 and 114.

79 *See* Zipes, *supra* note 67, at 866.

80 *See* Kamenetsky, *supra* note 9, at 116; *See also* Zipes, *supra* note 67, at 866.

81 *See* Zipes, *supra* note 67, at 866; Kamenetsky, *supra* note 9, at 118–21.

82 *See* Velten, *supra* note 67, at 959.

83 *See* Kamenetsky, *supra* note 9, at 143.

84 *See id.* at 143–44.

85 *See* Bottigheimer, *supra* note 4, at 35–36; Velten, *supra* note 67, at 963.

86 *Compare* Kamenetsky, *supra* note 9, at 142–143, *with* Velten, *supra* note 67, at 968.

reverted to earlier written work in order to collect some of his fairy tales.[87] No specific evidence shows Basile utilized this tactic, but it is presumed he did so.[88]

The myth further propagates the notion of literal transcription of oral tales by the collectors without any creative intervention.[89] Under such circumstances, the fairy tale collectors would respect community involvement. However, once transcribed, the Brothers Grimm, Perrault and Basile (the latter two to a lesser extent) showed quite some infidelity to their sources.[90] Departure from original sources should not necessarily be understood as a negative point. To that end, intangible cultural heritage is a living heritage and thus can change.[91] Whenever the community indicates that a fairy tale evolves, a fairy tale collector should respond. However, changes within fairy tale collections, not driven by community involvement, are problematic, as the intangible cultural heritage does not present anymore the spirit of that community. Without indicating any reason, the Brothers Grimm changed the villain of the *Hansel and Gretel* fairy tale from the mother to the stepmother.[92] Identically, the Brothers Grimm leave out the fairy godmother in *Cinderella* from their second edition of *Kinder- und Hausmärchen*

---

87 *See* VELTEN, *supra* note 67, at 968 (indicating that the *Decamerone* from Giovanni Boccaccio was an inspirational source for Perrault).

88 Even though Basile may have got inspiration from Straparola, this would not have affected his community involvement as much as with the other collectors. At the end, both Basile and Straparola were relying on Venetian tales; *see* ZIPES, *supra* note 67, at 855.

89 The collectors themselves created a part of this myth. At the end, they claimed to be faithful to their sources; *see* NEUMANN, *supra* note 14, at 971 n.7.

90 *See, e.g.*, TATAR, *supra* note 7, at 6 ("The changes made from the first to the second edition ... show just how keen the Grimms must have been to give added prominence to violent episodes") or 7 ("what they did their best to eliminate from the collection through vigilant editing"); CROCE, *supra* note 22, at 891 (stating that "Basile managed ... to make the Neapolitan dialect even more Neapolitan than it really is"); VELTEN, *supra* note 67, at 967 ("Perrault may have reported a mutilated variant."). Worse than creative interventions of the collectors, was intervention by Georg Reimer, the publisher of several early editions of *Kinder- und Hausmärchen*; *see* KAMENETSKY, *supra* note 9, at 167 ("In spite of their principled approach to the editing task, the Grimms sometimes encountered circumstances beyond their control. This referred specifically to the interference of their publisher, Georg Reimer, in Berlin, who was responsible for all editions of the *Kinder- und Hausmärchen* until 1832. ... Ironically, one of the Grimms' supposedly most authentic tales, 'The fisherman and his Wife,' underwent a strange transformation for which they were not responsible. ... Reimer assumed the authority to edit the folktale by himself.").

91 The living nature of intangible cultural heritage is often depicted in the sense that documentation is able to freeze it; *see, e.g.*, Chapter [OGUAMANAM] of the present volume; M.F. BROWN, "Heritage Trouble: Recent Work on the Protection of Intangible Cultural Property", 12 *Int. J. Cult. Prop.* 40, 45 (2005). The Brothers Grimm allude to the living nature in their first edition. They hold that "fairy tales are 'never fixed and always changing from one region to another, from one teller to another"; *see* NEUMANN, *supra* note 14, at 975. However, some of their changes belong to the Brothers Grimm's moral perception than to the living nature of the fairy tales; *see* TATAR, *supra* note 7, at 11.

92 *See* M. TATAR, *The Annotated Classic Fairy Tales*, 2002, 45. Similarly, the villain in the original Snow White was not the stepmother, but Snow White's mother; *see* TATAR, *supra* note 7, at 36–37.

onwards. The role of the fairy godmother is taken over by Cinderella's biological parents.[93]

Whereas the myth of searching and transcribing fairy tales told by illiterate peasants closely links with the present day thinking of community involvement, the real practice reveals several problematic issues. It would be problematic if an inventory made today referenced fairy tales that the inventory maker knows and includes. Verification of community support requires further historical and empirical research. In fact, the Brothers Grimm did this for most of their fairy tales.[94]

Once the link between a fairy tale and a community is made, the inventory maker seeks community consent. Likely, this can only be obtained if the community fully understands the project.[95] In this respect, all three of the mentioned fairy tale collectors fail. None of them took steps at developing a collection of fairy tales with a community in mind. This probably also explains why they showed indifference towards making alterations or adjustments. This especially applies to the Brothers Grimm's successive editions, which changed little over time. Inventories in a contemporary world should, given the emphasis on the importance of communities and their involvement, reflect changes related to community practice.

The ICH Convention includes community involvement, specifically in Articles 11 and 15. The former demands "the participation of communities, groups and relevant non-governmental organizations." The latter, however, uses softer language. This article only requires that States "endeavour to ensure the widest possible participation of communities". Even though these two articles seem to be in direct conflict with each other, a logical explanation can be given if one dissects the term safeguarding into different steps. The hard obligation of Article 11 applies to the initial stage of the safeguarding, specifically the identification and definition stage. For all later stages of safeguarding, the State Parties have discretion in seeking community involvement. In this sense, both provisions can stand next to each other.

The soft wording of Article 15 affects implementation of Article 11. During the preparatory stage of the ICH Convention, it was pointed out that forcing the State

93 *See* BOTTIGHEIMER, *supra* note 4, at 36.

94 *See* KAMENETSKY, *supra* note 9, at 143–44.

95 *See* Chapter [ARANTES] of the present volume (pointing out that paying respect to communities is essential in the present day context of inventory making). This importance was stressed again at the expert meeting held by the United Nations Educational, Scientific and Cultural Organization (UNESCO) and Asia/Pacific Cultural Centre for UNESCO (ACCU) in 2006 in relation to community involvement as part of the preparatory work for the convention's entry into force. The community must receive an explanation about the project they are cooperating with, what the ultimate purpose is, how they will be involved and how they will benefit. Giving the community in advance this kind of information allows them to give their prior and informed consent to the project.

Parties to set up participation policies would conflict with the sovereign right of these States. Germany, along with Australia, Turkey, France and India, warned that including this kind of obligation required State willingness to comply, regardless of effects on sovereignty. Even though these countries worried about unwillingness to participate, Vanuatu, Bangladesh, Austria and Mauritius all supported an approach advocating community participation.[96]

Without a bedrock definition, different interpretations of the word "participation" could arise amongst members. Given the soft law obligation of community participation in Article 15[97] and a sovereignty enforcing Article 12(1) in relation to inventory making[98], certain State Parties will give a minimalist interpretation to participation. These State Parties might opt for a purely consultative role of the communities, without giving them any decisive rights. The only way to induce State Parties to increase the involvement of the communities would be via the Operational Directives on the condition that the lack of involvement would have some repercussions.

The Operational Directives could contain the "community involvement" as a selection criterion for the Representative List. On the contrary, the lack of proper community involvement or the disappearance of it could either reason for not listing the intangible cultural heritage at all or a criteria to inscribe the intangible cultural heritage on the *List of Intangible Cultural Heritage in Need of Urgent Safeguarding* (List in Need for Urgent Safeguarding). Limiting or denying international assistance represents another realistic repercussion for not involving communities in the application process or the management of the intangible cultural heritage.

Analyzing the language of the Operational Directives regarding the Representative List[99], the List in Need for Urgent Safeguarding[100] and, maybe to a lesser extent, international assistance[101], the Operational Directives reveal a similar tone as the ICH Convention. The politically sensitive issue of granting

---

96 *See* Blake, *supra* note 32, at 62.

97 *See supra* text accompanying note 70.

98 *See supra* Section 2.

99 The Operational Guidelines, however, leaves the examiners with quite a lot of discretion; *see* Operational Directives, *supra* note 29, par. 19, R.4 ("The element has been nominated following the widest possible participation of the community, group or, if applicable, individuals concerned and with their free, prior and informed consent.").

100 The text for the List in Need for Urgent Safeguarding is identical to the one for the Representative List; *see* Operational Directives, *supra* note 29, par. 1, U.4 ("The element has been nominated following the widest possible participation of the community, group or, if applicable, individuals concerned and with their free, prior and informed consent.").

101 *See* Operational Directives, *supra* note 29, par. 67 (One of the selection criteria for international assistance is that "The community, group and/or individuals concerned participated in the preparation of the request and will be involved in the implementation of the proposed activities, and in their evaluation and follow-up as broadly as possible").

rights to communities[102], as it is reflected in the ICH Convention, is also found in the Operational Directives. This implies that in certain cases State Parties have to be given the opportunity to overcome the political obstacles attached to empowering communities with legal rights. Such can be done by creating flexibility as to how State Parties incorporate the communities in the inventory making process. Like the Brothers Grimm, Perrault and Basile, State Parties will only rely on community involvement to the fullest extent possible or needed.

Further, State Parties find some guidance in Article 15 of the ICH Convention, regarding how community involvement can materialize. The ending of this article, phrased as "... and to involve them actively in its management,"[103] allows us to construe two important guidelines. First, management presupposes information. If State Parties involve communities in the management of their intangible cultural heritage, these State Parties should share long-term plans. Indirectly, this provision embeds the idea of prior and informed consent. The Operational Directives externalize this concept. In fact, they suggest that prior and informed consent is the key to community involvement.[104] Second, once inventories are created, community involvement ensures needed updates as intangible cultural heritage evolves. Doing so prevents intervention from the inventory maker, unlike methods of the Brothers Grimm, Perrault and Basile, who actively changed stories as needed and outright disregarded the natural evolution of tales. These steps maintain the integrity of intangible cultural heritage.

4. THE SCOPE OF INVENTORIZATION

4.1. INTANGIBLE CULTURAL HERITAGE EMBEDDED IN A BROADER CONTEXT

The primary technique employed by the Brothers Grimm, Perrault and Basile for creating collections of fairy tales was transcribing orally transmitted stories. In doing so, they wrote down complete fairy tales. For example, the fairy tale *Hansel and Gretel*[105] tells us a story of two children of a poor woodcutter, who, egged on

---

102 *See* BLAKE, *supra* note 32, at 62 and 76–77.

103 ICH Convention, *supra* note 8, Article 15.

104 *See* Operational Directives, *supra* note 29, par. 1, U.4, and par. 19, R.4.

105 Dortchen Wild passed the fairy tale *Hansel and Gretel* to the Brothers Grimm. The first part of the Brothers Grimm's version of this fairy tale resembles closely *Le Petit Poucet* written by Perrault in 1679. Madame d'Aulnoy published in 1721 a story *Finette Cendron* in which she also depicts the abandonment of children in the deep wood, but who manage to find their way back by leaving a trail. The house build of delicious foodstuff has resemblance with a fourteenth century manuscript, telling the story of the *Utopian Land of Cockayne*; *see* OPIE and OPIE, *supra* note 67, at 308–11 (history part of this fairy tale) and 312–19 (the fairy tale of *Hansel and*

by his wife, leads his children into the forest to abandon them. Hansel and Gretel try to leave a trail home, but instead arrive at a house made of bread. An old woman invites them to her house. She is in fact a witch and wants to fatten the children to eat them. Gretel saw through the scheme and was able to outwit the witch by tricking her to climb in the oven and close the door. She then liberates Hansel, and the two escape back home to their (relieved) father.

It is less well known that different parts of the fairy tale have changed over the time. The wife of the woodcutter appears in the early versions of the fairy tales as a mother of the two children. Later versions of the fairy tail depict her as the stepmother of the children. The house made of bread turns into a house made of gingerbread in later versions. By the time of the last edition, *Hansel and Gretel* had become twice as long as the original version in 1810.[106] Similar alterations happen in other fairy tales as well.[107] The collections of fairy tales do not contain an explanation of why these changes occur. Similarly, these collections lack social background information to contextualize their nuance. In other words, these collections limit their scope to the intangible cultural heritage as such. No attention is paid to the environment surrounding the intangible cultural heritage. There exists only one exception.[108] The Brothers Grimm, with their comprehensive

Gretel as it appeared translated in the 1853 *Household Stories collected by the Brothers Grimm*).

106 *See The Great Fairy Tale Tradition*, *supra* note 14, at 699.

107 The beginning of *The Frog King*, for example, changed over time. What follows is a quotation out of the beginning of this fairy tale from the 1812, 1819 and the 1857 edition respectively:

> Once upon a time there was a king's daughter who went into the forest and sat down on a cool well. She had a golden ball that was her favorite toy. She would throw it up and catch it in the air and was amused by this ...
>
> Once upon a time there was a king's daughter who was so bored she didn't know what to do. So she took a golden ball that she often played with and went into the forest. Now in the middle of the forest there was a clear, cool well and she sat down next to it, threw the ball into the air, and she would play this way ...
>
> In olden times, when wishing still helped, there lived a king whose daughters were all beautiful, but the youngest was so beautiful that the sun itself, which had seen so many things, was always filled with amazement each time it cast its rays upon her face. Now, there was a great dark forest near the king's castle, and in this forest, beneath an olden linden tree, was a well. Whenever the days were hot, the king's daughter would go into the forest and sit down by the edge of the cool well. If she became bored, she would take her golden ball, throw it into the air, and catch it. More than anything else she loved playing with this ball ...

See NEUMANN, *supra* note 14, at 973–74. For a comparison of *Cinderella*'s versions, *see* BOTTIGHEIMER, *supra* note 4, at 44–45 and 177–78. *See also supra* text accompanying notes 92 and 93.

108 Tatar indicates that the study of variants is a necessary condition in order to speak meaningfully about the context surrounding a fairy tale. She describes this issue with the words "[a]ny attempt to unearth the hidden meaning of fairy tales is bound to fail unless it is preceded by a rigorous, if not exhaustive, analysis of a tale type and its variants." *See* TATAR, *supra* note 7, at

comparative notes, provided the reader with the insight that similar sociological, psychological, anthropological, educational or any other kind of concern may have existed in various other communities.[109]

Though mostly ignored, some contextual debate occurred outside the publications. The Brothers Grimm found frequent criticism of their belief that the fairy tales were appropriate, understandable and digestible for children, as the title of their collection seems to imply.[110] In their response, the Brothers Grimm took a balanced approach to indicate that there was not a clear "either-or"[111] answer. Pleased by the appeal of their fairy tales to children's imagination, they strongly believed that children should be given the chance to read them without the interference of an adult, be it as a parent or a teacher.[112] The wisdom of the fairy tales illuminate and spark what a child already knows. The incomprehensible elements should be left for the future, alluding to the potential of these fairy tales for adults. The fairy tales, according to the Brothers Grimm, reflect the substance of life as they combine history, mythology, poetry, moral values and the like.[113]

The wider context of the fairy tales inspired many adults' imaginations. The fairy tales were researched from a diversity of perspectives. Anthropologist research shows that the fairy tales are a reflection of social customs, beliefs and rituals formed by an animated view of nature and the world.[114] Contrary to this literal view, scholars advocate a symbolic meaning of the fairy tales, of which the psychological perspective would be one example.[115] The fairy tales represent the conscious and unconscious forces of the world in human terms. Somewhere in

---

43. The reason why the comparative analysis is so important, according to Tatar, lies in the fact that it will enable the "interpreter to distinguish essential features from random embellishments and to identify culturally determined elements that vary from one regional version of a tale to the next." *See id.*

109 Tatar eloquently describes that all these variants indicate different meanings by stating that

> One of the chief sources of irritation for the interpreter of fairy tales is the nature of folkloric sources. For nearly every tale, there are at least a dozen versions, in some cases hundreds of extant variants. In other words, rather than a single, stable literary text in which even the finest points of detail may function as bearers of significance, we have an infinite number of corrupt "texts," spoken and written, each representing one version of a single tale type, and an imperfect version. *See id.* at 42.

110 *See* Kamenetsky, *supra* note 9, at 192–95.

111 *Id.* at 192.

112 *See id.* at 192–93.

113 *See id.* at 193.

114 *See, e.g.*, A. Lang, "Household Tales; Their Origin, Diffusion, and Relation to higher Myths", in *Grimm's Household Tales*, *supra* note 68, Introduction; B. Malinowsky, "Myth in Primitive Psychology", in B. Malinowsky (ed.), *Magic, Science, and Religion and other Essays*, 1954, 99.

115 *See, e.g.*, B. Bettelheim, *The Uses of Enchantment: The Meaning and Importance of Fairy Tales*, 1977; C.G. Jung, "On the Relation of Analytical Psychology to Poetry", in *The Portable Jung*, 301–22 (J. Campbell (ed.) and F.C. Hall (trans.), 1983) (1922).

between these extremes, we can find a feminist[116] or socio-historical perspective.[117] Others see a nationalistic reading of the fairy tales.[118] Still others agree with Perrault's assessment that the fairy tales are nothing else than a way of expressing moral and ethical claims.[119]

These perspectives developed after the Brothers Grimm, Perrault or Basile finalized their collections. Because a contextual vacuum preceded analysis, these different perspectives flourished. Such an array of post-publishing viewpoints can be tempered by taking Antonio A. Arantes's view on inventory making, presented elsewhere in this volume. Arantes stipulates that an inventory must encompass the broader context or environment in which intangible cultural heritage is embedded.[120] An inventory is not just the transcription of a storyteller's fairy tale; *e.g.*, besides a story of Hansel and Gretel, the inventory needs to contain elements that place the story in its context. Arantes lists several elements in this respect. Among these are issues of the origin and the historical continuity, social life and social memory, and attributed.[121] In doing so, Arantes seeks to externalize the notion of intangible cultural heritage, an expression of a community to the outside world in general, into a practical instrument, the inventory.

4.2. FEARING ALL-ENCOMPASSING INVENTORIES

Including context in inventory making creates all-encompassing inventories. Modern techniques of documentation create thorough results in terms of visibility and accessibility. Such deep reach may alienate some communities of their intangible cultural heritage. Michael F. Brown concludes Indigenous communities may not be eager to cooperate with the extensive documentation of their intangible cultural heritage.[122] He asserts that communities' preferred strategy will be, and

116 *See, e.g.*, K.F. Stone, "Feminist Approaches to the Interpretation of Fairy Tales", in R.B. Bottigheimer (ed.), *Fairy Tales and Society: Illusion, Allusion and Paradigm*, 1986, 229.

117 *See, e.g.*, Zipes, *supra* note 57 (1988); J. Zipes, *The Brothers Grimm: From Enchanted Forests to the Modern World*, 1988; O. Kahn, "Rumpelstilz hat wirklich geleb. Textvergleichende Studie über das Märchen vom Rumpelstilzchen und eine Erklärung mit Hilfe der Rechtsgeschichte [Rapunzel has actually lived. A Textual Comparative Study of the Rapunzel Fairy Tale and an Explanation by Using Legal History]", 17/18 *Rheinisches Jahrbuch für Volkskunde* 143 (1966/67).

118 *See, e.g.*, Chr. Kamenetsky, *Children's Literature in Hitler's Germany: The Cultural Policy of National Socialism*, 1984; Snyder, *supra* note 49; Siecke, *supra* note 48; Kamenetsky, *supra* note 54.

119 *See, e.g.*, K.-H. Hiemesch, *Der Gesinnungsunterricht [Ideological Teachings]*, 1925.

120 *See* Chapter [Arantes] of the present volume.

121 *Id.*

122 *See* Brown, *supra* note 91, at 48.

he quotes the words of the anthropologists Eric C. Kansa, "security through obscurity".[123]

Brown's critique of extensively documented inventories is justified. It might not be what the communities want. This possibility exists when States implement Article 12(1) of the ICH Convention. This particular provision, being silent on many aspects of inventory making, is revealing on one particular issue. The inventory should enable the identification of the intangible cultural heritage present in a State's territory. From a purely legalistic point of view, State Parties are not obliged to extend their inventories beyond a stage in which the identification is ensured. This minimalist approach can then be brought in line with Brown's comment that anthropology presently recognizes the modest role of documentation in the preservation of culture.[124]

On points left silent in the ICH Convention, some clarification comes from expert meetings held by UNESCO in 2005 and 2006 dealing with inventory making as part of the preparatory work for the ICH Convention's entry into force.[125] Except for being minimalist, the scope of the national inventories is an open question.[126] Nothing has been stipulated in regard to the criteria for listing in the national inventories.[127] The ownership of the inventories is also not addressed.[128] It is further not determined how the communities, who according to Article 11(2) of the ICH Convention have a role within the identification process, should be involved.[129] Another issue not discussed in the expert meetings, but put forward by Janet Blake, is whether the national inventories should be disclosed to the public.[130]

Focusing on the issues of the inventory itself, scope, openness, and listing criteria, ignores one central question; that is, how does the ICH Convention leave it up to State Parties to develop inventories according to the necessity of the intangible cultural heritage and their ability. No one method of inventory exists, as should be obvious from flexibility afforded under Article 12. Even though the first Operational Directives prepared by the Intergovernmental Committee for the Safeguarding of the Intangible Cultural Heritage do not do so[131], next versions

---

123 *Id.* at 56 n. 26.

124 *Id.* at 48.

125 *See* UNESCO, *Report of the Expert Meeting on Inventorying Intangible Cultural Heritage* (17–18 March 2005), *available at* www.unesco.org/culture/ich/doc/src/00036-EN.pdf (last visited 31 July 2008).

126 *See id.* at 12 (summary of keynote speech by Marcia Sant'Anna).

127 *See id.* at 16 (summary of keynote speech by Chérif Khaznadar).

128 *See id.* at 29–30 (summary of keynote speech by Wend B. Wendland).

129 *See id.* at 32–33.

130 The concerns of the community or group should be the determinant factor on whether the State creates an open inventory or a closed one; *cf.* Blake, *supra* note 32, at 63 (suggesting that the disclosure of the national inventories seems to be instigated by the broad flexibility of ICH Convention, *supra* note 8, Article 12).

131 *See* Operational Directives, *supra* note 29.

could formulate principles on national inventories. To avoid jeopardizing strengths provided by flexibility, the Operational Directives could contain a non-exhaustive list of non-binding guidelines for national inventorization. The more binding the rules, the more likely the inventorization ends up in the unfortunate situation depicted by Brown.[132]

5. INVENTORIES EMBEDDED IN A BROADER POLICY FRAMEWORK

5.1. INTELLECTUAL PROPERTY ISSUES

Perrault and Basile, and to a lesser extent the Brothers Grimm[133], wrote in an era without intellectual property rights, copyrights specifically. All their collections of fairy tales developed from borrowing intangible cultural heritage from communities and from each other. Within their time, this appropriation of the intangible cultural heritage and the subsequent alterations were not considered exploitation or misuse. Moreover, as Fiona Macmillan illustrates in relation to Hans Christian Andersen, a contemporary to the Brothers Grimm, that it was common practice to make use of the cultural commons either as collections or recreated as new stories at that time.[134]

The Brothers Grimm, Perrault, Basile were in no sense different than their peers. They understood it as their right to collect, transcribe, adapt or transform what was out there. The difference between the Brothers Grimm on the one side, and Perrault and Basile on the other, was how they perceived their role as collector. For Perrault and Basile, being a collector was equal to being author. Perrault published his collection under the pseudonym Pierre Perrault Darmancourt.[135] Basile's sister published the work under the pseudonym Gian Alessio Abbattutis.[136] The Brothers Grimm, however, identified their final product as "collected by the

132 *See* Brown, *supra* note 92, at 48–49.

133 The issues of copyright receive vigorous discussion during the early 19th century; *see* U. Suthersanen, "'Bleak House' or 'Great Expectations'?: The Literary Author as a Stakeholder in nineteenth-Century International Copyright Politics", in H. Porsdam (ed.), *Copyright and other Fairy Tales: Hans Christian Andersen and the Commodification of Creativity*, 2006, 40.

134 *See* F. Macmillan, "What Might Hans Christian Andersen Say About Copyright Today?", in H. Porsdam (ed.), *Copyright and other Fairy Tales*, 2006, *supra* note 133, at 83. It has to be stipulated that, unlike the Brothers Grimm, Perrault and Basile, Hans Christian Andersen did not use the cultural commons extensively. Rather than transcribing fairy tales known within Scandinavian communities, Hans Christian Andersen made "transformative use" of the existing folk tales or other literary works; *see id.* at 85. *See also* D.C. Frank and J. Frank, *The Stories of Hans Christian Andersen*, 2004.

135 *See The Great Fairy Tale Tradition*, *supra* note 14, at 839.

136 *See id.* at 824.

Brothers Grimm".[137] This *belonging to others* manifests another awareness of the community's importance. As earlier indicated in this Chapter, this stage of awareness was still embryonic in the sense that the Brothers Grimm did not systematically reveal community origins.[138] Consequently, the *Kinder- und Hausmärchen* collections are usually identified with the Brothers Grimm rather than with the community behind it.

Placing the ICH Convention within the Brothers Grimm's time framework would still allow leeway for the appropriation and use of the fairy tales. Nothing in the ICH Convention stipulates that the inventory belongs to the community.[139] The inventory maker can, just as Perrault or Basile did, identify himself with the inventory. Differently, the inventory maker can stipulate that he has been in charge of putting together the information, just as the Brothers Grimm did. Moreover, the ICH Convention does not prohibit profiting from inventory making. There is no provision in the convention limiting the rights of third persons in respect to either the inventory maker or the community. The development of intellectual property laws often provide basis for criticism of the ICH Convention that lacks attention to the inventory's information protection.[140] The ICH Convention is therefore often seen as a missed opportunity to merge intellectual property law issues with heritage law issues.[141]

Wend B. Wendland, elsewhere in this volume, indicates that one should not perceive the ICH Convention in this way. The ICH Convention is safeguarding orientated, in which the viability of the intangible cultural heritage is the central issue. Intellectual property law, on the contrary, aims at protection.[142] Protection refers to the protection of intangible creations and innovations from illegitimate exploitation and misuse. Since the aim of both laws is different, they complement rather than contradict. Even though intellectual property issues arise in connection with the process of inventorying and the management of the inventories, they should not present obstacles for inventorying. Wendland points out that only some legal and practical steps have to be taken to overcome the intellectual property issues. Wendland indicates that the World Intellectual

---

137 The editions of the *Kinder- und Hausmärchen* were always published with the indication "collected by the Brothers Grimm"; *see, e.g.*, Brüder Grimm, *supra* note 1 ("gesammelt durch die Brüder Grimm") (author's translation).

138 *See supra* Section 3.

139 *See* ICH Convention, *supra* note 8.

140 *See* P. Kuruk, "Cultural Heritage, Traditional Knowledge and Indigenous Rights: An Analysis of the Convention for the Safeguarding of Intangible Cultural Heritage", 1 *Macquarie J. Int'l & Comp. Env'l. L.* 111, 129 (2004), *available at* www.law.mq.edu.au/html/MqJICEL/vol1/vol1_5.pdf (last visited 31 July 2008).

141 *See id.* at 129.

142 *See* Chapter [Wendland] of the present volume. *See also* W.B. Wendland, "Intangible Cultural Heritage and Intellectual Property: Challenges and Future Prospects", 56 *Museum Int'l* 97, 99 and 101 (2004).

Property Organization (WIPO) has done an effort by setting up the *Creative Heritage Project*[143] in which they give best practices and guidelines for recording, digitizing and disseminating intangible cultural heritage.

Interestingly, Wendland seems to be willing to clinically separate the ICH Convention from any of intellectual property law aspect.[144] Given the intellectual property law related statement in Article 3 of the ICH Convention, this analysis seems to be plausible. It states that the ICH Convention may not be interpreted as affecting a State Party's rights or obligation under an intellectual property rights instrument. However, it cannot be the purpose of the ICH Convention to set up systems that directly jeopardize the viability of intangible cultural heritage. There must be an element in the ICH Convention that obliges State Parties to act to ensure the viability of the intangible cultural heritage, even in the inventory phase. This element emerges from a combined reading of Articles 2(3) and 11(a). An argument in favour of creating a broad legal and policy framework to which intellectual property law, in its present or future form, belongs comes from these articles. In this way, the ICH Convention does still not touch upon intellectual property law. It only requires the State Parties to adopt the appropriate intellectual property law scheme for the ICH Convention's purposes.

5.2. INTELLECTUAL PROPERTY ISSUES AS PART OF A POLICY FRAMEWORK

A broad policy framework aiming at the viability of fairy tales did not drive the early collectors. The Brothers Grimm placed their engagement in collecting fairy tales and other literature within the framework of their quest into the development of language and various sorts of linguistic phenomena.[145] The collections were a by-product of their research related to language. Having received positive reactions towards their collection of fairy tales from various sides, they decided to continue their process of collecting fairy tales and even older stories and legends.[146] Perrault's interest in fairy tales is related to the education of his children and to his belief that France should develop into a modern nation, something that was only possible by taking folklore, among others, into account.[147] Basile, as a courtier, mainly wrote his fairy tales for performances at the court.[148] Even

143 *See* WIPO, *Creative Heritage Project: IP Guidelines for Documenting, Recording and Digitizing Intangible Cultural Heritage*, www.wipo.int/tk/en/folklore/culturalheritage/index.html (last visited 31 July 2008).

144 *See* Chapter [Wendland] of the present volume. *See also* Wendland, *supra* note 142, at 101.

145 *See* Kamenetsky, *supra* note 9, at 100.

146 *See id.* at 41–45.

147 *See The Great Fairy Tale Tradition*, *supra* note 14, at 838–39.

148 *See id.* at 824–25; Croce, *supra* note 22, at 880–81.

though these collections contributed to the viability of this specific part of intangible cultural heritage, the collectors' main focus was their contemporary generation and not the one beyond.

The obvious consequence of this emphasis on the contemporary generation is that the collections of fairy tales represented an endpoint. They were not meant to be the starting-point for further action. This is understandable given the private nature of the collections. Nevertheless, the Brothers Grimm tried to spark interest in fairy tales around Europe. By corresponding with several scholars, such as Sir Walter Scott, Henry Weber, Peter Christian Asbjörnsen, Jörgen Moe, Berhard Thiele or Stepanovic Karadcik[149], they encouraged these people to search for their nation's native fairy tales. Many of them were motivated and followed the Brothers Grimm's path. The 1850 edition of the *Kinder- und Hausmärchen* contained a list of all the collections of fairy tales that had come into existence since 1812.[150] This bibliography encompassed several hundred entries. Most of these cited works had given the Brothers Grimm credit for their example either in their preface acknowledgements or in letters.

Whereas the private initiatives furthest extent was nothing more than encouraging other scholars to engage in similar activities, much more is expected from the ICH Convention's inventories. The inventory making process and its outcome is part of a public effort to ensure the viability of intangible cultural heritage, called safeguarding. Within this complex process, inventory making functions as the first step. The inventory only enhances the visibility of the intangible cultural heritage. In turn, visibility becomes viability when inventories join other policies. This is implied in the wording of Arantes when he writes "... in order to be socially sustainable, safeguarding action plans should promote the inclusion of the ICH in public policies".[151] Some authors seem to loose focus in this respect. Brown, for example, questions the inventory making as being potentially successful.[152] By first pointing out that "documentation has only a modest role in the preservation of culture,"[153] his objections become obvious. He further states, "there is obviously nothing harmful about the [ICH Convention]s ambitious program of cultural documentation, one struggles to imagine how it

149 *See* Kamenetsky, *supra* note 9, at 27.

150 *See id.* at 28.

151 A.A. Arantes, *ICH Inventories in Context: Purpose, Methodology and Functionality*, at 5 (25–26 March 2007) (paper presented at the conference on *Intangible Cultural Heritage and Intellectual Property under the 2003 Convention: Seeking a Collaborative Interface between ICH and IP*, New Delhi, India) (on file with author).

152 *See* Brown, *supra* note 91, at 48. A similar view has been mentioned by Kurin; *see* R. Kurin, "Safeguarding Intangible Cultural Heritage in the 2003 UNESCO Convention: A Critical Appraisal", 56 *Museum Int'l* 66, 71–72 (2004).

153 Brown, *supra* note 91, at 48.

will protect cultures as living, dynamic systems,"[154] his scepticism towards inventory making is clearly shared.

Brown's scepticism towards inventory making is not only embedded in his distrust for the digital media, but also in his belief that Indigenous people seek either greater secrecy or become anxious about exploitation. What Brown's vision partly lacks, is that inventory making is just one step in the process of safeguarding intangible cultural heritage. The belief that the ICH Convention is flawed, for it tries to reduce heritage to a mere list of items, most likely has its origin in the drafting of the ICH Convention. Indeed, the inventory making is expressly stressed in Article 12(1). The obligation of inventory making is formulated as a hard law provision in the form of a "shall" sentence. The other safeguarding mechanism are then summed up in Article 13, but not anymore as a "shall" sentence, but as a "shall to endeavor" sentence. The latter is commonly viewed as soft law according to the content. The fact that one of the safeguarding measures is so visually prominent in the ICH Convention definitely impacted perceptions of the ICH Convention.[155] This visually prominent safeguarding measure distracts the attention from the other provisions dealing with safeguarding. In particular, more attention should be paid to a combined reading of Articles 2(3), 11(a) and 12(1). Based on this combination of articles, we cannot but conclude that the ICH Convention explicitly recognizes that much more has to be done than only inventory making.

Article 12(1) stipulates that the drawing up of one or more inventories has to be done "[t]o ensure identification *with a view* to safeguarding".[156] Safeguarding is defined earlier in the Convention, namely in Article 2(3). Besides the identification and documentation of intangible cultural heritage, to which inventory making belongs, safeguarding of intangible cultural heritage is also research, preservation, promotion, enhancement, and transmission.[157] Article 11(a) of the ICH Convention, consecutively, makes this safeguarding into an obligation for the State Parties. The different aspects of safeguarding are not further defined in the ICH Convention's definition of safeguarding, leaving several issues open. For the purposes of the latter mentioned obligations, the inventory becomes an instrument of positive state action. By using the technique

154 *Id.* at 48.

155 The reason for formulating soft law provisions could be that the ICH Convention, *supra* note 8, is a *general* convention. It does not aim to regulate in detail what every concept means to protect the sovereignty of the State Parties. Therefore, it transfers the further development of what the best safeguarding measures are for their intangible cultural heritage to the State Parties. A critique of this system has been given by Kuruk; *see* Kuruk, *supra* note 141, at 129–30.

156 ICH Convention, *supra* note 8, Article 12(1) (emphasis added).

157 ICH Convention, *supra* note 8, Article 2(3).

of a framework convention[158], the ICH Convention shifts the burden for this action to the State Parties. They are forced to adopt several legislative approaches. It can be argued that intellectual property law must be one of these legislative approaches.

Wendland's argument of complementarily action by different regimes is very promising for the project envisioned by the ICH Convention. One of the safeguard measures happens to be protection. What kind of protection is not further stipulated in the ICH Convention, giving an argument that any kind of protection imaginable, including intellectual property law, should be included. At the end, the viability of a certain intangible cultural heritage might be jeopardized when a community cannot react to misappropriation or misuse with a fear that the respective community might abandon its intangible cultural heritage. In this sense, the concept of protection is not only complementary to safeguarding, but also supportive. Without the intellectual property law protection, talking about safeguarding might become obsolete to a certain extent.

6. CONCLUSION

Activities of the Brothers Grimm, who engaged in a project of collecting 200 fairy tales, sparked an interest in this form of intangible cultural heritage all over the world. No one at that time would have dared to think that one and a half centuries after their efforts UNESCO would set up a legal instrument, the ICH Convention, putting the Brothers Grimm's activities in a broader perspective of safeguarding. At the same time, the most eye-catching obligation for State Parties in the ICH Convention resembles the Brothers Grimm's activities. State Parties must inventory their intangible cultural heritage. In this perspective, this Chapter has explored this new standard setting instrument in the light of the early intangible cultural heritage collections and the activities surrounding these collections.

This explorative exercise reveals that the ICH Convention affords State Parties a considerable amount of freedom in framing their national legislation. This discretion led to the conclusion that 200-year-old practices of safeguarding intangible cultural heritage are still possible under the ICH Convention. Hence, the State Parties may disregard communities in various respects. Their involvement should not necessarily be pursued. Prior and informed consent does in principle

---

[158] As we have just indicated, the ICH Convention, *supra* note 8, evolved as a general text with only a few specifications. The other specifications need to be either developed in the operational directives, national legislations or other treaties. The Operational Directives, *supra* note 29, 77, cover some of duties of State Parties in relation to their national inventories and the safeguarding measures that should be developed based on that information. However, intellectual property law issues are not part of. Hence, they will most likely have to be addressed in national legislations or another international treaty.

not have to be obtained for the inventory making. Besides this, nothing is stipulated about the scope of the inventory, implying that it can be minimalistic, maximalistic or anything in between. Similarly, the ICH Convention is silent about intellectual property law issues, leaving the possibility to the State Parties to provide no protection at all, stick to their existing intellectual property law or to customize their intellectual property law to the specific needs of the intangible cultural heritage.

Legal flexibility offered by the ICH Convention should not necessarily be regarded as a negative point. Within 19 months after its adoption, the ICH Convention entered into force. 30 States ratified the ICH Convention by 20 January 2006. A rigid working framework could have made the ICH Convention less attractive to these ratifying States. Various reasons may be cited for this. Safeguarding techniques vary according to the intangible cultural heritage. Further, political and cultural sensitivities within a State Party may require the necessary flexibility to develop appropriate safeguarding schemes. State Parties have also different financial abilities for safeguarding. All this calls for a framework convention, what the ICH Convention is.

PART THREE CONCEPTUALIZATION OF COMMUNITY

CONCEPTUALIZATION OF COMMUNITY AS A HOLDER OF INTANGIBLE CULTURAL HERITAGE

Branislav HAZUCHA and Toshiyuki KONO*

The main objective of the *Convention for the Safeguarding of the Intangible Cultural Heritage* (ICH Convention)[1] is to safeguard intangible cultural heritage.[2] However, its adequate and appropriate incorporation into individual safeguarding measures and their subsequent effective implementation can be hampered by several challenges. These challenges are inherent in the definition of intangible cultural heritage and must be overcome. Intangible cultural heritage does not exist on its own. Individual cultural practices, representations and other expressions become part of cultural heritage only when they are recognized by particular communities, groups or, in some cases, individuals.[3] Accordingly, it is essential to define and identify "communities", "groups" and "individuals" as essential constitutive elements of intangible cultural heritage.[4]

In addition, formation of cultural heritage through its recognition by a community implies some proprietary nuances and implications. This raises

* Branislav Hazucha is Assistant Professor of Law, Kyushu University Faculty of Law; Toshiyuki Kono is Professor of Law, Kyushu University Faculty of Law.

1 Convention for the Safeguarding of the Intangible Cultural Heritage, 17 October 2003, U.N. Doc. MISC/2003/CLT/CH/14 (2003), *available at* http://unesdoc.unesco.org/images/0013/001325/132540e.pdf (last visited 31 July 2008) [hereinafter "ICH Convention"].

2 *See* ICH Convention, *supra* note 1, Article 1(a).

3 *Id.*, Article 2(1) ("practices, representations, expressions, knowledge, skills – as well as the instruments, objects, artefacts and cultural spaces associated therewith – that communities, groups and, in some cases, individuals recognize as part of their cultural heritage"). *See also* G.J. ASHWORTH, B. GRAHAM and J.E. TUNBRIDGE, *Pluralising Pasts: Heritage, Identity and Place in Multicultural Societies*, 2007, 3.

4 *See, e.g.*, UNESCO/ACCU, *Expert Meeting on Community Involvement in Safeguarding Intangible Cultural Heritage: Towards the Implementation of the 2003 Convention*, at 9, *available at* http://unesdoc.unesco.org/images/0014/001459/145919e.pdf (last visited 31 July 2008).

questions concerning the content and scope of relationships within and between communities, groups or amongst individuals in relation to their intangible cultural heritage. Do communities or their members have any rights and obligations with regard to their cultural traditions?[5] If so, what is the actual scope and extent of such rights *vis-à-vis* other stakeholders such as other members and non-members of the concerned community, neighbouring communities and humankind? These intricate issues are scrutinized by the contributors to this Part.

This introductory Chapter attempts to provide a broader perspective for the individual contributions that follow. This Chapter starts by outlining the mutual relationship and interaction between communities and their cultural heritage. This mutual interdependence between communities and their cultural traditions implies that cultural heritage belongs to communities and thus communities can exercise control over an access to, or use of, their traditional knowledge and cultural expressions. Since adequate and efficient safeguarding of intangible cultural heritage requires recognition of communities and their intangible cultural heritage, this Chapter concludes by describing the conundrums that arise in giving limited legal recognition to communities and their cultural traditions and the possible negative outcomes of such limited recognition.

1. COMMUNITY AND CULTURAL HERITAGE

The notion of "community" is heavily criticized as a vague and useless term in social sciences.[6] In law, it causes similar problems.[7] The reason is that there are

---

5 In this Chapter, the terms "intangible cultural heritage" and "cultural traditions" are used interchangeably, unless it is provided otherwise. The former is used in the way as it is defined by the ICH Convention, *supra* note 1, Article 2(1). The latter is employed in more informal sense than the former. However, the authors acknowledge that some authors strictly distinguish between "heritage" and "traditions" so that the former is not in practice anymore, while the latter is still alive and practiced by communities. *See, e.g.*, U. Kockel, "Reflexive Traditions and Heritage Production", in U. Kockel and M.N. Craith (eds.), *Cultural Heritages as Reflexive Traditions*, 2006, 19. Although this distinction is often perceived in practice, the reason why it is disregarded for the purpose of this Chapter is that the ICH Convention requires to safeguard intangible cultural heritage in its living form; *see* ICH Convention, *supra* note 1, Article 2(3) (defining "safeguarding" of intangible cultural heritage as "measures aimed at ensuring the viability of the intangible cultural heritage ... as well as the revitalization of the various aspects of such heritage.").

6 *See, e.g.*, G. Hillery, "Definitions of Community: Areas of Agreement", 20 *Rural Society* 111 (1955); M.J. Watts, "Contested Communities, Malignant Markets, and Gilded Governance: Justice, Resource Extraction, and Conservation in the Tropics", in Ch. Zerner (ed.), *People, Plants, and Justice: The Politics of Nature Conservation*, 2000, 21; V. Amit and N. Rapport, *The Trouble with Community: Anthropological Reflections on Movement, Identity and Collectivity*, 2002.

7 *See, e.g.*, J. Gibson, *Community Resources: Intellectual Property, International Trade and Protection of Traditional Knowledge*, 2005. For an inquite into conceptualization of community

various types of communities and it is hard to define the term "community" in such a way as to fit all possible cases and for all purposes. To define community in a simple way, it may be suggested that a community is a body of people which are united by a certain social network of interrelationships.[8] The bonds and relationships between individual members are reinforced by social norms which are buttressed by social sanctions.[9]

Although the term "community" is used broadly and has a variety of meanings, this volume focuses on communities which are bodies of people sharing history, habits, customs, rituals, traditional knowledge, cultural expressions and other social practices – intangible cultural heritage. The intangible cultural heritage is reflection of a community's natural and social habitat. It helps members of a community to identify themselves with the community and to exclude the "others". Put it more clearly, individual members of the community are allowed to clearly define who they are and who the others are, through their traditional knowledge and cultural expressions.[10] Culture traditions thus play a crucial role in the formation of communities themselves and in the preservation of their integrity.

Cultural heritage is often employed to build up communities and their common shared identity. History is full of examples where carefully selected cultural traditions were used to strengthen the identity of certain communities whether on a local, regional, national or international level.[11] For this purpose, some traditions and cultural expressions are overemphasized and given new meanings, significance and strength, while the others are marginalized in order to achieve the image of unity and integrity. Stressing shared historical and cultural experience reinforces social ties within and outside a community. The perception of shared roots aids to establish a social network between individual members of a community by providing them with a feeling of closeness with each other. In

---

in a broader perspective within international law, *see, e.g.* A. Meijknecht, *Towards International Personality: The Position of Minorities and Indigenous Peoples in International Law*, 2001; S.J. Anaya, *Indigenous Peoples in International Law*, 2nd ed., 2004; P.G. McHugh, *Aboriginal Societies and the Common Law: A History of Sovereignty, Status, and Self-Determination*, 2004.

8 *See, e.g.*, R. Tyler, "Comprehending Community", in S. Herbrechter and M. Higgins (eds.), *Returning (to) Communities: Theory, Culture and Political Practice of the Communal*, 2006, 21, 26.

9 *See id.* For literature on social norms, *see generally* R.C. Ellikson, *Order Without Law: How Neighbors Settle Disputes*, 1991; L. Lessig, "The Regulation of Social Meaning", 62 *U. Chi. L. Rev.* 943 (1995); C.R. Sunstein, "Social Norms and Social Roles", 96 *Colum. L. Rev.* 903 (1996); R.H. McAdams, "The Origin, Development and Regulation of Norms", 96 *Mich. L. Rev.* 338 (1997); E.A. Posner, *Law and Social Norms*, 2000.

10 *See* N. Douglas, "Political Structures, Social Interaction and Identity Change in Northern Ireland", in B. Graham (ed.), *In Search of Ireland: A Cultural Geography*, 1997, 151–52; Ashworth, Graham and Tunbridge, *supra* note 3, at 4–5.

11 *See* Ashworth, Graham and Tunbridge, *supra* note 3.

this way, cultural heritage supports the integrity, coherence and convergence between individual members of a respective community.

Accordingly, there is a close mutual interaction between communities and their intangible cultural heritage. While communities and their members create their cultural traditions over long time period, particular cultural traditions simultaneously shape communities and their individual members. Changes in any of them then have considerable consequences on the other. We can find many examples in the past and present, such as the impact of colonization or social phenomena brought by modernity – rapid urbanization, large-scale migration, severe environmental change and pervasive globalization – on Indigenous, traditional, local and other cultural communities and their cultures. The result is slow, but steady alterations of social values, norms and preferences, which cause weakening of social structures and ties within communities. Simultaneously, this also influences communities' cultures and causes modifications and adjustments to their intangible cultural heritage.[12]

The close interaction between a community and its intangible cultural heritage implies some notions of "belonging" – cultural traditions belong to the community. This claim can be supported by several justificatory explanations. Although most of them sound quite similar, there are minor nuances which can play an important role in defining the content and scope of rights and obligations in relation to intangible cultural heritage.

One line of justification is based upon the concepts of "inheritance" and "legacy". Cultural traditions are deemed to be created by ancestors of the current community members. They are passed down from one generation to another. Accordingly, a conventional view on habits, customs and other traditional cultural practices is that they were given to current community members by their ancestors for the benefit of past, current and future generations. Individual members are thus deemed to be only custodians or trustees of a community's intangible cultural heritage on behalf of past and future generations. When any decision concerning cultural traditions is under consideration, the interests of past and future generations must also be taken into account.

Another justification stems from recognizing a community as a living entity capable of collective creativity. A community is an entity distinctive from its individual members. It is an imaginary living creature capable of creating its own cultural traditions by maintaining them for a long time. Intangible cultural heritage then reflects the communal spirit of a particular community. This argument is a nuanced modification of labour theory adjusted to specific features of communities. Labour theory, stemming from John Locke's writing, is the

12 *See, e.g.*, L.J. Sears, "Comment", 43 *Current Anthropology* 146, 147 (2002) (describing changes in Javanese "classical" shadow theatre by introducing instruments and comic interludes which were new and not used traditionally in this context).

foundation for the traditional liberal concept of ownership.[13] When somebody takes something from its state of nature, he becomes the owner of such a thing. He uses his labour, mixes it with the thing and therefore he becomes the owner of the result. The modified argument applicable to culture and cultural patrimony was often used in the case of creating modern nations. A particular culture was alleged to reflect nation's spirit.[14] Accordingly, it was thought that a particular culture belongs to the nation which created it. Similar arguments are recently put forward in relation to Indigenous, traditional and other cultural communities.[15] This approach implies that a community is a holder or even owner of its cultural traditions. The community is therefore seen to be allowed to control access to, and use of, its traditional knowledge and cultural expressions.

Each line of argument leads to a different scope of entitlements which are supposed to be enjoyed by communities, groups of people or particular individuals. The question then arises who controls access to, and use of, particular traditional knowledge or cultural expressions and on whose behalf and account. Are communities, groups of people, or individuals the actual owners or holders of cultural traditions? Can they freely dispose of their cultural traditions for the benefit of their current members or particular individuals? Or, are they just the custodians or trustees who administer, maintain and preserve cultural traditions for the entire community, including their ancestors and future generations?

2. CONTROL OVER CULTURAL TRADITIONS

One thing is to attribute culture or cultural patrimony to a particular group of people or community. Another is to claim that such a group or community is entitled to control or even to restrict an access to, or use of, its intangible cultural heritage. This claim clashes with other important public values and interests, such as freedom of expression and personal autonomy. It thus goes, to a certain extent, against modern Western liberal traditions which are built around individualism and the notion of freedom. Zygmunt Bauman puts it tersely:

> There is a price to be paid for the privilege of "being in a community" – and it is inoffensive or even invisible only as long as the community stays in the dream. The price is paid in the currency of freedom, variously called "autonomy," "right of self-assertion," "right to be yourself."[16]

---

13 *See, e.g.*, A. Mossoff, "What Is Property? Putting the Pieces Back Together", 45 *Ariz. L. Rev.* 371, 385–89 (2003).

14 *See, e.g.*, Ashworth, Graham and Tunbridge, *supra* note 3, at 94–101.

15 *See generally* M.F. Brown, *Who Owns Native Culture?*, 2004, 94.

16 Z. Bauman, *Community: Seeking Safety in an Insecure World*, 2001, 4.

Pursuant to the traditional Western view, cultural traditions are in the public domain.[17] Anyone can then grab some parts of the public domain and can use them as building blocks for his own creativity and inventiveness. It is conventionally accepted that when someone invests his time, labour, financial and other resources, he should be allowed to control the result of his creative intellectual labour to a certain degree.[18] He is deemed to be entitled to exclude others from access to a particular work of authorship or invention under certain conditions.[19]

However, people do not only re-create their surroundings, but they are also shaped by their surrounding. Accordingly, there is a close relationship between individuals and their natural, social and other environments. As Ikechi Mgbeoji shows in his contribution, the members of Indigenous and traditional communities are heavily influenced by their environment, religion, beliefs, traditions, rituals and so on.[20] The same applies to any author. Each author is formed by his natural and social environment, his education, upraising, traditions and so on.[21] The difference is only that in certain societies, this influence is higher or felt to be more present than in others. And this is the case of Indigenous and traditional communities. As Terri Janke points out in her contribution, some communities do not even have a term to describe an author.[22] The persons who create traditional art are considered to be persons who follow traditions. They create the given artistic creations, which are held and preserved for generations by communities. They are deemed to be only guardians of cultural traditions passed on by their ancestors.[23]

At the same time, it should be noted that individuals are not only passive absorbers of influences from their environment. They also actively change their surroundings. They re-create cultural traditions.[24] In addition, there is also active

---

17 *See generally* A. Chander and M. Sunder, "The Romance of the Public Domain", 92 *Calif. L. Rev.* 1331, 1346–7 (2004) (discussing problems concerning traditional knowledge). For discussion on public domain; *see generally* Symposium, "The Public Domain", 66 *Law & Contemp. Prob.* 1 (2003); P. Samuelson, "Enriching Discourse on Public Domains", 55 *Duke L. J.* 783 (2006).

18 *See, e.g.*, J. Hughes, "The Philosophy of Intellectual Property", 77 *Geo. L. J.* 287, 296–330 (1988) (analysing Locke's labour theory); A.C. Yen, "Restoring the Natural Law: Copyright as Labour and Possession", 51 *Ohio St. L. J.* 517 (1990); P. Drahos, *A Philosophy of Intellectual Property*, 1996, 41–69.

19 Intellectual property right holders are granted certain types of exclusive rights to their intellectual property. Their scope and extent depends upon the particular type of intellectual property rights.

20 *See* Chapter [Mgbeoji] of the present volume.

21 *See, e.g.*, M. Foucault, "What Is an Author?", in V. Harari (ed.), *Textual Strategies: Perspectives in Post-Structuralist Criticism*, 1979, 141.

22 *See* Chapter [Janke] of the present volume.

23 *See id.*

24 *Id.* (analyzing *Bulun Bulun v. R & T Textiles*, where Justice von Doussa recognizes ownership of bark painting to its author Johnny Bulun Bulun).

exchange and communication between neighbouring communities through cross-cultural borrowings.[25]

In order to unravel the conundrum concerning the level a community can control access to, and use of, their cultural traditions, some guidance may be found by looking at actual practice within communities with regard to their intangible cultural heritage. Each community has its own norms regulating these aspects. This kind of approach is expressly incorporated in a report prepared by the United Nations Office of the High Commissioner for Human Rights, where it is put succinctly that Indigenous and traditional communities' "ownership and custody of their heritage must continue to be collective, permanent and inalienable, as prescribed by the customs, rules and practices of each people."[26]

Although cultural traditions are held in common, certain knowledge or cultural expressions are accessible to different groups of people within a community. To put it more bluntly, some parts of intangible cultural heritage are held in common only for a fraction of a particular community. Hence, communities are not homogenous groups of people. They are structured in a certain way. The position of individual members of a community may depend upon various characteristics, such as race, sex, age, knowledge, skills and so on. The differentiation within communities also has an impact on access to, and knowledge of, some parts of intangible cultural heritage. Certain types of rituals and other cultural traditions are accessible only to a limited part of a community or even to particular individuals. For instance, some traditional knowledge and cultural expressions are accessible only to elders or healers. The others are excluded from access to them. Mgbeoji provides an example of the Igbo people's cultural traditions in which certain knowledge and rituals are accessible only to elders, men, women, or healers and the like.[27] Wim van Zanten, elsewhere in the present volume, provides an example of Baduy epic *pantun* story which is accessible only to the "knowledgeable".[28]

Differential access to cultural traditions creates several layers within communities. Differential access to individual parts of cultural traditions within communities is the reason why the ICH Convention refers to "communities, groups and, in some cases, individuals".[29] This reflects the three-layer system normally maintained in many Indigenous and traditional communities. For

---

25 *See, e.g.*, Brown, *supra* note 15, at 19 (describing the case of "*kachina* dolls" which caused friction between Navajo nation and the Hopis).

26 United Nations, Economic and Social Council, *Discrimination against Indigenous Peoples: Protection of the Heritage of Indigenous People*, Annex 1, par. 5, U.N. Doc. E/CN.4/Sub.2/1995/26 (21 June 1995) (*prepared by* E.-I.A. Daes) (containing *Principles and Guidelines for the Protection of the Heritage of Indigenous People*).

27 *See* Chapter [Mgbeoji] of the present volume.

28 *See* Chapter [van Zanten] of the present volume.

29 ICH Convention, *supra* note 1, Articles 1(b), 2(1), 11(b) and 15.

instance, Walter E.A. van Beek and Fabiola Jara describe the three-layer social organization in Kapsiki society in relation to the access to medicinal information in the following way. The first layer is composed from the general public which has access to general health and medicinal information. The second layer is represented by specific specialized groups, *e.g.* blacksmiths. They have access to so-called "official secrets" which are accessible within the respective group. Finally, at the top there are a few individuals who can handle the preparation and application of a particular medicine which can have life-threatening side-effects for a patient if the person administering such medicine lacks the necessary skills and information.[30]

Consequently, discrimination concerning the access to some cultural traditions is often justified by practical considerations. In many cases, a person needs to achieve a certain level of skills, knowledge or mental capabilities in order to be able to comprehend or perceive the cultural traditions in their entirety. If such knowledge was disclosed to a person who has not achieved such a level, it might be dangerous for the receiving person, other members of the community, the entire community or nature.[31] The members of a particular group – guardians of certain knowledge – must therefore be careful when they decide to whom they may disclose such knowledge.

3. RECOGNITION OF COMMUNITIES AND THEIR INTANGIBLE CULTURAL HERITAGE

In order to achieve efficient safeguarding of intangible cultural heritage, it is important "to ensure respect for the intangible cultural heritage of the communities, groups and individuals concerned".[32] This does not mean only respect for the intangible cultural heritage, but also the recognition of such communities, groups and individuals concerned, as well as social norms regulating the access to, and use of, particular parts of heritage. As Mgbeoji shows in his contribution[33], Indigenous and traditional communities were taken as savage and uncivilized when the Europeans started to colonize the territories where such communities lived. The colonizers did not take the local communities as equal. They considered Indigenous people to be at an inferior stage of evolution. Their view of the local population was that it had to be educated and civilized. The

30 *See* W.E.A. van Beek and F. Jara, ""Granular Knowledge": Cultural Problems with Intellectual Property and Protection", in F.W. Grosheide and J.J. Brinkhof (eds.), *Intellectual Property Law 2002: Articles on the Legal Protection of Cultural Expressions and Indigenous Knowledge*, 2002, 35, 48–49. *See also* W.E.A. van Beek, *The Kapsiki of the Mandara Hills*, 1987.

31 *See* Chapter [van Zanten] of the present volume.

32 ICH Convention, *supra* note 1, Article 1(b).

33 Chapter [Mgbeoji] of the present volume.

colonizers did not deem traditions, habits, customs and rituals maintained by local communities as being equal to or at least comparable to the ideas and values accepted by the Western civilization. The Western culture was seen to be superior. Mgbeoji opines that by respecting their intangible cultural heritage, such communities and groups will be finally given the same position as the Westernized dominant culture.

He thus urges that the rules and customs of communities should be recognized by laws which regulate safeguarding, dealing, use and appropriation of intangible cultural heritage. Further, he suggests that in respect to the conceptualization of the community as a holder of intangible cultural heritage, it is also important to enquire whether our contemporary understanding of legal personality can accommodate such a notion. Based upon the analysis of how intangible cultural heritage is created and preserved, as well as how it operates, amongst the Igbo community of south-eastern Nigeria, he questions the applicability of the Western concept of authorship in the context of Indigenous or traditional communities. The national laws in the majority of the countries of the world are heavily influenced by the Western legal traditions: Anglo-American common law traditions, and the French and German civil codes. Mgbeoji thus emphasizes that it is essential to rethink the Western notion of legal personality in a way which would be able to encompass the idea that various legal personalities could be capable of exercising ownership and control over intangible cultural heritage. He posits that a variety of entities recognized by communities, but not by Western legal traditions, should also be recognized by laws, whether made by legislatures or judges. The question remains how to do it.

As shown above, communities have their norms which regulate access to, or use of, intangible cultural heritage within and outside the respective communities. In many cases, the ability of a community to exercise control stems from the fact that traditional knowledge or cultural expression is kept in secret among certain groups of people or individuals. Although recognizing such social norms seems to offer a simple solution to protect and safeguard intangible cultural heritage, there are several problems with this approach. First, social norms are often hidden. They are habitually invisible unless they are breached. Second, there may be a different understanding and perception of the content and scope of norms among individual members. For instance, van Zanten depicts a situation where several members of community had different views on what the community's stance to a particular problem should be.[34] Finally, as Michael F. Brown puts it succinctly, "groups have a strong tendency to define their external boundaries more rigidly than is warranted by actual social practice, especially when they feel threatened."[35]

---

34 *See* Chapter [van Zanten] of the present volume.

35 M.F. Brown, "Reply", 49 *Current Anthropology* 379, 380 (2008).

It may then happen that individual members may present stronger claims than those which are actually supported by particular social norms.

This can have a considerable impact on other public interests especially in case of those parts of intangible cultural heritage, which are accessible by all members of respective ethnic, Indigenous or traditional communities, or even by outsiders. With regard to these cultural traditions, any communal claims to exclude others from access to them should be taken with caution. This can be seen in Janke's contribution.[36] She points out the main problems with granting proprietary rights over intangible cultural heritage to Indigenous and traditional communities in Australia by showing how the concept of Indigenous and traditional communities and their recognition as holders of intangible cultural heritage have developed there.

On the other hand, when traditional knowledge and cultural expressions which are not held in secret are used by non-members, they should be at least properly and adequately attributed to the concerned community. For example, when someone publishes a collection of fairytales, he should clearly attribute the collected fairytales to a particular community.[37] The requirements of this kind are included in numerous codes of conduct concerning use of cultural traditions for commercial and other purposes. Janke refers to several of them in different fields of creative intellectual productions which were adopted in Australia.[38]

4. AWARENESS RAISING AND INVENTION OF TRADITIONS

The approach based upon respect for communities and their cultural traditions is also reflected in the ICH Convention. As dealt with in more detail in the previous part of the present volume, the process of safeguarding intangible cultural heritage under the Convention includes "the identification, documentation, research, preservation, protection, promotion, enhancement, transmission, particularly through formal and non-formal education, as well as the revitalization of the various aspects of such heritage."[39] In this process, Article 11(b) of the ICH Convention requires an active participation of communities, groups and relevant non-governmental organizations, especially in the process of identifying and

36 Chapter [Janke] of the present volume.

37 *See, e.g.*, J.V. Emberly, *Threshold of Difference: Feminist Critique, Native Women's Writings, and Postcolonial Theory*, 1993, 94 (referring to the case of A. Cameron, *Daughters of Copper Woman*, 1981) where Anne Cameron collected stories told her by the Nuu-Chah-Nulth women of Vancouver Island). *See also* Chapter [Wendland] of the present volume.

38 *See* Chapters [Janke] and [Wendland] of the present volume.

39 ICH Convention, *supra* note 1, Article 2(3).

defining "the various elements of the intangible cultural heritage" present in the territory of the State Parties.

At the same time, the drafters of ICH Convention were aware that ensuring respect for intangible cultural heritage of various communities and groups is not enough for its safeguarding. It is equally important to "raise awareness at the local, national and international levels of the importance of the intangible cultural heritage, and of ensuring mutual appreciation thereof".[40] Article 14 of the ICH Convention thus requires the State Parties to focus on the general public and especially young people, on the one side, and on the concerned communities and groups, on the other side, by various educational, training, awareness-raising and information programmes.[41] Such programmes can play a vital role in achieving the recognition "that communities, in particular indigenous communities, groups and, in some cases, individuals, play an important role in the production, safeguarding, maintenance and re-creation of the intangible cultural heritage".[42] This can assist the accomplishment of the final goal which is enrichment of "cultural diversity and human creativity".[43] The State Parties are therefore required under Article 15 of the ICH Convention to "endeavour to ensure the widest possible participation of communities, groups and, where appropriate, individuals that create, maintain and transmit such heritage, and to involve them actively in its management" within the framework of their safeguarding activities of the intangible cultural heritage.

Experiences from different countries, however, urge to be cautious in this regard. Many of well-thought out legal instruments had negative effects on communities, including their lifestyle, development, cultural traditions and so on. The problem arises when such measures are constructed and enforced by courts in a manner which do not completely reflect the actual reality. It often happens that the current situation of Indigenous, traditional, local and other cultural communities is not fully taken into account. For instance, in Australia several laws were drafted with an intention to recognize Indigenous and traditional communities under certain conditions. Nonetheless, a significant part of Aborigines moved during the last fifty years to the suburbs of large cities and towns[44], where they created new forms of communities within the suburban populace. As this part of the Aboriginal population does not satisfy the statutory requirements, they are excluded from the recognition as Indigenous and traditional communities. The result is that the law divides the Aboriginal

40 *Id.*, Article 1(c).
41 *Id.*, Article 14(a).
42 *Id.*, Preamble, par. 6.
43 *Id.*
44 *See, e.g.*, G. Morgan, "Aboriginal Politics, Self-Determination and the Rhetoric of Community", in S. Herbrechter and M. Higgins (eds.), *Returning (to) Communities: Theory, Culture and Political Practice of the Communal*, 2006, 367.

population into several groups. This creates barriers and friction amongst Aborigines.[45] Similar problems are faced by Indigenous, traditional and other cultural communities in many other countries.[46]

Furthermore, when the law recognizes traditions, habits and rules, it does so within certain limits. Article 2(1) of the ICH Convention recognizes only "such intangible cultural heritage as is compatible with existing international human rights instruments, as well as with the requirements of mutual respect among communities, groups and individuals, and of sustainable development." Similar limited approaches are adopted by national laws in many countries. For instance, in several cases Australian courts refused to recognize traditions and customs which were against universally recognized values.[47]

Although the rules on limited recognition are justified by protection of other important public interests, it should be noted that they can have side effects on communities and their cultural traditions. The rules on recognition set up certain patterns of, and requirements for, communities when they want to be recognized by law. These effects go in two directions. First, they force communities to stay on a certain level of development. The communities are supposed to be frozen at that moment. This precludes further development of communities as response to a changing environment, be it natural or man-made. In addition, the patterns of Indigenous and traditional communities are often heavily influenced by Western ideas and images of what such communities should be and how they should look. This view depicts such communities as centralized structures, like Indian clans and tribes in the Americas. However, there are many Indigenous and traditional communities found all around the world that do not fit this view.[48] The organization of Aboriginal communities in Australia can be taken as an example. Their organization caused many inconveniences to the British colonizers when they came to Australia, especially because they were not able to reach a viable agreement with the local Aboriginal groups. And many of these problems still persist there to the present time.

The second type of side effects of limited recognition on communities and their intangible cultural heritage is the adjustment of certain cultural traditions to universally recognized values and norms which are heavily influenced by Western civilization. The cause of such changes is the rejection of recognizing

---

45 *See id.*

46 *See, e.g.*, B.D. Haley and L.R. Wilcoxon, "Anthropology and the Making of Chumash Tradition", 38 *Current Anthropology* 761 (1997); L.W. Field, "Complicities and Collaborations: Anthropologists and the "Unacknowledged Tribes" of California", 40 *Current Anthropology* 193 (1999).

47 *See, e.g.*, E.A. Povinelli, "At Home in the Violence of Recognition", in K. Verdery and C. Humphrey (eds.), *Property in Question: Value Transformation in the Global Economy*, 2004, 185, 202–3 (referring to *Barnes v. the Queen, 1997*, rejecting receiving traditional punishment).

48 *See, e.g.*, van Beek, *supra* note 30 (describing Kapsiki/Higi people).

certain cultural expressions and practices. This gives the concerned communities, expressly or implicitly, a message that a particular part of their intangible cultural heritage is banned or not appreciated by a majority of the population or humankind. In this way, some customs, habits and traditions are considerably shaped by outside pressure.

To sum up, automatic application of legal concepts foreign to respective Indigenous, traditional or local communities can lead to invention of traditions[49] and proprietary claims to them. This occurs especially when actual norms which are maintained by communities and which regulate access to, and use of, their cultural traditions are not taken into account. Invention of proprietary claims to traditional knowledge and cultural expressions can have negative impacts on the preservation of intangible cultural heritage and its dissemination, as well as on future creativity. By examining the notion of the community as the holder of intangible cultural heritage in the Indian context, Shubha Chaudhuri, in her contribution[50], advises the use of caution before applying legal mechanisms and models from other countries and cultures, which do not always fit the historical, social and cultural environment in the receiving country. She warns that creating artificial boundaries and placing legal tools into the wrong hands may have a negative impact on the preservation and development of intangible cultural heritage. She thus suggests that it would be unwise to protect community traditions if a communal sense of ownership or protection does not already exist within such community. At the same time, she stresses the importance of education in preservation efforts. Furthermore, she advocates that the successful dissemination of intangible cultural heritage may create an audience for such arts.

As shown above, the main difficulty in the search for regulatory solutions to any social, economic or legal problem is whether to adopt a "one size fits all" solution or to take a piecemeal approach by slicing up the problem into several issues and searching for a solution issue by issue. In this regard, Branislav Hazucha, in his contribution[51], warns against any quest for a universal definition of, and scope of entitlements held by, a community as holder of its intangible cultural heritage. He draws attention to the fact that individual legal regimes and mechanisms may be appropriate, adequate and efficient only for certain types of communities or their cultural heritage. He thus advocates a multidimensional approach to safeguarding intangible cultural heritage. He urges that distinct legal regimes and mechanisms may fit different notions of communities and specific sets of entitlements to their cultural traditions.

---

49 *See, e.g.*, Haley and Wilcoxon, *supra* note 46; Erlandson, "The Making of Chumash Tradition: Replies to Haley and Wilcoxon", 39 *Current Anthropology* 477 (1998); Brown, *supra* note 15, at 189–90.

50 Chapter [Chaudhuri] of the present volume.

51 Chapter [Hazucha] of the present volume.

INDIGENOUS INTANGIBLE CULTURAL HERITAGE AND OWNERSHIP OF COPYRIGHT

Terri JANKE*

* Terri Janke is an Indigenous lawyer who specializes in Indigenous heritage, copyright and intellectual property. She is an expert in her field and is a world renowned legal expert on Indigenous cultural and intellectual property issues. She is Solicitor/Director of her own law firm Terri Janke and Company Pty Ltd located in Sydney, Australia. Terri Janke would like to acknowledge the assistance of Sonia Cooper, paralegal, and Anastasia Charles, admin assistant. She would also like to thank the editor for comments and feedback on the paper.

1. INTRODUCTION

In 2003, the United Nations Educational, Scientific and Cultural Organization (UNESCO) adopted the *Convention for the Safeguarding of Intangible Cultural Heritage* (ICH Convention).[1] The ICH Convention asks each signatory country to "identify and define the various elements of the intangible cultural heritage present in its territory, with the participation of communities, groups and relevant non-governmental organizations."[2] In this way, the ICH Convention requires countries to develop inventories of their traditional cultural expressions and traditional knowledge. There is therefore an emphasis on community inventory-making. The ICH Convention, however, also states that its text cannot be interpreted as "affecting the rights and obligations of State Parties deriving from any other international instrument relating to intellectual property rights ... to which they are parties."[3] This means that in the recording, collation and development of databases and inventories of intangible cultural heritage, the state members will need to consider how intellectual property law impacts on the ownership of Indigenous cultural heritage. They will have to adopt appropriate measures for recognizing "ownership" of intangible cultural heritage by its traditional custodians.

This Chapter explores the ownership of intangible cultural heritage from the perspective of Australian intellectual property law, an area in which I have practiced and developed an expertise. While Australia is not a signatory to the ICH Convention, the recording, dissemination, digitization and commercial use of intangible cultural heritage raises issues relevant to Indigenous Australians. One of their concerns is that the intellectual property which is generated as a result of such processes is often not owned by them. In the past 15 years there have been a number of important cases, as well as the development of new protocols and policy, that may provide some insight for other countries.

In this Chapter I will examine Indigenous cultural heritage and ownership of copyright provisions, referring to Australian law. Recording intangible cultural heritage means that copyright will be created in oral traditions and expressions that are the heritage of a people. Section 2 looks at the content and nature of

---

1 Convention for the Safeguarding of the Intangible Cultural Heritage, 17 October 2003, U.N. Doc. MISC/2003/CLT/CH/14 (2003), *available at* http://unesdoc.unesco.org/images/0013/001325/132540e.pdf (last visited 31 July 2008) [hereinafter "ICH Convention"].

2 *See id.*, Article 11(b).

3 *See id.*, Article 3(b).

Intangible cultural heritage and intellectual property. Section 3 examines how copyright laws recognize ownership of the expressed form in individuals. Section 4 provides case studies to exemplify the issues. Section 5 concludes that there are shortfalls in the copyright law and how Indigenous people seek to control and manage their intangible cultural heritage. This leads to the overall conclusion that there is a need for frameworks beyond copyright and intellectual property to deal with the protection of intangible cultural heritage.

2. INTANGIBLE CULTURAL HERITAGE AND INTELLECTUAL PROPERTY

2.1. WHAT IS INTANGIBLE CULTURAL HERITAGE?

Intangible cultural heritage, as defined by the ICH Convention, consists of non-physical characteristics, practices, representations, expressions as well as knowledge and skills that identify and define a group or civilization.[4] This category includes the following cultural manifestations:

(a) oral traditions and expressions, including language as a vehicle of the intangible cultural heritage;
(b) music, dance, drama and other performing arts;
(c) social practices, rituals and festive events;
(d) knowledge and practices concerning nature and the universe;
(e) foods and clothing; and
(f) traditional craftsmanship.[5]

According to UNESCO, "Intangible Cultural Heritage is transmitted from generation to generation, and is constantly recreated by communities and groups, in response to their environment, their interaction with nature and their historical conditions of existence. It provides people with a sense of identity and continuity. Its safeguarding promotes, sustains and develops cultural diversity and human creativity.

Through the existence and transmission of this intangible cultural heritage, a group or community is able to associate itself with a communal identity."[6]

"Folklore" or "traditional cultural expressions" are intangible cultural heritage. It is described as being socially based. Its ownership or custodianship is often collective. This is enshrined in the *Recommendation on the Safeguarding of*

---

4 *See* UNESCO, *Intangible Cultural Heritage*, www.unesco.or.id/activities/culture/general/258.php (last visited 15 October 2007).

5 *Id.*

6 *Id.*

Traditional Culture and Folklore: "Folklore, as a form of cultural expression, must be safeguarded by and for the group (familial, occupational, national, regional, religious, ethnic, etc.) whose identity it expresses."[7]

2.2. WHAT IS INTELLECTUAL PROPERTY?

"Intellectual property" refers to the bundle of rights that the law grants to individuals for the protection of creative intellectual, scientific and industrial activity, such as ideas (expressed in a material or immaterial form) and inventions. The *Convention Establishing the World Intellectual Property Organization* defines "intellectual property" as:

> the rights relating to
> - literary, artistic and scientific works;
> - performances of performing artists, phonograms, and broadcasts;
> - inventions in all fields of human endeavour;
> - scientific discoveries;
> - industrial designs;
> - trademarks, service marks, and commercial names and designations;
> - protection against unfair competition;
>
> and all other rights resulting from intellectual activity in the industrial, scientific, literary or artistic fields.[8]

Intellectual property rights are designed to inspire creative innovation by granting specific economic rights to inventive persons as a reward for sharing their contributions and to stimulate further inventive activities. Through international treaties, such as the *Berne Convention for the Protection of Literary and Artistic Works* (Berne Convention)[9], intellectual property rights are enforced internationally in countries that are signatories to such treaties.

In Australia, copyright protects Indigenous traditional cultural expressions where Indigenous people meet the requirements set out in the *Copyright Act 1968* (Cwlth).[10] The ability of copyright law to protect Indigenous traditional cultural expressions will be explored in Section 3.

---

7 UNESCO, *Recommendation on the Safeguarding of Traditional Culture and Folklore*, 15 November 1989, *available at* http://portal.unesco.org/en/ev.php-URL_ID=13141&URL_DO=DO_PRINTPAGE&URL_SECTION=201.html (last visited 31 July 2008).

8 Convention Establishing the World Intellectual Property Organization, Article 2(viii), 14 July 1967, 828 U.N.T.S. 3 (1967), *available at* www.wipo.int/treaties/en/convention/trtdocs_wo029.html (last visited 31 July 2008).

9 Berne Convention for the Protection of Literary and Artistic Works, 9 September 1886, as amended on 28 September 1979, 828 U.N.T.S. 222 [hereinafter "Berne Convention"].

10 Copyright Act 1968 (Cwlth) (Austl.), *available at* www.comlaw.gov.au/ComLaw/Legislation/ActCompilation1.nsf/framelodgmentattachments/8F4161B3394B2E08CA25748F00049DE0

2.3. WIPO DRAFT PROVISIONS

Since 2000, the World Intellectual Property Organization (WIPO) has convened the Intergovernmental Committee on Intellectual Property and Genetic Resources, Traditional Knowledge and Folklore (Intergovernmental Committee).[11] The Intergovernmental Committee has developed two documents:

(a) *Revised Draft Provisions for the Protection of Traditional Cultural Expressions: Policy Objectives and Core Principles*[12]; and
(b) *Revised Draft Provisions for the Protection of Traditional Knowledge: Policy Objectives and Core Principles.*[13]

It is expected that the draft guidelines will shape future laws and policies relating to traditional cultural expressions and traditional knowledge. This paper focuses on traditional cultural expressions. Traditional cultural expression incorporates songs, stories, ceremonies, rituals, dance and art. The latter category includes rock art, face and body painting, sand sculptures and bark paintings.

3. COPYRIGHT AND TRADITIONAL CULTURAL EXPRESSIONS

In Australia, the Copyright Act 1968 provides copyright owners with the right to control the use and dissemination of literary, dramatic, artistic and musical works,[14] as well as certain listed subject matter including sound recordings[15], cinematograph films, television and sound broadcasts, and published

(last visited 31 July 2008).

11 *See* WIPO, Intergovernmental Committee, www.wipo.int/tk/en/igc/(last visited 31 July 2008).

12 *See* WIPO, Intergovernmental Committee on Intellectual Property and Genetic Resources, Traditional Knowledge and Folklore, *The Protection of Traditional Cultural Expressions/Expressions of Folklore: Draft Objectives and Principles*, Annex, WIPO/GRTKF/IC/10/4 (2 October 2006), *available at* www.wipo.int/edocs/mdocs/tk/en/wipo_grtkf_ic_10/wipo_grtkf_ic_10_4.pdf (last visited 31 July 2008).

13 *See* WIPO, Intergovernmental Committee on Intellectual Property and Genetic Resources, Traditional Knowledge and Folklore, *The Protection of Traditional Knowledge: Draft Objectives and Principles*, Annex, WIPO/GRTKF/IC/10/5 (2 October 2006), *available at* www.wipo.int/edocs/mdocs/tk/en/wipo_grtkf_ic_10/wipo_grtkf_ic_10_5.pdf (last visited 31 July 2008).

14 While the Copyright Act 1968, *supra* note 10, does not define these terms, Section 10 provides guidance on what these categories include.

15 *Id.*, sec. 10(1) (defining a "sound recording" as "the aggregate of the sounds embodied in a record").

editions. There are certain requirements that must be met before protection is granted.

3.1. THE REQUIREMENT OF A MATERIAL FORM

Copyright protection does not require registration. It exists automatically if a work or subject matter is created in a material form.[16] Copyright law protects the form in which ideas are expressed rather than the ideas themselves.[17]

Many generations contribute to the creation of traditional cultural expression. A song, dance, story or traditional design may have been created many generations ago. When traditional cultural expression is first reduced to a material form – an oral story is put in writing; a "creation being" is etched on paper; body paintings are shifted on to canvas; an initiation song is recorded on tape or a sacred ceremony is filmed – copyright is created. This means that ephemeral and performance forms of traditional cultural expressions, such as oral stories, songs and dances that are performed at ceremonies and have never been recorded will not be protected under Australian copyright law.

Some commentators state that the recording of traditional cultural expressions has the effect of freezing or stifling a living traditional culture. In some Indigenous communities, there are songs or stories that have so far been considered too sacred to be committed to a written form. Culture is continuously evolving. The ephemeral nature of traditional cultural expression is fundamental to the manner in which the next generation of cultural practitioners will interact with it, re-interpret it and revitalize it within their context and contemporary situation.

Many Indigenous Australian forms of cultural expression are oral. Traditional songs and stories told and passed on through the generations were not recorded in material form. Some forms of art are transient such as body painting and sand sculptures. These do not meet the material form requirement of copyright, unless they are photographed or filmed.[18]

The traditional stories of Indigenous peoples have been written up in books, theatre and film without their prior informed consent. Indigenous people have been concerned about incidents where non-Indigenous authors have written down previously unpublished "traditional stories" and then claimed a copyright without giving proper recognition to the source of the story.

---

16 *Id.*, sec. 10(1) (defining "material form" in relation to a work or an adaptation of a work, as including "any form (whether visible or not) of storage" from which the work or adaptation, or a substantial part of the work or adaptation, can be reproduced).

17 *See, e.g.*, Walter v. Lane, [1900] AC 539.

18 *See* Australian Copyright Council, *Protecting Indigenous Intellectual Property: A Copyright Perspective* (March 1997) (*prepared by* I. McDonald).

The requirement that there be a material form places considerable limitations on any attempt to protect oral works. Much Indigenous and other non-fixed forms of intangible cultural heritage will fall outside of this copyright protection requirement. The Berne Convention states that the "expression literary and artistic works" includes "every production in the literary, scientific and artistic domain, whatever may be the mode or form of its expression".[19] It is, however, up to each country to decide whether to prescribe within its copyright laws the requirement that a work be fixed in some material form.[20] In France, works do not have to be fixed in a material form to be copyright protected. The criterion for protection of a work under French copyright law is that it be an *œuvre d'esprit*, a work of the mind (Article L112–1). Article L111–2 of *le Code de la propriété intellectuelle* (Intellectual Property Code) states "a work shall be deemed to have been created, irrespective of any public disclosure, by the mere fact of realization of the author's concept, even if incomplete."[21] It must be 'fixed' in a certain way. There is no restriction under the Berne Convention to the protection of intangible and unfixed forms of expression. Legislators have enough scope to extend copyright protection to intangible cultural heritage.

3.2. PROTECTION FOR A LIMITED TIME

Copyright protects works and other subject matter only for a limited time period.[22] After this, the work, film or sound recording can be used without the need to obtain consent or the payment of royalties.

---

19 Berne Convention, *supra* note 9, Article 2(1).

20 *Id.*, Article 2(2).

21 *Code de la propriété intellectuelle* [C.P.I.] Article L111–2 (Fr.), *available at* www.legifrance.gouv.fr/(last visited 31 July 2008) ("L'oeuvre est réputée créée, indépendamment de toute divulgation publique, du seul fait de la réalisation, même inachevée, de la conception de l'auteur.").

22 In accordance with the Australia-U.S. Free Trade Agreement signed at Washington, D.C., on 18 May 2004, Australian copyright protection was extended from 50 years to 70 years to be consistent with U.S. copyright laws. The 70 years duration period applies to non-government produced works and materials produced after 1 January 2005, as well as works and materials still under copyright on 1 January 2005; *see* Australia-US Free Trade Agreement, Article 17.4(4). The period of "70 years *post mortem auctoris*" originally stems from the German copyright law; *see* Urheberrechtsgesetz [UrhG] [Copyright Law 1965], Article 64, 9 September 1965, BGBl. 1 at 1273 (F.R.G.), *available at* www.iuscomp.org/gla/statutes/UrhG.htm#64 (last visited 31 July 2008). This standard was taken from the German law for the European Union harmonization. In the U.S., the Copyright Term Extension Act 1998 (also referred to as Sony Bono Act) adopted the 70 year period. Currently, similar discussions for extending the term to 70 years are occurring in Japan.

In Australia, published literary, dramatic, musical and artistic works are protected for 70 years after the author's death.[23] As for unpublished literary, musical and dramatic works, not previously broadcast or publicly performed works, as well as records of work that have not been offered or exposed for sale to the public (such as those released after the death of the artist), they are protected for 70 years from the first date of publication, performance or broadcast, whichever occurs first.[24] Importantly, protection is indefinite if the work is not published. Finally, subject matter other than works, films[25] and sound recordings are copyright protected for 70 years from the date of production.[26]

When the period of copyright protection ends, anyone can copy or make use of the work, film or sound recording without seeking permission from the copyright owner.

Traditional cultural expressions have a long history, often stretching over many generations. Despite their antiquity, Indigenous people have a continuing cultural connection to these forms of expression. This connection may have been severed or threatened in the past as a result of colonization or disenfranchisement. Therefore, reclaiming, revitalizing and strengthening traditional cultural expression is important for the identity of Indigenous people.

Indigenous people argue that the right to culturally practice their traditional cultural expressions should last forever and should not stop with the end of the copyright.[27] The limited time frame of copyright protection does *not* adequately reflect the nature of traditional cultural expressions, which are created as part of an ongoing process of passing cultural knowledge to future generations. Indigenous rights to cultural works are recreated in perpetuity and therefore cultural consent to their use should always be necessary, even if a work is no longer copyright protected.

---

23 Pursuant to the Copyright Act 1968, *supra* note 10, sec. 33(2), copyright in a literary, dramatic, musical or artistic work continues to subsist until the expiration of seventy years after the end of the calendar year in which the author dies.

24 *See id.*, sec. 33(3).

25 After 1 May 1968.

26 It is important to note that the copyright duration rules for Government copyright did not change after 1 January 2005. Material made under the direction and control of the Government is generally protected for 50 years from the date of publication. *See* Australian Copyright Council, *Information Sheet G23: Duration of Copyright* (Sep. 2005), *available at* www.copyright.org.au/publications/infosheets.htm (last visited 31 July 2008).

27 *See* T. Janke, *Our Culture: Our Future: Report on Australian Indigenous Cultural and Intellectual Property Rights*, 1998, 59, *available at* www.frankellawyers.com.au/media/report/culture.pdf (last visited 31 July 2008).

3.3. ORIGINAL WORKS FROM THE OLD AND ANCIENT

Another rule of copyright law is that a work must be original.[28] It cannot be copied from another work. The creator needs to have put into the work the necessary degree of labour, skill and judgement to give it some quality or character which the original raw materials did not possess. However, it is in the very nature of traditional cultural expressions and practices that the cultural group uses pre-existing designs to create its art. Members imitate ceremonies and retell stories as best as they can recollect them, in the manner handed down from their forebears. The copying or mimicking of styles and performance is a necessary means of learning cultural practices.

This mode of transmission has lead to speculation as to whether an artist who reproduces a traditional or pre-existing design or story is in fact creating an original work. The cultural requirement of "painting" iconic themes in accordance with tradition limits the scope for interpretation and individuality.[29] While the issue depends on the particular facts at hand, Justice von Doussa in *Milpurrurru v. Indofurn* (*Carpets Case*)[30] stated that "[a]lthough the artworks follow traditional Aboriginal form and are based on dreaming themes, each artwork is one of intricate detail and complexity reflecting great skill and originality."[31] Based on the specific facts of the case, Justice von Doussa considered that there was sufficient scope for individual artistic interpretation, notwithstanding that the Indigenous artworks in question followed pre-existing traditional designs.

One of the works discussed in the *Carpets Case* was a linocut by the Aboriginal artist Banduk Marika, entitled *Djanda and the Sacred Waterhole*. This work depicted two sand goannas, representing the creation place of Marika's clan. According to the ruling, she had the right to depict this scene by virtue of her birth into her family and clan. Before her, her brother was entitled to depict the image and, before that, one of her ancestors. Every generation painted and depicted the story, each bringing it greater clarity and development.

3.4. CREATORS ARE INDIVIDUALS

Under copyright law, the individual person or persons recording or writing down the form of the traditional cultural expression will be recognized as the author and copyright owner. Unless there is some joint authorship by way of collaboration,

---

28 *See* Copyright Act 1968, *supra* note 10, sec. 32.

29 Department of Home Affairs and Environment, *Report of the Working Party on the Protection of Aboriginal Folklore*, 1981, par. 1403.

30 Milpurrurru & Ors v. Indofurn Pty Ltd. & Ors, 30 I.P.R. 209 (1995).

31 *Id.* at 216.

the law does not recognize the trans-generational development of traditional cultural expressions. According to Anthony Seeger, the individual nature of rights in Western copyright laws has its origins in the Enlightenment, where the focus of philosophy shifted from the group to the individual as the basic element of society.[32] Michael Dodson, an Australian Indigenous member of the United Nations Permanent Forum on Indigenous Issues, noted that this was the main difficulty in using intellectual property laws to protect Indigenous knowledge. According to Dodson, "Western constructs of intellectual property focus on individual knowledge and creativity, rather than on communal trans-generational knowledge."[33]

3.5. SPIRITUAL BEINGS ARE NOT "AUTHORS" OF COPYRIGHT WORKS

Art, stories, songs and other traditional cultural expressions are manifestations of religious and spiritual beliefs. Chants from ceremonies and sacred images on rock walls are believed by Indigenous people to have been created by ancestral or spiritual beings. The spiritual creators of rock art would not be considered 'authors' under copyright because they are no longer living. According to an Indigenous custodian from Warradjan Aboriginal Cultural Centre:

> Rock Art shows our life
>
> Rock art is an important part of Aboriginal people's lives. Mimi[[34]] spirits were the first of the Creation Ancestors to paint on rock. They taught some Aboriginal people how to paint and other Aboriginal people learned by copying Mimi art.
>
> At the end of their journeys, some Creation Ancestors put themselves on rock walls as paintings and became djang (Dreaming places). Some of these paintings are andjamun (sacred and dangerous) and can be seen only by senior men or women; others can be seen by all people.[35]

---

32 *See* A. Seeger, "Intellectual Property and Audiovisual Archives and Collections", in Council on Library and Information Resources (ed.), *Folk Heritage Collections in Crisis*, 2001, 32, 37.

33 United Nations Economic and Social Council, Permanent Forum on Indigenous Issues, *Indigenous Forum Discusses Implementation of Fourth Session's Recommendations: Possible Study on Proper Protection of Traditional Knowledge*, 30 May 2007, *available at* www.un.org/News/Press/docs/2007/hr4924.doc.htm (last visited 31 July 2008).

34 D. Horton, *The encyclopaedia of Aboriginal Australia*, Volume 2 M-Z, 698 (1994) ("Mimi is the name given to an art style found in the Arnhem Land plateau. They are human figures and are small, usually less than 50cm high and rarely exceeding one metre.").

35 The Australian Government Department of the Environment and Water Resources, *Aboriginal Art*, www.environment.gov.au/parks/kakadu/artculture/art/(last visited 31 July 2008) (quoting Warradjan Aboriginal Cultural Centre).

Some rock art sites can only be painted or depicted by certain people with the relevant ritual knowledge and the right to do so under customary law. Archaeologist George Chaloupka notes that in the language of Indigenous clans of Arnhem Land, an area world famous for its rock art, there is no special category for those who paint. It is the act of creation that is considered as most important:

> everybody is aware that the person carrying it out is only an agent of the Dreamings, which institutes all the aspects of their cultures. Creativity of one kind or another is expected of every person throughout his or her life. 'Art' is an integral part of the Aborigines' social and religious life, in which individual artists share and interpret the traditions of the group.[36]

This contrasts with Western forms of contemporary art where the individual rather than the group experience is the underlying philosophy. For rock art figures or images, there may be no identifiable individual creator. Therefore, copyright is never asserted by any individual.

Rock art is being reproduced in an increasing variety of ways. It is being photographed or redrawn. It is finding its way onto postcards, websites and books. Some of its uses, especially where the rock art images are altered or shown to wider audiences than allowable under customary laws, are inappropriate and cause offence to the Indigenous custodians.

3.6. FILMS AND SOUND RECORDINGS

Copyright also subsists in cinematograph films. The maker of the film is usually recognized as the owner of the copyright in the film, after its completion for the production of the first copy.[37] There is also a separate type of copyright recognized in sound recordings.[38] Before 1 January 2005 the maker of a sound recording was the recognized owner of copyright. This had an effect on Indigenous cultures, because the owner of the tape could freely say how the tape was used. If the performed song was outside of copyright protection, or was a traditional Indigenous song, there was no copyright recognized in the content, and no rights recognized in the performers or traditional song owners.

In Australia, there is no such thing as a performer's copyright and performers do not have a proprietary right over their performance. Under the Copyright Act 1968, certain provisions do relate to performers rights, such as the ability to prevent certain unauthorized uses of recordings of their performances. Also,

36 G. Chaloupka, *Journey in Time: The World's Longest Continuing Art Tradition: The 50,000 Year Story of the Australian Aboriginal Rock Art of Arnhem Land*, 1993, 45.

37 *See* Copyright Act 1968, *supra* note 10, sec. 90.

38 *Id.*, sec. 89.

since 1 January 2005, performers share with the recording company part of the copyright in a sound recording of a live performance, if they were not paid for it.[39] Changes to the law were also made to include "folklore" in the definition of a "live performance".[40] Depending on the facts, an Aboriginal who performs "folklore" (without a fee) and is recorded by another person will have a partial copyright interest in the recording of their performance.[41]

3.7. AUTHORS HAVE EXCLUSIVE RIGHTS

Once the requirements for a copyright are met, the copyright owner has exclusive permission to exploit the copyright in the work or subject matter. This includes the right to reproduce and authorize reproduction of the work or subject matter, as well as to deal with the copyright in a number of ways, depending on the nature of the work or subject matter, such as performing the work in public[42], communicating the work to the public[43] and making an adaptation of the work.[44]

In the case of traditional cultural expressions that have been recorded by outsiders, the copyright owners of these recordings are freely able to exploit and control their documents, books, tapes, films and other copyright materials, without observing any cultural restrictions.[45]

In the Copyright Act 1968, the creator is referred to as "the author". The general rule is that the author of a work is the first owner of the copyright in that work.[46] However, there are circumstances where this will not be the case and it is not unusual for the author and the owner of the copyright to be different entities. These exceptions include the following situations:

---

39 Australian Copyright Council, *Information Sheet G22: Performers' Rights* 4 (February 2005), *available at* www.copyright.org.au/publications/infosheets.htm (last visited 31 July 2008).

40 Copyright Act 1968, *supra* note 10, sec. 84.

41 This would depend on the circumstances of the case. It should also be noted that there are "exempt recordings" with regard to this provision. They include indirect film and sound recordings of performances, made for private and domestic use only or for the purposes of research or study; *see id.*, sec. 248A.

42 *Id.*, sec. 31(1)(a)(iii). A public performance refers to any form of presentation to the public, whether visual and aural, or even merely aural. The definition of performance includes not only performances of works encompassed in films, CDs, etc., but extends to live performances, speeches, addresses, lectures and sermons, for example. The right to make a public performance of material protected by copyright is separate from the right to communicate to the public.

43 *Id.*, sec. 31(1)(a)(iv).

44 Copyright Act 1968, *supra* note 10, sec. 31(1)(a)(v).

45 *See* Janke, *supra* note 27, at 54.

46 Copyright Act 1968, *supra* note 10, sec. 35(2).

(a) where a work is produced by an employee under a contract of employment (the employer will own the copyright)[47];
(b) where the work is produced under the direction and control of the Crown (that is, state or commonwealth government);
(c) where the work is produced under commission and there may be a contract assigning copyright in the work to the commissioning body;
(d) where a copyright has been assigned or exclusively licensed in writing.[48]

3.8. MORAL RIGHTS FOR INDIVIDUALS NOT COMMUNITIES

Since 2000, Australian creators have enjoyed moral rights in their works and films. Sound recordings, however, are not included in the moral rights regime. The Copyright Act 1968 provides creators the following unalienable rights:

(a) the right of attribution of authorship;
(b) the right not to have authorship falsely attributed; and
(c) the right of integrity of authorship.[49]

These rights, like copyright itself, belong to the individual creators who "create" the work or film, by making or fixing it in a material form.[50] In this respect, moral rights do not extend collectively to an Indigenous clan group or community.

Moral rights cannot be assigned or sold and remain with the author even when the latter does not own the copyright. For instance, employees hold moral rights in created works, even if the copyright is vested with the employer. An important thing to note, however, is that it is possible for a creator to consent to the infringement of his moral rights. In some industries, contracts are presented to creators that include a wide-ranging consent to such infringement.

3.8.1. Rights of Attribution/Against False Attribution

The Indigenous artist of a painting has the right to be named as the author[51] of the work. This is the author's right of attribution of authorship in respect of his or her work.[52] The right to be recognized as the community or source of clan imagery is

47 *Id.*, sec. 35(6).
48 *Id.*, sec. 96.
49 *Id.*, sec. 189.
50 *Id.*, sec. 190.
51 The term "author" used here refers to creator, as the term is defined in the Copyright Act 1968, *supra* note 10.
52 *Id.*, sec. 193.

important for cultural works. Information, images and knowledge incorporated in the painting may be linked to identity, land ownership and kinship. One interesting question is whether the use of a form of traditional cultural expression in a painting by an outsider should create rights of attribution for the clan. This danger of false attribution through the misuse of traditional cultural expression also exists in relation to artistic works and cinematograph films.[53]

3.8.2. Rights of Integrity

The moral right of integrity provides creators with a right to bring an action if their work is subjected to derogatory treatment. "Derogatory treatment" refers to anything that results in a material distortion, mutilation or alteration of the work[54] or film[55] that is prejudicial to the author's honour or reputation. It also applies to "an exhibition in public of the work that is prejudicial to the author's honour or reputation because of the manner or place in which the exhibition occurs."[56] Additionally, it includes doing anything else in relation to the work[57] or film which is prejudicial to the author's reputation.

The right of integrity is important for Indigenous artists. Preserving the overall integrity of the work and the underlying story or ritual knowledge is crucial to the proper representation of Indigenous art and film. Greater access to artistic works and films, once they are in digital form, increases the ways in which they can be distorted, mutilated and altered. The right of integrity, including the right to bring an action for infringement, is useful to protect the integrity of Indigenous works.

The right of integrity is not infringed if the alleged derogatory treatment can be proved to have been reasonable in view of the particular circumstances[58], or if the author consented to the treatment.[59] Indigenous creators should be cautious when considering commercial agreements and contracts of employment. They must seek wide consent to their moral rights. However, even if consent was not given, the fact of employment[60] and industry practice may be taken into account when deciding whether the derogatory treatment was reasonable.[61]

---

53 *Id.*, secs. 195AE and 195AF.
54 *Id.*, secs. 195AJ(a) and 195AK(a).
55 *Id.*, sec. 195AL.
56 *Id.*, sec. 195AK(b).
57 *Id.*, secs. 195AJ(c), 195AK(c) and 195AL(b).
58 *Id.*, sec. 195AS. Certain matters must be taken into account when determining if the treatment was reasonable. These are listed in Section 195AS(2) for literary, dramatic, musical and artistic work and in Section 195AS(3) for films.
59 *Id.*, sec. 195AW (film or work included in a film) and sec. 195AWA (work that is not a film or included in a film).
60 *Id.*, sec. 195AS(2)(e)(f)(g) (for literary, dramatic, musical or artistic works) and sec. 195AS(3)(f)(g)(h) (for films).
61 *Id.*, sec. 195AS.

One of the deficiencies in the provisions dealing with moral rights is that like copyright protection their duration is limited.[62] For works of important cultural significance, Indigenous peoples assert cultural rights, including those of attribution and reproduction, which will last in perpetuity.

Indigenous people are intent upon keeping the cultural integrity of their heritage. They collectively wish to be recognized as the primary guardians and interpreters of their cultures, arts and sciences, both those created in the past and developed in the future. The right for all members of the group to prevent derogatory treatment of Indigenous traditional cultural expression is critical.

The rising demand for Indigenous visual arts has led to wide-scale copying of Indigenous designs, motifs, symbols and artworks for commercial gain. Indigenous art has been copied onto carpets[63], dresses, fabrics[64] and t-shirts[65] without the knowledge or permission of the Indigenous artists or their community. In many instances, the designs are altered. Indigenous Australians complain that such uses are inappropriate, derogatory and culturally offensive. The Australian laws with regard to moral rights entitle individual artists to protect their works against derogatory treatment, but the works must be protected by a copyright and artists must seek to assert their rights.

3.8.3. Proposals for Indigenous Communal Moral Rights

The Commonwealth Government has drafted amendments of the Copyright Act 1968 for Indigenous communal moral rights. These amendments are not published but were circulated on a confidential basis to a number of Indigenous arts and community organizations. The current proposed model introduces the concept of Indigenous communal moral rights as existing alongside individual moral rights. It is proposed that the Indigenous communal moral rights will be exercisable independently of the individual author's moral rights. Indigenous communal moral rights will exist in works and films drawn from a traditional base.[66] They will apply if, before the first dealing of the work or film, there is a voluntary agreement between the creator and the Indigenous community.[67] There must also

---

62 The right of integrity in a film lasts until the death of the author; *see id.*, sec. 195AM(1). The right of integrity in works other than film continues for the duration of the copyright, which is fifty years after the death of the author; *see id.*, sec. 195AM(2).

63 *See, e.g.*, *Milpurrurru v. Indofurn*, 30 I.P.R. 209.

64 *See, e.g.*, John Bulun Bulun & Anor v. R & T Textiles Pty Ltd., [1998] 1082 F.C.A. (3 Sep. 1998).

65 *See, e.g.*, Bulun Bulun v. Nejlam Pty Ltd., unreported (settled) (1989) (*Flash T-Shirts Case*).

66 "Drawn from a traditional base" means that the work or film must be drawn from the "particular body of traditions, observances, customs or beliefs held in common by the Indigenous community.".

67 A "community" is defined loosely and can include an individual, family, clan or community group.

be acknowledgement of the community's association with the work.[68] Furthermore, all interest holders in the work (*i.e.* copyright owners) need to have consented to the Indigenous communal moral rights existing in the work or film.

An Indigenous community that has communal moral rights in respect of a work may exercise those rights only through an individual who is the authorized representative in respect of the work. This authorized representative may be designated by the community according to its cultural practices or may be appointed according to decision making processes.[69]

Another limitation of the proposed Bill is that Indigenous communal moral rights would only exist for the term of the copyright period. As discussed above, Indigenous people see their rights to traditional cultural expression as extending in perpetuity for the sake of their continuing cultural practice.

The Bill is not yet law, however, the government intends to introduce it for consideration shortly. The draft has been criticized as being ineffective. According to Jane Anderson, "the draft Bill is highly complicated and legalistic, presenting serious practical hurdles for Indigenous people and communities seeking to protect their knowledge and its use".[70] Anderson says there is a glaring difference between the Government's stated objective and its current draft, adding that it is difficult to see where a remedy might arise for infringement.

The Arts Law Centre of Australia also considered that the Bill required further work, in respect of the voluntary agreement requirement for Indigenous communal moral rights to exist. Their opinion is that the Indigenous communal moral rights should arise automatically when the work is made, and when it draws from a community's traditions, customs or beliefs.[71]

Another perturbing issue is the government's limited consultation with Indigenous peoples on the draft Bill. The government has failed to engage Indigenous stakeholders in a meaningful debate on the contents of the Bill. This seems to be a major oversight if the main impetus for introducing the Bill was to benefit Indigenous communities. Robynne Quiggin criticizes the Bill as predominantly protecting third parties in their dealing with Indigenous art, rather than recognizing the nature of communal ownership and protecting its content.[72] Unless an Indigenous community's moral rights can be established in

---

68 Draft Copyright Amendment (Indigenous Communal Moral Rights) Bill 2003, secs. 195AZZL and 195AZZM.

69 T. Janke, "The Moral of the Story: Indigenous Communal Moral Rights", *Bulletin*, No. 3/2005, at 1, 2, 7 and 8.

70 J. Anderson, "Indigenous Communal Moral Rights: The Utility of an Ineffective Law", *Indigenous Law Bulletin*, February 2004, at 8.

71 Arts Law Centre of Australia, *Indigenous communal moral rights*, www.artslaw.com.au/_documents/files/ICMRLetterAndExecutiveSummary2006.pdf (last visited 31 July 2008).

72 *See* R. Quiggin, *The Contribution of Protocols and Moral Rights* (5 August 2004) (paper presented at *Snapshot 2*, AMAG, Melbourne, Australia).

a work or film prior to the first dealing (which is limited as discussed above), then a person who deals with the work or film, such as a publisher or film maker is not legally obliged to recognize any Indigenous cultural sensitivities in dealing with the work or film.

3.9. COPYRIGHT AND THE RESPONSIBILITY OF THE TRADITIONAL CULTURAL EXPRESSION ARTIST

The exclusive rights granted to copyright owners to use, adapt and reproduce their works without conditions are at odds with Indigenous cultural heritage material. In many Indigenous clans, strict rules are applied to the responsibility for cultural heritage in order to ensure that it is maintained, protected and passed on to future generations. An individual or group of individuals may be empowered to act as the caretaker of a particular item of heritage.[73] However, these traditional custodians may only make decisions that are in harmony with the best interests of the community as a whole.

3.9.1. Bulun Bulun v. R & T Textiles

The Federal Court case of *Bulun Bulun v. R & T Textiles*[74] examined the issue of custodianship. Johnny Bulun Bulun was the artist and copyright owner of the bark painting *At the Waterhole*. The painting embodied traditional ritual knowledge of the Ganalbingu people. Johnny Bulun Bulun's right to use ritual knowledge to produce the artworks was given to him under Ganalbingu customary law. This right was based on the trust and confidence of the clan in the artist personally. R & T Textiles Pty Ltd. had imported and sold within Australia fabric which copied parts of *At the Waterhole*. When issued with a statement of claim from the artist, the textile company was quick to negotiate a settlement. However, the case still went to court to consider the issues relating to the clan's interests in the copyright work.

Justice von Doussa, the same judge who presided over the *Carpets Case*, found that there was no native title right to the painting. He also considered that there was no equitable interest in the work, nor was this a case of joint ownership because there was no evidence that anyone other than Johnny Bulun Bulun had created the bark painting.[75] Von Doussa also considered that the artist had not created the work as part of an implied legal trust, which would have made his clan

73 In some groups, this may not be the case, due to the disruption of cultural practices and customary laws since colonization.

74 *Bulun Bulun v. R & T Textiles*, [1998] 1082 F.C.A.

75 *See* M.F. Brown, *Who Owns Native Culture?*, 2003, 64.

an equal owner. The witnesses and affidavit evidence showed that "on many occasions paintings which incorporate to a greater or lesser degree parts of the ritual knowledge of the Ganalbingu people are produced by Ganalbingu artists for commercial sale for the benefit of the artist concerned."[76]

Justice von Doussa found that there was a fiduciary relationship between the artist and the clan. Customary laws impacted on the rights of the artist to deal with the work embodying the ritual knowledge. He had to discuss and negotiate the use of the traditional knowledge with relevant persons in authority within his clan. Evidence given by Djardie Ashley discussed how the Ganalbingu laws dealt with the consent procedures. Ashley noted that in some circumstances, such as the reproduction of a painting in an art book, the artist might not need to consult widely with the group. In other circumstances, such as the mass-reproduction of a painting as merchandize, Bulun Bulun could be required to consult extensively. Ashley further noted that

> the question in each case depends on the use and the manner or the mode of production. But in the case of a use which is one that requires direct consultation, rather than one for which approval has been already given for a class of uses, all of the traditional Aboriginal owners[[77]] must agree. There must be total consensus. Bulun Bulun could not act alone to permit the reproduction of 'at the Waterhole' in the manner as was done.[78]

The relationship between the artist and the clan imposed the obligation on Johnny Bulun Bulun "not to exploit the artistic work in a way that is contrary to the laws and custom of the Ganalbingu people, and, in the event of infringement by a third party, to take reasonable and appropriate action to restrain and remedy infringement of the copyright in the artistic work."[79] If the artist had been unable or unwilling to take copyright action, equity would have allowed the clan leader to take action to stop the infringement.

3.9.2. Fiduciary Duty and Its Potential Extent

The fiduciary obligation imposed on the copyright owner artist has sparked much interest among Indigenous people. The question is whether the clan can use this legal principle to bring an action based in equity to stop the unauthorized use by a third party of an image or an aspect of traditional ritual knowledge embodied in a copyright work.

---

76 *Bulun Bulun v R & T Textiles*, [1998] 1082 FCA.

77 The notion "traditional owners" refers to the group, clan, community of people in whom the custody and protection of cultural heritage is entrusted in accordance with the customary law and practices.

78 *Bulun Bulun v. R & T Textiles*, [1998] 1082 F.C.A.

79 *Id.*

Sally McCausland has considered the potential repercussions of the decision in *Bulun Bulun v. R & T Textiles* and whether the fiduciary obligation may extend in certain circumstances where notice of the "Bulun Bulun equity" is given by the clan to outsiders. For example, a third party licensee of an Indigenous artwork, who is notified of the custodial interest of an Indigenous clan, may be open to claims by the latter that it has a fiduciary duty to safeguard the integrity of the work when using its copyright.[80] McCausland further enquires into whether the Bulun Bulun equity applies to other copyright works incorporating "traditional ritual knowledge":

> It is possible that any person who has acquired copyright in a work embodying traditional ritual knowledge with notice is a fiduciary under Australian law. If so, the person would be bound to act in accordance with the fiduciary duty (that is, respect customary law concerning reproduction and adaptation of the work.) If a person breaches the fiduciary duty, the situation might be analogous to the breach of confidence case of *Foster v Mountford*, in which the Federal Court granted an order to stay sales of a book containing traditional knowledge of the Pitjantjatjara people.[81]

McCausland speculates that a third party fiduciary duty might arise where traditional custodians allow access to a filmmaker to interview community members. If the filmmaker is given notice of the custodians' interest in the traditional ritual knowledge communicated in the interviews, he may owe a fiduciary duty to the custodians when dealing with copyright in the filmed interviews. She says that notice of the custodians' interest incorporated in the access permit would help to establish this duty.[82] In other areas too, where outsiders come into communities to record traditional cultural expression, an Indigenous community could use written agreements to state the fiduciary obligations of third parties when they access traditional ritual knowledge. For example, where a researcher wants access to traditional ritual knowledge for a particular project, the community could enter into a written agreement with that person, requiring her to consult on an ongoing basis about the project. It could also require her to display a custodians' interest notice on any copyright material created. McCausland further states, "the community could even require copyright in the project to be jointly owned or held on trust for its benefit."[83]

In my opinion, this line of thought has implications for scholars, authors, filmmakers, people who record sound, compilers, researchers and other

---

80 *See* S. McCausland, "Protecting Communal Interests in Indigenous Artworks after the Bulun Bulun Case", *Indigenous Law Bulletin*, July 1999, at 4–6.

81 *Id.* at 5.

82 *Id.*

83 *Id.*

documenters of Aboriginal traditional knowledge and traditional cultural expression where copyright is created.

Michael F. Brown notes the legal potential for this precedent to be applicable to other traditionally based, non-Indigenous groups, and the potential for claims against urban based Indigenous artists. He states: "Beyond enthusiasm for the recognition of communal rights in art, then, lie unexplored legal paths, some of which hint at troubling possibilities."[84]

4. CASE STUDIES DEALING WITH COPYRIGHT FORMS OF TRADITIONAL CULTURAL EXPRESSIONS

4.1. ROCK ART ON T-SHIRTS CASE STUDY

Copyright rewards the person who imparts skill and labour into existing material to create an original work. When the raw material is traditional cultural expression or work in the public domain, this can result in a new copyright vesting in the diligent author. In the *Unauthorized Reproduction of Indigenous Rock Art* case study in *Minding Culture*[85], it was determined that, under the law, the skill and labour of a researcher in redrawing rock art images was arguably enough to create a new original copyright work in the resulting photographs and illustrations.[86] This matter was settled before the commencement of court action. However, it provides a good basis to examine the ownership of copyright over intangible cultural heritage.

In 1997, Riptide Churinga, a Sydney based t-shirt manufacturer, produced a range of t-shirts with *Mimi* rock art figures. The t-shirts were discovered on sale to the surprise of a descendant of the Badmardi clan and Vivien Johnson, an Aboriginal art lecturer. The use of the *Mimi* figures is guarded carefully under customary law and they are still significant to Indigenous cultural beliefs. For cultural heritage purposes, stories and information surrounding the sites, the sites themselves and the right to touch up or depict images like those embodied in rock form should, in theory, belong to the owners of the cultural images that are depicted. The rock art is estimated to be about 4,000 years old and therefore not the subject of copyright.[87] How could the clan stop the t-shirt maker from transgressing their laws?

84 M.F. Brown, *supra* note 75, at 65.

85 T. Janke, *Minding Culture: Case Studies on Intellectual Property and Traditional Cultural Expressions*, 2003, *available at* www.wipo.int/tk/en/studies/cultural/minding-culture/studies/finalstudy.pdf (last visited 31 July 2008).

86 *Id.* at 100–13.

87 *Id.* at 106.

In the 1970s, Eric Brandl was funded by the Australian Institute of Aboriginal Studies (now the Australian Institute of Aboriginal and Torres Strait Islander Studies or AIATSIS) to visit and record certain rock art sites in the Northern Territory. His methods of recording involved photographing the various rock art sites, which were in almost inaccessible places in the Deaf Adder Creek region. He then returned to his office, where he projected the images onto a wall and traced the works out with his hand in Indian ink.

These drawings and photographs of the *Mimi* rock art were published by the Australian Institute of Studies in 1973.[88] There was copyright in the book, the photographs and the drawings. In line with the originality principles of copyright, the skill and labour applied by Brandl to the original rock art created a copyright interest in the derived sketches. It was obvious that Riptide Churinga had taken images directly from the book to produce its t-shirts.

The Australian Institute of Aboriginal and Torres Strait Islander Studies, the Brandl Estate and the Badmardi clan were able to demand that the t-shirt company stop production. They entered into a settlement which included damages and the delivery up of unsold items. There was also a public apology posted in *The Australian*, a national newspaper.

The case illustrates that copyright owners had the right to take legal action. The "cultural owners" were able to enlist the holders of the copyright to commence action, even though the "cultural owners" had no copyright ownership rights. Anderson notes that "had the images of the *Mimi* reproduced on tee-shirts been copied straight from the rock-art itself, there would have been no grounds for complaint by [the Australian Institute of Aboriginal and Torres Strait Islander Studies], the Brandl Estate or the Badmardi clan, for the material would be classified as being in the public domain and therefore open to use. The problem of protecting rock art has existed as a pertinent complaint about the biases of copyright in relation to Indigenous knowledge."[89]

4.2. WRITING TRADITIONAL STORIES

Under copyright laws, if an individual storyteller writes down an oral story, the individual is recognized as the owner of at least that version of the story. What if that story is sacred and not suitable for wide circulation? A story or ceremony may

88 E.J. Brandl, *Australian Aboriginal Paintings in Western and Central Arnhem Land: Temporal Sequences and Elements of Style in Cadell River and Deaf Adder Creek Art*, 1973.

89 J. Anderson, *Access and Control of Indigenous Knowledge in Libraries and Archives: Ownership and Future Use*, 24 (5–7 May 2005) (paper presented at the conference *Correcting Course: Rebalancing Copyright for Libraries in the National and International Arena*, Columbia University, New York, United States), *available at* http://conservationcommons.org/media/document/docu-i64cij.pdf (last visited 31 July 2008).

be unsuited to wider access and limited to the initiated, as was the case in *Foster v. Mountford*.[90] The right to maintain the secrecy of Indigenous knowledge and other cultural practices is important.

What if the storyteller is not from the traditional owner group? What are the rights of the story owners to stop publication? This is a big issue for Indigenous groups where traditional cultural expressions are recorded by outsiders. In many instances where outsiders have come to research or record oral stories, the recorder became the owner of the copyright in that written form. A large amount of recorded traditional cultural expressions is in written reports, books, field notes and language dictionaries compiled by a range of outsiders including linguists, anthropologists and university researchers.

The Australia Council for the Arts[91] has developed protocols for writing Indigenous Australian literature, which aim to recognize Indigenous ownership of traditional stories. The protocols state that if writing up traditional stories involves the verbatim transcription of an oral story from specific informants, then permission, attribution and ownership of the material should always be recognized.[92] There are also protocols for other art forms – music, drama/dance, visual arts and media art. These protocols promote ethical conduct, and respect for Indigenous cultural heritage. Whilst they are recommended use for all projects involving Indigenous cultural heritage, it is a condition of Council funding that the protocols be met for Council funded projects.

4.3. MUSIC

When traditional cultural expressions are recorded on tape or compact disc (CD) by outsiders such as researchers and ethnomusicologists, there is a copyright in the sound recording that is created. This copyright will generally belong to the maker of the recording. In the past, sound recordings of oral stories and performances have been taken by outsiders to the cultural group. These tapes and

---

90 Foster v. Mountford & Rigby Ltd., 14 A.L.R. 71 (1976).

91 The Australia Council is the Australian Government's arts funding and advisory body. It directly supports young, emerging and established artists, as well as new and established organizations. The Council provides over 1700 grants each year to artists and arts organisations across the country in the fields of Aboriginal and Torres Strait Islander arts, community cultural development, dance, literature, music, new media arts, theatre and visual arts/craft. Aboriginal and Torres Strait Islander Arts (ATSIA) supports the Aboriginal and Torres Strait Islander Arts Board, which is the leading authority for Indigenous arts. The division manages the established grant assessment process, together with devising strategies and policies to assist Indigenous artform development. *See* www.ozco.gov.au (last visited 31 July 2008).

92 *See* AUSTRALIA COUNCIL FOR THE ARTS, *Writing Cultures: Protocols for Producing Indigenous Australian Literature*, 2002 (*prepared by* T. JANKE), *available at* www.ozco.gov.au/arts_resources/publications/writing_cultures/files/315/proto_writing.pdf (last visited 31 July 2008).

recordings are taken away from the cultural setting and their use is controlled by the outsider. Who can use, reproduce or adapt the content contained in the recordings? Who has the right to stop the unauthorized use of a "traditional song"?

In his article *pygmy POP: A Genealogy of Schizophonic Mimesis*[93], Steven Feld notes that the music of the group Deep Forest was based on several ethnographic recordings of traditional music from Africa and a CD entitled *Polyphony of the Deep Rain Forest.*[94] Deep Forest gained use of the recordings with permission from the relevant archives and copyright owners, but did not obtain the consent of the traditional song performers or owners. In fact, the latter were not recognized as copyright holders. In a Western legal sense, the originality of the traditional song may have been questionable because, presumably, the performers did not write the song. However, the rights of the song performers, who are the traditional people from which the traditional cultural expression originates, remain vital for their cultural identity.

The Australia Council for the Arts has developed protocols for the development of Indigenous music, in an effort to recognize Indigenous cultural rights. The protocols include protecting the secrecy of Indigenous cultural material that is not suitable for wide dissemination, such as the use of the bullroarer, an Indigenous ceremonial instrument. The bullroarer has been reproduced in a number of sound recordings. The protocols advise musicians "to exercise extra vigilance when it comes to consultation and consent for any proposed use."[95]

4.4. FILMS

In a report on film and Indigenous people, Michael Leigh and Walter Saunders state that the first film about Indigenous Australians was made by Alfred C. Haddon, a visiting academic from England. It was made on Mer (Murray) Island in the Torres Strait in 1898.[96] Since then, the cameras have captured a lot of Indigenous content. This includes ethnographic accounts of culture, sacred

93 *See* S. Feld, "pygmy POP: A Genealogy of Schizophonic Mimesis", 28 *Yearbook for Traditional Music* 1 (1996).

94 *See id.* at 24.

95 Australia Council for the Arts, *Song Cultures: Protocols for Producing Indigenous Australian Music*, 2002 (*prepared by* R. Quiggin), *available at* www.ozco.gov.au/arts_resources/publications/song_cultures/files/313/proto_song.pdf (last visited 31 July 2008).

96 *See* M. Leigh and W. Saunders, *Hidden Pictures: Colonial Camera*, 1995, 7; University of Cambridge, *View First Ever Cambridge Film*, www.screenmedia.group.cam.ac.uk/film.html (last visited 31 July 2008).

ceremonial practices, personal histories and Indigenous knowledge about land, animals, plants and events.[97]

As a result, the film archives have inherited a lot of films that are of significant Indigenous content. Issues now confront the archives about how to manage this material and to whom it should be made available. Often the depositors or the copyright owners are not the Indigenous people, even thought they are the owners of the cultural expression embodied in the film. This is because the filmmaker is recognized as the owner of the copyright in the film.[98] Or, where films are made for another person and fees are paid, the copyright belongs to the person who commissioned it.[99]

This is a concern for Indigenous people whose stories and knowledge have been recorded in the past without proper consent. There is no copyright recognized in a performance and the person who made the recording is often the controller of the material.[100]

An interesting story told by Anderson exemplifies the sort of issues that may arise. Anderson accompanied her friend Joe, an Indigenous man from the Gupapyyngu clan, on a visit to the National Film and Sound Archives in Canberra. They came across a film which recorded Joe's father teaching the *Djawa*[101] in the 1950s. Now 50 years on, Joe was able to view the film, his father and, for the first time, himself as a child. Joe, like other Indigenous Australians, is reclaiming this material, taking it back to his community so that it can establish its own archive.[102] For Indigenous Australians, there are concerns about the uses of film footage of such ceremonies. From a legal standpoint, the copyright owners and depositors have the right to control access, but the Indigenous cultural owners do not. Indigenous people seek to have a say over how these important materials are used, and who gets access to them.

Archives like the National Film and Sound Archive (NFSA) have developed policies and protocols for the access and reproduction of its Indigenous film materials. The NFSA holds a large collection of Indigenous content in the form of films, photographs, videotapes, audio tapes and other forms of media. According to the *NFSA Collection Policy* (September 2006), there are an estimated 15,000 or

---

97 T. Janke, *Captured Images: Film Archives and Indigenous Cultural and Intellectual Property Rights* (27 February 2003) (paper presented at *Culture & Ethics: Who decides?*, a forum hosted by Film Australia, Lindfield, Australia), *available at* www.filmaust.com.au/about/publications/cultureandethics_transcript.pdf (last visited 31 July 2008).

98 Copyright Act 1968, *supra* note 10, sec. 98(2).

99 *Id.*, sec. 98(3).

100 *See* T. Janke and R. Quiggin, "Indigenous Cultural and Intellectual Property and Customary Law", in Law Reform Commission of Western Australia (ed.), *Aboriginal Customary Laws: Background Papers* 451, 460 (January 2006), *available at* www.lrc.justice.wa.gov.au/2publications/reports/ACL/BP/BP-12.pdf (last visited 31 July 2008).

101 *Djawa* is a clan dancing ceremony from Arnhem Land; *see* Anderson, *supra* note 89, at 3.

102 *See id.*

3.5% of films, recordings and programs held at NFSA that include depictions of Indigenous peoples, cultures, and experiences from a range of perspectives and historical attitudes.[103]

The NFSA's *Indigenous Collection Policy* set out good professional practice procedures for the access and use of Indigenous materials, including for description and classification, staffing, education, and training for professional practice.[104]

The collection comprises sensitive materials that depict traditional cultural ceremonies or practices. The policy notes:

> In relation to Indigenous subject matter, sensitivities have greater force when the works and other materials accessed include recordings and/or depictions of secret and/or sacred events recorded with or without permission. In the past, some Aboriginal peoples have given secret information to respected researchers, not realising this information would be published and made available to the general public. In such circumstances, an item need not be readily available to everyone simply by virtue of its prior publication, and may require specific permission from the relevant peoples of association.[105]

The Australian Institute of Aboriginal and Torres Strait Islander Studies Audiovisual Archives (AIATSIS Audiovisual Archives) also developed a Code of Ethics in 2005, the *Collections Management Policy Manual*.[106] The Code is a statement of professional conduct and values which seek to clarify mandatory standards of practice within the AIATSIS Audiovisual Archive.[107] The Code addresses personal conduct relating to archived materials, the standard of care for the collections and the access to secret and sacred materials. It also recognizes the rights of Indigenous communities and individuals by requiring that they consent to publication of archival material. For example, the Australian Institute of Aboriginal and Torres Strait Islander Studies' Audiovisual Code of Ethics states that "[c]opies of material will only be provided for publication purposes if the requestor has consulted with the relevant Indigenous community or individual(s) and has received written permission to proceed, even in such cases where the copyright owner has approved publication."[108]

---

103 National Film and Sound Archive, *Collection Policy and Statement of Cultural Values*, 2006, 31–36, *available at* www.nfsa.afc.gov.au/docs/collectionpolicy.pdf (last visited 31 July 2008) (containing Indigenous Collections Policy).

104 *Id.*

105 *Id.* at 34.

106 The Australian Institute of Aboriginal and Torres Strait Islander Studies Audiovisual Archive's Code of Ethics was examined and endorsed by the AIATSIS Council in August, 2005; *see* Australian Institute of Aboriginal and Torres Strait Islander Studies, *Code of Ethics*, www.aiatsis.gov.au/audiovisual_archives/audiovisual_archives_collection_management_policy_manual/code_of_ethics (last visited 31 July 2008).

107 *See id.*, sec. 10.3.2(b).

108 *Id.*, sec. 10.3.2 (Access to the collections).

4.5. INDIGENOUS LANGUAGES

The past work of non-Indigenous linguists has generated a large amount of materials dealing with Indigenous languages, including sound recordings, films, field notes and dictionaries. The question of who owns a language becomes a problem when you consider the issues that are being raised in Australia with regard to the revival of languages with only a limited number of speakers. Linguists may, by virtue of their own skills, labour and effort become the copyright owners of dictionaries and tapes that become important after the death of the living speakers they consulted to gain their information.

Aboriginal Language Centres and Organizations[109], which are responsible for language maintenance and revitalization, have to negotiate the right to use and adapt the dictionaries which were produced by past linguists on the basis of the oral information provided to them by the speakers of now extinct languages. The living speakers have currently passed on but the dictionary has copyright which belongs to the linguist. In some cases, these linguists live overseas and are retired. Others have passed on and Aboriginal Language Centres now have to engage with the linguist's descendants, or the relevant universities, just to get copies of the materials and to reproduce them for the purposes of language maintenance.[110]

In light of the lessons from the past and the growing knowledge Indigenous people have of copyright laws, Aboriginal Language Centres are now employing their own linguists. The copyright of any resulting works are owned by the Aboriginal Language Centres by virtue of the employee/employer ownership provisions of copyright law. They are also entering into written contracts which assign copyright to organizations owned and operated on behalf of the speaker community. This approach makes use of Section 196 of the Copyright Act 1968, which provides that copyright can be assigned in writing.

5. CONCLUSION: REDRESSING THE IMBALANCE

In conclusion, the focus of Western intellectual property laws is to provide economic incentives for the production of intellectual and creative effort. These objectives stand in contrast to customary laws and the rights of Indigenous peoples to promote cultural maintenance, claim custodial rights and protect the

---

109 These centres are community based organisations established to run language programs to assist with the recording and maintenance of Indigenous languages. They rely on government funding to undertake this important work.

110 *See* JANKE, *supra* note 27, at 22 (quoting concerns raised by Wangka Maya Pilbara Aboriginal Language Centre in its submission to the report).

integrity and the sources of their traditional cultural expressions and intangible cultural heritage. There are some fundamental shortfalls to be found in the use of copyright to protect Indigenous peoples' traditional cultural expressions. These are summarized in the table below:

Table: Comparison of non-indigenous laws and indigenous customary laws dealing with rights to intangible cultural heritage

Non-indigenous laws	Indigenous customary law
* Emphasis on material form.	* Generally orally transmitted.
* **Limited in time eg: copyright for 70 years after the death of the artist; patent rights are 20 years.**	* **Emphasis on preservation and maintenance of culture.**
* Individually based – created by individuals.	* Socially based – created through the generations via the transmission process.
* **Intellectual property rights are owned by individual creators or their employers and research companies.**	* **Communally owned but often custodians are authorised to use and disseminate.**
* Intellectual property can be freely transmitted and assigned – usually for economic returns – for a set time, in any medium and in any territory.	* Generally not transferable but transmission, if allowed, is based on a series of cultural qualifications.
* **Intellectual property rights holders can decide how or by whom the information can be transmitted, transferred or assigned.**	* **There are often restrictions on how transmission can occur, particularly in relation to sacred or secret material.**
* Intellectual property rights are generally compartmentalised into categories such as tangible, intangible, arts and cultural expression.	* A holistic approach, by which all aspects of cultural heritage are inter-related.
* **Emphasis on economic rights.**	* **Emphasis on preservation and maintenance of culture.**
* No special protection of sacred secret material or gender restrictions.	* Specific laws on gender and sacred secret material.

Source: Terri Janke, *Looking Out for Culture*, Workshop Materials (2003).

The introduction of moral rights law into Australia in 2000 has allowed the protection of the integrity of a copyright work, as well as the right of attribution. These rights, however, belong to individual creators. There are proposals to recognize Indigenous communal moral rights by amending the Copyright Act 1968 but there is a requirement that there be a voluntary agreement between the copyright owner and the Indigenous community before these rights arise. This will therefore have limited application.

In Australia, Indigenous people are making use of three main legal tools:

(a) use of contracts to ensure that the ownership of the copyright vests with Indigenous people, or that some rights relating to traditional cultural expression protection are provided for;
(b) conditions of access to archives – putting requirements that users of content must get the consent of traditional cultural expression owners;
(c) protocols for respecting Indigenous people's rights to culture. A range of protocols has been developed in visual arts, song, music, writing, new media and film.

Despite the widespread use of the above measures, Indigenous people still call for the Australian law to recognize their rights to traditional cultural expressions, in the same way that recognition is given to the rights of copyright owners, by requiring that their prior informed consent be obtained before use.

The WIPO's *Revised Draft Provisions on Traditional Cultural Expressions/ Folklore and Traditional Knowledge* developed by the WIPO Intergovernmental Committee on Intellectual Property and Genetic Resources, Traditional Knowledge and Folklore illustrate some perspectives and approaches for dealing with traditional cultural expressions. Its objects include preventing the misappropriation of traditional cultural expressions/expressions of folklore, and supporting customary practices and community cooperation.[111] Wend B. Wendland notes that "[i]n line with the views of many indigenous and traditional communities, the draft provisions do not require the assertion of new exclusive property rights over ... [traditional cultural expressions], but accommodate this option should communities wish to take it up."[112]

The *Pacific Regional Framework for the Protection of Traditional Knowledge and Expressions of Culture* proposes a framework for "traditional cultural rights" for owners of traditional knowledge and cultural expressions.[113] The prior and informed consent of the traditional owners is required to reproduce, publish,

---

111 WIPO, Intellectual Property and Genetic Resources, Traditional Knowledge and Traditional Cultural Expressions/Folklore: Information Resources, at 3, WIPO/ GRTKF/INF/1 (2006).

112 W.B. Wendland, *Safeguarding Intangible Heritage and Protecting Creativity: Practical Mechanisms for Complementarity* (13–16 December 2005) (paper presented at the Sub-Regional Experts Meeting in Asia on *Intangible Cultural Heritage: Safeguarding and Inventory-Making Methodologies*, Bangkok, Thailand), *available at* www.accu.or.jp/ich/en/pdf/ c2005subreg_WIPO.pdf (last visited 31 July 2008).

113 South Pacific Community, *Model Law for the Protection of Traditional Knowledge and Expressions of Culture*, sec. 6, July 2002 (*drafted by* K. Puri and C. Peturu), *available at* www. wipo.int/tk/en/laws/pdf/spc_framework.pdf (last visited 31 July 2008).

perform, display, make available on line and electronically transmit traditional knowledge or expressions of culture.

Using this model as a guide, Palau has drafted a *Bill for the Protection and Promotion of Traditional Knowledge and Expressions of Culture*.[114] The Bill aims to establish a new form of intellectual property identified as "traditional knowledge and expressions of culture" and to vest ownership of this new property in the appropriate traditional groups, clans, and communities. "Ownership" is defined as "the manner of collective property control recognized in traditional law and does not create or imply non-traditional property interests for individual members of the owner."[115] The Palauan proposed law requires prior and informed consent for all non-customary uses of traditional knowledge and expressions of culture.

Whilst these models are being explored by our neighbours in the Pacific, it is unlikely that we will see such laws in Australia for some time.

114 Reprinted *in* Asia/Pacific Cultural Centre for UNESCO (ACCU), *2004 Workshop on Inventory-Making for Intangible Cultural Heritage Management: Final Report*, at 143 (2005), *available at* www.accu.or.jp/ich/en/pdf/2004_Tokyo.pdf (last visited 31 July 2008).

115 "Owner" is defined as, depending on the context: (i) the Republic of Palau; (ii) the Palauan group, clan, or community determined by Palauan tradition and provisions of this Act to be the unique source or sole custodian of a particular item of traditional knowledge or expression of culture; and (iii) the individual officially recognized as the representative of the Palauan group, clan or community for the purposes of taking actions under this Act.

WHO IS THE "HOLDER" OF INTANGIBLE CULTURAL HERITAGE?

Revisiting the Concept of Community from an Intangible Cultural Heritage Perspective

Shubha CHAUDHURI*

Issues of intellectual property rights are at the centre of the concerns that face those working in the area of safeguarding intangible cultural heritage as indeed in many other areas. There is an increased awareness of these issues in all sectors today. The increase of broadcasting channels, digital technology and the Internet have all contributed to this situation, leading to many questions and not many answers.

I am discussing these issues not only as one who works in this area but as one providing a perspective from India, from the standpoint of an archivist who is involved in the documentation, preservation and dissemination of forms of intangible cultural heritage including music and oral traditions, rituals and other forms of performance.

Archives have an important role and the viewpoint of archivists provides a bridge between performers, practitioners and users of these materials – actual or potential.[1] They are therefore in a position to influence the attitude of both sides in which they interact. By being part of an institutional structure, they are an

* Archives and Research Centre for Ethnomusicology, American Institute of Indian Studies.

1 By this we mean that the use of archival material is what we can describe, but we have to be prepared for all kinds of uses in the future as technology and communication change.

appropriate agency to formulate policies, create guidelines and serve as intermediaries. Archives also for the most part do not have any financial benefit and thus can be seen as impartial parties.

Within the vast area that is referred to as "intangible cultural heritage" there is a major division between the intangible and ephemeral element of the intangible cultural heritage and the tangible outcome. For example, a song that is sung or a ritual that is performed exists only in the moment and remains only a memory for those who have participated in or observed it. The tangible outcomes of these are recordings, or documentation – electronic or otherwise. In the case of crafts, the tangible crafts are based on intangible elements, such as motifs and designs, or forms of traditional knowledge. Intangible cultural heritage thus includes the products and performance of oral and performative traditions, in the case of songs and rituals, for example, and process in the area of crafts and other traditional arts. Though there is a lot in common, there is a need to emphasize that there are also a lot of differences in how these play out. Copying a motif of a ritual drawing on to a mill printed textile or a bath towel has implications that are different from using a melody of one genre by practitioners of another genre. These are based on how the communities function and how they interact, and how they have done so through the generations.

1. THE INDIAN SCENARIO

Those of us who have been working with what has been called "expressions of folklore" in the last few decades faced a situation where we were working without the aid of any legal instruments. Few if any institutions had a system of contracts and agreements and this void caused confusion and lack of clarity among both practitioners and administrators. It is only the commercial recording and broadcasting industries which were restricted to the national All India Radio which employed a system of royalties and contracts. Collection agencies, a common element in Western countries, are not existent in any tangible fashion, or not really known to those who work in the field. Against this backdrop, the introduction in 1997 of two elements of intellectual property law – the performer's rights and fair dealing property – has been very significant.

Performer's rights protect the performer by the very act of recording, and this protection extends to the recordings made of the recording. This makes no claim to the ownership of the content or composition when we talk of traditional expressions, but the performer has individual rights that flow from the act of performing.

We have all regretted that we have no legal instrument to deal with community ownership and rights. And yet as we examine the existing models and examples of communities working with intellectual property issues, there seems to be only a longer list of unresolved issues. So today we are able to use performer's rights to protect the performance itself and recordings that may result from it. Where the community comes in is at the level of composition or performance style which is traditionally held. We have no way of dealing with traditional compositions which are part of the oral traditions.

Expressions of folklore in India cover not only the myriad regional traditions but the highly evolved classical traditions of Hindustani and Karnatak music as well as dance traditions which have today moved out of the concept of community. Traditions such as *Bharat Natyam*, *Kuchipudi* and *Odissi* dances did belong to particularly well defined communities but are today part of the urban stage and are not linked any more to the concept of community. There is thus in the history and evolution of Indian dance in post-independent India, an existing model towards which we can see many regional genres moving.

2. DEFINITION OF COMMUNITY: WHO IS THE OUTSIDER?

At this point we need to review what the definitions of "community", "group" and "individual" are. The Report from the *Expert Meeting on Community Involvement in Safeguarding Intangible Cultural Heritage* provides the following definitions:

> *Communities* are networks of people whose sense of identity or connectedness emerges from a shared historical relationship that is rooted in the practice and transmission of, or engagement with, their ICH;
> *Groups* comprise people within or across communities who share characteristics such as skills, experience and special knowledge, and thus perform specific roles in the present and future practice, re-creation and/or transmission of their intangible cultural heritage as, for example, cultural custodians, practitioners or apprentices.
> *Individuals* are those within or across communities who have distinct skills, knowledge, experience or other characteristics, and thus perform specific roles in the present and future practice, re-creation and/or transmission of their intangible cultural heritage as, for example, cultural custodians, practitioners and, where appropriate, apprentices.[2]

The definition of community has been kept flexible as it must and thus the large and overlapping categories of what can be considered "community" in terms of

2 UNESCO/ACCU, *Expert Meeting on Community Involvement in Safeguarding Intangible Cultural Heritage: Towards the Implementation of the 2003 Convention*, at 9 (13–15 March 2006), *available at* http://unesdoc.unesco.org/images/0014/001459/145919e.pdf (last visited 31 July 2008).

ownership or stake holders of intangible cultural heritage in India can at the very least be summed up as follows:

in terms of social organization:
- caste and subcastes;
- tribe;

in terms of cultural entities:
- region, linguistic and cultural area;
- religion, sect and cult;
- *gharana*, *Akhara* and other forms of stylistic affiliation as applies to performance traditions;

political boundaries or geographic zones:
- village, state or nation.

Each of the above is a community in some sense, and there are examples of genres of performance, craft or costume that belong to each. Each community in a village would have its life cycle rituals and songs, devotional music, and rituals and songs associated with festivals. There are festivals which are national in scope, those that are on the regional level, and finally those that are much more local in nature. The rituals and songs associated with even those that are national or belong to large regions are celebrated in a highly localized manner. Similarly, we have rituals and devotional music for the gods and goddesses of mainstream religions, as well as for the scores of local deities which lie outside the organized religious structures. In most areas we have forms of ritual theatre, ritual dance and other performances, ritual story telling and the performance of oral epics for ritual purposes. Ritual contexts are further part of religious or secular practices.

To make this more complex, there are myriad traditions of music, theatre, storytelling and other folklore such as mimicry, and the telling of jokes and riddles that exist in the sphere of entertainment. Thus in the case of intangible cultural heritage, one village in India has enough material for a lifetime of research and documentation, as these traditions change and are moulded by each successive generation, as social and cultural practices change with globalization, *i.e.*, the accelerating of these process by media and communication.

Further in each community and group, there are nested relationships of traditional trade and exchange, patron-client relationships, and borrowing that come from contact due to migration and acculturation. It thus becomes very challenging if not impossible to attribute cultural ownership across the board to most if not all expressions of intangible cultural heritage.

With increasing acceptance of the notion of diasporic communities in India and outside, it becomes difficult to attribute ownership even on national lines. Today the borders are dissolving in each of these categories as the context of performance or of making ritual objects changes. This is part of social change that we cannot control.

3. "INAPPROPRIATE" USE OR CHANGE OF CONTEXT

Today in India as in other countries, the status of traditional forms has changed from their original contexts. With the increasing availability of media and television in rural areas, people no longer rely on story telling or local theatre for their entertainment. Many of these genres were performed night-long and went on for as long as a week. Though the forms continue to exist in most places, they are now turned into "capsules" – shortened for public consumption. On the other hand, while many social rituals are being performed less in the original context, the performances that were associated with them are getting converted to staged performances. The state governments and tourism agencies, in the search for portraying "local culture", support this trend which results in the creation of groups that can be commissioned to perform. State governments followed by other agencies have also started holding competitions for traditional forms in an attempt to promote them. This has of course brought in many changes, as an informal group becomes formalized, costumes and instruments get added for enhancement, and then increasingly the practitioners are not restricted to the community with which they were initially associated. Though it is not uniform and it would be wrong to generalize, there is a dilution between the community and the arts with which they were associated.

In the more tangible realm of crafts the situation is as much in a state of flux as the practitioners themselves, perhaps aided by designers and non-governmental organizations, using ritual wall decoration patterns and adapting them to fabric prints, paper panels and contemporary furnishing: The case of Warli and Madhubani painting is an example of this. These traditional wall decorations, two of many such traditions in India, are examples where the painting has moved on to paper panels, greeting cards, textiles – hand painted and printed by mills, transposed on ceramic tiles and so on. These are not the only examples of this kind of change but are significant as they are traditions that were more regionally and culturally demarcated than most.

In this case, it is the practitioners inside the community who have been part of this movement, aided by well meaning efforts of those who wanted to give greater visibility to the beauty of these traditions and perhaps saw this as a way of financially sustaining these traditions. Clearly then, these communities, on the whole, do not see this as abusing the ritual motifs. With such a mass proliferation of these products, there is nothing to protect other communities from copying these motifs, and thus it does happen. Craftspeople at an exhibition or fair need little time in contact before borrowing begins and the crafts become assimilated based on the perception of what will sell better.

These factors have not only diluted clear lines of community but have also resulted in artistic dilution, as forms and skills developed over generations also develop a community based aesthetic, different from that of the individual artist.

We cannot ignore the fact that these communities have used their own ritual arts to create products which have now gained commercial value. We also see that women who were decorating the walls of their homes for rituals or to merely beautify them, or identify the caste or community, are income-earning members of the community and are being recognized as *craftspeople* rather than housewives. The significance of the fact that "Warli" and "Madhubani" are terms that are known to the general public today cannot be overlooked. Their coming into vogue may have caused others from copying their motifs but it has also served to highlight them. This popularity creates a space for the traditional practitioners to promote themselves as genuine for the discerning buyer.

4. PROTECTING WHAT DEMANDS PROTECTION

This then brings us to the issue of protection of rights or a community against commercial exploitation or cultural misuse. For example, if a ritual is sacred in a specific community and sharing it outside is not allowed by the community, this certainly needs protection. There are instances where some forms are restricted within a village, subcaste or by gender. However this is not the case for many parts of India, nor is it the case for most communities. There are numerous genres of performance that are identified by community such as by caste or within a region, but there is also a great amount of borrowing even traditionally.

Can we then say that there is no sense of community identity? That is again not really the case. For example, when musician castes discuss repertoire, they are aware that the "style" of their community is different from another which they see as their specialty and as their identity. I have had interviews with the *Rao* and *Manganiar* musician castes in Rajasthan on this topic at length in an attempt to elicit caste repertoire or arrive at a sense of musical ownership.

Traditionally, even in Hindustani classical music, transmission was oral and occurred within what is called the *guru-shisya parampara*, where a disciple (*shisya*) is tied in a close relationship with a teacher (*guru*) and hence the term "*gharana*" – a musical lineage; there was thus a great deal of secrecy about the teaching, and much that would not be shared until the *guru* or teacher was sure about the loyalty of the disciple. However this situation is much more diluted today as musicians train with more than one *guru* and often move from one *gharana* to another. This is also due to the greater number of musicians from middle class families entering the field – a field which was earlier largely restricted to hereditary musicians. It must, however, be stated that there is an established code of acknowledgment of compositions in this tradition, where a musician acknowledges a *bandish* (composition) learned from the teacher or another musician.

The case of Australia[3] is often mentioned in this regard, where we know that ownership of songs was and is closely tied to the identity of the tribe or moiety, and thus sound recordings have been used for substantiating land claims. There are similar instances in the Amazonian tribes.[4] However we need to exercise caution to extend these ideas of protection in areas where it may not be appropriate. There is then a danger of applying models from other countries and cultures that may provide a negative effect by creating artificial boundaries, stifling creativity and placing legal tools in the wrong hands.

5. INDIVIDUAL AND COMMUNITY OWNERSHIP

In the vast area of knotty problems and unresolved issues, the issue of individual versus community ownership is perhaps the one that rears its head at regular intervals!

In my experience, when objections are made to the use of intangible cultural heritage (*e.g.* use in film or popular music), they are usually made by an individual, as the compositions are seen as individual, either by the individual in question, their family or community. Interestingly, there seem to be few if any objections on behalf of communities.

It is necessary to recognize for each tradition what is considered within the right of an individual and what is considered community property. Creating an "artist" of an individual from within a group has the same problems.

Similarly in the case of professional and non-professional genres, there are songs sung by everybody such as wedding songs, or those related to domestic ritual and those sung by professionals. Some genres are restricted to a caste and some are not.

3 *See* Chapter [JANKE] of the present volume. *See also* T. JANKE, *Our Culture: Our Future: Report on Australian Indigenous Cultural and Intellectual Property Rights*, 1998, 59, *available at* www.frankellawyers.com.au/media/report/culture.pdf (last visited 31 July 2008).

4 *See, e.g.*, A. SEEGER, "Ethnomusicology and Music Law", 36 *Ethnomusicol.* 345 (1992).

As a researcher in West Rajasthan, I have been working with a few musician castes intensively and yet I am not able to pin down what the community repertoire is. To some extent, there are some melodies or songs that seem to be part of one community or there are some that they consider more theirs than others, but in the few communities that I worked with – *Manganiars*, *Langas*, and *Hurkals* or *Raos* – the communities seem to share a fair amount of their repertoire. However what is distinct is the melodic structure and the style of singing. This is something of which they are aware.

I would like to share two experiences in this regard. One is the case that attracted some attention – that of Gazi Khan – a highly accomplished singer of the musician caste *Manganiar* of Rajasthan. He became famous for a major hit in Rajasthani "folk music" for a song called *Nimbuda*. All the musicians of the *Manganiar* community we have interviewed agree it is Gazi Khan's composition and not a traditional composition. It has been widely sung and Gazi Khan was very proud of its success. He told me how every child in each village of Rajasthan was singing it! The problem came up when the song was turned into a film song in the Hindi film *Hum dil de chuke sanam*. The song was automatically copyrighted by the "composer" of the film song, and today Gazi Khan would have to pay royalty to sing his own composition, if we were to follow the law.

However since Gazi Khan has recorded this song commercially long before the film got released, a claim by the film song "composer" would not stand.

The film song seeks to evoke "Rajasthan" in a vague sense by the presence of turbaned musicians, a dance which is based on the dancing of Kalbeliya women and uses the main motif of the *Nimbuda* song though it has additional text and melody as well.

This is not the first time, by any means, that a folk song has found its way into the Hindi film world to become a hit. This case has been viewed differently within the *Manganiar* community as it was an individual composition and not traditional. Also since Gazi Khan is a *Manganiar*, the *Manganiar* community feel a sense of ownership towards it. We need to recognize however that there is no way for a casual visitor or "outsider" to know that the song is not an old traditional one but an individual composition. Perhaps many who sing it in Rajasthan also do not know the original. Arguably, a composer who wants to use a folk tune cannot afford to be a casual outsider. When questioned on this at a workshop, Gazi Khan said that this song was like a daughter who is now married and has her own life. Her parental home remains her home but she has to make her own life and destiny. It is also worthy of noting that the controversy and publicity has helped Gazi Khan to be publicly acknowledged as the composer, which may otherwise not have happened, and the publicity also has helped him as he acknowledges.

A more recent example is one I faced during a field trip to Goa. As I was recording a group of young musicians who were singing what is accepted as the more Christian repertoire, they described the *Dekhni*, a song and dance form that is today an accepted stage genre in Goa. This song which is in Konkani was adapted in a Hindi film *Bobby* – with the lyrics loosely translated into Hindi and retaining just a line of the refrain in Konkani. I asked the assembled group of perhaps 20 young musicians how they felt about it. From the silence that faced me I realized that this was the first time they had faced the question. I then had to elaborate that I wanted to know if they had resented the song being adapted into a film song: did they feel good about it? Did they feel it had been mutilated? Or, had it portrayed Goan culture in a way that was not acceptable? After some discussion they said they were happy – they felt that it had put something of Goa on a national screen – it made people happy listening to it – so what could possibly be wrong? One member of the group however said that he would have been happier had they sung it more accurately. The consensus was summed up by the group leader who said: "That is a film song, it was a hit of yester years and *Dekhni* continues to be *Dekhni* in Goa and we go on singing it and the film song has nothing to do with us".

I am aware that this cannot be called a representational opinion, but by and large we find that the long history of borrowing and drawing on traditions in India has created a situation where the use of community based forms by another community or in a film has gained some sort of acceptance. Film composers like Sachin Dev Burman or Bhupen Hazarika have used traditional songs in their compositions and are greatly respected. It is perhaps different as they themselves belonged to the region from which the music originates.

Acknowledgment or attribution is what is required by most people. On the other hand, it is certain that if a recording was used without payment or acknowledgment, the performers would have not found it acceptable.

The all pervasive nature of film music in India also means that the borrowing is not only one way, *i.e.*, unidirectional. We also have examples in urban situations where religious songs are sung to film tunes, and where brass bands play in weddings and ceremonies using a repertoire that is almost totally made up of film tunes. Thus borrowing in performance and practice seems less of an issue within most communities. As in most cases, it is where a claim of ownership is made by another party or where there is income arising out of a published recording that there is likely to be a dispute or a feeling of injustice.

However the problem that arises in the area of individual versus community is that of an individual claiming personal rights over what is traditional and is seen as belonging to the community. With legal instruments entering the picture, this is a form of misuse that is a matter of grave concern.

We have increasing cases – even in classical music – of a musician copyrighting a traditional *bandish*. Though I do not know of cases where such a musician has demanded royalties on this basis, the attribution of composer in this case is problematic. Similarly, as in the case described earlier, a traditional melody may be taken by a composer and or music director in Hindi films and then the film version becomes the canonical version.[5] The folk melody is then viewed as borrowing from a film tune as of course film music is highly accessible. To add to the confusion, traditional music forms tend to also borrow film tunes. However the issue here is that an individual gets the composition rights for a borrowed traditional melody.

Another way that this happens is the process of publication. When a recording is made, a copyright notice for the music and lyrics is put in automatically with little or no regard for the fact that it is not the property of one who is performing it. This is further extended to popular singers of "folk songs" who do not belong to the community but have "collected" the song. For the most part this has not caused great problems, because it is ignored and there is little litigation in this area.

It is often well meaning agencies that are responsible for creating an "artist" out of a practitioner of a traditional art or craft. For example, I heard of a craftsman who received an award for his work, and when he returned to his village, he was attacked, and made to share the prize money with the rest of the community, who of course engaged in the same craft. Similarly, publishing a recording or broadcasting confers special status on a practitioner although the practitioner may be no different from many in his or her community. This then, creates a tension between the individual and the community of which they are a part.

6. CONCLUSION

We see thus that there are various issues and problems in trying to deal with the concept of a community as owners of a tradition. It is possible at the level of a village where there is a head, or at times of a tribe or subcaste in a small area. Some communities are spread over a very large area – encompassing several states. How do we, in such cases, identify the representatives? This has been a significant problem in dealing with community rights.

If I release a recording of traditional music, I can make sure that the performers get a due share for their performance as the music itself and thus the rights of composition belong to the community. But how can this be done, when there are

5 The Hindi film music industry has had a long history of "borrowing" without too much modification not only melodies from Indian traditional genres, but Western classical music, rock and pop for many years.

several thousand performers or "composers" spread over four districts? The option of creating representational organizations is also fraught with problems. We may satisfy our consciences at a superficial level by doing so but it is not possible to do so fairly for the purpose for which it is intended.

According to the *Convention for the Safeguarding of the Intangible Cultural Heritage*[6] inventorying should follow these criteria:

- requiring proper identification of communities/groups and their representatives;
- ensuring that only ICH that is recognised by communities and groups is inventoried, or proposed for listing;
- ensuring that the permission of communities and groups is obtained for inventorying;
- ensuring the prior consent of communities when involving non community members;
- respecting customary practices governing the access to ICH;
- ensuring the free, prior and informed consent of communities and groups for nominating their ICH for the lists of the Convention.[7]

Given the issues and problems discussed, this seems to be an impossible task even though it is desirable. Inventories and lists can perhaps work within small areas. The approach is that which is borrowed from tangible cultural heritage, where the numbers of monuments do not change, and buildings do not change shape of their own volition! What then could be the solution to supporting traditional arts and protecting them against misuse and economic exploitation?

Though they seem to be the "soft" options, and not punitive in nature, there are some factors that can be considered:

Support documentation and archiving

Though concerns have been voiced about this freezing traditions, we do not see any evidence in all the countries where archives exist. An important factor then would be to make sure that communities and individual practitioners have access to archives, so that repertoire is preserved. Even if today a tradition is seen as endangered, future generations may want to revive it, or extend their repertoire, and archived material can assist in that. This may be seen as passive but as we cannot force social change, the least we can do is to preserve and document it.

---

6 Convention for the Safeguarding of the Intangible Cultural Heritage, 17 October 2003, U.N. Doc. MISC/2003/CLT/CH/14 (2003), *available at* http://unesdoc.unesco.org/images/0013/001325/132540e.pdf (last visited 31 July 2008).

7 UNESCO/ACCU, *supra* note 2, at 10.

Acknowledge and attribute

A policy of acknowledging not only borrowing but influences, attributing the source of shared materials, would go a long way in supporting and protecting intangible cultural heritage. Apart from providing the respect that is due, it creates a structure and documents the influences.

Moral rights are not negligible and though this may not be possible through an inventory, attribution would create value for the intangible cultural heritage.

Educate and not ban

Promoting intangible cultural heritage can be done through many avenues. As information is made available, and people are informed of the importance and value of these, it will create a discerning market that will appreciate the difference between genuine and knocked off articles.

Publication of materials – through books, recordings or the Internet – of "genuine" objects of intangible cultural heritage can work to create respect and appreciation.

By preventing others from using motifs or melodies, we are not able to sustain the many thousands of practitioners. The occasional successful legal case may help a few and may distract a few more. If the use of traditional material is made more and more difficult, it will not lead to its support, but will leave the way only for mass manufactured globalized products.

Guidelines not punishments

The compiling and publication of guidelines and manuals can go a great way to protect and promote the use of intangible cultural heritage. Those who use such materials can be sensitized to the issues of which they may not be aware. Those who run museums and archives or those who carry out documentation projects may not be aware of the many issues of rights of those they work with. Most people are not averse to doing the right and ethical thing, but they have often not thought about it and are not aware of the legal implications.

Ethical and moral rights are discussed and many organizations are working towards these, but these need to be interpreted and worked at on a local level by organizations such as non-governmental organizations for them to be more effective in practical terms.

Similarly, communities and individuals who are engaged in the performance and production of intangible cultural heritage should have access to manuals that make them aware of their rights and give them guidelines to protect their own rights.

It is also essential that communities and individuals are involved in the process of creating guidelines and contracts that protect not only their materials but also respect their feelings and beliefs.

There is no doubt that successful dissemination is what creates an audience, and patronage for the arts. If we restrict the dynamic nature of these traditions, we will not be punishing those who break the law alone, but those who would benefit by them.

ON THE SHOULDERS OF THE "OTHER'ED"

Intellectual Property Rights in Intangible Cultural Heritage and the Persistence of Indigenous Peoples' Texts and Inter-Texts in a Contextual World

Ikechi MGBEOJI*

This Chapter explores the problematic issue of the ownership and control of intangible cultural heritage. The context for this analysis is the emerging revival of Indigenous peoples'[1] cultures and practices in contemporary

* LL.B. (Nig.), B.L. (Lagos), LL.M., J.S.D. (Dalhousie). Associate Professor, Osgoode Hall Law School of York University, Toronto. This Chapter is dedicated to my newborn son, Nnazimizu. May his shadows be larger than his father's.

1 The definition of Indigenous peoples is a matter of debate. However, this Chapter adopts the generally accepted definition of Dr. Martinez Cobo which describes Indigenous peoples as "those which, having a historical continuity with pre-invasion and pre-colonial societies that developed on their territories, consider themselves distinct from other sectors of the societies now prevailing in those territories, or parts of them"; *see* United Nations, Sub-Commission on Prevention of Discrimination and Protection of Minorities, *Study of the Problem of Discrimination Against Indigenous Populations*, Part III, at 50, par. 379, E/CN.4/Sub.2/1983/21/ Add.8 (1983) (*prepared by* J. MARTÍNEZ COBO), *available at* www.un.org/esa/socdev/unpfii/ documents/MCS_xxi_xxii_e.pdf (last visited 31 July 2008).

times.[2] Indigenous peoples' cultures and traditions were hitherto considered non-existent or, at best, savage.[3] More recently, the main challenge has been to reconcile dominant systems or narratives of intellectual property rights with non-Western concepts, practices and protocols governing the creation, dissemination, sharing and transmission of intangible cultural heritage. Therefore the emphasis of this Chapter is on the control and ownership of intangible cultural heritage *vis-à-vis* notions of individual authorship, especially in the context of copyright law. As a result of space constraints, the related issues of patents and trademarks need not detain us here.

In modern legal systems, copyright is generally described as a form of legal protection provided to the creators of original works of authorship. This umbrella of protection covers literary and artistic works, whether published or unpublished, insofar as such works are fixed in a tangible or material form. A copyright affirms the exclusive right of the author to reproduce, perform, distribute and display a work publicly. Central to this concept of rights is the idea of individual authorship, which is anchored in the Romantic individualism of eighteenth century Britain.[4] The regime of individual authorship was the philosophical offspring of European writers such as Immanuel Kant, William Wordsworth and John Keats. They contended that their works sprung spontaneously from their minds and, as such, were their individual creations. In the words of Martha Woodmansee, as authors constructed themselves into creators rather than producers, "[the] work was made peculiarly and distinctively the product – and property – of the writer."[5] According to this narrative, the author is the sole originator of the ideas expressed in a copyrighted work.

In this Chapter, I question the prevalent doctrine of authorship as a solitary effort, especially within the context of intangible cultural heritage. My argument proceeds from the proposition that creators and authors are essentially social beings, deriving their muse and inspiration from the milieu and context in which they live and interact with the environment. Of course, individual interventions and interpretations significantly shape the output, but authors and creators nonetheless remain interpreters.

---

2 *See, e.g.*, World Intellectual Property Organization (WIPO), *Intellectual Property Needs and Expectations of Traditional Knowledge Holders: WIPO Report on Fact-Finding Missions on Intellectual Property and Traditional Knowledge (1998–1999)*, at 28 (April 2001), *available at* www.wipo.int/tk/en/tk/ffm/report/final/index.html (30 October 2007) [hereinafter "*WIPO Report*"].

3 *See, e.g.*, Convention on Biological Diversity, 5 June 1992, 31 I.L.M. 818, *available at* www.biodiv.org/convention/convention.shtml (last visited 31 July 2008) [hereinafter "CBD"].

4 *See* An Act for the Encouragement of Learning, by Vesting the Copies of Printed Books in the Authors or Purchasers of such Copies, during the Times therein mentioned (Statute of Anne), 1709, 8 Anne, c. 19 (Eng.). *See also* M. Woodmansee, "The Genius and the Copyright: Economic and Legal Conditions of the Emergence of the "Author"", 17 *Eighteenth Century Stud.* 425 (1984).

5 *Id.* at 427.

My analysis makes use of well-known intangible cultural expressions among the Igbos of South-Eastern Nigeria and is based upon methods favoured under the Third World Approaches to International Law (TWAIL).[6] This Chapter is divided into four Sections. Section 1 introduces the subject of intangible cultural heritage. Section 2 examines the binary concept of civilization and the influence of Western imperialism on global legal attitudes towards the intangible cultural expressions of Indigenous peoples. The phases of colonialism and cultural imperialism are explicated, not as epochs in human history but as radical structural re-configurations of the globe. Section 3 uses an exploration of ceremonies among the Igbo people in order to explain the inadequacies of attributing authorship among Indigenous peoples on the basis of Romantic individualism. Section 4 wraps up the analysis by highlighting the various legal persons capable of exercising ownership and control over intangible cultural heritage.

1. INTANGIBLE CULTURAL HERITAGE

It is generally recognized that, throughout the world, there are diverse cultural expressions, such as dance, music, craft techniques, rituals, traditional customs and ceremonies, which are emblematic of certain communities and have been recognized as such for countless generations. Such cultural expressions, often conveyed in immaterial forms, may be described as intangible cultural heritage. In 2003, the United Nations Educational, Scientific and Cultural Organization (UNESCO) adopted the *Convention for the Safeguarding of the Intangible Cultural Heritage* (ICH Convention).[7] According to Article 2(2) of the ICH Convention, intangible cultural heritage is manifested in the domains of

(a) oral traditions and expressions ... ;
(b) performing acts;
(c) social practices, rituals and festive events;

---

6 On the Third World Approaches to International Law (TWAIL), *see* M. WA MUTUA, "What is TWAIL?", 94 *ASIL Proc.* 31 (2000); K. MICKELSON, "Rhetoric and Rage: Third World Voices in International Legal Discourse", 16 *Wis. Int'l L.J.* 353 (1998); A. ANGHIE *et al.*, (eds.), *The Third World and International Order: Law, Politics and Globalization*, 2003; A. ANGHIE, "Francisco De Vitoria and the Colonial Origins of International Law", 5 *Soc. & Legal Stud.* 321 (1996); J. THUO GATHII, "International Law and Eurocentricity", 9 *Eur. J. Int'l L.* 184 (1998); J. THUO GATHII, "Alternative and Critical: The Contribution of Research and Scholarship on Developing Countries to International Legal Theory", 41 *Harv. Int'l L.J.* 263 (2000); O. CHINEDU OKAFOR, "Newness, Imperialism, and International Legal Reform in Our Time: A Twail Perspective", 43 *Osgoode Hall L.J.* 171, 174–80 (2003).

7 Convention for the Safeguarding of the Intangible Cultural Heritage, 17 October 2003, U.N. Doc. MISC/2003/CLT/CH/14 (2003), *available at* http://unesdoc.unesco.org/images/0013/001325/132540e.pdf (last visited 31 July 2008) [hereinafter "ICH Convention"]. The Convention entered into effect on 20 April 2006.

(d) knowledge practices concerning nature and the universe; [and]
(e) traditional craftsmanship.[8]

Article 2(1) defines intangible cultural heritage as

> [T]he practices, representations, expressions, knowledge, skills – as well as the instruments, objects, artefacts and cultural spaces associated therewith – that communities, groups and, in some cases, individuals recognize as part of their cultural heritage. This intangible cultural heritage, transmitted from generation to generation, is constantly recreated by communities and groups in response to their environment, their interaction with nature and their history, and provides them with a sense of identity and continuity, thus promoting respect for cultural diversity and human creativity. For the purposes of this Convention, consideration will be given solely to such intangible cultural heritage as is compatible with existing international human rights instruments, as well as with requirements of mutual respect among communities, groups, and individuals, and of sustainable development.[9]

Unlike artefacts, historical objects, archaeological ruins, and other tangible manifestations and embodiments of culture, intangible cultural heritage is peculiarly vulnerable to insidious but powerful changes in lifestyle and social values caused by globalization. Another crucial aspect of intangible cultural heritage is the central role that communities play in its creation, modification, sustenance and demise, even though there are cases where communal intangible cultural heritage is vested in the memory or practice of an individual. A community may be defined as groups of people with a "shared history, shared experience, shared practice, shared knowledge, [and] shared values".[10] Hence, in numerous communities, the intellectual rights in intangible cultural heritage often belonged to the community, not to individuals. The authorship of songs, oral traditions, music, dance, *etc.*, are construed as manifestations of shared values and a common worldview. However, the colonial encounter set the stage for a radical remaking of the cultural world, particularly because of the pre-eminence accorded by the Western powers to the role of individuals in the authorial process. This fundamental phenomenon is examined in some detail in Section 2.

---

8 *Id.*, Article 2(2).

9 *Id.*, Article 2(1).

10 D. Baird N'Diaye, *Community in the Context of UNESCO's Convention on Intangible Cultural Heritage*, at 3 (13–15 March 2006) (paper presented at the *UNESCO-ACCU Expert Meeting on Community Involvement in Safeguarding Intangible Cultural Heritage: Towards the Implementation of the Convention for the Safeguarding of the Intangible Cultural Heritage*, Tokyo, Japan), *available at* www.accu.or.jp/ich/en/pdf/c2006Expert_NDIAYE.pdf (last visited 31 July 2008).

2. INTANGIBLE CULTURAL HERITAGE AND THE COLONIAL EXPERIENCE

2.1. INTANGIBLE CULTURAL HERITAGE IN THE COLONIAL ENCOUNTER

Embedded in the mindset of imperialist colonizing cultures in the last two centuries was the fundamental notion that Western civilization was superior to other manifestations of human creativity, insights and civilization. As I have argued elsewhere[11], cultural chauvinism is not endemic to any given society. However, human history has never witnessed a more successful subordination and near extirpation of cultures and communities as the one carried out by Western imperialists.

The colonial narrative thrived on a division of peoples and cultures into opposed camps: the "civilized" versus the barbaric "other". According to this diametric logic, the non-European communities were largely depicted as anarchic and primitive. Hence, the prevalent notion that it was Europe's "duty" to bring light and civilization to the benighted multitudes.[12] The task of "civilizing" the "other" often involved brutal violence.[13] The infantilization of the global South was inscribed and codified in several international legal instruments dealing with intellectual property rights protection.[14] The global North[15], became the source of culture, laws and parameters for measuring enlightenment. Arguably, the most subtle but potent assault on the

---

11 *See* I. Mgbeoji, "The Civilised Self and the Barbaric Other: Imperial Delusions of Order and the Challenges of Human Security", 27 *Third World Q.* 855 (2006).

12 *See* M.F. Lindley, *The Acquisition and Government of Backward Territory in International Law: Being a Treatise on the Law and Practice Relating to Colonial Expansion*, (Negro Universities Press 1969) (1926).

13 For a useful approach to understanding the meaning of the expression "Third World" or the "global South", *see* B. Rajagopal, "Locating the Third World in Cultural Geography", 1998–99 *Third World Legal Stud.* 1; K. Mickelson, "Rhetoric and Rage: Third World Voices in International Legal Discourse", 16 *Wis. Int'l L.J.* 353, 360 (1998).

14 *See e.g.*, Treaty of Peace with Germany (Treaty of Versailles), 28 June 1919, arts I-XXVI, 2 Bevans 43 [hereinafter "League of Nations Covenant"]; Convention (No. 107) concerning the Protection and Integration of Indigenous and Other Tribal and Semi-Tribal Populations in Independent Countries, 26 June 1957, 328 U.N.T.S. 247, *available at* www.ilo.org/ilolex/cgi-lex/convde.pl?C107 (last visited 31 July 2008). *See also* M. Bedjaoui, "Poverty of the International Order", in R. Falk, F. Kratochwil and S.H. Mendlovitz (eds.), *International Law: A Contemporary Perspective*, 1985, 152; R. Coombe, "The Cultural Life of Things: Anthropological Approaches to Law and Society in Conditions of Globalization", 10 *Am. U. J. Int'l L. & Pol'y* 791 (1995); D. Slater, "Contesting Occidental Visions of the Global: The Geopolitics of Theory and North-South Relations", *Beyond Law*, December 1994, at 97.

15 For an excellent analysis of the nature of the economic and cultural divide between the North and South, *see* N.A. Adams, *Worlds Apart: The North-South Divide and the International System (1993);* G. Lundestad, *East, West, North and South: Major Developments in International Politics, 1945–1986* (G.A. Kvam (trans.)), 1988.

colonized was the deterioration of their intangible cultural heritage brought about by the forces of empire.[16] The result has been a physical and cultural conquest of "othered" societies by Europe since the eighteenth century.

2.2. EUROCENTRIC NOTIONS OF AUTHORSHIP AND COLONIAL INTERTEXTUALITY

In his review of Martha Woodmansee and Peter Jaszi's influential text on the contested concept of authorship[17], Lionel Bently, acknowledged the immense influence of Michel Foucault's[18] penetrating critique of the myth of the individual author.[19] Foucault observed that the literary author was an invention of eighteenth century capitalism. Taking the argument a few notches further, Roland Barthes announced the death of the author.[20] In his view, "[a]ny text is a new tissue of past citations. Bits of code, formulae, rhythmic models, fragments of social languages, *etc.* pass into the text and are redistributed within it, for there is always language before and around the text."[21] Although there are voices of dissension[22] from the Foucault/Barthes thesis on authorship, contemporary scholarship strongly reinforces its credibility and legitimacy, particularly with regard to the social context and jurisprudence of Indigenous peoples. It is now beyond doubt that a characteristic feature of Indigenous peoples' intangible cultural heritage is the primacy of communal institutions and systems over individual preferences and identities.[23] Individual authors are more or less agents or custodians, as well as interpretive voices, of communal cultural heritage.[24] In a recent piece, Megan M. Carpenter highlighted the inadequacies and huge cultural gaps between the Eurocentric and Indigenous conception of authorship.[25]

---

16 *See* I. Seidl-Hohenveldern, *International Economic Law*, 1989, 4; W.E. Langley, "The Third World: Towards A Definition", 2 *B.C. Third World L.J.* 1 (1981).

17 *See* M. Woodmansee and P.R Jaszi (eds.), *The Construction of Authorship: Textual Appropriation in Law and Literature*, 1994.

18 *See* M. Foucault, "What is an Author?", in V. Lambropoulos and D.N. Miller (eds.), *Twentieth Century Literary Theory: An Introductory Anthology*, 1987.

19 *See* L. Bently, "Copyright and the Death of the Author in Literature and Law", 57 *Mod. L. Rev.* 973 (1994).

20 *See* R. Barthes, *Image, Music, Text* 142–48 (S. Heath (ed. and trans.), Fontana Press 1977).

21 R. Barthes, *Theory of the Text, in Untying the Text: A Post-Structuralist Reader* 31, 39 (R. Young (ed.), 1981).

22 For traditional defence of authorship, *see* E.D. Hirsch, Jr., *Validity in Interpretation*, 1967, 1.

23 *See* Milpurrurru & Ors v. Indofurn Pty Ltd. & Ors, 30 I.P.R. 209 (1995).

24 *See* T. Janke, *Minding Culture: Case Studies on Intellectual Property and Traditional Cultural Expressions*, 2003, 9–27, *available at* www.wipo.int/tk/en/studies/cultural/minding-culture/studies/finalstudy.pdf (last visited 31 July 2008) (*prepared for* WIPO).

25 *See* M.M. Carpenter, "Intellectual Property Law and Indigenous Peoples: Adapting Copyright Law to the Needs of a Global Community", 7 *Yale Hum. Rts & Dev.* L.J. 51 (2004).

Notwithstanding the historicity and existence of Indigenous peoples' protocols governing the creation, use, and transmission of diverse forms of intangible cultural heritage, the cultural assault by imperialist forces on the "developing countries", or "Third World", has not attracted as much scholarly attention and moral outrage as the physical dispossession and depredations of colonialism. As noted above, the colonial repression of Indigenous peoples' laws, customs and practices was a phenomenal success[26], more enduring than the holocausts of post-Columbian America.[27]

In full bloom, European colonialism was at heart an economic and cultural project. At the cultural level, the "savage" had to acquire or internalize Eurocentric norms, values, institutions and ways of life in order to be regarded as "civilized". As Makau wa Mutua notes, within this colonialist logic, "history is a linear, unidirectional progression with the *superior* and *scientific* Western civilization leading and paving the way for others to follow."[28] The cultural refurbishment of colonized peoples led to the emergence of Western-style intellectual property rights regimes in most parts of the colonized world. Western norms and ideas on authorship, creativity, epistemology and culture were alone in being considered as rational, empirical and universal ideals, attainable by all regardless of differences in culture.[29] In contrast, Indigenous knowledge systems and juridical protocols were dismissed as barbarous rituals lacking a normative and legal character.

Although the colonialists asserted that there were frameworks available for articulating and protecting intellectual property among the colonized peoples of the global South[30], the fact is that Indigenous knowledge systems and cultural expressions cover a wide range of lifestyles, cultural experiences, epistemologies and empiricisms. Intangible cultural heritage and Indigenous knowledge systems involve such domains as ecology, agronomy, agriculture, medicine, animal husbandry, music, story-telling and cloth-weaving, across several thousands of different cultures and peoples.

Prior to the colonial encounter, there were thousands of different protocols, norms and practices regulating the acquisition, use, transfer and alienation of intangible cultural heritage and Indigenous knowledge among Indigenous healers, poets, griots, story-tellers, dancers, artistes, *etc.* A characteristic feature

---

26 *See* Editors Report, *Cerebrating on Columbus and His Legacy: Protest Obscures the Large Point: Repeating Pattern of European Conquest*, Indian Country Today, 17 October 2005, *available at* www.msnbc.msn.com/id/9664359/(last visited 31 July 2008).

27 *See* G.F. Margadant, "Official Mexican Attitudes Toward the Indians: An Historical Essay", 54 *Tul. L. Rev.* 967 (1980). *See also*, E. Williamson, *The Penguin History of Latin America*, 1992.

28 M. wa Mutua, "Savages, Victims, and Saviours: The Metaphor of Human Rights", 42 *Harv. Int'l L.J.* 201, 201 n.2 (2001) (emphasis added).

29 *See* V. Shiva, *Staying Alive: Women, Ecology And Development*, 1989.

30 *See* F. Cohen, "The Spanish Origin of Indian Rights in the Law of the United States", 31 *Geo. L.J.* 1, 12 (1942).

of creativity among Indigenous cultures is the influence of their cosmological worldview on their cultural expressions. The rules, protocols and norms regulating the acquisition, use, transfer, sharing and transmission of diverse intangible cultural heritage were often unwritten, yet they possessed binding effect and authority over those concerned.

The fact that the modern nomenclatures of Western jurisprudence were absent in pre-colonial Indigenous communities often leads to the unfounded notion that such regimes, if they are acknowledged at all, were primitive, inchoate and lacking in their ability to obtain obedience from their members. A more tenable and truthful position is that, even without adopting Western nomenclatures on intellectual property rights, such Indigenous regimes often embodied the concepts of social justice, legitimacy of the law, public participation in governance, integrity of the human person and protection of communal values.[31] More importantly, such Indigenous legal regimes were autochthonous, deriving their legitimacy from the daily lives and worldview of the communities concerned.

2.3. CEREMONIES AND INTANGIBLE CULTURAL HERITAGE

Indigenous norms on the regulation of intangible and tangible cultural heritage were often reiterated, modified and transmitted in the course of diverse ceremonies. These traditional ceremonies are the vehicle through which intangible cultural expressions are enjoyed, created, modified, and transmitted. To the ignorant observer, however, they exist merely for the indulgence of primitive appetites for excitement. Nothing could be further from the truth. Indeed, beyond merry-making, ceremonies among Indigenous communities are norm-bearing activities which reinforce intangible cultural heritage and afford an opportunity for its creation, enjoyment, modification and transmission.

It must be recognized that a large number of intangible cultural heritage encompasses various commemorative and iterative ceremonies and prescriptions including taboos, customs and art. In short, the house of intangible cultural heritage is an abode with many mansions. None of the individual aspects of these diverse forms of expressions fully narrates the entire grandeur, depth and diversity of Indigenous peoples' worldview. Intangible cultural heritage is often exemplified in various rites and ceremonies interwoven with institutions of governance that defy rigid compartmentalization.

---

31 *See* J. Donelly, *Universal Human Rights in Theory and Practice* 49–65 (1989). For a critique of this school of thought, *see* O.M. Ejidike, "Human Rights in the Cultural Traditions and Social Practice of the Igbo of South-Eastern Nigeria", 43 *J. Afr. L.* 71 (1999).

Consequently, an inquiry into the ownership of intangible cultural heritage in Indigenous peoples' communities requires an understanding of their social order and ways of life.[32] Intangible cultural heritage is thus part of the expressed worldview and value-system of communities, as generated and reinvigorated through diverse modes of expressions and festivities. As forums for conveying the thoughts, concerns, values, fears and triumphs of local communities, these transactions or expressions of intangible cultural heritage are social creations. They are often geared towards social control, the facilitation of social interaction and the transmission of beliefs and values in fairly predictable modes.[33] For this reason, most critics of the application of Western intellectual property rights to Indigenous peoples' intangible cultural heritage argue that these rights, with their emphasis on the property rights of the Romantic solitary author or artist, are incompatible with the values and culture of traditional and Indigenous peoples.

Expressions of intangible cultural heritage often embody rules, which shape and direct inter-personal conduct and the group's reciprocal relationship with the rest of humanity and the spirit world in a dynamic regime. The norms and values embedded and narrated through ceremonies are thus aimed at preserving individual and group dignity and maintaining a state of equilibrium in the midst of changing circumstances. In this context, individual agency may add impetus to, or help shape, the accommodation of change.

The worldview of many Indigenous communities of the global South is predominantly holistic rather than analytic. These cultures "tend to see the total picture, not parts of it."[34] The central thrust of such a holistic conception of the world is that manifestations of intangible cultural heritage are often inspired by the concept of maintaining a dynamic duality and balance between opposites, as well as responding to the interactive roles of the entities and spiritual forces active in both the cosmic and temporal realms. The spirit world, an animate and inanimate place, is the abode of both the creator and the ancestral spirits. The temporal world is construed as a marketplace for both the dead and the living. It is in a constant state of birth, death and rebirth. In this dynamic equilibrium, the dead are expected to come back to life to join the community. Life is thus a cycle in which all created beings – animate and inanimate – are in a constant cycle and interact with each other.

Events that could upset the equilibrium include natural disasters, such as long droughts, famines, epidemics, sorcery and other antisocial forces, including

---

32 Open exchange of ideas among practitioners of intangible cultural heritage is often the norm; *see* S.B. Brush, "Is Common Heritage Outmoded?", in S.B. Brush and D. Stabinsky (eds.), *Valuing Local Knowledge: Indigenous People and Intellectual Property Rights*, 1996, 143, 149.

33 *See* M.J. Adler, "Legal Certainty", 31 *Colum. L. Rev.* 91 (1931).

34 A.O. Anya, *The Environment of Isolation or the Ecology and Sociology of Igbo Cultural and Political Development*, 1982 Ahiajoku Lecture, *available at* http://ahiajoku.igbonet.com/1982/ (last visited 31 July 2008).

litigation, homicide, violation of taboos, as well as other incidents deemed to be infractions of the natural balance of life forces.[35] Maintaining or restoring the social and cosmological equilibrium may take the form of several types of sacrifices, ceremonies, rituals, dances, and other means.

Another radical feature of most Indigenous communities of the global South, particularly in the context of the creation and sharing of intangible cultural heritage, is that most of these societies were in fact "closed" with regard to certain types or aspects of their intangible cultural heritage, despite an appearance of "openness". Not all forms of intangible cultural heritage are open and available to everyone for unregulated use, transfer or transmission. Consequently, only those members of society that participate in the inner workings and dynamics of its various aspects or parts can speak with authority on how they are configured, used or transmitted.[36] For example, unless one is a member of a particular art group or cult, one cannot speak authoritatively about its inner workings.

In effect, Indigenous communities, contrary to the extravagant claims by some colonial historians, were often secretive in the way and manner in which several manifestations of intangible cultural heritage were created, enjoyed and transmitted. On the one hand, there was the façade, which everyone could see. Beyond, however, were several layers of exclusion and social ordering. The only ones who could participate in and, more importantly, speak about these matters were those whose age, class, cult-membership, gender, *etc.*, qualified them to do so. As John Anenechukwu Umeh aptly observed with regard to the Igbos:

> [T]heirs' is essentially a participatory society. You can't know the inside facts about Mmanwu (masquerade) unless you are admitted to Mmanwu and participate in operating Mmanwu. You cannot say much about the various Ozo titled societies unless you are admitted to them and participate in their rituals and activities. You can't know the implications of various socialization rites, ceremonies, including rites of passage unless you participate in them.[37]

Ceremonies and festivities among Indigenous communities often function as communal signals indicating or iterating the occurrence of certain important events, which affect social bonds and involved complex inter-relationships. Such ceremonies are not merely artistic, purposeless, bacchanals or empty acts of primitive excitability or meaningless gestures by idle natives. Rather, they are complex norm-building and rule-modifying regimes.

Given that culture is dynamic, it follows that the relevance of these ceremonies is not necessarily limited to times past. They are living historical processes that

---

35 *See* V.C. Uchendu, *The Igbo of Southeast Nigeria*, 1965, 11.

36 *See* A.A. Dike, *The Resilience of Igbo Culture: A Case Study of Awka Town*, 1985, 157.

37 J.A. Umeh, *Igbo People: Their Origin and Culture Area*, 1999, ii.

reinvent themselves. They derive their vitality and legitimacy from popular acceptance and participation.[38] A key feature of West African native custom is its flexibility and "unquestionable adaptability to altered circumstances without entirely losing its individual characteristics."[39] As fountains from which certain forms of intangible cultural heritage emanate or are iterated, such ceremonies, festivals, *etc.*, create new or validate existing obligations which members of society could not unilaterally deviate from without sanction.[40] At the hub of these traditions is a sense of common weal.

Traditional and communal activities, from which a diverse range of intangible cultural heritage are created or iterated, tend to focus on birth, marriage, coming of age, title-taking, environmental sanitization, cosmological balance, treaty-making, war, religious rites, games, professional engagements, dancing, burials and story-telling. This list of ceremonies and festivities is not an exhaustive inventory of the panoply of intangible cultural heritage practiced by the pre-colonial Igbo nation. The "closed" nature of intangible cultural heritage means that knowledge and diverse practices are not always in the public domain. The appearance of open access for members of local communities to intangible cultural heritage, such as dances, songs, stone/woodcarving and masquerades, has led to the unfounded notion that such intangible cultural heritage is always in the public domain and is available for the unrestricted use of all members of the community.

Such a notion is unfounded and gives rise to a misconception with regard to the character and functions of the diversity of intangible cultural heritage. While many local people may have common knowledge of intangible cultural heritage, there are circumstances and types of intangible cultural heritage whose use, creation, transfer and enjoyment is restricted on the basis of such factors as occasion, class, gender, age, season and initiation into a group. Indigenous communities are ancient and diverse and a chapter of this length can hardly do justice to the variety, richness and complexity of such communities and the resultant complexity of intangible cultural heritage. Certain forms of intangible cultural heritage are peculiar to specific cultures and areas. It also has to be emphasized that some intangible cultural heritage is no longer viable or alive and that those which survived European conquest and colonialism have witnessed significant adulteration and Westernization.[41]

---

38 *See* Eshugbayi Eleko v. Government of Nigeria, [1931] A.C. 662, 673 (Lord Atkin). Walter Ullmann has also demonstrated that the same quality of general acceptance pervaded medieval customary laws of Europe; *see* W. Ullmann, *Law and Politics in the Middle Ages: An Introduction to the Sources of Medieval Political Ideas*, 1975.

39 Lewis v. Bankole, 1 N.L.R. 81, 101 (1908).

40 *See* E. Isichei, *A History of the Igbo People*, 1976, 3.

41 *See* Barimah Balogun and Scottish Nigeria Mortgage and Trust Co. v. Saka Chief Oshodi, 10 N.L.R. 36 (1931); Ewa Inyang v. Ekeng Ita, 9 N.L.R. 84 (1929); Balogun v. Balogun, 9 W.A.C.A. 73 (1943).

The factors which influence the character of intangible cultural heritage are not constant but dynamic and evolving mechanisms. They often work in symbiotic relationships with a myriad of external and domestic stimuli.[42] Against such a background, old facts have often had to acquire new meanings and have ultimately impacted on the processes of expression in both their tangible and intangible forms.[43] In the modern age, the important lesson that this teaches us is that any rational study of the nature of intangible cultural heritage must *ex necessitate* be "an essay in descriptive sociology".[44] It must now be clear that intangible cultural heritage is living phenomena and not "a kind of museum piece offering an object of serious study only to anthropologists curious about the ways of tribal peoples."[45]

2.4. EXPRESSIONS AND OWNERSHIP OF INTANGIBLE CULTURAL HERITAGE AMONG THE IGBOS OF NIGERIA

The typology of intangible cultural heritage as depicted above is largely representative of the Igbos of Nigeria. Among the Igbos, certain ceremonies afford opportunities for the expression and revitalization of intangible cultural heritage. These include ceremonies on birth and death, child-naming and religious worship. External stimuli such as geography, ecological factors and weather-patterns have been known to influence and mediate the character and function of intangible cultural heritage. None of these factors, however, impede the overriding influence of group action, as well as communal cooperation and achievements.[46]

The nuclear and extended family is often of great importance to Indigenous communities. It is common for elders to tell tales to children in the evenings. This reinforces the bonds of family but, more importantly, it also drills into the minds of the young the normative values and worldview held by the community[47], as

42 *See* A.E. Afigbo, *The Age of Innocence: The Igbo and Their Neighbours in the Pre-Colonial Times*, 1981 Ahiajoku Lecture, *available at* http://ahiajoku.igbonet.com/1981/(last visited 31 July 2008); A.E. Afigbo, *The Igbo and Their Neighbours: Inter-Group Relations in Southeastern Nigeria*, 1987.

43 *See* M. Chanock, "Neo-Traditionalism and Customary Law in Malawi", 16 *Afr. Legal Stud.* 80, 83 (1978).

44 *See, e.g.*, H.L.A. Hart, *The Concept of Law*, 1961, vii; J.G. March, "Sociological Jurisprudence Revisited: A Review (More or Less) of Max Gluckman", 8 *Stan. L. Rev.* 499, 518 (1956).

45 L.L. Fuller, "Law as an Instrument of Social Control and Law as a Facilitation of Human Interaction", 1 *B.Y.U. L. Rev.* 89 (1975).

46 *See* J.E. Eberegbulam Njoku, *The Igbos of Nigeria: Ancient Rites, Changes, and Survival*, 1990, 1.

47 *See* E. Obiechina, *Nchetaka: The Story, Memory and Continuity of Igbo Culture*, 1994 Ahiajoku Lecture, *available at* www.kwenu.com/igbo/igbowebpages/Igbo.dir/Ahiajoku_Lectures/ahiajoku_Lec94.htm#lecture (last visited 31 July 2008).

well as instilling in them[48] the values of their society.[49] In some cases, intangible cultural heritage is meant to act as a means of social control. Such concepts are sometimes expressed in the signs and symbols of secret societies and masquerade groups. In these cases, the "art" embodied in the masks and songs have alternate meanings. Similarly, land has often inspired songs, masks, dances, folklore, mores and communal rights.

Thus, for many Indigenous peoples, ceremony is at the heart of culture.[50] Whether the ceremonies are simple or elaborate, there is often an element of the sublime and spiritual in them.[51] Intangible cultural heritage is a complex and sophisticated web of norms, practices and prescriptions of social and cosmic ordering. Intangible cultural heritage affords avenues for modifying the worldview and dramatizing the peoples' beliefs and value systems. Relevant members of society participate in forms of intangible cultural heritage such as ceremonies, songs and dances in varied ways. The communal input and interventions in the continued vitality and evolution of these forms of intangible cultural heritage strongly suggest that the notion of solitary authorship is inappropriate in this context.

3. CEREMONIES AND OWNERSHIP OF INTANGIBLE CULTURAL HERITAGE

Igbos place a high premium on children. The ceremonies surrounding childbirth follow traditional notions of clan continuity and solidarity with the ancestors. The birth of a child is usually announced to the father by the mother of the bride.[52] The celebration is largely an affair for the extended family as well as the village. Every man on having his first child plants a ritual tree in front of his house. This is the *Ogbu Chi* which represents the child's *Chi* (an agent of the Creator), a sort of guardian. The parents usually select the names of the newborn. Shortly afterwards, the child will be taken out of the closed room and introduced to the lineage group. Again, this is an event that is not limited to the immediate relatives but extends to all the clan and kindred. The naming of the child marks its formal admission into the family and lineage.

There are also various ceremonies surrounding the process of maturation into adulthood. The teething ceremony comes first. It is a taboo for a child to be born

48 *See* E. Isichei, *The Ibo People and the Europeans: The Genesis of a Relationship, to 1906*, 1973, 18.

49 *See* M.O. Chijioke, *Ugwumba: The Greatness of a People*, 1989 Ahiajoku Lecture.

50 *Id.*

51 *See* O. Equiano, *The Interesting Narrative of the Life of Olaudah Equiano, or Gustavus Vassa, the African*, 1794, 34.

52 *See* R. Nna Umeasiegbu, *The Way We Lived: Igbo Customs and Stories*, 1969, 1.

with any dentition. The first person to notice the child's teeth is obliged to give the latter a hen. The offspring from the hen are shared between the child and the benefactor. This establishes a relationship between them. Apart from these bonds, the teething ceremony, known as *Ifu Eze*, serves the purpose of notifying the larger family that the child may now eat certain types of adult food. This is not an otiose ceremony because in Igbo societies, children are generally given food by extended family members or even by members of the village. The teething ceremony therefore signals to the community which types of food they may give to the child.

Of all rites of passage among the Igbos, it is probable that the most dramatic is the Cloth Wearing ceremony, referred to as *Iwa Akwa*. It is designed to initiate Igbo males into adulthood. All children born in the same year invariably belong to the same age grade and undertake their rites of passage contemporaneously. The Cloth Wearing ceremonies involve elaborate rituals which place the entire community on notice that the young adult male has attained maturity and is now a sane, full-fledged, member of the society. After the *Iwa Akwa*, the young male is expected to move out and create his own household.

The initiation into adulthood may also take the form of another rite of passage known as *Itu Anya* (opening of the eyes). This is a moment of privation, challenges and entrance into manhood. The *Itu Anya* is often done by a native healer, the *dibia*.[53] The young adult male passes through many stages designed to equip him with power, knowledge and courage.

For Igbo women, the analogous ceremony marking passage into adulthood is the ceremony of the first menstruation, called the *Ihu Nso*. Prior to this, no serious talk of marriage can ever be entertained between the girl's family and any interested parties. The *Ihu Nso* ceremony usually involves a noticeable change in the dressing and hairstyle of the newly menstruating woman. The second arm of the rite of passage into adulthood is the ceremony of *Iru Mgbede* (fattening of a woman before marriage). Here, the woman is separated from her usual household or abode under the sponsorship of the proposed groom.[54]

No self-respecting Igbo family would publicly acknowledge that their daughter has been married without first performing traditional marriage rites. Generally speaking, no parent or groom may approach a girl's family for marriage talks without first securing the "tentative consent of the girl".[55] The next step is the *Mmanyi Ajuju* (wine for inquiries) whereby the groom, accompanied by at least two close friends, publicly declares his interest and initiates an open inquiry as to whether the girl would publicly accept him as a husband. It is at this stage that the

53 In Igbo culture, the *dibia* is in contact with the spirit world. With dignified but austere looks, he or she is in fact a walking library.

54 J.T. Agbasiere, *Women in Igbo Life and Thought*, 2000, 2.

55 *Id.* at 45.

families mutually probe their genealogy to determine whether the marriage is precluded by rules of consanguinity. Family reputation and the health history of the family are also important. Families with a record of insanity, epilepsy and genetic diseases are often avoided.

Marriage ceremonies in the Indigenous community are a public event. The wide publicity attendant on such ceremonies is the legal equivalent of a marriage certificate or a license issued by modern-day authorities. As Lon L. Fuller observed, "certainly, among a people who have no state-kept official records to show who is married to whom, the elaborate wedding ceremonies found in some customary system can be said to serve a purpose of communication and clarification."[56]

Among the Igbo, the payment of a price for the bride is a gesture of appreciation for the loss of a daughter. This gesture is made as part of the marriage contract. It is done before the bride's father, mother and relatives, as well as the family the bridegroom. This payment seals the transaction and is followed by the singing of lewd songs harping on the expectation that there will be children from the marital conjugation. For the groom's family, the ceremony celebrates the addition of a new daughter, wife and sister. Another significant character of the bride's price is that it cements the groom's right to any offspring from the marriage.

I referred previously to the influence of ecology on intangible cultural heritage. This is true for the Igbo, whose land is often infertile and a challenge to the skills of the farmers. It is therefore unsurprising that pre-colonial Igbos had elaborate ceremonies, songs and rituals surrounding the planting and harvesting of crops. Among Igbos, harvest time at a rural farm was always the most spectacular occasion for joy and festivities. The most important and prestigious crop in Igbo culture is the yam. Yam and palm oil have defined the political economy of the Igbo since time immemorial.[57]

Yam formed the economic basis of Igbo civilization.[58] The harvest of yam is preceded by and suffused with religious ceremonies. This is known as *Iri Ji Ohuu* (eating of yams) ceremonies. After the harvest, the farmer with a surplus may take the title of *Ezeji*. His male children are called *Osuji* and his daughters *Nmaji*. After this, he automatically receives the honorary title of *Ogaranya* in the community. Sometimes, yams can occupy the position of deities in Igbo culture. In Igbo jurisprudence, oaths could be taken with yams.[59]

Warfare and the negotiation of post-conflict disagreements were also governed by certain forms of intangible cultural heritage. Elaborate precautions and ceremonies were often adopted to minimize the impact of wars. Prior to the

---

56 FULLER, *supra* note 45.

57 AFIGBO, *supra* note 42. Botanists estimate that Igbo yams are the result of at least three millennia of cultivation and development involving the improvement of local varieties, increasing their yield and, in some cases, reducing their toxicity.

58 *See* ISICHEI, *supra* note 40.

59 *See* J.P. JORDAN, *Bishop Shanahan of Southern Nigeria*, 1971, 41.

commencement of any armed conflict, the parties would entrust the negotiations to sagacious intermediaries, especially elders and titled personages. These intermediaries were diplomats of great wisdom, whose powers of elocution and discretion were well-known and acclaimed. If these efforts failed, a formal declaration of war followed.

The declaration of war had to contain a notice of the nature of the weapons to be used. These were usually long sticks, hence the use of the term *Ogu Osisi* (war of sticks) to refer to these conflicts. The declaration also specified the days when the battles might be fought and other rules of engagement. In other words, not all wars were designed for bloodshed. Only in the *Ogu Egbe* (war with guns) or *Ogu Nma* (war of machetes) could blood be shed.[60]

In all wars, women and children were exempt. Markets, and those visiting them, were left in peace. Similarly, shrines and places of religious and cultural significance were exempt from war. Wars were never fought during religious festivals, such as the New Yam festival. Given the high rate of intermarriage between villages, the pursuit of warfare was a tricky, awkward business. Deliberate attempts were made to ensure that the casualty rates were low and also to ensure that the vanquished were only defeated, not humiliated. The ending of wars also made use of ceremonies and peace treaties. According to Elizabeth Isichei:

> [W]hen a community desired to make peace; it sent a delegation carrying palm fronds which symbolize peace. Typically, women played a key role as a pressure group for peace, because of their unique role as daughters and sisters in one community, and wives and mothers in another.[61]

Pre-colonial Igbo jurisprudence and culture was very familiar with the fundamental principle of *pacta sunt servanda*.[62] This was apparent in Igbo treaties and pacts sealed in blood and otherwise known as *Igbandu*. This was a traditional and religious ceremony in which associations were consummated by "mixing drops of participants' blood and eating kola nuts dipped therein. Once concluded, they regarded themselves as clansmen."[63]

These blood pacts, or *Igbandu*, were treaties in their own rights and no one was permitted to shirk obligations created by duly appointed representatives of the participating mini-states or clans.[64] It is equally instructive that most blood pacts or treaties were concluded in the "presence" of great oracles or at *Ihu Ala*, a

60 *See* Isichei, *supra* note 40, at 79.
61 *Id.*
62 *See* Vienna Convention on the Law of Treaties, Article 26, 23 May 1980, 1155 U.N.T.S. 331.
63 Ejidike, *supra* note 31, at 91.
64 *Id.* at 77.

sacred location known as "the face of the earth"[65] and which Igbos hold in great reverence.

Another significant form of intangible cultural heritage among the Igbos are the ceremonies, rituals and songs that often precede the felling and "burial" of giant trees. This custom is predicated upon the Igbo belief that natural things have agency. There is no hierarchy in the Igbo construction of life forms and inanimate things. Elaborate rituals analogous to the burial of humans or the establishment of a shrine often preceded the felling of big trees.[66] As Donatus Ibe Nwoga noted in his 1984 Ahiajoku lecture:

> [W]hen villagers want to cut down a big and aged tree, they take four sticks of *ogilisi* [a flower tree used to demarcate borders in Igbo land] and plant them in a small square, put the neck of a pot in-between and put some stones around the pot-neck and call upon the tree to move to that place and not be angry with them for removing him from its earlier habitation ...[67]

Finally, there are forms of intangible cultural heritage associated with death and burials. Those who are wealthy bury their departed with pomp and pageantry. Those who are poor bury theirs with as much festivity as they can eke out. It would seem that preparations for grandiose funerals often precede the actual death of those to be buried. For example, a sick man or woman of prominence immediately receives financial contributions from his or her peers towards the medical expenses. If the person dies, the *ikoro*, a gigantic wooden drum whose sound can travel about 15 kilometres, is beaten early in the morning according to a distinctive pattern. An interval of at least ten minutes elapses before the next sound of the *ikoro*. Its sound can be interpreted by members of the community. Indeed, listening to the *ikoro*, a member of the community can tell the name of the deceased, the funeral date and other information.[68] The variations of the music of the *ikoro* also tell people whether the deceased died rich and whether the latter raised successful children or not. The *Ese*, a type of music performed by professional musicians on the death of an elderly and important person, may also be played. Family members or relations of the deceased are not permitted to weep or cry in public unless and until the *ikoro* or *Ese* have formally announced the demise of their relative.

---

65 Virtually all Igbo communities have myths or sentimental tales about their settlement. The first settlers are almost always said to have founded *Ihu Ala* which thus became a sacred spot for the people. No agreement, decisions, or judgments made at the *Ihu Ala* could be lightly deviated from. *See* Uchendu, *supra* note 35, at 96.

66 *See* Ejidike, *supra* note 31, at 96.

67 D. Ibe Nwoga, *Nka na Nzere: The Focus of Igbo Worldview*, 1984 Ahiajoku Lecture, *available at* http://ahiajoku.igbonet.com/1984/(last visited 31 July 2008).

68 *See* Umeasiegbu, *supra* note 52, at 5.

4. WHO OWNS INTANGIBLE CULTURAL HERITAGE?

In view of the foregoing examples of some of the notable cultural practices and intangible cultural heritage among the Igbos, the question of who owns intangible cultural heritage can hardly be resolved in favour of the individual. The reality is that manifestations of intangible cultural heritage often embody complex accretions of communal values, beliefs, social ordering, *etc.*[69] These manifestations are generally inconsistent with absolute individual ownership. The complex social processes by which such forms of intangible cultural heritage are acquired, transmitted and modified have been posited as one of the grounds for denying them protection according to Eurocentric intellectual property rights.[70] There is merit in this argument.[71] The alleged boundary between individual and collective creativity mistakes communalism with the notion of collective inventions. Local artists may derive inspiration from pre-existing knowledge to create new interpretations of the old.[72]

The difficulty with fitting intangible cultural heritage into the straitjacket of Western-inspired intellectual property rights is that Indigenous peoples recognize certain institutions and legal persons that are considered invalid and irrelevant according to Eurocentric norms and legal rules. Under customary law and the jurisprudence of traditional communities and Indigenous peoples, legal personality is extended to individuals, families, compounds, villages, clans, stools, age grades, the spirits of the unborn, ancestral spirits and other forms and categories unknown to or unrecognized by the colonizing institutions and powers. These forms of legal personality have, over the millennia, proven themselves relevant and convenient for Indigenous communities across the world. Unfortunately, rather than being recognized, they have been construed as mere exotic curiosities or examples of savage superstition and primitivism.

In conclusion, the discourse on the ownership of intangible cultural heritage is one that must first recognize the limitations of imperialist legal narratives.[73] The significance of intangible cultural heritage is that it embeds, transmits and modifies the normative prescriptions and worldviews of Indigenous peoples. In

69 *See* A.N. Okoro, *Chukwu Ka Dibia*, 1988 Ahiajoku Lecture.

70 *See* R.L. Gana, "Has Creativity Died in the Third World? Some Implications of the Internationalization of Intellectual Property", 24 *Denv. J. Int'l L. & Pol'y* 109 (1995).

71 *See* K. Petersen, "Note, Recent Intellectual Property Trends in Developing Countries", 33 *Harv. Int'l L.J.* 277 (1992); M. Hannig, "An Examination of the Possibility to Secure Intellectual Property Rights for Plant Genetic Resources Developed by Indigenous Peoples of the NAFTA States: Domestic Legislation Under the International Convention for New Plant Varieties", 13 *Ariz. J. Int'l & Comp. L.* 175 (1996).

72 *See Milpurrurru v. Indofurn*, 30 I.P.R. at 216 (von Doussa J.).

73 *See* A. Sawyerr, "Internal Conflict of Laws in East Africa", in A. Sawyerr (ed.), *East African Law and Social Change*, 1967, 110, 134.

considering these difficult issues, it must be borne in mind that the passage of time and contemporary realities often modify the jurisprudence on intangible cultural heritage, especially aspects of ownership, the social nature of the creative process, legal personality and other features. All of these underpin the Indigenous protocols for the regulation of intangible cultural heritage.[74] Thus, a conception of intellectual property rights as a policy instrument of states[75] is crucial in fashioning a contemporary response to intangible cultural heritage's marginalized status.[76] The intangible cultural heritage of Indigenous populations contains invaluable methods of communicating and transferring meaning, knowledge and information among citizens and in their relationships with the larger universe.[77] The authorial process is shared. The mythic image of the solitary author is the exception rather than the rule.

74 The literature on this burgeoning school of thought is quite remarkable; *see generally* T. Greaves (ed.), *Intellectual Property Rights for Indigenous Peoples: A Source Book*, 1994.

75 *See* D. Vaver, "Intellectual Property Today: Of Myths and Paradoxes", 69 *Can. B. Rev.* 98 (1990).

76 *See* E. Tilton Penrose, *The Economics of the International Patent System*, (Greenwood Press 1973) (1951).

77 *See* A. Odi, "As It Was in the Beginning: The Influence of Traditional Elements in Igbo Information Systems", 28 *Int'l Info. & Libr. Rev.* 193 (1996).

COMMUNITY AS A HOLDER OF INTANGIBLE CULTURAL HERITAGE

A Broader Public Policy Perspective

Branislav HAZUCHA*

Previous chapters in this Part raise many essential, yet intricate, points concerning interrelations between communities and their cultural traditions[1], such as

* LL.M. 1999 (Commenius University); Dr. jur. 2002 (Trnava University); LL.D. 2005 (Kyushu University); Assistant Professor of Law, Kyushu University. The author would like to acknowledge, with thanks, the insights and comments of Steven Van Uytsel and other participants of the *Conference on Intangible Cultural Heritage and Intellectual Property under the 2003 Convention: Seeking a Collaborative Interface between ICH and IP*, held on 25–26 March 2007 in New Delhi, India. All the remaining shortcomings and omissions are of the author's sole responsibility.

1 In this Chapter, the terms "intangible cultural heritage" and "cultural traditions" are used interchangeably, unless it is provided otherwise. The former is used in the way as it is defined by the *Convention for the Safeguarding of the Intangible Cultural Heritage* (ICH Convention); *see* Convention for the Safeguarding of the Intangible Cultural Heritage, 17 October 2003, Article 2(1), U.N. Doc. MISC/2003/CLT/CH/14 (2003), *available at* http://unesdoc.unesco.org/images/0013/001325/132540e.pdf (last visited 31 July 2008) [hereinafter "ICH Convention"]. The latter is employed in a more informal sense than the former. However, the author acknowledges that some authors strictly distinguish between "heritage" and "traditions" so that the former is not in practice anymore, while the latter is still alive and practiced by communities. *See, e.g.*, U. KOCKEL, "Reflexive Traditions and Heritage Production", in U. KOCKEL and M. NIC CRAITH (eds.), *Cultural Heritages as Reflexive Traditions*, 2006, 19. Although this distinction is often perceived in practice, the reason why it is disregarded for the purpose of this Chapter is that the ICH Convention requires to safeguard intangible cultural heritage in its living form; *see* ICH Convention, *supra* note 1, Article 2(3) (defining "safeguarding" of intangible cultural heritage as "measures aimed at ensuring the viability of the intangible cultural heritage ... as well as the revitalization of the various aspects of such heritage.").

traditional knowledge and traditional cultural expressions.[2] This Chapter addresses some additional aspects concerning how to define a "holder" of intangible cultural heritage.[3] The main question tackled in this Chapter is who actually holds cultural traditions? How can we define such holders, and how does such a definition affect the operation of different legal regimes aiming to protect, preserve and safeguard[4] intangible cultural heritage in a living form?

The obvious answer is that intangible cultural heritage "belongs" to the community who created, maintains and still practices individual forms of traditional knowledge or cultural expressions. It is a truism that expresses a proprietary relationship that exists within, and outside, the community in relation to its intangible cultural heritage. It is therefore often reflected in foundations and justifications of many proposals made by proponents of the protection of

2 In this Chapter, the terms "cultural traditions" and "intangible cultural heritage" are used in the way that they cover the notions of "traditional knowledge" and "traditional cultural expressions" as defined by the World Intellectual Property Organization (WIPO); *see* WIPO, Intergovernmental Committee on Intellectual Property and Genetic Resources, Traditional Knowledge and Folklore, *The Protection of Traditional Knowledge: Draft Objectives and Principles*, Annex, Article 3(2), WIPO/GRTKF/IC/10/5 (2 October 2006), *available at* www.wipo.int/edocs/mdocs/tk/en/wipo_grtkf_ic_10/wipo_grtkf_ic_10_5.pdf (last visited 31 July 2008) [hereinafter "*Draft TK Principles*"]; WIPO, Intergovernmental Committee on Intellectual Property and Genetic Resources, Traditional Knowledge and Folklore, *The Protection of Traditional Cultural Expressions/Expressions of Folklore: Draft Objectives and Principles*, Annex, Article 1(a), WIPO/GRTKF/IC/10/4 (2 October 2006), *available at* www.wipo.int/edocs/mdocs/tk/en/wipo_grtkf_ic_10/wipo_grtkf_ic_10_4.pdf (last visited 31 July 2008) [hereinafter "*Draft TCE Principles*"]. However, the author acknowledges that the notion of "traditional knowledge", as used in academic literature, covers forms of collective knowledge and heritage which are not covered by the term "intangible cultural heritage".

3 In literature, the terms "custodian", "holder" or "owner" are often used to explain the relationship between communities and their intangible cultural heritage. Although the terms partially overlap each other, each of them describes a slightly different position of a community in relation to its intangible cultural heritage. The analysis of their nuances is omitted here for reasons of space. However, it should be noted that the actual relationship between communities and their intangible cultural heritage heavily depends upon social norms accepted and recognized by these communities in relation to creation, preservation and re-creation of their cultural traditions. In this sense, the term "holder" of intangible cultural heritage is used for the purposes of this Chapter.

4 Pursuant to ICH Convention, the term of "safeguarding" also covers the notions of "protection" and "preservation"; *see* ICH Convention, *supra* note 1, Article 2(3) (defining "safeguarding" of intangible cultural heritage as "measures aimed at ensuring the viability of the intangible cultural heritage, including the identification, documentation, research, preservation, protection, promotion, enhancement, transmission, particularly through formal and non-formal education, as well as the revitalization of the various aspects of such heritage"). Nonetheless, there might be legal regimes aiming at protection and preservation of intangible cultural heritage, which are clearly not covered by the Convention. In order to avoid the narrowing down of the scope of such regimes for purposes of this Chapter, the author employs all the three terms.

traditional knowledge and cultural expressions in the form of *sui generis*[5] intellectual property rights or through other types of regimes based upon the communities' proprietary interests in their intangible cultural heritage.[6]

Such an instant and instinctive answer, however, faces a significant challenge to overcome. It ignores the fact that "belonging" is a vague, indistinct, unclear and blurry concept. An answer of this kind fails to clearly define the scope of such relationships, *i.e.* the community's entitlements to its intangible cultural heritage and duties owed within and outside the concerned community. Put another way, it does not provide a clear scope or parameters for what the community can do with its cultural traditions and to what extent the community can exclude its members or non-members from the access to, and the usage of[7], its traditional knowledge and cultural expressions.

Accordingly, this Chapter argues that the concept of "belonging" can hardly justify any one-size-fits-all solution based upon conventional views which assume that a community's entitlements to its cultural traditions are identical for all types of communities.[8] This Chapter argues that, in order to properly scrutinize this conundrum relating to the "holdership" of intangible cultural heritage, it is necessary to take into account the web of relationships that exists between various stakeholders (such as the communities, their members and non-members, and all of humankind) with regard to individual components of cultural traditions as a social product. This facilitates the recognition of diversity and vibrancy emerging amongst Indigenous, traditional, local and other cultural communities. Ensuring adequate and sufficient importance is placed on networks of social relationships, which occur within and outside communities relative to their intangible cultural heritage, is a key to designing an efficient legal framework for the protection, preservation and safeguarding of cultural traditions.

---

5 As Wend B. Wendland accurately pointed out in private discussion with the author, it should be noted that intellectual property rights are already *sui generis* proprietary rights. The author acknowledges this feature, but throughout this Chapter, the term is used in its conventional way stressing the difference of these new forms of intellectual property rights which do not fit to conventional intellectual property rights, such as copyrights, patents and trademarks.

6 *See, e.g.*, WIPO, INTERGOVERNMENTAL COMMITTEE ON INTELLECTUAL PROPERTY AND GENETIC RESOURCES, TRADITIONAL KNOWLEDGE AND FOLKLORE, *The Protection of Traditional Cultural Expressions/Expressions of Folklore: Updated Draft Outline of Policy Options and Legal Mechanisms*, Annex, par. 20, WIPO/GRTKF/IC/9/INF/4 (27 March 2006), *available at* www.wipo.int/edocs/mdocs/tk/en/wipo_grtkf_ic_9/wipo_grtkf_ic_9_inf_4.pdf (last visited 31 July 2008) [hereinafter "*Updated Draft TCE Legal Mechanisms*"].

7 The right to exclude an access to a thing and the right to exploit a thing are conventional proprietary entitlements of the owner.

8 *See, e.g.*, A.R. RILEY, "Recovering Collectivity: Group Rights to Intellectual Property in Indigenous Communities", 18 *Cardozo Arts & Ent. L.J.* 175 (2000) (proposing an Indian Copyright Act); L. GRAHAM and S. MCJOHN, "Indigenous People and Intellectual Property", 19 *Wash. U. J.L. & Pol'y* 313 (2005) (proposing adjustment to intellectual property laws to fit cultural traditions).

This is especially indispensable when we take into account the fact that each regime aimed at the protection, preservation or safeguarding of cultural traditions only works well with certain types of communities and their organizational structures and not with others. The ways of defining a "community" as a holder of intangible cultural heritage and the community's role in the entire process of its preservation, safeguarding and survival are thus considerably dependant upon the specific features and mechanisms of particular regimes. Each regime sets out different conditions and requirements for a person to become entitled. The configuration, or definition, of an entitled entity thus differs between individual regimes which can range from those based upon the granting of communal property rights[9] or the imposing of liability for the expropriation of intangible cultural heritage by non-members of affected communities[10], to those aimed at the safeguarding of intangible cultural heritage through the implementation of measures financed by private or public funds.[11] Some of them are currently in the preliminary stages of their proposal[12], while others are in the final stages of adoption or implementation[13] such as the system under the *Convention for the Safeguarding of the Intangible Cultural Heritage* (ICH Convention).[14] As the efficiency of a particular regime depends upon its suitability to particular types of communities and their intangible cultural heritage, the preservation of myriad cultural traditions in living incarnation requires the designing of efficient networks of legal regimes. These must be tightly connected to an understanding of the web of relationships concerning cultural traditions within and outside the concerned communities as a social product.

---

9 *See, e.g.*, *Updated Draft TCE Legal Mechanisms*, *supra* note 6, Annex, par. 20. For an analysis of conditions under which property right or liability rights should be granted, *see* G. Calabresi and A.D. Melamed, "Property Rules, Liability Rules, and Inalienability: One View of the Cathedral", 85 *Harv. L. Rev.* 1089 (1972).

10 *See, e.g.*, *Updated Draft TCE Legal Mechanisms*, *supra* note 6, Annex, par. 21. *See also* J.H. Reichman and T. Lewis, "Using Liability Rules to Stimulate Local Innovation in Developing Countries: Application to Traditional Knowledge", in K.E. Maskus and J.H. Reichman (eds.), *International Public Goods and Transfer of Technology Under a Globalized Intellectual Property Regime*, 2005, 337, 354–66 (proposing a liability regime for the protection of traditional knowledge).

11 *See, e.g.*, ICH Convention, *supra* note 1, Articles 11–15.

12 *See Draft TK Principles*, *supra* note 2; *Draft TCE Principles*, *supra* note 2.

13 *See Updated Draft TCE Legal Mechanisms*, *supra* note 6; WIPO, Intergovernmental Committee on Intellectual Property and Genetic Resources, Traditional Knowledge and Folklore, *The Protection of Traditional Knowledge: Revised Outline of Policy Options and Legal Mechanisms*, WIPO/GRTKF/IC/9/INF/5 (27 March 2006), *available at* www.wipo.int/edocs/mdocs/tk/en/wipo_grtkf_ic_9/wipo_grtkf_ic_9_inf_5.doc (last visited 31 July 2008).

14 *See* ICH Convention, *supra* note 1.

1. DEFINING A "COMMUNITY" AS A HOLDER OF INTANGIBLE CULTURAL HERITAGE

Examining the etymology of the word "community", uncovers two similar meanings with somewhat different nuances. Departing from the etymology of the English word "community", the search leads to the Latin prefix *con-*, which means "together", and the word *munus*. As Michael V. McGinnis, Freeman House and William Jordan present, the Latin word *munus* "has an extremely interesting range of meanings, including service or duty; gift; and sacrifice."[15] This understanding allows them to identify the following implications in relation to the notion of community:

> The word "community" ... is a metaphor. At its root is the idea of an exchange of services – out of duty, it may be, but also pointing to another dimension of the idea, freely, even affectionately, as a gift, or even a sacrifice. A community, then, is the assemblage of individuals to whom one is bound by this kind of relationship – one defined, we might even say constituted, by mutual obligation and by an exchange of gifts.[16]

Another etymological inquiry, stressing foundational aspects of interrelationships between the members of community, may stem from the German term *Gemeinschaft*. Although the German counterpart of the English word "community" does not originate from the same Latin roots, the elements of identity, relationship and solidarity can be found in earlier German writings about *Gemeinschaft*. More than hundred years ago, Ferdinand Tönnies distinguished between *Gemeinschaft* and *Gesellschaft* (society). While the former is founded on long standing traditional links between its members, the latter is composed of people who are drawn together by impersonal and instrumental relations.[17] Accordingly, James Brow, following Max Weber, puts forward tersely:

> "Community" refers simply to "a sense of belonging together" ... Since the term is often very loosely applied either to a place or to a collection of people, it is necessary to insist that ... community is defined by nothing more or less than this subjective state. The sense of belonging together typically combines both *affective* and *cognitive* components, both a feeling of solidarity and an understanding of shared identity.[18]

---

15 M.V. McGinnis, F. House and W. Jordan III, "Bioregional Restoration: Re-Establishing an Ecology of Shared Identity", in M.V. McGinnis (ed.), *Bioregionalism*, 1999, 205, 213.

16 *Id.* at 213.

17 *See* F. Tönnies, *Gemeinschaft und Gesellschaft: Grundbegriffe der reinen Soziologie*, (3th ed.), 1920.

18 J. Brow, "Notes on Community, Hegemony, and the Uses of the Past", 63 *Anthropological Q.* 1 (1990) (emphasis added).

The sense of "belonging together" gives the impression of a certain degree of uniformity between individual communities. However, the image of community, as perceived by particular individuals, diverges to some extent. This divergence can sometimes even be on very minor and highly nuanced points. This can be observed in notions of communities presented elsewhere in this volume[19] stemming from the huge diversity of communities around the world. We can take, as an example, Indigenous communities and how their organizational structures differ in time and from a place to another. When the Europeans colonized the Americas, they encountered centralized structures of local populations, which could not be found later amongst the Aborigines in Australia[20], or amongst some other Indigenous or traditional communities elsewhere.[21] Moreover, due to external forces having a significant impact on Indigenous communities for centuries of colonization, their organizational structure and strength of ties between their members changed considerably throughout time. Many of their members currently live in fringe settlements, inner city ghettos or white suburban areas together with descendants of settlers' populations. This simultaneously causes new social frictions between majority populations and minority groups, as well as within Indigenous and traditional communities.[22] The Indigenous people who moved and settled outside their original communities often no longer find themselves considered as members of their traditional communal structures.[23] Problems and frictions related to creating suburban communities are not unique to Indigenous communities, and can also be found in many developed countries with higher levels of population mobility amongst traditional rural communities.

Consequently, a definition that would cover all possible types of communities with diverse internal and external social bonds can oversimplify the necessary implications of the term "community". Such difficulties crop up within the long and detailed history of attempts to create an appropriate and adequate definition. Over a half-century ago, George A. Hillery counted 94 different definitions of community.[24] Doubtlessly, many more exist at present.

---

19 *See, e.g.*, Chapters [Janke], [Chaudhuri] and [Mgbeoji] of the present volume.

20 *See, e.g.*, G. Morgan, "Aboriginal Politics, Self-Determination and the Rhetoric of Community", in S. Herbrechter and M. Higgins (eds.), *Returning (to) Communities: Theory, Culture and Political Practice of the Communal*, 2006, 367, 371.

21 *See* W.E.A. van Beek and F. Jara, ""Granular Knowledge": Cultural Problems with Intellectual Property and Protection", in F.W. Grosheide and J.J. Brinkhof (eds.), *Intellectual Property Law 2002: Articles on Cultural Expressions and Indigenous Knowledge*, 2002, 35, 42–43 (referring to the Kapsiki/Higi people, inhabitants of the Mandara mountains in the North of Cameroon and the North-East of Nigeria).

22 *See, e.g.*, Morgan, *supra* note 20 (discussing the current situation of Australian Aborigines who moved to the suburbs of Australian towns and cities over the last 50 years).

23 *See id.*

24 *See* G.A. Hillery Jr., "Definitions of Community: Areas of Agreement", 20 *Rural Sociology* 111 (1955).

With so many types of communities all around the world varying in their features and characteristics, several scholars question the usefulness of this notion.[25] This problem is even magnified by the fact that a person may consider herself to be a member of several different communities. Vered Amit and Nigel Rapport thus conclude that the notion of community is very slippery. They believe that it is "too vague, too variable in its applications and definitions to be of much utility as an analytical tool".[26] The reason why it is used so often together with terms such as culture in anthropology and other social sciences is seen by them in the fact that the terms "evoke a thick assortment of meanings, presumptions and images."[27] Michael J. Watts puts it succinctly: "[community] is often invoked as a unity, as an undifferentiated thing with intrinsic powers that speaks with a single voice".[28] But actual communities in workaday life are "nothing of the sort".[29] Amit and Rapport therefore come to the conclusion that such a vague term persists in usage only because it provides "a convenient conceptual haven, a location from which to safely circumscribe potentially infinite webs of connection."[30]

By drawing on this critical literature, I want neither to enter to this controversial academic discussion, nor to question the definition of community or the usefulness of the notion. Scholars criticizing the notion of community because of its vagueness and indeterminacy, however, draw our attention to an often neglected, underestimated or even purposely-simplified fact. They stress that there is no universal concept of community characterized by certain types of relationships within and outside the community. On the contrary, a wide-ranging and complex "webs of connection(s)" defines a community.

Another way this critical scholarship enlightens our endeavour is through its successes in understanding the core elements or features of community. Although individual authors diverge in the number and classification of core elements or features of community[31], the three main groups of them can be clustered. First, communities are bound together by something, be it *locus*, history, culture, values, interests or other perspectives giving a community a sense of being in

---

25 *See* M.J. Watts, "Contested Communities, Malignant Markets, and Gilded Governance: Justice, Resource Extraction, and Conservation in the Tropics", in Ch. Zerner (ed.), *People, Plants, and Justice: The Politics of Nature Conservation*, 2000, 21; Vered Amit and Nigel Rapport, *The Trouble with Community: Anthropological Reflections on Movement, Identity and Collectivity*, 2002.

26 Amit and Rapport, *supra* note 25, at 13.

27 *See id.*

28 Watts, *supra* note 25, at 37.

29 *See id.*

30 Amit and Rapport, *supra* note 25, at 17.

31 *Compare* K.M. MacQueen *et al.*, "What is Community? An Evidence-Based Definition for Participatory Public Health", 91 *Am. J. Public Health* 1929 (2001), *with* D. Patrick and T. Wickizer, "Community and Health", in B. Amick *et al.* (eds.), *Society and Health*, 1995, 46.

time, place or social networks. Unifiers of this kind allow for the raising of boundaries around communities in order to exclude others from their membership. Their members are thus provided with a criterion for distinguishing between "Us" (members) and "Others" (non-members). Second, in this way, individuals and groups of people also recognize their social ties within and outside their communities. Such internal and external social bonds and networks form the second important group of core elements for characterizing a community, and allow individuals to identify with their respective communities and give a community a sense of coherence and identity. Third, diversity and often multiplicity of communities bring a sense of co-existence between various communities. Membership in one community does not preclude simultaneous membership in another. This occurs because members may differ in perceptions of the importance of core elements giving the identity to communities.

The identification and characteristics of abovementioned features are very useful tools for analysis and classification of diverse communal entities. Especially, in relation to the last two groups, the emphasis should be laid on the fact that the creation, use, preservation and re-creation of traditional knowledge and cultural expressions within individual communities are governed by internally recognized social norms. However, such social norms are often hidden from non-members. They are habitually deeply embedded in organizational structure of communities. Their normative characters usually appear only when the norms are overtly violated. Antony Taubman puts it tersely: "[W]here the customary laws and protocols are deeply embedded in the way of life of a community, it may only be the sense of violation that arises when [traditional knowledge] is alienated or misused that enables the truly normative character of these practices to crystallize and become fully recognized and articulated, in retrospect, as a binding norm."[32]

Additionally, not all parts of intangible cultural heritage are accessible to all community members. Especially with regards to sacred rituals or knowledge, only a limited group, sometimes just a few chosen individuals, can have access to them and thus be acquainted with the respective social norms governing the creation, use, preservation and re-creation of these types of cultural traditions.[33] The differences in access to information on such cultural traditions and respective social norms may even cause clashes and conflicts concerning some sacred rituals, knowledge and social norms within and outside communities.[34] In some cases,

---

32 A. Taubman, "Saving the Village: Conserving Jurisprudential Diversity in the International Protection of Traditional Knowledge", in *International Public Goods*, *supra* note 10, at 521, 527.

33 *See*, *e.g.*, van Beek and Jara, *supra* note 21, at 48–51.

34 *See* M.F. Brown, *Who Owns Native Culture?*, 2003, 173–85 (describing an Australian case where a few Ngarrindjeri women claimed sacred knowledge and women-only rituals on Hindmarsh Island).

the divergence or discrepancy in the knowledge of cultural traditions and social norms between individual members of community may also be explained by the third feature characteristic for communities, *i.e.* individual members may differently perceive the role, position and importance of information and norms in question.

To sum up, there is a variety in types of communities, which have complex "webs of connection" amongst individual members of such communities, and between them and other members of society. Since relationships within and outside communities created by these cultural traditions are social products, they can differ from one type of community to another. Accordingly, it is almost impossible to design a one-size-fits-all solution, which would aim at the protection, preservation and safeguarding of cultural traditions in a living form and which would work adequately and properly with all types of communities or their intangible cultural heritage. The more feasible solution is to attempt to efficiently combine several different legal regimes in order to maximize their pros and to minimize their cons. To do so, it is essential to adjust individual regimes to particular types of communities and social networks built around the creation, preservation and further re-creation of their intangible cultural heritage.

2. SEARCH FOR APPROPRIATE REGIME: IDENTIFICATION OF COSTS AND BENEFITS

This brings us to the main question of this Chapter. Who is the "holder" of intangible cultural heritage and to what extent can this concept work in relation to different legal regimes? When one attempts to tackle the question, several related queries arise. What role should a community play as a "holder" of its intangible cultural heritage in relation to protection, preservation and safeguarding of its cultural traditions? Should a community be granted any property rights, be they in form of intellectual property rights we currently recognize or *sui generis* rights? Should it be entitled only under some type of liability regime when someone encroaches into the domain of intangible cultural heritage by appropriating some of its parts? Or, should it be granted no rights allowing for controlling access to, and usage of, its cultural traditions in order to avoid any restrictions to freedom of expression enjoyed by other members of society?

The adoption of any of the abovementioned legal regimes, or combinations thereof, requires careful and accurate adjustment, calibration and tuning to justly and efficiently protect and preserve the community's intangible cultural heritage while not harming other important social values of individuals within and outside the concerned community. For instance, granting communal rights that exclude non-members from access to, or use of, cultural traditions can have a negative impact on other important public interests recognized by modern societies, *i.e.* the legitimate interest of affected individuals in freedom of expression and access to information. As Robert K. Paterson and Dennis S. Karjala warn us, when "any group, indigenous or otherwise, does not share the free speech and building-block approach to the development of culture, there is a conflict of fundamental importance that is not easily resolved."[35] Consequently, any legal regime aiming to protect, preserve or safeguard intangible cultural heritage must also be considered in a broader public policy perspective. Compared with other possible mechanisms, its negative consequences and the social costs for individual communities and society can be minimized while benefits are maximized.

The central question of such cost-benefit analysis is why and at what cost we should protect cultural traditions, be they the result of individual or communal intellectual labour. Cultural diversity is considered to be an important value for humankind. Although numerous communities and cultural traditions exist all around the world, many individual traditional knowledge and cultural expressions are heavily influenced by communal cultural traditions or cross-cultural borrowings from other cultural groups, be they neighbours or complete outsiders.[36] The processes of historical selection, separation and cross-cultural communication between diverse communities brought a huge variety of cultural expressions worldwide. Cultural diversity is thus deemed as a "common heritage of humanity"[37] and essential for further sustainable development.[38]

The last decades can, however, be characterized by slow, but steady, changes in cultural traditions and communal organization. Many people see liberalization of world trade and removal of national border barriers as the cause of these changes. These critics argue that the disappearance of national barriers brings harsher competition to sales of goods and provision of services, but also to cultures, habits and values of particular communities. While economic competition leads either to adaptation of goods and services by their producers or providers in order to cope with the changed economic reality, or to vanishing of non-competitive entrepreneurs, the cultural competition causes even more far-reaching consequences. As its result, our habits, values and cultures undergo considerable changes. Some decry that in this way, communities lose their

35 R.K. Paterson and D.S. Karjala, "Looking Beyond Intellectual Property in Resolving Protection of the Intangible Cultural Heritage of Indigenous Peoples", 11 *Cardozo J. Int'l & Comp. L.* 633, 657 (2003).

36 *See* Chapter [Van Uytsel] of the present volume (describing cross-cultural borrowings in relation to fairy tales).

37 *See* Convention on the Protection and Promotion of the Diversity of Cultural Expressions, 20 October 2005, Preamble, par. 2, U.N. Doc. CLT-2005/CONVENTION DIVERSITE-CULT REV., *available at* http://unesdoc.unesco.org/images/0014/001429/142919e.pdf (last visited 31 July 2008) [hereinafter "CD Convention"].

38 *See id*, Preamble, par. 3.

uniqueness and become increasingly similar.[39] They even suggest that this process may even lead to the disappearance of certain cultures, the identity loss of certain communities and, at the end, to lower cultural diversity.[40]

However, I think that the abovementioned negative effects on cultural diversity are often a bit exaggerated. Although trade liberalization and cross-cultural communication has some negative impacts on marginal cultures, it creates long-term benefits for exposed communities' identities and cultural diversity worldwide.[41] When people can face other cultures, they learn that different communities have similar habits. The awareness of similarities and differences between cultures can help individuals understand others. In the long run, the tolerance of other cultures may help us to improve our postmodern societies. We become more open-minded and tolerant to persons from other cultural environments. It helps us to fight against hatred and xenophobia. The more culturally diverse our societies are, the freer and more tolerant they are.

Well, why is it then so important to protect intangible cultural heritage by specific legal regimes for future generations? Why is it crucial to recognize or grant any communal property or liability rights, or to set up a welfare system aiming at the protection, preservation or safeguarding of cultural traditions? Although this topic may appear a bit far from the main focus of this Chapter, the enquiry of this sort is vital for a proper and adequate calibration of cost-benefit analysis in a broader public policy perspective. By addressing the reason and justifications for the protection of cultural traditions, I will come back to the main topic, *i.e.* the position of community as a "holder" of intangible cultural heritage. The proper understanding of this issue plays a significant role in designing an efficient combination of specific legal regimes.

The key argument in favour of safeguarding intangible cultural heritage is that market works only for some cultural traditions, especially those from mainstream cultures, which are valuable for specific groups of customers. But in many cases, individual traditional knowledge or cultural expressions are valuable only for the members of concerned communities and not in any economic way. Accordingly, the market habitually fails in relation to marginal cultures, especially because of its distortions. Market failures magnified by globalization and economic progress may facilitate disintegration of traditional communities. By

39 *See, e.g.*, F. Jameson, "Globalization and Political Strategy", *New Left Rev.*, No. 4, at 49, 51 (2000) ("The standardization of world culture, with local popular or traditional forms driven out or dumbed down to make way for American television, American music, food, clothes and films, has been seen by many as the very heart of globalization.").

40 *See, e.g.*, J. Tunstall, *The Media are American*, 1977, 57 (defining "cultural imperialism thesis" as the view that "authentic, traditional and local culture in many parts of the world is being battered out of existence by the indiscriminated dumping of large quantities of slick commercial and media products, mainly from the United States").

41 *See, e.g.*, T. Cowen, *Creative Destruction: How Globalization Is Changing the World's Cultures*, 2002 (seeing the long-term benefits of globalization in hybridization).

loosening social bonds and communal structures, such communities may lose their identity or even disappear. The question is whether we should try to prevent such disintegration processes.

Leaving the solutions to the market without any legal intervention may cause deeper negative consequences for affected communities and their cultural traditions. It may give communities the incentive to preserve and re-create only those cultural traditions with market value. As pointed out elsewhere in this volume, there is a mutual interdependency between community and its intangible cultural heritage.[42] Culture and especially intangible cultural heritage, on one side, and community, on the other, are inherently entangled and mutually dependent systems. A community creates culture, and culture, including cultural traditions, forms and shapes the community. Put it more bluntly, while the intangible cultural heritage, or, as defined by the ICH Convention, "the practices, representations, expressions, knowledge, skills – as well as the instruments, objects, artefacts and cultural spaces associated therewith"[43], is the product of a particular community, any community is simultaneously formed and shaped by the practices, representations and expressions.[44] Accordingly, neither a community nor its intangible cultural heritage is static and motionless. They are dynamic, mutually-shaped and influenced phenomena. This feature is also mirrored in the definition of intangible cultural heritage in Article 2(1) of the ICH Convention, which provides that "intangible cultural heritage, transmitted from generation to generation, is constantly recreated by communities and groups in response to their environment, their interaction with nature and their history, and provides them with a sense of identity and continuity".[45]

Consequently, if no action is taken to prevent the further deformation of communities and their intangible cultural heritage, we may lose other important cultural entities which may extinguish due to modern global social phenomena such as migration, modernization or globalization. The objection to such line of thinking can be that nobody can be forced to stay intact and solid. Nevertheless, avoiding distortions caused by market failures requires intervention by law for the protection, preservation and safeguarding of cultural traditions. Yet simultaneously, we should be careful with any intervention due to the fragile interdependency between communities and their cultural traditions. Each legal regime has positive and negative impacts on important social values, interests and norms. Such social costs and benefits[46] can occur both within and outside communities and on the local, national, regional and worldwide level. At this

---

42 *See* Chapters [Hazucha and Kono] and [Mgbeoji] of the present volume.

43 ICH Convention, *supra* note 1, Article 2(1).

44 *See, e.g.*, Kockel, *supra* note 1.

45 ICH Convention, *supra* note 1, Article 2(1).

46 By the application of cost-benefit analysis, the author does not refer to its form as presented by some schools of law and economics which advocate the neo-liberal economic theory, but the

point, it should be made clear that it is essential to consider all social costs and benefits as valued by particular communities and societies, and not by an economist with a certain degree of prejudice inherited in his political orientation, values and believes.[47]

For the assessment of particular regulatory mechanisms, we can modify the evaluation system designed by David Throsby in relation to tangible cultural heritage.[48] Throsby identifies individual values of cultural heritage considered as social benefits for communities, societies or humankind. Accordingly, there are *use* and *non-use values* of intangible cultural heritage.[49] While the former consist of benefits brought to particular communities and its members, the latter are composed of *existence value* (the benefit derived form the existence of intangible cultural heritage as such), *option value* (the benefit that the members of other communities have option to get acquainted with intangible cultural heritage of other communities) and *bequest value* (the benefit that intangible cultural heritage will be preserved for other generations).[50] In addition to *use* and *non-use value*, there are other cultural values attributed to intangible cultural heritage and benefits derived from its preservation by communities, its members and also non-members. We may refer to (a) *aesthetic value*; (b) *spiritual value*; (c) *social value*; (d) *historical value*; (e) *symbolic value*; (f) *authenticity value* and so on.[51]

However, legal regimes also bring other costs and benefits which should be taken into consideration. Their creating, maintaining and enforcing require certain expenditures (*administrative costs*) on the side of communities and also broader society. As individual regimes fit only to certain types of communities and their intangible cultural heritage, they can have negative effects on other concerned stakeholders and their activities. For instance, the level of integrity and cohesion within a community heavily influences the efficiency of regimes based upon granting any communal property rights or upon imposition of liability for misappropriation of certain forms or expressions of cultural traditions. In case of corroded and deteriorated communities, the efficiency of such regimes decreases due to their increasing administration costs and loss of legal certainty between affected stakeholders. In this regard, property rights require a higher degree of certainty concerning an entitled entity for their efficient operation. In case of highly integrated communities, the identification of the holder of intangible cultural heritage would bring less uncertainty for affected stakeholders than in

---

author refers to the cost-benefit analysis which takes into account all social benefits and costs as valued by the respective communities, society or humankind.

47 *See, e.g.*, W.M. Landes and R.A. Posner, *The Economic Structure of Intellectual Property Law*, 2003, 12–24 (referring only to "economic" benefits and costs).

48 *See* D. Throsby, *Economics and Culture*, 2001, 83–86.

49 *Id.* at 78.

50 *Id.* at 78–79.

51 *Id.* at 84–85.

case of disintegrated communities. The more decentralized and disorganized the community is, the less efficient the regime based on granting such community any communal property rights to its intangible cultural heritage is. Other legal regimes aimed at the protection, preservation or safeguarding of cultural traditions have similar drawbacks.

In addition to administrative costs, a legal regime which does not fit well with particular communities and their cultural traditions also causes social costs in the form of artificial changes to the communal organization and intangible cultural heritage. Such an inefficient legal regime often induces the concerned communities to undergo changes in their organization, cultural traditions or respective social norms so that they would be able to maximize benefits gained under the concerned regulation. The artificial creation of traditions and traditional communal structures is, in academic literature, a well-known and examined phenomenon called "invention of traditions"[52], which can be considered as a negative consequence of respective regulation. Accordingly, understanding all the respective social costs and benefits of individual legal regimes which are aimed at the protection, preservation or safeguarding of intangible cultural heritage is essential for designing an efficient legal framework.

3. "LIMITED COMMONS" AND LAW

Legal regimes are neither static nor changeless. Social interests in resources and their management practices can change over time from simple and emerging regimes of entitlements to well defined, clear and refined property regimes. Based upon the conventional economic understanding, Carol M. Rose suggests that "we may predict alterations in property – and specifically, more refined property – under certain conditions."[53] She identifies the following three conditions which have impact on "alterations in property": (a) increase in social benefits and interests; (b) decrease of social costs; and (c) taking into account other cultural and to some degree political considerations. The first condition relates to overall social benefits. In this regard, Rose stresses the importance of property rights in their clarity and certainty. She puts it succinctly: "[W]e gain greater benefits if we use property to manage conflict and encourage investment."[54] The second condition concerns the administrative costs of a particular legal regime. The less costly the administration, the more refined and sophisticated the regulation can

52 *See, e.g.*, E. Hobsbawm and T. Ranger (eds.), *The Invention of Tradition*, 1983.

53 *See* C.M. Rose, "The Several Futures of Property: Of Cyberspace and Folk Tales, Emission Trades and Ecosystems", 83 *Minn. L. Rev.* 129, 143 (1998).

54 *Id.*

be.[55] The final condition trumps the previous two by considering the actual political climate and reasons behind adopting a particular regime. She suggests that cultural, and to some degree political, circumstances cause alterations in property regimes because they take "notice [of] unconventional forms of property, or property among previously under-acknowledged persons and groups".[56]

With regard to the "holdership" of cultural traditions, it should be noted that they are conventionally deemed to be in the public domain. In Rose's opinion the major problem with regard to the legal recognition of community "holdership" over its intangible cultural heritage are the traditional prejudices against property rights. She notes that "[s]ome things get treated as property, some things do not; some persons get treated as owners, some do not."[57] She explains these possible negative outcomes as follows:

> [C]ertain property claims do not make it onto our property radar screen, or appear only dimly there. At best this pattern creates an imbalance in favor of the kinds of claims that we do recognize, while at worst it may foster violence and dissipate wealth.[58]

Although conventional wisdom considers intangible cultural heritage to be in the public domain[59], reality often differs. Particular forms of intangible cultural heritage are held "in common" but only within certain groups of people. While some forms are accessible to the entire community, others can be employed only by members of certain professions. A further, more limited, number of sacred traditions and rituals are accessible to elite individuals.[60] Likewise, different information or parts of a cultural tradition can be accessible by different groups. This kind of division occurs in cases of specific rituals which can be performed only when all the concerned stakeholders or members of one community participate in such rituals.[61] Accordingly, information or cultural tradition is held in common, but only within that particular community or group of people. Circumstances like these exclude non-members, partially or completely, from access to such information or cultural traditions.[62]

---

55 *Id.* ("we should expect to see more refined property where technological or administrative advances make it cheaper for us to organize property regimes.").

56 *Id.*

57 *Id.* at 152.

58 *Id.* at 143.

59 *See generally* P. Samuelson, "Enriching Discourse on Public Domain", 55 *Duke L.J.* 783 (2006) (reviewing thirteen possible definitions for the public domain).

60 *See, e.g.*, van Beek and Jara, *supra* note 21, at 48–51.

61 *See* Brown, *supra* note 34, at 28 ("Information is nearly everywhere held differentially along lines of age, gender, social class, kinship, and occupation. It may be acquired through interactions with other peoples.").

62 *Id.* at 23 (quoting a Hopi spokesperson arguing that some ideas are "the birthrights of the Hopis, to be shared only under strict religious standards by those vested with that religious authority to do so").

Rose defines such a situation as "limited common property".[63] She characterizes it as "property on the outside, commons on the inside."[64] It is "property held as a commons among the members of a group, but exclusively vis-à-vis the outside world."[65] She puts forward that many such regimes "are held together by custom rather than private 'constitutions'."[66] The membership in communities and access to such informal communal property regimes is based upon a "web of connections", which include "long residence, kinship and local friendships, proven skills, and acceptance of local norms."[67] This brings some scholars to advocate a regime based on mutual recognition of customary laws recognized by individual communities. Erica-Irene A. Daes advocates "[that] the solution is to resolve any disputes over the acquisition and use of indigenous people's heritage according to the customary laws of the indigenous peoples concerned".[68]

Among other factors, amorphous membership and the evolving direction of the community create a problem central to "limited commons". This problem is the difficulty in recognizing, monitoring, transferring and enforcing claims of entitlement.[69] It is especially true since social norms of this kind are often deeply hidden in the organization and life of community.[70] This causes considerable problems identifying customary rules and norms. Furthermore, interpretation and application may be difficult in unique economic, political, social and cultural environments. As Taubman states, "[a] court would need to bridge wide legal and cultural gaps to interpret and apply customary law that is rooted in a traditional culture unfamiliar in the country where relief is sought."[71] But it would not be an insurmountable problem when we take into account that the majority of such cases would take place in countries where the concerned community lives.

Furthermore, certain proprietary interests in individual forms of traditional knowledge and cultural expressions are already recognized by current national laws. For instance, craftsmen and their folk art or musicians and their performances are usually protected by law in some way. In this regard, it should be noted that such artistic creations, artefacts and performances are not exact copies of previous forms. The new generations of artisans, practitioners and performers usually add aspects and perspectives to traditional forms and expressions, and thus give cultural traditions a re-created life of their own. We can then distinguish two types of

---

63 *See* Rose, *supra* note 53, at 132.
64 *Id.* at 144.
65 *Id.* at 132.
66 *Id.* at 139 (reference omitted).
67 *Id.* at 140.
68 E.-I.A. Daes, *Defending Indigenous People's Heritage* (23–26 February 2000) (keynote address presented at the *Conference on Protecting Knowledge: Traditional Resources Rights in the New Millennium*, Union of British Columbian Indian Chiefs, Vancouver, Canada).
69 *Id.*
70 *See supra* text accompanying note 32.
71 Taubman, *supra* note 32, at 530.

traditional cultural production. In the first type, individual practitioners and performers put something new, original and creative into performances and products of folk art. Conventionally, the copyrightability requirements are quite low and many of such drawings, carvings, fabrics or performances easily pass the threshold and are entitled to copyright protection. Unless the expressions of author's thoughts are mundane and routine[72], copyright law can protect them. Time limits on such rights show the main flaw in this method. After their expiry, individual forms and expressions of cultural traditions become part of the public domain.

The second type is composed of copies of traditional cultural forms and motives. Although the works of this type rarely satisfy the requirement of originality and creativity for obtaining copyright by their creators, they may still be entitled to a weaker protection under certain conditions. Only the members of affected communities can claim the authenticity of their products. The concept of "authenticity" means that particular goods and services are produced or provided by members of a concerned community, or that the community, at least, authorizes their production. Non-members should not be allowed to claim that their products were produced by the community in question. Many countries therefore have established regimes aimed at protecting consumers who buy such cultural products and services and their producers or providers against unfair trade practices.[73] National laws prohibit misrepresentation, confusion and other unfair trade practices, which may trick, mislead and deceive the consumers who value the authentic products, and thus cause distortions on the market.[74] The drawback of this approach is identifying who is entitled to claim the authenticity of goods and services.

To solve this problem, some authors[75] propose, and some countries[76] adopted various "authenticity" mark systems similar to trademark regimes. Although the advantage of such proposals is clarity based upon registration, the formalization occurring through an administrative act of registration may create a considerable barrier to some Indigenous, traditional and local communities. Thus, these regimes work with different success in particular jurisdictions. While the U.S. regulation under the *Indian Arts and Crafts Act of 1990* is considered as successful[77], some scholars see the Australian "authenticity" mark system as a

72 The majority of national copyright laws requires that the works of authorship are to be original in order to be copyrightable. Put it otherwise, such works cannot be mundane or routine.

73 *See, e.g., Updated Draft TCE Legal Mechanisms, supra* note 6, Annex, par. 59.

74 *See id.*, Annex, 25. *See also generally* A. Kamperman Sanders, *Unfair Competition Law: The Protection of Intellectual and Industrial Creativity*, 1997.

75 *See, e.g.*, S. Scafidi, "Intellectual Property and Cultural Products", 81 *B.U. L. Rev.* 793, 817–20, 842 (2001).

76 *See, e.g., Updated Draft TCE Legal Mechanisms, supra* note 6, Annex, par. 59(a).

77 *See, e.g.*, S.D. Osborne, "Protecting Tribal Stories: The Perils of Propertization", 28 *Am. Indian L. Rev.* 203, 222 (2003); Scafidi, *supra* note 75, at 818–19; Paterson and Karjala, *supra* note 35, at 666–67.

failure.[78] Perhaps Australian Aborigines are weakly organized and dispersed, so many stakeholders want to exclude others to use the respective "authenticity" marks. Further, consumers may reject higher prices on "authorized" goods on the grounds of their low value in the eyes of consumers. The main disadvantage of attempting to regulate the authenticity of products (through authenticity marks or bans on misrepresentation, confusion or other unfair trade practices) is that such legal regimes work only in cases of actual misrepresentation or confusion. These methods do not cover vendors who do not pretend that their products are authentic, or that put an express disclaimer on their goods to avoid confusion.

Accordingly some scholars suggest, as a solution, granting communities proprietary rights to their cultural traditions. There are several problems with this approach and an incompatibility with regard to the application of such rights to the relationship between the community and other stakeholders. Notwithstanding this, the proponents of this solution argue that simple adjustments to current intellectual property laws could accommodate communal proprietary claims to traditional knowledge and cultural expressions. In this way, individual items and cultural traditions can be protected against misappropriation by non-members of the concerned communities.[79]

The first obstacle to overcome is that copyright and patent laws are supposedly built around the importance of individual authors or inventors, which is expressed in the Romantic notion of authorship. Some scholars think that its importance as a foundation of intellectual property laws is confuted by the deconstruction of authorship, which takes into account cultural influences on the author.[80] Some of them even suggest that protecting authorship is only used to cover up other unpopular outcomes of the application of intellectual property laws. Paterson and Karjala put it tersely: "Vague appeals to natural rights of authorship are almost invariably a political smoke screen aimed at reducing the public benefits of copyright in favor of greater monetary returns to copyright owners."[81]

Regardless of this criticism, authors can creatively express there thoughts, feelings and emotions despite the heavy influence of their surroundings. In addition, the notion of authorship is often used to justify expanding the scope of, and strengthening the force of, intellectual property laws, especially copyright and patent laws.[82] Accordingly, it is essential to scrutinize whether the notion of

---

78 *See* P. Drahos, "A Networked Responsive Regulatory Approach to Protecting Traditional Knowledge", in D. Gervais (ed.), *Intellectual Property, Trade and Development: Strategies to Optimize Economic Development in a TRIPS-Plus Era*, 2007, 385, 403 (referring to the failure of the authenticity mark in Australia).

79 *See, e.g.*, Riley, *supra* note 8; Graham and McJohn, *supra* note 8.

80 *See* M. Foucault, "What Is an Author?", in J.V. Harari (ed.), *Textual Strategies: Perspectives in Post-Structural Criticism*, 1979, 141.

81 *See* Paterson and Karjala, *supra* note 35, at 647.

82 *See id.*

"community" as a "holder" of intangible cultural heritage can pass through the test. After careful survey of contemporary copyright and patent laws, it is clear that they also recognize corporate creativity, through the concepts of joint authorship or inventorship.[83] Intellectual property laws grant exclusive rights to joint authors and inventors, yet it is hard to ignore the difference between the two types of entities. Joint authors or inventors are often identified or easily identifiable, contrary to amorphous entities such as Indigenous, traditional, local or other cultural communities. In many cases, communities lack clear authorities to administer such rights and solve conflicts arisen during collective administration of exclusive rights. Consequently, the granting of exclusive intellectual property rights to such communities would not bring the necessary level of legal certainty and clarity intended through these protections.

The second obstacle is that intellectual property rights are time limited.[84] Traditional knowledge and cultural expressions have their own life. They develop by slow, steady adaptations and re-creation during long time. Granting time-limited intellectual property rights to communities prevents long-term control to individual items of their intangible cultural heritage. After their expiry, cultural traditions become a part of the public domain to which anyone around the world would be allowed to access and use without restriction. On the other hand, the granting or recognition of perpetual intellectual property rights might completely negate the foundations of contemporary intellectual property laws and might bring negative outcomes for other social interests such as freedom of expression and access to information. One might argue that protection of geographical indications may be a model for intellectual property protection of traditional knowledge and cultural expressions.[85] The scope and application of geographical indications is narrower, however, than any respective proprietary interests in cultural traditions. And while protection of geographical indications is easier in terms of operation, administration and enforcement, it also creates considerable friction amongst affected actors. Accordingly, to design a system based upon communal proprietary rights to cultural traditions, legislature or judges must carefully balance the legitimate interests of concerned stakeholders. The communities' interests in protecting their cultural traditions represent one side with the other by a society interested in a broad and rich public domain accessible

83 *See, e.g.*, Graham and McJohn, *supra* note 8, at 330.

84 *See, e.g.*, Agreement on Trade-Related Aspects of Intellectual Property Rights, Articles 12, 14(5), 18, 26(3), 33 and 38, 15 April 1994, Marrakesh Agreement Establishing the World Trade Organization, Annex 1C, Legal Instruments – Results of the Uruguay Round, 33 I.L.M. 1125 (1994).

85 *See, e.g.*, S. Ragavan, "Protection of Traditional Knowledge", 2 *Minn. Intell. Prop. Rev.* 1, 24 (2001); S. Subbiah, "Reaping What They Sow: The Basmati Rice Controversy and Strategies for Protecting Traditional Knowledge", 27 *B.C. Int'l & Comp. L. Rev.* 529 (2004); M. Sunder, "IP3", 59 *Stan. L. Rev.* 257, 297–303 (2006).

to anyone as a source for further creativity.[86] Paterson and Karjala suggest the following solution of the problem:

> Where privacy and confidentiality are legitimately present, there is nothing in the Western legal tradition antithetical to protection carefully tailored to these concerns. On the other hand, where knowledge of old works (i.e., those no longer protected by copyright) is publicly available, the creation of new exclusive rights somehow restricting the use of those designs, and all designs based on them, to a single group is fundamentally antithetical to basic notions of free expression and the overall dissemination and development of culture. At this point, [they] believe that indigenous cultural tradition must give way to the modern creative spirit.[87]

Another argument against any significant adjustments of intellectual property laws is that intellectual property rights are designed for the market. They create a monopoly intended to spur further creativity. In this way, investments are protected against reaping by others where they have not sown. But in many cases Indigenous, traditional and other local communities do not want to put their traditions on the market. They do not wish to grant access to non-members. They want to partially or completely exclude access to some forms of their cultural traditions.[88] This goes against the main spirit of intellectual property laws which are designed to spur innovation and a steady flow of new literary, artistic and scientific works, inventions and other intellectual creative endeavours to the public domain after their expiry.

Some scholars see adoption of liability rules as another way to accommodate the communities' claims to their intangible cultural heritage. These regimes allow all members of society, not only members of affected communities, to come and use communities' traditional knowledge and cultural expressions without considerable restriction. However, the payment of a fee, either a lump sum or a certain percentage from the turnover, to concerned communities is required. The regimes proposed by several scholars[89] and already adopted by some developing countries[90] differ. One commonality is a licence agreement, whether actually

86 *See* Paterson and Karjala, *supra* note 35, at 668 ("the scope of legislation or even an incrementally developed judicial definition of cultural heritage rights must involve a careful balance of the legitimate interests both of source communities in controlling their cultural heritage and society as whole in maintaining a rich and growing public domain that promotes basic values of free thought and expression in all individuals").

87 *Id.* at 670.

88 *See, e.g.*, Brown, *supra* note 34, at 30–31.

89 *See, e.g.*, Reichman and Lewis, *supra* note 10, at 354–66.

90 *See, e.g.*, *Updated Draft TCE Legal Mechanisms*, *supra* note 6, Annex, 21; E.R. Harvey, "The Domaine Public Payant in Comparative Law with Special Reference to Argentina", 28(4) *Copyright Bull.* 29 (1994); P. Kuruk, "Protecting Folklore under Modern Intellectual Property Regimes: A Reappraisal of the Tensions between Individual and Communal Rights in Africa and the United States", 48 *Am. U. L. Rev.* 769, 831 (1999).

concluded between the entrepreneurs, on one side, and communities or organizations representing their interests, on the other, or implied by statutes which allow the entrepreneurs to commercially exploit traditional knowledge or cultural expressions in exchange for contributing to a fund established for the promotion and benefits of Indigenous, traditional, local or other cultural communities. These regimes are administered by governmental agencies or non-governmental associations. However, such programs often suffer a general failure to accrue revenues sufficient to cover their high administrative expenses. Furthermore, they provide room for bribery and fraud. Despite their inherent flaws and shortcomings, the regimes based on the collective administration of the communal rights to intangible cultural heritage should not be *a priori* dismissed or rejected. Communities may gain significant benefits from the collected funds, which may be used for building necessary social infrastructure, such as hospitals, schools and the like.

Another imperfection in these regimes is that they are applicable only to certain forms of cultural traditions. They scale quite well in relation to traditional knowledge and cultural expressions, which are already available to the broader population or shared by more communities and groups. In such a case, they do not cause further degradation of social norms recognized by affected communities.

Regimes of this kind are inapplicable, however, to those parts of intangible cultural heritage which are habitually kept in secrecy and are not accessible to outsiders. Accessibility under such regimes often disregards social norms recognized and applied by communities which regulate access to and use of cultural traditions. Moreover, many argue protecting intangible cultural heritage through property or liability rules degrades its value and spirit.[91] Some cultural traditions supposedly originated from gods. Divine origin is the main reason for their preservation for future generations. Treating them as property is seen as eliminating their sanctity.

Building a welfare system to protect, preserve and safeguard cultural traditions in a living form is thus another solution. Preservation could occur directly through various preservation actions[92] or indirectly through educating and inducing the spirit of communal identity and integrity.[93] Funding could be private or public. Welfare programmes receive opposition and problems similar to those of regimes based on collective administration of the communal rights to intangible cultural heritage. Costs are high, especially administrative, and securing sufficient funds poses barriers. Furthermore, the spending of public funds habitually brings opportunism and provides a room for corruption. Finally, welfare systems may be considered by communities as outside elements, *e.g.* as an instrument of central

91 *See, e.g.*, Scafidi, *supra* note 75, at 828–31.
92 *See, e.g.*, ICH Convention, *supra* note 1, Article 11.
93 *See id.*, Article 14.

government or majority population for intrusion into its internal private matters. This can cause such regimes to lack the expressive and persuasive power that is vitally needed to enflame the communal spirit.

To sum up, each legal regime aiming at the protection, preservation or safeguarding of intangible cultural heritage has its pros and cons. Their benefits can be maximized and social cost minimized by an efficient combination of several regimes. During this endeavour, it should be kept in mind that openness, cross-cultural communication and respect for other cultures may play a crucial role for further re-creation of cultural traditions and for enrichment of cultural diversity. In this way, members of communities may comprehend the distinctiveness of their intangible cultural heritage from other communities. This can help deepen self-recognition and self-esteem. The more the members of particular communities realize the value of their unique cultures, the more they will return to their traditions, cultures and values. It may help not only to preserve intangible cultural heritage, but also to develop it further.

4. CONCLUSION

To answer the questions raised at the beginning, the definition of "holders" of intangible cultural heritage should not be intended to provide a one-size-fits-all model of protection, preservation and safeguarding cultural traditions in a living form. It is more fruitful to expand our search outward for an efficient combination of different ways and methods of their safeguarding which would maximize social benefits and would, at the same time, minimize social costs for communities, societies and entire humankind. Such multidimensional legal regimes can fit a range of individual communities and their particular stages of integration and cohesion.

For the adoption of such a legal framework, there is a basis in the form of two recent United Nations Educational, Scientific and Cultural Organization (UNESCO) conventions – the ICH Convention and the *Convention on the Protection and Promotion of the Diversity of Cultural Expressions*[94] – which may provide a sufficient framework for national regimes. Since several states already adopted their national regimes based either on communal property rights or on liability for misappropriation of intangible cultural heritage, it might be valuable to collect data on their implementation. Empirical data of this kind would be especially fruitful now because it is time to implement the two conventions and find a balanced and efficient combination of legal approaches to the protection, preservation and safeguarding of intangible cultural heritage, and thus to keep and induce cultural diversity on a local, national and worldwide level.

94 CD Convention, *supra* note 37.

PART FOUR
COMMUNITY'S PRIOR INFORMED CONSENT

PRIOR INFORMED CONSENT

Empowering the Bearers of Cultural Traditions

Joël-David DALIBARD and Toshiyuki KONO*

Determining how to effectively protect intangible cultural heritage involves the careful weighing of many different policy objectives. Among these competing considerations, two are particularly difficult to reconcile. They are the need to give holders of traditional knowledge and cultural expressions effective control over their know-how, while still creating a framework whereby this knowledge and expressions can be made available to the general population.

The previous Part of this volume explained one of the main obstacles to the delicate balance between accessibility and protection, namely, the difficulty in defining a "community" as a collective bearer of traditional knowledge and cultural expressions. The chapters that follow, by Graham Dutfield, Wim van Zanten and Ryu Kojima, continue to address the role of the community, but from a different angle. They consider whether the misappropriation of traditional knowledge or cultural expressions by outsiders can be prevented by requiring that the latter first obtain the "prior informed consent" of the relevant community.

The basic principle of prior informed consent is that outsiders should be required to properly explain their intentions before they can use the traditional know-how of a community. The latter is entitled to approve or deny the requested

* Joël-David R. Dalibard, LL.B.-B.C.L. (McGill), Barrister & Solicitor (Ontario, Canada), a Foreign Service Officer with the Canadian Department of Foreign Affairs and International Trade. Toshiyuki Kono is the Professor of Law, Kyushu University Faculty of Law. The views expressed in the text are the authors' own and do not reflect the positions of the Governments of Canada or Japan.

use. Such a system is intended to benefit both parties. It entitles communities to veto the misuse of their traditions, thereby placing them in a good bargaining position. If the intended application of the knowledge or cultural expression is commercial, a community can make its approval conditional upon receiving a share of any profits. Outsiders, on the other hand, benefit by having clear ethical guidelines for the proper steps to follow before making use of traditional knowledge or cultural expressions. They would have access to these cultural traditions as long as they could obtain the community's consent to their activities.

In the present essay, we try to clarify a few of the issues surrounding the concept of prior informed consent. We briefly consider its origins and relevance, before looking more closely at its meaning and some of the challenges surrounding its implementation. This analysis is facilitated by the fact that prior informed consent has already been invoked and used in several project where researchers sought to patent inventions based on traditional knowledge. Hopefully, this Chapter provides some context for the more focused analyses of Dutfield, van Zanten and Kojima.

1. ORIGINS AND RELEVANCE

The term "prior informed consent" appears to have been drawn from the medical field.[1] It refers to the practice of informing patients, particularly participants in clinical trials, of the risks that they will incur by agreeing to undergo a specific treatment. The intention is to emphasize the respect for human dignity, rather than follow purely practical considerations.[2] The movement to protect traditional knowledge and cultural expressions is based on a somewhat similar philosophy. Just as a patient's body should not be used for experiments without permission, a community's identity has an inviolable quality that takes priority over any practical or commercial benefits that might be derived from their exploitation. Respecting the integrity of traditional cultures is a way to show appreciation for the unique qualities and abilities of the societies that created them. The *Convention on Biological Diversity* (CBD)[3] was the first international document to reflect this

1 *See* Chapter [Kojima] of the present volume; L.A. Firestone, "You Say Yes, I Say No; Defining Community Prior Informed Consent under the Convention on Biological Diversity", 16 *Geo. Int'l Envtl. L. Rev.* 171, 181–83 (2003) (tracing the origins of prior informed consent also back to international agreements on hazardous substances).

2 *See* J.P. Rosenthal, "Politics, Culture, and Governance in the Development of Prior Informed Consent in Indigenous Communities", 47 *Current Anthropology* 119, 120 (2006); Chapter [Dutfield] of the present volume.

3 Convention on Biological Diversity, 5 June 1992, 31 I.L.M. 818, *available at* www.biodiv.org/convention/convention.shtml (last visited 31 July 2008) [hereinafter "CBD"].

attitude by suggesting the need to consult traditional communities about decisions affecting their lifestyle.

According to Article 8(j) of the CBD, the proper management of biodiversity requires the involvement of the "indigenous and local communities embodying traditional lifestyles relevant for the conservation and sustainable use of biological diversity".[4] The Convention also indicates that these communities should receive a share of the benefits derived from the use of their knowledge. While the term "prior informed consent" does not actually appear in Article 8(j)[5], the wording of the provision strongly suggests the need to empower Indigenous communities. Dutfield, in the next Chapter, explains the evolution that led from the vague terms of the CBD to the explicit mention of prior informed consent in such documents as the 2002 *Bonn Guidelines on Access to Genetic Resources and Fair and Equitable Sharing of the Benefits Arising out of their Utilization.*[6] Prior informed consent is now widely recognized as a relevant consideration when dealing with Indigenous communities and other holders of traditional knowledge and cultural expressions.[7]

---

4 Rosenthal, *supra* note 2, at 120.

5 The term "prior informed consent" does appear in CDB, *supra* note 3, Article 15.5, which gives the contracting parties control over their genetic resources.

6 Conference of the Parties to the Convention on Biological Diversity, *Bonn Guidelines on Access to Genetic Resources and Fair and Equitable Sharing of the Benefits Arising out of their Utilization,* Annex I, Decision VI/24/A at 262, UNEP/CBD/COP/6/20 (7–19 April 2002), *available at* www.cbd.int/doc/decisions/COP-06-dec-en.pdf (last visited 31 July 2008). *See also* Chapter [Dutfield] of the present volume.

7 *See, e.g.,* Biodiversity Law, sec. 63(1), Law No. 7788 (1998) (Costa Rica), *available at* www.grain.org/brl/?docid=475&lawid=1859 (last visited 31 July 2008) [hereinafter "Costa Rican Law"]; Indigenous Peoples Rights Act, sec. 3(g), Republic Act No. 8371 (1997) (Philippines), *available at* www.grain.org/brl/?docid=801&lawid=1508 (last visited 31 July 2008) [hereinafter "Philippines Law"]; Law Introducing a Protection Regime for the Collective Knowledge of Indigenous Peoples Derived from Biological Resources, sec. 6, Law No. 27811 (2002) (Peru), *available at* www.grain.org/brl/?docid=81&lawid=2041 (last visited 31 July 2008) [hereinafter "Peruvian Law"]. *See also* African Model Legislation for the Protection of the Rights of Local Communities, Farmers and Breeders, and for the Regulation of Access to Biological Resources, Article 18 (adopted by the Organisation of African Unity during 2000 in Algeria), *available at* www.grain.org/brl/?docid=798&lawid=2132 (last visited 31 July 2008) [hereinafter "African Model Legislation"]; Common Regime on Access to Genetic Resources, Article 7, 2 July 1996, Decision 391 (Andean Community), *available at* www.sice.oas.org/trade/JUNAC/decisiones/DEC391e.asp (last visited 31 July 2008) [hereinafter "Andean Decision 391"]; Association of South East Asian Nations, *ASEAN Framework Agreement on Access to Biological and Genetic Resources* (draft, 2000), Article 10, *available at* www.grain.org/brl/?docid=785&lawid=1261 (last visited 31 July 2008) [hereinafter "ASEAN Framework"]; *Free Trade Agreement of the Americas* (draft, 2003), ch. XX, subsec. B.2.f., Article 2.1, *available at* www.grain.org/brl/?docid=868&lawid=1924 (last visited 31 July 2008) [hereinafter "FTAA"]; Pacific Forum, *Model Law for the Protection of Traditional Ecological Knowledge, Innovations and Practices* (draft, 2001), Article 10, *available at* www.grain.org/brl/?docid=698&lawid=1430 (last visited 31 July 2008) [hereinafter "Pacific Forum Model Law"].

It has been discussed in many international forums, such as the World Intellectual Property Organization (WIPO) and the World Trade Organization (WTO).[8]

As a result of its origins in the CBD, the application of prior informed consent has often been limited to very specific forms of traditional knowledge tied to the protection of biodiversity. Community approval is necessary when, for example, modern researchers want to study the use of a medicinal plant or the cultivation of a particular crop by an Indigenous group. The requirement of prior informed consent is intended to promote "ethical bioprospecting"[9] as opposed to "biopiracy".[10] The latter term encompasses the misappropriation of traditional ecological knowledge, usually by corporate entities, for the purpose of creating new patents.

The fight against biopiracy is, of course, an important aspect of efforts to protect the intangible cultural heritage of traditional groups. In the present volume, however, the applicability of prior informed consent goes far beyond biodiversity. It extends to all aspects of traditional knowledge and cultural expressions that can be misappropriated, including its many artistic manifestations. Indeed, Indigenous creations in such fields as paintings[11], music and clothing have occasionally become very popular with the broader public and have been exploited commercially without proper community authorization and benefit-sharing. The chapter by van Zanten illustrates the diversity of situations where it might be useful to require prior informed consent before granting access to traditional cultural expressions.[12] His description of the ethical dilemmas he faced while recording Indigenous songs and stories in Indonesia demonstrates that consent can be an issue even in a context that is seemingly harmless, such as the collection of data for academic purposes.

---

8 *See* Chapter [Dutfield] of the present volume. *See also, e.g.*, World Intellectual Property Organization (WIPO), *Intellectual Property Needs and Expectations of Traditional Knowledge Holders: WIPO Report on Fact-Finding Missions on Intellectual Property and Traditional Knowledge (1998–1999)* (April 2001), *available at* www.wipo.int/tk/en/tk/ffm/report/index.html (last visited 31 July 2008); World Trade Organization (WTO), Council for Trade-Related Aspects of Intellectual Property Rights, *The Relationship between the TRIPS Agreement and the Convention on Biological Diversity (CBD) and the Protection of Traditional Knowledge-Elements of the Obligation to Disclose Evidence of Prior Informed Consent under the Relevant National Regime*, IP/C/W/438 (10 December 2004) (submission from Bolivia, Brazil, Cuba, Ecuador, India, Pakistan, Peru, Thailand and Venezuela); WTO, Council for Trade-Related Aspects of Intellectual Property Rights, *The Relationship between the TRIPS Agreement and the Convention on Biological Diversity: Summary of Issues Raised and Points Made*, IP/C/W/368/Rev.1 (8 February 2006) (*prepared by* the WTO Secretariat), *available at* www.wto.org/english/tratop_e/trips_e/ipcw368_e.doc (last visited 31 July 2008).

9 Rosenthal, *supra* note 2, at 120.

10 Chapter [Dutfield] of the present volume (defining the term "biopiracy").

11 *See* Chapter [Janke] of the present volume (discussing the *Bulun Bulun* case). *See also* M.F. Brown, *Who Owns Native Culture?*, 2003, 48–54.

12 *See* Chapter [van Zanten] of the present volume.

Van Zanten mentions the unintended consequences resulting from the efforts of ethnomusicologist Hugo Zemp to document the music of the Solomon Islands natives.[13] Their tunes were recorded as part of a research project. Without permission from either the natives or Zemp, some of this music was used by a French artist in a CD entitled *Deep Forest*. It would seem that none of the benefits from the sale of the CD ever reached the Solomon Islands.[14] This situation might have been avoided had the composer of *Deep Forest* been obligated to consult with the native population. It seems that a requirement of prior informed consent could have provided a clear standard for determining whether a non-member was entitled to use the community's traditional knowledge or cultural expressions.

2. WHAT CONSTITUTES PRIOR INFORMED CONSENT?

In order to properly appreciate whether a requirement of prior informed consent can effectively enhance the protection of traditional knowledge and cultural expressions, it is important to understand how to measure this consent. In the following paragraphs we attempt to briefly enumerate the criteria that must be satisfied before an outsider can claim to have obtained a community's prior informed consent. These requirements are grouped into three categories.

First, it is essential that there be a free and frank dissemination of information between outsiders and the community. The former must explain the origins, intended mode of operation and likely consequences, including benefits and drawbacks, of any project involving traditional knowledge or cultural expressions.[15] New details should be shared with the community as they emerge. The exchange of information is therefore not a one-time obligation, but rather part of an extended process stretching over the whole duration of a project.[16] It is also necessary to ensure that the community is aware of all the alternatives courses of action that are available to it, both on an operational and a legal level.[17] Outsiders should not seek to manipulate the community by providing incomplete data. Naturally, all this information must be communicated in a manner that is

---

13 *Id.*

14 *See* Brown, *supra* note 11, at 62.

15 *See* Firestone, *supra* note 1, at 186–92, 195–97; A. Perrault, K. Herbertson and O. Lynch, "Partnerships for Success in Protected Areas: The Public Interest and Local Community and Rights to Prior Informed Consent", 19 *Geo. Int'l Envtl. L. Rev.* 475, 522 (2007); M. Hassemer, "Genetic Resources", in S. von Lewinski (ed.), *Indigenous Heritage and Intellectual Property: Genetic Resources, Traditional Knowledge and Folklore*, 2004, 151, 179.

16 *See* Firestone, *supra* note 1, at 190; Perrault, Herbertson and Lynch, *supra* note 15, at 522.

17 *See* Firestone, *supra* note 1, at 190–91; Perrault, Herbertson and Lynch, *supra* note 15, at 522.

intelligible to community members at large.[18] In some cases, all that will be required is the translation of documents. In others, it will be necessary to develop much more creative ways of communicating.[19] The terms of an agreement might involve very complex scientific and legal notions, but they must nonetheless be conveyed with sufficient clarity. In short, every effort must be made to ensure that consent can truly be described as "informed".

The second broad criterion for ensuring prior informed consent is related to the decision-making process of the community. One of the most basic principles in this regard is that the decision to consent must be taken according to a procedure that is recognized by community members.[20] Several international documents and national laws have noted the importance of letting Indigenous groups follow their customary practices when deciding whether to share their traditional knowledge or cultural expressions.[21] Obviously, outside interference could compromise the validity of any decision and must be avoided.[22] In this regard, it is important to remember that consent must come "prior" to any outside use of cultural traditions.[23] It would be inappropriate to put community members before an ultimatum or a *fait accompli*.

The final requirement is an implicit one because it is not referred to in the term "prior informed consent". It is the obligation to ensure adequate benefit-sharing between the community and any outsiders authorised to make use of the traditional knowledge or cultural expressions.[24] There is no universal standard as to what constitutes acceptable compensation[25], but it is reasonable to expect that the bearers of cultural traditions will receive some form of advantage when they agree to share their secrets. Provisions to this effect appear in almost all laws and international agreements dealing with prior informed consent.[26] Furthermore, if

---

18 *See* Firestone, *supra* note 1, at 192–94; Hassemer, *supra* note 15, at 179.

19 *See, e.g.*, *infra* Section 3 (describing the Mayan project).

20 *See* Firestone, *supra* note 1, at 194–95; Perrault, Herbertson and Lynch, *supra* note 15, at 522.

21 *See, e.g.*, African Model Legislation, *supra* note 7, Article 21; ASEAN Framework, *supra* note 7, Article 10; Philippines Law, *supra* note 7, sec. 3(g).

22 *See* Perrault, Herbertson and Lynch, *supra* note 15, at 521–22.

23 *See id.* at 521–22; Firestone, *supra* note 1, at 200–1.

24 *See* Firestone, *supra* note 1, at 189–190.

25 Some texts do provide for specific percentages that must be remitted to Indigenous communities. For instance, African Model Legislation, *supra* note 7, Article 22, provides as follows:

> 1) The State shall ensure that at least fifty per cent of benefits provided for in Article 12.2 shall be channelled to the concerned local community or communities in a manner which treats men and women equitably.
> 2) The sharing the benefits in paragraph 1) above shall involve the full participation and approval of the concerned local community or communities.

26 *See, e.g.*, Provisional Measure on Access to Genetic Resources and Traditional Knowledge, sec. 24–25, 23 August 2001, Provisional Measure No. 2.186–16 (Brazil), *available at* www.grain.

the knowledge or cultural expressions are being used for a research project, there is an assumption that the results of any studies will be made available to the community.[27] While the details of specific arrangements are up to the parties involved, it is important to remember that one of the fundamental purposes of prior informed consent is to prevent the exploitation of traditional communities.

Prior informed consent sets a very high standard in order to provide strong protection. Theoretically, it should empower communities in such a way that they will be able to prevent the misuse of their intangible cultural heritage. Implementing the above requirements should also improve their living conditions by letting them enjoy the commercial benefits that can be derived from their traditional knowledge. The question, however, is whether prior informed consent is effective in practice.

3. THE CHALLENGE OF DECISION-MAKING: WHO GRANTS PRIOR INFORMED CONSENT?

Past experiences and scholarly analysis have revealed a number of obstacles that can hamper efforts to obtain prior informed consent. Even the best-intentioned research projects face considerable difficulties. The biggest potential impediment is perhaps the fact that it is not always clear who has the authority to grant access to traditional knowledge or cultural expressions. As was discussed earlier in this volume, it can be very difficult to define the limits, membership and rights of a traditional community.[28] Even if the community has a clear identity, its leadership structure may be hard to identify. This is particularly true in the case of Indigenous and traditional communities.

Indigenous and traditional groups do not necessarily have the same clearly defined hierarchical system as modern states. Power may be dispersed among the members or various subgroups. In the following chapter, Dutfield describes the complicated situation that arose in Peru when a joint American-Peruvian research team sough to negotiate a deal with the Aguaruna people in order to study plants used in their traditional medicine.[29] One of the major problems that the project faced was identifying an organization that could effectively speak for the entire

org/brl/?docid=850&lawid=1768 (last visited 31 July 2008); Costa Rican Law, *supra* note 7, Article 10(4); Peruvian Law, *supra* note 7, sec. 7; African Model Legislation, *supra* note 7, Articles 12(2) and 22; Andean Decision 391, *supra* note 7, Article 2(a); ASEAN Framework, *supra* note 7, Article 11; FTAA, *supra* note 7, ch. XX, subsec. B.2.f., Article 2.2; Pacific Forum Model Law, *supra* note 7, Article 10.

27 Firestone, *supra* note 1, at 190, 196.

28 *See* Part on "Conceptualization of Community", earlier in the present volume.

29 *See* Chapter [Dutfield] of the present volume; Rosenthal, *supra* note 2, at 122–123; Brown, *supra* note 11, at 112–114.

Aguaruna community. Negotiations with one body failed, but researchers finally reached a deal with a rival group. This provoked a bitter dispute between the two organizations, both of which claimed to better represent the Aguarunas.[30] In the end, the project went ahead, but it excluded those community members who did not belong to the group that had reached an agreement with the research team.

In spite of the bickering that characterized the research on the Aguarunas, at least it was able to go ahead. A similar project to collect data on medicinal plants used by the Highland Mayas of the Chiapas region in Southern Mexico ended in complete failure. The scheme was organized by Brent Berlin, an anthropologist who had considerable experience working with the Mayas. He was backed by two academic institutions, the University of Georgia and El Colegio de la Frontera Sur (ECOSUR), as well as one corporate entity, Molecular Nature Ltd. As with the aforementioned research on the Aguarunas, funding for the project was provided under a United States government program called International Cooperative Biodiversity Groups.[31]

The organizers of the project went to great lengths to obtain prior informed consent and to design an adequate benefit-sharing mechanism. As Micheal F. Brown explains:

> [E]fforts included translation of background material into the Tzeltal and Tzotzil languages and even the scripting of a play that explained issues of intellectual property and biodiversity in terms local farmers could understand. Twelve percent of the project budget would go to salaries for two dozen Maya field assistants, most of whom the project had already trained in "linguistic transcription of their own languages, field botanical survey techniques, computer literacy, laboratory techniques, plant propagation, marketing, and intellectual property rights issues." The project committed itself to finding practical uses for Maya knowledge that could be put to work immediately to benefit Indian participants ... Finally, the project specified that Maya communities would receive one-quarter of any royalties that emerged from the research. This put the Maya on an even financial footing with the project's three institutional partners ... The Maya share was to be paid to a non-profit organization called PROMAYA. Even communities that refused to collaborate with the project were to be eligible for PROMAYA funds.[32]

In the context of this elaborate preparation, it appears that PROMAYA may have been the weakest link. It was meant to fulfil the role of a representative body

30 *See* Rosenthal, *supra* note 2, at 123.

31 For information on the International Cooperative Biodiversity Groups (ICBG) program, *see* U.S. National Institutes of Health, J.E. Fogarty International Center, *International Cooperative Biodiversity Groups (ICBG)*, www.fic.nih.gov/programs/research_grants/icbg/index.htm (last visited 31 July 2008). *See also* Rosenthal, *supra* note 2, at 119; Brown, *supra* note 11, at 109–110.

32 Brown, *supra* note 11, at 119–120. *See also* Rosenthal, *supra* note 2, at 123–124.

expressing the will of the Mayan community. PROMAYA, however, did not exist prior to the beginning of the project. Mayan society in Chiapas lacked a clear leadership structure[33], in part because the region has been mired in civil war since 1994.[34] The organizers of the research project founded PROMAYA themselves, apparently in order to create a Mayan interlocutor where none existed. On this subject, Berlin himself writes:

> In our original proposal, we outlined a viable solution to the lack of an institutionalized Highland Maya political structure beyond traditional community-level governing bodies – the establishment of PROMAYA. As a civil organization under Mexican law PROMAYA, made up of elected indigenous representatives from the original 46 communities plus any others that joined later, would have had full legal status in all commercial negotiations and management of any future income through a trust fund.[35]

PROMAYA never really caught on with the Indigenous community. This failure to establish itself as a strong representative institution had significant implications for the research project. Indeed, two other organizations, opposed to the project, managed to convince public opinion that they were the true defenders of the interests of the Mayas. The first was an association of practitioners of traditional medicine, the Consejo de Médicos y Parteras Indígenas Tradicionales de Chiapas (Consejo). The other was a Canadian non-governmental organization, the Rural Advancement Foundation International (RAFI). The latter launched a publicity campaign that successfully undermined the credibility of Berlin's project, largely by arguing that the consultations with the Mayas had been inadequate. RAFI claimed that consent to the use of Mayan traditional knowledge would be invalid unless all Mayan communities had been consulted. The public controversy following Consejo and RAFI's denunciations eventually led the Mexican government and ECOSUR to withdraw their support from the project, causing its collapse.[36]

There is considerable irony in the failure of the Mayan project. When one compares the list of requirements for prior informed consent with the measures that were actually taken by the project's organizers, it would seem that they made very significant efforts to fulfil their obligations. Commentators have questioned both the reasoning as well as the legitimacy of Consejo and RAFI in this affair.[37]

---

33 *See* Rosenthal, *supra* note 2, at 123.

34 *See* Brown, *supra* note 11, at 115–119.

35 *See* B. Berlin and E.A. Berlin, "Comment", 47 *Current Anthropology* 129 (2006).

36 For details on these events, *see* Rosenthal, *supra* note 2, at 124; Brown, *supra* note 11, at 120–125.

37 *See* Brown, *supra* note 11, at 122–25; Rosenthal, *supra* note 2, at 124; Berlin and Berlin, *supra* note 35, at 130; E.S. Hunn, "Comment", 47 *Current Anthropology* 133–34 (2006).

These two organizations could hardly claim to be representative of the Mayan population. Furthermore, it is difficult to accept RAFI's allegation that consultations were woefully insufficient. It is hard to imagine how one could realistically have expected Berlin and his colleagues to obtain the consent of all two millions Mayas living in Mexico and Guatemala.[38] The standard that RAFI required for prior informed consent seems to have been deliberately set at an impossibly high level. Indeed, in a document released during the dispute over the Mayan project, RAFI stated that it "regards all bioprospecting agreements to be biopiracy."[39] It seems the non-governmental organization considered that no degree of sensitivity to Mayan needs could make Berlin's project ethical.

RAFI's obstructionism notwithstanding, Joshua P. Rosenthal argues that the fundamental reason behind the failure of the project was the absence of a clear leadership structure among the Mayas.[40] If there had been a body capable of speaking in their name, it could have granted the necessary prior informed consent and would have had the legitimacy to deny allegations of biopiracy. In order to avoid the collapse of future projects such as the one with the Mayas, Rosenthal suggests that financially motivated research involving traditional knowledge should never be undertaken in collaboration with communities that do not have a Western-style governance system.[41]

Rosenthal probably goes too far in singling out Western governance as the prerequisite for effective negotiations on the use of community traditional knowledge and cultural expressions by outsiders.[42] He does, however, make a valid point when he underlines the difficulty of obtaining adequate prior informed consent from a community that lacks some form of centralized authority. This was apparently what happened with the Mayas. Even with the Aguarunas in Peru, where governance structures did exist, the outcome could hardly be termed satisfactory. The competition between the two representative bodies of the Aguarunas created a rift within the tribe. This precedent makes it clear that outsiders cannot artificially rearrange a community's governance simply to suit their needs. To do so would be completely inconsistent with the philosophy that inspired prior informed consent in the first place. If there is to be any reform of

---

38 Population figures taken from ROSENTHAL, *supra* note 2, at 124.

39 *See* RURAL ADVANCEMENT FOUNDATION INTERNATIONAL (RAFI), *Messages from the Chiapas "Bioprospecting" Dispute: An Analysis of Recent Issues Raised in the Chiapas "Bioprospecting" Controversy with Reflections on the Message for BioPiracy*, at 2 (22 December 1999), *available at* www.etcgroup.org/upload/publication/pdf_file/344 (last visited 31 July 2008).

40 *See* ROSENTHAL, *supra* note 2, at 125–26.

41 *Id.* at 126–27.

42 For critical responses, *see* "Comments", 47 *Current Anthropology* 128–137 (2006). It is quite difficult to know it advance whether a project will lead to a commercial product; *see* P.A. MARSHALL, "Comment", 47 *Current Anthropology* 134, 135 (2006); Chapter [VAN ZANTEN] of the present volume (presenting several cases from ethnomusicology field).

community governance, it must be guided by the needs and culture of the members.

Fostering new governance structures in a non-intrusive way is a long term undertaking that falls beyond the scope of most research projects involving traditional knowledge and cultural expressions. The creation of PROMAYA could be described as an attempt at such a reform, but ended in failure. Perhaps more time and better circumstances might have allowed this organization to gain legitimacy and become a proper advocate for community members. It might also have helped if state institutions in Mexico had done more to favour governance among the Mayas in the first place.

States have an important role to play in the protection of the traditional knowledge and cultural expressions of communities living on their territory. If governments do not require prior informed consent within their legal system, the concept will have little force. Communities by themselves are not equipped to penalize those who misuse their cultural traditions. Furthermore, any state that endorses prior informed consent should assist traditional groups in developing decision-making procedures. In this regard, Laurel A. Firestone writes:

> Arguably, governments have a duty under Article 8(j) of the CBD to develop the capacities of indigenous and local communities to play equal roles in any decision-making process regarding traditional knowledge. Capacity building programs could include the provision of "legal and scientific advice [or] the help of a linguist and/or anthropologist, in order to accurately assess: (a) How their traditional knowledge is to be used (practical use, publication); (b) The implications of such use; (c) What conditions they should attach to its use (secret/sacred knowledge); (d) The most suitable means to protect their traditional knowledge (e.g., legal contract, mou [memorandum of understanding]); and (e) How they can benefit from its application." More generally, capacity programs could focus on building the skills necessary within communities to conduct inventories of genetic resources or traditional knowledge, negotiate contracts, draft legal documents, and navigate through relevant intellectual property systems. Again, non-governmental organizations should be encouraged to serve this role as well.[43]

Naturally, the lack of a clear leadership structure is not the only obstacle that may impede the use of prior informed consent. We have already alluded to the logistical challenges involved. In the case of the Mayas, obtaining consent from the entire community rather than just the members living in Chiapas would have meant consulting a large number of people spread over extremely remote regions in two different countries. Similar logistical obstacles are likely to emerge in many future

43 Firestone, *supra* note 1, at 204 (quoting from the Convention on Biological Diversity Working Group on Article 8(j), *Meeting Docs: Participatory Mechanisms for Indigenous and Local Communities,* P11 UNEP/CBD WG8J/2/4 (2001)) (footnotes omitted).

cases. Traditional lifestyles are mostly found off the beaten track. Also, it is important not to forget the many difficulties that can arise when trying to effectively explain to traditional groups the implications of consenting to the use of their knowledge. Because of the differences in lifestyle and culture, there is considerable scope for misunderstandings. For example, van Zanten mentions the fact that Indigenous communities often have exaggerated expectations with regard to the royalties they are likely to receive.[44] Finally, one must not forget that a particular tradition is not necessarily limited to a single community. It may belong to two or more groups who share the same knowledge. In such a situation, it would be necessary to determine whether the approval of one community is sufficient, or if it is necessary to appeal to each group separately.

The difficulties surrounding community governance reveal a fundamental weakness in the concept of prior informed consent. Indeed, the latter is premised on the assumption that a community's intentions can somehow be ascertained. If this is not the case, then prior informed consent becomes impossible to implement.

4. A PATH WORTH FOLLOWING?

In light of what we have just said, it is tempting to conclude on a low note by dismissing prior informed consent as impractical. This is in fact the conclusion that has been reached by certain experts. Klaus Hoeyer, in his response to Rosenthal's analysis of the governance issues in the Aguaruna and Mayan projects, suggests that prior informed consent is a theoretical dead-end:

> As I read Rosenthal's two case studies, I am convinced by his assertion that it is a "critical question" to figure out how to "maximize the benefits to indigenous societies" in this type of research collaboration, but I have found nothing to support his claim that prior informed consent "is a fundamental part of the answer to this question." In fact, it remains a puzzle why a study of a "sophisticated" but *failed* consent process should make us want to put more emphasis on it, not least considering that it is expensive and fits only the project cycles of funding agencies. Is prior informed consent simply becoming a new mantra, replacing other organizational recipes such as participatory rural appraisal? Has the need for a "solution", an *answer*, limited the opportunity for critical judgement?[45]

Hoeyer's words clearly underline the weaknesses revealed by prior informed consent's ambivalent results. It is far from being an ideal solution. Nonetheless, it

44 *See* Chapter [van Zanten] of the present volume.
45 K. Hoeyer, "Comment", 47 *Current Anthropology* 132, 133 (2006).

has received widespread recognition as a method for allowing traditional communities to control access to their intangible heritage. At least on a symbolic level, the fact that it appears in numerous laws and international documents represents a growing consensus in favour of the recognition of the rights of communities with regard to their traditional knowledge and cultural expressions. Furthermore, for those communities that do have the necessary governance structures to reach a decision, prior informed consent appears to be a very useful standard.[46] It is certainly a considerable improvement over the previous practice of simply leaving intangible cultural heritage to the public domain and not even considering benefit-sharing with traditional communities.

46 *See, e.g.*, BROWN, *supra* note 11, at 132.

PRIOR INFORMED CONSENT AND TRADITIONAL KNOWLEDGE IN A MULTICULTURAL WORLD

Graham DUTFIELD*

The best laid schemes o' Mice an' Men,
Gang aft agley,
An' lea'e us nought but grief an' pain,
For promis'd joy!
"To a Mouse" – Robert Burns, 1785

1. INTRODUCTION

This Chapter explores the prior informed consent concept as applied to the knowledge and biological resources of indigenous peoples. The discussion is confined mainly to such transactions involving, on one side, people to whom

* Professor of International Governance, University of Leeds.

International Labour Organization Convention 169[1] applies, namely "indigenous and tribal peoples in independent countries"[2], and on the other, commercial, governmental and scientific entities. Accordingly, we cover prior informed consent in the context of consent being sought from members of groups very different from the seekers in terms of culture, worldview, expertise and power.

It is not self-evident that a concept originating in modern healthcare situations should have any relevance to the search for fairer ways to trade in traditional knowledge and associated biological resources. Nonetheless, many people have come to believe strongly that it does. What are the concerns that led to the promotion of prior informed consent as a means of ensuring fairness in transactions involving traditional knowledge and biological resources found in developing countries, including those known about, used, and in many cases managed and improved, by indigenous peoples? And how have such concerns translated into law and policy? As this Chapter explains, these concerns all tend to be regarded as aspects of "biopiracy", a popular catchall phrase that has focused attention on perceived inequities in the ways that the benefits of biodiversity-based commerce are distributed. As to the development of responsive law and policy, this Chapter shows that prior informed consent tends, as a consequence of seeing the problem through the "lens" of biopiracy, to be linked to proposals to reform patent law in ways that are meant to make the patent system more transparent and fair. The benefits for indigenous peoples of this approach are far from clear. Having said that, this need not be a cause for concern if prior informed consent for indigenous peoples continues to be seen as a fundamental right to which they are entitled, and not an issue to be pursued exclusively in the context of patent reform.

It is of course one thing to demand that prior informed consent be central to the achievement of equitable relationships between business, government and universities on the one side and indigenous peoples on the other; it is quite another to put such a demand into practice. In fact, prior informed consent advocates

---

1 Convention (No. 169) concerning Indigenous and Tribal Peoples in Independent Countries, 27 June 1989, 28 I.L.M. 1382, *available at* www.ilo.org/ilolex/cgi-lex/convde.pl?C169 (last visited 31 July 2008) [hereinafter "ILO Convention 169"].

2 ILO Convention 169, *supra* note 1, Article 1, defines them in the following way:

> This Convention applies to:
> (a) tribal peoples in independent countries whose social, cultural and economic conditions distinguish them from other sections of the national community, and whose status is regulated wholly or partially by their own customs or traditions or by special laws or regulations;
> (b) peoples in independent countries who are regarded as indigenous on account of their descent from the populations which inhabited the country, or a geographical region to which the country belongs, at the time of conquest or colonisation or the establishment of present state boundaries and who, irrespective of their legal status, retain some or all of their own social, economic, cultural and political institutions.

appear often to have little understanding of how to implement it or even of what it actually means.

In order to assist the process of effective prior informed consent implementation, this Chapter assesses the meaning, origins and uses of prior informed consent, and the assumptions underlying its application to traditional knowledge and biological resource transactions. Basically, the key assumption is that communities, or groupings of communities, are bounded political entities with systems of governance that allow for direct and definitive negotiating and deal-making between indigenous groups and bioprospectors. The Chapter also faces up to the complexities that need to be overcome before prior informed consent can become a workable policy tool in the present context. Using a case study approach, the Chapter shows why applying prior informed consent requirements in very diverse and extremely different cultural settings, and in very tense political contexts, can be immensely challenging. Even with the best intentions and the most carefully drawn up plans, things go wrong, and misunderstanding, confusion, inappropriate exclusion, disappointment, resentment and even internal conflict can ensue.

The Chapter also shows that as a consequence of the manifold and complicated linkages between drug discovery and marketing, the prior informed consent concept may do little to resolve biopiracy in its broadest sense. This is not to suggest that prior informed consent is not a useful concept. In my view, indigenous peoples have a right to expect that bioprospectors will formally request their prior informed consent. However, prior informed consent is not a substitute for respect of their basic human rights as individuals and as peoples. Prior informed consent should be seen as a necessary but not sufficient requirement for the establishment of more equitable bioprospecting arrangements; but only if it is acquired according to procedures that are effective, culturally appropriate, transparent and flexible.

2. "BIOPIRACY"

The vast majority of countries formally recognize that cross-border exchange of genetic resources and traditional knowledge must be carried out in compliance with the principles of the *Convention on Biological Diversity* (CBD).[3] For a number of reasons, intellectual property rights, particularly patents but also plant variety protection, have become central to discussions on this matter. The reasons for the centrality of intellectual property rights relate to the following:

---

3 Convention on Biological Diversity, 5 June 1992, 31 I.L.M. 818, *available at* www.biodiv.org/convention/convention.shtml (last visited 31 July 2008) [hereinafter "CBD"].

1. The conviction – widely held among developing countries and non-governmental organizations (NGOs) – that biodiversity and associated traditional knowledge have tremendous economic potential;
2. The fact that patent claims in various countries may incorporate biological and genetic material including life forms within their scope;
3. The belief, also shared by developing countries and NGOs, that this feature of the patent system enables corporations to misappropriate genetic resources and associated traditional knowledge, or at least to unfairly free-ride on them;[4]
4. The ability of modern intellectual property law to protect innovations produced by industries based mainly in the developed world, and its *in*ability to protect adequately those innovations in which developing countries are relatively well-endowed;
5. The perception that as a consequence of reasons 2–4, the unequal distributions and concentrations of patent ownership and the unequal share of benefits obtained from industrial use of biogenetic resources are closely related.

"Biopiracy" has emerged as a term to describe the ways that corporations from the developed world free ride on the genetic resources and traditional knowledge and technologies of developing countries. While corporations complain about "intellectual piracy" in developing countries, the latter group of nations counters that their biological, scientific and cultural assets are being "pirated" by these same businesses. Intellectual piracy is a political term, and as such is inaccurate and deliberately so. The assumption behind it is that the copying and selling of pharmaceuticals, music compact discs (CDs) and films anywhere in the world is intellectual piracy irrespective of whether the works in question had patent or copyright protection under the domestic laws. After all, if drugs cannot be patented in a certain country, copying them by local companies for the domestic market, or overseas markets where the drugs in question are also not patented, is hardly piracy in the legal sense of the word.

Similarly, biopiracy is an imprecise term, and there are good reasons to keep it so, at least in the international arena. But such "strategic vagueness" is not a helpful approach for those working on legal solutions in such forms as national laws, regulations or international conventions.

Let us start by elucidating, as far as we can, the actual meaning of the word. To start with the obvious, "biopiracy" is a compound word consisting of "bio", which is an abbreviation for "biological", and "piracy". According to the *Concise Oxford*

---

4 The distinction I seek to draw between misappropriation and unfair free-riding is that with misappropriation, there must be victims as well as beneficiaries for the word to apply. However free-riding is not necessarily harmful to anybody, and there is likely to be considerable disagreement about where to draw the line between fair and unfair free-riding.

Dictionary[5], "piracy" means the following: (1) the practice or an act of robbery of ships at sea; (2) a similar practice or act in other forms, especially hijacking; and (3) the infringement of copyright.

Apart from the use of "piracy" for rhetorical effect, the word does not seem to be applicable to the kinds of acts referred to as biopiracy. But let us now turn to the verb "to pirate". The two definitions given are: (1) appropriate or reproduce (the work or ideas *etc.* of another) without permission for one's own benefit; and (2) plunder.

These definitions seem to be more appropriate since inherent to the biopiracy rhetoric are misappropriation and theft. In essence, "biopirates" are those individuals and companies accused of one or both of the following acts: (i) the misappropriation of genetic resources or traditional knowledge through the patent system; and (ii) the unauthorized collection for commercial ends of genetic resources or traditional knowledge. But since biopiracy is not just a matter of law, but also of morality and fairness, we need to acknowledge that the line between an act of biopiracy and a legitimate practice may not always be easy to draw. The difficulty in drawing the line is compounded by the vagueness in the way the term is applied.

To illustrate this point, a wide range of acts listed below have been considered acts of biopiracy of traditional knowledge.

Collection and use:
- The unauthorized use of common traditional knowledge;
- The unauthorized use of traditional knowledge only found among one indigenous group;
- The unauthorized use of traditional knowledge acquired by deception or failure to fully disclosure the commercial motive behind the acquisition;
- The unauthorized use of traditional knowledge acquired on the basis of a transaction deemed to be exploitative;
- The unauthorized use of traditional knowledge acquired on the basis of a conviction that all such transactions are inherently exploitative ("all bioprospecting is biopiracy");
- The commercial use of traditional knowledge on the basis of a literature search.

Patenting:
- The patent claims traditional knowledge in the form in which it was acquired;
- The patent covers a refinement of the traditional knowledge;
- Patent covers an invention based on traditional knowledge *and* other modern or traditional knowledge.

5 J. Pearsall (ed.), *The Concise Oxford Dictionary* (10th rev. ed.), 2001.

It is by no means clear how much biopiracy actually goes on. Apart from lack of information, the answer depends on how one differentiates between legitimate and unfair exploitation. The distinction is not always obvious. The answer also depends on whether resources are considered to be wild and unowned or domesticated and owned. A common view among critics of conventional business practice is that most companies do not recognize that they may have a moral obligation to compensate communities providing genetic material for their intellectual contribution, *even when* such material is assumed to be "wild". Often genetic resources considered "gifts of nature" are in fact the results of many generations of selective crop breeding and landscape management. Essentially the argument is that failing to recognize and compensate for the past and present intellectual contributions of traditional communities is a form of intellectual piracy.

The likely response from industry is that this is not piracy since the present generation may have done little to develop or conserve these resources. The argument might continue that this is, at worst, a policy failure, and that measures outside the intellectual property rights system could be put into place to ensure that traditional communities are rewarded.

As for the patent-related version of "biopiracy", there is little doubt that companies are in an advantageous position in the sense that, while a useful characteristic of a plant or animal may be well-known to a traditional community, the community cannot obtain a patent even if it could afford to do so or could describe the phenomenon in the language of chemistry or molecular biology.[6] While it is unlikely that a company could then obtain a patent simply by describing the mode of action or the active compound[7], it could claim a synthetic version of the compound or even a purified extract. In the absence of a contract or specific regulation, the company would have no requirement to compensate the communities concerned.

It is important to understand that the emergence of the prior informed consent concept is tightly linked to the emergence of the biopiracy concept and the concerns behind biopiracy. Without biopiracy concerns, we would not be talking about prior informed consent, whether of developing country governments or of indigenous peoples. But if biopiracy is such a vague and elastic notion, how can prior informed consent do anything about it? That is a question that has not yet been answered. Arguably this is because very few people have even thought to pose the question in the first place!

---

6 It may be able to if it can describe a specific formulation, even in fairly non-technical terms.

7 In some circumstances this may be allowable under the U.S. patent system.

3. THE CONCEPT OF PRIOR INFORMED CONSENT

As is well known, informed consent has its origins in medical practice. Anybody undergoing medical treatment in a hospital, especially surgery, is likely to be requested to sign a consent form. Thus, prior informed consent in its original context concerns information exchange between *individuals*. Informed consent turned out to be useful in other contexts and consequently found its way into international environmental law. Thus, while the term "prior informed consent" was not actually used, the principle was incorporated into the *Basel Convention on the Control of Transboundary Movements of Hazardous Wastes and Their Disposal*[8], and then more explicitly into the CBD. Article 15(5) of the latter agreement states: "Access to genetic resources shall be subject to prior informed consent of the Contracting Party providing such resources, unless otherwise determined by that Party." As should be clear, there is no intention to apply the prior informed consent principle to indigenous peoples, but only to the competent government agency. Nonetheless, Article 8(j) requires Contracting Parties to:

> respect, preserve and maintain knowledge, innovations and practices of indigenous and local communities embodying traditional lifestyles relevant for the conservation and sustainable use of biological diversity and promote their wider application with the approval and involvement of the holders of such knowledge, innovations and practices and encourage the equitable sharing of the benefits arising from the utilization of such knowledge, innovations and practices; ...

"Approval and involvement" is clearly not the same as prior informed consent. While "approval" may be synonymous with "consent", there is no explicit requirement that such approval must be based on the full disclosure of relevant information beforehand.

However, in response to lobbying from indigenous peoples' organizations and their supporters, at the Fifth Ordinary Meeting of the Conference of the Parties to the Convention on Biological Diversity (Conference of the Parties) in Nairobi in 2000, a Decision V/16[9] was adopted. This stated as a general principle that:

> Access to traditional knowledge, innovations and practices of indigenous and local communities should be subject to prior informed consent or prior informed approval from the holders of such knowledge, innovations and practices.[10]

---

8 Basel Convention on the Control of Transboundary Movements of Hazardous Wastes and Their Disposal, 22 March 1989, 28 I.L.M. 657, *available at* www.basel.int/text/con-e-rev.pdf (last visited 31 July 2008).

9 Conference of the Parties (COP) to the CBD, *Article 8(j) and related provisions*, Decision V/16, UNEP/CBD/COP/5/23 (15–26 May 2000), *available at* www.cbd.int/doc/decisions/COP-05-dec-en.pdf (last visited 31 July 2008).

10 *Id.* at 143.

But how can one operationalize the concept? In a 1996 book, the esteemed ethnoecologist and campaigner for indigenous peoples' rights, Darrell Posey, with the author, came up with a working definition in the hope that it would contribute to effective implementation:

> Prior informed consent is consent to an activity that is given after receiving full disclosure regarding the reasons for the activity, the specific procedures the activity would entail, the potential risks involved, and the full implications that can realistically be foreseen. Prior informed consent implies the right to stop the activity from proceeding, and for it to be halted if it is already underway. The following types of activity should be subject to the [prior informed consent] condition:
>
> - Medical or other research carried out on a human body, whether or not it involves extraction of material, such as organs, body fluids, etc., and whether or not it is for commercial purposes;
> - Medical treatment, especially where it entails risk;
> - The extraction of biogenetic material and minerals from local communities or the territories of traditional communities, whether or not the communities have legal title to these lands;
> - The acquisition of knowledge from a person or people;
> - All projects affecting local communities, such as construction works, colonization schemes, and protected areas.
>
> Requests for consent should be accompanied by full disclosure of the following, in writing **in the local language**:
>
> - The purpose of the activity;
> - The identity of those carrying out the activity and its sponsors, if different;
> - The benefits for the people or person whose consent is being requested and for the sponsors;
> - The costs and disadvantages for the people whose consent is being requested;
> - Possible alternative activities and procedures;
> - Any risks entailed by the activity;
> - Discoveries made in the course of the activity that might affect the willingness of the people to continue to cooperate;
> - The destination of knowledge or material that is to be acquired, its ownership status, and the rights of local people to it once it has left the community;
> - Any commercial interest that the performers and sponsors have in the activity and in the knowledge or material acquired; and
> - The legal options available to the community if it refuses to allow the activity.[11]

Few efforts have been made since then to further elaborate the concept as a clear set of guidelines for well intentioned scientists to follow. One shining exception to

[11] D.A. Posey and G. Dutfield, *Beyond Intellectual Property: Toward Traditional Resource Rights for Indigenous Peoples and Local Communities*, 1996, 47–8.

this is the International Society of Ethnobiology, which over a decade developed and adopted a code of ethics that was mainly drafted by Maui Solomon, an indigenous lawyer from New Zealand.[12]

4. RECENT INTERGOVERNMENTAL NEGOTIATIONS ON PIC, TRADITIONAL KNOWLEDGE PROTECTION AND BIOCULTURAL RESOURCES

4.1. THE CONVENTION ON BIOLOGICAL DIVERSITY

The international negotiations on the CBD that deal with legal solutions to traditional knowledge protection have considered, *inter alia*, the following: (i) national and international *sui generis* regimes; (ii) legally and non-legally binding instruments and agreements including contracts, guidelines and codes of conduct; (iii) specific protection measures such as traditional knowledge databases and disclosure of the origin of genetic resources and associated traditional knowledge in patent applications; (iv) principles such as prior informed consent and respect for customary law; and (v) the incorporation of traditional knowledge protection provisions in the international regime on access and benefit sharing (ABS). We now turn to the details of these negotiations.

At the Sixth Meeting of the Conference of the Parties (COP-6), which took place in The Hague in 2002, the *Bonn Guidelines on Access to Genetic Resources and Fair and Equitable Sharing of the Benefits Arising out of their Utilization* (Bonn Guidelines)[13] were officially adopted. The Guidelines are intended to be used when developing and drafting legislative, administrative or policy measures on ABS and contracts. COP-6 Decision VI/24, to which the Bonn Guidelines were annexed, also called for further information gathering and analysis regarding several matters including:

> (b) Role of customary laws and practices in relation to the protection of genetic resources and traditional knowledge, innovations and practices, and their relationship with intellectual property rights;
>
> ...

---

[12] International Society of Ethnobiology, *Code of Ethics* (as adopted in November 2006), *available at* http://ise.arts.ubc.ca/_common/docs/ISECodeofEthics2006_000.pdf (last visited 31 July 2008).

[13] COP, *Bonn Guidelines on Access to Genetic Resources and Fair and Equitable Sharing of the Benefits Arising out of their Utilization*, Decision VI/24 A, UNEP/CBD/COP/6/20 (7–19 April 2002), *available at* www.biodiv.org/decisions/default.aspx?m=cop-06&d=24 (last visited 31 July 2008).

(d) Efficacy of country of origin and *prior informed consent* disclosures in assisting the examination of intellectual property rights application and the re-examination of intellectual property rights granted; ...[14]

In addition, the Decision invited the World Intellectual Property Organization (WIPO), which is actively engaged in these same issues,

> to prepare a technical study, and to report its findings to the Conference of the Parties at its seventh meeting, on methods consistent with obligations in treaties administered by the World Intellectual Property Organization for requiring the disclosure within patent applications of, *inter alia*:
> (a) Genetic resources utilized in the development of the claimed inventions;
> (b) The country of origin of genetic resources utilized in the claimed inventions;
> (c) Associated traditional knowledge, innovations and practices utilized in the development of the claimed inventions;
> (d) The source of associated traditional knowledge, innovations and practices; and
> (e) Evidence of *prior informed consent*.[15]

In a separate COP-6 Decision V/10 on *Article 8 (j) and related provisions*, the Conference of the Parties invited

> Parties and Governments, with the approval and involvement of indigenous and local communities representatives, to develop and implement strategies to protect traditional knowledge, innovations and practices based on a combination of appropriate approaches, respecting customary laws and practices, including the use of existing intellectual property mechanisms, *sui generis* systems, customary law, the use of contractual arrangements, registers of traditional knowledge, and guidelines and codes of practice...[16]

It also requested "the Ad Hoc Open-ended Inter-Sessional Working Group on Article 8(j) and Related Provisions of the Convention on Biological Diversity[[17]] to address the issue of *sui generis* systems for the protection of traditional knowledge".[18]

---

14 COP, *Role of intellectual property rights in the implementation of access and benefit-sharing arrangements*, at 284, Decision VI/24 C, UNEP/CBD/COP/6/20 (7–19 April 2002), *available at* www.biodiv.org/decisions/default.aspx?m=cop-06&d=24 (last visited 31 July 2008) (emphasis added).

15 *Id.* at 284–85 (second emphasis added).

16 COP, *Article 8(j) and related provisions*, at 161, Decision VI/10, UNEP/CBD/COP/6/20 (7–19 April 2002), *available at* www.cbd.int/doc/decisions/COP-06-dec-en.pdf (last visited 31 July 2008).

17 This body was established by the COP in 1998.

18 COP, *supra* note 16, at 161.

The Seventh Meeting of the Conference of the Parties (COP-7), which took place in Kuala Lumpur in 2004, adopted Decision VII/16 on *Article 8(j) and related provisions*.[19] Section H of the Decision was on the development of elements of *sui generis* systems for the protection of traditional knowledge, innovations and practices. Drawing on the work of the Working Group on Article 8(j) and Related Provisions, its annex offered the following list of potential elements for a *sui generis* system. It should be noted here that the prior informed consent concept is not explicitly linked to patents.

1. Statement of purpose, objectives and scope.
2. Clarity with regard to ownership of traditional knowledge associated with biological and genetic resources.
3. Set of relevant definitions.
4. Recognition of elements of customary law relevant to the conservation and sustainable use of biological diversity with respect to: (i) customary rights in indigenous/traditional/local knowledge; (ii) customary rights regarding biological resources; and (iii) customary procedures governing access to and *consent* to use traditional knowledge, biological and genetic resources.
5. A process and set of requirements governing *prior informed consent*, mutually agreed terms and equitable sharing of benefits with respect to traditional knowledge, innovations and practices associated with genetic resources and relevant for the conservation and sustainable use of biological diversity.
6. Rights of traditional knowledge holders and conditions for the grant of rights.
7. The rights conferred.
8. A system for the registration of indigenous/local knowledge/Systems for the protection and preservation of indigenous/local knowledge.
9. The competent authority to manage relevant procedural/administrative matters with regard to the protection of traditional knowledge and benefit-sharing arrangements.
10. Provisions regarding enforcement and remedies.
11. Relationship to other laws, including international law.
12. Extra-territorial protections.[20]

Activities relating to traditional knowledge are being carried out not just by the aforementioned Working Group on Article 8(j) and Related Provisions, but also by the Working Group on Access and Benefit Sharing (ABS Working Group), another body set up by the Conference of the Parties, most importantly in the context of the international regime on access to genetic resources and benefit sharing. Agreement that there should be such a regime was reached at the *2002*

19 COP, *Article 8(j) and related provisions*, at 253, Decision VII/16, UNEP/CBD/COP/7/21 (9–20 and 27 February 2004), *available at* www.cbd.int/doc/decisions/COP-07-dec-en.pdf (last visited 31 July 2008).

20 *Id.* at 283 (emphasis added).

World Summit on Sustainable Development, specifically to "[n]egotiate within the framework of the Convention on Biological Diversity, bearing in mind the Bonn Guidelines, an international regime to promote and safeguard the fair and equitable sharing of benefits arising out of the utilization of genetic resources".[21] The international regime is currently under negotiation and the Conference of the Parties is the body mandated by the United Nations General Assembly to be the principle forum to develop the regime. As indicated in COP-7 Decision VII/19 Section D, a number of elements the ABS Working Group is required to consider are relevant to traditional knowledge protection. Again, prior informed consent is delinked from patents:

> (x) Measures to ensure compliance with *prior informed consent* of indigenous and local communities holding traditional knowledge associated with genetic resources, in accordance with Article 8(j);
>
> ...
>
> (xiv) Disclosure of origin/source/legal provenance of genetic resources and associated traditional knowledge in applications for intellectual property rights;
>
> (xv) Recognition and protection of the rights of indigenous and local communities over their traditional knowledge associated to genetic resources subject to the national legislation of the countries where these communities are located;
>
> (xvi) Customary law and traditional cultural practices of indigenous and local communities;
>
> (xviii) Code of ethics/code of conduct/models of prior informed consent or other instruments in order to ensure fair and equitable sharing of benefits with indigenous and local communities; ...[22]

At the Eighth Meeting of the Conference of the Parties (COP-8), which took place in March 2006, two relevant decisions were adopted, Decision VIII/4 on *Access and benefit sharing*[23], and Decision VIII/5 on *Article 8(j) and related provisions*.[24] Decision VIII/4 requested the ABS Working Group "to continue the elaboration and negotiation of the international regime"[25] and instructed it "to complete its work at the earliest possible time before the tenth meeting of the Conference of

---

21 United Nations, *Plan of Implementation of the World Summit on Sustainable Development*, par. 42(o), 23 September 2002, *available at* www.un.org/jsummit/html/documents/summit_docs/2309_planfinal.htm (last visited 31 July 2008).

22 COP, *Access and benefit-sharing as related to genetic resources (Article 15)*, at 302, Decision VII/19, UNEP/CBD/COP/7/21 (9–20 and 27 February 2004), *available at* www.cbd.int/doc/decisions/COP-07-dec-en.pdf (last visited 31 July 2008) (emphasis added).

23 COP, *Access and benefit-sharing*, Decision VIII/4 (20–31 March 2006), *available at* www.cbd.int/decisions/cop-08.shtml?m=COP-08&id=11016&lg=0 (last visited 31 July 2008).

24 COP, *Article 8(j) and related provisions*, Decision VIII/5 (20–31 March 2006), *available at* www.cbd.int/decisions/cop-08.shtml?m=COP-08&id=11017&lg=0 (last visited 31 July 2008).

25 COP, *supra* note 23, Section A, par. 6.

the Parties".[26] The Tenth Meeting of the Conference of the Parties (COP-10) is likely to take place in 2010. It will be interesting to see how prior informed consent is covered.

4.2. THE WORLD INTELLECTUAL PROPERTY ORGANIZATION

For the 25th Session of WIPO General Assembly in 2000, the Secretariat prepared a document which invited member states to consider the establishment of an Intergovernmental Committee on Intellectual Property and Genetic Resources, Traditional Knowledge and Folklore (Intergovernmental Committee). The WIPO Secretariat suggested that the Intergovernmental Committee constitute a forum for members to discuss three themes that it had identified during the consultations. These were "intellectual property issues that arise in the context of (i) access to genetic resources and benefit sharing; (ii) protection of traditional knowledge, whether or not associated with those resources; and (iii) the protection of expressions of folklore."[27] This suggestion was enthusiastically supported by a large number of developing countries and was approved without formal opposition from any member.

In the early years, most of the Intergovernmental Committee's work on traditional knowledge and on folklore (nowadays referred to more often as "traditional cultural expressions") concentrated on defensive protection. More specifically, the Committee has been considering ways to improve the availability to patent examiners of traditional knowledge and of publications describing traditional knowledge. In addition, much discussion has covered disclosure of the origin of genetic resources or related traditional knowledge in patent applications, as at the World Trade Organization (WTO) and the meetings of the Conference of the Parties to the CBD.

However, positive protection is increasingly being discussed in a substantive manner. The first shift in this direction came at the Third Session of the Intergovernmental Committee in June 2002, for which WIPO prepared a paper called *Elements of a* Sui Generis *System for the Protection of Traditional Knowledge*.[28] It was given further impetus in Autumn 2003 when the WIPO

---

26 *Id.*

27 WIPO, Permanent Committee on Cooperation for Development Related to Intellectual Property, *Protection of Traditional Knowledge and Intellectual Property in Developing Countries: Progress Report*, at 4, PCIPD/2/7 (25 January 2001) (*prepared by* the International Bureau), *available at* www.wipo.int/documents/en/document/pcipd/doc/pcipd2_7.doc (last visited 31 July 2008).

28 WIPO, Intergovernmental Committee on Intellectual Property and Genetic Resources, Traditional Knowledge and Folklore, *Elements of a* Sui Generis *System for*

General Assembly decided that the Intergovernmental Committee's new work would focus particularly on the international dimension of the relevant issues and agreed that "no outcome of its work is excluded, including the possible development of an international instrument or instruments."[29]

The Intergovernmental Committee has drafted two sets of provisions: the *Provisions for the Protection of Traditional Knowledge*[30], and the *Provisions for the Protection of Traditional Cultural Expressions/Expressions of Folklore.*[31] Both of these were presented first at the Eighth Session of the Intergovernmental Committee and further deliberated on at the Ninth and subsequent Sessions.

The *Provisions for the Protection of Traditional Knowledge* as revised in April 2005 pay extensive attention to the principle of prior informed consent, and reserve an entire article to it. Thus, Article 7 states:

> 1. The principle of prior informed consent should govern any access of traditional knowledge from its traditional holders, subject to these principles and relevant national laws.
> 2. The holder of traditional knowledge shall be entitled to grant *prior informed consent* for access to traditional knowledge, or to approve the grant of such consent

the Protection of Traditional Knowledge, WIPO/GRTKF/IC/3/8 (29 March 2002) (*prepared by* the Secretariat), *available at* www.wipo.int/edocs/mdocs/tk/en/wipo_grtkf_ic_3/wipo_grtkf_ic_3_8.pdf (last visited 31 July 2008). An updated version was prepared for the following session of the Intergovernmental Committee on Intellectual Property and Genetic Resources, Traditional Knowledge and Folklore (Intergovernmental Committee); *see* WIPO, Intergovernmental Committee on Intellectual Property and Genetic Resources, Traditional Knowledge and Folklore, *Elements of a* Sui Generis *System for the Protection of Traditional Knowledge*, WIPO/GRTKF/IC/4/8 (30 September 2002) (*prepared by* the Secretariat), *available at* www.wipo.int/edocs/mdocs/tk/en/wipo_grtkf_ic_4/wipo_grtkf_ic_4_8.pdf (last visited 31 July 2008).

29 WIPO General Assembly, *Report*, at 19, WO/GA/30/8 (1 October 2003), *available at* www.wipo.int/documents/en/document/govbody/wo_gb_ga/pdf/wo_ga_30_8.pdf (last visited 31 July 2008).

30 As revised for the Eighth Session of the Intergovernmental Committee, *see* WIPO, Intergovernmental Committee on Intellectual Property and Genetic Resources, *The Protection of Traditional Knowledge: Revised Objectives and Principles*, Annex, WIPO/GRTKF/IC/8/5 (8 April 2005); and reproduced in WIPO, Intergovernmental Committee on Intellectual Property and Genetic Resources, *The Protection of Traditional Knowledge: Revised Objectives and Principles*, Annex, WIPO/GRTKF/IC/9/5 (9 January 2006), *available at* www.wipo.int/edocs/mdocs/tk/en/wipo_grtkf_ic_9/wipo_grtkf_ic_9_5.pdf (last visited 31 July 2008) [hereinafter "*Draft TK Principles*"].

31 As revised for the Eighth Session of the Intergovernmental Committee, *see* WIPO, Intergovernmental Committee on Intellectual Property and Genetic Resources, *The Protection of Traditional Cultural Expressions/Expressions of Folklore: Revised Objectives and Principles*, Annex, WIPO/GRTKF/IC/8/4 (8 April 2005); and reproduced in WIPO, Intergovernmental Committee on Intellectual Property and Genetic Resources, *The Protection of Traditional Cultural Expressions/Expressions of Folklore: Revised Objectives and Principles*, Annex, WIPO/GRTKF/IC/9/4 (9 January 2006), *available at* www.wipo.int/edocs/mdocs/tk/en/wipo_grtkf_ic_9/wipo_grtkf_ic_9_4.pdf (last visited 31 July 2008) [hereinafter "*Draft TCE Principles*"].

by an appropriate national authority, as provided by applicable national legislation.

3. Measures and mechanisms for implementing the principle of *prior informed consent* should be understandable, appropriate, and not burdensome for all relevant stakeholders, in particular for traditional knowledge holders; should ensure clarity and legal certainty; and should provide for mutually agreed terms for the equitable sharing of benefits arising from any agreed use of that knowledge.[32]

It would be fair to say that the *Provisions for the Protection of Traditional Cultural Expressions/Expressions of Folklore* as revised in April 2005 pay less attention to prior informed consent, which is mainly covered in the context of acts of misappropriation (Article 3). Here the prior informed consent concept is applied in support of rights in relation to cultural expressions that are very similar to the moral rights existing within the copyright laws of many countries:

(a) In respect of traditional cultural expressions/expressions of folklore of particular cultural or spiritual value or significance to a community, and which have been registered or notified as referred to in Article 7, there shall be adequate and effective legal and practical measures to ensure that the relevant community can prevent the following acts taking place without its free, *prior and informed consent*:

(i) in respect of such traditional cultural expressions/expressions of folklore other than words, signs, names and symbols:
   - the reproduction, publication, adaptation, broadcasting, public performance, communication to the public, distribution, rental, making available to the public and fixation (including by still photography) of the traditional cultural expressions/expressions of folklore or derivatives thereof;
   - any use of the traditional cultural expressions/expressions of folklore or adaptation thereof which does not acknowledge in an appropriate way the community as the source of the traditional cultural expressions/expressions of folklore;
   - any distortion, mutilation or other modification of, or other derogatory action in relation to, the traditional cultural expressions/expressions of folklore; and
   - the acquisition or exercise of IP rights over the traditional cultural expressions/expressions of folklore or adaptations thereof;

(ii) in respect of words, signs, names and symbols which are such traditional cultural expressions/expressions of folklore, any use of the traditional cultural expressions/expressions of folklore or derivatives thereof, or the acquisition or exercise of IP rights over the traditional cultural expressions/expressions of folklore or derivatives thereof, which disparages, offends or falsely suggests a connection with the community concerned, or brings the community into contempt or disrepute; ...[33]

---

32 *Draft TK Principles, supra* note 30, Annex, at 31 (emphasis added).

33 *Draft TCE Principles, supra* note 31, Annex, at 19 (emphasis added).

Past experience suggests that the odds of these sets of provisions being turned into international treaties are very long indeed. Few developed countries are at all supportive. On the other hand, WIPO has gone further than many would have expected, and some kind of settlement is definitely possible though this is more likely to take the form of a non legally-binding declaration than a treaty.

4.3. THE WORLD TRADE ORGANIZATION AND THE TRIPS AGREEMENT

The *Agreement on Trade-Related Aspects of Intellectual Property Rights* (TRIPS Agreement)[34] is silent on traditional knowledge. Nonetheless, discussions on traditional knowledge have come up, mostly at the TRIPS Council. These initially took place in the context of the review of implementation of Article 27.3(b). The 2001 launching of the Doha Development Agenda has made traditional knowledge and folklore, as well as the relationship between the TRIPS Agreement and the CBD, integral to the TRIPS Council's work.

Specifically, at the Fourth Session of the WTO Ministerial Conference in Doha, a *Ministerial Declaration* was adopted according to which the WTO member states instructed:

> the Council for TRIPS, in pursuing its work programme including under the review of Article 27.3(b), the review of the implementation of the TRIPS Agreement under Article 71.1 and the work foreseen pursuant to paragraph 12 of this Declaration, to examine, *inter alia*, the relationship between the TRIPS Agreement and the Convention on Biological Diversity, the protection of traditional knowledge and folklore, and other relevant new developments raised by Members pursuant to Article 71.1. In undertaking this work, the TRIPS Council shall be guided by the objectives and principles set out in Articles 7 and 8 of the TRIPS Agreement and shall take fully into account the development dimension.[35]

As at the Conference of the Parties to the CBD and at WIPO, disclosure of origin has been debated at some length, and several proposals have been tabled.[36] The

---

34 Agreement on Trade-Related Aspects of Intellectual Property Rights, 15 April 1994, Marrakesh Agreement Establishing the World Trade Organization, Annex 1C, Legal Instruments – Results of the Uruguay Round, 33 I.L.M. 1125 (1994) [hereinafter "TRIPS Agreement"].

35 WTO Ministerial Conference, *Ministerial Declaration*, par. 19, 14 November 2001, WT/MIN(01)/DEC/1 (20 November 2001), *available at* www.wto.org/english/thewto_e/minist_e/min01_e/mindecl_e.pdf (last visited 31 July 2008).

36 These are summarised and listed by the World Trade Organization (WTO) Secretariat; *see* WTO, Council for Trade-Related Aspects of Intellectual Property Rights, *The Relationship between the TRIPS Agreement and the Convention on Biological Diversity: Summary of Issues Raised and Points Made*, IP/C/W/368/Rev.1, (8 February 2006) (*prepared by* the WTO Secretariat), *available at* www.wto.org/english/tratop_e/trips_e/ipcw368_e.doc

most recent of these, in May 2006 was submitted by Brazil, Pakistan, Peru, Thailand and Tanzania.[37] Annexed to this document is text that would form an additional section of TRIPS Agreement, namely Article 29*bis* ("Disclosure of Origin of Biological Resources and/or Associated Traditional Knowledge"). The most substantial part is paragraph 2, which states as follows:

> Where the subject matter of a patent application concerns, is derived from or developed with biological resources and/or associated traditional knowledge, Members shall require applicants to disclose the country providing the resources and/or associated traditional knowledge, from whom in the providing country they were obtained, and, as known after reasonable inquiry, the country of origin. Members shall also require that applicants provide information including evidence of compliance with the applicable legal requirements in the providing country for *prior informed consent* for access and fair and equitable benefit-sharing arising from the commercial or other utilization of such resources and/or associated traditional knowledge.[38]

It hardly needs to be mentioned that prior informed consent is, again, linked to the patent system.

5. PRIOR INFORMED CONSENT IN PRACTICE: IS IT WORKABLE? AND WHAT GOOD WOULD IT DO ANYWAY?

5.1. THE PERU INTERNATIONAL COOPERATIVE BIODIVERSITY GROUPS PROJECT

The first case study, which is meant to address the first question ("is it workable?"), is a project titled *Peruvian medicinal plant sources of new pharmaceuticals*. It ran from 1994 to 2000 and was funded by four United States government agencies under a programme known as the *International Cooperative Biodiversity Groups* (ICBG).[39] The funding agencies were the National Institutes of Health, the

(last visited 31 July 2008). *See also* IPRsonline.org, Official Submissions to the WTO, www.iprsonline.org/submissions/article273.htm (last visited 31 July 2008).

37 *See* WTO, Council for Trade-Related Aspects of Intellectual Property Rights, *Doha Work Programme – The Outstanding Implementation Issue on the Relationship between the TRIPS Agreement and the Conventional on Biological Diversity*, WT/GC/W/564/Rev.2 (5 July 2006), *available at* http://docsonline.wto.org/DDFDocuments/t/ip/c/w474.doc (last visited 31 July 2008) (containing the draft of Article 29*bis* of TRIPS Agreement as proposed by Brazil, China, Columbia, Cuba, India, Pakistan, Peru, Thailand and Tanzania).

38 *Id.* at 2 (emphasis added).

39 This case study draws heavily on Shane Greene's work; *see* S. Greene, "Indigenous People Incorporated?: Culture as Politics, Culture as Property in Pharmaceutical Bioprospecting", 45 *Current Anthropology* 211 (2004).

National Science Foundation, and the U.S. Department of Agriculture. The ICBG programme was intended to support the principles of the CBD while promoting industrial use of biodiversity. As the anthropologist Shane Greene explains: "ICBG grants are based on a collaborative funding, research, and mutual-benefits relationship between U.S. and developing-country institutions, commercial partners, and, in a few cases, specific indigenous/local communities."[40]

One of the awardees was Washington University in St Louis, Missouri, whose consortium included the Universidad Peruana Cayetano Heredia, the Museo de Historia Natural de la Universidad San Marcos, G. D. Searle & Co., a pharmaceutical firm then part of Monsanto, and the Aguaruna people. The Aguaruna are a large Amazonian population, over 45,000 strong inhabiting over 180 communities, most of which are affiliated to at least 13 organizations run by the Aguaruna alone or jointly with neighbouring ethnic groups. The primary aim of the project was to collect and study medicinal plants used by the Aguaruna for both scientific and commercial ends.

It soon became apparent that prior informed consent would be a major challenge. Initially, Walter Lewis of Washington University, who was the project leader, had identified the Organización Central de Comunidades Aguarunas del Alto Marañon ("the Organización") as a potential partner organization. Presumably, the consent of this organization would have been taken to mean the consent of the whole Aguaruna people. However, once the grant was awarded, Lewis was apparently advised to approach a bigger and better known organization, the Consejo Aguaruna Huambisa ("the Consejo"), which he did. A rather basic written agreement was made between the ICBG team and the Consejo promising annual payments for plant collections and royalties. Having done this deal, Washington University negotiated a more formal arrangement with Searle according to which the University would receive the payments due from Searle and then pass on a share to the Consejo. The latter organization was unhappy that such a separate deal was made without their direct involvement, and they began to make objections. Once the two agreements were made public, Washington University and Searle found themselves being condemned as biopirates for offering the Aguaruna too small a share of the proceeds, for keeping them out of the substantial negotiations, and for not being transparent with them. One issue apparently overlooked at the time was that the Consejo was hardly sufficiently representative to negotiate on behalf of the entire population of 45,000 plus Aguarunas anyway.

The following year, 1995, the Consejo withdrew from the project, leaving the consortium without any Aguaruna representation. Washington University decided to approach the Organización, which turned out to be much more receptive, and a detailed written agreement was signed enabling the Organización

40 *Id.* at 214.

to join the ICBG consortium. The Consejo publicly condemned this, but the Organización came out in defense of the ICBG's activities with the support of two other Aguaruna organizations, which jointly rejected the representativeness of the Consejo's leader.

At this point, a national indigenous peoples' confederation, to which the Organización and the other two organizations were affiliated, became involved. This was the Confederación de Nacionalidades Amazónicas del Perú ("the Confederación", or CONAP). The Confederación organized a meeting of community and organization leaders including representatives of the Organización and several other Aguaruna organizations and one from a neighbouring group, the Huambisa (but not the Consejo), and representatives of the ICBG consortium, including Searle and other interested individuals. The outcome was the formation of a consortium comprising the Confederación and several Aguaruna organizations, and an agreement that three individuals go to the headquarters of Searle in St. Louis to directly negotiate a contract.

Putting to one side the question of to what extent the parties represented all Aguaruna people (in fact, less than half), did these organizations have sufficient legitimacy to give the consent of members of communities that *were* represented? On this question, Greene has this to say:

> Acceptance by CONAP and Affiliates [a consortium of Aguaruna organizations] of course did not automatically mean acceptance by all Aguaruna communities formally affiliated with those organizations. In many instances, individual communities challenged CONAP and Affiliates' authority to accept the project on their behalf and refused to permit the ICBG researchers to work in their communal territory despite their affiliation with one of the participating organizations. While there is not enough space to document all this local dissent, it is important that it be mentioned, since even the apparent incorporation of these organizations provoked substantial internal debate, discussion, and disagreement among Aguaruna community leaders.[41]

In the end, a contract was agreed including a know-how license agreement. Members of the Confederación-led consortium formed the parties on the Aguaruna side. The agreement provided for payments for plant samples, and license fees paid as long as Searle uses plant extracts accompanied by the collective medicinal know-how of the Aguaruna people. Also promised were milestone payments and royalties dependent on the research and development progress of discovered therapeutic agents acquired from these plants. Can this be right? Despite the formality of the agreement, one can argue that it was presumptuous of the Confederación and its partners to license the collective know how of *all* the Aguaruna people.

41 *Id.* at 214 n. 9.

There was a separate biological collection agreement with the ICBG researchers. However, to meet the objection that the Confederación group was unfairly monopolizing the benefits of the unrepresented Aguaruna people, the agreement expressly committed to "ensur[ing] the fair and equitable sharing of benefits among the Aguaruna People".[42] As Greene explains:

> The agreement thus remains open to other Aguaruna communities, provided that they apply for inclusion by affiliating themselves with an existing Aguaruna organization, and to other Aguaruna organizations, provided that they are approved by CONAP and Affiliates in a traditional assembly and dialogue called the Ipaamamu that has become central to CONAP's strategy for dealing with the local constituency.[43]

This does not seem sufficient since "[t]he legal arrangement clearly moves in the direction of contractual and financial legitimation of CONAP and Affiliates as representatives of the 'Aguaruna People.'"[44]

In the event, financial benefits were generated from the project. Most of these went to the two Peruvian universities involved. However, money did get channelled to the Aguaruna. Of the money from Searle, the Confederación and its Aguaruna consortium used part of it to support themselves. The rest went "to their affiliated communities in the form of small loans, scholarships for Aguaruna students, and individual reimbursement to field informants who worked with the ICBG researchers in identifying medicinal plants."[45] Needless to say the Consejo was frozen out. However, it turned out that Searle, while keen to screen the plants, was not interested in the associated traditional knowledge. Its agreement with the Aguaruna was good public relations for the company, but scientifically it contributed nothing to the company, which chose not to renew the agreement when it expired in 2000.

There are some very positive things to say about this project. First, the direct negotiations between an indigenous group and a major pharmaceutical corporation were an undoubtedly groundbreaking development. Second, the know-how license was unprecedented and had some significant implications in terms of knowledge ownership. As Brendan Tobin, legal counsel to the Aguarunas explained to Greene, "the know-how license is a truly novel step in contract law, for the first time giving a group of indigenous peoples control and full ownership of its traditional knowledge."[46] On the negative side, for all the efforts to put the

---

42 *Id.* at 218 (quoting Article 3.01 of the agreement).
43 *Id.* (referring to Article 7).
44 *Id.*
45 *Id.* at 219.
46 *Id.* at 217.

prior informed consent concept into practice, the results were sharp divisions among the Aguaruna, and decidedly unsatisfactory levels of representation.

5.2. THE ROSY PERIWINKLE

That leaves us with the second question posed above: what good would prior informed consent do anyway? In the 1950s the rosy periwinkle (*Catharanthus roseus*), a plant originally found in Madagascar, yielded two anti-cancer alkaloids, Vincristine and Vinblastine, which have generated huge profits for Eli Lilly since they came on the market around four decades ago. To some this is the classic biopiracy case with Madagascar and its people the unfortunate victim.[47] In fact, while the plant is thought to originate from Madagascar, it exists throughout the tropics and has grown in the Caribbean long enough to be considered as a native plant there. It has been many years since the company relied on Madagascar for supplies of the plant, and most now come from plantations in Texas. The Eli Lilly researchers who discovered and patented Vincristine[48] and its anti-cancer properties decided to study the plant when a literature search uncovered its use by rural populations in the Philippines. Those at the University of Western Ontario who discovered and patented Vinblastine[49] received plant samples from Jamaica that were considered worth testing, again, because people used the plant for therapeutic purposes. In both countries the plant was used by rural communities not to treat cancer but diabetes.[50] Neither of the research teams made any secret in their publications of the fact that they were inspired by traditional knowledge. On the other hand, only the University of Western Ontario team was reliant both upon overseas sources of plant material and unpublished ethnobotanical information when it began research on the periwinkle. Since then two further vinca compounds have come on the market: GlaxoSmithKline's *Vinorelbine* and Eli Lilly's *Vindesine.*

---

47 *See* R. Stone, "The Biodiversity Treaty: Pandora's Box or Fair Deal?", 256 *Sci.* 1624 (1992).

48 *See* U.S. Patent No. 3,205,220 (issued 7 September 1965) ("Leurosidine and Leurocristine and their production").

49 *See* U.S. Patent No. 3,097,137 (issued 9 July 1963) ("Vincaleukoblastine"). The patent was assigned by the inventors, Charles T. Beer, James H. Cutts and Robert L. Noble, to Canadian Patents and Development, Ltd., who made a deal with Eli Lilly allowing the latter company to commercially exploit the invention.

50 As expressed by three medical researchers at the University of Western Ontario, "the disease of cancer was certainly far from our thoughts when we learned of a tea made from the leaves of a West Indian shrub that was supposedly useful in the control of diabetes mellitus"; *see* R.L. Noble, Ch.T. Beer and J.H. Cutts, "Role of Chance Observation in Chemotherapy: Vinca Rosea", 76 *Ann. N.Y. Acad. Sci.* 882 (1958).

The rosy periwinkle case exemplifies the reality that portraying pharmaceutical development as a linear process taking place over a relatively short period[51] is a gross simplification with many if not most drugs. It also suggests that in many cases, a prior informed consent requirement would not be applicable. It was only with Vinblastine that ethnobiological information and plant samples were directly acquired from local people. In that case a prior informed consent requirement could have benefited the local healers and their communities. But not in the other cases.

6. CONCLUSIONS

Some will argue, justifiably, that I have cherry-picked my cases in a way deliberately to cast the prior informed consent "solution" in a sceptical light. They are right. I have. But I maintain that my reasons for doing so are sound. Methodological scepticism is the only way to assess the true potential of prior informed consent. We need to get our doubts and objections out of the way first. In my view we still have not done that. The case studies highlight the point that, first, we are still some way from developing workable prior informed consent procedures for equitable cross-cultural traditional knowledge transactions. Even the most sincere and painstakingly worked out efforts to do prior informed consent right can lead to unfortunate unforeseen complications. As Burns reminds us, even "[t]he best laid schemes o' Mice an' Men, Gang aft agley".[52] Second, we cannot expect prior informed consent alone to put the world right. Indeed, emphasizing prior informed consent over other approaches may be unhelpful. Prior informed consent should be part of a broader regulatory framework; it should not be mistaken for the framework itself.

---

51 A common estimate of the average duration is 10–15 years from initial discovery to marketing.

52 The best laid schemes of Mice and Men often go awry.

PRIOR INFORMED CONSENT

Experiences with Ethnomusicology Recordings

Wim VAN ZANTEN*

This Chapter addresses the practical problems of obtaining prior informed consent for ethnomusicology field recordings. While the relationship between ethnomusicologists and their informants implies a degree of consent, the contours of that consent remain undefined by law or custom. Recently, ethnomusicology societies and others have moved towards formalizing the relationship between researchers and informants. Though such measures address an important problem, numerous practical difficulties remain. In this contribution, I shall use my experiences with the Baduy – an Indigenous community – and the Minangkabau people to illustrate some of the lingering difficulties of obtaining consent from rural communities in Indonesia.

---

* Wim van Zanten was a staff member at the Department of Cultural Anthropology and Development Sociology, Leiden University, from 1971–2007 and did ethnomusicology fieldwork in Malawi (1969–1971) and Indonesia (1976 - present). Most of his publications are based on this fieldwork and some are about methodological issues in anthropology and ethnomusicology, including statistics for the social sciences. Filming for documentary purposes has been part of his fieldwork since 1976 and he published two films about Minangkabau performing arts in West Sumatra. Presently he is preparing a book about the music of the Baduy minority group in West Java and another book on Tembang Sunda Cianjuran music from West Java, both accompanied by film and audio CDs. More information may be found at his website (www.xs4all.nl/~wvzant27/).

1. BETWEEN TRUST AND LEGAL PROTECTION

In ethnomusicology fieldwork, like in anthropological fieldwork, the relationship between researcher and informants should be based on trust. In order to establish a relationship of trust, the informants and recorded musicians need to understand the researcher's purpose in asking questions and making audiovisual recordings. Such a relationship of trust will contribute to the validity of the data obtained. Simply said, collected data are valid when we have measured what we wanted to measure: questions should be understood properly, answers should be reliable, apparatus should record precisely and accurately, *etc.* This validity of the data can only be achieved if the relation between researcher and informants is based on trust: trust is a necessary condition for obtaining valid data. Hence for the data collection and recordings to begin, the informants must offer their informed consent, at least implicitly. However, this does not mean that the content of that consent has been clearly defined.

The issue becomes even more complicated when the aspects concerning benefits and rewards obtained from fieldwork recordings are taken into account. Ethnomusicologists mostly collect data for documentary and not for financial reasons, except perhaps for the important but indirect reward of enhancing the academic career of the researcher. Where the informants are concerned, fieldwork practices of their payment vary amongst social science disciplines. In anthropological fieldwork the informants are seldom paid for the information they supply, because payment could easily jeopardize the documentation process and thus lead to collecting invalid information, which may have been supplied purely to gain financial profit. Almost all informants accept that they are not being paid. On the contrary, they are quite often eager to talk about their social situation and problems with an outsider whom they trust.

In ethnomusicology fieldwork, the standard today is that individual musicians and music groups are paid for the recordings of their performances. Payment for recording music is quite often acceptable, because playing music has a technological component that is valued in most societies. However, payment does not always happen in a direct way. For instance, the recording may be made during a ritual in which, apart from the – often non-professional – musicians, many other people are involved. In such cases, a financial contribution to the organizers of the ritual may be the most appropriate form of payment. The process of paying for the recordings in the field is therefore often unclear from a legal perspective. Moreover, financial reward is not the only issue. Ritual music is not just for entertainment; it may have power that should only be dealt with by knowledgeable people. Sometimes it may even be better not to use money as a reward, because it may be considered an insult. I have experienced this several times, and in such cases I have shown my appreciation by offering gifts or paying for medicines, children's school fees or other such indirect forms of compensation.

A further complication in relation to ethnomusicology recordings stems from the fact that scientific knowledge should, by its very nature, be public. Field recordings should therefore be easily accessible in archives and commercial publications, as well as through public lectures and media broadcasts. Because of this public accessibility, the question arises of how best to protect the intellectual property rights of the individuals and communities who performed the music, while also guaranteeing the public interest in access to knowledge and information.[1] Intellectual property related questions of this kind may often only come up many years after the recordings have been made, as these audiovisual documents tend to have a long life.[2] How should this influence the way the recordings are obtained?

When researchers decide to make their research data publicly available, they must also take into account other circumstances than those under which the recordings were made. Since the whole process of collecting data and recording music is based mostly on trust rather than legal contracts, researchers should never publish data that may damage their informants. On the other hand, once sound or audiovisual recordings are released for commercial purposes, musicians should not be excluded from any financial benefits obtained from recordings of their music.

Many misunderstandings about the legal issues related to ethnomusicology recordings stem from the fact that intellectual property laws are mainly based on Western ideas about protecting individual rights and their financial interests, rather than the rights of communities. Moreover, differences remain between national regulations of rights held by the recorded performer and the person making recordings of his performance. For instance, American copyright law for recordings is more directed to the recorder than to the recorded musicians.[3]

As strong legal protection often brings negative and unexpected outcomes, one must ask whether the safeguarding of living culture (also called intangible cultural heritage) will benefit from a stricter legal framework. Such stricter legal guidelines may be counterproductive and have unintended consequences: they may hamper the process of creativity and intercultural exchange. In

1 *See also, e.g.*, World Intellectual Property Organization (WIPO), *WIPO Intellectual Property Handbook: Policy, Law and Use*, (2nd ed.), 2004, 3, *available at* www.wipo.int/about-ip/en/iprm/index.html (last visited 31 July 2008) (stating that one of two main reasons why countries have laws to protect intellectual property is "to give statutory expression to the moral and economic rights of creators in their creations and the rights of the public in access to those creations").

2 *See also* A. Seeger, "Lost Lineages and Neglected Peers: Ethnomusicologists outside Academia", 50 *Ethnomusicol.* 214, 223 (2006).

3 *See* S. Mills, "Indigenous Music and the Law: An Analysis of National and International Legislation", 28 *Yearbook for Traditional Music* 57, 67–68 (1996).

ethnomusicology fieldwork, an international ethical code and the establishment of an international ethical commission on the use of audiovisual recordings may be a better solution, if only a temporary one, for controversies and disputes.

2. RECORDING MUSIC: THE ROLE OF INSTITUTIONS AND COMMERCIALIZATION

For several years, two of the most important societies for ethnomusicologists – the Society for Ethnomusicology (SEM) and the International Council for Traditional Music (ICTM) – have focused on the ethical and legal issues of fieldwork as they relate to copyright protection and intellectual property rights. The SEM published *A Manual for Documentation, Fieldwork, and Preservation for Ethnomusicologists* (SEM Manual) in 1994, with a second edition released in 2001.[4] The ICTM has also recently started on the construction of an ethical code for ethnomusicologists. In 1996 it published several articles in its *Yearbook for Traditional Music* on ethics, copyright issues and the recording industry.[5]

The studies made by both societies outline several conceptual and practical problems when applying current copyright law to ethnomusicology recordings. The first problem is that "the concept of copyright is essentially a business concept".[6] The ethnomusicology context differs from the business context in several meaningful respects. Field recordings are frequently obtained in a non-commercial setting, where the informants may consider some materials "too sacred, personally meaningful, or even shameful to commit to tape."[7] Also, perceptions of ownership over music may differ significantly among indigenous peoples. Copyright law "does not take into account community ownership of indigenous material, spirit authorship, or other more traditional concepts a researcher may encounter."[8] Finally, the relationship between the recorder and the performer is different in the ethnomusicology context. Ethnomusicologists have a long-term commitment to the rights and concerns of the individuals and their communities.

The second problem in applying copyright law to the ethnomusicology context is that "intellectual property [laws] are constantly changing, through legislation

4 *See* J. Topp Fargion (ed.), *A manual for Documentation, Fieldwork, and Preservation for Ethnomusicologists*, (2nd ed.), 2001 [hereinafter "*SEM Manual*"].

5 *See* Mills, *supra* note 3; A. Seeger, "Ethnomusicologists, Archives, Professional Organizations, and the Shifting Ethics of Intellectual Property", 28 *Yearbook for Traditional Music* 87 (1996); H. Zemp, "The/An Ethnomusicologist and the Record Business", 28 *Yearbook for Traditional Music* 36 (1996).

6 *See SEM Manual*, *supra* note 4, at 15.

7 *Id.* at 13.

8 *Id.* at 15.

and through interpretation by the courts, both of which are expanding the areas covered by the law".[9] This mutability in copyright law makes it difficult to apply by ethnomusicologists, who cannot remain specialists in the current state of the law.

Nevertheless, ethnomusicologists must remain aware of their role in safeguarding the rights to music. They should realize that their responsibility will extend beyond the fieldwork setting. In the future, there may be unanticipated, possibly exploitative, uses of recording and other documentation.[10] Yet the absence of an appropriate legal framework leaves the ethnomusicologists to rely largely on their own judgement.

The SEM Manual attempts to address the vacuum of guidance by offering a set of ethical principles. Instead of imposing a legalistic regime on the ethnomusicologist, the manual suggests that "the current professional standards of ethical field conduct are [an ethnomusicologist's] best guide."[11] In Appendix VI, entitled *Ethical Considerations*, it advises ethnomusicologists, among other things, to:

1. uphold "honesty in the representation of oneself and one's work"[12];
2. build relationships "based on informed consent, rights of privacy and confidentiality, and mutual respect"[13];
3. maintain "awareness of the connection between proprietary concerns and economic interests."[14]

These maxims are interconnected. In order to obtain informed consent, an ethnomusicologist must be honest about himself and his work. In turn, the function of prior informed consent is to establish the rights to the recordings, which govern the economic interests. In order to set out the rights clearly, the SEM Manual advises the ethnomusicologist to "[a]pply the concept of informed consent to all his dealings with his informants".[15] It further suggests how best to formalize that consent, in order to clarify the relationship between the parties and avoid future conflict:

> [Ethnomusicologists should p]repare recording agreement forms or develop a format for recording permissions. [Researchers] may obtain permission in writing or verbally

9 *Id.* at 14.
10 *Id.* at 86–87.
11 *Id.* at 14.
12 *Id.* at 86.
13 *Id.* at 86.
14 *Id.* at 86.
15 *Id.* at 12.

> (with the tape recorder running), but it's best to keep written records of these transactions in either case.[16]

Though these recommendations should be acceptable to most ethnomusicologists, putting them into practice is more difficult. Ethnomusicologists are aware of the importance of a respectful relation with their informants and musicians, and they are increasingly becoming aware of copyright issues. In the words of Hugo Zemp, ethnomusicologists "are more and more involved in the web of the world market."[17] Nevertheless, there remain very few publications explicitly dealing with copyright issues in ethnomusicology journals and books. For instance, in the index of the widely known book on fieldwork edited by Gregory F. Barz and Timothy J. Cooley words like "copyright", "legal issues" or "entertainment law" are missing, as are the economic issues of music making.[18] Despite this dearth of publications, we could learn from the legal issues in popular music, for example. As Anthony Seeger mentions:

> [S]ome of the most in-depth research on western song seems to have been done under the sting of a lawsuit. It probably pays better than most research grants; the stakes are higher. ... [O]ne could argue that the lawcourts are as good a place to define the minimum definition of a musical theme.[19]

There are several reasons why ethnomusicologists pay little attention to legal issues. The ethnomusicologist, like other social scientists, is often placed in the "schizophrenic" position of sharing experiences with his informants at certain moments, and becoming an outside observer at other moments. The ethnomusicologist must withdraw for reflection in order to publish research findings. These moments of reflection are mostly carried out in an educational institution or research institute, and those institutions want scientific production in the form of publications. In the Western world articles and books are still considered the best products; while CDs and films are only slowly gaining some scientific recognition. Because of this focus on publication, the institutions often pay little regard to the legal implications of the recorded music.

Nevertheless, evolving technologies demonstrate the urgent need for institutions and ethnomusicologists to pay greater regard to the legal implications of the recordings. It should be standard practice for ethnomusicologists to leave recordings behind in the local institution of the country or region where the music was recorded. However, in the past this could not easily be achieved because

---

16 *Id.* at 21.

17 *See* Zemp, *supra* note 5, at 53.

18 *See* G.F. Barz and T.J. Cooley (eds.), *Shadows in the Field: New Perspectives for Fieldwork in Ethnomusicology*, 1997.

19 *See* A. Seeger, "Ethnomusicology and Music Law", 36 *Ethnomusicol.* 345, 354 (1992).

of the costs involved, time required to make the copy by the researcher, and the limited facilities for storage and accessibility in the local institutions that would receive a copy. Moreover, conforming to this practice may have infringed the copyright of the sponsoring institution, since the sponsoring institution typically retains the rights to the recording.

While copying technology for analogue recordings remained cumbersome and expensive, the ethnomusicologists and institutions did not perceive that the requirements to deposit copies of recordings raised many significant legal problems. Nowadays, in the digital era, the technology involved in making copies has become much less of a burden as copying digital files is much faster than copying analogue recordings (for instance, on reels, cassette tape or film). Some hard-disk (audio) recorders are already able to record on hard-disk and at the same time make a copy on a memory-card (CompactFlash card) and also externally via a FireWire connection. Hence in today's world, digital recordings and the great facility of dissemination magnify the potential for legal implications.

Despite the urgency and importance of these issues, ethnomusicologists are only slowly becoming aware of the complicated copyright problems involved in making field recordings, archiving them and publishing samples with a book or on a separate CD or DVD. This can partially be attributed to the fact that making field recordings and publishing these is usually not a financial success. On the contrary, quite often the researcher has to pay a considerable sum out of his own pocket to achieve the required results. I estimate that during my academic life I have paid for about one third of the apparatus needed to record and analyse the music for my research, because I could not borrow or obtain the appropriate apparatus from any institution. I think in this regard I am not an exception.[20]

Moreover, when copies of some of my recordings were presented to institutions, there was no payment for the time I spent on making the copies of tapes and documentation. Further, I was not asked to sign a contract with conditions for the use of my recordings in future, when I left a copy of the Malawian music recordings with the University of Malawi in 1971. This was repeated when I presented the University of Amsterdam with a copy of these Malawian music recordings and later with copies of audio recordings made from Baduy music in West Java between 1976 and 1979. Of course, these institutions, like the researcher, usually do not make money from these recordings and probably therefore did not bother to think seriously about copyright issues.

Seeger describes a similarly lamentable situation in the U.S.A.[21], and on the whole, the conditions in the Netherlands are still much worse for the few ethnomusicologists in and out of university departments. There are signs of

20 *See also, e.g.*, Zemp, *supra* note 5, at 36–37.

21 *See* Seeger, *supra* note 19, at 350–51.

improvement on a European scale, for instance, with the modest start of the Training for Audiovisual Preservation in Europe (TAPE) project, coordinated by the European Commission on Preservation and Access (ECPA).[22] The TAPE project describes itself as "primarily concerned with preservation and access issues of [audiovisual (AV)] materials in non-dedicated institutions, i.e. collections not specializing in audiovisual that happen to have AV collections."[23] This includes audiovisual materials collected by linguists, anthropologists and ethnomusicologists for their research.

Although ethnomusicologists generally cannot count on much understanding and help from the institutions for their problems, this does not mean that they can neglect the copyright problems. Ethnomusicologists have treated this too casually in the past. They were innocent and now they are gradually realizing that there are many possibilities for misuse of their recorded music.

Zemp's experiences on how he dealt with prior informed consent and royalties in the Solomon Islands can be taken as an example.[24] When he arrived in 1969 there was a discussion with traditional leaders about his research project. He did not pay for the recording of music with shell money, because that would be too expensive for him as an outsider. In the end, they agreed on paying each musician the amount that the government paid for labour, for example, for building a road or a school, which was US$ 1 per day in 1969. This was compensation for the time that the musicians would have worked in their gardens, since the leaders explained to Zemp that he could never "buy" their music. The leaders insisted that any profit from producing records should come back to the musicians. However, this money would not be given to the individual musicians, but to the 'Are'are council of chiefs, "who were responsible for custom and development, since the music belonged to the 'Are'are people as a whole." After the fieldwork, Zemp returned to France and published three gramophone records with 'Are'are music in 1971–73. Although the received royalties were sent to the chiefs, on Zemp's next trip it appeared that they were not pleased at all. Apparently, they thought that he had been cheating them, like a record company had been cheating an 'Are'are pop musician. Zemp easily solved the problem by providing the chiefs with a copy of all the royalty payments. This shows that often the expectations for royalties are too high, especially when they are compared to royalties for pop music. Sometimes ethnomusicologists receive no royalties at all. For instance, I personally have not received any royalties for my book and cassette tape on Cianjuran music.[25]

---

22 *See generally* TAPE – Training for Audiovisual Preservation in Europe, *available at* www.tape-online.net/index.html (last visited 31 July 2008).

23 *Id.*

24 *See* Zemp, *supra* note 5, at 37–39.

25 *See* W. van Zanten, *Sundanese Music in the Cianjuran Style: Anthropological and Musicological Aspects of Tembang Sunda*, 1989.

Zemp also describes how samples of music recorded by him were included in Western songs without asking permission. The first case he describes is by a French composer and interpreter, Michel Portal, who used a lullaby from the 'Are'are people in one of his compositions. In his letter to Portal on 21 January 1996, Zemp[26] acknowledges that, according to French law, "traditional music is a matter of the public domain and, consequently, on the legal level, you have the right to use a tune without paying royalties to the true owners," but then admonishes Portal on the moral level. Zemp asks for a voluntary payment of part of the royalties to the 'Are'are people, and he supplies the address and bank account of their official representatives. Zemp did not receive a reply, but heard that "Portal did receive the letter and that he said that he was irreproachable".[27]

The second case described by Zemp is the *Deep Forest* CD published in 1992.[28] The musicians involved in this project used a sample of his *Solomon Islands: Malaita Fataleku and Baegu Music* CD, re-issued by Auvidis-UNESCO on CD in 1990, without any permission given by Zemp or the United Nations Educational, Scientific and Cultural Organization (UNESCO) to use it. Furthermore, no credit was even given to the recorded musicians nor were royalties paid to Auvidis or UNESCO. In fact, the *Deep Forest* CD liner went so far as to state that UNESCO, as well as the two musicologists Hugo Zemp and Simha Arom, had supported this enterprise. Zemp protested in a letter to the two musicians involved, Michel Sanchez and Eric Mouquet. These musicians replied in a letter dated 1 October 1996, and they told Zemp that his position was erroneous and that they had done the right thing.[29] This affair with the *Deep Forest* CD, of which 2 million copies were sold by May 1995, is now well-known by many ethnomusicologists as a cautionary tale.

I have published far fewer audiovisual recordings than Hugo Zemp. My own audiovisual recordings were mainly made for documentary reasons and musical analysis. However, copyright issues remain prominent both in my own work and in the field of ethnomusicology. Below I shall give a few examples of prior informed consent in my own fieldwork in Indonesia since 1976 and discuss some of the problems encountered.

3. PRIOR INFORMED CONSENT OF BADUY MINORITY GROUP

The Baduy are an ethnic group of 7,500–8,000 people living in Kanékés, which is an area of about 51 square kilometres located some 100 km southwest of Jakarta,

26 *See* Zemp, *supra* note 5, at 43–44.
27 *Id.* at 44.
28 *Id.* at 44–49.
29 *Id.* at 54.

in West Java. They have been recognized as an Indigenous community (*masyarakat adat*) with collective land rights (*hak ulayat*) by the local government of the Lebak Regency since 2001. The Baduy have been living in Kanékés village for at least several hundred years, and no other groups are allowed to live there. They speak a Sundanese dialect and are in this respect not very different from other Sundanese peoples.

However, Baduy social organization and religion (called *Sunda Wiwitan*) are different from those of the surrounding Islamic Sundanese. According to the dictates of their religion, the Baduy live in an ascetic way for the well-being of the world. Their life is regulated by many duties and prohibitions, as handed down by former generations. For instance, they are not allowed to attend school, or to have irrigated rice fields, buffalo or fishponds. They cannot grow cloves or tea, nor can they use electricity, radio or television. The Baduy live mainly from agricultural products, such as rice, vegetables, and fruits, but they also sell products like palm sugar, knives and woven cloths.

The Indonesian government recognizes Kanékés as the area where only Baduy people live, and where they can have their own regulations.[30] For instance, the Baduy do not pay taxes to the Indonesian government. They also do not vote in general elections[31], nor send their children to school, which is compulsory for other Indonesians. The secular village head of Kanékés (*jaro pamaréntah*; literally "village head of the government") mediates between the Baduy, especially the spiritual leaders, and the Indonesian authorities. Although the village head of Kanékés is formally appointed by the Indonesian authorities, with consent of the spiritual leaders of the Baduy, he is not paid by the government, like other village heads. The same holds true for the secretary (*carik*) to the village head, who is always a non-Baduy person. The secretary's role today involves handling identification cards, registration of births and deaths, and the census.

The Baduy way of life has recently come under great pressure, caused by the increase of their number and the interaction with the modernizing outside world. Baduy social organization, their religion and their music making are greatly affected by the developments in the last decades. In 2003 the Baduy ascetics seemed to have given in to some of the many temptations that the surrounding world offers them. Ukang Sukarna, the secretary of Kanékés since 1970, told me in 2003 that "the law was already weak" (*hukum sudah lemah*), meaning that the leaders, who were supposed to maintain the religious law, already frequently broke the law themselves.[32]

---

30 In colonial times the Dutch-Indies government had also recognized the special status of the Baduy.

31 If not, too much pressure is put on them by government officials.

32 *See* W. van Zanten, "Les tentations des ascètes: Patrimoine culturel immatériel des Baduy dans le Banten du sud (Indonésie)", in J. Duvignaud and Ch. Khaznadar (eds.), *Le patrimoine culturel immatériel: Les enjeux, les problématiques, les pratiques*, 2004, 124, 135–36.

In order to protect Baduy social organization and way of life, there are strict restrictions imposed on outsiders who want to visit Kanékés. They must first report to the village head. It is difficult to get permission to stay in Kanékés village for longer periods and to be present at rituals. Some Western researchers were even forbidden from staying in the village for longer than one night.[33] My own experiences with the attitude of the Baduy towards research and audiovisual recordings are rather positive. In June and again in July 1976 my wife and I were allowed to stay in the Baduy hamlet of Gajéboh, though only for a few days. Talsim, the Baduy official (*jaro dangka*) who had made arrangements for my research, said that he was pleased with the recordings I had made. In this way the outer world would become acquainted with Baduy music. Watching my Super 8 film some time later in Jakarta, he said he very much enjoyed the visual documentation as well.

Though I succeeded in establishing a good relationship with the Baduy, I always remained subject to their restrictions in terms of time, place and manner of recording. At the time of our visits to Kanékés village in June and July of 1976 the set of shaken bamboo idiophones (*angklung*) could not be played, as those instruments are forbidden (*pamali*) outside the season for planting rice. These instruments can only be played from the end of August until December. For that reason, Talsim came to our house in Jakarta in September 1976 with a group of Baduy to play *angklung* and xylophone (*calung* and *gambang*) music. He again showed his interest in having Baduy music recorded when he turned up at our house in Jakarta in January 1977. This time he had brought a storyteller with him to have an epic *pantun* story recorded. Within the Baduy territory the recitation of a *pantun* story can take place only in a ritual context and it is, for instance, performed for curing the rice and at circumcisions. Accordingly, before the *pantun* could begin, some necessary ritual measures were taken. The storyteller burned incense and made a kind of tent (*lawon bodas*) from a white sheet under which he was sitting while performing. Then a magic formula was recited. However, there was no offering made, as I had always seen when recording *pantun* stories in Bandung from 1981 to 1989[34] and near the Baduy area in Margaluyu in 2003. In 1992 several musicians were willing to recite a *pantun* story for a recording, but only outside Kanékés village. Unfortunately, at that time I did not have the opportunity to arrange such *pantun* recordings outside Kanékés village. My recordings of *gamelan* music in 1976 were also subject to some restrictions. The Baduy *gamelan* may only be played during the 2–3 months after the *Seba*

33 *See* W. van Zanten, "Aspects of Baduy Music in its Sociocultural Context, with Special Reference to Singing and Angklung", 151 *Bijdragen tot de Taal-, Land- en Volkenkunde* 516, 519 (1995).

34 *See* W. van Zanten, "Sung Epic Narrative and Lyrical Songs: Carita Pantun and Tembang Sunda", in B. Arps (ed.), *Performance in Java and Bali: Studies of Narrative, Theatre, Music and Dance*, 1993, 144, 145.

ceremony[35], a period which falls between June and August. That is the season for weddings and circumcisions, and the *gamelan* groups perform on these occasions. To record a *gamelan* ensemble playing in the Gajéboh hamlet of Kanékés village, I could only place microphones inside the house near the *gamelan*, and then record outside with the recording apparatus during the performance (*see* Figure 1). Most probably this was because modern and foreign technology could not come too close to the fireplace of a Baduy house (kitchen), positioned behind the room where the *gamelan* was played, which is a place for family members and close friends only. Most other recordings took place on the veranda of Baduy houses, which is the place for receiving guests.[36]

Figure 1: The author with a tape recorder outside of the Baduy house where a *gamelan* ensemble is being recorded. The recording apparatus had to stay outside the house, and only the microphones were allowed inside. Gajéboh, Kanékés, West Java, 19 July 1976.

As the Baduy community knew me from my fieldwork there between 1976 and 1979, it was relatively easy to arrange my next time in Kanékés village in 1992. In October and November 1992 I was allowed to stay with the secular village head (*jaro pamaréntah*), Asrab, for nearly twenty days at a stretch, and later on for

35 The harvest ceremonies are concluded with the *Seba* ceremony, in May – beginning of June. It is a presentation of agricultural products by several hundred to a thousand Baduy men and women to some rulers outside the Baduy area. The *Seba* ceremony revives the relationship between the "elder brothers" (Baduy) and their "younger brothers", the worldly rulers. The ascetic Baduy advise their "younger brothers", who for their part protect the Baduy.

36 *See* van Zanten, *supra* note 34, at 519–21.

another four days. With the special permission of Asrab, I was able to record the ceremonial playing of *angklung* on digital audio tape (DAT) from inside a house. While doing this, I was able to witness this very important ritual of "wakening" the rice goddess Asri and announcing her "marriage" through a hole in the wall. The following morning I was allowed to follow the procession in which the rice was carried to a special field where it was planted. During this ceremony the rice goddess Asri was "married" to the Earth. However, I was again restricted by Baduy custom: I could not, together with some other non-Baduy people, cross the river and enter the rice field, but rather had to watch from a distance of about 500 meters.[37]

These experiences illustrate that, for ritual music, the place and time of performance are meaningful. This makes it difficult to interpret the prior informed consent of the Baduy community outside of the particular context in which the music was performed. For instance, could my recordings be played outside of the appropriate season? Would a secular audience be allowed to hear them? In the extreme, could the recordings be used for commercial gain? The nuances of prior informed consent for ethnomusicology recordings often leave these questions unanswered.

As a further complication, communities seldom speak with one voice. The leaders of the community agreed to my recordings, and the recordings quite often took place at their houses. However, this does not necessarily mean that each individual member of the society agreed to the recordings. For instance, in 1976 two Baduy whom I had accidentally filmed in the Baduy area (Kanékés) ran away from the camera, and obviously did not consent to being filmed. As an additional problem, it is sometimes difficult to discern which leaders are representative of the community. For example, some apparent leaders may represent only part of the population, or the composition of leadership may change such that the consenting leaders no longer represent the people.

The nature of prior informed consent is also confounded by the form of payment for ethnomusicology recordings. In 1992 I agreed to contribute 4 million rupiah (about US$ 2,000) for buying farmland outside the Baduy area of Kanékés[38] to be used by the village head in office (*jaro pamaréntah*). This land was not for private use, but attached to the office of the village head, like other communal land attached to Baduy officials (*see* Figure 2). When I visited the Baduy again in 2003 I heard that the money had been used to buy the piece of land. However, they alleged that the owner had tricked the Baduy, as his land had already been sold to another person as well. I have no proof of all this, but I believe that this is indeed

37 *Id.* at 532–35.

38 Due to land pressure the Baduy have bought much land surrounding Kanékés village for many decades. If there is much work to do on these fields, they will stay there overnight in a shelter and only go back to Kanékés for one or two days per week.

what happened. It would have been very difficult for the Baduy to get that money back, if they had tried this via a legal procedure. The lost money was paid from my own pocket, and it would have been impossible to charge an institute for it. Nevertheless, the gift was part of my research. This is how the complicated issue of prior informed consent works.

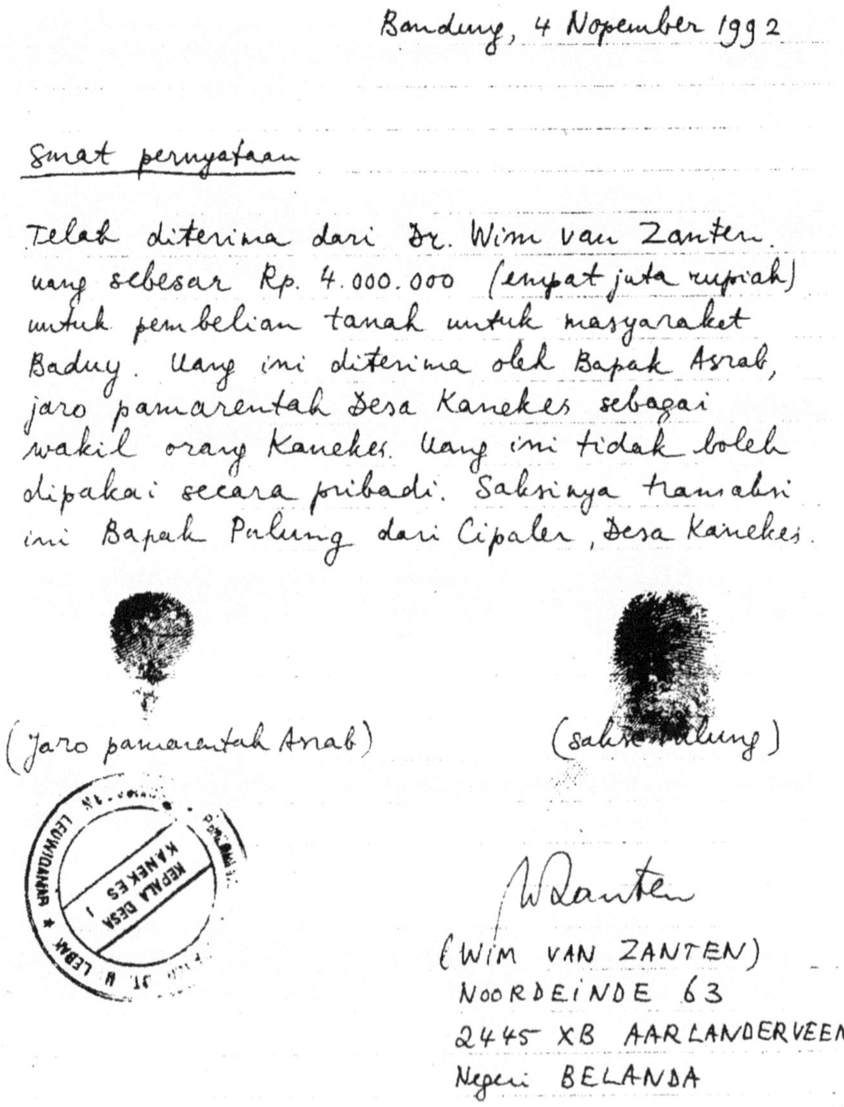

Bandung, 4 Nopember 1992

Surat pernyataan

Telah diterima dari Dr. Wim van Zanten uang sebesar Rp. 4.000.000 (empat juta rupiah) untuk pembelian tanah untuk masyarakat Baduy. Uang ini diterima oleh Bapak Asrab, jaro pamarentah Desa Kanekes sebagai wakil orang Kanekes. Uang ini tidak boleh dipakai secara pribadi. Saksinya transaksi ini Bapak Pulung dari Cipaler, Desa Kanekes.

(Jaro pamarentah Asrab) (saksi Pulung)

KEPALA DESA KANEKES

W Zanten

(WIM VAN ZANTEN)
NOORDEINDE 63
2445 XB AARLANDERVEEN
Negeri BELANDA

Figure 2: A contract between the author and the Baduy secular village head for the donation of money.

Bandung, 4 November 1992

Contract/statement.

[We have] received from Dr Wim van Zanten the amount of Rp 4.000.000 (4 million rupiah) for buying land for the Baduy community. This money was received by Mr. Asrab, head of Kanekes village, as representative of the Baduy people. This money may not be used for private purposes. Witness of this transaction was Mr. Pulung from Cipaler, Kanekes village.

[left thumb print]
(village head Asrab)

[left thumb print]
(witness Pulung)

[official stamp head of Kanekes village]

[signature]
(Wim van Zanten)
[address in the Netherlands]

From my work in 1976, I only intended to make one or two gramophone records with Baduy music. For several reasons this did not happen, and in the 1970s and 1980s I only used my recordings as documentation for scholarly work and for teaching purposes. However, in the early 1990s, I started to realize that the audiovisual recordings of the Baduy were rather unique and I developed the idea of publishing a book on Baduy music combined with the audiovisual recordings on CD and DVD. In considering whether to publish such recordings, I immediately encountered the problem of prior informed consent. What permission do I have to distribute the music of the Baduy? To what did the Baduy consent by allowing me to record? Could I publish all of the audiovisual materials, or only some of them? Also, was the consent I obtained still binding on the Baduy? The Baduy leaders and the individual musicians had approved of these recordings, and I had paid for most of them in direct form or *via* several gifts to the community. However, the recordings might be heard and seen by people with little understanding of the religious setting of the music. Can I pass these recordings on to them?

The Baduy tradition suggests otherwise. When a bard first begins an epic *pantun* story, he explains that this story from heaven should be told only by those who are knowledgeable:

From where is this story?
From where does it come that will be told?
Its place is in the abode of the gods.
Caught in a [magical] jewel-box, ...
Put down on the large road,
Opened by a passer-by,

By someone who is acquainted with what is found,
By someone who is knowledgeable and wise,
By someone whose knowledge is many-sided.
When it is opened there is great joy (?)
With them who asked for the performance.[39]

The Baduy have received my two articles about their music[40], but they cannot read or write (at least most of them cannot) and certainly not in English or French. So, do they agree with what I wrote about them? The last time I visited the Baduy was in March and April of 2003. At that time, they also expressed no objections to my recordings, even though my visit fell within a three-month period that is normally unsuitable for receiving visitors (*Kawalu* harvest rituals). In fact, instead of limiting my use of the recordings, the village head at that time, Daénah, remarked that it would be good if people would see this music on Dutch television: It would be much better than looking at "images of a war with dead bodies". He made this remark at the end of March 2003, a few days after the invasion of Iraq by the U.S.A. and its allies. This event was frequently discussed by the Baduy, because they were afraid of a Third World War that, according to them, would be a war about religion.

I had chosen to visit the Baduy during these fasting months, as I had never been there during this period. I was less interested in audiovisual recordings and more in checking many details about the data collected during earlier fieldwork periods. Apparently the Baduy respected me enough to allow me and two of my companions[41] to stay at the house of the village head, Daénah. There were some restrictions, though. I could not just walk freely around in the Baduy area. However, I was allowed to make audio and video recordings, even during this period that is not suitable for such activities.

Hence it seems that the Baduy did not object to my publishing the recorded music and film. However, does the same consent apply to my recordings of *pantun* storytelling or *angklung* music, both of which are used in Baduy rituals? In the end, there seems to be no clear answer to this question, and no law or framework to guide my decision. Such determinations ultimately rest on my personal judgement and ethics.

39 *See* VAN ZANTEN, *supra* note 35, at 156–57.

40 *See* VAN ZANTEN, *supra* note 34, and VAN ZANTEN, *supra* note 33.

41 A Dutch student of mine who happened to be studying for a year at the conservatory of performing arts (STSI) in Bandung and a student of theatre at this conservatory, who was born near the Baduy area and assisted me in my research.

4. A CONTRACT ON PAPER: STORY OF A BADUY GAMELAN

The ethical guidelines proposed by the SEM appear to remedy such ambiguities, at least somewhat, by advising ethnomusicologists to obtain permission "in writing or verbally (with the tape recorder running)".[42] In theory, such explicit documentation should clarify the nature of the informants' consent. However, the realities of contracting with Indigenous peoples like the Baduy create a much murkier picture, as illustrated by my experiences.

From 1976–79 I worked at the Faculty for Social Sciences of the University of Indonesia in Jakarta. In April 1976 I bought a small old *gamelan* from the Baduy minority group (*see* Figure 3, depicting another Baduy *gamelan*) for about US$ 1,200. The instruments were offered for sale to me in Jakarta by the Baduy official Talsim, because the owner had died and the family needed money to pay their debts. I was interested in Baduy music, as I had already been planning to make audiovisual recordings, but had no real interest in purchasing a *gamelan*. However, at that time I felt, it would be better to buy the *gamelan* myself than to allow a tourist unfamiliar with Baduy music to buy it.

Figure 3: A Baduy *gamelan* played in Kompol, 25 July 1976 (still photo captured from a movie)

---

42 *SEM Manual*, *supra* note 4, at 21.

A *gamelan* is a set of (mainly) bronze instruments, in this case consisting of hanging and lying gongs, metallophones, and small cymbals. The Baduy *gamelan* are of the type of the Sundanese small "village" *gamelan*. The one I bought was said to be tuned according to the *pélog* tone system[43] and estimated to date back to the first half of the nineteenth century. Not every Baduy hamlet is allowed to have a *gamelan*. In 2003 there were at least 4 Baduy *gamelan*[44], and the total number today may be 6 or 7.

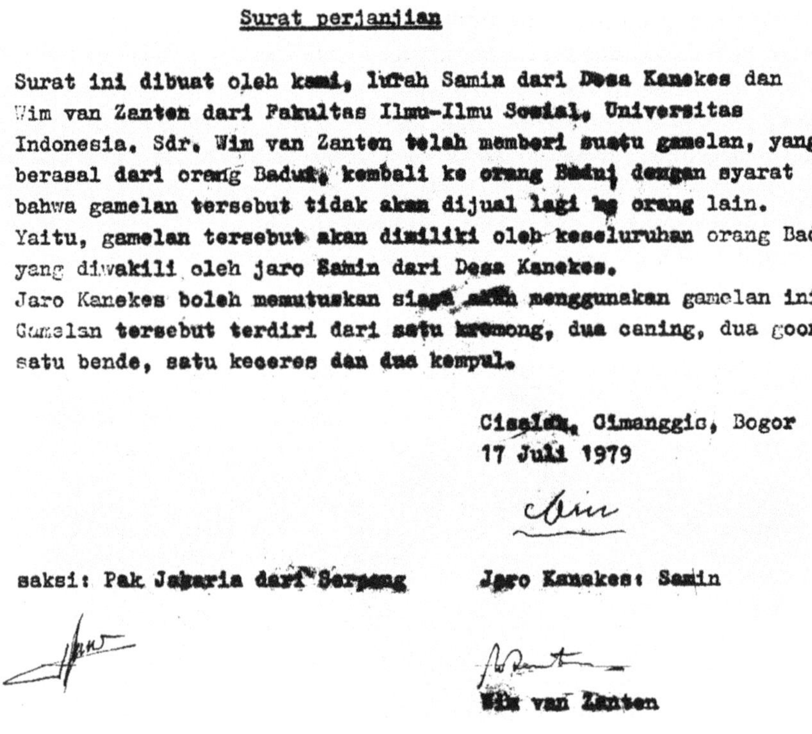

Surat perjanjian

Surat ini dibuat oleh kami, lurah Samin dari Desa Kanekes dan Wim van Zanten dari Fakultas Ilmu-Ilmu Sosial, Universitas Indonesia. Sdr. Wim van Zanten telah memberi suatu gamelan, yang berasal dari orang Badui, kembali ke orang Badui dengan syarat bahwa gamelan tersebut tidak akan dijual lagi ke orang lain. Yaitu, gamelan tersebut akan dimiliki oleh keseluruhan orang Badui, yang diwakili oleh jaro Samin dari Desa Kanekes. Jaro Kanekes boleh memutuskan siapa [illegible] menggunakan gamelan ini. Gamelan tersebut terdiri dari satu kromong, dua caning, dua goong, satu bende, satu kecores dan dua kempul.

Cisalak, Cimanggis, Bogor
17 Juli 1979

saksi: Pak Jakaria dari Serpong

Jaro Kanekes: Samin

Wim van Zanten

Figure 4: A contract between the author and the Baduy secular village head for the donation of a *gamelan*.

---

43 There are several tone systems for *gamelan* in West Java of which the *saléndro* and the *pélog* tone system are the most common. *Saléndro* is conceptually an equidistant pentatonic system and a *saléndro gamelan* is used for the accompaniment of the *wayang golék* puppet theatre. *Pélog* is a pentatonic system with unequal distances between the notes and this tone system is used in the *gamelan degung*. The Sundanese *gamelan* do not combine both tone systems in one ensemble, as in the Central-Javanese *gamelan*, and are therefore smaller. The tone systems of Baduy instruments need to be studied in more detail and we cannot take for granted that these are the same as those used in the urban *gamelan*.

44 This figure includes the gamelan that I bought and later returned in 1979, as described below.

> Contract ["letter of agreement"]. This contract is made by us, Samin, head of Kanékés village, and Wim van Zanten of the Faculty of Social Sciences, University of Indonesia. Mr. Wim van Zanten has a *gamelan* that came from the Baduy community, now returned to the Baduy community, with the condition that this gamelan will not be sold again to other people. That means, this *gamelan* will be owned by the whole Baduy community that is represented by Samin, village head of Kanekes.
> The village head of Kanekes may decide who shall be using this *gamelan*.
> This *gamelan* consists of one *kromong* [set of lying gongs], two *caning* [metallophones], two gongs, one *bende* [small gong], one *keceres* [small cymbals] and two *kempul* [single lying gongs, kept in the hand].
>
> Cisalak, Cimanggis, Bogor
> 17 July 1979
> [signature]
>
> witness: Mr. Jakaria from Serpong
> [signature]
>
> Head of Kanékés village: Samin
> [signature]
> Wim van Zanten

When I planned to leave Indonesia in July 1979, I needed to decide what to do with this *gamelan*. I did not want to export the *gamelan*, and most probably I would not have been permitted to do so by the Indonesian government, as the *gamelan* was old. The second possibility was to donate it to the *gamelan* museum in Subang, West Java. Then it would probably not be played. Hence I presented this *gamelan* to Samin, secular village head of Kanékés, as a representative of the Baduy people, with the hope that it would be played again by them. The village head came to my house in Cisalak to collect the *gamelan*, and we made a simple "contract" on paper that stated that this *gamelan* was returned to the Baduy community with the sole condition that it could never be sold again to outsiders (*see* Figure 4).

I did not return to the Baduy area until 1992. Samin, the former village head of Kanékés, had died in December 1991, and the *gamelan* instruments were no longer played. It was no longer possible to play the *gamelan*, because the different instruments were no longer kept together in one place, but were divided between the houses of two of Samin's sons, who lived in villages outside the Baduy area (Cipangembar and Margaluyu). The sons remembered that I had presented the *gamelan* to their father, but they did not know anything about the conditions. They did not have a copy of my contract with their father. They also told me that they were put under great pressure to give the *gamelan* to the Regent of Rangkasbitung (non-Baduy area: seat of the Lebak Regency), as had happened before with other Baduy instruments. I made clear, that my intention had been to have the *gamelan* played by the Baduy people, and that I had returned it to the Baduy community, with the sole condition that it could not be sold again or disappear from the Baduy area. I asked for the *gamelan* to be returned to Kanékés village, which only happened at the end of 2002. The *gamelan* is now in the hamlet of Kadujangkung in the Baduy area, where I saw it in April 2003. By that time, the wooden frames for the different gongs and metallophones had wasted away and I donated Rp 600,000 (about EUR 65) to have new ones made. The *gamelan* was going to be played in the first coming *gamelan* season of June-August 2003.[45]

Part of the confusion around this *gamelan* was that in 1979 the Baduy society was upset by the transmigration project that had started in 1978. In fact, Samin was in 1979 still officially secular village head of the Baduy area, that is, of Kanékés village. However, because he moved to the transmigration village Cipangembar with about 80 Baduy families and no longer lived according to Baduy rules, he was at the same time no longer part of the Baduy society. I did not understand this situation very well in 1979, otherwise I might have transported the *gamelan* immediately to Kanékés village, which is the Baduy region.[46]

This example demonstrates the problems of contracting with rural communities like the Baduy. Even though a contract may be clear by international standards, the community may not safeguard the contract, and more broadly, it may not feel bound by the contract across generations or geographies. The example also illustrates the monitoring difficulties of contracts with Indigenous peoples. Many Indigenous peoples would find it extremely difficult, if not impossible, to determine whether a Western ethnomusicologist has violated the terms of their consent. In this case, the difficulty of enforcement fell to me rather than the Baduy, but in general the same limitations apply. If I had not returned to Kanékés in 1992, there would have been no way to discover that my contract had been breached. Finally, the example illustrates the problem of representation among Indigenous peoples. I had assumed that by contracting with Samin, I could validly bind the Baduy community, but the facts on the ground proved otherwise. The challenges of accurately assessing the appropriate representative of an Indigenous community, compounded by potential changes in leadership, cast doubt on the enforceability and validity of any contract with an Indigenous community. So even though a contract with the Baduy for the use of their music may, in theory, alleviate many of the ambiguities of their consent, the practical problems of executing and enforcing such contracts render the requirement of written consent an imperfect solution, at best.

---

45 For more details, *see* VAN ZANTEN, *supra* note 33, at 143–45.

46 For more details, *see id.* at 130–32, 137–41 and 143–44.

5. A TAPE RECORDED CONTRACT IN MINANGKABAU

The above example illustrates the difficulty of executing a written agreement with Indigenous peoples. As an alternative, the SEM Manual also advocates recording verbal consent. Yet recorded consent bears its own problems, as the following example demonstrates. In 1996, with Bart Barendregt, I made video recordings of Minangkabau[47] performing arts in West Sumatra, Indonesia. From this material we made a film about the Randai theatre[48] and I made a film about solo singing with a bamboo flute.[49] In the early morning of 19 November 1996, I had recorded the recitation of an epic story (*sijobang*) by *Datuk* Kodo, also known as As. *Datuk* Kodo was the leader of a Randai theatre group that we had filmed a few times. The performance of the *sijobang* episode lasted for about two hours and ended around 2:30 in the morning. *Datuk* Kodo accompanied his singing rhythmically by tapping a matchbox. The story was about the hero Anggun Nan Tungga. After this *sijobang* performance, we discussed the purpose of my recordings and copyright issues in a relaxed setting, when most other people in the room were sleeping. I recorded this discussion on my DAT recorder, and below you find the most important sections of our discussion, translated from Indonesian.

[WvZ]: It would be nice if a Randai group could come to Europe, because it seems that Europeans will like this type of theatre [which includes dialogue, music,

---

47 There are about 6 million Minangkabau people. More than 4 million still live in West Sumatra, and about two million are living in cities outside West Sumatra, like Medan and Jakarta, and also in the nearby country Malaysia. Padang, the largest Minangkabau city lying at the sea coast, numbers close to one million people, but the inland cities like Bukittinggi and Payukumbuh each have about one hundred thousand inhabitants. Traditionally the young, unmarried Minangkabau men left their home town for an extended period to acquire knowledge, experience and wealth, and sometimes married in foreign regions. This (temporary) migration is called *marantau*, and many of the Randai theatre stories and the *sijobang* epic stories are about such travels of the hero.

48 Randai theatre involves a kind of circular dancing (*galombang*), based on movements of the martial arts (*pencak silat*), a dialogue between actors and sung poetry. During the intervals in a Randai performance popular songs may be played, a dance like the *tari piring* – with earthenware plates – may be performed, there may be a comical sketch, or a demonstration of the martial art. *See* W. van Zanten and B. Barendregt, *Told in Heaven to Become Stories on Earth: A Study of Change in Randai Theatre of the Minangkabau in West Sumatra using Visual Documentation from the 1930s* (educational film accompanied by a documentation book, 2000).

49 This type of songs is called *saluang jo dendang* – singing (*dendang*) that is accompanied by a bamboo flute (*saluang*). In these songs the singers express different moods and sing about topics like love, nature and the past. *See* W. van Zanten, *Play the Saluang Flute, Use Your Fifth Finger: Lyrical Songs from Payakumbuh, West Sumatra* (educational film accompanied by a documentation book, 2002).

dance and comic sections]. The *sijobang* epic story telling would probably be too difficult.

[DK]: I agree. When we performed in Jakarta, many Europeans liked Randai, although they did not understand the words and the story. However, the movements were funny, so they laughed. Yes, we wait until you arrange something for us in Europe! [He laughs, then continues.] In fact we need only to come with three players, that is enough. [A normal performance has about 12–20 players].

[WvZ]: A few years ago I could arrange that my teacher of West Javanese Cianjuran music came to stay for almost half a year in the Netherlands to teach. I assisted him, because I knew about the music [since my PhD dissertation was about that music], and the effect was great. It would be nice if such thing could be organized with Randai theatre. I shall try.

[DK]: Here in Indonesia, you need help from others; otherwise it would be impossible to succeed for people like us, who belong to the lower strata. Take the recordings by the television. How many local people have been recorded by the [Indonesian] TV? None. They only record the performing arts from Java. Not from the Minangkabau [West Sumatra]! [He then corrects himself.] Well, *Saluang jo dendang* [solo singing with a bamboo flute] has been on TV, and that made us very happy. The TV is run by Javanese people!

[WvZ]: If we succeed in getting a Randai group to Europe or America, it would be nice, because then the people in Jakarta would realize that there are interesting performing arts in West Sumatra.

[DK]: Some time ago people from Malaysia came here to film. They wanted to pay us 2 million rupiah [in 1996, about US$ 880]. But for how many millions would they sell this in Malaysia? ... With ASKI dance and music conservatory [in the nearby city of Padang Panjang] it is different: we allow them to record, but that does not mean that they may use it commercially.

[WvZ]: Yes for scientific reasons it is different: only for documentation. If you make a [scientific] CD there are usually no royalties, it will sell only in small quantities, and the expenditure is higher than the income. But if the CD is sold commercially, then you have to be careful, because it is not easy to make these documentations. Then you have to ask permission. I do not know how it is here, but in West Java, when recorded for a commercial cassette tape, the [Cianjuran] musicians usually get a lump sum, each about Rp 50 000 to Rp 100 000 [in 1996, about US$ 22–44]. Then they get nothing more, whatever the number of copies sold may be, a hundred or a million. There is no system of royalties. I think that when the company sells many copies, the musicians should also get more money.

[DK]: Yes, Yes.

[WvZ]: In Europe and America the situation is that when the person who recorded gets a profit, the musicians should have their share.

[DK]: Yes, that is how it should be.

[WvZ]: We, scientists, are usually not able to help financially in a direct way. In an indirect way we may be able to help by our publications, such as the publication of Nigel Phillips about *sijobang* epic story telling.[[50]] It may attract the attention of people and then they may want to get musicians to perform in Europe.

[DK]: There were people who said, "The recordings of your performance will be sold on cassette tape in the Netherlands." I said, "Let him go ahead." If people like the music, it will be impossible for them to learn *sijobang* from these cassettes; that is impossible.

[WvZ]: Yes, this is just a start, to draw their attention ...

[DK]: [interrupting] Yes, that is it! When they hear it, they want to know more, meet the people and go to Indonesia. That is good. People here in the village have only limited experience. Yes, I am a farmer with only primary school education, but I know what happens in the outside world. Coming back to the 2 million rupiah offered by the Malaysians, well many people said to me: "Don't do this; for 2 million rupiah it will be sold commercially in Malaysia." Well, I replied, "Let them go ahead, whatever the number of cassettes that will be sold." I know that some time the Malaysians want to know about us here!

[WvZ]: It is a kind of promotion.

[DK]: Yes, promotion. Sometimes other people who record us want to be paid, but we don't want that! It once happened that the Indonesian TV wanted to be paid for filming our performance. So we would perform and we had to pay the TV crew for filming us!

[WvZ]: They wanted money from the Randai group? The Randai group should be receiving money!

[DK]: Yes, the performers should receive money. Like the performance in Sungai Baringin [which had occurred three days before, and I had also attended and filmed]. The Indonesian TV was also there in the morning [to film the installation of an *adat* chief]. ... They said that they were also willing to come in the evening to film the Randai performance, but then we would have to pay. I said that they could film if they wanted, but that we would not pay them.[51]

This recorded discussion took place in an informal setting, and it is not at all clear that the musician intended it as an expression of his consent. However, it is certainly a spoken "letter of intent" and helpful in possible discussions about intellectual property rights. The question is of course whether we should aim for a more formalized form of contract. It is clear that *Datuk* Kodo wants pupils who are genuinely interested in the Minangkabau performing arts, in particular Randai and *sijobang*. This is a general attitude of musicians. They are not only

50 *See* N. Phillips, *Sung narrative poetry of West Sumatra*, 1981.

51 W. van Zanten, DAT 96-9 (19 November 1996) (unpublished sound recording) (on file with author) (part of the discussion in the last 15 recorded minutes on the 2-hour tape).

interested in financial reward, but rather in the recognition that their "technology of enchantment"[52] deserves respect. Therefore, musicians are concerned about the transmission of their musical knowledge.

It was difficult for me to promise *Datuk* Kodo that I would arrange pupils from the Netherlands for him. However, I gave him a VHS copy of the Randai film in February 2001.[53] In addition, as at that time his son was enrolled as a student in an Islamic university (STAIN), I bought a bicycle for him and several books, including dictionaries English-Indonesian and Indonesian-English. *Datuk* Kodo first refused to accept this for his son. He did not want to become dependent, but he eventually accepted, as I made clear that his contribution to my film was very valuable. The total amount of money was only about US$ 150 (in 2001, about 1.3 million rupiah). By Indonesian standards it was a lot of money, but by Western standards it was not. As already remarked above, it is often difficult to put such money on the budget of a Western institute. Although on my budgets there has always been a modest post "presents for musicians", this was only for the time of recording. The strict division between business and private matters in the Netherlands clashes with the local culture in the Minangkabau and other parts of Indonesia.

This example illustrates both the practical difficulties of discerning consent from a recording and the ambiguous nature of indirect payment to musicians. More importantly, it demonstrates that the (individual) intellectual property rights are not really a concern. The musicians want to be remunerated, but they are much more concerned about the transmission of their cultural knowledge, as it is part of the heritage of the Minangkabau community.

6. CONCLUSION: WHO BENEFITS FROM THE RECORDINGS?

I have tried to show that, although prior informed consent is necessary, we should not think of it as a final solution to the problem of intellectual property rights in the field of ethnomusicology. There should be a long-term commitment to the rights of musicians and their communities, especially because the copyright laws give disproportionate power to the person making recordings of performed music. One can take as an example Seeger's long-time involvement with the Suyá

52 *See* A. Gell, "The Technology of Enchantment and the Enchantment of Technology", in E. Hirsch (ed.), *The Art of Anthropology: Essays and Diagrams*, 1999, 159, 163 (stating that "[t]he enchantment of technology is the power that technical processes have of casting a spell over us so that we see the real world in an enchanted form").

53 *See* van Zanten and Barendregt, *supra* note 49.

minority group in Brazil, which he researched in the early 1970s and to whom he returned in the 1990s and 2000s.[54]

The Baduy allowed me to record their music and daily life because they knew me as someone interested in their culture, who returned a *gamelan* to them in 1979 and donated money to buy communal land for the village head in 1992. My dealings in this were all based on my own judgements of fairness. It would have been preferable to have the guidance of a more concrete code for researchers. However, it seems that the present copyright laws are so biased toward Western standards of music production that it would be better to leave things as they are, and tell our students: "[T]he current professional standards of ethical field conduct are your best guide."[55] Sherylle Mills suggests that ethnomusicologists could establish a complaint board so that they could file complaints against their colleagues when breaches of trust occur.[56]

World Intellectual Property Organization (WIPO) could play a role in dispute settling resolution concerning intellectual property issues via the WIPO Arbitration Centre. However, I think there is more needed. UNESCO and WIPO should think about an easily accessible dispute settling body about problems such as I have described and possibly in the context of the *Convention for the Safeguarding of the Intangible Cultural Heritage* (ICH Convention).[57]

It is strange to hear that the Dutch organization that looks after intellectual property rights of composers, BUMA-STEMRA, has charged the Tropentheater in Amsterdam for "traditional" music performed by, for instance, Indian and Indonesian groups. Does BUMA-STEMRA have a list of composers of the performed music to whom they will send royalties? On the other hand, some Indonesian musicians do not realize that researchers seldom get royalties for CDs, and that already for some years the market for "traditional music" has been saturated with CDs. In fact UNESCO closed down its *Collection of Traditional Music*[58] in May 2005, because in this situation it did not have the money and time to go on with the series. As the editor at the ICTM responsible for this series since the beginning of 2004, I had the sad task to convey this message to my colleagues.

My own fieldwork examples presented above came from small rural groups in Indonesia. It would be somewhat different when talking about groups involved

54 *See* A. SEEGER, *Why Suyá Sing: A Musical Anthropology of an Amazonian People*, 2004.

55 *SEM Manual*, *supra* note 4, at 14.

56 *See* MILLS, *supra* note 3, at 82.

57 Convention for the Safeguarding of the Intangible Cultural Heritage, 17 October 2003, U.N. Doc. MISC/2003/CLT/CH/14 (2003), *available at* http://unesdoc.unesco.org/images/0013/001325/132540e.pdf (last visited 31 July 2008).

58 The UNESCO Collection of Traditional Music was a series of CDs with music from different parts of the world and edited by the International Council for Traditional Music (ICTM). This CD series was a continuation of the famous UNESCO Collection called *Musical Sources* on gramophone records, edited by Alain Daniélou and starting in the 1960s.

with pop music, as this branch is more organized according to the Western model. They are closer to understanding contracts and its implications. However, also in pop music the Indonesian (and generally Asian) situation is different from the Western situation. Critical voices have been raised in the Indonesian press, claiming that intellectual property rights are only meant to enlarge the profits of multinational companies in the richest parts of the world.[59]

Also in the West, the voices critical of copyright became much stronger in the last decades. Joost Smiers writes in the section of his book entitled *The meltdown and abolition of copyright*:

> [C]opyright is no longer an undisputed concept and also... the practice is not beneficial to most artists, to Third World countries and to the public domain.... It should also not be forgotten that the copyright system is rooted in a romantic concept of originality, which is disadvantageous for the public domain.... Why shouldn't we take the next step and abolish the whole system of authors' rights and copyright and replace it with a system that provides better payment to artists in Western and Third World countries alike, gives due respect to their work and brings the public domain back to a central place in our lives?[60]

After the mortgage crisis and the food crisis we are apparently waiting for the crisis of copyright that may have much more serious financial implications than the first two. However, this will not affect the musicians, dancers and actors so much, but rather the large conglomerates that deal with intellectual property rights. The performers may be better off when they negotiate directly with producers and distributors.

For the musicians the most important issue is respect for their music, not ownership. The 'Are'are leaders explained to Zemp that he could never "buy" their music.[61] Of course not, because in many cultures music, dance and theatre are, as in West Java, "outer manifestations... of inner life... or thought... It cannot be separated from the patterns of thought in Sundanese culture about human existence, society and the cosmic powers."[62] Only the devil buys a soul.

---

59 *See* B. Barendregt and W. van Zanten, "Popular Music in Indonesia since 1998, in Particular Fusion, Indie and Islamic Music on Video Compact Discs and the Internet", 34 *Yearbook for Traditional Music* 67, 86 (2002).

60 *See* J. Smiers, *Arts Under Pressure: Promoting Cultural Diversity in the Age of Globalization* 2003, 205, 207.

61 *See infra* Section 2.

62 *See* W. van Zanten, "Inner and Outer Voices: Listening and Hearing in West Java", 39(2) *The World of Music* 48 (1997).

PRIOR INFORMED CONSENT
An Intellectual Property Law Perspective

Ryu KOJIMA*

1. INTRODUCTION: THE MOORE CASE AND INTANGIBLE CULTURAL HERITAGE

Related to previous chapters written by Graham Dutfield and Wim van Zanten which address several aspects of prior informed consent in relation to documenting, researching or even exploiting intangible cultural heritage, this Chapter examines this issue from an intellectual property law perspective.

When I first heard the terminology of "prior informed consent" in the context of intangible cultural heritage, one issue that came to my mind was the concept of "fiduciary duty", especially in the context of the doctor-patient relationship. A particularly famous court judgment with regard to this topic in the United States is *Moore v. Regents of the University of California*.[1]

The plaintiff, John Moore, had an incurable disease, so called, "hairy cell leukemia". At the treatment stage, the defendant, Doctor David W. Golde realized that Moore's spleen cell had great research value. Although Doctor Golde informed Moore that the splenectomy was related to medical research, he did not tell his

* LL.B. (University of Tokyo Faculty of Law, 2000); LL.M. (Harvard Law School, 2003); Associate Professor, Kyushu University Faculty of Law.

1 Moore v. Regents of the University of California, 51 Cal. 3d. 120 (1990). *See also* J. BOYLE, *Shamans, Spleens and Software: Law and the Construction of the Information Society*, 1996, 97–108; J.A. POTTS, "Note, Moore v. Regents of the University of California: Expanded Disclosure, Limited Property Rights", 86 *Nw. U. L. Rev.* 453 (1992); Sh.N. PERLEY, "Note, From Control over One's Body to Control over One's Body Parts: Extending The Doctrine of Informed Consent", 67 *N.Y.U. L. Rev.* 335 (1992); Sh.F. Kurtz, "The Law of Informed Consent: From "Doctor is Right" to "Patient Has Rights"", 50 *Syracuse L. Rev.* 1243 (2000).

intention of using Moore's cell for scientific research. Later, Doctor Golde got a patent from Moore's cell, then the patent right was assigned to the defendant, the Regents of University of California. Issues argued in this case were whether the defendant, Doctor Golde, was (i) engaged in "conversion" of the cell, and (2) breached the "fiduciary duty" in the context of a "conflict of interest".

The California Supreme Court held that the plaintiff had no *property* on his spleen therefore the requirement of conversion was not met. This is partly because the property right – patent right – was different from the physical objects of the plaintiff's cell. Seen from the perspective of fiduciary duty, however, prior informed consent was necessary because the doctor used the patient's cell to a totally irrelevant purpose and gain profit without any information disclosure.

It is difficult to go into the details of the argument of conversion due to the space limitations, however, the issue discussed in the *Moore* case has some relevance in the context of safeguarding intangible cultural heritage.[2] One of the reasons why it is difficult to incorporate prior informed consent into the legal framework is that the patent rights to an invention derived from traditional knowledge qualitatively differs from any possible rights to the original intangible cultural heritage.

The range of acts which Dutfield listed elsewhere in this volume is reminiscent to the similar situation of third party's unlawful acquisition of the patent right – misappropriated application. Under the *Japanese Patent Act*[3], for example, it is difficult to acknowledge as a general principle that the true right holder – true inventor – would be able to demand that the person who filed the misappropriated application should return the right to obtain the patent right.[4] The rationale behind this is that the patent right is different from the original invention and the applicant also makes a substantial contribution for obtaining the patent right. German law admits the return of the patent right to the true inventor, and Japanese law also has certain exceptions such as if the third party falsely transfers the registration of the patent right after the patent application by the original inventor was already made.[5] In this circumstance, the original inventor also contributes to the patent application and it should be taken into account.

The discussion concerning intangible cultural heritage is not necessarily related to the issue of fiduciary duty because the parties sometimes do not have any contact with each other. It also contains more considerable aspects in addition

---

2 James Boyle argued these topics under the overarching framework in his book; *see* Boyle, *supra* note 1, at 97–108, 119–143.

3 Patent Act, Law No. 121 (1959) (as amended) (Japan).

4 *See* N. Nakayama, *Industrial Property Law: Patent Law*, Vol. I, (2nd rev. ed.), 2000, 56 *available at* www.iip.or.jp/translation/nakayama/part3.PDF (last visited 31 July 2008).

5 55 *Minshu* 793 (Sup. Ct., 12 June 2001) (Japan), *available at* www.courts.go.jp/english/judgments/text/2001.06.12-1997.-O-.No.1918.html (last visited 31 July 2008).

to the ordinary civil law issues, such as the existence of the community[6], the difficulty of finding the legitimate representatives[7], the necessity of an appropriate profit allocation system[8], and so forth. These arguments, especially the relationship with the *Convention on Biological Diversity* (CBD)[9], are clearly explained elsewhere in this volume.[10]

I do not want to go to the details of conversion and fiduciary duty in this Chapter. However, I would like to emphasize that the issue of prior informed consent can already be seen in an ordinary property or civil law context. Although the discourse should be more meticulously articulated, we should not forget that the discussion of prior informed consent in relation to intangible cultural heritage should also be situated in a broader perspective at the same time.

The discussion of prior informed consent is also an applied question for intellectual property law. There are many issues to be discussed regarding prior informed consent, however, I would like to focus on two points: One is the role of *trust* between the parties, and the other is the meaning of "consent". Although not exclusive to each other, the first issue mainly corresponds to the stage of inventory making and the second to the stage of exploitation. Based upon Dutfield's taxonomy, the debate on prior informed consent with regard to inventory making seems to be situated at the stage of *defensive protection* because it tries to prevent granting patent rights to inventions derived from intangible cultural heritage. However, a more substantive manner of prior informed consent should be introduced in the exploitation of intangible cultural heritage and profit sharing.

2. THE ROLE OF TRUST

Van Zanten emphasizes the significance of *trust* between ethnomusicologists and Indigenous people when conducting research. I fully agree with him on this point. At the stage of disclosure or sharing of information, certain categories of information definitely require mutual trust between the parties.[11] Typical examples include confidential or sensitive information. In intellectual property law, trade secrets fall in this category.

Imagine when you disclose your secrets to others. Secret information obviously loses secrecy once it is open to the public. Although trade secret protection supports this anti-dissemination motive, it only gives legal protection to bolster

6 *See, e.g.*, Part on "Conceptualization of Community", earlier in the present volume.

7 *See, e.g.*, Chapters [Dalibard and Kono] and [Dutfield] of the present volume.

8 *See, e.g.*, Chapters [Dutfield] and [de Werra] of the present volume.

9 Convention on Biological Diversity, 5 June 1992, 31 I.L.M. 818, *available at* www.biodiv.org/convention/convention.shtml (last visited 30 October 2008) [hereinafter "CBD"].

10 *See, e.g.*, Chapter [Dutfield] of the present volume.

11 S. Bok, *Secrets: On the Ethics of Concealment and Revelation*, 1989.

self-help. If the information is widely spread such as the dissemination through the Internet, you cannot retrieve the secrets in an exclusive fashion and all you can do is require monetary damages. Injunctive relief does not work any more. This is why you are required to estimate who is trustworthy when sharing your secrets.

Under the *Convention for the Safeguarding of the Intangible Cultural Heritage*[12], an inventory is being made for the purpose of preservation of culture, which means that the original purpose of inventory-making had no relationship with intellectual property. Nevertheless, inventory-making inevitably affects the area of intellectual property since the patent application may be negated because of the existence of the inventory.[13] Moreover, you can exploit the use of traditional knowledge once the legitimate entitlement is set.

Likewise in the case of patent registration, the inventory plays a role of public notification, which requires accuracy, credibility, and comprehensiveness, then also contributes to the reduction of search costs of the public. Third parties access that information and based upon it they develop future inventions or creative expressions. Usually, it is expected that government or government-related agencies make a commitment in inventory making.

If the government takes a paternalistic attitude, no prior informed consent is necessary. There seems to be no problem of trust when necessary information is gathered from the public domain, such as the current stage of Traditional Knowledge Digital Library (TKDL) in India.[14] If the database consists of confidential information, however, the story is going to be different. In order to get information, the inventory maker and local Indigenous people should co-operate with each other. Without mutual trust, how can the project be successful? Van Zanten's experience with the Baduy people clearly illustrates this complex situation.

The distinctive feature of *trust* is that it is extremely difficult to ensure and very easy to lose. According to micro-economic theory (game theory), the peaceful relationship among the people can be maintained to some extent based on the mutual trust without legal enforcement, which is strengthened under the so-called "tit-for-tat" strategy. If you break the promise and a bad reputation spreads out among stakeholders, it is extremely difficult for you to regain trust – sometimes you may be ousted from the interest groups – and make a deal among the parties. The same thing may happen when inventory makers gather information.

---

12 Convention for the Safeguarding of the Intangible Cultural Heritage, 17 October 2003, U.N. Doc. MISC/2003/CLT/CH/14 (2003), *available at* http://unesdoc.unesco.org/images/0013/001325/132540e.pdf (last visited 30 October 2007).

13 *See, e.g.*, Chapter [de Werra] of the present volume.

14 *See, e.g.*, Chapter [Gupta] of the present volume.

If inaccurate, or false information is listed in the inventory, it does not also serve the purpose of preserving culture and jeopardizes the credibility of the inventory. This may eventually cause great harm also from the perspective of intellectual property law because the issue of patent rights also relies on the credibility of the inventory. In inventory-making, therefore, we should be extremely careful about the interests of each stakeholder, namely the inventory makers, local people and the public.

As is already pointed out elsewhere in this volume by van Zanten[15], we should bear in mind that Indigenous people do not always prefer monetary rewards since they may feel insulted. It is natural that we want to be respected with our achievement, and monetary rewards do not always play the most important role. In extreme cases, monetary reward distorts our behaviour or obscures the ultimate goal of creativity. I believe this is a universal phenomenon and not only applies to what van Zanten experienced.

If we take a look at the area of intellectual property law, the argument mentioned above is often associated with the fact that open-source software has increasingly come to the forefront over recent years. The structure of open-source is totally different from proprietary software.[16] In addition to the technical issues, several advocates of the open-source movement clearly declared that they are engaged in the creation not for pursing profit but "just for fun".[17]

The argument of open-source software strongly urges the re-examination of our modern way of thinking, such as the dominant view toward labour, market mechanism, underlying rationale of property law, and so on. It is extremely interesting to find a similar way of thinking from a totally different angle, namely, traditional communal creativity embodied in intangible cultural heritage.

3. THE MEANING OF "CONSENT"

Another issue I would like to raise here is the meaning of "consent". The question is (1) to whom and (2) to what extent the power of controlling information should be given. This is because the ease in acquisition of consent affects the entire flow of information. This is an analogy from the discussion of gaining a license from the right holders of an intellectual property right.

A preliminary question is to whom we should give the power of controlling the information. In Dutfield's presentation, he introduced the example of a

15 *See* Chapter [van Zanten] of the present volume.

16 *See* S. Weber, *The Success of Open Source*, 2004.

17 *See* L. Torvalds and D. Diamond, *Just for Fun: The Story of an Accidental Revolutionary*, 2001; P. Himanen, L. Torvalds and M. Castells, *The Hacker Ethic and the Spirit of the New Economy*, 2001.

Peruvian medical plant as a source of new pharmaceuticals. In this case, 45,000 Aguarunas, over 180 communities and 13 representative organizations can be regarded as stakeholders.

Dutfield pointed out controversies concerning the following issues: (1) who should be contacted and informed; (2) how many people's or organizations' consent is sufficient; and (3) what should be done when neighbouring ethnic groups share the same knowledge but are not the parties to the bio-prospecting agreement.

If the contact persons are not easily accessible and dispersed throughout the region, it is extremely difficult to get their all consent. This issue has been already discussed in academic literature as the "tragedy of the anticommons".[18] Too many right holders bring high transaction costs, which eventually brings about negative externality and a chilling effect toward licensing. Therefore, non-profit or small-scale creators have a great influence. In order to solve this situation, one possibility may be unifying the holders or other custodians of intangible cultural heritage. If we are allowed to borrow similar concepts from intellectual property law, "bundling rights" between the right holders such as making patent pools, then distributing profits among the stake holders would be the strategy to be adopted. In this regard, similar problems were also raised by Dutfield[19] and van Zanten.[20] The latter experienced a great difficulty in identifying the appropriate representative of the Baduy people during his ethnomusicology research.

A second question is to what extent the power of controlling information should be given. This is important once the *entitlement* in intangible cultural heritage is set.

Guido Calabresi's analysis already pointed out more than 35 years ago that the amount of transaction costs will affect the choice between "property rules" (property rights with injunctive relief) and "liability rules" (property rights without injunctive relief).[21] One possible derivative of liability rules may be a collective management system or levy system that is widely adopted in the music industry and so on.

This argument is closely related to information transactions. Take a look at the discussion of "fair use" in copyright law in the United States, for example. Transaction costs, which are again counted as an element to be considered in determining the establishment of fair use, play an important role. It is said that if

---

18 M.A. Heller and R.S. Eisenberg, "Can Patents Deter Innovation?: The Anticommons in Biomedical Research", 280 *Sci.* 698 (1998). *See also* M.A. Heller, "The Tragedy of the Anticommons: Property in the Transition from Marx to Markets", 111 *Harv. L. Rev.* 621 (1998); G. Hardin, "The Tragedy of the Commons", 162 *Sci.* 1243 (1968).

19 *See* Chapter [Dutfield] of the present volume.

20 *See* Chapter [van Zanten] of the present volume.

21 *See* G. Calabresi and A.D. Melamed, "Property Rules, Liability Rules, and Inalienability: One View of the Cathedral", 85 *Harv. L. Rev.* 1089 (1972).

the license is easy to acquire from the right holders, it is more difficult to tilting on the fair use.[22] In Japan, we do not adopt fair use but statutory codified exemptions[23], therefore, it is not easy to permit fair use even if the license is extremely difficult to acquire, such as the right holders never say "yes" in the licensing negotiations. In this case, the possibility of compulsory license – using third party's adjudication[24] – should be seriously considered.

Seen from the perspective of transaction costs, the abovementioned two questions are closely intertwined with each other. In order to get a license or consent (regardless of with or without payment), there exists a "negative externality". Users are required to consider whether the future benefit surmounts the current transaction cost. Therefore, how easily we can get consent from the intangible cultural heritage holders is crucial in information flow and also the distribution of welfares among the Indigenous people.

This issue also relates the following question, namely who wins or who receives the benefit from the protection of intangible cultural heritage in the long run? Even if the inventory and the scheme of profit allocation – benefit sharing – are made, it may just bring benefit to strong intellectual property holders. For example, the local community may be swallowed up by the music industry if the royalties are set extremely low. On the other hand, if the amount of royalties is relatively higher, small-scale or non-profit creators cannot get a license for negative externality reasons. As long as the level of protection reflects who takes an initiative in information transactions[25], how to strike a balance between the stakeholders should be closely examined. This also applies to the relationship between intangible cultural heritage and intellectual property.

Another interesting remark made by van Zanten is that stricter legal guidelines may hamper the process of creativity and intercultural exchange. Therefore, he advocates the introduction of a code of conduct as a "soft" approach.[26] Because of space limitation, we cannot go into an in-depth analysis of this issue. One thing I

---

22 American Geophysical Union v. Texaco, Inc., 60 F.3d 913 (2nd Cir. 1994); Princeton University Press v. Michigan Document Services, Inc., 99 F.3d 1381 (6th Cir. 1996) (*en banc*), *cert. denied*, 117 S. Ct. 1336 (1997). *See also* W.J. Gordon, "Fair Use as Market Failure: A Structural and Economic Analysis of the Betamax Case and Its Predecessors", 82 *Colum. L. Rev.* 1600 (1982); U.S. Dep't of Commerce, *Working Group on Intellectual Property Rights, Intellectual Property and the National Information Infrastructure: The Report of the Working Group on Intellectual Property Rights*, 1995; T.W. Bell, "Fair Use vs. Fared Use: The Impact of Automated Rights Management on Copyright's Fair Use Doctrine", 76 *N.C. L. Rev.* 557 (1998).

23 Copyright Act, Articles 30–50, Law No. 48 (1970) (as amended) (Japan).

24 *See* D.L. Burk and J.E. Cohen, "Fair Use Infrastructure for Rights Management Systems", 15 *Harv. J.L. & Tech.* 41 (2001).

25 *See* Y. Benkler, "Free as the Air to Common Use: First Amendment Constraints on Enclosure of the Public Domain", 74 *N.Y.U. L. Rev.* 354 (1999); Y. Benkler, "Through the Looking Glass: Alice and the Constitutional Foundations of the Public Domain", 66 *Law & Contemp. Probs.* 173 (2003).

26 *See* Chapter [van Zanten] of the present volume.

can remark is that the recent hot debates on soft law, corporate social responsibility, and self-regulation are closely connected with this topic. The current difficulty in an international forum is how to codify the "moral obligation"[27] to compensate the Indigenous community. However, van Zanten's experience shows this is not the only way of solving the problem.[28]

4. CONCLUDING REMARK

This Chapter is a rough sketch of the problems of intangible cultural heritage seen from the perspective of intellectual property law. As van Zanten accurately pointed out, we have to concede that applying Western concepts of intellectual property law to the field of intangible cultural heritage cannot grasp the whole picture. If we persist with this attitude, it leads to the conclusion of the superiority of Western concepts to that of Indigenous people. This does not serve to achieving the goal of cultural diversity.

Nevertheless, it seems to me that the debate on the interrelationship between safeguarding intangible cultural heritage and intellectual property law is still somewhat underdeveloped. The discourse which has emerged in the field of intellectual property law may be helpful in conceptualizing the issues concerning the safeguarding intangible cultural heritage more clearly and that is exactly the purpose of this short comment.

---

27 *See* Chapter [Dutfield] of the present volume.

28 *See* Chapter [van Zanten] of the present volume.

PART FIVE
BENEFITS AND POTENTIAL HARMS TO COMMUNITIES AND THEIR INTANGIBLE CULTURAL HERITAGE

SAFEGUARDING OF INTANGIBLE CULTURAL HERITAGE
Benefits and Potential Harms

Branislav HAZUCHA and Toshiyuki KONO*

1. INTRODUCTION

Previous chapters in this volume addressed issues concerning the design of intangible cultural heritage inventories. They inquired into particular issues and controversies which arise during the safeguarding of intangible cultural heritage. As mentioned several times earlier in this volume, there are several possible approaches to safeguarding. Each of them has its pros and cons. The question which is before us here is how to design particular safeguarding regimes so that their benefits are maximized. At the same time, any possible expected or unexpected negative consequences on communities and their intangible cultural heritage should be minimized or even eliminated. The aim of the contributions to this Part is to scrutinize these benefits and potential harms which may arise from currently proposed regimes for safeguarding intangible cultural heritage. Some of the benefits or potential harms may be anticipated by a particular safeguarding regime, while other potential harms reflect more or less obvious or even unexpected shortcomings and flaws which should be prevented.

So far, most of the discussion on safeguarding cultural traditions has been focussed on a so-called *defensive*, anti-appropriative approach to the protection of traditional knowledge and cultural expressions. Both contributions in this Part criticize this minimalist approach. Its limitation is that it focuses only on the protection of cultural traditions by banning and preventing their misappropriation

* Branislav Hazucha is the Assistant Professor of Law, Kyushu University Faculty of Law; Toshiyuki Kono is the Professor of Law, Kyushu University Faculty of Law.

by non-members of the affected Indigenous, traditional or other cultural communities. The problem is that patent cancellation and other legal sanctions for misappropriation of traditional knowledge or cultural expressions rarely help those whom they are supposed to protect. The final outcome of such sanctions – the disclosure of traditional knowledge or cultural expressions which were kept in secrecy – goes against the interests of concerned communities. When these types of cultural traditions become a part of the public domain, Indigenous, traditional or other cultural communities end up in an even worse situation than they were in before. Hence, the approach based upon threatening such sanctions has "little chance of ensuring proper compensation" for concerned communities.[1]

In their contributions, Jacques de Werra[2] and Chidi Oguamanam[3] suggest that the passive, defensive approach is not enough. They urge that something more can be done to protect the interests of Indigenous, traditional and other cultural communities. They propose positive, *proactive* approaches to ensure that communities can truly benefit from measures aiming at safeguarding their intangible cultural heritage. It is only through more proactive approaches to safeguarding communities' cultural traditions that their further flourishing and thriving can be guaranteed for future generations and thus for all humankind. At the same time, it should be noted that both contributions concentrate only on certain limited aspects of benefits and potential harms of safeguarding measures on Indigenous, traditional and other cultural communities and their intangible cultural heritage. There is still plenty of work before us and further research should be conducted to better understand these intricate issues.

2. EMPOWERMENT OF COMMUNITIES

It is simple to grant rights or to declare protection to certain public interests when the possibility and outcome of implementing such laws are not taken into account. However, such laws often end only on paper. They seldom provide any actual and efficient protection for those who need it. This is the key motive which drives de Werra to put forward a "balanced and flexible approach" to protection of traditional knowledge and cultural expressions as an alternative to regimes based only upon the obligation to disclose the source of the invention. These regimes are currently proposed at several fora such as World Trade Organization (WTO), World Intellectual Property Organization (WIPO) and others. De Werra shows that they do not do enough for Indigenous, traditional and other local communities.

1 Chapter [DE WERRA] of the present volume.
2 *Id.*
3 Chapter [OGUAMANAM] of the present volume.

In order to avoid the flaws of existing proposals, de Werra's proposal is based upon a combination of three different mechanisms: (i) databases of intangible cultural heritage; (ii) compulsory licensing schemes; and (iii) efficient access to justice. By combining these mechanisms, he believes that the protection of communities and their cultural traditions can be actually achieved "without overly burdening other stakeholders".

The first step in de Werra's proposal is to guarantee legal certainty for all affected stakeholders: inventors, investors, communities and the public. When someone invests his human, financial, technical and other resources in research and development, he should be protected unless he actually knows or should have known that the invention in question is based upon particular traditional knowledge. Hence, the regime aiming to protect traditional knowledge against its misappropriation by non-members of affected communities should protect those who acted with due diligence. In order to achieve this, de Werra suggests the deployment of databases similar to those used under the *UNIDROIT Convention on Stolen or Illegally Exported Cultural Objects*.[4] Making an analogy to the protection of tangible cultural heritage allows him to outline a possible regime for the protection of traditional knowledge in broad strokes.

Under the proposed regime, patent applicants should be required to consult registries of intangible cultural heritage. If they did so, they would be deemed to have acted in good faith and the law should then protect their legitimate interests. This would not mean shielding respective patent applicants from any claims from the side of concerned communities. Actually, it would only protect patent applicants from legal sanctions for intentional or negligent misappropriation of traditional knowledge. It is also essential to take into account that pure traditional knowledge is often not enough for granting a patent. Certain inventive activity is normally required in order to obtain a patent for a new invention. Therefore, it is important to protect persons who acted in good faith. They should be allowed to keep profits gained from exploitation of their inventions under certain conditions. At the same time, they would be required to enter into a benefit-sharing agreement with the affected community.

Second, de Werra discusses the possibility of applying a co-ownership regime to inventions based upon traditional knowledge. He sees several disadvantages of this regime for Indigenous and traditional communities. Communities might be required to contribute more, especially financially. For example, they may be required to contribute: to research and development activities; to the cost of obtaining a patent; and later to costs related to prosecution and maintenance of a patent. If somebody infringes the patent, they might also be asked to bear a share

4 UNIDROIT Convention on Stolen or Illegally Exported Cultural Objects, 24 June 1995, 34 I.L.M. 1322 (1995), *available at* www.unidroit.org/english/conventions/1995culturalproperty/1995culturalproperty-e.htm (last visited 31 July 2008).

of the enforcement expenses. On the other hand, if the invention infringes other persons' proprietary rights, they might be sued for damages.

As to sharing profits gained from exploitation of an invention, it should be noted that patents are territorial rights. Patents holders have rights that are regulated by individual jurisdictions. In this regard, co-ownership regimes can diverge from one jurisdiction to another. For instance, some jurisdictions provide that co-owners do not need to share their profits gained from the exploitation of an invention amongst themselves.

Although some of these problems can be overcome by contractual solutions, the negotiating position of Indigenous and traditional communities is often weaker than that of Western multinational enterprises. The principle of contractual freedom may not serve the interests of the weaker parties very well. However, regardless of any contractual solution between patent co-owners, communities can still face some liability in case of infringing another person's patent. De Werra therefore suggests as a solution the adoption of compulsory licensing schemes for the use of traditional knowledge. In this way, the interests of investors would be protected while the interests of communities in fair benefit sharing would be guaranteed.

Finally, no rights and interests of communities can be efficiently guaranteed without actual access to justice. De Werra criticizes the failure, so far, of policy makers to pay any real attention to settling disputes concerning misappropriation of traditional knowledge. As a solution, he suggests providing for a stay of a patent application when an Indigenous or traditional community files a lawsuit or initiates any other alternative dispute resolution mechanism. This would put pressure on the patent applicants to find a solution that is mutually beneficial to them and to the relevant communities.

Another aspect related to access to justice is that disputes should be resolved in a quick and cost-effective manner. To achieve this goal, de Werra proposes several options: (i) specialized international courts; (ii) arbitration; and (iii) other flexible alternative dispute resolution mechanisms such as mediation. The advantage of the first option is that specialized courts established at the international level would be entrusted with the exclusive jurisdiction for deciding disputes regarding misappropriation of traditional knowledge. This would prevent forum shopping and initiating lawsuits in jurisdictions which would be unfriendly to communities' claims or where it would be too expensive and difficult for communities to protect their legitimate interests. The advantage of the last two options is greater flexibility. In the case of arbitration, a patent applicant may be required to agree on an arbitration clause at the time of filing a patent application. Of all three options, the most flexible is mediation. De Werra suggests that the proposed dispute resolution mechanisms should also cover disputes between communities themselves in relation to disputed traditional knowledge.

Although the proposed "balanced and flexible approach" is scrutinized in case of misappropriating traditional knowledge, de Werra suggests that its application should not be limited only to patent law. Its flexibility allows efficient application of his proposal to various forms of cultural traditions.

3. REGIONAL INVENTORIES OF INTANGIBLE CULTURAL HERITAGE

While de Werra focuses on ensuring fair benefit sharing for communities with regard to any exploitation of their cultural traditions, Oguamanam directs his attention to completely different aspects of safeguarding intangible cultural heritage, namely, documentation and digitization of intangible cultural heritage. He agrees with de Werra that documentation and digitization should be seen as part of a "broader vision" that "transcends its present thrust as a defensive and anti-appropriative strategy".[5] He sees the way forward as involving greater stress on the importance of a "regional approach to documentation". This might solve the main problem faced by documentation and digitization of cultural traditions – insufficient financial, human, material and other resources. Only a few countries, mainly developed countries, have sufficient resources for safeguarding their intangible cultural heritage.

Through the regional approach to documentation and digitization, many of the disadvantages of documentation and digitization may be avoided. The limited resources might be used in a more efficient way. This would also help to limit disputes and controversies when cultural traditions are shared by several communities in different countries or when a particular community inhabits a territory divided between two or more countries. Most of the tensions concerning shared cultural traditions between neighbouring countries might be reduced by agreement and mutual co-operation. Simultaneously, the possibility of duplication and thus of wasting limited resources would be avoided.

However, a regional approach to documentation and digitization of intangible cultural heritage also has its own drawbacks and obstacles. One of them occurs when there is a rivalry between countries within a region. In addition, some countries can free ride on investment of others in documentation and digitization of their cultural traditions. This can cause friction between participating countries.

Although there are certain downsides of, and impediments to, a regional approach to documentation and digitization, Oguamanam suggests that we should make the most of this endeavour. He sees it as a great source of further

---

[5] Chapter [OGUAMANAM] of the present volume.

creativity. When people have access to their cultural traditions, they can build upon them. At the end, this can lead to cultural creolization and cosmopolitanism. On this point, the approaches proposed by de Werra and Oguamanam considerably differ.

Under the regime proposed by de Werra, public access to inventories is to be limited. This restriction is supposedly justified by the fact that much information and traditional knowledge contained in inventories is sacred or is kept secret by concerned communities. Accordingly, de Werra suggests that inventories should be operated by "accessible agencies" which would have the *duty of secrecy* with respect to their content. Patent applicants would not be allowed to search for information and knowledge contained in inventories. This would prevent them from making a shopping list for their private commercial purposes. They would be allowed only to ask the respective agency to examine whether their inventions interfere with any prior traditional knowledge. This would protect such knowledge against disclosure and potential misappropriation by non-members of the affected communities. On the other hand, patent applicants would receive a certificate that their invention is not based upon any traditional knowledge contained in the inventories.

Although it might seem that the approaches proposed by de Werra and Oguamanam are irreconcilable, digital technologies allow for differential individual access to stored information by different users. In co-operation with communities, the agencies assigned with the safeguarding intangible cultural heritage can restrict access to certain information only to particular individuals or all members of concerned communities. Digitization of the intangible cultural heritage thus has significant potential, and it is now upon individual agencies to efficiently employ digitization in designing credible strategies to prevent rapid weakening of Indigenous, traditional and other cultural communities, as well as of their languages, habits, rituals and other cultural traditions.

FIGHTING AGAINST BIOPIRACY

Moving from the Obligation to Disclose to Effective Benefit Sharing

Jacques DE WERRA*

* Professor of intellectual property law and contract law at the Law School of the University of Geneva (Switzerland); LL.M (Columbia 2001); co-director of the Geneva Art Law Centre (www.art-law.org); jacques.dewerra@droit.unige.ch.

1. INTRODUCTION

In the global fight against "biopiracy"[1], one of the key issues, as identified in the report entitled *The Protection of Traditional Knowledge: Draft Objectives and Principles*[2], prepared under the auspices of the WIPO Intergovernmental Committee on Intellectual Property and Genetic Resources, Traditional Knowledge and Folklore, is to "[p]reclude the grant of improper [intellectual property] rights to unauthorized parties".[3] More specifically the goal is to:

> curtail the grant or exercise of improper intellectual property rights over traditional knowledge and associated genetic resources, by requiring, in particular, as a condition for the granting of patent rights, that patent applicants for inventions involving traditional knowledge and associated genetic resources disclose the source and country of origin of those resources, as well as evidence of prior informed consent and benefit-sharing conditions have been complied with in the country of origin.[4]

According to the Draft TK Principles, "[t]raditional knowledge shall be protected against misappropriation".[5] To accomplish this, "legal means should be provided to prevent ... false claims or assertions of ownership or control over traditional knowledge, including acquiring, claiming or asserting intellectual property rights over traditional knowledge-related subject matter when those intellectual property rights are not validly held in the light of that traditional knowledge and any conditions relating to its access".[6]

Proposals have been formulated by various countries advocating the inclusion of such a disclosure obligation in a variety of international patent law conventions[7],

---

1 *See generally* I. Mgbeoji, *Global Biopiracy: Patents, Plants, and Indigenous Knowledge*, 2006; A. Mushita and C.B. Thompson, *Biopiracy of Biodiversity: Global Exchange as Enclosure*, 2007; for practical examples, *see* J. McGown, *Out of Africa: Mysteries of Access and Benefit Sharing*, 2006, *available at* www.edmonds-institute.org/outofafrica.pdf (last visited 31 July 2008) and the examples listed in the document filed by Peru with the World Trade Organization, *Combating Biopiracy - the Peruvian Experience*, IP/C/W/493 (19 September 2007), *available at* http://docsonline.wto.org/DDFDocuments/t/ip/c/w493.doc (last visited 31 July 2008).

2 *See* WIPO, Intergovernmental Committee on Intellectual Property and Genetic Resources, Traditional Knowledge and Folklore, *The Protection of Traditional Knowledge: Draft Objectives and Principles*, WIPO/GRTKF/IC/10/5 (2 October 2006), *available at* www.wipo.int/edocs/mdocs/tk/en/wipo_grtkf_ic_10/wipo_grtkf_ic_10_5.pdf (last visited 31 July 2008) [hereinafter "*Draft TK Principles*"].

3 *Id.*, Annex, at 4.

4 *Id.*, Annex, at 4–5, xiii and xiv.

5 *Id.*, Annex, Article 1(1).

6 *Id.*, Annex, Article 1(3)(iii).

7 Other proposals have been formulated in scientific publications; *see, e.g.*, N. Pires de Carvalho, "Requiring Disclosure of the Origin of Genetic Resources and Prior Informed Consent in Patent Applications Without Infringing the TRIPS Agreement: The Problem and the Solution", 2 *Wash. U. J.L. & Pol'y* 371 (2000) (pleading for an application of the "unclean hands" doctrine). *See also* United Nations Conference on Trade and Development

while national regulations have already been adopted or are being discussed in different countries.[8] Three different proposals for implementing this obligation at the international level can be distinguished.[9] These proposals are (i) the *TRIPS Disclosure Proposal*[10], (ii) the *PCT Disclosure Proposal*[11] and (iii) the *Mandatory Disclosure Proposal.*[12]

The most protective of the three is the TRIPS Disclosure Proposal, which was made by Brazil and India, together with other countries. Under its terms, a patent can be granted, provided that the patent application included information regarding, or evidence of, (i) the source of the invention, its country of origin and the country of origin of the biological resource and of the traditional knowledge used in the invention; (ii) the obtainment of prior informed consent from the authorities under the relevant national regime; and (iii) fair and equitable benefit sharing under the relevant national regime.[13] In case of violation of these obligations by the patent applicant, the potential sanctions would include, among others, the revocation of the patent, the narrowing of the scope of the patent and the "full or partial transfer of the rights to the invention would also follow where full disclosure

---

(UNCTAD), *Analysis of Options for Implementing Disclosure of Origin Requirements in Intellectual Property Applications*, UNCTAD/DITC/TED/2005/14 (15 February 2006) (*prepared by* J.D. Sarnoff and C.M. Correa), *available at* www.unctad.org/en/docs/ditcted200514_en.pdf (last visited 31 July 2008) (discussing various available policy options).

8 *See, e.g.*, Ch.C. Liu and J.J. Liu, *Waves of Changes in Chinese Patent Law and Regulations–Part IV, available at* www.chinabiotoday.com/articles/20080131_1 (last visited 31 July 2008) (describing the draft changes contemplated in the Chinese patent law on this issue); D. Cochrane, "Africa: Patents Act amended to protect genetic resources", *Managing Intell. Prop.*, March 2008, *available at* www.managingip.com/Article/1886062/Patents-Act-amended-to-protect-genetic-resources.html (last visited 31 July 2008) (describing the situation in South Africa); Swiss Patent Act, Article 49a, *available at* www.admin.ch/ch/f/ff/2007/4363.pdf (visited 30 March 2008) (introduced by the amendments to the Swiss Patent Act which were adopted by the Swiss Parliament on 22 June 2007 and entered into force on 1 July 2008).

9 This tripartite division is based on a note which was drafted by the World Trade Organization (WTO) Secretariat; *see* WTO, Council for Trade-Related Aspects of Intellectual Property Rights, *The Relationship between the TRIPS Agreement and the Convention on Biological Diversity: Summary of Issues Raised and Points Made*, IP/C/W/368/Rev.1 (8 February 2006) (*prepared by* the WTO Secretariat), *available at* www.wto.org/english/tratop_e/trips_e/ipcw368_e.doc (last visited 31 July 2008) [hereinafter "*WTO Summary*"]. For the summary of the different approaches, *see also* WTO, *TRIPS: Reviews, Article 27.3(b) and Related Issues: Background and the Current Situation*, www.wto.org/english/tratop_e/trips_e/art27_3b_background_e.htm (last visited 31 July 2008). For an updated status of the negotiation process at the WTO as of June 2008, *see* WTO, *Issues Related to the Extension of the Protection of Geographical Indications Provided for in Article 23 of the TRIPS Agreement to Products Other than Wines and Spirits and those Related to the Relationship between the TRIPS Agreement and the Convention on Biological Diversity*, WT/GC/W/591 (9 June 2008), *available at* www.wto.org/english/tratop_e/trips_e/giextension_cbd_dgreport_9jun08_e.pdf (last visited 31 July 2008).

10 *See infra* text accompanying notes 13–16.

11 *See infra* text accompanying notes 17–23.

12 *See infra* text accompanying notes 24–26.

13 *See WTO Summary, supra* note 9, at 28, par. 71.

would have shown that another person or community or governmental agency is the inventor or part inventor".[14] The TRIPS Disclosure Proposal is meant to be formally implemented in the *Agreement on Trade-Related Aspects of Intellectual Property Rights* (TRIPS Agreement)[15] in a new Article 29*bis*.[16]

The PCT Disclosure Proposal, which was made by Switzerland[17], is based on a proposed amendment to the *Regulations under the Patent Cooperation Treaty* (PCT Regulations).[18] Under this amendment, national patent law *could*[19] require a patent applicant to declare the source of genetic resources and traditional

---

14 *Id.* at 29, 75. *See also* WTO, Council for Trade-Related Aspects of Intellectual Property Rights, *The Relationship between the TRIPS Agreement and the Convention on Biological Diversity (CBD) and the Protection of Traditional Knowledge - Elements of the Obligation to Disclose Evidence of Benefit-Sharing under the Relevant National Regime*, 4, par. 14, IP/C/W/442 (18 March 2005), *available at* http://docsonline.wto.org/DDFDocuments/t/IP/C/W442.doc (last visited 31 July 2008), for the submission by India, Brazil and other countries to the WTO:

> Where the failure to provide evidence of benefit-sharing is discovered after the grant of a patent, the legal effect could include:
> - Revocation of the patent where it is determined that there is fraudulent intention behind the failure to provide evidence of benefit-sharing. In addition to, or as an alternative to revocation, criminal and/or administrative sanctions may also be imposed, in particular, to ensure adequate compensation where it is eventually determined that no benefits were shared or are intended to be shared;
> - Full or partial transfer of the rights to the invention, also as an alternative to revocation, as a means of promoting fair and equitable benefit-sharing; ...

15 Agreement on Trade-Related Aspects of Intellectual Property Rights, 15 April 1994, Marrakesh Agreement Establishing the World Trade Organization, Annex 1C, Legal Instruments - Results of the Uruguay Round, 33 I.L.M. 1125 (1994) [hereinafter "TRIPS Agreement"].

16 WTO, Council for Trade-Related Aspects of Intellectual Property Rights, *Doha Work Programme - The Outstanding Implementation Issue on the Relationship between the TRIPS Agreement and the Conventional on Biological Diversity*, WT/GC/W/564/Rev.2 (5 July 2006), *available at* http://docsonline.wto.org/DDFDocuments/t/ip/c/w474.doc (last visited 31 July 2008) (containing the draft of Article 29*bis* of TRIPS Agreement as proposed by Brazil, China, Colombia, Cuba, India, Pakistan, Peru, Thailand and Tanzania). It appears that this approach is gaining momentum and support among members States of the WTO; *see* K. Mara, *TRIPS Council: Half Of WTO Membership Backs Biodiversity Amendment, available at* www.ip-watch.org/weblog/index.php?p=961 (last visited 31 July 2008).

17 *See* WIPO, Working Group on Reform of the Patent Cooperation Treaty, *Proposals by Switzerland Regarding the Declaration of the Source of Genetic Resources and Traditional Knowledge in Patent Applications*, PCT/R/WG/4/13 (5 May 2003), *available at* www.wipo.int/edocs/mdocs/pct/en/pct_r_wg_4/pct_r_wg_4_13.pdf (last visited 31 July 2008); *see also* WIPO, Working Group on Reform of the Patent Cooperation Treaty, *Proposals by Switzerland Regarding the Declaration of the Source of Genetic Resources and Traditional Knowledge in Patent Applications*, PCT/R/WG/5/11 Rev. (19 November 2003), *available at* www.wipo.int/edocs/mdocs/pct/en/pct_r_wg_5/pct_r_wg_5_11_rev.pdf (last visited 31 July 2008).

18 Regulations under the Patent Cooperation Treaty, 19 June 1970, *available at* www.wipo.int/pct/en/texts/pdf/pct_regs.pdf (last visited 31 July 2008) (as in force from 1 April 2007) [hereinafter "PCT Regulations"].

19 The PCT Disclosure Proposal is optional and is left to the decision of the individual countries.

knowledge in a patent application.[20] The absence of compliance by the patent applicant with such a formal requirement could lead to the refusal of the patent by the relevant patent office.[21] However, if the applicant's failure to disclose the source of the invention or its submission of false information were only to be discovered after the granting of the patent, the latter's validity would only be affected if the applicant were found to have had fraudulent intentions.[22] In such a case, other sanctions outside patent law could also be imposed.[23]

The third proposal, the Mandatory Disclosure Proposal, was made by the European Union. Pursuant to this proposal, each country *shall* require all patent applicants to disclose information on the country of origin or source of genetic resources in the invention which applicants know or have reason to know.[24] Under this proposal, the failure or refusal by the patent applicant to provide the required information would stop the processing of the patent application. However, after the grant of the patent, the sanction imposed on an applicant who provided incorrect or incomplete information would lie outside patent law. Therefore, each country would keep the ability to decide on the sanctions to be

---

20 *See WTO Summary*, *supra* note 9, at 31, par. 80. *See also* WIPO, Working Group on Reform of the Patent Cooperation Treaty, *Additional Comments by Switzerland on Its Proposals Regarding the Declaration of the Source of Genetic Resources and Traditional Knowledge in Patent Applications*, PCT/R/WG/6/11 (21 April 2004), *available at* www.wipo.int/edocs/mdocs/pct/en/pct_r_wg_6/pct_r_wg_6_11.doc (last visited 31 July 2008), for the new proposed Rule 51*bis*.1(g) of PCT Regulations, *supra* note 18, which would read as follows:

> (g) The national law applicable by the designated Office may, in accordance with Article 27, require the applicant
> (i) to declare the source of a specific genetic resource to which the inventor has had access, if an invention is directly based on such a resource; if such source is unknown, this shall be declared accordingly;
> (ii) to declare the source of knowledge, innovations and practices of indigenous and local communities relevant for the conservation and sustainable use of biological diversity, if the inventor knows that an invention is directly based on such knowledge, innovations and practices; if such source is unknown, this shall be declared accordingly.

21 *See* WTO, Council for Trade-Related Aspects of Intellectual Property Rights, *Additional Comments by Switzerland on Its Proposals Submitted to WIPO Regarding the Declaration of the Source of Genetic Resources and Traditional Knowledge in Patent Applications*, IP/C/W/423 (14 Jun. 2004) (containing the document submitted by Switzerland to the WTO); *WTO Summary*, *supra* note 9, at 32, par. 84.

22 *See* Patent Law Treaty, Article 10(1), 1 June 2000, 39 I.L.M. 1047 (2000), *available at* www.wipo.int/treaties/en/ip/plt/trtdocs_wo038.html (last visited 31 July 2008) [hereinafter "PLT"] (providing that "[n]on-compliance with one or more of the formal requirements referred to in Articles 6(1), (2), (4) and (5) and 8(1) to (4) with respect to an application may not be a ground for revocation or invalidation of a patent, either totally or in part, except where the non-compliance with the formal requirement occurred as a result of a fraudulent intention").

23 *WTO Summary*, *supra* note 9, at 32, par. 85.

24 *Id.* at 33, par. 87.

imposed in the case of a violation of the disclosure requirement.[25] As expressed in a submission of the European Union, this proposal supposes that

> [m]eaningful and workable sanctions should be attached to the provision of incorrect or incomplete information. Where it is proved that the patent applicant has disclosed incorrect or incomplete information, effective, proportionate and dissuasive sanctions outside the field of patent law should be imposed on the patent applicant or holder. ... For reasons of legal certainty, the submission of incorrect or incomplete information should not have any effect on the validity of the granted patent or on its enforceability against patent infringers.
>
> It must be left to the individual Contracting State to determine the character and the level of these sanctions, in accordance with domestic legal practices and respecting general principles of law.[26]

Among the three options mentioned above, the TRIPS Disclosure Proposal is obviously the most protective of the interests of local communities (hereinafter "communities"), in view of its extensive reach.[27] Indeed, it presupposes the conclusion of a benefit-sharing agreement between the applicant and the relevant stakeholders. Therefore, if one were to try to answer the question raised in the title of this Chapter as to whether the obligation to disclose truly helps communities[28],

---

25 WTO, Council for Trade-Related Aspects of Intellectual Property Rights, *Communication from the European Communities and Their Member States*, IP/C/W/383 (17 October 2002) [hereinafter "*EU Proposal*"]; *WTO Summary*, *supra* note 9, at 33, par. 88. This also results from the recital 27 of the *Directive 98/44/EC on the legal protection of biotechnological inventions* which provides: "Whereas if an invention is based on biological material of plant or animal origin or if it uses such material, the patent application should, where appropriate, include information on the geographical origin of such material, if known; whereas this is without prejudice to the processing of patent applications or the validity of rights arising from granted patents"; *see* Directive 98/44/EC of the European Parliament and of the Council of 6 July 1998 on the legal protection of biotechnological inventions, OJ L 213, 30 July 1998, p. 13.

26 WIPO, Intergovernmental Committee on Intellectual Property and Genetic Resources, Traditional Knowledge and Folklore, *Disclosure of Origin or Source of Genetic Resources and Associated Traditional Knowledge in Patent Applications*, Annex, at 4, par. 6, WIPO/GRTKF/IC/8/11 (17 May 2005) (containing the document submitted by the European Union and its Member States).

27 For a definition of the concept of the communities, *see Draft TK Principles*, *supra* note 2, Annex, Article 5 ("Protection of traditional knowledge should benefit the communities who generate, preserve and transmit the knowledge in a traditional and intergenerational context, who are associated with it and who identify with it in accordance with Article 4. Protection should accordingly benefit the indigenous and traditional communities themselves that hold traditional knowledge in this manner, as well as recognized individuals within these communities and peoples. Entitlement to the benefits of protection should, as far as possible and appropriate, take account of the customary protocols, understandings, laws and practices of these communities and peoples.").

28 This Chapter does not address the complex issue of the determination of the ownership over the traditional knowledge and simply considers that communities should be treated as the

it could be considered that the TRIPS Disclosure Proposal would effectively help them because it requires the patent applicant to prove benefit sharing with communities when filing a patent application. However, in spite of its appeal, the TRIPS Disclosure Proposal seems unlikely to be implemented at the global level in view of the opposition it faces in political spheres and because of the delicate legal issues that it raises.[29]

On this basis, the goal of this Chapter is to assess whether the *obligation to disclose* the use in an invention of traditional knowledge and of associated genetic resources (hereinafter jointly referred to as "traditional knowledge") truly helps communities that create and own traditional knowledge. For this purpose, the Chapter focuses on whether the obligation to disclose (as resulting in particular from the PCT Disclosure Proposal and from the Mandatory Disclosure Proposal), as well as the sanctions attached to its violation, can be deemed to provide a suitable legal framework for allowing effective benefit sharing for the communities.

In view of this focus, this Chapter does not discuss the other complex issues relating to the implementation of the obligation to disclose, such as the so-called "trigger of the disclosure"[30] (*i.e.* what connection needs to exist between the traditional knowledge and the invention for which the patent application has been filed in order to trigger the obligation to disclose)[31], nor does it discuss the compliance of the obligation to disclose with international instruments (most specifically with the TRIPS Agreement).[32] Instead, it focuses on assessing the effectiveness of the obligation to disclose, which can be viewed as a *defensive* protection measure[33] (*i.e.* as an element of "anti-appropriation initiatives"[34]), and does not discuss the creation of a potential new exclusive right (*sui generis* right) to be adopted for the purpose of positively protecting traditional knowledge.[35]

---

owners, even though other stakeholders may be involved (such as the states from which the traditional knowledge originates, as may be inferred from the wording of the CBD, *infra* note 36, Article 15).

29 *See WTO Summary*, *supra* note 9, at 44, par. 118; M.A. Girsberger, "Transparency Measures under Patent Law Regarding Genetic Resources and Traditional Knowledge: Disclosure of Source and Evidence of Prior Informed Consent and Benefit-Sharing", 7 *J. World Intell. Prop.* 451, 485 (2004).

30 *WTO Summary*, *supra* note 9, at 50, par. 125.

31 *See* the discussion in the *WTO Summary*, *supra* note 9, at 50, par. 125.

32 On this issue, *see* G. Dutfield, "Sharing the Benefits of Biodiversity: Is there a Role for the Patent System?", 5 *J. World Intell. Prop.* 899, 922 (2002); *see generally* N. Pires de Carvalho, "From the Shaman's Hut to the Patent Office: In Search of a TRIPS-Consistent Requirement to Disclose the Origin of Genetic Resources and Prior Informed Consent", 17 *Wash. U. J.L. and Pol'y* 111 (2005).

33 *See* G. Dutfield, *Protecting Traditional Knowledge: Pathways for the Future*, 2006, 25.

34 *See* Chapter [Oguamanam] of the present volume.

35 This issue is also intensively discussed in the WIPO Intergovernmental Committee on Intellectual Property and Genetic Resources, Traditional Knowledge and Folklore.

This Chapter is structured as follows: Section 2 describes the origins and the limits of the obligation to disclose and concludes that the obligation to disclose is not sufficient to protect communities; Section 3 then discusses alternative approaches to the obligation to disclose which may ensure real benefit sharing for communities. In this context, an analogy is drawn with the legal protection of tangible cultural property in order to see how that regime could serve as a model for the protection of traditional knowledge (*see* Section 3.1. below). This Section also examines how the goal of benefit sharing could be achieved, both at the level of substantive law (*see* Section 3.2. below) and procedural law (*i.e.* enforcement and dispute resolution; *see* Section 3.3. below).

2. ORIGINS AND LIMITS OF THE OBLIGATION TO DISCLOSE

2.1. ORIGINS

The debate about the obligation to disclose can be considered to have been initiated in the context of the *Convention on Biological Diversity* (CBD)[36], which was concluded on 5 June 1992 in Rio de Janeiro and has 190 contracting parties.[37] The CBD provides for the obligations of access to, benefit-sharing of, as well as prior informed consent with regard to, traditional knowledge.[38] Article 8 of the CBD provides that

> [e]ach Contracting Party shall, as far as possible and as appropriate:
>
> ...
>
> (j) Subject to its national legislation, respect, preserve and maintain knowledge, innovations and practices of indigenous and local communities embodying traditional lifestyles relevant for the conservation and sustainable use of biological diversity and promote their wider application with the approval and involvement of the holders of such knowledge, innovations and practices and *encourage the equitable sharing of the benefits arising from the utilization of such knowledge, innovations and practices.* (Emphasis added.)

Article 15(7) of the CBD further provides that

---

36 Convention on Biological Diversity, 5 June 1992, 31 I.L.M. 818, *available at* www.biodiv.org/convention/convention.shtml (last visited 31 July 2008) [hereinafter "CBD"].

37 For the list of contracting parties with status of adhesion or ratification, *see* Convention on Biological Diversity, *List of Parties*, www.cbd.int/convention/parties/list.shtml (last visited 31 July 2008).

38 CBD, *supra* note 36, Articles 8(j), 10(c), 15, 16, and 19.

> [e]ach Contracting Party shall take legislative, administrative or policy measures, as appropriate, and in accordance with Articles 16 and 19 and, where necessary, through the financial mechanism established by Articles 20 and 21 *with the aim of sharing in a fair and equitable way the results of research and development and the benefits arising from the commercial and other utilization of genetic resources* with the Contracting Party providing such resources. Such sharing shall be upon mutually agreed terms. (Emphasis added.)

In the context of the implementation of these goals, the Conference of the Parties to the CBD (COP) adopted the *Bonn Guidelines on Access to Genetic Resources and Fair and Equitable Sharing of the Benefits Arising out of their Utilization* (Bonn Guidelines)[39] at its sixth meeting which took place in The Hague from 7 to 19 April 2002. The Bonn Guidelines, which only provide guidance and can be implemented on a voluntary basis by the stakeholders, are intended to "serve as inputs when developing and drafting legislative, administrative or policy measures on access and benefit-sharing with particular reference to provisions under Articles 8(j), 10 (c), 15, 16 and 19" of the CBD.[40]

With respect to the issue of benefit sharing, the Bonn Guidelines contain a non-exhaustive list of potential ways of implementing it. Appendix II of the Guidelines provides a selection of monetary and non-monetary benefits.[41]

At its sixth meeting, the COP further set the framework for the obligation to disclose by inviting "Parties and Governments to encourage the disclosure of the country of origin of genetic resources in applications for intellectual property rights, where the subject matter of the application concerns or makes use of genetic resources in its development, as a possible contribution to tracking compliance with prior informed consent and the mutually agreed terms on which access to those resources was granted".[42] The COP also invited "Parties and Governments to encourage the disclosure of the origin of relevant traditional knowledge, innovations and practices of indigenous and local communities relevant for the conservation and sustainable use of biological diversity in applications for intellectual property rights, where the subject matter of the application concerns or makes use of such knowledge in its development".[43]

---

39 Conference of the Parties to the CBD (COP), *Bonn Guidelines on Access to Genetic Resources and Fair and Equitable Sharing of the Benefits Arising out of their Utilization*, Decision VI/24 A, UNEP/CBD/COP/6/20 (7–19 April 2002), *available at* www.biodiv.org/decisions/default.aspx?m=cop-06&d=24 (last visited 31 July 2008) [hereinafter "*Bonn Guidelines*"].

40 *Id.*, Annex, par. 1.

41 *Id.*, appendix II.

42 COP, *Role of intellectual property rights in the implementation of access and benefit-sharing arrangements*, at par. 1, Decision VI/24 C, UNEP/CBD/COP/6/20 (7–19 April 2002), *available at* www.biodiv.org/decisions/default.aspx?m=cop-06&d=24 (last visited 31 July 2008).

43 *Id.*, par. 2.

The obligation to disclose in patent applications can thus be conceived as "a possible contribution to tracking compliance with prior informed consent and the mutually agreed terms on which access to those resources was granted".[44] According to this interpretation, disclosure essentially aims at creating transparency in the patent application process.[45] However, although the obligation to disclose has raised awareness about the CBD and the issue of benefit sharing, experiences from various countries suggest that it is uncertain that the goal of transparency has been achieved.[46] It is thus important to consider the limitations of the obligation to disclose.

2.2. LIMITS

Even though the obligation to disclose and the sanctions for its violation, both in the PCT Disclosure Proposal and in the Mandatory Disclosure Proposal, could deter potential violators in many circumstances, it appears that in some instances they are insufficient in ensuring benefit sharing for communities. This situation essentially results from the fact that, except for in very specific circumstances (*i.e.* circumstances in which – further to the scenario envisaged under the PCT Disclosure Proposal – the fraudulent intent of the patent applicant can be established under Article 10 of the *Patent Law Treaty*[47]), the validity of a patent could not be challenged by communities once it had been granted, even though the patented invention would misappropriate traditional knowledge.

In addition, the fact that bad faith patent applicants might incur criminal sanctions may not prove deterrent to the extent that criminal sanctions would be imposed on physical persons and not on corporate entities (which is generally the case in civil law countries). Such corporate entities might thus remain unpunished even though they would receive the financial benefits resulting from the grant of a patent based upon an undue use of traditional knowledge.[48]

In addition, any criminal or even civil[49] sanctions would generally suppose the showing of tortious intent (wilful or negligent). Consequently, these sanctions

44 *Id.*, par. 1.

45 Transparency being one of the key principles underpinning the *Bonn Guidelines*, *supra* note 39, Annex, par. 7(h).

46 *See* A.L. Hoare and R.G. Tarasofsky, "Asking and Telling: Can "Disclosure of Origin" Requirements in Patent Applications Make a Difference?", 10 *J. World Intell. Prop.* 149, 158 (2007).

47 For the text of Article 10(1) of the PLT, *see supra* note 22.

48 Criminal sanctions could thus be imposed on outside patent agents who have been hired and instructed by corporate entities (the future owners of the patents), even though sanctions should essentially target these entities themselves and not their patent agents.

49 According to a submission by the European Union, a "civil claim for compensation" could be considered; *see EU Proposal*, *supra* note 25, par. 54–56.

would not be applicable in a scenario in which the patent applicant was effectively unaware of pre-existing traditional knowledge, even after having conducted a proper due diligence.[50] In such a case, the applicant, even while acting in good faith, would not have disclosed the presence of any traditional knowledge during the patent application process. Such an applicant could escape any criminal or civil sanctions and might also avoid any risk of cancellation of the patent, since there would have been no fraudulent behaviour. A perhaps more realistic scenario is that an entity could acquire a patent or a patent application in good faith from a third party, which may itself have misappropriated traditional knowledge when filing the patent application. In these circumstances too, criminal or civil sanctions might not be easily imposed on such a patent holder if there is no evidence of any bad faith behaviour.

Furthermore, it is also questionable whether the cancellation of a patent, which various proposals envisage as a potential sanction, would bring any benefit to communities or allow any benefit sharing. As was accurately noted by Norway in a submission to the WTO,

> revoking a patent as a consequence of non-compliance with the disclosure obligation would not benefit those who consider themselves to be entitled to a share of the benefits of the inventions. Once patent protection is revoked, there are no exclusive rights from which benefits could be derived.[51]

Quite to the contrary, it has been emphasized that "the issuing of a patent could trigger benefit sharing."[52] As a result, the point was made that the obligation to disclose should be coupled with additional protective measures in order to meet the goal of benefit sharing[53], particularly in view of the fact that such an approach has apparently been adopted with some success in real cases.[54]

---

50 On this issue, *see infra* Section 3.1.2.

51 WTO, Council for Trade-Related Aspects of Intellectual Property Rights, *The Relationship between the TRIPS Agreement, the Convention on Biological Diversity and the Protection of Traditional Knowledge – Amending the TRIPS Agreement to Introduce an Obligation to Disclose the Origin of Genetic Resources and Traditional Knowledge in Patent Applications*, 8, IP/C/W/473 (14 June 2006) (containing the statement of Norway).

52 M. Walløe Tvedt, "Elements for Legislation in User Countries to Meet the Fair and Equitable Benefit-Sharing Commitment", 9 *J. World Intell. Prop.* 189, 197 (2006).

53 *Id.* at 204 ("This information [about the origin of the genetic material] will not necessarily convert into any distribution of benefits. ... Therefore, disclosure requirements of any kind must be paired with enforcement mechanisms to be a successful strategy.").

54 *See* WIPO/UNEP, *WIPO-UNEP Study on the Role of Intellectual Property Rights in the Sharing of Benefits Arising from the Use of Biological Resources and Associated Traditional Knowledge*, 156 (2004) (*prepared by* A.K. Gupta), *available at*: www.wipo.int/tk/en/publications/769e_unep_tk.pdf (last visited 31 July 2008) ("Without the protection [by patent] sought and obtained in the second and third case studies, the technology would not have been licensed for potential commercial exploitation and thus benefits would not have been obtained and shared.

Furthermore, it is important to emphasize that judicial proceedings for the purpose of obtaining the cancellation of patents issued in spite of the misappropriation of traditional knowledge would be quite burdensome for communities, should they wish to initiate such actions. It is a well-known and unfortunate fact that litigation in general, and patent litigation in particular, is quite costly.[55] As a result, should patents for the same invention be granted in different countries (potentially after having been filed on the basis of a centralized patent filing system such as the *Patent Cooperation Treaty*[56]), then separate patent cancellation proceedings would have to be initiated in each of the relevant countries or regional areas, such as the region subject to the *Convention on the Grant of European Patents* (European Patent Convention).[57] The costs to be incurred by communities would consequently be quite substantial. Communities cannot reasonably be expected to incur these extremely high costs in order to litigate against the owners of patents that have been improperly registered in different countries.[58] From this perspective, the sanction of patent cancellation does not appear an appropriate means of protecting the communities.

It can thus be concluded that the obligation to disclose and the use of punitive measures, such as criminal sanctions and the cancellation of patents in case of a violation of the obligation to disclose, do not generally offer an efficient guarantee of benefit sharing for communities. In that sense, the obligation to disclose may not be sufficiently protective. As a result, it is appropriate to discuss what "legal means"[59] should be made available to communities in order "to provide remedies

To this extent, the use of existing patent laws enabled the generation and sharing of benefits.").

55 More generally, from an economic perspective, the present patent system is considered to unduly favour patent owners over third party litigants. Indeed, patent owners are likely to incur lesser costs than third parties challenging the validity of a patent. *See* J.R. Robledo, "Strategic Patents and Asymmetric Litigation Costs as Entry Deterrence Instruments", *Econ. Bull.*, Vol. 15, No. 2 (2005).

56 Patent Cooperation Treaty, 19 June 1970, 1160 U.N.T.S. 231.

57 After the expiry of the nine-month time limit for filing an opposition at the European Patent Office (EPO); *see* Convention on the Grant of European Patents (European Patent Convention), Article 99, 5 October 1973, 13 I.L.M. 270, *available at* www.epo.int/legal/epc/e/ma1.html (last visited 31 July 2008). *See also* EPO, *Assessment of the impact of the European patent litigation agreement (EPLA) on litigation of European patents*, 1 (February 2006), *available at* www.european-patent-office.org/epo/epla/pdf/impact_assessment_2006_02_v1.pdf (last visited 31 July 2008).

58 *See* S.A. Hanson, "Intellectual Property and Traditional Ecological Knowledge: Institutionally Globalized Biopiracy?", *Prof. Ethics Rep.*, summer 2002, at 1, 2, *available at* www.aaas.org/spp/sfrl/per/per30.pdf (last visited 31 Jul. 2008) (noting that the "prohibitive costs of registering, maintaining and defending patents against infringement" have the end effect of deterring holders of indigenous knowledge from filing patent applications should they have wished to do so).

59 This terminology is taken from the *Draft TK Principles*, *supra* note 2, Article 1(1) and (3), which provide that "[t]raditional knowledge shall be protected against misappropriation", whereby "*legal means* should be provided to prevent ... false claims or assertions of ownership or control

for traditional knowledge holders in cases where the fair and equitable sharing of benefits ... has not occurred".[60]

3. MOVING FROM TRANSPARENCY TO BENEFIT SHARING

Based on the analysis made above, it appears that in order to enable communities to truly share the benefits derived from the exploitation of their traditional knowledge it is necessary to move beyond the obligation to disclose, which essentially ensures the transparency of the patent application process. From a policy perspective, it was accurately noted that probably too much attention has been paid to the obligation to disclose and not enough to benefit sharing.[61] As accurately expressed by Emanuela Arezzo, "even if such measures [*i.e.* the obligation to disclose] were adopted and indigenous people were able to discover which patents are based on their misappropriated property, there is little chance of ensuring proper compensation pursuant to CBD's principles."[62]

In terms of a potential *shift of paradigms*, the point could be made that it is desirable to move from a *punitive and defensive* approach (*i.e.* the threat of patent cancellations and criminal sanctions in the case of a violation of the obligation to disclose) to a *positive and proactive* approach aimed at ensuring that communities will truly benefit[63] from the exploitation of traditional knowledge by third parties.[64] In discussing the methods to ensure benefit sharing for communities, it is interesting to assess whether lessons could be learnt from the legal protection of tangible cultural property (*see* Section 3.1. below). The focus will then turn to the potential modalities of ensuring benefit sharing at the level of both substantive law (*see* Section 3.2. below) and procedural law (*see* Section 3.3. below).

---

over traditional knowledge, including acquiring, claiming or asserting intellectual property rights over traditional knowledge-related subject matter when those intellectual property rights are not validly held in the light of that traditional knowledge and any conditions relating to its access" (emphasis added).

60 *Draft TK Principles*, *supra* note 2, Article 6(4).

61 *See* TVEDT, *supra* note 52, at 207 ("A dangerous strategy for developing countries is to put a too high a stake in the disclosure requirements or in the certificate systems if they are not developed as part of a total package of implementation of enforceable benefit-sharing commitments upon the beneficiaries. The discussions in the WIPO and the CBD indicate that there is too much of a focus on these tools, and too little focus upon other more legally binding mechanisms. Countries must be aware of the limits embedded in these strategies regarding the potential to create any benefit sharing.").

62 E. AREZZO, "Struggling Around the "Natural" Divide: The Protection of Tangible and Intangible Indigenous Property", 25 *Cardozo Arts & Ent. L.J.* 367, 414 (2007).

63 Not only at the financial level.

64 *See also* AREZZO, *supra* note 62, at 387 (showing the insufficiency of defensive mechanisms).

3.1. ARE THERE LESSONS TO BE LEARNT FROM THE LEGAL PROTECTION OF TANGIBLE CULTURAL PROPERTY?

The protection of *tangible* cultural property differs by the very nature of its object from the protection of traditional knowledge. However, it is worth considering whether some legal concepts which have been developed for and applied to the protection of tangible cultural property goods could be implemented by analogy in a system of benefit sharing related to the exploitation of traditional knowledge.[65] For this purpose, several concepts drawn from the protection of tangible cultural property will be presented (*see* Section 3.1.1. below). Their potential application by analogy will then be assessed (*see* Section 3.1.2. below).

3.1.1. Relevant Aspects of the Legal Protection of Tangible Cultural Property

Among the various international conventions protecting tangible cultural property goods, the *UNIDROIT Convention on Stolen or Illegally Exported Cultural Objects* (UNIDROIT Convention)[66], signed in Rome on 24 June 1995, contains some features which are worth discussing in the context of this Chapter. The UNIDROIT Convention applies to international claims for the restitution of cultural objects stolen or removed from the territory of a contracting state contrary to its cultural heritage protection laws regulating the export of cultural objects.[67]

First, with regard to the restitution of stolen cultural objects, the basic rule anchored in the UNIDROIT Convention is that the possessor of such objects shall return them.[68] A claim for restitution of a cultural object is subject to time limitations[69], which include specific and more favourable rules for cultural objects that are part of a "public collection".[70]

65 For an interdisciplinary approach between cultural property and traditional knowledge (limited, however, to the issue of the definition of traditional knowledge), *see* S. Harding, "Defining Traditional Knowledge – Lessons from Cultural Property", 11 *Cardozo J. Int'l & Comp. L.* 511 (2003).

66 UNIDROIT Convention on Stolen or Illegally Exported Cultural Objects, 24 June 1995, 34 I.L.M. 1322 (1995), *available at* www.unidroit.org/english/conventions/1995culturalproperty/1995culturalproperty-e.htm (last visited 31 July 2008).

67 *Id.*, Article 1.

68 *Id.*, Article 3(1).

69 *Id.*, Article 3(3) ("Any claim for restitution shall be brought within a period of three years from the time when the claimant knew the location of the cultural object and the identity of its possessor, and in any case within a period of fifty years from the time of the theft.").

70 *Id.*, Article 3(4) ("However, a claim for restitution of a cultural object forming an integral part of an identified monument or archaeological site, or belonging to a public collection, shall not be subject to time limitations other than a period of three years from the time when the claimant knew the location of the cultural object and the identity of its possessor.").

Pursuant to Article 3(7) of the UNIDROIT Convention, a public collection is defined as "a group of inventoried or otherwise identified cultural objects owned by: (a) a Contracting State; (b) a regional or local authority of a Contracting State; (c) a religious institution in a Contracting State; or (d) an institution that is established for an essentially cultural, educational or scientific purpose in a Contracting State and is recognised in that State as serving the public interest." In addition, Article 3(8) provides that "a claim for restitution of a sacred or communally important cultural object belonging to and used by a tribal or indigenous community in a Contracting State as part of that community's traditional or ritual use, shall be subject to the time limitation applicable to public collections."

The UNIDROIT Convention further protects – to a certain extent – the good faith possessor of a stolen cultural object by providing that "[t]he possessor of a stolen cultural object required to return it shall be entitled, at the time of its restitution, to payment of fair and reasonable compensation provided that the possessor neither knew nor ought reasonably to have known that the object was stolen and can prove that it exercised due diligence when acquiring the object."[71] With respect to the measures to be taken by the possessor of a stolen cultural object in order to be entitled to such payment (by showing its good faith), Article 4(4) provides that

> in determining whether the possessor exercised due diligence, regard shall be had to all the circumstances of the acquisition, including the character of the parties, the price paid, whether the possessor consulted any reasonably accessible register of stolen cultural objects, and any other relevant information and documentation which it could reasonably have obtained, and whether the possessor consulted accessible agencies or took any other step that a reasonable person would have taken in the circumstances.

Based on this provision, a good faith possessor can be protected if – among other factors to be taken into account – he has consulted "any reasonably accessible register of stolen cultural objects" or "accessible agencies". In such cases, the possessor may obtain "fair and reasonable compensation" if required to return the stolen cultural object to its legitimate owner.

Regarding the return of illegally exported cultural objects, Article 5(3) of the UNIDROIT Convention provides that "the court or other competent authority of the State addressed shall order the return of an illegally exported cultural object if the requesting State establishes that the removal of the object from its territory significantly impairs one or more of the following interests", which include "the traditional or ritual use of the object by a tribal or indigenous community". It

71 *Id.*, Article 4(1).

further provides for a similar system of compensation of the good faith possessor of the cultural object[72] and mentions that "[i]nstead of compensation, and in agreement with the requesting State, the possessor required to return the cultural object to that State may decide", in particular, "to retain ownership of the object".[73]

Finally, with respect to the mechanisms for dispute settlement, Article 8(2) of the UNIDROIT Convention provides for the ability of the litigating parties to consensually choose a judicial or arbitration forum for solving disputes relating to claims for recovering stolen or illegally exported cultural property (by stating that "[t]he parties may agree to submit the dispute to any court or other competent authority or to arbitration").

3.1.2. Are There Analogies to the Protection of Traditional Knowledge from Misappropriation?

Based on this description of selected aspects of the protection of cultural property goods under the UNIDROIT Convention, the question is whether any of them may be applied by analogy in the context of the protection of traditional knowledge from misappropriation.

The starting point of this analysis is the fact that the misappropriation of traditional knowledge and, most specifically, the unauthorized patenting of inventions which are derived from traditional knowledge, can conceptually be compared with the unauthorized traffic and export of cultural objects to the extent that in both cases the goal of the legal protection is to ensure that the legitimate right holders shall recover the control over their misappropriated goods (*i.e.* traditional knowledge or cultural property goods). Such a connection cannot be denied, even though differences obviously exist between the two situations. It could, however, be argued that the position of a patent owner (whose patent would be based on traditional knowledge) is more legitimate than that of someone in possession of a stolen or illegally exported cultural property good. Indeed, the grant of a patent presupposes an inventive activity which justifies the grant of the exclusive right, whereas by contrast, such respectable inventiveness is, obviously, lacking in the context of the traffic and export of tangible cultural objects.

In any case, it appears that some elements of the UNIDROIT Convention could be of interest in the context of the discussion over the potential legal remedies against the misappropriation of traditional knowledge in patent applications.

First of all, it is worth noting that the protection of cultural objects, as implemented in the UNIDROIT Convention, is strengthened for an object which

---

72 *Id.*, Article 6(1) and (2).
73 *Id.*, Article 6(3).

belongs to a public collection or which is a "sacred or communally important cultural object belonging to and used by a tribal or indigenous community in a Contracting State as part of that community's traditional or ritual use".[74] Such increased protection for a "communally important cultural object" which is used "as part of the community's traditional or ritual use" is quite interesting from the perspective of the protection against the misappropriation of traditional knowledge because it shows a clear convergence with the protection of traditional knowledge (which also targets the traditional use of local resources). With respect to the increased level of protection of cultural goods belonging to public collections, this derives in particular from the fact that these goods are inventoried or otherwise identified.[75]

From the perspective of traditional knowledge, it could similarly be expected that the level of protection against unauthorized misappropriation should be increased with respect to knowledge for which there exists some publicity.[76] This raises the issue of the potential role of databases and registries of traditional knowledge. On this subject, it can be reminded that Article 11(2) of the Draft TK Principles provides that

> [i]n the interests of transparency, certainty and the conservation of traditional knowledge, relevant national authorities may maintain registers or other records of traditional knowledge, where appropriate and subject to relevant policies, laws and procedures, and the needs and aspirations of traditional knowledge holders. Such registers may be associated with specific forms of protection, and should not compromise the status of hitherto undisclosed traditional knowledge or the interests of traditional knowledge holders in relation to undisclosed elements of their knowledge.

These databases and registries could thus have an important role to play in preventing the misappropriation of traditional knowledge.[77] In the same way that an acquirer or possessor of a cultural object under the UNIDROIT Convention is expected to conduct due diligence by consulting relevant registries[78] to ensure that a cultural object has not been reported to have been stolen, a company

---

74 *Id.*, Article 3(4), (7) and (8).

75 *Id.*, Article 3(7).

76 An aspect of the increased level of protection resulting from the publicity of traditional knowledge is the fact that such disclosed knowledge would belong to the prior Article. This would potentially bar the patentability of inventions based on this traditional knowledge for lack of novelty or non-obviousness.

77 This is precisely the goal of the remarkable project of the Indian government with the Traditional Knowledge Digital Library (TKDL); *see* Traditional Knowledge Digital Library, http://203.200.90.6/tkdl/langdefault/common/home.asp (last visited 31 July 2008).

78 Including the databases of the Art Loss Register (www.artloss.com/) and of INTERPOL (www.interpol.com/Public/WorkOfArt/Default.asp).

wishing to file a patent application relating to traditional knowledge should be required to check all relevant available registries and databases. It would thereby be possible to ensure that the invention that is the subject of a patent application is not unduly derived from any traditional knowledge. Even though this may impose a difficult task on patent applicants and their agents, as well as on patent offices, the use of databases and registries of traditional knowledge can be viewed positively.[79] However, the issue of broad access to databases and registries of traditional knowledge is complex. It can be argued that excessively broad access would be detrimental given that it could facilitate the misappropriation of traditional knowledge, rather than help the fight against it.[80] On the other hand, the legitimate point has been made that the identification of the owner of traditional knowledge, which could potentially be achieved through the consultation of the relevant databases and registries, is obviously required in order to allow benefit sharing.[81]

In this respect, the similarity between databases of lost tangible cultural property objects and those of traditional knowledge can be evidenced by the following sentence which, although relating to databases of lost cultural property objects, can be perfectly applied by analogy to databases of traditional knowledge:

> Access is therefore a double-edged sword. The publication of inventories on the Internet makes it very easy for potential thieves to browse and make their shopping lists. It makes insiders of outsiders. On the other hand, the Internet can offer a very good support in the recovery of stolen objects.[82]

In spite of these similarities, the databases of traditional knowledge raise additional questions in connection with the issue of prior art.[83] In order to avoid any misuse of databases and registries of traditional knowledge, they could be

---

79 One question relates to the accessibility of these databases to the patent applicants; on this issue, *see* WIPO, Intergovernmental Committee on Intellectual Property and Genetic Resources, Traditional Knowledge and Folklore, *Practical Mechanisms for the Defensive Protection of Traditional Knowledge and Genetic Resources Within the Patent System*, WIPO/GRTKF/IC/5/6 (14 May 2003).

80 *See* G. Dutfield, *supra* note 32, at 927; *see generally* T.J. Krumenacher, "Comment, Protection for Indigenous Peoples and Their Traditional Knowledge: Would a Registry System Reduce the Misappropriation of Traditional Knowledge?", 8 *Marq. Intell. Prop. L. Rev.* 143 (2004).

81 *See* Tvedt, *supra* note 52, at 202 (discussing the existence of "credible information" on the provider or origin of the genetic resources).

82 T. Cremers, "Theft, the Internet and Museum Objects: Threats and Opportunities", *ICOM News*, No. 4/2006, at 4, *available at* http://palimpsest.stanford.edu/icom/pdf/E_news2006/p4_2006-4.pdf (last visited 31 July 2008).

83 *See* UNU-IAS, *The Role of Registers and Databases in the Protection of Traditional Knowledge: A Comparative Analysis* 38 (2004), *available at* www.ias.unu.edu/binaries/UNUIAS_TKRegistersReport.pdf (last visited 31 July 2008) ("Databases can play an important role in defensive protection of TK. However, existing law and policy regarding sources of prior art is insensitive to the nature of TK, its confidentiality, and the rights and interests of indigenous

made accessible only to specific international or national entities (which would be bound by a duty of secrecy with respect to the content of the databases) and not directly to potential patent applicants. Patent applicants would then be obliged to consult these "accessible agencies" (in reference – by analogy – to the terminology of Article 4(4) of the UNIDROIT Convention). Applicants would submit to them their patent applications and these independent "agencies" would check whether the applications related to or contained traditional knowledge. They could then inform the patent applicants whether this would be the case, without disclosing to them the full content of the searched databases or the full results of their searches. This would avoid giving patent applicants an opportunity to misappropriate traditional knowledge by accessing privileged data to which only the "agencies" would have access on a secured basis.

Another interesting feature of the UNIDROIT Convention relates to the legal consequences when a possessor of a stolen cultural object has demonstrated good faith when acquiring the object by conducting sufficient due diligence. In such a case, the UNIDROIT Convention provides that the possessor may be financially compensated in exchange for the obligation to return the cultural object (Article 4(1)).

By analogy, it could be accepted that a proper and sufficient due diligence by a patent applicant could have an impact on the sanctions imposed, should it appear at a later stage that his invention is based on traditional knowledge. It should be acknowledged that it could be difficult for patent applicants to trace the origins of genetic resources.[84] As a result, it would be legitimate to take into account the interests of a patent owner when deciding on the modalities of benefit sharing. This is particularly true in the case of owners to whom the patent has been transferred and who, consequently, cannot be blamed for violating the obligation to disclose at the time of filing the patent application. The legitimate interests of such patent owners may deserve some protection in the shaping of remedies to be granted against them, should the patent at issue involve a misappropriation of traditional knowledge.[85] However, the protection of such good faith patent owners (by analogy to the good faith possessor of a cultural object) shall in no way constitute an absolute shield which would prevent the efficient protection of communities against the misappropriation of their traditional knowledge, unless the communities shall accept that the patentee shall keep the benefits from the patent (by analogy to the ability of the possessor of an illegally exported cultural good to retain ownership of the object with the agreement of the state from which

---

peoples over its future uses. Requiring that TK be placed in the public domain as a condition for recognising it as prior art is a double-edged sword.").

84 *See* Carvalho, *supra* note 32, at 186.

85 This raises the issue of the flexibility of the sanctions to be imposed in a particular case; *see infra* Section 3.3.2.

the object was illegally exported, as provided for by Article 7(3) of the UNIDROIT Convention). As a result, the fact that a patent owner may have legitimate reasons for not having identified the traditional knowledge in the patented invention and, thus, may not have disclosed it in the course of the application process would not bar granting certain rights[86] to communities over the patented invention.

Finally, the UNIDROIT Convention also offers to the parties the ability to solve their disputes by recourse to alternative dispute resolution mechanisms and, most specifically, by arbitration. This is something which could and should be encouraged with regard to disputes arising from cases of misappropriation of traditional knowledge.[87]

On this basis, it can be considered that valuable concepts are provided by the law governing the protection of tangible cultural property goods. These concepts could help shape an appropriate system of protection against the misappropriation of traditional knowledge. The question now is to see how such protection could be implemented in order to ensure true benefit sharing.

3.2. POTENTIAL MODALITIES FOR SHARING BENEFITS WITH THE COMMUNITIES

Various solutions have been discussed at the international level[88], or adopted at the national level[89], in order to implement the sharing of benefits resulting from the use of traditional knowledge. In spite of the differences between these regimes, benefit sharing should in all cases include both monetary and non-monetary[90] elements, as properly emphasized in the Bonn Guidelines.

86 The potential nature and extent of which are discussed below; *see infra* Section 3.2.

87 *See infra* Section 3.3.1.

88 *See Bonn Guidelines*, *supra* note 39; *see also* WIPO, Intergovernmental Committee on Intellectual Property and Genetic Resources, Traditional Knowledge and Folklore, *Draft Guidelines on Access and Benefit Sharing Regarding the Utilisation of Genetic Resources*, WIPO/GRTKF/IC/1/9 (27 April 2001) *available at* www.wipo.int/edocs/mdocs/tk/en/wipo_grtkf_ic_1/wipo_grtkf_ic_1_9.pdf (last visited 31 July 2008) [hereinafter "*Swiss Draft ABS Guidelines*"] (containing the document submitted by the Government of Switzerland).

89 For instance, the regulation adopted in India to implement the CBD, *supra* note 36; *see* Act to provide for conservation of biological diversity, sustainable use of its components and fair and equitable sharing of the benefits arising out of the use of biological resources, knowledge and for matters connected therewith or incidental thereto, sec. 21, 5 February 2003, No. 18 of 2003, *available at* www.nbaindia.org/act/act_english.htm (last visited 31 July 2008) [hereinafter "Biological Diversity Act, 2002"] (requiring equitable benefit sharing); Biological Diversity Rules, 2004, Rule 20, 15 April 2004, G.S.R. 261, *available at* www.nbaindia.org/rules.htm (last visited 31 July 2008) (implementing, *inter alia*, Section 21 of the Biological Diversity Act, 2002 by setting up the criteria for equitable benefit sharing).

90 *See* CBD, *supra* note 36, Articles 16(3) and 19(1) and (2) (referring to non-monetary benefit sharing in terms of transfer of technology to the countries providing genetic resources).

Among the potential modalities for benefit sharing which have been evoked, the co-ownership of patents is frequently listed as a privileged option.[91] Consequently, it is necessary to assess the appropriateness of this solution (*see* Section 3.2.1. below). In view of the potential drawbacks of a co-ownership regime, which will be described below, it may be wondered whether another regime for benefit sharing, potentially based on a compulsory licensing system, should not be encouraged (*see* Section 3.2.2. below).

3.2.1. Co-Ownership of the Patents

The proposal that communities shall be co-owners of the patents has been mentioned in the Bonn Guidelines[92] and has also been discussed in the legal literature.[93] As a matter of principle, one potential advantage of the co-ownership regime is that it would allow benefit sharing in terms of both monetary and non-monetary aspects. As co-owners of the relevant patents, communities would indeed be generally entitled to derive financial benefits from this status, as well as potentially non-financial (*i.e.* technological) benefits, particularly as a result of an exchange of information with their co-owner(s).[94]

However, it can be wondered whether the communities truly deserve to claim co-ownership of the patented invention. A claim of co-ownership would only be justified if the co-owner had actively participated in the creation of the patented invention. In a situation in which a patent is derived from pre-existing traditional knowledge, it is uncertain that the owner or creator of the underlying traditional knowledge could, in all circumstances, claim to be the co-inventor of the patented invention.

Irrespective of this issue, the status of co-ownership further raises the difficult question of how to define the persons or entities which should be considered as co-owners.[95] This key issue, however, is not limited to the specific case of the potential co-ownership of patents but, rather, arises generally in the debate surrounding the protection of traditional knowledge as such. As a result,

---

91 *See* Biological Diversity Act, 2002, *supra* note 89, sec. 21(2)(a) (listing the "grant of joint ownership of intellectual property rights to the National Biodiversity Authority, or where benefit claimers are identified, to such benefit claimers" as the first available option); *see also* WTO, *supra* note 14, at 4, par. 14 (stipulating that "[w]here the failure to provide evidence of benefit-sharing is discovered after the grant of a patent, the legal effect could include ... [f]ull or partial transfer of the rights to the invention, also as an alternative to revocation, as a means of promoting fair and equitable benefit-sharing").

92 *See Bonn Guidelines*, *supra* note 39, appendix II, pars. 1(j) and 2(q).

93 *See* M. Kohls, "Blackbeard or Albert Schweitzer: Reconciling Biopiracy", 6 *Chi.-Kent J. Intell. Prop.* 108, 122 (2007).

94 This double aspect of the regime of co-ownership may explain why the joint ownership of intellectual property rights is listed in the *Bonn Guidelines* both as a monetary *and* as a non-monetary benefit; *see Bonn Guidelines*, *supra* note 39, appendix II, Pars. 1(j) and 2(q).

95 Kohls, *supra* note 93, at 123.

uncertainty regarding the definition of the persons or entities to be treated as co-owners should not, in and of itself, block the adoption of a co-ownership model.

In any case, even though co-ownership over a patent is generally understood as meaning that the co-owners will share the benefits deriving from its commercial exploitation, co-ownership also means sharing the associated costs. These costs relate first to the prosecution and maintenance of the patent, but they also cover the potential costs which may result from its judicial enforcement or, more generally, from any patent litigation (such as patent cancellation proceedings). As already emphasized[96], these costs can be quite substantial. From this perspective, co-ownership may not be the most favourable system of benefit sharing for communities.

Co-owners of intellectual property rights may be free to contractually allocate the profits and losses between them, based on the general principle of freedom of contract, so that it is conceivable that a community might obtain only profits without having to share the costs of filing, maintaining and enforcing the patent which would be borne exclusively by its industrial partner. It however appears somehow unlikely that communities would be in a position to claim co-ownership of patents and obtain only the benefits from such co-ownership without bearing at least a fraction of the relevant costs. In addition, it is quite uncertain that such internal contractual agreements could be validly opposed to third parties that wished to sue all the co-owners of the relevant patent in the course of patent infringement or patent cancellation proceedings, particularly as a result of mandatory rules of civil procedure making it compulsory that all co-owners be sued.

Furthermore, it is a fact that co-ownership of intellectual property rights is frequently difficult to manage, most particularly in an international context.[97] The legal rules defining the respective rights and obligations of the co-owners may indeed diverge widely at the national level. This means that, assuming that a regime of co-ownership were to exist with respect to national patents issued in various countries, the respective rights and obligations of the co-owners might be different in each of these countries. While in some countries each of the co-owners could validly use and license out the patented invention for use by third party licensees and might also be able to keep the profits thus generated for themselves, without having to share them with their co-owner(s)[98], it is possible that national

96 *See supra* text accompanying notes 55–58.

97 *See* T.J. Calame and J. de Werra, "Co-titularité des droits de propriété intellectuelle (tout particulièrement des brevets) dans le cadre de projets de recherche et développement conjoints: un piège à éviter?", 2003 *Anwaltsrevue* 10.

98 This is the case under US patent law; *see* U.S. Patent Act, 35 U.S.C. § 262 (2007) ("[i]n the absence of any agreement to the contrary, each of the joint owners of a patent may make, use, offer to sell, or sell the patented invention within the Unites States, or import the patented

patent regulations applicable in other countries would prevent such acts.[99] This discrepancy of national patent regimes, and the resulting legal uncertainty, would obviously be detrimental to the interests of the co-owners, most specifically communities.

Even though part of the issue may be addressed by way of contractual provisions between the co-owners, it is still important to emphasize that such contractual solutions will not solve all issues. This is particularly true with respect to mandatory principles of civil procedure which impose that all co-owners be parties to litigation proceedings. It is likely that communities will still risk facing some liabilities as co-owners of patents.

As a result of these features and potential liabilities resulting from co-ownership over patents, this regime does not appear to be the most appropriate in order to reach the goal of benefit sharing for communities.

3.2.2. *Compulsory Licensing Scheme for the Use of Traditional Knowledge?*

As noted above[100], communities may not have an interest in obtaining the cancellation of a patent covering an invention which unduly misappropriated traditional knowledge. They may in fact have an interest in keeping such patents alive in order to try to share potential benefits which could result from their commercial exploitation. In the same line of argument, it has been argued that the exploitation of a patent shall not be blocked by the owner of relevant pre-existing traditional knowledge. On this basis, scholars have suggested that a compensatory liability regime should be adopted, in contrast to the recognition of exclusive property rights for communities. Such a regime might indeed "entitle indigenous people to procure compensation from third party exploitation; however, it would not grant them the right to block access to third parties."[101]

For the purpose of such a scheme, an application by analogy of Article 31(l) of the TRIPS Agreement, which defines the status of dependent patents, has been evoked.[102] With regard to protection from the misappropriation of traditional

invention into the United States without the consent of and without accounting to the other owners").

99 This is, for instance, the case under Swiss patent law; *see* Swiss Patent Act, Article 34 para. 2 ("Where a patent application or the patent itself is owned by several persons, a license may not be granted without the consent of all co-owners").

100 *See supra* text accompanying notes 51–52.

101 Arezzo, *supra* note 62, at 391–92 (presenting and discussing the proposal made by Jerome H. Reichman and Tracy Lewis on a compensatory liability regime); *see also* J.H. Reichman and T. Lewis, "Using Liability Rules to Stimulate Local Innovation in Developing Countries: Application to Traditional Knowledge", in K.E. Maskus and J.H. Reichman (eds.), *International Public Goods and Transfer of Technology Under a Globalized Intellectual Property Regime*, 2005, 337.

102 Arezzo, *supra* note 62, at 391 n.111; *see also* G. Ghidini and E. Arezzo, "Patent and Copyright Paradigms vis-à-vis Derivative Innovation: The Case of Computer Programs", 36 *Int'l Rev. of*

knowledge, the status of communities could be similar to that of owners of a pre-existing patent. The latter may have to tolerate the commercial exploitation of a subsequent patent (*i.e.* the patent unduly incorporating their traditional knowledge) provided that the new patent shall "involve an important technical advance of considerable economic significance in relation to the invention claimed in the first patent"[103], that communities shall "be paid adequate remuneration in the circumstances of each case, taking into account the economic value of the authorization"[104] and they shall "be entitled to a cross-licence on reasonable terms to use the invention claimed in the second patent"[105], among the others conditions set forth under Article 31 of the TRIPS Agreement.

Such a compulsory license scheme could thus offer an appropriate legal framework under which the validity of a patent incorporating traditional knowledge would not be threatened, given that the cancellation of the patent would not bring benefits to the relevant community. At the same time, the exploitation of such a patent would still be made subject to the authorization of a court and to the payment to the community of compensation to be fixed, or at least reviewed, by an independent authority.[106]

Such a proposal could allow the sharing of benefits with communities, both at the financial and technological levels, as a result of the cross-license to be granted by the patent owners.

This approach is quite promising, even though it would require some adaptations in order to address more effectively the specificities of the issue of the misappropriation of traditional knowledge. This need for adaptation particularly relates to the matter of the "triggering event" necessary for granting a compulsory license. In the system of dependent patents under Article 31(l)(i) of the TRIPS Agreement, the new patent shall "involve an important technical advance of considerable economic significance in relation to the invention claimed in the first patent" in order to deserve the grant of a compulsory license on the pre-existing patent. How shall this requirement be adapted to the case of misappropriation of traditional knowledge?

As a matter of principle, it may appear inappropriate to refer essentially to the "considerable economic significance" of the patent as the relevant criterion, given that the economic significance would only relate to monetary benefit sharing. This approach would not address the non-monetary aspects, which are essential

---

Intell. Prop. & Competition L. 159, 162–63 (2005) (proposing the use of a compensatory liability regime for computer programs).

103 TRIPS Agreement, *supra* note 15, Article 31(l)(i).

104 *Id.*, Article 31(h).

105 *Id.*, Article 31(l)(ii).

106 *See id.*, Article 31(j) ("any decision relating to the remuneration provided in respect of such use shall be subject to judicial review or other independent review by a distinct higher authority in that Member").

in the context of the discussion about potential legal remedies against the misappropriation of traditional knowledge. Similarly, the mere ability to grant a financial remuneration and a cross license to a community, as set forth under Article 31(l) of the TRIPS Agreement, may not sufficiently reflect the broad range of monetary and, more importantly, non-monetary benefits that communities would deserve to obtain in the context of a benefit sharing system. This system would consequently need to be further adapted and fine-tuned in order to provide a valuable solution for allowing benefit sharing.

3.3. IMPLEMENTATION OF THE BENEFIT SHARING SYSTEM

Beyond the definition of the potential modalities which may ensure efficient benefit sharing at the level of substantive law, it is critical to keep in mind that an effective enforcement system should be made available to communities. This is why, in a paragraph entitled *Principle of effectiveness and accessibility of protection*, the Draft TK Principles provide that

> [m]easures for protecting traditional knowledge should be effective in achieving the objectives of protection, and should be understandable, affordable, accessible and not burdensome for their intended beneficiaries, taking account of the cultural, social and economic context of traditional knowledge holders. Where measures for the protection of traditional knowledge are adopted, appropriate enforcement mechanisms should be developed permitting effective action against misappropriation of traditional knowledge and supporting the broader principle of prior informed consent.[107]

A similar concern was also expressed in the context of the CBD in which the need to ensure "access to justice" was expressly identified.[108]

On this basis, the practical implementation of an efficient benefit sharing system requires an effective enforcement and dispute resolution mechanism (*see* Section 3.3.1. below) as well as a flexible approach in the design of the available remedies (*see* Section 3.3.2. below).

---

107 *Draft TK Principles*, *supra* note 2, Annex, at 8–9 (general guiding principles).

108 In the context of the creation of an international regime on access and benefit-sharing, *see* COP, *Access and benefit-sharing*, Decision VIII/4, UNEP/CBD/COP/8/31 (20–31 March 2006), *available at* www.cbd.int/decisions/cop-08.shtml?m=COP-08&id=11016&lg=0 (last visited 31 July 2008) (providing, under a specific chapter entitled "Access to justice", "[m]easures to [facilitate][ensure] access to justice and redress" and "[m]easures to [guarantee and] facilitate access to justice and redress, including administrative and judicial remedies, as well as alternative dispute resolution mechanisms [by providers and users]").

3.3.1. *Efficient Enforcement and Dispute Resolution System*

It is widely acknowledged that a global solution to the problem of the misappropriation of traditional knowledge should be found at the international level, in order to cover the countries from which traditional knowledge has been unduly "exported", as well as importing countries and systems (*i.e.* countries in which traditional knowledge would have been commercially used and patented).[109] However, relatively little attention has so far been paid to the ways in which one may settle disputes arising from cases of misappropriation of traditional knowledge in patent applications.[110]

In the context of this discussion about potential ways to improve the efficient enforcement of protection against the misappropriation of traditional knowledge and to ensure access to justice for communities, various mechanisms adopted in existing patent law instruments deserve to be mentioned. It is worth considering their application, by analogy, to the use of traditional knowledge.

From this perspective, it is interesting to note that under the system of the European Patent Convention a claim raised by a third party, challenging the entitlement of the patent applicant to the invention, may lead to the stay of the patent application proceedings. Rule 13(1) of the *Implementing Regulations to the Convention on the Grant of European Patents* (EPC Implementing Regulations)[111] states that "[i]f a third party provides proof to the European Patent Office that he has opened proceedings against the applicant for the purpose of seeking a judgment that he is entitled to the grant of the European patent, the European Patent Office shall stay the proceedings for grant unless the third party consents to the continuation of such proceedings."

This system of staying patent application proceedings might also be used in the context of protection against the misappropriation of traditional knowledge. A stay of patent application proceedings would be imposed if a community were to initiate a legal action against the patent applicant in order to try to obtain some benefit sharing on the patent at issue. This system could be quite promising for communities, given that it would put pressure on patent applicants to find a solution to disputes (given that patent applications would not be processed until

---

109 *See* HOARE and TARASOFSKY, *supra* note 46, at 159.

110 Some commentators consider that the existing international dispute resolution system is sufficient for this purpose; *see* T. COTTIER and M. PANIZZON, "Legal Perspectives on Traditional Knowledge: The Case for Intellectual Property Protection", 7 *J. Int'l Econ. L.* 371, 399 (2004). On this issue, *see* HOARE and TARASOFSKY, *supra* note 46, at 163 (confirming that it is very difficult to challenge a patent which has been granted in a foreign jurisdiction in violation of the principles of the CBD, *supra* note 36).

111 Implementing Regulations to the Convention on the Grant of European Patents, 5 October 1973, *available at* www.european-patent-office.org/legal/epc/e/ma2.html (as last amended by Decision of the Administrative Council of the European Patent Organisation of 9 December 2004).

they had been solved), without however threatening the validity of the patents. If an agreement could be found with the relevant community, the patent could be granted, provided of course that the conditions of patentability were met.

In addition, and perhaps more importantly, the efficient enforcement of the rights of communities would require setting up specialized courts or other dispute resolution authorities for the purpose of allowing quick and, ideally, cheap resolutions to disputes. In this context, it is also worth noting that the system implemented under the European Patent Convention provides for specific exclusive forums for litigating claims relating to the potential rights of claimants on a disputed European patent. The exclusive jurisdiction of these specialized courts, subject to specific exceptions defined on the basis of the place of residence or place of business of the parties, involves claims relating to the entitlement to a patent under the *Protocol on Jurisdiction and the Recognition of Decisions in Respect of the Right to the Grant of a European Patent* (Protocol on Recognition).[112]

By analogy, it could thus be imagined that specific courts would be entrusted with the exclusive task of deciding disputes regarding the misappropriation of traditional knowledge. The exclusive jurisdiction of these courts, which could be instituted at the national level or preferably at the international level[113], might avoid the costs and hassles resulting from the otherwise inevitable obligation to initiate separate legal actions in each and every country in which a disputed patent application had been filed or granted. In the absence of specialized courts, this strictly local approach would be imposed by virtue of the principle of territoriality which governs patent law (*i.e.* each national state has the sovereign power to decide on its national patents).

Another potential approach would be to use arbitration for solving these cases, bearing in mind that arbitration is a well established method of solving international disputes. In this respect, it is worth noting that arbitration is mentioned in Article 27(3)(a) and Part 1 of Annex II of the CBD, as well as in other CBD related documents.[114] Furthermore, arbitration has gained significant

---

112 Protocol on Jurisdiction and the Recognition of Decisions in Respect of the Right to the Grant of a European Patent (Protocol on Recognition), 5 October 1973, *available at* www.european-patent-office.org/legal/epc/e/ma4.html#REC (last visited 31 July 2008).

113 *See* G.B. Dinwoodie, *Towards an International Framework for the Protection of Traditional Knowledge*, 15 (4–6 February 2004) (paper presented at UNCTAD-Commonwealth Secretariat workshop on the *Elements of National Sui Generis Systems for the Preservation, Protection and Promotion of Traditional Knowledge: Innovations and Practices and Options for an International Framework*, Geneva, Switzerland), *available at* http://ssrn.com/abstract=707002 (last visited 31 July 2008) (considering that an "international institution could be authorized to make determinations regarding traditional knowledge claims").

114 COP, *Access and benefit-sharing as related to genetic resources (Article 15)*, Decision VII/19, UNEP/CBD/COP/7/21 (9–20 and 27 February 2004), *available at* www.cbd.int/decisions/cop-07.shtml?m=COP-07&id=7756&lg=0 (last visited 31 July 2008) (mentioning that disputes can be solved by "dispute settlement and/or arbitration" which constitutes a somewhat unclear

momentum for intellectual property-related disputes, as confirmed by the successful expert services and documents provided by the WIPO Arbitration and Mediation Center in this field (which may serve as a reference).[115]

However, arbitration requires an arbitration agreement between the parties, which may not be easy to obtain in all cases. This could potentially be achieved by obligating all patent applicants (including those having misappropriated traditional knowledge) to submit to the jurisdiction of specific courts in the course of the patent application process (*i.e.* by requesting patent applicants to accept such jurisdiction at the time of filing of the patent applications). Patent applicants could be obliged, already at the time of filing, to accept that any claim potentially raised by communities against them on the basis of an alleged misappropriation of traditional knowledge should be litigated before a specific court, based on a specific dispute resolution system.

This approach could be inspired by the system successfully implemented at the quasi-worldwide level for so-called "cybersquatting" cases, arising about the misappropriation of Internet domain names.[116] Under this system, registrants of domain names are required to accept, in the terms and conditions of the domain name registrars at the time when they register a domain name, to submit to administrative proceedings which may be initiated against them at a later time by trademark owners trying to obtain the transfer or cancellation of the disputed domain name under the *Uniform Domain Name Dispute Resolution Policy* (UDRP)[117] or other similar policies.[118] The implementation by analogy of such a system in the international patent arena could potentially be achieved by imposing a similar obligation on persons and bodies filing international patent applications in the PCT Regulations or European patent applications in the EPC Implementing Regulations.

Beyond these relatively formal dispute resolution systems, it is probable that informal and more flexible dispute resolution mechanisms, such as mediation, may constitute the best approach for solving disputes relating to the misappropriation of traditional knowledge.[119] It is consequently not a surprise

---

formulation given that arbitration is a method of dispute settlement so that the terms "and/or" which are used in this provision may not reflect the real nature of arbitration).

115 *See* D. Gervais, "Traditional Knowledge & Intellectual Property: A TRIPS-Compatible Approach", 2005 *Mich. St. L. Rev.* 137, 165.

116 For a discussion about such a potential analogy and limits thereto, *see* Dinwoodie, *supra* note 113, at 15–16.

117 *See* ICANN, Uniform Domain Name Dispute Resolution Policy, www.icann.org/dndr/udrp/policy.htm (last visited 31 July 2008).

118 On Internet domain name disputes, *see* WIPO, *Domain Name Dispute Resolution Service*, www.wipo.int/amc/en/domains/(last visited 31 July 2008) (the dedicated website of the WIPO Arbitration and Mediation Center).

119 On this issue, *see* J.Chr. Wichard and W.B. Wendland, "Mediation as an Option for Resolving Disputes between Indigenous/Traditional Communities and Industry Concerning

that the recourse to mediation was recommended in the context of the negotiation of fair and equitable benefit sharing agreements regarding the use of traditional knowledge[120], as well as regarding disputes between contracting parties to the CBD.[121]

Finally, it is also quite essential that any dispute settlement mechanisms not only address the disputes between communities and patent applicants or patent owners, but also cover potential disputes between communities themselves, in cases where they may raise competing and conflicting claims on the same traditional knowledge.[122] For the sake of efficiency, it would appear convenient that all disputes relating to an alleged case of misappropriation of traditional knowledge in a patent application process be solved globally in one forum.

3.3.2. Flexible Approach

In view of the widely diverging interests of the stakeholders (and most specifically of the victims of acts of misappropriation of traditional knowledge), it would be counterproductive to set rigid methods and sanctions for solving all legal issues on the basis of a predefined scheme. This suggests the necessity, as seen above[123], of adopting flexible dispute resolution systems, such as mediation.

In other words, there is not and there cannot be a single solution to the various claims and interests of the stakeholders. Any and all acts of misappropriation of traditional knowledge shall consequently not *automatically* lead to the same sanction. Quite to the contrary, a balanced and flexible approach is required in order to better reflect the specific interests of the relevant stakeholders.[124] This flexibility is essential in view of the fact that victims of acts of misappropriation of traditional knowledge have different views on the potential ways in which to cure or solve the violation of their interests.[125] While some consider that their

Traditional Knowledge", in B.T. HOFFMAN (ed.), *Art and Cultural Heritage: Law, Policy and Practice*, 2006, 475.

120 *See Swiss Draft ABS Guidelines*, *supra* note 88, Article 15.

121 *See* CBD, *supra* note 36, Article 27(1) and (2):

> 1. In the event of a dispute between Contracting Parties concerning the interpretation or application of this Convention, the parties concerned shall seek solution by negotiation.
> 2. If the parties concerned cannot reach agreement by negotiation, they may jointly seek the good offices of, or request mediation by, a third party.

122 GERVAIS, *supra* note 115, at 165.

123 *See supra* text accompanying notes 119–120.

124 *See also* Chr. B. GRABER and M.A. GIRSBERGER, "Traditional Knowledge at the International Level: Current Approaches and Proposals for a Bigger Picture that Includes Cultural Diversity", in J. SCHMID and H. SEILER (eds.), *Recht des ländlichen Raums: Festgabe für Paul Richli zum 60. Geburtstag*, 2006, 243, 265–66 (acknowledging that there cannot be a "one size fits all" solution).

125 *See* KOHLS, *supra* note 93, at 110.

resources are sacred and should remain secret, so that no patents shall be granted at all[126], others believe that indigenous communities should obtain equitable benefit sharing in the profits generated from the exploitation of their resources resulting from a patent.[127]

This variety of positions calls for flexibility in the solutions to be adopted. This is the reason why such flexibility was expressly mentioned in the Bonn Guidelines which provide under Paragraph 49 that "[m]echanisms for benefit-sharing may vary depending upon the type of benefits, the specific conditions in the country and the stakeholders involved. The benefit-sharing mechanism should be *flexible* as it should be determined by the partners involved in benefit-sharing and will vary on a case-by-case basis."[128]

4. CONCLUSION

The goal of this Chapter was to discuss whether the obligation to disclose was effectively protecting communities. As was noted, this obligation may not be sufficient, as it merely creates transparency in the patent application process but does not directly ensure benefit sharing for communities. This is the reason why some thought must be given to additional protective measures which could be implemented in order to turn benefit sharing into reality. For this purpose, different legal approaches may be considered, including ones derived from other legal fields, as shown in the analysis of the potential application by analogy of protection mechanisms existing for stolen tangible cultural property objects. In addition to the measures to be implemented at the level of substantive law, the practical enforcement of the claims of communities shall in no way be forgotten and left aside. From this perspective, the issues of access to justice and efficient dispute resolution methods must not be neglected given that they will condition the practical efficiency of the protection of communities against the misappropriation of their traditional knowledge.

In any case, irrespective of the potential protection mechanisms which could be implemented in the field of patent law, it should not be forgotten that the misappropriation of traditional knowledge is not limited to cases of its unauthorized use in inventions for which patent protection has been sought. It can, more generally, arise in all cases of unauthorized use of traditional knowledge, whether or not such use leads to the filing of patent applications and, potentially,

126 *Id.* at 110 (referring to this group as the "romantic bio-opponents").

127 *See id.*; Chr. Haight Farley, "Protecting Folklore and Indigenous Peoples: Is Intellectual Property the Answer?", 30 *Conn. L. Rev.* 1, 14–15 (1997) (noting the potential difference of views of local communities).

128 *See, e.g.*, *Swiss Draft ABS Guidelines*, *supra* note 88, Annex C (emphasis added).

to the grant of patents.[129] Therefore, a solution which would be anchored in patent law would not solve all the potential disputes, given that misappropriation could occur even if no patent applications are filed to the detriment of communities. Any global solution will consequently require an interdisciplinary approach combining different legal[130] (including intellectual property[131], unfair competition, biodiversity and, potentially, tangible[132] and intangible cultural property laws) and non-legal fields.[133] Such an interdisciplinary approach should ideally create mutually beneficial interactions between the respective fields, as well as between the people and institutions, both national and international, involved in them. This could constitute a most welcome and quite important emanation (or *avatar*) of mutual "benefit sharing", which may pave the way toward the implementation of an effective benefit sharing system over traditional knowledge, which could ensure the protection of communities without overly burdening other stakeholders.[134]

---

129 *See* AREZZO, *supra* note 62, at 388.

130 *See Draft TK Principles*, *supra* note 2, Annex, Article 2(1) ("The protection of traditional knowledge against misappropriation may be implemented through a range of legal measures, including: a special law on traditional knowledge; laws on intellectual property, including laws governing unfair competition and unjust enrichment; the law of contracts; the law of civil liability, including torts and liability for compensation; criminal law; laws concerning the interests of indigenous peoples; fisheries laws and environmental laws; regimes governing access and benefit-sharing; or any other law or any combination of those laws.").

131 The interaction between the protection of traditional knowledge and the protection of intellectual property rights is already by itself a complex issue; *see* Ch. OGUAMANAM, *International Law and Indigenous Knowledge: Intellectual Property, Plant Biodiversity, and Traditional Medicine*, 2006; S. VON LEWINSKI (ed.), *Indigenous Heritage and Intellectual Property: Genetic Resources, Traditional Knowledge and Folklore*, 2004; C.J. VISSER, "Making Intellectual Property Laws Work for Traditional Knowledge", in J.M. FINGER and Ph. SCHULER (eds.), *Poor People's Knowledge: Promoting Intellectual Property in Developing Countries*, 2004, 207 *available at* www.worldbank.org/research/Poor_Peoples_Knowledge.pdf (last visited 31 July 2008).

132 This approach was tentatively adopted with respect to the potential analogies between regulations protecting cultural property and the ones drafted to govern traditional knowledge; *see supra* Section 3.1. It is interesting to note that the protection of traditional knowledge is considered as a part of cultural heritage; *see Art and Cultural Heritage*, *supra* note 119, at 325 (Part 7 devoted to traditional knowledge).

133 Such as anthropology; *see* Sh. GREENE, "Indigenous People Incorporated?: Culture as Politics, Culture as Property in Pharmaceutical Bioprospecting", 45 *Current Anthropology* 211 (2004).

134 *See* HOARE and TARASOFSKY, *supra* note 46, at 164–65 (noting in their conclusion that a balanced system of obligation to disclose should be adopted in order to prevent the appropriation of genetic resources without deterring research and development activities based on such resources).

DOCUMENTATION AND DIGITIZATION OF TRADITIONAL KNOWLEDGE AND INTANGIBLE CULTURAL HERITAGE

Challenges and Prospects

Chidi OGUAMANAM*

* LL.M., Ph.D. (British Columbia), Assistant Professor and Director, Law and Technology Institute, Dalhousie University Law School, Halifax, Nova Scotia, Canada. This contribution is dedicated to Professor Teresa Scassa, of the University of Ottawa, a treasured colleague and mentor.

For many in the developing world, TRIPS – the Agreement on Trade Related Aspects of Intellectual Property Rights – ... establishes both Western property rights and the right of foreigners to own [Indigenous] property ... [and] is leading to a steady transfer of the "ownership" of intellectual "products" from the developing world to the developed world.[1]

1. INTRODUCTION

The *Agreement on Trade-Related Aspects of Intellectual Property Rights* (TRIPS Agreement)[2] represents a bold attempt to universalize the Western system of intellectual property rights. Some have gone so far as to characterize it as potentially "one of the most effective vehicles of Western imperialism in history."[3] Indeed, the TRIPS Agreement provides a critical legal platform for consolidating the long-standing inequities in intellectual property rights between the industrialized world and the Indigenous and local communities of both the South and North. These inequalities have been aggravated by the simultaneous appearance of the so-called "Information Age", which has led to the emergence of a major shift in scientific and industrial approaches to the exploitation of plants, animals and the diverse ecological and biological resources at humanity's disposal. This new era has made the ability to control information central to the generation, application, management and appropriation of knowledge by means of intellectual property rights.[4] The TRIPS system, however, has left the traditional knowledge of Indigenous communities vulnerable to misappropriation by outsiders.[5]

According to Anupam Chander and Madhavi Sunder, the TRIPS Agreement "transformed a global public domain in information by propertizing the information resources of the West ... but leaving in the commons the information resources of the rest of the world, such as genetic resources and traditional knowledge."[6] Left in the public domain, traditional knowledge and intangible

1 *See* A. Chander and M. Sunder, "The Romance of the Public Domain", 92 *Calif. L. Rev.* 1331, 1346–7 (2004).

2 Agreement on Trade-Related Aspects of Intellectual Property Rights, 15 April 1994, Marrakesh Agreement Establishing the World Trade Organization, Annex 1C, Legal Instruments – Results of the Uruguay Round, 33 I.L.M. 1125 (1994) [hereinafter "TRIPS Agreement"].

3 *See* M.A. Hamilton, "The TRIPS Agreement: Imperialistic, Outdated, and Overprotective", 29 *Vand. J. Transnat'l L.* 613, 614 (1996).

4 *See* G. Takach, *Computer Law,* (2nd ed.), 2003, 48–58.

5 *See* P.K. Yu, "Currents and Crosscurrents in the International Intellectual Property Regime", 38 *Loy. L.A. L. Rev.* 323 (2004); A.S. Oddi, "The International Patent System and Third World Development: Reality or Myth?", 63 *Duke L.J.* 831 (1987).

6 *See* Chander and Sunder, *supra* note 1, at 1331–2.

cultural heritage are open to appropriation by second comers or diverse external forces, especially Western based multinational corporations with little regard for the interests of holders and custodians of such knowledge and cultures. A glaring consequence of this TRIPS-driven international intellectual property regime is the endangerment of traditional knowledge and the intangible cultural heritage[7] of Indigenous and local communities across the world. Interestingly, Western scientific interest in the value of such knowledge forms has only intensified. That interest is particularly relevant in the context of the multi-disciplinary and applied knowledge domain known as biotechnology.[8] Not surprisingly, in the TRIPS era, the intellectual property or knowledge protection regime has come to represent a source of tension, resistance, regime-shifting and debate without historical parallel.[9]

This Chapter explores the discourses emerging from diverse international legal and institutional endeavours implicated in the search for a knowledge protection mechanism that can stem the unbridled appropriation of the intangible cultural heritage of Indigenous and local communities. The chapter explains how the present initiatives for the documentation and digitization of intangible cultural heritage[10] are controversial and revolutionary aspects of the new intangible cultural heritage protection campaign. I explore the documentation project and its challenges, reflecting on how it potentially advances or undermines the agenda of Indigenous and local communities in the intellectual property or knowledge protection debate.

I locate intangible cultural heritage documentation within the "new public domain movement"[11] in intellectual property discourse, which advocates the need to protect goods held in common from private enclosure. The public domain movement has not resolved the issue of distributional disequilibrium in the exploitation of resources in the public domain, particularly with regard to the risk of misusing traditional knowledge. I argue that the documentation initiative can

7 On the conflated nature of the concepts of traditional knowledge and intangible cultural heritage, *see infra* notes 10, 14, 16 and 17 and accompanying text.

8 Biotechnology generally refers to the use of biological and technological processes in the exploration and exploitation of the complex chemistry of biological systems for food, pharmaceuticals, health promotion and therapeutic applications and other industrial ends.

9 *See* L.R. Helfer, "Regime Shifting: The TRIPs Agreement and New Dynamics of International Law Making", 29 *Yale J. Int'l L.* 1 (2004).

10 Generally, the discourses on documentation refer to traditional knowledge only but the definition of intangible cultural heritage adopted here takes into account the fusion of the concepts of traditional knowledge and intangible cultural heritage. More importantly, the Convention for the Safeguarding of the Intangible Cultural Heritage now includes intangible cultural heritage in the documentation or inventory making process. *See* Convention for the Safeguarding of the Intangible Cultural Heritage, 17 October 2003, U.N. Doc. MISC/2003/CLT/CH/14 (2003), *available at* http://unesdoc.unesco.org/images/0013/001325/132540e.pdf (last visited 31 July 2008) [hereinafter "ICH Convention"].

11 *See infra* note 75 and accompanying text.

be used to plug this dangerous loophole by enhancing equitable access to the public domain and promoting anti-enclosure programs. Furthermore, in order to maximize the promise of the documentation program, it must be re-thought to transcend its current status as a defensive and anti-appropriative initiative. I contend that a regional approach to documentation, as well as the use of digital technology[12] as a preferred documentation option, has the potential to address the knotty issue of distributional inequity and can enhance the ability of Indigenous and local communities to benefit from the expected results of the documentation of their intangible cultural heritage.

For clarity, reference to Indigenous and local communities in this Chapter is made in the broadest sense. It includes Indigenous peoples in the developed countries of the world whose claims to indigeneity are already recognized, as well as their counterparts in the developing countries whose claims to indigeneity may be inchoate and contested but who fit within the less technical category of "local communities", as used in the *Convention on Biological Diversity* (CBD).[13] In the same way, references to traditional knowledge and intangible cultural heritage are made in accordance to their respective definitions by World Intellectual Property Organization (WIPO) and United Nations Educational, Scientific and Cultural Organization (UNESCO). In this regard, traditional knowledge refers to "content or substance of knowledge resulting from intellectual activity in a traditional context".[14] The intangible cultural heritage, on the other hand, refers to elaborated and identified "practices, representations, expressions, knowledge, skills – as well as instruments, objects, artefacts and cultural spaces associated therewith" deployed by communities and groups to foster human creativity in the relevant ecological and diverse cultural contexts and affirmative of their identity.[15] Similarly, this chapter adopts, for analytical convenience, WIPO's definition of "traditional cultural expressions" and "expressions of folklore"[16] which includes

---

12 Digitization is a pivotal application in computing technology that translates all informational representations onto an optimal medium or into electronically recordable numeric-based signals. *See* Takach, *supra* note 4, at 35.

13 Convention on Biological Diversity, 5 June 1992, 31 I.L.M. 818, *available at* www.biodiv.org/convention/convention.shtml (last visited 31 July 2008) [hereinafter "CBD"]. *See also* N. Roht-Arriaza, "Of Seeds and Shamans: The Appropriation of the Scientific and Technical Knowledge of Indigenous and Local Communities", 17 *Mich. J. Int'l L.* 919, 946 (1996).

14 *See* WIPO, Intergovernmental Committee on Intellectual Property and Genetic Resources, Traditional Knowledge and Folklore, *The Protection of Traditional Knowledge: Draft Objectives and Principles*, Annex, Article 3(2), WIPO/GRTKF/IC/10/5 (2 October 2006), *available at* www.wipo.int/edocs/mdocs/tk/en/wipo_grtkf_ic_10/wipo_grtkf_ic_10_5.pdf (last visited 31 July 2008) [hereinafter "*Draft TK Principles*"].

15 *See* ICH Convention, *supra* note 10, Article 2(1).

16 WIPO uses both terms interchangeably. The term "traditional cultural expressions" is more novel. It is adopted in recognition of the sensitivity and perceived negative connotations of the word "folklore" in Indigenous communities.

"any forms, whether tangible and intangible, in which traditional culture and knowledge are expressed, appear or are manifested".[17]

A marriage of these overlapping definitions affirms the received wisdom in Indigenous circles that, for the most part, knowledge and the objects that embody it have intricate and interdependent affinities. Up until now, Indigenous knowledge forms have been cast to fit into a fragmentary Western epistemological and pedagogic framework which divides tangible and intangible heritage, yet the border between these two knowledge forms is a faint one, casting doubt as to the enduring or practical value of distinguishing them. The knowledge base of an Indigenous or local community flows naturally from the inherent intellectual processes in their dynamic relationships with natural phenomena, ecological forces, the environment, cultural properties or artefacts and other natural and artificial creations and objects. In Indigenous circles, there is a unity of purpose between the creator or maker of a thing and the process of creation, and the resulting object. Knowledge is generated through constant interaction between these entities. Every object is a domain of knowledge in a holistic order; the tangible is fused with the intangible and vice versa.

This Chapter is divided into three sections. Section 2 explores trends in the discourses emanating from the diverse forums that debate alternative strategies for the protection of intangible cultural heritage outside of intellectual property regime. Section 3 focuses on the documentation and digitization of intangible cultural heritage as a defensive and anti-appropriative mechanism. The section also examines the place of documentation within the existing public domain movement for knowledge protection. Section 4 is a partial critique of the public domain movement. It highlights the "*romance of the public domain*"[18] as an issue being raised by the new public domain campaign and its potential danger for the documentation project. Here, I point to a regional approach to documentation as one possible way around the distributional inequity implicated in the *romance of the public domain*. Also, I highlight the potential benefits of digitization as a preferred documentation option. In conclusion, I call for a broader vision of documentation that transcends its present thrust as a defensive and anti-appropriative strategy.

---

17 *See* WIPO, Intergovernmental Committee on Intellectual Property and Genetic Resources, Traditional Knowledge and Folklore, *The Protection of Traditional Cultural Expressions/Expressions of Folklore: Draft Objectives and Principles*, Annex, Article 1(a), WIPO/GRTKF/IC/10/4 (2 October 2006), *available at* www.wipo.int/edocs/mdocs/tk/en/wipo_grtkf_ic_10/wipo_grtkf_ic_10_4.pdf (last visited 31 July 2008) [hereinafter "*Draft TCE Principles*"].

18 *See* Chander and Sunder, *supra* note 1.

2. OPTIONS FOR THE PROTECTION OF INTANGIBLE CULTURAL HERITAGE: BEYOND INTELLECTUAL PROPERTY

For a number of reasons, intangible cultural heritage has difficulty fitting within the Western forms of intellectual property rights universalized for global application by the TRIPS Agreement. These obstacles include its communal and informal nature, its deep cultural orientation in a socio-cultural and economic framework outside the market economic matrix and, perhaps most important, its systemic devaluation and exclusion from formal science. Elsewhere, I have articulated, in a detailed fashion, the major arguments and counterarguments regarding the inoperability of conventional intellectual property rights in the intangible cultural heritage context.[19] That debate need not detain us here. The fitness and equity gap separating intangible cultural heritage from conventional intellectual property rights, now bolstered by the TRIPS Agreement, "have provided the platform for marginalized stakeholders (mainly indigenous peoples, local communities in developing and developed countries, and their sympathizers around the globe) to challenge not only TRIPS' legitimacy, but also to amass counter-regime pressures on the [international intellectual property system]."[20] These pressures translate, to a significant extent, into the search for an alternative or *sui generis* regime of knowledge protection. Such a regime would be conditioned by equity and fairness concerns, especially in regard to a unidirectional transfer of ownership of intangible cultural heritage and other intellectual assets, tangible and intangible, to the developed world. It requires examining the pattern of developments and the outcome of discussions in some key international legal and institutional arenas that supervise the search by Indigenous and local communities for the diversification of the conceptual frameworks for knowledge protection.

---

19 *See* Ch. Oguamanam, "Localizing Intellectual Property in the Globalization Epoch: The Integration of Indigenous Knowledge", 11 *Ind. J. Global Legal Stud.* 135 (2004); *see also* Ch. Oguamanam, "The Protection of Traditional Knowledge: Towards a Cross-Cultural Dialogue on Intellectual Property Rights", 15 *Aust. Intell. Prop. J.* 34 (2004).

20 *See* Ch. Oguamanam, "Agro-Biotechnology and Food Security: Biotechnology and Traditional Agricultural Practices at the Periphery of International Intellectual Property Regime Complex", 2007 *Mich. St. L. Rev.* 215, 217; *see also* B.S. Simon, "Intellectual Property and Traditional Knowledge: A Psychological Approach to Conflicting Claims of Creativity in International Law", 20 *Berkeley Tech. L.J.* 1613 (2005).

2.1. EQUITABLE ACCESS, PRIOR INFORMED CONSENT AND DISCLOSURE OF THE SOURCE OF ORIGIN

2.1.1. *The CBD and Other Forums*

The pilfering of intangible cultural heritage alluded to above appears to pitch two directly relevant international legal regimes against each other, at least in their respective approaches. They are the CBD and the TRIPS Agreement. While the CBD embodies international environmental law's response to the global biodiversity crisis, the TRIPS Agreement is a long-arm extension of the World Trade Organization (WTO) neo-liberal economic program. The TRIPS is an instrument for the global enclosure of intellectual endeavours by private property rights. Quite unlike the latter agreement, which makes no direct mention of intangible cultural heritage, the CBD shows perhaps more sensitivity than any other instrument to such forms of knowledge as well as to the practices that are relevant to the conservation of biological diversity. Even though the CBD's approach to traditional knowledge is rooted in the market economy model[21], the instrument's empowerment of traditional knowledge is a marked departure from the way in which it has usually been neglected by the conventional intellectual property system.

The CBD acknowledges that holders of intangible cultural heritage are entitled to rewards and incentives. It provides for the twin frameworks of access and benefit-sharing, as well as endorsing prior informed consent and technology transfers as useful tools for negotiating, under mutually agreed terms[22], the entitlements that should be granted to intangible cultural heritage holders.

More than any instrument before it, the CBD provides an impetus for the recognition of Indigenous and local communities' claims for the equitable distribution of the benefits of genetic resources and for preventing the appropriation of embedded intangible cultural heritage. One suggested method for preventing such appropriation is to require the disclosure of the origin of genetic resources in patent applications. This idea has continued to be debated and elaborated in many forums outside the CBD. For instance, thanks to the input of Switzerland, this issue is being hotly debated in the course of the ongoing discussions for the reform of the WIPO-supervised *Patent Cooperation Treaty*.[23] These discussions may have

---

21 *See* G.T. Martin and S. Vermeylen, "Intellectual Property, Indigenous Knowledge, and Biodiversity", 16 *Capitalism Nature Socialism* 27 (2005).

22 CBD, *supra* note 13, Articles 8(j), 10 (c), 15, 16, 17 and 19.

23 *See* WIPO, Working Group on Reform of the Patent Cooperation Treaty, *Proposals by Switzerland Regarding the Declaration of the Source of Genetic Resources and Traditional Knowledge in Patent Applications*, PCT/R/WG/5/11 REV (19 November 2003); WIPO, Working Group on Reform of the Patent Cooperation Treaty, *Additional Comments by Switzerland on Its Proposals Regarding the Declaration of the Source of Genetic Resources*

a ripple effect on the *Patent Law Treaty*. Indeed, according to the Swiss proposal, failure to comply with the disclosure requirements should attract extant sanctions under both these treaties.

Spurred by the unfolding debates at the CBD regarding the disclosure of the source of origin of genetic resources and associated intangible cultural heritage, developing countries have demanded an amendment to the TRIPS Agreement to accommodate this concern.[24] They have proposed that the disclosure of genetic resources and traditional knowledge be made compulsory, as opposed to a Swiss initiative which makes disclosure optional. These two proposals also differ in terms of the sanctions envisaged and the scope of the new rule's application.[25] Nonetheless, both proposals share the objective of achieving the efficient resolution of controversies associated with genetic resources-driven patents and the entrenchment of an equitable access and benefit sharing regime. Perhaps most important is the fact that they extend the disclosure requirement to tangible and intangible resources corresponding roughly to genetic resources *per se*, as well as to associated traditional knowledge and aspects of intangible cultural heritage.

2.1.2. The European Community (EC)

Since 1995, the EC has expressed support for the application to genetic resources of the CBD's provisions on access and benefit sharing.[26] In fact, the EC played an active role in the adoption of the *2002 Bonn Guidelines on Access to Genetic Resources and Fair and Equitable Sharing of the Benefits Arising out of their Utilization*.[27] The issue of the disclosure of the source of origin of genetic materials

---

and Traditional Knowledge in Patent Applications, PCT/R/WG/6/11 (21 April 2004); WIPO, Working Group on Reform of the Patent Cooperation Treaty, *International Publication an PCT Gazette in Electronic Form*, PCT/R/WG/7/8 (5 April 2005); WIPO, Working Group on Reform of the Patent Cooperation Treaty, *Declaration of the Source of Genetic Resources and Traditional Knowledge in Patent Applications*, PCT/R/WG/8/7 (21 April 2006).

24 *See* WTO, Council for Trade-Related Aspects of Intellectual Property Rights, *Doha Work Programme – The Outstanding Implementation Issue on the Relationship between the TRIPS Agreement and the Conventional on Biological Diversity*, WT/GC/W/564/Rev.2 (5 July 2006) (containing the draft of Article 29*bis* of TRIPS Agreement as proposed by Brazil, China, Columbia, Cuba, India, Pakistan, Peru, Thailand and Tanzania).

25 Under the Swiss proposal, the requirement of disclosure applies if the invention is directly based on a particular source, whereas the proposal of the developing countries states that a minimal application of tangible or intangible resources triggers the disclosure requirement.

26 The EC commissioned a study group in 1995 to explore the best possible measures for implementing the CBD, *supra* note 13, Articles 15 and 16.

27 COP, *Bonn Guidelines on Access to Genetic Resources and Fair and Equitable Sharing of the Benefits Arising out of their Utilization*, Decision VI/24 A, UNEP/CBD/COP/6/20 (7–19 April 2002), *available at* www.biodiv.org/decisions/default.aspx?m=cop-06&d=24 (last visited 31 July 2008).

is not entirely novel to EC law. However, the objective of existing rules is not directly linked to the underlying motivations of Indigenous and local communities for access and benefit sharing. The EC legislative requirement of the extra-disclosure of the origin of biological materials in patent applications, in the *Directive 98/44/EC on the legal protection of biotechnological inventions*[28], is contingent upon many constraining factors.[29] It is couched in non-obligatory language and failure to disclose is not necessarily prejudicial to the applicant's ability to obtain a patent or exercise incidental rights.[30]

While the EC is amenable to the modification of the Patent Cooperation Treaty, the Patent Law Treaty and the regional regime of the *Convention on the Grant of European Patents* (European Patent Convention) in order to accommodate the disclosure requirement, it does not envision the same for the TRIPS Agreement. This is contrary to the demands of developing countries. Thus, the EC's sympathy for the disclosure requirement is cosmetic because it is circumscribed in all crucial respects.

2.1.3. The WIPO's Intergovernmental Committee

In addition to the foregoing forums, perhaps the most important channel today for the sharing of ideas regarding the protection of intangible cultural heritage, as well as access and benefit sharing, is WIPO's Intergovernmental Committee.[31] Established in 2000 by WIPO's General Assembly, the Intergovernmental Committee provides a platform for WIPO member states to explore issues regarding access to genetic resources and benefit sharing, as well as the protection of traditional knowledge, innovations, creativity and traditional cultural expressions. The Intergovernmental Committee fosters a holistic approach to intangible cultural heritage whether as traditional cultural expressions or traditional knowledge in their diverse nuances, ramifications and manifestations.

Some of the important issues on the Intergovernmental Committee's agenda, particularly with regard to the subject of genetic resources, are informed to a large degree by developments at the CBD, especially through the activities of the latter's

---

28 Directive 98/44/EC of the European Parliament and of the Council of 6 July 1998 on the legal protection of biotechnological inventions, OJ L 213, 30. July 1998, p. 13 [hereinafter "Directive 98/44/EC"].

29 *See id.*, recital 27 (articulating these constraints).

30 Even where the disclosure requirement is obligatory (as under the Community plant variety rights regime established by Council Regulation (EC) No. 2100/94), only the geographic origin of the particular plant variety and not the parent material is required; *see* Council Regulation (EC) No. 2100/94 of 27 July 1994 on Community plant variety rights, OJ L 227, 1. Sep. 1994, p. 1.

31 *See* WIPO, Intergovernmental Committee on Intellectual Property and Genetic Resources, Traditional Knowledge and Folklore, www.wipo.int/tk/en/igc/(last visited 31 July 2008).

Working Group on Article 8(j).[32] The topics that are being addressed include: the documentation of traditional knowledge, the compilation of contractual practices involving the use of traditional knowledge and the auditing of contractual clauses regarding access and benefit sharing.[33] All of these measures are discussed in parallel with the initiative of the Working Group on Article 8(j).[34] Along with other independent national initiatives, the Intergovernmental Committee was instrumental in securing the formal recognition of the documentation of intangible cultural heritage in the *Convention for the Safeguarding of Intangible Cultural Heritage* (ICH Convention).[35]

Since its inception, the Intergovernmental Committee has continued to supervise discussions on various ways to better protect intangible cultural heritage, whether as genetic resources or folklore and other cultural expressions. From the evolving debates as articulated in its principal documents, entitled *The Protection of Traditional Knowledge: Draft Objectives and Principles*[36] and *The Protection of Traditional Cultural Expressions/Expressions of Folklore: Draft Objectives and Principles*[37], we see attempts to elaborate a policy framework and principles for ensuring this protection. We can also notice efforts to clarify conceptual and definitional issues, as well as to identify appropriate stakeholders.

In spite of these efforts, there is lack of consensus in regard to specific forms of protection. It would seem that the emerging approaches do not support the creation of a new regime of intellectual property rights even though they endorse protection within a holistic policy context.[38] There is, however, little disagreement over the need to protect traditional knowledge or traditional cultural expressions

32 The Working Group on Article 8(j) is established to supervise and provide guidelines on the implementation of Article 8(j) which creates obligation on contracting parties to preserve and maintain the knowledge and innovations and practices of Indigenous and local communities embodying traditional life styles relevant to conservation of biological diversity.

33 *See* WIPO, *Contracts Database*, www.wipo.int/tk/en/databases/contracts/index.html (last visited 31 July 2008); *see also* WIPO, *Creative Heritage Project: IP Guidelines for Recording, Digitizing and Disseminating Intangible Cultural Heritage*, www.wipo.int/tk/en/folklore/culturalheritage/index.html (last visited 31 July 2008).

34 *See* Ch. Oguamanam, *International Law and Indigenous Knowledge: Intellectual Property, Plant Biodiversity, and Traditional Medicine*, 2006, 212.

35 The ICH Convention, *supra* note 10, Article 2(3), provides that the identification, documentation, research, preservation, protection, promotion, enhancement, transmission are strategies to safeguard intangible cultural heritage. The campaign for a registration system for traditional knowledge and innovations seen in diverse propositions has been ongoing since the 1990s. For instance, *see* A.K. Gupta, *Conserving Biodiversity and Rewarding Associated Knowledge and Innovation Systems: Honey Bees Perspective, available at* www.maharashtra.gov.in/english/signs/info_honeybee/berne-goa.pdf (last visited 10 August 2007). In a way, the Honey Bee provided impetus for India's Traditional Knowledge Digital Library (TKDL) Project.

36 *Draft TK Principles*, *supra* note 14.

37 *Draft TCE Principles*, *supra* note 17.

38 *See id.* at pars. 16 and 17.

against exploitation or misappropriation by unfair or otherwise illegal means. For the most part, interested parties endorse a regime of negative rights. In relation to traditional knowledge, such rights are premised mainly on unfair competition principles with specific reference to Article 10*bis* of the *Paris Convention for the Protection of Industrial Property.*[39] The principal aim is to prevent external interests or second comers from exploiting or appropriating traditional knowledge or traditional cultural expressions. In a word, it is an anti-appropriation treatise.

Meanwhile, along with the continuing elaboration of the details of the CBD-initiated access and benefit sharing in diverse forums, many legal and policy initiatives on a national and regional scale have been aimed at addressing the opposition of Indigenous and local communities to the appropriation of traditional knowledge and genetic resources.[40] Also, a number of similar individual-inspired or independent private sector practices have appeared, sometimes without any support of national governments or specific legislation.[41] For example, Indian scholar Anil K. Gupta's metaphoric Honey Bee Network, as well as the Indian Society for Research and Initiatives for Sustainable Technologies (SRIST)[42], exemplify an ethical commitment to a sustainable use of traditional knowledge innovation by those who benefit from it.[43] The Network acknowledges the owners of the knowledge that it uses. It shares with them the benefits it receives while it builds and facilitates for the use of traditional knowledge innovation and knowledge sharing among the local communities. While some of these programs are independent of institutional or state support, many of them are inspired by the CBD's access and benefit sharing scheme, various common initiatives of WIPO and UNESCO, and especially the Intergovernmental Committee. The ICH Convention provides a further impetus.

Like the Intergovernmental Committee, a number of these initiatives are not overtly enthusiastic about the creation of a new rights regime in order to enhance the protection of the intangible cultural heritage of Indigenous communities.[44]

---

39 Paris Convention for the Protection of Industrial Property, 20 March 1883, 828 U.N.T.S. 305 (as revised on 14 July 1967 in Stockholm). *See also Draft TK Principles*, *supra* note 14, Annex, Article 1(4).

40 For a database of what the Genetic Resources Action International (GRAIN) calls Biodiversity Rights Legislation (BRL) at national and regional levels, *see* GRAIN, *Biodiversity Rights Legislation (BRL)*, www.grain.org/brl/(last visited 31 July 2008).

41 Notable among these are the moribund Sharman Pharmaceutical Model, the MERCK/INBio deal with the Costa Rica Government, the U.S. National Cancer Institute initiatives with developing countries that are sources of vital genetic resources, the UK Commission on Intellectual Property Rights, the ICBG-Peru program, the agreement between Indian Kani People (Karala) and the Tropical Botanic Garden and Research Institute (TBGRI).

42 *See* www.sristi.org/or www.sristi.org/honeybee.html.

43 *See* Gupta, *supra* note 35.

44 There is no consensus as to the definite attitude of some of these institutional interveners on the issue of a new rights regime for traditional knowledge. Signals from the two major reports

The implication of this trend is that, except for measures aimed at preventing misappropriation and a variety of private contracting devices, not very much has happened in practical terms to challenge the decision under the TRIPS Agreement to exclude intangible cultural heritage. Even on the theoretical front, the anti-appropriation school appears to be entrenched in its search for legal hybrids outside the conventional intellectual property models. It is exemplified by Jerome H. Reichman's compensatory liability model[45] for Indigenous knowledge, the elaboration of which is outside the scope of the present discourse.[46] In the face of this resistance to the anti-appropriation approach to intangible cultural heritage, perhaps the best countermeasures available are documenting, digitizing and inventory-making. They are the subject of the next section.

3. DOCUMENTATION AND DIGITIZATION OF INTANGIBLE CULTURAL HERITAGE

One increasingly important development in the response of Indigenous and local communities to the appropriation of their intangible cultural heritage is the initiative toward the documentation of such knowledge forms. This originally controversial idea originated in India. It is a strategic response by that country to the pilfering of its rich traditional medicinal knowledge by second comers who capitalize on the gaps in the conventional patent system, specifically its narrow approach to novelty and "prior art".[47] Documentation has engaged WIPO's attention and arguably received its unofficial support, as well as the support of the Special Union for the International Patent Classification[48] and leading patent

---

of the Intergovernmental Committee on this subject are mixed; *see supra* notes 14 and 17.

45 *See* J.H. Reichman, "Legal Hybrids Between the Patent and Copyright Paradigms", 94 *Colum. L. Rev.* 2432 (1994); J.H. Reichman, "Of Green Tulips and Legal Kudzu: Repackaging Rights in Subpatentable Innovation", 53 *Vand. L. Rev.* 1743 (2000), J.H. Reichman and T. Lewis, "Using Liability Rules to Stimulate Local Innovation in Developing Countries: Application to Traditional Knowledge", in K.E. Maskus and J.H. Reichman (eds.), *International Public Goods and Transfer of Technology Under a Globalized Intellectual Property Regime*, 2005, 337.

46 However, for a partial critic and overview of Reichman's compensatory liability model, *see* E. Arezzo, "Struggling Around the "Natural" Divide: The Protection of Tangible and Intangible Indigenous Property", 25 *Cardozo Arts & Ent. L.J.* 367, 407–410 (2007).

47 *See infra* note 72 and accompanying text.

48 Established pursuant to the 1971 Strasbourg Agreement concerning International Patent Classification (IPC), the IPC is a system for common classification of patents for invention and incidental claims. Under the system, implicated innovations and patent applications are divided into recognized technological categories and subcategories to facilitate retrieval of appropriate documentation for confirmation of their novelty and state of prior art in a particular field.

offices.[49] It has also been adopted, at least, in principle, by other countries and regional bodies.[50] In addition to the support already provided under the unique approach to documentation adopted by WIPO's Intergovernmental Committee, the ICH Convention directly provides that inventory-making (which is a form of documentation) is a vital means for safeguarding intangible cultural heritage.[51] Specifically, in Article 12(1), it is provided that "[t]o ensure identification with a view to safeguarding [intangible cultural heritage], each State Party shall draw up, in a manner geared to its own situation, one or more inventories of the intangible cultural heritage present in its territory." The implication of this is that those in favour of the intangible cultural heritage documentation project have received further support from the Convention.

While the practice of India, China (and indeed potentially several other countries that have so far expressed interest in the documentation initiative)[52] has been to focus on documenting in detail the theories and applications of their intangible cultural heritage in its cultural setting, the Intergovernmental Committee's approach to documentation involves a different conceptual model. The latter encompasses the recording of emerging global trends in intangible cultural heritage protection, including the collation of relevant publications, databases or inventories that document, *inter alia*, contractual practices and specific legislative provisions that deal with issues such as access and benefit sharing, prior informed consent and other patterns of protection of intangible cultural heritage. Thus, there is more than one conceptual approach to documentation. However, to this day, traditional knowledge documentation projects, specifically those falling into the first category outlined above (*i.e.* detailed recording of traditional knowledge), have not been fully embraced in Indigenous and local community circles, especially in the developed countries, despite the success of this approach in India.[53] There are a few readily available arguments against the project.

---

49 There are 57 Contracting Parties to the Strasbourg Agreement, including the U.S., Japan and countries of the European Community, which collectively hold the most patents globally. These countries are by implication bound by the test of novelty of patents of invention and state of prior art using the IPC model.

50 *See* OGUAMANAM, *supra* note 34, at 151.

51 ICH Convention, *supra* note 10, Article 2(3); *see also Draft TCE Principles*, *supra* note 17, at par. 16.

52 For example, countries of the South Asian Association for Regional Cooperation (SAARC): Bangladesh, Bhutan, India, Maldives, Nepal, Pakistan and Sri Lanka.

53 There are credible arguments in general as to why that is. For example, the Indian government initiative could be tantamount to state appropriation of traditional knowledge with no guarantee to benefit its local custodians or to enhance sustainable development of that knowledge. Perhaps most importantly, however, this state of affairs is also a consequence of the diverging objectives that Indigenous and local communities of the South (such as India) and their counterparts in the North attach to the protection of their traditional knowledge and intangible cultural heritage. This theme is discussed further in Section 3.1.

3.1. THE CHALLENGES TO DOCUMENTATION

The first reason for opposing documentation is best understood if one compares this process to vaccination. Indeed, it potentially attracts consequences similar to those of a failed vaccine. Documentation creates more awareness and increases the accessibility of traditional knowledge by entrenching it in the public domain. Undoubtedly, documentation may serve the purpose of scuttling biopiracy and other acts of appropriation of intangible cultural heritage. If not well handled, however, it is capable of backfiring and, like a failed vaccine, of infecting its victim with the disease it was meant to prevent. In the case of intangible cultural heritage, this would mean revealing for public consumption knowledge about forms of traditional knowledge which are still secret and should have remained undisclosed.[54]

Making intangible cultural heritage easily accessible raises an important question. Who is better equipped to exploit documented knowledge? Is it the holders or custodians of this knowledge or their Western industrial counterparts and other second comers? Admittedly, if documentation succeeds on a global scale, exclusive patent claims on traditional-knowledge-based inventions may no longer be a viable option. However, patents (or other intellectual property rights for that matter) are hardly the only avenue for exploiting useful knowledge. In this regard, developed countries are better placed than their developing counterparts due to their advantage in terms of financial, technical, industrial and other resources.

Second, the documentation of traditional knowledge could potentially lead to a divisive confrontation between Indigenous and local communities of the global South and their counterparts in the North. Without a doubt, the campaign for the protection of intangible cultural heritage has fostered solidarity among the rank and file of non-Western peoples.[55] However, as between Indigenous and local communities of the South and the North, the motivation for knowledge protection can differ. Because the Indigenous identity of most communities in the Northern industrialized world has already been internationally recognized, their claim to traditional knowledge is essentially an aspect of their demands for self-determination, which is to them a matter of enormous priority.[56] For these

54 *See* WIPO, Intergovernmental Committee on Intellectual Property and Genetic Resources, Traditional Knowledge and Folklore, *Recognition of Traditional Knowledge within the Patent System: Interim Draft*, par. 14, WIPO/GRTKF/IC/9/8 (15 March 2006); *see also* WIPO, Intergovernmental Committee on Intellectual Property and Genetic Resources, Traditional Knowledge and Folklore, *Recognition of Traditional Knowledge within the Patent System*, WIPO/GRTKF/IC/11/7 (6 June 2007).

55 *See* Ch. Oguamanam, "Protecting Indigenous Knowledge in International Law: Solidarity Beyond the Nation State", 8 *Law Text Culture* 191 (2004).

56 *See* R.J. Coombe, "The Recognition of Indigenous Peoples' and Community Traditional Knowledge in International Law", 14 *St. Thomas L. Rev.* 275, 277 (2001).

communities, the significance and sanctity of Indigenous knowledge is determined by its contribution to the objectives of cultural preservation and self-determination.[57] They draw upon the symbiotic relationship between knowledge and culture as a crucial aspect of Indigenous self-determination, human dignity, identity and cultural survival.[58]

Presently, the documentation project is promoted mainly by nation states and embedded local communities of the global South. The indigeneity of most of these constituent communities is not internationally recognized or, at best, it is inchoate. However, as compared to their Northern counterparts, they are organized mostly as independent states and not under the domination of a single hybrid or Creole culture such as European-Native.[59] As a result, the issue of self-determination is not quite as contentious. Their interest in knowledge protection is driven by a strategic quest for international political leverage, legitimation and economic considerations.[60] Thus, the documentation of traditional knowledge is designed more to secure some economic leverage than to address the political issue of self-determination and cultural survival for local knowledge holders. As a trade-off, this means that the overall campaign for traditional knowledge protection is unintentionally divorced from the issue of self-determination. In this regard, it does not seem to matter if traditional knowledge is rid of its cultural content and subjected to Western "scientification" (which the documentation process facilitates) as a condition for its validation[61] so long as the economic objective is realized. To sum up, the dominant considerations for documentation are not commonly shared across Indigenous and local communities. Documentation has the potential to advance the priorities of the Indigenous and local communities of the South who approach the issue of traditional knowledge for mainly economic objectives. However, it does not necessarily hold the same promise for their Northern counterparts who prioritize the objectives of self-determination and cultural survival in their traditional knowledge campaign.

The third problem with documentation initiatives is that they evoke the division in Indigenous circles over the effects of using conventional intellectual property regimes (which are largely based on documentation processes) to protect intangible cultural heritage. Documentation tends to support the views of the pro-economic interest groups with regard to the appropriate objective when

---

57 *See* B. Kingsbury, "Self-Determination and "Indigenous Peoples"", 86 *ASIL Proc.* 383 (1992).

58 *See* Oguamanam, *supra* note 55, at 205.

59 *See* S. Brush, "Whose Knowledge, Whose Genes, Whose Rights?", in S.B. Brush and D. Stabinski (eds.), *Valuing Local Knowledge: Indigenous Peoples and Intellectual Property Rights*, 1996, 1, 5.

60 *See* Coombe, *supra* note 56, at 277–8; *see also* Oguamanam, *supra* note 34, at 187.

61 Through the use of technologies, such as digital devices, and exposure to foreign languages, Indigenous knowledge can be rid of its cultural content and readily transposed into the Western scientific epistemological domain.

protecting intangible cultural heritage. According to Christine Haight Farley, within Indigenous circles there are two competing views regarding how to deal with traditional knowledge: the traditionalist group and the realist group.[62] Traditionalists are opposed to the economic exploitation of traditional knowledge and culture which would be facilitated by documentation and the use of concepts drawn from the conventional intellectual property system. They prefer to preserve without compromise the sacredness of traditional knowledge as the heart of Indigenous social and cultural identity. Realists, on the other hand, support the exploitation of the economic potential that can be found in traditional cultural resources, a position which the documentation of traditional knowledge facilitates.

The last difficulty caused by documentation relates to its relationship with intellectual property rights. As noted, some groups oppose the application of intellectual property rights to traditional knowledge and intangible cultural heritage. However, they may find the use of documentation as a viable anti-appropriation strategy. This position fails to take into consideration that documentation or inventory-making is inherently an intellectual property facilitating mechanism. In fact, to a large measure, documentation is a necessary step in drawing intangible cultural heritage into the conventional intellectual property system. This promise of documentation naturally finds favour with the opposing group of those who support the application of intellectual property rights to intangible cultural heritage.

It can however be argued that inventory-making provided for under the ICH Convention (which may or may not include documentation) is a safeguarding strategy only. But the question is safeguarding to what end? Indeed, intangible cultural heritage documentation or inventory-making is hardly an exercise carried out in isolation or an end in itself. Somehow, it will be difficult to ignore the link between inventory-making or documentation and intellectual property rights. It is instructive that India expects that one of the results of its massive documentation program will be to place it in a position of strength when negotiating the joint ownership of intellectual property rights arising from its documented *ayurvedic*, *sidha* and *unani* traditional medical heritage. Clearly, the relationship between intellectual property rights and the documentation of intangible cultural heritage is enigmatic and requires rigorous exploration.

The various drawbacks to documentation certainly demonstrate how it may become a threat to the integrity of traditional knowledge. First, unless documentation promises to be comprehensive, it may only help those knowledge forms which are targeted for inclusion, while exposing undocumented knowledge

62 *See* Chr. Haight Farley, "Protecting Folklore and Indigenous Peoples: Is Intellectual Property the Answer?", 30 *Conn. L. Rev.* 1, 14–15 (1997).

forms to a greater risk of appropriation.[63] Indigenous and local communities have an interest in sustaining the secrecy of local knowledge forms that are not, so far, part of the public domain. They reserve the option to determine if and when they want to make such knowledge part of the public domain and on what terms.[64]

Second, documentation is capable of freezing traditional knowledge, and as such, undermines its incremental process of evolution. Third, because of its static nature, documentation facilitates the erosion of traditional knowledge in its essentially oral or unfixed character. Fourth, documentation aids the translocation of traditional knowledge from its cultural environment and geographically embedded sensitivity, symbolism and spirituality. Fifth, documentation imposes an artificial categorization on intangible cultural heritage and presses it into pre-determined and narrow epistemic groupings with the risk of undermining its holistic appeal. Any attempt to categorize the essence and symbolism of "fluid social and communal creative processes"[65] in Indigenous and local communities is, most likely, an imprecise science.

Because different kinds of traditional knowledge require different forms of protection, documentation may not always be appropriate.[66] Indeed, the sixth problem with documentation is that practical issues arise when trying to match documented traditional knowledge with patented scientific innovations. In addition to determining the appropriate "person skilled in the art" and the particular "art" in question, WIPO has noted that "[a] wide range of possible linkages between a claimed invention [and traditional knowledge] may arise when a patent application is examined."[67] Lastly, as a practical matter, the actual process of digitization and documentation raises issues of duplication, conflicting claims[68], funding challenges and concerns regarding the scope of the information to be incorporated. The latter concerns are all too real given the differences in

---

63 According to India, the TKDL "involves documentation of the knowledge available in the public domain on traditional knowledge from existing literature related to Ayurveda, Unani and Sidha in digitalized format in five international languages"; *see* http://203.200.90.6/tkdl/langdefault/common/AboutTKDL.asp#Intro (last visited 5 Sept. 2007). It does not seem that the project is involved with discovery of uncodified forms of traditional knowledge and those that are not yet in the public domain which are the ones in dire need of protection.

64 They could also insist on making such knowledge forms or improvements thereto eligible for patent. *See* Gupta, *supra* note 35.

65 *See supra* note 17 and accompanying text.

66 There are multiple layers of claims by complex stakeholders in traditional knowledge which may be compounded or undermined by documentation.

67 *See* WIPO, *supra* note 54, Annex, at par. 3.

68 Gupta proposes the adoption of a universal system like ISBN and use of postal pin code to identify contributing individuals and communities in a registry of traditional knowledge and an indexing system for geo-referencing of innovations to facilitate the cross-referencing and cross connecting of communities having identical ecological situations. *See* Gupta, *supra* note 35.

epistemological narratives within Indigenous cultures that are generally presumed to be monolithic.

3.2. PROSPECTS AND PROMISES OF DOCUMENTATION

Despite the inherent risks of the documentation project, there is no denying that it has remained popular since 1999 when the idea first drew attention. India, the pioneering country for this project, has become a Mecca of sorts for countries and regional organizations wishing to document their intangible cultural heritage. Also, as we have seen, the documentation of traditional knowledge as a policy option has been endorsed and entrenched in important institutions and forums. A number of reasons account for this enthusiasm for the documentation of intangible cultural heritage.

At the top of the list is the unprecedented rise in the provocative appropriation of intangible cultural heritage through the patent process by Northern multinational corporations, a practice often depicted as "biopiracy".[69] Related to that is the rapid pace of technological transformations in the digital and biotechnological arenas since the late 20th century. These two mutually complementary technological sectors have simplified the process of isolation, manipulation, exploitation and ultimate appropriation, otherwise known as "e-piracy", of traditional knowledge relating to genetic resources. Ironically, these technological in-roads, especially digital technology, provide the critical support and impetus to the documentation process.

Another development that fuels the documentation project is the encroachment of market economic practices in Indigenous localities as a result of the neoliberal forces of globalization[70], particularly the WTO's free trade regime. Today, it is increasingly possible for external interests and second comers to commodify the products of traditional knowledge, as well as various other cultural properties.[71] Under fanciful labels, these products are then put back into the original local market, often to the exclusion of traditional knowledge holders. These practices have awakened many in the local communities to the lack of legitimacy of conventional intellectual property structures, as well as the tyranny of the TRIPS Agreement and of the larger neoliberal economic system.

---

69 India's dogged fight to revoke foreign patents on some of its notable genetic resources, including neem, turmeric, and basmati, provides the impetus for the TKDL project. For a treatise on biopiracy, *see* I. Mgbeji, *Global Biopiracy: Patents, Plant and Indigenous Knowledge*, 2005.

70 *See* R. Kiely and Ph. Marfleet (eds.), *Globalisation and the Third World*, 1998.

71 This was exemplified in two famous Australian cases; *see* Yumbul v. Reserve Bank of Australia, 21 I.P.R. 481 (1991), and Milpurrurru & Ors v. Indofurn Pty Ltd & Ors, 30 I.P.R. 209 (1995). *See also* Chapter [Janke] of the present volume.

A critical weakness in the TRIPS Agreement is its indifference to the role of unwritten and undocumented traditional knowledge as prior art.[72] Among the many problems caused by this approach, it is to be blamed for the fact that intangible cultural heritage is left in the public domain. Thanks to the efforts of many Indigenous, environmental and general public interest non-governmental organizations, as well as certain intergovernmental bodies, the sense of urgency over the need to counteract the rapid appropriation of local knowledge has become irresistible. Consequently, digitization and documentation established themselves as possible tools for protecting and rewarding intangible cultural heritage and its holders, while combating the current practice of *prior art discrimination*.

As a desperate intervention program, the documentation of traditional knowledge is justified especially as it applies to those Indigenous peoples under threat of extinction. Statistical accounts of the rapid waning of Indigenous communities, languages, cultures and knowledge systems underscore the urgency of traditional knowledge documentation as a potential rescue strategy.[73] A similar argument was made in support of the human genome project.[74] It was, however, dismissed by many in the Indigenous communities as self-serving. Indigenous peoples will continue to see documentation and similar projects as opportunistic and exploitative as long as they are not linked to a credible strategy to reverse the tide of their predicted annihilation, real or imagined. Ironically, while the ICH Convention endorses documentation as one of the safeguarding measures aimed at ensuring the viability of intangible cultural heritage[75], it remains silent on the need to safeguard the custodians and repositories of the community's traditional knowledge. Despite these reservations, the main point is that documentation has an attractive potential for making possible the preservation of Indigenous oral or written traditions in ways that will make them accessible to support future enrichment within and across the cultures that developed them.

The traditional knowledge holders have been incorporated into the global knowledge economy. As such, the insistence by those in the traditionalist camp upon maintaining the uncompromised sanctity of intangible cultural heritage may lack pragmatism.[76] Indeed, the idea of epistemic purity is utopian. In the

---

72 A national test of novelty premised on written publication which excludes most of the world's traditional knowledge base is the norm in U.S. and Japan – two countries with the highest number of patents globally.

73 At the beginning of the 21century, many Indigenous goups have undergone a rapid decline in population, some are threatened with extinction. Few have recorded any sort of population growth. Today, Indigenous peoples constitute an estimated 5–6 *per cent* of global population.

74 *See* the Declaration of Indigenous Peoples of the Western Hemisphere Regarding the Human Genome Diversity Project, 19 February 1995, *available at* www.ankn.uaf.edu/IKS/declaration.html (last visited 31 July 2008).

75 *See* ICH Convention, *supra* note 10, Articles 2(3) and 12.

76 *See* A. Agrawal, "Dismantling the Divide Between Indigenous and Scientific Knowledge", 26 *Dev. & Change* 413 (1995).

globalized free market, the holders and custodians of intangible cultural heritage, like all other participants, are challenged to explore the resilience of their own knowledge systems while interacting with other epistemic traditions. In this exchange, something has to give. No knowledge system has ever existed in isolation.[77] Knowledge systems exist and intermesh on a dynamic scale and this is healthy for their survival.

The hard question is whether Indigenous and local communities can afford to ignore the idea of documenting their intangible cultural heritage. In the present global order, most (but emphatically not all) of the arguments against the documentation of intangible cultural heritage may be indicative of the trade-offs necessary for the survival of those treasured resources. However, the practical importance of the documentation project for the protection of intangible cultural heritage can be evaluated according to how it will deal with the pressure from a new movement aimed at expanding the knowledge placed in the public domain rather than limiting it. The *romance of the public domain* is founded on the presumption that knowledge should be equitably accessed to everyone. In the next section, I examine the *romance of the public domain vis-à-vis* the intangible cultural heritage documentation initiative.

4. INTANGIBLE CULTURAL HERITAGE DOCUMENTATION AND THE ROMANCE OF THE PUBLIC DOMAIN

Traditionally, intellectual property regimes are based on enclosure and appropriation. To some extent, it is an important capitalist response to the so-called "*tragedy of the commons*", a celebrated catch-phrase for designating the danger posed by the over or underutilization of resources that are not subject to property rights.[78] According to economists, as well as law-and-economics theorists, the propertization of the commons is the key to their efficient management and utilization, though private property rights must be kept in constant balance with other competing claims.[79] Like classical property jurisprudence, the intellectual property regimes seek to strike a balance between the competing private and public claims over the commons, specifically to ensure that the public and private domains are mutually enriching. That balancing act is a major bone of contention in intellectual property jurisprudence.

77 See T.S. Kuhn, *The Structure of Scientific Revolutions*, (2nd ed.), 1970; S. Harding, *Whose Science? Whose Knowledge?: Thinking from Women's Lives*, 1991.

78 See G. Hardin, "The Tragedy of the Commons", 162 *Sci.* 1243 (1968).

79 See H. Dagan and M.A. Heller, "The Liberal Commons", 110 *Yale L.J.* 549 (2001).

Since the advent of digital and biotechnologies, or the so-called Information Age, developments in the intellectual property arena reflect a radical proprietary encroachment on the public domain, encompassing almost anything that is not already subject to a property right. Specifically, the TRIPS Agreement makes possible the extension of intellectual property claims to virtually all scientific, technological and informational resources[80] while it leaves out genetic resources and the traditional knowledge of non-Western peoples. The irony of the double standard is that by leaving intangible cultural heritage unenclosed, the TRIPS Agreement has created a framework for their progressive appropriation by Western industrial scientific complexes, who also maintain a firm grip on their original and appropriated intellectual resources. Despite leaving intangible cultural heritage unenclosed, the global intellectual property order in the Information Age thus reflects a victory for the enclosure movement.

But that victory has fuelled the rise of a countermovement. There is increasing scholarly support for the freeing up of the public domain through anti-enclosure campaigns based upon a number of well-thought, practical and theoretical propositions. And rightly so. The "creative commons" movement and "open source" software are symbolic examples of this trend in intellectual property which aims at creating balance and moderation between private enclosure and public domain considerations. By trying to stem the increasing tide of public domain erosion and private enclosure, the new public domain movement insists upon free, or at best, liberal access to culture, knowledge and other products of intellectual endeavour. Thus, according to some commentators, "[t]he public domain is now the cause célèbre among progressive intellectual property and cyber law scholars."[81] At its most extreme, it is depicted as the antithesis of (intellectual) property.[82]

The need to balance private and public stakes in the commons is obvious. The same is true of the need for a robust public domain, because of the latter's intricate affinity with private innovation and creativity. However, Chander and Sunder warn that the new public domain movement must be wary of what they characterize as "the *romance* of the commons: the belief [or more accurately presumption] that because a resource is open to all by force of law, it will indeed be equally exploited by all."[83] The intangible cultural heritage documentation project is caught in the middle of the public domain debate and is highly susceptible to the *romance* of the commons in at least two obvious and yet unsuspecting ways.

---

80 See generally TRIPS Agreement, supra note 2, Article 27(1).

81 See Chander and Sunder, *supra* note 1, at 1334.

82 See J. Boyle, "Foreword: The Opposite of Property?", 66 *Law & Contemp. Prob.* 1 (2003); *see also* Symposium, "The Public Domain", 66 *Law & Contemp. Prob.* 1 (2003) (providing a compendium of perspectives on the pubic domain discourse).

83 See Chander and Sunder, *supra* note 1, at 1332.

In the first place, ironically, the process of documentation is akin to a scramble for the appropriation of intangible cultural heritage, especially if the latter is presently in the public domain. Consequently, the documentation process makes intangible cultural heritage susceptible to the *romance* of the commons. Obviously, countries have differing leverages in their ability to take advantage of the documentation process. Countries with a natural endowment of genetic resources and a rich intangible cultural heritage are not necessarily commensurably endowed in relation to the expertise, knowledge, economic power, human resources, and skills required for documenting them. For instance, aside from its rich, albeit nonexclusive, *ayurvedic*, *sidha* and *unani* traditional medical heritage, India's pioneering and outstanding success in the documentation project is mainly due to its rich and talented human resources. It has access to people with the diverse and specialized skills required for the documentation project. Admittedly, a nation's documentation project is limited to the intangible cultural heritage and resources within its boundaries. However, because nation states are artificial creatures born of politico-historical experiences, intangible cultural heritage and other natural resources are not affected by artificial geographic and political boundaries. Association with a particular form of intangible cultural heritage is a matter of national, group or communal pride and identity. Therefore, a state's documentation of trans-boundary or shared intangible cultural heritage will have implications for other countries.

The second way in which documentation interacts with the *romance* of the commons has to do with the ability of countries to exploit documented intangible cultural heritage. The narrow logic of documentation is that placing traditional knowledge in the public domain curtails its exploitation and appropriation, as well as limiting incidences of biopiracy. Everyone is free to exploit the knowledge without excluding other stakeholders, especially the original owners of the knowledge. This raises the *romance* of the commons scenario, namely, the presumption that when intangible cultural heritage are placed in the public domain, original holders or owners and second comers can equitably access such resources. In reality, that is hardly the case. Access to intangible cultural heritage in the public domain is beset by the question of distributional equity.

The process of the documentation of traditional knowledge may, in some cases, facilitate a shift from one epistemological domain to another. For example, it could transform an oral culture into a written one. As in the Indian case, it can translate traditional knowledge into several languages alien to its original owners.[84] Also, documentation follows a convenient categorization and classification model that facilitates the epistemological transposition of traditional

84 The Indian documentation initiative (via the TKDL) aims at fixing knowledge from existing literature in regard to *ayurveda*, *unani* and *sidha* in digitized format in five languages: English, German, French, Japanese and Spanish.

knowledge into Western science.[85] The documentation project radically enhances the ability of the Western industrial complex to access intangible cultural heritage. Already, because of their long-standing technological edge, their capitalist orientation and market efficiency, developed countries of the West do not scoop information from the public domain with shovels the same size as those of their developing counterparts. The main point is that when intangible cultural heritage is documented and officially incorporated into the public domain, the ability of countries to exploit it is affected by many considerations that tend to favour Western industrialized countries.[86] The documentation of traditional knowledge is a potential double-edged sword that is highly susceptible to the distributional disequilibrium associated with accessing resources in the commons.

4.1. WANTED: A REGIONAL APPROACH TO THE DOCUMENTATION OF INTANGIBLE CULTURAL HERITAGE

There is an urgent need to ensure that the documentation project plugs the loopholes in the new public domain movement. The project should not be allowed to short-change communities and nations that do not have the necessary resources, wealth, power and ability to identify, inventory and document their otherwise rich intangible cultural heritage. A regional approach to documentation is one effective way to fix the inequality inherent in allowing better endowed or powerful countries to single-handedly undertake the initiative. It is instructive that since the launch of India's efforts to document traditional knowledge, some regional associations have indicated interest in doing the same on a regional level. Using its Traditional Knowledge Digital Library (TKDL) as a model, India is supporting the creation of a composite database comprising country-specific digital libraries of traditional knowledge in the areas of traditional medicine, foodstuffs, architecture and culture from South Asian countries. The groundwork for a regional approach appears to have been laid by the post-CBD regional push for an equitable access and benefit sharing strategy for traditional knowledge and genetic resources. This is exemplified by the African Union, the Association of South East Asian Nations, the Pacific

85 The Indian model of documented traditional knowledge follows a new regime known as Traditional Knowledge Resource Classification (TKRC) which is now reconcilable to, and forms part of, the international patent classification system.

86 It may be argued that because intangible cultural heritage is already owned by Indigenous and local communities, they have no problem with accessing them. Although this may be true, documentation opens up intangible cultural heritage to industrial exploitation, epistemological transposition, and complex opportunities for exploitation beyond the sophistication of original holders.

Regional Environmental Program and the Andean Pact initiatives.[87] This is a promising trend for the documentation project to build upon.

In addition to tackling the distributional draw-backs of the *romance* of the commons, a regional approach to documentation better reflects the shared ecological, historical, social and cultural heritage of states, communities and nations within a regional group. It is also a better approach if one wishes to lessen the risk of duplication and create a more efficient and comprehensive identification of the variations in epistemological details across different areas of traditional knowledge. Regionalism has the potential to facilitate a productive deployment of specialized, albeit scarce, resources and skills crucial for the success of any documentation project. In all, a regional framework for traditional knowledge documentation will generate less tension and will probably be able to resolve those conflicts that may arise between peoples or states having important cultural ties within a regional grouping.

It attractions notwithstanding, the success of the regional option will, in part, depend on the determination of the cooperating countries and the international community to tackle some inherent challenges. These include financing, competition and rivalry between cooperating countries within a regional bloc. It is not unexpected that some of these countries may be lured by tempting offers from external interests to undermine their regional commitment. Other drawbacks may stem from the historically rooted divisive tendencies among countries within a geopolitical or regional group.[88] Also, the variegated complexities in compositions of local knowledge holders and the diverging relationships they have with their host states may mar the ability of a state to fully participate in, or undertake regional commitments.

4.2. DIGITIZATION: A DOCUMENTATION OPTION WITH IMMENSE POTENTIALS

As many Indigenous communities are enmeshed in the knowledge economy, the documentation of traditional knowledge helps make up for the technological gap that gives industrialized countries a disproportionate access to documented and undocumented forms of intangible cultural heritage, as well as genetic resources. For example, India's TKDL makes it evident that digitizing has become the most efficient documentation option. Digital technology gradually exposes owners and

---

87 *See* Oguamanam, *supra* note 34, at 89-90.

88 It is reassuring that despite the occasional political tensions between India and Pakistan, both countries enjoy some measure of cooperation on the subject of documentation of their shared traditional medicinal knowledge systems. *See* V.K Gupta (this volume) in answer to a remark by Ikechi Mgbeoji (this volume) during my presentation.

custodians of intangible cultural heritage from different regions to the phenomenal possibilities in regard to knowledge transformation, translation and knowledge democratization. Thus digitizing intangible cultural heritage has the potential to assist countries and communities in making the most of documentation. Gupta has rightly noted that:

> Modern science and technology could supplement the efforts of the [Indigenous and local] people[s] ...[89]
>
> Information Technologies like any other technology can help bridge as well as widen the gaps between haves and have-nots. What is very encouraging about the new possibilities that IT trends offer is the scope for democratizing knowledge, which was never so high as now.[90]

Using digitization for documenting traditional knowledge will enable local knowledge holders to access and build upon subsequent transformations of their knowledge by others. Documentation thereby represents an important step in re-positioning Indigenous and local communities to make the most of the opportunities that are likely to emerge as a result of placing their knowledge in the public domain. In sum, documentation through digitization has the potential to bridge the distributional inequity which the new public domain movement appears to neglect.

The application of digital technology in the documentation project will, over time, initiate Indigenous and local communities to that technology's phenomenal possibilities. It could potentially empower them not only to exploit their knowledge system but also to identify the sorts of multifarious opportunities which second comers have been so good at using. This, however, is not as simple as it seems. First, the documentation of traditional knowledge must expand its narrow objective and be able to accommodate educational and human resource capacity-building, as well as epistemologically transformative contents. Detailing the new vision of traditional knowledge documentation is outside the scope of the present discussion. It is, however, tempting to drop a few snippets of such a vision. Documentation would assist in a strategic empowerment of traditional knowledge holders to not only appreciate their contribution but also to leverage their negotiating ability in the new knowledge economy. Perhaps most important, documentation signifies Indigenous and local communities' ability to respond to and participate in the knowledge and cultural creolization process. Opposition to their claims to traditional knowledge harps on the insensitivity of such claims to

89 Gupta, *supra* note 35, at 7.

90 Gupta, *supra* note 35, at 15.

the phenomenon of cultural creolization and cosmopolitanism.[91] Overall, documentation must be aimed at mitigating the inequity in the ability of Indigenous and local communities to access and benefit from the exploitation of their intangible cultural heritage by second comers.

5. CONCLUSION

Indigenous and local communities are searching for a knowledge protection mechanism which can accommodate the peculiar nature of their intangible cultural heritage. Working from the fringes and with great pragmatism, they have come to appreciate the shortcomings and potentials of the conventional intellectual property regime. It would also seem that they are mindful of the tradeoffs that come with any potential protection mechanism. Several options for the protection of intangible cultural heritage are being suggested at diverse institutional, policy and even scholarly forums. Out of these initiatives arises an emerging consensus in favour of adopting defensive and anti-appropriative measures, rather than attempt to create a new rights regime. One of those defensive options is the documentation of intangible cultural heritage.

The next step in this evolution is to determine how the documentation project could mitigate the dangers of global distributional inequity. In agreement with Chander and Sunder, I argue that this problem is neglected by the new public domain movement. A regional approach to documentation, however, might be a good solution. In addition, for the documentation of intangible cultural heritage to be successful, it must transcend the narrow objectives of its proponents as an anti-biopiracy and anti-appropriation device. Documentation will make it easier to identify the uses for which interests outside Indigenous and local communities have employed intangible cultural heritage. It will allow these communities the opportunity for a healthy exchange of ideas across diverse knowledge domains. In a way, the documentation project provides an opportunity for introspection and self-rediscovery by Indigenous and local communities who are being coerced into participating in the global knowledge economy.[92]

This Chapter has focused largely on an increasingly important, albeit controversial, defensive and anti-appropriative model for intangible cultural heritage protection namely, the documentation of intangible cultural heritage. The documentation program has already received recognition from many institutions with a stake in the protection of intangible cultural heritage. Most

91 *See, e.g.*, M.F. Brown, "Can Culture be Copyrighted?", 39 *Current Anthropology* 193 (1998).

92 See T.J. Krumenacher, "Comment, Protection for Indigenous Peoples and Their Traditional Knowledge: Would a Registry System Reduce the Misappropriation of Traditional Knowledge?", 8 *Marq. Intell. Prop. L. Rev.* 143, 147 and n. 27 (2004).

significantly, it has been endorsed by the ICH Convention. Clearly, there is no denying the reality of documentation and the arguments in its favour. We need to re-think it thoroughly and expand its underlying objectives beyond their present narrow confines with a view to making the best of the opportunities it presents, especially for the use of digital technology as a documentation option.

It is interesting, for instance, to note that India's documentation project aims, in part, to facilitate the interaction between Indigenous communities and second comers in such areas as the joint ownership of intellectual property in intangible cultural heritage products and processes, collaborative research and development around intangible cultural heritage, technology transfers, as well as local institutional capacity building in infrastructure, manpower training and access to advanced science and hi-tech.[93] The possibilities created by documentation are a source of optimism. The realization of those objectives will ensure that documentation eschews the present and real danger of making intangible cultural heritage vulnerable to the *romance* of the commons. Although the documentation of intangible cultural heritage, regardless of how it is carried out, has an enigmatic relationship with intellectual property, it is clear that it has intellectual property implications, on top of its safeguarding objectives. The relationship between the documentation process and the many complex rationales for safeguarding traditions and applying intellectual property regimes to the safeguarding of intangible cultural heritage requires a more thorough exploration, both within and outside the context of the ICH Convention.

---

93 See Chapter [Gupta] of the present volume.

TABLE OF INTERNATIONAL TREATIES AND CONVENTIONS

Agreement on Trade-Related Aspects of Intellectual Property Rights, 15 April 1994, Marrakesh Agreement Establishing the World Trade Organization, Annex 1C, Legal Instruments – Results of the Uruguay Round, 33 I.L.M. 1125 (1994).

Basel Convention on the Control of Transboundary Movements of Hazardous Wastes and Their Disposal, 22 March 1989, 28 I.L.M. 657, *available at* http://www.basel.int/text/con-e-rev.pdf (last visited 31 July 2008).

Berne Convention for the Protection of Literary and Artistic Works, 9 September 1886, 828 U.N.T.S. 221 (amended 28 Sept. 1979), *available at* http://www.wipo.int/export/sites/www/treaties/en/ip/berne/pdf/trtdocs_wo001.pdf (last visited 31 July 2008).

Convention for the Protection of Cultural Property in the Event of Armed Conflict, 14 May 1954, 249 U.N.T.S. 240 (1954).

Convention Establishing the World Intellectual Property Organization, 14 July 1967, 828 U.N.T.S. 3 (1967), *available at* http://www.wipo.int/treaties/en/convention/trtdocs_wo029.html (last visited 31 July 2008).

Convention on the Means of Prohibiting and Preventing the Illicit Import, Export and Transfer of Ownership of Cultural Property, 14 November 1970, 823 U.N.T.S 231, 10 I.L.M. 289 (1971).

Convention Concerning the Protection of the World Cultural and Natural Heritage, 16 November 1972, 1037 U.N.T.S. 151, 11 I.L.M. 1358 (1972).

Convention on the Grant of European Patents (European Patent Convention), 5 October 1973, 13 I.L.M. 270, *available at* http://www.epo.int/legal/epc/e/ma1.html (last visited 31 July 2008).

Convention on Biological Diversity, 5 June 1992, 31 I.L.M. 818, *available at* http://www.biodiv.org/convention/convention.shtml (last visited 31 July 2008).

Convention for the Safeguarding of the Intangible Cultural Heritage, 17 October 2003, U.N. Doc. MISC/2003/CLT/CH/14 (2003), *available at* http://unesdoc.unesco.org/images/0013/001325/132540e.pdf (last visited 31 July 2008).

Convention on the Protection and Promotion of the Diversity of Cultural Expressions, 20 October 2005, *available at* http://unesdoc.unesco.org/images/0014/001429/142919e.pdf (last visited 31 July 2008).

ILO Convention (No. 107) concerning the Protection and Integration of Indigenous and Other Tribal and Semi-Tribal Populations in Independent Countries, 26 June 1957, 328 U.N.T.S. 247, *available at* http://www.ilo.org/ilolex/cgi-lex/convde.pl?C107 (last visited 31 July 2008).

ILO Convention (No. 169) concerning Indigenous and Tribal Peoples in Independent Countries, 27 June 1989, 28 I.L.M. 1382, *available at* http://www.ilo.org/ilolex/cgi-lex/convde.pl?C169 (last visited 31 July 2008).

International Covenant on Economic, Social and Cultural Rights, 16 December 1966, 993 U.N.T.S. 3 (1966).

International Treaty on Plant Genetic Resources for Foods and Agriculture, 3 November 2001, *available at* ftp://ftp.fao.org/ag/cgrfa/it/ITPGRe.pdf (last visited 31 July 2008).

Paris Convention for the Protection of Industrial Property, 20 March 1883, 828 U.N.T.S. 305 (as revised on 14 July 1967 in Stockholm).

Patent Cooperation Treaty, 19 June 1970, 1160 U.N.T.S. 231.

Patent Law Treaty, Article 10(1), 1 June 2000, 39 I.L.M. 1047 (2000), *available at* http://www.wipo.int/treaties/en/ip/plt/trtdocs_wo038.html (last visited 31 July 2008).

UNIDROIT Convention on Stolen or Illegally Exported Cultural Objects, 24 June 1995, 34 I.L.M. 1322 (1995), *available at* http://www.unidroit.org/english/conventions/1995culturalproperty/1995culturalproperty-e.htm (last visited 31 July 2008).

Universal Copyright Convention, opened for signature 6 September 1952, 943 U.N.T.S. 311 (revised 24 July 1971).

Vienna Convention on the Law of Treaties, 23 May 1980, 1155 U.N.T.S. 331.

TABLE OF DECLARATIONS, RECOMMENDATIONS AND OPERATIONAL DIRECTIVES

Declaration of Indigenous Peoples of the Western Hemisphere Regarding the Human Genome Diversity Project, 19 February 1995, *available at* http://www.ankn.uaf.edu/IKS/declaration.html (last visited 31 July 2008).

Mataatua Declaration on Cultural and Intellectual Property Rights of Indigenous Peoples, 19 June 1993, U.N. Doc. E/CN.4/Sub.2/AC.4/1993/CRP.5 (1993).

Recommendation on the Safeguarding of Traditional Culture and Folklore, 15 November 1989, *available at* http://portal.unesco.org/en/ev.php-URL_ID=13141&URL_DO=DO_TOPIC&URL_SECTION=201.html (last visited 31 July 2008).

UN Declaration on the Rights of Indigenous Peoples, 13 September 2007, G.A. Res. 61/295, U.N. Doc. A/RES/61/295 (2007).

Universal Declaration on Cultural Diversity, 9 November 2001, *available at* http://unesdoc.unesco.org/images/0012/001271/127160m.pdf (last visited 31 July 2008).

Universal Declaration of Human Rights, 10 December 1948, G.A. Res. 217A(III), U.N. Doc. A/810 (1948).

UNESCO, General Assembly, *Operational Directives for the implementation of the Convention for the Safeguarding of the Intangible Heritage*, 16–19 June 2008, *available at* http://www.unesco.org/culture/ich/index.php?pg=00026 (last visited 31 July 2008).

BIBLIOGRAPHY

1. BOOKS

ADAMS, N.A., *Worlds Apart: The North-South Divide and the International System* (London: Zed Books, 1993).

AFIGBO, A.E., THE *Igbo and Their Neighbours: Inter-Group Relations in Southeastern Nigeria* (Ibadan: University Press, 1987).

AGBASIERE, J.T., *Women in Igbo Life and Thought* (New York: Routledge, 2000).

AMIT, V. and R., NIGEL, *The Trouble with Community: Anthropological Reflections on Movement, Identity and Collectivity* (London: Pluto Press, 2002).

ANAYA, S.J., *Indigenous Peoples in International Law* (Oxford: Oxford University Press, 2nd ed., 2004).

ANGHIE, A. *et al.* (eds.), *The Third World and International Order: Law, Politics and Globalization* (Leiden: Martinus Nijhoff, 2003).

ASHWORTH, G.J., B. GRAHAM and J.E. TUNBRIDGE, *Pluralising Pasts: Heritage, Identity and Place in Multicultural Societies* (London: Pluto Press, 2007).

AUST, A., *Modern Treaty Law and Practice* 122 (Cambridge: Cambridge University Press, 2nd ed., 2007).

BARTHES, R., *Image, Music, Text* (S. HEATH (ed. and trans.), London: Fontana Press 1977).

BARZ, G.F. and T.J. COOLEY. (eds.), *Shadows in the Field: New Perspectives for Fieldwork in Ethnomusicology* (New York: Oxford University Press, 1997).

BASILE, G., *Stories from the Pentamerone* (E.F. STRANGE (ed.), J.E. TAYLOR (trans.), London: Macmillan, 1911) (1847).

———, *Der Pentamerone* (K. RANKE (ed.), F. LIEBRECHT (trans.), Hindelheim: Georg Olm Verlag, 1973) (1846).

BAUMAN, Z., *Community: Seeking Safety in an Insecure World* (Cambridge: Polity, 2001).

BETTELHEIM, B., *The Uses of Enchantment: The Meaning and Importance of Fairy Tales* (New York: Vintage Books, 1977).

BLAKE, J., *Commentary on the UNESCO 2003 Convention on the Safeguarding of Intangible Cultural Heritage* (Leicester: Institute of Art and Law, 2006).

BOK, S., *Secrets: On the Ethics of Concealment and Revelation* (New York: Vintage Books, 1989).

BRANDL, E.J., *Australian Aboriginal Paintings in Western and Central Arnhem Land: Temporal Sequences and Elements of Style in Cadell River and Deaf Adder Creek Art* (Canberra: Australian Institute of Aboriginal Studies, 1973).

BROWN, M.F., *Who Owns Native Culture?* (Cambridge, Harvard University Press, 2003).

BOYLE, J., *Shamans, Software and Spleens: Law and the Construction of the Information Society* (Cambridge, Harvard University Press 1996).

BOTTIGHEIMER, R.B., *Grimms' Bad Girls and Bad Boys: The Moral and Social Vision of the Tales* (New Haven: Yale University Press, 1987).

CAMERON, A., *Daughters of Copper Woman* (Vancouver, Press Gang Publishers, 1981).

CHALOUPKA, G., *Journey in Time: The World's Longest Continuing Art Tradition: The 50,000 Year Story of the Australian Aboriginal Rock Art of Arnhem Land* (Chatswood, Reed, 1993).

COWEN, T., *Creative Destruction: How Globalization Is Changing the World's Cultures* (Princeton: Princeton University Press, 2002).

DIKE, A.A., *The Resilience of Igbo Culture: A Case Study of Awka Town* (East Lansig, Michigan: Michigan State University Press, 1985).

DONELLY, J., *Universal Human Rights in Theory and Practice* (Ithaca, Cornell University Press, 1989).

DRAHOS, P., *A Philosophy of Intellectual Property* (Aldershot: Dartmouth, 1996).

DRAHOS, P. with J. BRAITHWAITE, *Information Feudalism: Who Owns the Knowledge Economy?* (London: Earthscan, 2002).

ELLIKSON, R.C., *Order Without Law: How Neighbors Settle Disputes* (Cambridge, Harvard University Press, 1991).

ELLIS, J., *One Fairy Story Too Many: The Brothers Grimm and the Tales* (Chicago: University of Chicago Press, 1983).

EMBERLY, J.V., *Threshold of Difference: Feminist Critique, Native Women's Writings, and Postcolonial Theory* (Toronto: University of Toronto Press, 1993).

EQUIANO, O., *The Interesting Narrative of the Life of Olaudah Equiano, or Gustavus Vassa, the African* (Sollors, WERNER (ed.), New York: Norton, 2001) (1794).

FRANK, D. C. and J. FRANK, *The Stories of Hans Christian Andersen* (Boston: Houghton Mifflin, 2003).

FRANKE, C., *Die Brüder Grimm: Ihr Leben und Werk* [The Brothers Grimm: Their Life and Work] (Leipzig: Weidmannsche Buchhandlung, 1894).

FRAZER, J.G., *The Golden Bough: A Study in Magic and Religion* (London: Macmillan, 1922) (1890).

GIBSON, J., *Community Resources: Intellectual Property, International Trade and Protection of Traditional Knowledge* (Aldershot: Ashgate, 2005).

GREAVES, T. (ed.), *Intellectual Property Rights for Indigenous Peoples: A Source Book* (Ottawa: International Development Research Centre, 1994).

GRIMM, BRÜDER, *Deutsche Sagen* [*German Legends*], Vol. I, 1–5 (D. WARD (trans.), Philadelphia: Institute for the Study of Human Issues, 1981) (1816).

———, *Kinder- und Hausmärchen [Children and Household Tales*] (Frankfurt am Main: Deutscher Klassiker Verlag, 18th ed., 1999).

GRIMM, J. and W. GRIMM, *Grimm's Household Tales: with the Author's Notes,* Vol. I and II (M. HUNT (ed. and trans.), London: Georg Bell 1892).

———, *German Popular Stories* (C. BALDWYN (ed.), E. TAYLOR (trans.), Menston: Scolar Press 1971) (1823).

HARDING, S., *Whose Science? Whose Knowledge?: Thinking from Women's Lives* (Ithaca: Cornell University Press, 1991).

HART, H.L.A., *The Concept of Law* (Oxford: Clarendon Press, 1961).

HIEMESCH, K.-H., *Der Gesinnungsunterricht* [Ideological Teachings] (Leipzig: Wunderlich, 1925).

HIMANEN, P., L. TORVALDS and M. CASTELLS, *The Hacker Ethic and the Spirit of the New Economy* (New York: Random House, 2001).

HIRSCH, E.D., Jr., *Validity in Interpretation* (New Haven: Yale University Press, 1967).

HOBSBAWM, E. and T. RANGER (eds.), *The Invention of Tradition* (Cambridge: Cambridge University Press, 1983).

HORTON, D., *The encyclopaedia of Aboriginal Australia* (Canberra: Aboriginal Studies Press, 1994).

ISICHEI, E., *The Ibo People and the Europeans: The Genesis of a Relationship, to 1906* (London: Faber and Faber, 1973).

———, *A History of the Igbo People* (London: Macmillan, 1976).

JORDAN, J.P., *Bishop Shanahan of Southern Nigeria* (Dublin: Dublin Echo Press, 1971).

KAMENETSKY, Chr., *Children's Literature in Hitler's Germany: The Cultural Policy of National Socialism* (Athens, Ohio: Ohio University Press, 1984).

———, *The Brothers Grimm and their Critics, Folktales and the Quest for Meaning* (Athens, Ohio University Press, 1992).

KIELY, R. and Ph. MARFLEET (eds.), *Globalisation and the Third World* (London: Routledge, 1998).

KUHN, T.S., *The Structure of Scientific Revolutions* (Chicago: University of Chicago Press, 2nd ed., 1970).

LANDES, W.M. and R.A. POSNER, *The Economic Structure of Intellectual Property Law* (Cambridge, Belknap Press of Harvard University Press, 2003).

LINDLEY, M.F., *The Acquisition and Government of Backward Territory in International Law: Being a Treatise on the Law and Practice Relating to Colonial Expansion* (New York: Negro Universities Press 1969) (1926).

LUNDESTAD, G., *East, West, North and South: Major Developments in International Politics*, 1945–1986 (G. -A. KVAM (trans.), Oslo: Norwegian University Press, 1988).

MALINOWSKI, B., *The Sexual Life of Savages in North-Western Melanesia: An Ethnographic Account of Courtship, Marriage, and Family Life Among the Natives of the Trobriand Islands British New Guinea* (London: Routledge & Kegan Paul, 1968) (1929).

MCGOWN, J., *Out of Africa: Mysteries of Access and Benefit Sharing* (Washington: Edmonds Institute, 2006), *available at* www.edmonds-institute.org/outofafrica.pdf (last visited 31 July 2008).

MCHUGH, P.G., *Aboriginal Societies and the Common Law: A History of Sovereignty, Status, and Self-Determination* (Oxford: Oxford University Press, 2004).

MEIJKNECHT, A., *Towards International Personality: The Position of Minorities and Indigenous Peoples in International Law* (Antwerp: Intersentia, 2001).

MGBEOJI, I., *Global Biopiracy: Patents, Plants, and Indigenous Knowledge* (Vancouver: University of British Colombia Press, 2006).

MUSHITA, A. and C.B. THOMPSON, *Biopiracy of Biodiversity: Global Exchange as Enclosure* (Trenton: Africa World Press, 2007).

NAKAYAMA, N., *Industrial Property Law: Patent Law* (Tokyo: Koubundou Publishers, Vol. I, 2nd rev. ed., 2000), *available at* www.iip.or.jp/translation/nakayama/ (last visited 31 July 2008).

NIGEL Ph., *Sung narrative poetry of West Sumatra* (Cambridge: Cambridge University Press, 1981).
NJOKU, J.E.E., *The Igbos of Nigeria: Ancient Rites, Changes, and Survival* (Lewiston: E. Mellen Press, 1990).
OPIE, I. and P. OPIE, *The Classic Fairy Tales* (London: Oxford University Press, 1974).
OGUAMANAM, Ch., *International Law and Indigenous Knowledge: Intellectual Property, Plant Biodiversity, and Traditional Medicine* (Toronto: University of Toronto Press, 2006).
PENROSE, E.T., *The Economics of the International Patent System* (Westport, Connecticut: Greenwood Press 1973) (1951).
PERRAULT, Ch., *Histoire ou Contes de Temp passé* (P. DURAND (ed.), Paris: Editions des Deux Coqs d'Or, 1971) (1679).
POSEY, D.A. and G. DUTFIELD, *Beyond Intellectual Property: Toward Traditional Resource Rights for Indigenous Peoples and Local Communities* (Ottawa: International Development Research Centre, 1996).
POSNER, E.A., *Law and Social Norms* (Cambridge, Harvard University Press, 2000).
PROTT, L.V. and P.J. O'KEEFE, *Law and Cultural Heritage: Discovery and Excavation* (Abingdon, Oxon: Professional Books, 1984).
RICOEUR, P., *Memory, History, Forgetting* (Chicago: University of Chicago Press, 2004).
RÖLLEKE, H. (ed.), *Grimms Märchen wie sie nicht im Buche Stehen* [Grimm's Fairy Tales as They are not Portrayed in the Books] (Frankfurt am Main: Insel, 1993).
SANDERS, A.K., *Unfair Competition Law: The Protection of Intellectual and Industrial Creativity* (Oxford: Clarendon Press, 1997).
SCHOTT, G., *Weissagung und Erfüllung im deutschen Volksmärchen [Fortune Telling and its Realization in German Folk Tales]* (München: Ehen Verlag, 1936).
SEEGER, A., *Why Suyá Sing: A Musical Anthropology of an Amazonian People* (Urbana: University of Illinois Press, 2004).
SEIDL-HOHENVELDERN, I., *International Economic Law* (Dordrecht: Martinus Nijhoff, 1989).
SEITEL, P. (ed.), *Safeguarding Traditional Cultures: A Global Assessment* (Washington D.C.: Center for Folklife and Cultural Heritage Smithsonian, 2001).
SELL, S.K., *Private Power, Public Law: The Globalization of Intellectual Property rights* (Cambridge: Cambridge University Press, 2003).
SHIVA, V., *Staying Alive: Women, Ecology And Development* (London: Zed Books, 1989).
SMIERS, J., *Arts Under Pressure: Promoting Cultural Diversity in the Age of Globalization* (The Hague: Hivos, 2003).
SNYDER, L.L., *Roots of German Nationalism* (Bloomington: Indiana University Press, 1978).
STRATHERN, M., *Property, Substance, and Effect: Anthropological Essays on Persons and Things* (London: New Brunswick, 1999).
TAKACH, G., *Computer Law* (Toronto: Irwin Law, 2nd ed., 2003).
TATAR, M., *The Hard Facts of the Grimms' Fairy Tales* 11 (Princeton, N.J.: Princeton University Press, 1987).
———, *The Annotated Classic Fairy Tales* (New York: Norton, 2002).
THROSBY, D., *Economics and Culture* (Cambridge: Cambridge University Press, 2001).

TÖNNIES, F., *Gemeinschaft und Gesellschaft: Grundbegriffe der reinen Soziologie* (Berlin: Curtius, 3rd ed., 1920).

TOPP FARGION, J. (ed.), *A Manual for Documentation, Fieldwork, and Preservation for Ethnomusicologists* (Bloomington, Society for Ethnomusicology, 2nd ed., 2001).

TORREMANS, P.L.C. (ed.), *Copyright and Human Rights: Freedom of Expression - Intellectual Property - Privacy* (The Hague, Kluwer Law International, 2004).

TORVALDS, L. and D. DIAMOND, *Just for Fun: The Story of an Accidental Revolutionary* (New York: Harper Business, 2001).

TUNSTALL, J., *The Media are American* (New York: Columbia University Press, 1977).

TYLOR, E.B., *Primitive Culture: Researches into the Development of Mythology, Philosophy, Religion, Language, Art, and Custom* (London: J. Murray, 1871).

UCHENDU, V/C., *The Igbo of Southeast Nigeria* (New York: Holt, Rinehart and Winston 1965).

ULLMANN, W., *Law and Politics in the Middle Ages: An Introduction to the Sources of Medieval Political Ideas* (Ithaca, N.Y.: Cornell University Press, 1975).

UMEASIEGBU, R.N., *The Way We Lived: Igbo Customs and Stories* (London: Heinemann Educational 1969).

UMEH, J.A., *Igbo People: Their Origin and Culture Area* (Enugu, Nigeria: Gostak Print & Publisher, 1999).

UNESCO INSTITUTE FOR STATISTICS, INTERNATIONAL FLOWS OF SELECTED CULTURAL GOODS AND SERVICES, *1994–2003: Defining and Capturing the Flows of Global Cultural Trade* 9 (Montreal: UNESCO UIS, 2005), *available at* www.uis.unesco.org/template/pdf/cscl/IntlFlows_EN.pdf (last visited 31 July 2008).

VAN BEEK, W.E.A., *The Kapsiki of the Mandara Hills* (Long Grove: Waveland Press, 1987).

VAN ZANTEN, W., *Sundanese Music in the Cianjuran Style: Anthropological and Musicological Aspects of Tembang Sunda* (Dordrecht: Foris Publication Holland, 1989).

VON LEWINSKI, S. (ed.), *Indigenous Heritage and Intellectual Property: Genetic Resources, Traditional Knowledge and Folklore* (The Hague: Kluwer Law International, 2004).

WEBER, S., *The Success of Open Source* (Cambridge, Mass.: Harvard University Press 2004).

WILLIAMSON, E., *The Penguin History of Latin America* (London: Penguin, 1992).

WIPO, *The Berne Convention for the Protection of Literary and Artistic Works from 1886 to 1986* (Geneva: WIPO Publications, 1986).

———, *WIPO Intellectual Property Handbook: Policy, Law and Use* (Geneva: WIPO Publication, 2nd ed., 2004), available at www.wipo.int/about-ip/en/iprm/index.html (last visited 31 July 2008).

WOODMANSEE, M. and P. JASZI (eds.), *The Construction of Authorship: Textual Appropriation in Law and Literature* (Durham: Duke University Press, 1994).

ZIPES, J., *The trials and Tribulations of Little Red Riding Hood: Versions of the Tale in Sociocultural Context* (South Hadley, Bergin & Garvey Publishers, 1983).

———, *The Brothers Grimm: From Enchanted Forests to the Modern World* (New York: Routledge, 1988).

2. JOURNAL ARTICLES, BOOK CHAPTERS AND PRESENTATIONS

Adler, M.J., "Legal Certainty", 31 *Columbia Law Review* 91 (1931).

Afigbo, A.E., "The Age of Innocence: The Igbo and Their Neighbours in the Pre-Colonial Times", 1981 Ahiajoku Lecture, *available at* http://ahiajoku.igbonet.com/1981/ (last visited 31 July 2008).

Agrawal, A., "Dismantling the Divide Between Indigenous and Scientific Knowledge", 26 *Development & Change* 413 (1995).

Aikawa, N., "An Historical Overview of the Preparation of the UNESCO International Convention for the Safeguarding of the Intangible Cultural Heritage", 56 *Museum International* 140 (2004).

———, "Challenges for National Inventories of Intangible Cultural Heritage", in 2004 *Workshop on Inventory-making for Intangible Cultural Heritage Management: Final Report* 43 (2005), *available at* www.accu.or.jp/ich/en/pdf/2004_Tokyo.pdf (last visited 31 July 2008).

Aikawa-Faure, N., "UNESCO Convention for the Safeguarding of Intangible Cultural Heritage – from its Adoption to the First Meeting of the Intergovernmental Committee", in *Safeguarding Intangible Cultural Heritage: International Cooperation and the Role of Japan* 13 (Kokuritsu Bunkazai Kikou, Tokyo Bunkazai Kenkyujo and Mukei Bunka Isanbu (eds.), 2008), *available at* www.tobunken.go.jp/~geino/pdf/sympo/07KeynoteSpeech2Aikawa.pdf (last visited 31 July 2008).

American Anthropological Association, "Statement on Human Rights", 49 *American Anthropologist* 539 (1947).

Amnesty International, *Female Genital Mutilation and International Human Rights Standards*, ACT 77/014/97 (1 October 1997), *available at* www.amnesty.org/en/library/asset/ACT77/014/1997/en/dom-ACT770141997en.html (last visited 31 July 2008).

Anderson, J., "Indigenous Communal Moral Rights: The Utility of an Ineffective Law", *Indigenous Law Bulletin* 8 (February 2004).

———, *Access and Control of Indigenous Knowledge in Libraries and Archives: Ownership and Future Use*, at 4 (5–7 May 2005) (paper presented at the conference *Correcting Course: Rebalancing Copyright for Libraries in the National and International Arena*, Columbia University, New York, United States), *available at* www.conservationcommons.org/media/document/docu-i64cij.pdf (last visited 31 July 2008).

Anghie, A., "Francisco De Vitoria and the Colonial Origins of International Law", 5 *Socio-Legal Studies* 321 (1996).

Anya, A.O. *The Environment of Isolation or the Ecology and Sociology of Igbo Cultural and Political Development*, 1982 Ahiajoku Lecture, *available at* http://ahiajoku.igbonet.com/1982/ (last visited 31 July 2008).

Arantes, A.A., "Reconsidering the Social Aspects of Sustainability: Integrated Conservation and the Urban Environmental Heritage", in S.M. Zanchetti (ed.),

Conservation and Urban Sustainable Development: A Theoretical Framework, 1999, 41.

———, "Diversity, Heritage and Cultural Politics", 24 *Theory, Culture & Society* 290 (2007).

———, "Cultural Diversity and the Politics of Difference in Safeguarding Intangible Cultural Heritage", in J. Blake (ed.), *Safeguarding Intangible Cultural Heritage: Challenges and Approaches*, 2007, 85.

———, *ICH Inventories in Context: Purpose, Methodology and Functionality*, at 5 (25–26 March 2007) (paper presented at the conference on *Intangible Cultural Heritage and Intellectual Property under the 2003 Convention: Seeking a Collaborative Interface between ICH and IP*, New Delhi, India) (on file with the editor).

Arezzo, E., "Struggling Around the "Natural" Divide: The Protection of Tangible and Intangible Indigenous Property", 25 *Cardozo Arts & Entertainment Law Journal* 367 (2007).

Arizpe, L., "The Intellectual History of Culture and Development Institutions", in V. Rao and M. Walton (eds.), *Culture and Public Action*, 2004, 163.

Arts Law Centre of Australia, *Indigenous communal moral rights*, www.artslaw.com.au/_documents/files/ICMRLetterAndExecutiveSummary2006.pdf (last visited 31 July 2008).

Babalola J. Yaï, O., "Odo layé (éloge de la vie-fleuve): perspectives africaines sur le patrimoine culturel", in J. Blake (ed.), *Safeguarding Intangible Cultural Heritage: Challenges and Approaches*, 2007, 73.

Barendregt, B. and W. van Zanten, "Popular Music in Indonesia since 1998, in Particular Fusion, Indie and Islamic Music on Video Compact Discs and the Internet", 34 *Yearbook for Traditional Music* 67 (2002).

Barthes, R., "Theory of the Text", in R. Young (ed.), *Untying the Text: A Post-Structuralist Reader*, 1981, 3.

Bedjaoui, M., "Poverty of the International Order", in R. Falk, F. Kratochwil and S.H. Mendlovitz (eds.), *International Law: A Contemporary Perspective*, 1985, 152.

Bell, T.W., "Fair Use vs. Fared Use: The Impact of Automated Rights Management on Copyright's Fair Use Doctrine", 76 *North Carolina Law Review* 557 (1998).

Ben-Amos, D., "Toward a Definition of Folklore in Context", in A. Paredes and R. Bauman (eds.), *Toward New Perspectives in Folklore*, 1972, 10.

Benkler, Y., "Free as the Air to Common Use: First Amendment Constraints on Enclosure of the Public Domain", 74 *New York University Law Review* 354 (1999).

———, "Through the Looking Glass: Alice and the Constitutional Foundations of the Public Domain", 66 *Law & Contemporary Problems* 173 (2003).

Bently, L., "Copyright and the Death of the Author in Literature and Law", 57 *Modern Law Review* 973 (1994).

Berlin, B. and E.A. Berlin, "Comment", 47 *Current Anthropology* 129 (2006).

Blake, J., "Safeguarding Traditional Culture and Folklore: Existing International Law and Future Developments", in J. Blake (ed.), *Safeguarding Intangible Cultural Heritage: Challenges and Approaches*, 149.

———, *Developing a New Standard-setting Instrument for the Safeguarding of Intangible Cultural Heritage: Elements for consideration*, CLT-2001/WS/8 Rev. (2002), *available at* http://unesdoc.unesco.org/images/0012/001237/123744e.pdf (last visited 31 July 2008).

Boisson de Chazournes, L., "Treaty Law-Making and Non-Treaty Law-Making: The Evolving Structure of the International Legal Order", in R. Wolfrum and V. Röben (eds.), *Developments of International Law in Treaty Making,* 2005, 463.

Boyle, J., "Foreword: The Opposite of Property?", 66 *Law & Contemporary Problems* 1 (2003).

Braadland, J.F., "Echoes of the Brothers Grimm from Thule: A Short Introduction to Andreas Faye (1802–1869) and his 'Norske Sagn' (1833)", in H. Kugler, B. Lauer, F. Paul, L. Röhrich and R. Schmidt-Wiegand (eds.), *Jahrbuch der Brüder Grimm-Gesellschaft [Yearbook of the Brother's Grimm Association]*, 1995, 7.

Brow, J., "Notes on Community, Hegemony, and the Uses of the Past", 63 *Anthropological Quarterly* 1 (1990).

Brown, M.F., "Can Culture be Copyrighted?", 39 *Current Anthropology* 193 (1998).

———, "Safeguarding the Intangible, Cultural Commons", November 2003, *available at* www.culturalcommons.org/comment-print.cfm?ID=12 (last visited 31 July 2008).

———, "Heritage Trouble: Recent Work on the Protection of Intangible Cultural Heritage", 12 *International Journal of Cultural Property* 48 (2005).

———, "Cultural Relativism 2.0", 49 *Current Anthropology* 363 (2008).

———, "Reply", 49 *Current Anthropology* 379 (2008).

Brush, S., "Whose Knowledge, Whose Genes, Whose Rights?", in S.B. Brush and D. Stabinski (eds.), *Valuing Local Knowledge: Indigenous Peoples and Intellectual Property Rights*, 1996, 1.

———, "Is Common Heritage Outmoded?", in S.B. Brush and D. Stabinsky (eds.), *Valuing Local Knowledge: Indigenous People and Intellectual Property Rights*, 1996, 143.

Burk, D.L. and J.E. Cohen, "Fair Use Infrastructure for Rights Management Systems", 15 *Harvard Journal of Law & Technology* 41 (2001).

Calabresi, G. and A.D. Melamed., "Property Rules, Liability Rules, and Inalienability: One View of the Cathedral", 85 *Harvard Law Review* 1089 (1972).

Calame, T.J. and J. de Werra, "Co-titularité des droits de propriété intellectuelle (tout particulièrement des brevets) dans le cadre de projets de recherche et développement conjoints: un piège à éviter?", 2003 *Anwaltsrevue* 10.

Carpenter, M.M., "Intellectual Property Law and Indigenous Peoples: Adapting Copyright Law to the Needs of a Global Community", 7 *Yale Human Richts & Development Law Journal* 51 (2004).

Chander, A. and M. Sunder, "The Romance of the Public Domain", 92 *California Law Review* 1331 (2004).

Chanock, M., "Neo-Traditionalism and Customary Law in Malawi", 16 *African Legal Studies* 80 (1978).

Chijioke, M.O., *Ugwumba: The Greatness of a People*, 1989 Ahiajoku Lecture, *available at* http://ahiajoku.igbonet.com/1982/ (last visited 31 July 2008).

Chinkin, Chr., "Normative Development in the International Legal System", in D. Shelton (ed.), *Commitment and Compliance,* 2000, 21.

Cochrane, D., *Africa: Patents Act amended to protect genetic resources*, *Managing Intellectual Property*, March 2008, *available at* www.managingip.com/Article/1886062/Patents-Act-amended-to-protect-genetic-resources.html (last visited 31 July 2008).

Cohen, F., "The Spanish Origin of Indian Rights in the Law of the United States", 31 *Georgetown Law Journal* 1 (1942).

Committee of Governmental Experts on the Intellectual Property Aspects of the Protection of Expressions of Folklore, "Model Provisions for National Laws on the Protection of Expressions of Folklore Against Illicit Exploitation and Other Prejudicial Actions", 16(1/2) *Copyright Bulletin* 62 (1982).

Coombe, R.J., "The Cultural Life of Things: Anthropological Approaches to Law and Society in Conditions of Globalization", 10 *American University Journal of International Law & Policy* 791 (1995).

———, "The Recognition of Indigenous Peoples' and Community Traditional Knowledge in International Law", 14 *Saint Thomas Law Review* 275 (2001).

———, "Protecting Traditional Environmental Knowledge and New Social Movements in the Americas: Intellectual Property, Human Right, or Claims to an Alternative Form of Sustainable Development?", 17 *Florida Journal of International Law* 115 (2005).

Cottier, T. and M. Panizzon, "Legal Perspectives on Traditional Knowledge: The Case for Intellectual Property Protection", 7 *Journal International Economic Law* 371 (2004).

Cremers, T., "Theft, the Internet and Museum Objects: Threats and Opportunities", *ICOM News*, No. 4/2006, at 4, *available at* http://palimpsest.stanford.edu/icom/pdf/E_news2006/p4_2006-4.pdf (last visited 31 July 2008).

Croce, B., "The Fantastic Accomplishment of Giambattista Basile and his Tale of Tales", in J. Zipes (ed.), *The Great Fairy Tale Tradition: From Straparola and Basile to the Brothers Grimm*, 2001, 879.

Daes, E.-I.A., *Defending Indigenous People's Heritage* (23–26 Feb. 2000) (keynote address presented at the *Conference on Protecting Knowledge: Traditional Resources Rights in the New Millennium*, Union of British Columbian Indian Chiefs, Vancouver, Canada).

Dagan, H. and M.A. Heller, "The Liberal Commons", 110 *Yale Law Journal* 549 (2001).

Deacon, H., *Expert Report: Harriet Deacon* (13–15 March 2006) (paper presented at *UNESCO/ACCU Expert Meeting on Community Involvement in Safeguarding Intangible Cultural Heritage: Towards the Implementation of the 2003 Convention*, Tokyo, Japan), *available at* www.accu.or.jp/ich/en/pdf/c2006Expert_DEACON_1.pdf (last visited 31 July 2008).

de Carvalho, N.P., "Requiring Disclosure of the Origin of Genetic Resources and Prior Informed Consent in Patent Applications Without Infringing the TRIPS Agreement: The Problem and the Solution", 2 *Washington University Journal of Law and Policy* 371 (2000).

———, "From the Shaman's Hut to the Patent Office: In Search of a TRIPS-Consistent Requirement to Disclose the Origin of Genetic Resources and Prior Informed Consent", 17 *Washington University Journal of Law and Policy* 111 (2005).

Dinwoodie, G.B., *Towards an International Framework for the Protection of Traditional Knowledge* (4–6 February 2004) (paper presented at UNCTAD-Commonwealth Secretariat workshop on the *Elements of National Sui Generis Systems for the Preservation, Protection and Promotion of Traditional Knowledge: Innovations and Practices and Options for an International Framework*, Geneva, Switzerland), *available at* http://ssrn.com/abstract=707002 (last visited 31 July 2008).

Douglas, N., "Political Structures, Social Interaction and Identity Change in Northern Ireland", in B. Graham (ed.), *In Search of Ireland: A Cultural Geography*, 1997, 151.

Drahos, P., "A Networked Responsive Regulatory Approach to Protecting Traditional Knowledge", in D. Gervais (ed.), *Intellectual Property, Trade and Development: Strategies to Optimize Economic Development in a TRIPS-Plus Era*, 2007, 385.

Dutfield, G., *Sharing the Benefits of Biodiversity: Is there a Role for the Patent System?*, 5 *Journal of World Intellectual Property* 899 (2002).

———, *Protecting Traditional Knowledge: Pathways for the Future* (2006) *available at* www.iprsonline.org/unctadictsd/docs/Graham%20final.pdf (last visited 31 July 2008) (*prepared for* International Centre for Trade and Sustainable Development).

Early, J. and P. Seitel, "UNESCO Draft Convention For Safeguarding Intangible Cultural Heritage: "No Folklore Without the Folk", *Talk Story*, Fall 2002, No. 22:19, *available at* www.folklife.si.edu/resources/center/cultural_policy/pdf/TSFall2002 EarlySeitel.pdf (last visited 31 July 2008).

Ejidike, O.M., "Human Rights in the Cultural Traditions and Social Practice of the Igbo of South-Eastern Nigeria", 43 *Journal of African Law* 71 (1999).

Erlandson, J., "The Making of Chumash Tradition: Replies to Haley and Wilcoxon", 39 *Current Anthropology* 477 (1998).

Farley, Chr.H., "Protecting Folklore and Indigenous Peoples: Is Intellectual Property the Answer?", 30 *Connecticut Law Review* 1 (1997).

Feld, S., "pygmy POP: A Genealogy of Schizophonic Mimesis", 28 *Yearbook for Traditional Music* 1 (1996).

Field, L.W., "Complicities and Collaborations: Anthropologists and the "Unacknowledged Tribes" of California", 40 *Current Anthropology* 193 (1999).

Firestone, L.A., "You Say Yes, I Say No; Defining Community Prior Informed Consent under the Convention on Biological Diversity", 16 *Georgetown International Environmental Law Review* 171 (2003).

Foucault, M., "What Is an Author?", in J.V. Harari (ed.), *Textual Strategies: Perspectives in Post-Structuralist Criticism*, 1979, 141.

———, "What is an Author?", in V. Lambropoulos and D.N. Miller (eds.), *Twentieth Century Literary Theory: An Introductory Anthology*, 1987.

Fuller, L.L., "Law as an Instrument of Social Control and Law as a Facilitation of Human Interaction", 1 *Burnham Young University Law Review* 89 (1975).

Galla, A., *Museums and Intangible Heritage*, *available at* http://rspas.anu.edu.au/papers/heritage/museums_%20Intangible_Heritage_ARTery.pdf (last visited 31 July 2008).

GANA, R.L., "Has Creativity Died in the Third World? Some Implications of the Internationalization of Intellectual Property", 24 *Denver Journal of International Law & Policy* 109 (1995).
GATHII, J.T., "International Law and Eurocentricity", 9 *European Journal of International Law* 184 (1998).
———, "Alternative and Critical: The Contribution of Research and Scholarship on Developing Countries to International Legal Theory", 41 *Harvard International Law Journal* 263 (2000).
GELL, A., "The Technology of Enchantment and the Enchantment of Technology", in E. HIRSCH (ed.), *The Art of Anthropology: Essays and Diagrams*, 1999, 159, 163.
GERVAIS, D., "Traditional Knowledge & Intellectual Property: A TRIPS-Compatible Approach", *Michigan State Law Review* 137 (2005).
GHIDINI, G. and E. Arezzo, "Patent and Copyright Paradigms vis-à-vis Derivative Innovation: The Case of Computer Programs", 36 *International Review of Intellectual Property and Competition Law* 159 (2005).
GIRSBERGER, M.A., "Transparency Measures under Patent Law Regarding Genetic Resources and Traditional Knowledge: Disclosure of Source and Evidence of Prior Informed Consent and Benefit-Sharing", 7 *Journal of World Intellectual Property* 451 (2004).
GOODY, J.,"Literacy and Classification: On Turning the Tables", in J. GOODY (ed.), *The Domestication of the Savage Mind*, 1977, 52.
GORDON, W.J., "Fair Use as Market Failure: A Structural and Economic Analysis of the Betamax Case and Its Predecessors", 82 *Columbia Law Review* 1600 (1982).
GRABER, Chr.B. and M.A. GIRSBERGER, "Traditional Knowledge at the International Level: Current Approaches and Proposals for a Bigger Picture that Includes Cultural Diversity", in J. SCHMID and H. SEILER (eds.), *Recht des ländlichen Raums: Festgabe für Paul Richli zum 60. Geburtstag* 2006, 243.
GRAHAM, L. and S. MCJOHN, "Indigenous People and Intellectual Property", 19 *Washington University Journal of Law and Policy* 313 (2005).
GRAIN, *Biodiversity Rights Legislation (BRL)*, www.grain.org/brl (last visited 31 July 2008).
GREENE, Sh., "Indigenous People Incorporated?: Culture as Politics, Culture as Property in Pharmaceutical Bioprospecting", 45 *Current Anthropology* 211 (2004).
GUPTA, A.K., *Conserving Biodiversity and Rewarding Associated Knowledge and Innovation Systems: Honey Bees Perspective, available at* www.maharashtra.gov.in/english/signs/info_honeybee/berne-goa.pdf (last visited 10 August 2007).
HALEY, B.D. and L.R. Wilcoxon, "Anthropology and the Making of Chumash Tradition", 38 *Current Anthropology* 761 (1997).
HAMILTON, M.A., "The TRIPS Agreement: Imperialistic, Outdated, and Overprotective", 29 *Vanderbilt Journal of Transnational Law* 613 (1996).
HANNIG, M., "An Examination of the Possibility to Secure Intellectual Property Rights for Plant Genetic Resources Developed by Indigenous Peoples of the NAFTA States: Domestic Legislation Under the International Convention for New Plant Varieties", 13 *Arizona Journal of International & Comparative Law* 175 (1996).

Hanson, S.A., "Intellectual Property and Traditional Ecological Knowledge: Institutionally Globalized Biopiracy?", *Professional Ethics Report*, summer 2002, at 1 *available at* www.aaas.org/spp/sfrl/per/per30.pdf (last visited 31 July 2008).

Hardin, G., "The Tragedy of the Commons", 162 *Science* 1243 (1968).

Harding, S., "Defining Traditional Knowledge – Lessons from Cultural Property", 11 *Cardozo Journal of International & Comparative Law* 511 (2003).

Hartwig, O., "Zur ersten englischen Übersetzung der Kinder- und Hausmärchen der Brüder Grimm [About the First English Translations of the Children and Household Tales]", XV *Zentralblatt für Bibliothekswesen [Central Magazine for Libraries]* 1 (1898).

Harvey, E.R., "The Domaine Public Payant in Comparative Law with Special Reference to Argentina", 28(4) *Copyright Bulletin* 29 (1994).

Hassemer, M., "Genetic Resources", in S. von Lewinski (ed.), *Indigenous Heritage and Intellectual Property: Genetic Resources, Traditional Knowledge and Folklore*, 2004, 151.

Hastanto, S., *Inventory of Intangible Cultural Heritage in Indonesia* (13–16 December 2005) (paper presented at the Sub-Regional Experts Meeting in Asia on *Intangible Cultural Heritage: Safeguarding and Inventory-Making Methodologies*, Bangkok, Thailand), *available at* www.accu.or.jp/ich/en/pdf/c2005subreg_Indo.pdf (last visited 31 July 2008).

Helfer, L.R., "Human Rights and Intellectual Property: Conflict or Coexistence?", 5 *Minnesota Intellectual Property Review* 47 (2003).

———, "Regime Shifting: The TRIPs Agreement and New Dynamics of International Law Making", 29 *Yale Journal of International Law* 1 (2004).

Heller, M.A., "The Tragedy of the Anticommons: Property in the Transition from Marx to Markets", 111 *Harvard Law Review* 621 (1998).

Heller, M.A. and R.S. Eisenberg, "Can Patents Deter Innovation? The Anticommons in Biomedical Research", 280 *Science* 698 (1998).

Hillery, G., "Definitions of Community: Areas of Agreement", 20 *Rural Sociology* 111 (1955).

Hoare, A.L. and R.G. Tarasofsky, "Asking and Telling: Can "Disclosure of Origin" Requirements in Patent Applications Make a Difference?", 10 *Journal of World Intellectual Property* 149 (2007).

Hoeyer, K., "Comment", 47 *Current Anthropology* 132 (2006).

Hudson, E., *Cultural Institutions, Law and Indigenous Knowledge: A Legal Primer on the Management of Australian Indigenous Collections* (2006), *available at* www.wipo.int/export/sites/www/tk/en/folklore/creative_heritage/docs/aiatsis_ipria.pdf (last visited 31 July 2008).

Hughes, J., "The Philosophy of Intellectual Property", 77 *Georgetown Law Journal* 287 (1988).

Hunn, E.S., "Comment", 47 *Current Anthropology* 133 (2006).

International Council of Museums, *ICOM Code of Ethics for Museums*, *available at* www.wipo.int/export/sites/www/tk/en/folklore/creative_heritage/docs/icom_code.pdf (last visited 31 July 2008).

Jameson, F., "Globalization and Political Strategy", *New Left Review*, No. 4, at 49 (2000).

JANKE, T., *Our Culture: Our Future: Report on Australian Indigenous Cultural and Intellectual Property Rights* 59 (1998), *available at* www.frankellawyers.com.au/media/report/culture.pdf (last visited 31 July 2008) (report prepared for the Australian Institute of Aboriginal and Torres Strait Islander Studies).

———, *Captured Images: Film Archives and Indigenous Cultural and Intellectual Property Rights* (27 February 2003) (paper presented at *Culture & Ethics: Who decides?*, a forum hosted by Film Australia, Lindfield, Australia), *available at* www.filmaust.com.au/about/publications/cultureandethics_transcript.pdf (last visited 31 July 2008).

———, *Minding Culture: Case Studies on Intellectual Property and Traditional Cultural Expressions* (2003), *available at* www.wipo.int/tk/en/studies/cultural/minding-culture/studies/finalstudy.pdf (last visited 31 July 2008) (*prepared for* WIPO).

———, "The Moral of the Story: Indigenous Communal Moral Rights", 3 *Bulletin* 1 (2005).

JANKE, T. and R. QUIGGIN "Indigenous Cultural and Intellectual Property and Customary Law", in *Aboriginal Customary Laws: Background Papers* 451 (Law Reform Commission of Western Australia ed., January 2006), *available at* www.lrc.justice.wa.gov.au/2publications/reports/ACL/BP/BP-12.pdf (last visited 31 July 2008).

JUNG, C.G., "On the Relation of Analytical Psychology to Poetry", in J. Campbell (ed.), F.C. Hall (trans.), *The Portable* Jung, 1922, 1983, 301.

KAHN, O., "Rumpelstilz hat wirklich geleb. Textvergleichende Studie über das Märchen vom Rumpelstilzchen und eine Erklärung mit Hilfe der Rechtsgeschichte [Rapunzel has Actually Lived. A Textual Comparative Study of the Rapunzel Fairy Tale and an Explanation by Using Legal History]", 17/18 *Rheinisches Jahrbuch für Volkskunde* 143 (1966/67).

KAMENETSKY, Chr., "Folklore as a Political Tool in Nazi Germany", 85 *Journal of American Folklore* 221 (1972).

KINGSBURY, B., "Self-Determination and "Indigenous Peoples"", 86 *ASIL Proceedings* 383 (1992).

KIRSHENBLATT-GIMBLETT, B., "Intangible Heritage as Metacultural Production", 56 *Museum International* 52 (2004).

KOCKEL, U., "Reflexive Traditions and Heritage Production", in U. KOCKEL and M. NIC CRAITH (eds.), *Cultural Heritages as Reflexive Traditions*, 2007, 19.

KOHLS, M., "Blackbeard or Albert Schweitzer: Reconciling Biopiracy", 6 *Chicago-Kent Journal of Intellectual Property* 108 (2007).

KONO, T., "UNESCO and Intangible Cultural Heritage from the Viewpoint of Sustainable Development", in A.A. YUSUF (ed.), *Normative Action in Education, Science and Culture: Essays in Commemoration of the Sixtieth Anniversary of UNESCO*, 2007, 237.

KONO, T. and CORNETT, J., "What is Intangible Cultural Heritage? An Analysis of the Convention for the Safeguarding of Intangible Cultural Heritage and the Requirement of Compatibility with Human Rights", in J. BLAKE (ed.), *Safeguarding Intangible Cultural Heritage: Challenges and Approaches*, 2008, 143.

KREPS, Chr., "Indigenous Curation as Intangible Cultural Heritage: Thoughts on the Relevance of the 2003 UNESCO Convention", *Theorizing Cultural Heritage*, Vol.

1(2), *available at* www.folklife.si.edu/resources/center/cultural_policy/pdf/ChristinaKrepsfellow.pdf (last visited 31 July 2008).
KRUMENACHER, T.J., "Comment, Protection for Indigenous Peoples and Their Traditional Knowledge: Would a Registry System Reduce the Misappropriation of Traditional Knowledge?", 8 *Marquette Intellectual Property Law Review* 143 (2004).
KURIN, R., "Tangible Progress: A response to "Safeguarding the Intangible," a Cultural Comment essay by Michael F. Brown", *Cultural Commons*, December 2003, *available at* www.culturalcommons.org/kurin.htm (last visited 31 July 2008).
———, "Museums and Intangible Heritage: Culture Dead or Alive?", *ICOM News*, No. 4 (2004), *available at* http://palimpsest.stanford.edu/icom/pdf/E_news2004/p7_2004-4.pdf (last visited 31 July 2008).
———, "Safeguarding Intangible Cultural Heritage in the 2003 Convention: A Critical Appraisal", 56 *Museum International* 66 (2004).
KURTZ, Sh.F., "The Law of Informed Consent: From "Doctor is Right" to "Patient Has Rights"", 50 *Syracuse Law Review* 1243 (2000).
KURUK, P., "Protecting Folklore under Modern Intellectual Property Regimes: A Reappraisal of the Tensions between Individual and Communal Rights in Africa and the United States", 48 *American University Law Review* 769 (1999).
———, "Cultural Heritage, Traditional Knowledge and Indigenous Rights: An Analysis of the Convention for the Safeguarding of Intangible Cultural Heritage", 1 *Macquarie Journal of International & Comparative Environmental Law* 111 (2004), *available at* www.austlii.edu.au/au/journals/MqJICEL/2004/5.html (last visited 31 July 2008).
LANG, A., "Household Tales; Their Origin, Diffusion, and Relation to higher Myths", in M. HUNT (ed. and trans.), *Grimm's Household Tales: with the Author's Notes,* Vol. I, 1892.
LANGLEY, W.E., "The Third World: Towards A Definition", 2 *British Columbia Third World Law Journal* 1 (1981).
LAUER, B., "Die Brüder Jacob und Wilhelm Grimm im europäischen Kontext [The Brothers Jacob and Wilhelm Grimm in European Context]", in B. LAUER (ed.), *Die Brüder Grimm und die Geisteswissenschaften Heute [The Brothers Grimm and the Current Humanities]*, 1999, 146.
LESSIG, L., "The Regulation of Social Meaning", 62 *University of Chicago Law Review* 943 (1995).
LÉVI-STRAUSS, C., "Introduction à l'oeuvre de M. Mauss", in M. MAUSS (ed.), *Sociologie et anthropologie* 3d ed., 1966 (1950), I.
LIU, Ch.C. and J.J. LIU, "Waves of Changes in Chinese Patent Law and Regulations–Part IV", *available at* www.chinabiotoday.com/articles/20080131_1 (last visited 31 July 2008).
MACMILLAN, F., "What Might Hans Christian Andersen Say About Copyright Today?", in H. PORSDAM (ed.), *Copyright and other Fairy Tales: Hans Christian Andersen and the Commodification of Creativity*, 2006, 83.
MACQUEEN, K.M. *et al.*, "What is Community? An Evidence-Based Definition for Participatory Public Health", 91 *American Journal of Public Health* 1929 (2001).
MALINOWSKY, B., "Myth in Primitive Psychology", in B. MALINOWSKY (ed.), *Magic, Science, and Religion and other Essays*, 1954, 99.

MARA, K., "TRIPS Council: Half Of WTO Membership Backs Biodiversity Amendment", *available at* www.ip-watch.org/weblog/index.php?p=961 (last visited 31 July 2008).
MARCH, J.G., "Sociological Jurisprudence Revisited: A Review (More or Less) of Max Gluckman", 8 *Stanford Law Review* 499 (1956).
MARGADANT, G.F., "Official Mexican Attitudes Toward the Indians: An Historical Essay", 54 *Tulane Law Review* 967 (1980).
MARSHALL, P.A., "Comment", 47 *Current Anthropology* 134 (2006).
MARTIN, G.T. and S. VERMEYLEN, "Intellectual Property, Indigenous Knowledge, and Biodiversity", 16 *Capitalism Nature Socialism* 27 (2005).
MAUSS, M., "Essai sur le don", in M. MAUSS (ed.), *Sociologie et anthropologie*, 3d ed., 1966, 1950, 145.
MCADAMS, R.H., "The Origin, Development and Regulation of Norms", 96 *Michigan Law Review* 338 (1997).
MCCANN, A. *et al.*, "The 1989 Recommendation Ten Years On: Towards a Critical Analysis", in P. SEITEL (ed.), *Safeguarding Traditional Cultures: A Global Assessment*, 2001, 56.
MCCAUSLAND, S., "Protecting Communal Interests in Indigenous Artworks after the Bulun Bulun Case", *Indigenous Law Bulletin* 4 (July 1999).
MCGINNIS, M.V., "House, Freeman and Jordan, William III, Bioregional Restoration: Re-Establishing an Ecology of Shared Identity", in M.V. MCGINNIS (ed.), *Bioregionalism*, 1999, 205.
MGBEOJI, I., "The Civilised Self and the Barbaric Other: Imperial Delusions of Order and the Challenges of Human Security", 27 *Third World Quarterly* 855 (2006).
MICKELSON, K., "Rhetoric and Rage: Third World Voices in International Legal Discourse", 16 *Wisconsin International Law Journal* 353 (1998).
MILLS, Sh., "Indigenous Music and the Law: An Analysis of National and International Legislation", 28 *Yearbook for Traditional Music* 57 (1996).
MORGAN, G., "Aboriginal Politics, Self-Determination and the Rhetoric of Community", in S. HERBRECHTER and M. HIGGINS (eds.), *Returning (to) Communities: Theory, Culture and Political Practice of the Communal*, 2006, 367.
MOSSOFF, A., "What Is Property? Putting the Pieces Back Together", 45 *Arizona Law Review* 371 (2003).
MUTUA, M.w., "What is TWAIL?", 94 *ASIL Proceedings* 31 (2000).
———, "Savages, Victims, and Saviours: The Metaphor of Human Rights", 42 *Harvard International Law Journal* 201 (2001).
N'DIAYE, D.B., *Community in the Context of UNESCO's Convention on Intangible Cultural Heritage*, at 3 (13–15 March 2006) (paper presented at *UNESCO/ACCU Expert Meeting on Community Involvement in Safeguarding Intangible Cultural Heritage: Towards the Implementation of the 2003 Convention*, Tokyo, Japan), *available at* www.accu.or.jp/ich/en/pdf/c2006Expert_NDIAYE.pdf (last visited 31 July 2008).
NEUMANN, S., "The Brothers Grimm as Collectors and Editors of German Folktales", in J. ZIPES (ed.), *The Great Fairy Tale Tradition: From Straparola and Basile to the Brothers Grimm*, 2001, 969.
NOBLE, R.L., Ch.T. BEER and J.H. CUTTS, "Role of Chance Observation in Chemotherapy: Vinca Rosea", 76 *Annals of the New York Academy of Sciences* 882 (1958).

Nwoga, D.I., *Nka na Nzere: The Focus of Igbo Worldview*, 1984 Ahiajoku Lecture, *available at* http://ahiajoku.igbonet.com/1984/ (last visited 31 July 2008).

Obiechina, E., *Nchetaka: The Story, Memory and Continuity of Igbo Culture*, 1994 Ahiajoku Lecture, *available at* www.kwenu.com/igbo/igbowebpages/Igbo.dir/Ahiajoku_Lectures/ahiajoku_Lec94.htm#lecture (last visited 31 July 2008).

Oddi, A.S., "The International Patent System and Third World Development: Reality or Myth?", 63 *Duke Law Journal* 831 (1987).

Odi, A., "As It Was in the Beginning: The Influence of Traditional Elements in Igbo Information Systems", 28 *International Information & Library Review* 193 (1996).

Oguamanam, Ch., "The Protection of Traditional Knowledge: Towards a Cross-Cultural Dialogue on Intellectual Property Rights", 15 *Australia Intellectual Property Journal* 34 (2004).

———, "Localizing Intellectual Property in the Globalization Epoch: The Integration of Indigenous Knowledge", 11 *Indiana Journal of Global Legal Studies* 135 (2004).

———, "Protecting Indigenous Knowledge in International Law: Solidarity Beyond the Nation State", 8 *Law Text Culture* 191 (2004).

———, "Agro-Biotechnology and Food Security: Biotechnology and Traditional Agricultural Practices at the Periphery of International Intellectual Property Regime Complex", *Michigan State Law Review* 215 (2007).

Okafor, O.Ch., "Newness, Imperialism, and International Legal Reform in Our Time: A TWAIL Perspective", 43 *Osgoode Hall Law Journal* 171 (2003).

Oloka-Onyango, J. and D. Udagama, *The Realization of Economic, Social and Cultural Rights: Globalization and Its Impact on the Full Enjoyment of Human Rights*, U.N. Doc. E/CN.4/Sub.2/2000/13 (2000).

Osborne, S.D., "Protecting Tribal Stories: The Perils of Propertization", 28 *American Indian Law Review* 203 (2003).

Pacific Forum, *Model Law for the Protection of Traditional Ecological Knowledge, Innovations and Practices* (draft, 2001), *available at* www.grain.org/brl/?docid=698&lawid=1430 (last visited 31 July 2008).

Pacific Islands Museums Association, *PIMA Code of Ethics for Pacific Museums and Cultural Centres, available at* www.wipo.int/export/sites/www/tk/en/folklore/creative_heritage/docs/pima_code_ethics.pdf (last visited 31 July 2008).

Papuga, D.W., *A Taste of Intangible Heritage: Food Traditions Inside and Outside of the Museum* (2–8 October 2004) (paper presented at the *ICOM 2004 General Conference*, Seoul, South Korea), *available at* http://museumsnett.no/icme/icme2004/papuga.html (last visited 31 July 2008).

Paterson, R.K. and D.S. Karjala, "Looking Beyond Intellectual Property in Resolving Protection of the Intangible Cultural Heritage of Indigenous Peoples", 11 *Cardozo Journal of International and Comparative Law* 633 (2003).

Patrick, D. and T. Wickizer, "Community and Health", in B. Amick *et al.*, (eds.), *Society and Health* 1995, 46.

Perley, Sh.N., "Note, From Control over One's Body to Control over One's Body Parts: Extending The Doctrine of Informed Consent", 67 *New York University Law Review* 335 (1992).

PERRAULT, A., K. HERBERTSON and O. LYNCH, "Partnerships for Success in Protected Areas: The Public Interest and Local Community and Rights to Prior Informed Consent", 19 *Georgetown International Environmental Law Review* 475 (2007).

PETERSEN, K., "Note, Recent Intellectual Property Trends in Developing Countries", 33 *Harvard International Law Journal* 277 (1992).

PINNA, G., "Intangible Heritage and Museums", *ICOM News*, No. 4 (2003), *available at* http://icom.museum/pdf/E_news2003/p3_2003-4.pdf (last visited 31 July 2008).

POTTS, J.A., "Note, Moore v. Regents of the University of California: Expanded Disclosure, Limited Property Rights", 86 *Northwest University Law Review* 453 (1992).

POVINELLI, E.A., "At Home in the Violence of Recognition", in K. VERDERY and C. HUMPHREY (eds.), *Property in Question: Value Transformation in the Global Economy*, 2004, 185.

PROTT, L.V., "An International Legal Instrument for the Protection of Intangible Cultural Heritage?", in C.D. CLASSEN *et al.*, (eds.), *"In einem vereinten Europa dem Frieden der Welt zu dienen…": Liber amicorum Thomas Oppermann*, 2001.

———, "Some Considerations on the Protection of the Intangible Heritage: Claims and Remedies", in J. BLAKE (ed.), *Safeguarding Intangible Cultural Heritage: Challenges and Approaches*, 2008, 140.

QUIGGIN, R., *The Contribution of Protocols and Moral Rights* (5 Augustus 2004) (paper presented at *Snapshot 2*, AMAG, Melbourne, Australia).

RAGAVAN, S., "Protection of Traditional Knowledge", 2 *Minnesota Intellectual Property Review* 1 (2001).

RAJAGOPAL, B., "Locating the Third World in Cultural Geography", *Third World Legal Studies* 1 (1998–99).

REICHMAN, J.H., "Legal Hybrids Between the Patent and Copyright Paradigms", *94 Columbia Law Review* 2432 (1994).

———, "Of Green Tulips and Legal Kudzu: Repackaging Rights in Subpatentable Innovation," 53 *Vanderbilt Law Review* 1743 (2000).

REICHMAN, J.H. and T. LEWIS, "Using Liability Rules to Stimulate Local Innovation in Developing Countries: Application to Traditional Knowledge", in K.E. MASKUS and J.H. REICHMAN (eds.), *International Public Goods and Transfer of Technology Under a Globalized Intellectual Property Regime*, 2005, 337.

RILEY, A.R., "Recovering Collectivity: Group Rights to Intellectual Property in Indigenous Communities", 18 *Cardozo Arts & Entertainment Law Journal* 175 (2000).

ROBLEDO, J.R., "Strategic Patents and Asymmetric Litigation Costs as Entry Deterrence Instruments", 15/2 *Economic Bulletin* (2005).

ROHT-ARRIAZA, N., "Of Seeds and Shamans: The Appropriation of the Scientific and Technical Knowledge of Indigenous and Local Communities", 17 *Michigan Journal International Law* 919 (1996).

RÖLLEKE, H., "Entstehungs- und Veröffentlichungsgeschichte der Grimmschen Märchen [The Origin and the Publication History of the Grimm's Fairy Tales]", in *Kinder- und Hausmärchen [Children and Household Tales]* (18th ed.), 1999, 840.

ROSE, C.M., "The Several Futures of Property: Of Cyberspace and Folk Tales, Emission Trades and Ecosystems", 83 *Minnesota Law Review* 129 (1998).

ROSENTHAL, J.P., "Politics, Culture, and Governance in the Development of Prior Informed Consent in Indigenous Communities", 47 *Current Anthropology* 119 (2006).

RURAL ADVANCEMENT FOUNDATION INTERNATIONAL (RAFI), *Messages from the Chiapas "Bioprospecting" Dispute: An Analysis of Recent Issues Raised in the Chiapas "Bioprospecting" Controversy with Reflections on the Message for BioPiracy* (22 December 1999), *available at* www.etcgroup.org/upload/publication/pdf_file/344 (last visited 31 July 2008).

RÜSEN, J., "Human Rights from the Perspective of a Universal History", in W. SCHMALE (ed.), *Human Rights and Cultural Diversity: Europe, Arabic-Islamic World, Africa, China*, 1993, 28.

SAMUELSON, P., "Enriching Discourse on Public Domains", 55 *Duke Law Journal* 783 (2006).

SAWYERR, A., "Internal Conflict of Laws in East Africa", in A. SAWYERR (ed.), *East African Law and Social Change*, 1967, 110.

SCAFIDI, S., "Intellectual Property and Cultural Products", 81 *Boston University Law Review* 793 (2001).

SEALASKA HERITAGE INSTITUTE, *Cultural and Intellectual Property Rights Policy*, *available at* www.wipo.int/export/sites/www/tk/en/folklore/creative_heritage/docs/sealaska_cultural_policy.pdf (last visited 31 July 2008).

SEALASKA HERITAGE INSTITUTE, *Photography (Including Video and Film) Policy*, *available at* www.wipo.int/export/sites/www/tk/en/folklore/creative_heritage/docs/sealaska_photo_policy.pdf (last visited 31 July 2008).

SEARS, L.J., "Comment", 43 *Current Anthropology* 146 (2002).

SEEGER, A., "Ethnomusicology and Music Law", 36 *Ethnomusicology* 345 (1992).

———, "Ethnomusicologists, Archives, Professional Organizations, and the Shifting Ethics of Intellectual Property", 28 *Yearbook for Traditional Music* 87 (1996).

———, "Intellectual Property and Audiovisual Archives and Collections", in COUNCIL ON LIBRARY AND INFORMATION RESOURCES (ed.), *Folk Heritage Collections in Crisis*, 2001, 32.

———, "Lost Lineages and Neglected Peers: Ethnomusicologists outside Academia", 50 *Ethnomusicology* 214 (2006).

SEIFERT, L., "The Marvellous in Context: The Place of the Conte de Fées in Late Seventeenth-Century France", in J. ZIPES (ed.), *The Great Fairy Tale Tradition: From Straparola and Basile to the Brothers Grimm*, 2001, 902.

SHELTON, D., "Introduction: Law, Non-Law and the Problem of 'Soft Law'", in D. SHELTON (ed.), *Commitment and Compliance*, 2000, 1.

SHERKIN, S., "A Historical Study on the Preparation of the 1989 Recommendation on the Safeguarding of Traditional Culture and Folklore", in P. SEITEL (ed.), *Safeguarding Traditional Cultures: A Global Assessment*, 2001, 42.

SHIVA, B., "The Very Basis of World Food Production Is at Stake", *Humanscape Magazine*, August 2004, *available at* www.humanscape.org/Humanscape/new/aug04/thevery.htm (last visited 11 March 2007).

SIECKE, E., "Über die Bedeuting der Grimmschen Märchen für unser Volksthum: Rede, gehalten in der Ortsgruppe Berlin des Alldeutschen Verbandes am 15. März 1895 [On the Significance of Grimm's Folktales for our Nation: Speech held at the Berlin of the Pan-Germanic League]", in R. VIRCHOW and F. VON HOLTZENDORFF (eds.), *Sammlung gemeinverständlicher wissenschaftlicher Vorträge [Collection of Commonly Understandable Scientific Lectures]*, 1896.

SIMON, B.S., "Intellectual Property and Traditional Knowledge: A Psychological Approach to Conflicting Claims of Creativity in International Law", 20 *Berkeley Technology Law Journal* 1613 (2005).

SKRYDSTRUP, M., *Towards Intellectual Property Guidelines and Best Practices for Recording and Digitizing Intangible Cultural Heritage: A Survey of Codes, Conduct and Challenges in North America* (2006), *available at* www.wipo.int/export/sites/www/tk/en/folklore/culturalheritage/casestudies/skrydstrup_report.pdf (last visited 31 July 2008) (*prepared for* WIPO).

SLATER, D., "Contesting Occidental Visions of the Global: The Geopolitics of Theory and North-South Relations", *Beyond Law* 97 (December 1994).

SOLOMON, M., *The Long Journey Home: Return of Our Ancestors* (12 November 2005) (paper presented at *World Archaeological Congress*, Auckland, New Zealand), *available at* www.wipo.int/export/sites/www/tk/en/folklore/creative_heritage/docs/solomon_maui_ancestors.pdf (last visited 31 July 2008).

STOLL, P.-T. and A. VON HAHN, "Indigenous Peoples, Indigenous Knowledge and Indigenous Resources in International Law", in S. VON LEWINSKY (ed.), *Indigenous Heritage and Intellectual Property: Genetic Resources, Traditional Knowledge and Folklore*, 2004, 5.

STONE, K.F., "Feminist Approaches to the Interpretation of Fairy Tales", in R.B. BOTTIGHEIMER (ed.), *Fairy Tales and Society: Illusion, Allusion and Paradigm*, 1986, 229.

STONE, R., "The Biodiversity Treaty: Pandora's Box or Fair Deal?", 256 *Science* 1624 (1992).

SUBBIAH, S., "Reaping What They Sow: The Basmati Rice Controversy and Strategies for Protecting Traditional Knowledge", 27 *Boston College International and Comparative Law Review* 529 (2004).

SUNDER, M., "IP3", 59 *Stanford Law Review* 257 (2006).

SUNSTEIN, C.R., "Social Norms and Social Roles", 96 *Columbia Law Review* 903 (1996).

SUTHERSANEN, U., "'Bleak House' or 'Great Expectations'?: The Literary Author as a Stakeholder in nineteenth-Century International Copyright Politics", in H. PORSDAM (ed.), *Copyright and other Fairy Tales: Hans Christian Andersen and the Commodification of Creativity*, 2006, 40.

SYMPOSIUM, "The Public Domain", 66 *Law and Contemporary Problems* 1 (2003).

TAUBMAN, A., "Saving the Village: Conserving Jurisprudential Diversity in the International Protection of Traditional Knowledge", in K.E. MASKUS and J.H. REICHMAN (eds.), *International Public Goods and Transfer of Technology Under a Globalized Intellectual Property Regime*, 2005, 521.

TORSEN, M., *Sustaining Creativity, Safeguarding Cultural Heritage and Protecting Traditional Cultural Expressions: The Management of Intellectual Property Issues and Options – A Practical Guide for Museums and Archives* (forthcoming, 2008) (*prepared for* WIPO).

Turner, P., *Report on the Pocantico Conference for the International Journal of Cultural Property, available at* www.williams.edu/AnthSoc/IJCP/Synopsis.htm (last visited 31 July 2008).

Tvedt, M.W., "Elements for Legislation in User Countries to Meet the Fair and Equitable Benefit-Sharing Commitment", 9 *Journal of World Intellectual Property* 189 (2006).

Tyler, R., "Comprehending Community", in S. Herbrechter and M. Higgins (eds.), Returning (to) Communities: Theory, Culture and Political Practice of the Communal, 2006, 21.

van Beek, W.E.A. and J. Fabiola, ""Granular Knowledge": Cultural Problems with Intellectual Property and Protection", in F.W. Grosheide and J.J. Brinkhof (eds.), *Intellectual Property Law 2002: Articles on the Legal Protection of Cultural Expressions and Indigenous Knowledge*, 2002, 35.

van Zanten, W., "Sung Epic Narrative and Lyrical Songs: Carita Pantun and Tembang Sunda", in B. Arps (ed.), *Performance in Java and Bali: Studies of Narrative, Theatre, Music and Dance*, 1993, 144.

———, "Aspects of Baduy Music in its Sociocultural Context, with Special Reference to Singing and Angklung", 151 *Bijdragen tot de Taal-, Land- en Volkenkunde* 516 (1995).

———, "Inner and Outer Voices: Listening and Hearing in West Java", 39(2) *The World of Music* 48 (1997).

———, "Les tentations des ascètes: Patrimoine culturel immatériel des Baduy dans le Banten du sud (Indonésie)", in J. Duvignaud and Ch. Khaznadar (eds.), *Le patrimoine culturel immatériel: Les enjeux, les problématiques, les pratiques*, 2004, 124.

Vaver, D., "Intellectual Property Today: Of Myths and Paradoxes", 69 *Canadian Business Review* 98 (1990).

Velten, H., "The Influence of Charles Perrault's Contes de ma Mère L'oie on German Folklore", in J. Zipes (ed.), *The Great Fairy Tale Tradition: From Straparola and Basile to the Brothers Grimm*, 2001, 958.

Vetter, T. and K. Eddan, *Access to Knowledge in the Information Society* (September 2007), *available at* www.iisd.org/pdf/2007/igsd_access.pdf (last visited 31 July 2008) (*prepared for* International Institute for Sustainable Development).

Visser, C.J., "Making Intellectual Property Laws Work for Traditional Knowledge", in J.M. Finger and Ph. Schuler (eds.), *Poor People's Knowledge: Promoting Intellectual Property in Developing Countries*, 2004, 207.

Watts, M.J., "Contested Communities, Malignant Markets, and Gilded Governance: Justice, Resource Extraction, and Conservation in the Tropics", in Ch. Zerner (ed.), *People, Plants, and Justice: The Politics of Nature Conservation*, 2000, 21.

Wendland, W.B., "Intellectual Property and the Protection of Cultural Expressions: The Work of the World Intellectual Property Organization (WIPO)", in F.W. Grosheide and J.J. Brinkhof (eds.), *Intellectual Property Law 2002: Articles on Cultural Expressions and Indigenous Knowledge*, 2002, 101.

———, "Intangible Cultural Heritage and Intellectual Property: Challenges and Future Prospects", 56 *Museum International* 97 (2004).

———, *Safeguarding Intangible Heritage and Protecting Creativity: Practical Mechanisms for Complementarity* (13–16 December 2005) (paper presented at the Sub-Regional Experts Meeting in Asia on *Intangible Cultural Heritage: Safeguarding and Inventory-Making Methodologies*, Bangkok, Thailand), *available at* www.accu.or.jp/ich/en/pdf/c2005subreg_WIPO.pdf (last visited 31 July 2008).

———, "It's a Small World (After All): Some Reflections on Intellectual Property and Traditional Cultural Expressions", in Chr.B. GRABER and M. BURRI-NENOVA (eds.), *Intellectual Property and Traditional Cultural Expressions in a Digital Environment* (forthcoming 2008).

W.J. CHRISTIAN and W.B. WENDLAND, "Mediation as an Option for Resolving Disputes between Indigenous/Traditional Communities and Industry Concerning Traditional Knowledge", in B.T. HOFFMAN (ed.), *Art and Cultural Heritage: Law, Policy and Practice*, 2006, 475.

WOODMANSEE, M., "The Genius and the Copyright: Economic and Legal Conditions of the Emergence of the "Author"", 17 *Eighteenth Century Studies* 425 (1984).

WÜGER, D., "Prevention of Misappropriation of Intangible Cultural Heritage through Intellectual Property Laws", in J.M. FINGER and Ph. SHULER (eds.), *Poor People's Knowledge: Promoting Intellectual Property in Developing Countries*, 2004, 183.

YAÏ, O.B.J., "Odo layé (Éloge de la Vie-Fleuve): Perspectives Africaines sur le Patrimoine Culturel", in J. BLAKE (ed.), *Safeguarding Intangible Cultural Heritage: Challenges and Approaches*, 2007, 73.

YEN, A.C. "Restoring the Natural Law: Copyright as Labour and Possession", 51 *Ohio State Law Journal* 517 (1990).

YOUNGING, G., *Competing Jurisdictions over Traditional Knowledge in the Northern Americas* (2006), *available at* www.nationalimac.org/pt/Forums/tabid/59/Default.aspx?dnnbbfid=4&dnnbbtid=19 (last visited 31 July 2008) (paper submitted to Tenth Session of WIPO Intergovernmental Committee on Intellectual Property and Genetic Resources, Traditional Knowledge and Folklore, Geneva, Switzerland).

YU, P.K., "Currents and Crosscurrents in the International Intellectual Property Regime", 38 *Loyola L.A. Law Review* 323 (2004).

———, "Ten Common Questions About Intellectual Property and Human Rights", 23 *Georgia State University Law Review* 709 (2007).

ZEMP, H., "The/An Ethnomusicologist and the Record Business", 28 *Yearbook for Traditional Music* 36 (1996).

ZIPES, J., "The Grimms and the German Obsession with Fairy Tales", in R.B. BOTTIGHEIMER (ed.), *Fairy Tales and Society: Illusion, Allusion and Paradigm*, 1986, 272.

———, "Dreams of a Better Bourgeois Life: The Psychological Origins of the Grimms' Tales", in J.M. MCGLATHERY *et al.* (eds.), *The Brothers Grimm and Folktale*, 1988, 205.

———, "Cross-Cultural Connections and the Contamination of the Classical Fairy Tale", in J. ZIPES (ed.), *The Great Fairy Tale Tradition: From Straparola and Basile to the Brothers Grimm*, 2001, 845.

Zoogman, S., "Documentation Doesn't Keep My Heritage Alive!", *Tourist Productions*, 6 November 2005, *available at* www.nyu.edu/classes/bkg/touristblog/archives/2005/11/documentation_d.html (last visited 31 July 2008).

3. DOCUMENTS AND REPORTS PREPARED BY INTERNATIONAL ORGANIZATIONS

ACCU, *Workshop for Youth Participation for Safeguarding the Intangible Cultural Heritage and Community Development, Final Report*, (8–11 June 2007), *available at* www.accu.or.jp/ich/en/pdf/d2007Accenture.pdf (last visited 31 July 2008).

ASEAN, *ASEAN Framework Agreement on Access to Biological and Genetic Resources* (draft, 2000), *available at* www.grain.org/brl/?docid=785&lawid=1261 (last visited 31 July 2008).

Conference of the Parties (COP) to the CBD, *Article 8(j) and related provisions*, Decision V/16, UNEP/CBD/COP/5/23 (15–26 May 2000), *available at* www.cbd.int/doc/decisions/COP-05-dec-en.pdf (last visited 31 July 2008).

———, *Article 8(j) and related provisions*, Decision VI/10, UNEP/CBD/COP/6/20 (7–19 April 2002), *available at* www.cbd.int/doc/decisions/COP-06-dec-en.pdf (last visited 31 July 2008).

———, *Bonn Guidelines on Access to Genetic Resources and Fair and Equitable Sharing of the Benefits Arising out of their Utilization*, Decision VI/24 A, UNEP/CBD/COP/6/20 (7–19 April 2002), *available at* www.biodiv.org/decisions/default.aspx?m=cop-06&d=24 (last visited 31 July 2008).

———, *Role of intellectual property rights in the implementation of access and benefit-sharing arrangements*, Decision VI/24 C, UNEP/CBD/COP/6/20 (7–19 April 2002), *available at* www.biodiv.org/decisions/default.aspx?m=cop-06&d=24 (last visited 31 July 2008).

———, *Article 8(j) and related provisions*, Decision VII/16, UNEP/CBD/COP/7/21 (9–20 and 27 February 2004), *available at* www.cbd.int/doc/decisions/COP-07-dec-en.pdf (last visited 31 July 2008).

———, *Access and benefit-sharing as related to genetic resources (Article 15)*, Decision VII/19, UNEP/CBD/COP/7/21 (9–20 and 27 February 2004), *available at* www.cbd.int/doc/decisions/COP-07-dec-en.pdf (last visited 31 July 2008).

———, *Access and benefit-sharing*, Decision VIII/4 (20–31 March 2006), *available at* www.cbd.int/decisions/cop-08.shtml?m=COP-08&id=11016&lg=0 (last visited 31 July 2008).

———, *Article 8(j) and related provisions*, Decision VIII/5 (20–31 March 2006), *available at* www.cbd.int/decisions/cop-08.shtml?m=COP-08&id=11017&lg=0 (last visited 31 July 2008).

ECOSOC, *Discrimination against Indigenous Peoples: Protection of the Heritage of Indigenous People*, U.N. Doc. E/CN.4/Sub.2/1995/26 (21 June 1995) (*prepared by* E.-I.A. Daes).

———, Permanent Forum on Indigenous Issues, *Indigenous Forum Discusses Implementation of Fourth Session's Recommendations: Possible Study on Proper Protection of Traditional Knowledge*, 30 May 2007, *available at* www.un.org/News/Press/docs/2007/hr4924.doc.htm (last visited 31 July 2008).

ICTSD and UNCTAD, INTELLECTUAL PROPERTY RIGHTS: IMPLICATIONS FOR DEVELOPMENT 118 (Geneva: International Centre for Trade and Sustainable Development and United Nations Conference on Trade and Development 2003).

UN, *Plan of Implementation of the World Summit on Sustainable Development*, 23 September 2002, *available at* www.un.org/jsummit/html/documents/summit_docs/2309_planfinal.htm (last visited 31 July 2008).

———, Sub-Commission on Prevention of Discrimination and Protection of Minorities, *Study of the Problem of Discrimination Against Indigenous Populations*, Part III, E/CN.4/Sub.2/1983/21/Add.8 (1983) (*prepared by* J. MARTÍNEZ COBO), *available at* www.un.org/esa/socdev/unpfii/documents/MCS_xxi_xxii_e.pdf (last visited 31 July 2008).

UNCTAD, *Analysis of Options for Implementing Disclosure of Origin Requirements in Intellectual Property Applications*, UNCTAD/DITC/TED/2005/14 (15 February 2006) (*prepared by* J.D. SARNOFF and C.M. CORREA), *available at* www.unctad.org/en/docs/ditcted200514_en.pdf (last visited 31 July 2008).

UNESCO, *First Preliminary Draft of an International Convention for the Safeguarding of the Intangible Cultural Heritage*, CLT-2002/CONF.203/3 (26 July 2002), *available at* http://unesdoc.unesco.org/ulis/cgi-bin/ulis.pl?catno=127018&gp=0&mode=e&lin=1 (last visited 31 July 2008).

———, *Report of the Expert Meeting on Inventorying Intangible Cultural Heritage* (17–18 March 2005), *available at* www.unesco.org/culture/ich/doc/src/00036-EN.pdf (last visited 31 July 2008).

———, *Expert Meeting on Documenting and Archiving Intangible Cultural Heritage*, CLT/CH/ITH/DOCEM0106 (12–13 January 2006), *available at* http://unesdoc.unesco.org/images/0014/001445/144592e.pdf (last visited 31 July 2008).

———, *Presentation of a New Book: An Inventory of the Intangible Cultural Heritage in Cambodia*, http://portal.unesco.org/en/ev.php-URL_ID=19674&URL_DO=DO_PRINTPAGE&URL_ SECTION=201.html (last visited 12 March 2007).

———, *Proclamation of the Masterpieces of the Oral and Intangible Heritage of Humanity (2001–2005)*, www.unesco.org/culture/ich/index.php?pg=00103 (last visited 31 July 2008).

———, *Selection Procedure for the Masterpieces of the Oral and Intangible Heritage of Humanity (2001–2005)*, www.unesco.org/culture/ich/index.php?pg=00105 (last visited 31 July 2008).

UNESCO/ACCU, *Expert Meeting on Community Involvement in Safeguarding Intangible Cultural Heritage: Towards the Implementation of the 2003 Convention* (13–15 March 2006), *available at* http://unesdoc.unesco.org/images/0014/001459/145919e.pdf (last visited 31 July 2008).

———, *Expert Meeting on Transmission and Safeguarding of Intangible Cultural Heritage through Formal and Non-formal Education* (21–23 February 2007), *available at* www.accu.or.jp/ich/en/pdf/b2007Expert.pdf (last visited 31 July 2008).

UNHCHR, *Fact Sheet No.23, Harmful Traditional Practices Affecting the Health of Women and Children*, www.unhchr.ch/html/menu6/2/fs23.htm (last visited 31 July 2008).
———, *Intellectual Property Rights and Human Rights: Sub-Commission on Human Rights resolution 2000/7*, www.unhchr.ch/Huridocda/Huridoca.nsf/0/c462b62cf8a07b13c12569700046704e?Opendocument (last visited 31 July 2008).
WCED, *Our Common Future*, A/42/427, Annex (4 August 1987).
WIPO, *Contracts Database*, www.wipo.int/tk/en/databases/contracts/index.html (last visited 31 July 2008).
———, *Creative Heritage Project: IP Guidelines for Recording, Digitizing and Disseminating Intangible Cultural Heritage*, www.wipo.int/tk/en/folklore/culturalheritage/index.html (last visited 31 July 2008).
———, *Database of Existing Codes, Guidelines and Practices*, www.wipo.int/tk/en/folklore/creative_heritage/index.html (last visited 31 July 2008).
———, *Domain Name Dispute Resolution Service*, www.wipo.int/amc/en/domains/ (last visited 31 July 2008).
———, *Draft Provisions on Traditional Cultural Expressions/Folklore and Traditional Knowledge*, www.wipo.int/tk/en/consultations/draft_provisions/draft_provisions.html (last visited 31 July 2008).
———, *Intellectual Property Needs and Expectations of Traditional Knowledge Holders: WIPO Report on Fact-Finding Missions on Intellectual Property and Traditional Knowledge (1998–1999)* (April 2001), *available at* www.wipo.int/tk/en/tk/ffm/report/index.html (last visited 31 July 2008).
———, *Intergovernmental Committee on Intellectual Property and Genetic Resources, Traditional Knowledge and Folklore*, www.wipo.int/tk/en/igc/ (last visited 31 July 2008).
———, *Legislative Texts on the Protection of Traditional Knowledge and Traditional Cultural Expressions (Expressions of Folklore) and Legislative Texts relevant to Genetic Resources*, www.wipo.int/tk/en/laws/index.html (last visited 31 July 2008).
———, *Surveys of Existing Practices, Protocols and Policies*, www.wipo.int/tk/en/folklore/culturalheritage/surveys.html (last visited 31 July 2008).
———, *Traditional Knowledge, Genetic Resources and Traditional Cultural Expressions/Folklore*, www.wipo.int/tk/en/ (last visited 31 October 2007).
WIPO, General Assembly, *Report* WO/GA/30/8 (1 October 2003), *available at* www.wipo.int/documents/en/document/govbody/wo_gb_ga/pdf/wo_ga_30_8.pdf (last visited 31 July 2008).
WIPO, Intergovernmental Committee on Intellectual Property and Genetic Resources, Traditional Knowledge and Folklore, *Draft Guidelines on Access and Benefit Sharing Regarding the Utilisation of Genetic Resources*, WIPO/GRTKF/IC/1/9 (27 April 2001) *available at* www.wipo.int/edocs/mdocs/tk/en/wipo_grtkf_ic_1/wipo_grtkf_ic_1_9.pdf (last visited 31 July 2008).
———, *Elements of a* Sui Generis *System for the Protection of Traditional Knowledge*, WIPO/GRTKF/IC/3/8 (29 March 2002) (*prepared by* the Secretariat), *available at* www.wipo.int/edocs/mdocs/tk/en/wipo_grtkf_ic_3/wipo_grtkf_ic_3_8.pdf (last visited 31 July 2008).

———, *Elements of a* Sui Generis *System for the Protection of Traditional Knowledge*, WIPO/GRTKF/IC/4/8 (30 September 2002) (*prepared by* THE SECRETARIAT), *available at* www.wipo.int/edocs/mdocs/tk/en/wipo_grtkf_ic_4/wipo_grtkf_ic_4_8.pdf (last visited 31 July 2008).

———, *Practical Mechanisms for the Defensive Protection of Traditional Knowledge and Genetic Resources Within the Patent System*, WIPO/GRTKF/IC/5/6 (14 May 2003).

———, *Disclosure of Origin or Source of Genetic Resources and Associated Traditional Knowledge in Patent Applications*, WIPO/GRTKF/IC/8/11 (17 May 2005).

———, *Second Draft Report*, WIPO/GRTKF/IC/8/15. Prov. 2 (5 October 2005), *available at* www.wipo.int/edocs/mdocs/tk/en/wipo_grtkf_ic_8/wipo_grtkf_ic_8_15_prov_2.pdf (last visited 31 July 2008).

———, *Intellectual Property and Genetic Resources, Traditional Knowledge and Traditional Cultural Expressions/Folklore: Information Resources*, WIPO/GRTKF/INF/1 (2006).

———, *Recognition of Traditional Knowledge within the Patent System: Interim Draft*, WIPO/GRTKF/IC/9/8 (15 March 2006).

———, *The Protection of Traditional Cultural Expressions/Expressions of Folklore: Updated Draft Outline of Policy Options and Legal Mechanisms*, WIPO/GRTKF/IC/9/INF/4 (27 March 2006), *available at* www.wipo.int/edocs/mdocs/tk/en/wipo_grtkf_ic_9/wipo_grtkf_ic_9_inf_4.pdf (last visited 31 July 2008).

———, *The Protection of Traditional Knowledge: Revised Outline of Policy Options and Legal Mechanisms*, WIPO/GRTKF/IC/9/INF/5 (27 March 2006), *available at* www.wipo.int/edocs/mdocs/tk/en/wipo_grtkf_ic_9/wipo_grtkf_ic_9_inf_5.doc (last visited 31 July 2008).

———, *The Protection of Traditional Cultural Expressions/Expressions of Folklore: Draft Objectives and Principles*, WIPO/GRTKF/IC/10/4 (2 October 2006), *available at* www.wipo.int/edocs/mdocs/tk/en/wipo_grtkf_ic_10/wipo_grtkf_ic_10_4.pdf(last visited 31 July 2008).

———, *The Protection of Traditional Knowledge: Draft Objectives and Principles*, WIPO/GRTKF/IC/10/5 (2 October 2006), *available at* www.wipo.int/edocs/mdocs/tk/en/wipo_grtkf_ic_10/wipo_grtkf_ic_10_5.pdf (last visited 31 July 2008).

———, *Draft Report (Second Draft)* WIPO/GRTKF/IC/9/14. Prov.2 (5 November 2006), *available at* www.wipo.int/edocs/mdocs/tk/en/wipo_grtkf_ic_9/wipo_grtkf_ic_9_14_prov_2.pdf (last visited 31 July 2008).

———, *Recognition of Traditional Knowledge within the Patent System*, WIPO/GRTKF/IC/11/7 (6 June 2007).

WIPO, PERMANENT COMMITTEE ON COOPERATION FOR DEVELOPMENT RELATED TO INTELLECTUAL PROPERTY, *Protection of Traditional Knowledge and Intellectual Property in Developing Countries: Progress Report*, at 4, PCIPD/2/7 (25 January 2001) (*prepared by* THE INTERNATIONAL BUREAU), *available at* www.wipo.int/documents/en/document/pcipd/doc/pcipd2_7.doc (last visited 31 July 2008).

WIPO, SECRETARIAT, *Information Note* (13–15 March 2006) (paper presented at *UNESCO/ACCU Expert Meeting on Community Involvement in Safeguarding Intangible Cultural Heritage: Towards the Implementation of the 2003 Convention*, Tokyo,

Japan), *available at* www.accu.or.jp/ich/en/pdf/c2006Expert_UEMURA.pdf (last visited 31 July 2008).

WIPO, Working Group on Reform of the Patent Cooperation Treaty, *Proposals by Switzerland Regarding the Declaration of the Source of Genetic Resources and Traditional Knowledge in Patent Applications*, PCT/R/WG/4/13 (5 May 2003), *available at* www.wipo.int/edocs/mdocs/pct/en/pct_r_wg_4/pct_r_wg_4_13.pdf (last visited 31 July 2008).

———, *Proposals by Switzerland Regarding the Declaration of the Source of Genetic Resources and Traditional Knowledge in Patent Applications*, PCT/R/WG/5/11 Rev. (19 November 2003), *available at* www.wipo.int/edocs/mdocs/pct/en/pct_r_wg_5/pct_r_wg_5_11_rev.pdf (last visited 31 July 2008).

———, *Additional Comments by Switzerland on Its Proposals Regarding the Declaration of the Source of Genetic Resources and Traditional Knowledge in Patent Applications*, PCT/R/WG/6/11 (21 April 2004), *available at* www.wipo.int/edocs/mdocs/pct/en/pct_r_wg_6/pct_r_wg_6_11.doc (last visited 31 July 2008).

———, *International Publication a PCT Gazette in Electronic Form*, PCT/R/WG/7/8 (5 April 2005).

———, *Declaration of the Source of Genetic Resources and Traditional Knowledge in Patent Applications*, PCT/R/WG/8/7 (21 April 2006).

WIPO/UNEP, *WIPO-UNEP Study on the Role of Intellectual Property Rights in the Sharing of Benefits Arising from the Use of Biological Resources and Associated Traditional Knowledge* (2004) (*prepared by* A.K. Gupta), *available at* www.wipo.int/tk/en/publications/769e_unep_tk.pdf (last visited 31 July 2008).

WTO, *TRIPS: Reviews, Article 27.3(b) and Related Issues: Background and the Current Situation*, www.wto.org/english/tratop_e/trips_e/art27_3b_background_e.htm (last visited 31 July 2008).

———, *Issues Related to the Extension of the Protection of Geographical Indications Provided for in Article 23 of the TRIPS Agreement to Products Other than Wines and Spirits and those Related to the Relationship between the TRIPS Agreement and the Convention on Biological Diversity*, WT/GC/W/591 (9 June 2008), *available at* www.wto.org/english/tratop_e/trips_e/giextension_cbd_dgreport_9jun08_e.pdf (last visited 31 July 2008).

WTO, Council for Trade-Related Aspects of Intellectual Property Rights, *Communication from the European Communities and Their Member States*, IP/C/W/383 (17 October 2002).

———, *Additional Comments by Switzerland on Its Proposals Submitted to WIPO Regarding the Declaration of the Source of Genetic Resources and Traditional Knowledge in Patent Applications*, IP/C/W/423 (14 June 2004).

———, *The Relationship between the TRIPS Agreement and the Convention on Biological Diversity (CBD) and the Protection of Traditional Knowledge-Elements of the Obligation to Disclose Evidence of Prior Informed Consent under the Relevant National Regime*, IP/C/W/438 (10 December 2004).

———, *The Relationship between the TRIPS Agreement and the Convention on Biological Diversity (CBD) and the Protection of Traditional Knowledge – Elements of the Obligation to Disclose Evidence of Benefit-Sharing under the Relevant National*

Regime, IP/C/W/442 (18 March 2005), *available at* http://docsonline.wto.org/DDFDocuments/t/IP/C/W442.doc (last visited 31 July 2008).

———, *The Relationship between the TRIPS Agreement and the Convention on Biological Diversity: Summary of Issues Raised and Points Made*, IP/C/W/368/Rev.1 (8 February 2006) (*prepared by* the WTO Secretariat), *available at* www.wto.org/english/tratop_e/trips_e/ipcw368_e.doc (last visited 31 July 2008).

———, *The Relationship between the TRIPS Agreement, the Convention on Biological Diversity and the Protection of Traditional Knowledge – Amending the TRIPS Agreement to Introduce an Obligation to Disclose the Origin of Genetic Resources and Traditional Knowledge in Patent Applications*, IP/C/W/473 (14 June 2006).

———, *Doha Work Programme – The Outstanding Implementation Issue on the Relationship between the TRIPS Agreement and the Conventional on Biological Diversity*, WT/GC/W/564/Rev.2 (5 July 2006), *available at* http://docsonline.wto.org/DDFDocuments/t/ip/c/w474.doc (last visited 31 July 2008).

———, *Combating Biopiracy – the Peruvian Experience*, IP/C/W/493 (19 September 2007), *available at* http://docsonline.wto.org/DDFDocuments/t/ip/c/w493.doc (last visited 31 July 2008).

WTO, Ministerial Conference, *Ministerial Declaration*, 14 November 2001, WT/MIN(01)/DEC/1 (20 November 2001), *available at* www.wto.org/english/thewto_e/minist_e/min01_e/mindecl_e.pdf (last visited 31 July 2008).

4. OTHER SOURCES

Leigh, M. and W. Saunders, *Hidden Pictures: Colonial Camera*, 1995.

van Zanten, W., *Play the Saluang Flute, Use Your Fifth Finger: Lyrical Songs from Payakumbuh, West Sumatra* (educational film accompanied by a documentation book, Leiden: University of Leiden, 2002).

van Zanten, W. and B. Barendregt, *Told in Heaven to Become Stories on Earth: A Study of Change in Randai Theatre of the Minangkabau in West Sumatra using Visual Documentation from the 1930s* (educational film accompanied by a documentation book, Leiden: University of Leiden, 2000).

www.ingramcontent.com/pod-product-compliance
Ingram Content Group UK Ltd.
Pitfield, Milton Keynes, MK11 3LW, UK
UKHW051925100926
8556IPUK00022B/1377

9 789050 957588